# 1001 COOKIE RECIPES

# 1001
# COOKIE
# RECIPES

GREGG R. GILLESPIE

PHOTOGRAPHS BY PETER BARRY

BLACK DOG & LEVENTHAL PUBLISHERS
NEW YORK

Copyright © 1995 Gregg R. Gillespie

Photographs copyright © 1995 Black Dog & Leventhal

All rights reserved. No part of this book may be reproduced in any form or by any electronic or mechanical means including information storage and retrieval systems without written permission from the publisher.

Published by

Black Dog & Leventhal Publishers, Inc.
151 West 19th Street
New York, NY 10011

Distributed by

Workman Publishing Company
708 Broadway
New York, NY 10003

Designed by Martin Lubin

Typesetting by Brad Walrod/High Text Graphics

Food Styling by Clare Brean

Manufactured in United States of America

ISBN: 1-884822-35-5

h g f e d c

**Library of Congress Cataloging-in-Publication Data**
Gillespie, Gregg R., 1934–
    1001 cookie recipes / Gregg R. Gillespie : photographs by Peter Barry.
        p.     cm.
    Includes index.
    ISBN 1-884822-35-5 (hardbound)
    1. Cookies.   I. Title.
TX772.G54  1995
641.8′654—dc20                                                    95-40394
                                                                         CIP

# Acknowledgments

To thank everyone who has assisted me or has shown me kindnesses over the past thirty to forty years would be impossible. I would like to thank the Goodman family, Ros, Mel, and Michael Goodman of Portsmouth, New Hampshire, who was always ready to try the new things I came up with; and Gordon Allan for proofing my pages.

Thanks to J.P. Leventhal for believing in this tremendous amount of cookies. I would like to thank Pamela Horn for all her effort and commitment in editing this project. Thanks to Marty Lubin for his beautiful design; Peter Barry for his wonderful pictures; and Judith Sutton for her excellent copyediting job.

Specifically, I would like to thank my father, Peter G. Gillespie, and my mother, Elizabeth H. Gillespie. One showed the way, the other showed me the reason.

# TABLE OF CONTENTS

# INTRODUCTION

There is no record in history of when man first started to bake, but we can assume his first effort was a flat bread cooked over or near a flame or on a hot rock. We do know from primitive picture writings that many ancient civilizations baked something described as a honey cake. Barley flour was much in use during these early periods, as well as eggs, dates, and honey. With these four ingredients, it is quite possible honey cakes were the first cookies.

Jumping forward to the early Europeans, we find every developing country has its particular cookie—or, in Germany the *Keks*; in Holland, the *koekie*; in Italy, the *focaccina*; in Spain, the *galleta*, and across the Channel in England, the biscuit. One unusual fact stands out: The colder the climate, the greater the variety of cookies created.

England and Scotland, with their tradition of high tea, advanced the making of cookies to an art form. The British refer to their sweet treats as biscuits, and most of their biscuits are not-too-sweet, plain, small cookies. They may be eaten on their own but are usually served with tea or coffee.

In America, our cookie-baking traditions evolved from the early settlers. Our word

*cookie*, in fact, comes from the Dutch, *koekie*. The British influence over this country in pre-revolutionary days turned what was a *koekie* into a "biscuit." Then in revolutionary times, our ancestors rejected most things British and called the biscuit a wafer.

Cherished European cookie recipes came to this country with millions of immigrants. Many of those treasured cookies were named for nationalities or national regions, such as Grenze Keks (Swiss Border Cookie). They were handed down from mother to daughter, from aunt to niece, from friend to friend. Thus a recipe that started out as Grenze Keks soon became known as Priscilla's Charms or Mrs. Smith's Favorite Cookies.

The number of different cookies is so large that we sometime forget they are just combinations of flour, sugar, fat, and eggs. These four ingredients are the foundations of the cookie, although you can make cookies using just two of these items, for example meringues are made from just egg whites and sugar. With the addition of chocolate, fruits, spices, and other flavorings, the possibilities for variation are endless.

In this book, I present the best from a collection of baking information developed over forty to fifty years. The

recipes were accumulated by my father, also a baker, and myself. Some are original, and have never been made public before; and some are our versions and adaptations of classic recipes. Many of the recipes, especially those from other countries, date back to before 1900. And others were written on bits and pieces of paper and handed to us by friends, relatives, and even casual acquaintances. Ultimately, this is the definitive collection in that, if you are looking for a cookie recipe, there is no need to look anywhere else.

In this collection, I have tried to put together recipes that represent all the most popular cookies. In cases where the recipes were similar or even identical, I had to disregard many so-called original cookie formulations. (With brownie recipes alone, in fact, fifty-three were exactly the same as others I had already selected—identical, that is, in all except name.) When recipes were almost identical—e.g., one uses a quarter teaspoon of salt, the other used no salt—I baked both and chose the one I liked best. But with recipes that were almost identical, but the basic flavoring was different, I chose to include all my favorites. Thus you will find several listings for brownies, for example, or for chocolate chip cookies. The basic cookie may be similar, but the flavoring enhancers or additives contribute sufficiently to the taste or texture to result in a different cookie.

This is not the collection for you if you are merely looking to impress your guests with fancy decoration. I don't tell you how to make a house out of cookie dough. Instead this cookbook is for those who just want to make good, simple cookies at home. It is for you and your family, cookies to eat and cookies to give as gifts. Nothing more! This collection is designed to be *used*—day after day, year after year.

At all times I have adhered to the basic principles of good baking. But I have included short cuts and hints and insider baking tips. For instance:

☐ The more you handle a rolled-out dough cookie, the tougher the baked cookies will be; don't overwork the dough.

☐ The more flour you use when rolling out that cookie dough, the dryer the cookies will be; use a light hand.

☐ Plump raisins in a liquid such as boiling water or brandy before adding them to a cookie dough, to keep them from turning leathery when baked. (See Hints for Cookie Baking, xiii)

For rich cookies, butter, rather than margarine, lard, or shortening, is without question the best. It adds flavor and contributes to the texture. But

with the fine-quality shortening available today, not to mention price considerations, butter may not always be the first choice. For years, my father and I were in fierce competition to see who could produce the best chocolate chip cookie ever made. I always used butter. Sometimes I even churned my own butter! Despite my best efforts, I could never produce a chocolate chip cookie that was as good as my father's. Shortly before he died, he confided that all of the ingredients we used were identical—save one. I used butter, he used a high-quality vegetable shortening.

In choosing flavorings for cookies, one rule should always prevail: *Do not use imitations.* Pure extracts and oils are exciting and can make a baked product irresistible. Also keep in mind the fact that there are lots of other flavorings besides the ubiquitous vanilla extract. I guarantee that after trying some different flavorings, you will never limit yourself to vanilla extract again. (And I'll tell you a little secret: Dollar for dollar, you can purchase a whole bottle of fine liqueur or brandy for flavoring for far less than a two-ounce bottle of pure vanilla extract. See Alternative Flavorings, xxvii) You will find that there are few cookie recipes for which the flavoring ingredient is written in cement. Substitute almond extract or anise oil or even sherry for the vanilla in

a basic cookie recipe. One of my favorite flavorings for chocolate chip cookies is crème de menthe. The world of flavorings is almost without end. For those who love to bake—and love to see others enjoy what they bake—it is a world worth exploring.

This book is about exploring; about finding out what cookie making is all about. You can take any of the basic recipes offered here and change it. Substitute where you want to (or where you must). Create your own cookies using my recipes. Pick up an unusual ingredient and try it. If it doesn't work, throw your experiment away and try again. No one need ever know. If a recipe calls for baking powder and you don't have any, look at the list of substitutions (page xv) and see what can be used in its place. A member of your family doesn't like one of the spices you used in the cookie last time? Fine, use something else.

No one knows how many cookie recipes there are, but it would be safe to assume that there are more recipes for cookies than for any other food category! There is no prepared food product more universally accepted and eaten throughout the world. There isn't an hour, a minute, or even a second of any day that someone, someplace in the world, isn't eating a cookie. Do you want to make cookies that everyone will love to eat? Here are the recipes—the choice is yours.

## INGREDIENTS FOR A BASIC COOKIE

The basic ingredients needed to make a simple cookie are: flour, sugar, fat in one form or another, and, often, eggs. Baking powder and/or baking soda may be included, as may be salt. Proportions will vary from recipe to recipe and substitutions will be made; butter will be used in one recipe, vegetable shortening in another. Honey may be the sweetener rather than sugar. To change the taste and flavor of a basic cookie, we turn to the wide array of spices and other flavorings available. For example, look at a recipe for a basic cookie, Do-Everything Cookies.

### DO EVERYTHING COOKIES
**3 cups all-purpose flour**
**1½ cups granulated sugar**
**4 whole eggs**
**¾ teaspoon baking powder**
**¼ teaspoon salt**
**2½ teaspoons caraway seeds**

Flour, sugar, eggs, baking powder, and salt are there. But I omitted the shortening and added caraway seeds for a distinctive flavor. If you don't like the flavor of caraway seeds, you can add anise seeds, chocolate chips, or raisins, or add a liquid flavoring, such as vanilla or almond extract or liqueur. Finely chopped nuts could be added to the dough or sprinkled over the tops of the cookies. Add cocoa powder or powdered instant coffee to the dough—or sift cocoa or powdered sugar over the tops of the cookies.

In this collection there are hundreds of similar simple recipes that can be adapted to make a cookie with the ever-so-specific taste you want. From the dozens and dozens of recipes in this book, you can go on to create hundreds more. With the recipes, knowledge, and information presented here you will be able to give your family, your neighbors, and your friends any type of cookie they may desire.

## UTENSILS

**Baking pans**  For cookie baking, I would recommend that you have baking pans of the following sizes: 8-inch square, 9-inch square, 13 by 9-inch, 15 by 10-inch, 17 by 11-inch, 12 by 8-inch shallow baking pan.

You will find that throughout the book the yields give a range. These numbers are based on whether you cut bar cookies into large or small bars.

**Baking sheets/cookie sheets**  Have at least two baking sheets so you can be filling a sheet while the first is in the oven. If your oven is large enough to allow good heat circulation, you can bake two trays at once. The sheets should be bright and shiny, and they should fit in your oven leaving enough room all around the edges for heat to circulate between the baking sheets and the oven walls.

Although some people argue that flat sheets, without lips or sides, result in more even baking, others believe that rimmed baking sheets are just as effective. (And just about all bakeries use rimmed baking sheets.)

**Bowl scraper**  A rectangle of rubberized plastic, about the size of a 3 by 5-inch index card with one slightly rounded edge, is extremely handy in the kitchen.

**Cookie cutters** The variety of cookie cutters available is almost without end. Visit a few garage sales—you will probably find cookie cutters in all sizes and shapes: round, square, rectangular, octagonal, oblong, crescent, diamond, tree, flower, animal—I've even seen a dog bone shape. It's nice to have all sorts of styles, but I find a set of round cookie cutters to be particularly valuable. These sets come in round boxes, each containing six cutters of graduated sizes (or seven—if you would even use the box itself as a cutter). They range in size from ½ to 3 inches. Other collections, such as one of small animals, about the size of animal crackers, are fun to own too.

**Cookie molds** Cookie molds used to be more popular, but specialty cookware stores often have a wide selection of large and small molds for gingerbread men, birds, flowers, and Santa Clauses. For the most part, the use of cookie molds has remained a European tradition. A springerle rolling pin is another utensil used to mold cookies. These pins, available in various designs and size, are rolled over rolled-out dough to imprint it and mark it into cookies. Actually, almost anything in your kitchen—or your house—can be used as a cookie mold. Be imaginative.

**Cookie press/pastry bag** A cookie press is an efficient way to deposit soft cookie dough directly onto baking sheets. There is a wide variety of tips available for pressing out cookies, and most cookie presses come with a set of eight to ten tips or plates for forming different shapes. Some bakers prefer to pipe out soft doughs using a pastry bag. The best pastry bags are made of canvas and coated on the inside with plastic; and large bags are much more practical than small ones. Some come with a set of tips and a coupling attachment, or you can buy these separately in good housewares shops.

**Cooling racks** These wire racks allow air to circulate around cookies as they cool, preventing them from getting soggy. You'll want at least two racks.

**Flour sifter** A sifter is handy for sifting powdered sugar or even brown sugar, as well as flour.

**Large spoons** Large wooden spoons are preferable to those made of plastic or metal; I like to keep at least three large spoons at hand.

**Measuring cups** Good measuring cups may be the most important purchase you make for the kitchen. If the measuring cups you use are inaccurate, you will never get good results in baking. You need both a set of dry measuring cups (I like to have at least two sets of these) and at least a 1-cup glass measure for liquids. Larger sizes can be handy to have. Do not use liquid measuring cups for dry ingredients, or vice-versa—the measurements will not be accurate.

**Measuring spoons** Measuring spoons can make the difference between success and failure of any baked product you make. Buy the best set you can afford.

**Metal whisk** Useful for combining dry ingredients, whipping egg whites, and stirring a cooked custard.

**Mixing bowls** Invest in a good set of mixing bowls, either ceramic or stainless steel. (Plastic tends to absorb odors and becomes difficult to clean.) Most professional bakers prefer stainless steel bowls: they don't rust, they are easy to clean, and they certainly don't break. A set of three to five different sizes is most practical.

**Pastry blender** A wire pastry blender is convenient but not a necessity; a fork or two knives can be used effectively for cutting the butter or another fat into flour.

**Pastry Brush** A fine-bristle pastry brush is an absolute must for spreading on egg washes, glazes, or melted butter. You can also purchase good quality ½-inch or 1½-inch fine-bristle paintbrushes. Avoid using brushes with nylon bristles, as they will melt when used with hot liquids.

**Rubber spatula** Large rubber spatulas with wooden handles are useful for a multitude of kitchen tasks.

# HINTS FOR COOKIE BAKING

**1** Always read a recipe at least once before you attempt to make it.

**2** Be sure to allow adequate time for the oven to preheat before you begin baking.

**3** For the very delicate butter-type cookies, it is best to use butter to grease the cookie sheets.

**4** When measuring liquids, read the measure at eye level.

**5** To measure ⅛ teaspoon, first measure ¼ teaspoon of the ingredient, then remove half of what you have measured.

**6** An electric mixer will give cookies a more even texture than hand-beating.

**7** To cream any mixture by hand, use the back of a large wooden spoon and beat until the mixture is soft and smooth.

**8** Butter should always be creamed until it is light and fluffy before the sugar is beaten into it.

**9** Unless otherwise stated in the recipe, all baking powder will be double-acting type.

**10** Unless otherwise specified in the recipe, all of the ingredients should be at room temperature.

**11** When separating eggs, do not break them over the ingredients you have already placed in the mixing bowl.

Always crack them one at a time into a clean bowl. That way a piece of shell can easily be removed; and if you crack open a bad egg, it won't contaminate the other ingredients.

**12** Egg whites that are to be beaten should always be at room temperature.

**13** When beating egg whites, make sure the bowl and beaters are immediately clean and free of any grease or oil.

**14** For beating egg whites stiff, bowls made of copper are considered best and ceramic is better than aluminum and plastic.

**15** Roll a lemon back and forth on a countertop, pressing down with your hand; it will release more juice.

**16** When measuring honey, molasses, or corn syrup, lightly grease or oil the inside of the measuring cup first; the liquid will run out of the cup easily, making the measurement more accurate.

**17** To make chopping sticky dried fruit easier, heat the knife or food chopper blades before using them.

**18** To keep fruits and nuts from settling to the bottom of baked goods, dredge them in flour before adding them to any mixture.

**19** Store flour in an airtight container, not the bag it came in.

**20** To prevent brown sugar from hardening, store it in an airtight container. Place a

damp piece of cloth or paper towel in a small plastic bag, prick the bag all over with a needle, and add it to the container.

**21** To clean utensils used for dough and other mixtures containing flour, use warm water, not hot.

**22** It is not necessary to wash a flour sifter. Simply place it in a plastic bag for storage and tie it tightly closed.

**23** When deep-frying cookies, do not overcrowd the deep-fryer, or the cookies will absorb oil and be greasy.

**24** Chilled dough is usually easier to handle when making rolled cookies. Make sure the dough is thoroughly chilled.

**25** When making rolled cookies, cut as many cookies as possible the first time the dough is rolled out; the dough dries out a little more every time it is rerolled.

**26** The yield will always vary depending on the amount dropped from a spoon, the size of a cutter used, or the thickness it has been rolled out to. Bar-type cookies usually start at 12 and go up from there, depending on the size of the bar you cut.

**27** Any smooth drop-cookie dough can be piped out using a pastry bag or cookie press.

**28** If you are baking only one sheet of cookies at a time, place the rack in the center position. If you are baking two sheets at a time, remember that those on the rack closest to the heat have the greatest chance of browning or burning; rotate the baking sheets once or twice if necessary. It's also best to place the sheets so that one is on the left and one is on the right to allow maximum circulation of heat.

**29** Use a wide spatula to transfer cookies from the baking sheets to wire racks to cool. Don't overlap the cookies, or they will stick to each other as they cool.

**30** Let the baking sheets cool before reusing them.

**31** Most cookie doughs and baked cookies can be stored in the freezer for 4 to 6 weeks. Double-wrap the dough or cookies and carefully label each package with the name of the cookie and date.

**32** Always allow enough room for cookies to spread on cookie sheets.

**33** There should be at least 2 inches around all sides of any cookie sheet, baking pan, etc., in the oven to allow for air circulation and even baking.

**34** I prefer to cool cookies on clean newspapers; the paper absorbs any oils as the cookies cool; I turn the cookies upside down to cool. Be sure to use only newspaper that is at least a week old, and never use paper with colored printing.

**35** If you find yourself in a kitchen without a baking sheet, bake cookies on an upside-down baking pan.

**36** Always test cookies for doneness after the minimum amount of time (if a recipe tells you to bake something for 10 to 12 minutes, check after 10 minutes). Oven temperatures vary; to be safe, check the first tray of cookies a little before the minimum time has elapsed.

**37** Soft cookies should be stored in airtight containers and crisp cookies should be stored in containers with loosely fitting lids or covers. To help keep cookies soft, add a slice of apple to the container: be sure to change the apple frequently. For best results, when you store soft cookies, including bar cookies, layer them between waxed paper. Never store crisp and soft cookies in the same container.

# SUBSTITUTIONS

| INGREDIENT | AMOUNT | SUBSTITUTE |
|---|---|---|
| Allspice | 1 teaspoon | ½ teaspoon cinnamon plus ½ teaspoon cloves |
| Arrowroot | 1½ teaspoons | 1 tablespoon flour plus 1½ teaspoons cornstarch |
| Baking powder | 1 teaspoon | ⅓ teaspoon baking soda plus ½ teaspoon cream of tartar |
| | | ¼ teaspoon baking soda plus ½ cup milk (decrease the liquid in the recipe by ½ cup) |
| Butter | 1 cup | 1 cup shortening plus ½ teaspoon salt |
| | | ¾ cup plus 2 tablespoon lard plus ½ teaspoon salt |
| | | 1 cup margarine |
| Buttermilk | 1 cup | 1 cup plain yogurt |
| | | 1 cup minus 1 tablespoon milk plus 1 tablespoon fresh lemon juice or vinegar |
| Chocolate (semisweet) | 1⅔ ounces | 1 ounce unsweetened chocolate plus 4 teaspoons sugar |
| Chocolate chips | 6 ounces | 2 squares unsweetened chocolate plus 2 tablespoons shortening and ½ cup sugar |
| Chocolate | 1 ounce | 3 tablespoons unsweetened cocoa powder plus 1 tablespoon fat |
| Cocoa (semisweet) | ¼ cup | 1 ounce chocolate (reduce the amount of fat in the recipe by 1½ teaspoons) |
| Corn syrup | 1 cup | 1 cup honey |
| | | 1 cup sugar (increase the liquid in the recipe by ½ cup) |
| Egg | 1 large | 2 large egg yolks plus 1 tablespoon water |
| Flour, all-purpose | 1 cup | 1 cup plus 2 tablespoons cake flour |
| | | 1 cup minus 2 tablespoons unsifted flour |
| | | 1½ cups bread crumbs |
| | | 1 cup rolled oats |
| Lemon extract | 1 teaspoon | 2 teaspoons grated lemon zest |
| Maple sugar | ½ cup | 1 cup maple syrup |
| | | 1 cup brown sugar |
| Milk, whole | 1 cup | 1 cup reconstituted nonfat dry milk plus 2 teaspoons melted butter or margarine |
| | | ½ cup evaporated milk plus ½ cup water |
| | | 1 cup buttermilk plus ½ teaspoon baking soda |
| Molasses | 1 cup | 1 cup honey |
| Sour cream | 1 cup | 1 cup plain yogurt |
| | | ¾ cup plus 2 tablespoon sour milk plus ⅓ cup butter |
| Sour milk | 1 cup | 1 cup plain yogurt |
| | | 1 cup minus 1 tablespoon milk plus 1 tablespoon fresh lemon juice or vinegar |
| Sugar, granulated | 1 cup | 1 cup corn syrup (decrease liquid in recipe by ¼ cup) |
| | | 1⅓ cups molasses (decrease the liquid in the recipe by ⅓ cup) |
| | | 1 cup brown sugar |
| | | 1 cup honey (decrease the liquid in the recipe by ¼ cup) |
| | | 1¾ cups packed powdered sugar |
| Vegetable shortening, melted | 1 cup | 1 cup cooking oil |
| Yogurt, plain | 1 cup | 1 cup buttermilk |
| | | 1 cup pureed cottage cheese |
| | | 1 cup sour cream |

# WEIGHTS AND MEASURES

Dash = 2 to 3 drops (less than ⅛ teaspoon)
1 teaspoon = 5 milliliters
1 tablespoon = 3 teaspoons = 15 milliliters
⅛ cup = 2 tablespoons = 1 fluid ounce = 30 milliliters
¼ cup = 4 tablespoons = 2 fluid ounces = 60 milliliters
½ cup = 8 tablespoons = 4 fluid ounces = 120 milliliters
1 cup = 16 tablespoons = 8 fluid ounces = 240 milliliters
1 pint = 2 cups = 16 fluid ounces = 480 milliliters
1 quart = 4 cups = 32 fluid ounces = 960 milliliters (.96 liter)
1 gallon = 4 quarts = 16 cups = 128 fluid ounces = 3.84 liters
1 ounce = 28.35 grams
¼ pound = 4 ounces = 114 grams
1 pound = 16 ounces = 454 grams
2.2 pounds = 1,000 grams = 1 kilogram

## NUTS

| | |
|---|---|
| 1 pound almonds in shell | 1 to 1¼ cups shelled nuts |
| 1 pound shelled almonds | 3 cups |
| 1 pound almonds slivered | 5⅔ cups nutmeat |
| 1 pound brazil nuts in the shell | 1½ cups shelled nuts |
| 1 pound shelled brazil nuts | 3¼ cups |
| 1½ cups unshelled chestnuts | 1 pound shelled chestnuts |
| 1 pound hazelnuts in the shell | 1½ cups shelled nuts |
| 1 pound shelled hazelnuts | 3½ cups |
| 1 pound peanuts in the shell | 2 to 2½ cups shelled nuts |
| 1 pound shelled peanuts | 3 cups |
| 1 pound pecans in the shell | 2¼ cups shelled nuts |
| 1 pound shelled pecans | 4 cups |
| 1 pound walnuts in the shell | 2 cups shelled nuts |
| 1 pound shelled walnuts | 4 cups |

## SUGAR

| | |
|---|---|
| 1 cup white granulated sugar | 1 cup raw sugar |
| | 1 cup brown sugar |
| | 1 cup powdered sugar |
| | 1¾ cups confectioner's sugar |
| 1 pound granulated sugar | 2¼ cups sugar |
| 1 pound brown sugar | 2¼ cups brown sugar |
| 1 pound powdered sugar | 4 cups powdered sugar |
| 1 tablespoon maple sugar | 1 tablespoon granulated sugar |

## EGGS

| | |
|---|---|
| 1 egg | 2 egg yolks |
| 1 cup egg yolks | yolks of 12 to 14 large eggs |
| 1 cup egg whites | whites of 8 large eggs |

## MILK & DAIRY

| | |
|---|---|
| 1 cup heavy cream | 2 cups whipped cream |
| ⅓ cup evaporated milk | ⅓ cup dry milk plus 6 tablespoons water |
| One 14-ounce can evaporated milk | 1⅔ cups |

xvi

## WEIGHTS AND MEASURES

### MILK & DAIRY *(continued)*

| | |
|---|---|
| 8 ounces sour cream | 1 cup |
| 1 pound cheese | 4 cups grated cheese |
| 8 ounces cream cheese | 6 tablespoons |

### FATS

| | |
|---|---|
| 1 stick butter or margarine | ½ cup |
| | 8 tablespoons |
| 2 sticks butter or margarine | 1 cup |
| 4 sticks butter or margarine | 2 cups |
| 1 cup butter or margarine | ⅞ cup lard |
| 1 cup hydrogenated fat | 6⅔ ounces |

### FRUIT

| | |
|---|---|
| 4 medium apples | 4 cups sliced apples |
| 1 pound apples (2 medium) | 3 cups sliced apples |
| 1 pound dried apricots | 3 cups dried apricots |
| 1 pound banana (3 medium) | 2 cups mashed bananas |
| 1 pint of berries | 1¾ cups |
| 3½ ounces flaked coconut | 1⅓ cup plus 4 ounces shredded coconut |
| 1⅓ cup 1 pound candied cherries | 3 cups |
| 1 pound pitted dates | 2–2½ cups chopped |
| 1 pound figs | 2⅔ cups chopped |
| 1 medium lemon | 1½ teaspoons grated lemon zest |
| | 2 tablespoons juice |
| 1 medium orange | 3 teaspoons grated orange zest |
| 1 pound prunes | 2¼ cups pitted prunes |
| 1 pound raisins | 3 cups |

### CHOCOLATE

| | |
|---|---|
| 1 square baking chocolate | 1 ounce |
| 1 ounce unsweetened chocolate | 4 tablespoons grated |
| 6 ounces chocolate chips | 1 cup chocolate chips |
| 1 pound cocoa powder | 4 cups cocoa powder |

### SPICES & HERBS

| | |
|---|---|
| 2 teaspoons crystallized ginger | 1 teaspoon chopped fresh ginger |
| ¼ teaspoon ground ginger | 1 teaspoon chopped fresh ginger |
| | 2 teaspoons chopped crystallized ginger |

### GRAINS

| | |
|---|---|
| 1 cup rolled oats | 5 ounces |
| 1 cup rice | 7½ ounces |
| 1 cup uncooked rice | 2 cups cooked rice |

### MISC

| | |
|---|---|
| 1 inch-piece vanilla bean | 1 teaspoon vanilla extract |
| 13 ounces molasses | 3 cups |
| 7 coarsely crumbled crackers | approximately 1 cup |
| 30 vanilla wafers | 1 cup |

# GLOSSARY OF INGREDIENT AND BAKING TERMS

**All-Purpose Flour** "The everything flour" for the home kitchen. It is a white wheat flour, bleached or unbleached, enriched with various vitamins and minerals.

**Almond Extract** An extract of almonds.

**Almond Paste** A creamy mixture of ground almonds, sugar, and egg whites, used in some recipes to give an enhanced almond flavor. (See Marzipan.)

**Amaretto** A liqueur with a nutty flavor, which can be used as a flavoring in baking.

**Anise Extract** An extract of anise seeds, used in company with the seeds in breads and cookies.

**Anise Seeds** Also called aniseed. An aromatic spice used in baking. (See Spices and Herbs.)

**Apricot Butter** A flavorful blend of apricot puree and butter.

**Arrowroot** A starch used in many older European recipes; it is not in wide use today. Usually interchangeable with cornstarch and in some cases wheat flour. (See Substitutions.)

**Bake** To cook food in an oven using air.

**Baking Powder** A leavening agent added to batters and doughs to cause them to rise during baking. Baking powder is a combination of baking soda and cream of tartar. It is usually added to mixtures that contain acids, and reacts with the liquids in the batter or dough, producing gas-bubbles. Double-acting baking powder, the most common type, will produce the bubbling effect, first during mixing and then in the heat of the oven.

**Baking soda** Baking soda, or bicarbonate of soda, is a leavening agent used alone or in combination with baking powder. Doughs or batters containing baking soda should be baked as soon as they are mixed because the soda starts reacting as soon as it comes into contact with a liquid. Dissolving the soda in a small amount of water before adding it to the other ingredients ensures that it dissolves completely.

**Banana Chips** Dried thin banana slices.

**Batter** A thin combination of flour, liquid, and other ingredients, such as eggs and flavorings.

**Beat** To make a mixture smooth and uniform by combining the ingredients with a rapid motion, using an implement or utensil such as a wire whisk, a spoon, an egg beater, or an electric mixer.

**Beaten egg whites,** stages of: **Frothy** means the mass of eggs whites in the bowl has formed small bubbles. **Soft peaks** means the peaks of the beaten whites fall back on themselves when the beater is removed from the bowl. **Stiff peaks** means the peaks hold their shape when the beater is removed, and there is a uniform consistency.

**Blend** To thoroughly mix ingredients together.

**Boil** To heat liquid so bubbles rise from the bottom of the cooking vessel and break on the surface.

**Bread** In baking or cooking, to coat ingredients with a thin layer of flour, cracker crumbs, cookie crumbs or bread crumbs, or another such ingredient.

**Brown Sugar** is a refined sugar that is a combination of molasses and granulated sugar. The amount of molasses determines whether the sugar will be light or dark brown; dark brown sugar has a stronger flavor.

**Brush** To spread liquid mixture or coating over the surface of a solid food. It also refers to brushing on and coating over an ingredient with a (pastry) brush.

**Butter** A dairy by-product made from sweet or sour cream. Butter contains not less than 80 percent butter-fat. It can be purchased salted and unsalted, also called sweet butter. Most butter is artificially colored. Whipped butter should never be substituted for regular butter in a recipe. Unlike vegetable shortening, butter adds a flavor all its own to the baked goods. To butter means to spread a thin layer of butter over a surface in preparation for baking.

**Buttermilk** Originally the liquid left over after making butter. Today it is commercially produced. It is used in many baking recipes.

**Cake Flour** A superfine flour milled from a soft wheat. It is too soft for general use, but it produces fine-grained cakes.

**Candied Fruit** Candied fruit has been dried and coated with sugar syrup. (See page xxvi.)

**Canned Milk** See Evaporated milk.

**Caramelize** To cook sugar until it melts and turns golden brown.

**Carob** Also called St. John's Bread. Often used as a chocolate substitute. The pod of the carob tree is available toasted and untoasted. Unlike chocolate it is water-soluble.

**Chill** To place food in a refrigerator or other cold place, or in a bowl of ice or in ice water, until cold.

**Chocolate** A processed product derived from the cocoa bean.(See page xxv.)

**Chop** To cut an ingredient into smaller pieces.

**Chutney** A relish made from fruits, herbs, and/or spices. In some cookie recipes, it can be a good substitute for jam or jelly.

**Citron** A citrus fruit larger, than a lemon, it is also less

acidic with a thicker peel. The fruit is not usually considered edible, but the rind is made into jam or preserves or candied, to decorate baked goods.

**Coat** To sprinkle, dredge, roll, or cover with or dip into flour or other dry or liquid ingredients.

**Cocoa** The powdered, unsweetened form of the cocoa bean. It is a by-product of chocolate liquor. (See page xxv.)

**Coconut** The fruit of the tropical coconut palm. The meat is sold in shredded, flaked, or sometimes chunk form. Some recipes also call for **Coconut Milk:** The liquid from a coconut that also comes sweetened and canned.

**Combine** To mix ingredients together.

**Cookie Press** A device for dropping or otherwise placing cookie dough onto a baking sheet.

**Cooking Oil** (See Vegetable Oil.)

**Cool** To let food stand at room temperature until it is no longer warm to the touch.

**Cornmeal** Coarsely ground corn kernels. Cornmeal contributes a crumbly texture to baked good.

**Cornstarch** A thickener made from corn that can sometimes be used in place of flour.

**Corn Syrup** A thick liquid sweetener available in light and dark forms. (The difference in color has no effect on the taste of the cookie.) Corn

syrup is considered by some cooks and bakers to be interchangeable with honey and molasses.

**Cream** To make an ingredient such as butter, or a mixture such as butter and sugar, soft, smooth, and creamy by pressing on it with the back of a spoon or beating it with an electric mixer.

**Cream of Tartar** A water-soluble powder that is mixed with baking soda to make baking powder.

**Cube** To cut an ingredient into small cubes, usually ½ inch in size.

**Currants** A small dark seedless fruit similar to raisins. Dried currants are actually raisins.

**Cut in** To distribute a solid fat throughout flour or a flour mixture by using a pastry blender, two knives, or the back of a fork. Usually the resulting mixture looks crumbly. An electric hand mixer can also do the job, but overmixing is more likely.

**Dates** The sweet fruit of a palm tree.

**Dice** To cut something into very small cubes, ¼ inch in size or less.

**Dissolve** To liquefy a solid, by adding it to a liquid ingredient, or to melt a solid ingredient.

**Drop Cookies** Cookies made from a dough that is dropped, usually from the end of a spoon onto the baking sheet.

**Dust** To sprinkle an ingredient with a light coating of, for example, flour or sugar.

**Enriched** Refers to a food product which has been resupplied with vitamins and minerals lost during processing.

**Evaporated Milk** Milk that has been processed to remove a percentage of its water, then sterilized and canned.

**Fat** Butter, margarine, shortening, lard, and oil of any kind.

**Flake** To shave or break into small thin pieces.

**Flour** One of the primary ingredients in baking; In this book "flour" refers to enriched all-purpose flour unless otherwise specified in the recipe.

**Flute** To make a decorative edge on a pie tart or other pastry product before baking, usually using your fingers.

**Fold in** To combine delicate mixtures such as whipped cream or beaten egg whites and other ingredients. Using a gentle circular motion, cut down through the mixture near the side of the mixing bowl with a spatula or other such utensil, then across the bottom of the bowl and up the other side, to bring some of the mixture up and over the surface.

**Formed Cookies** Cookies that are shaped by hand; also cookies made using a cookie press or a pastry bag. (See also Molded Cookies.)

**Frost** To spread icing or frosting over a baked good.

**Frosting** A coating, usually sugar-based, that is spread over the tops of cookies, either as a decoration or flavor-enhancer. Frosting is generally spread in a thicker layer then icing. (See Icing.)

**Fry** To cook food in a small amount of fat over high heat. To **deep-fry** is to fry or boil by completely immersing food in a large quantity of fat.

**Garnish** To decorate, add color, etc. to a finished dish with fruits or other foods.

**Glaze** To coat a baked good or other food with a sugar-based mixture or liquid.

**Grate** To rub an ingredient across a food grater or chop in a blender or food processor to produce fine, medium, or coarse particles. Often refers to the process of shaving small amounts of zest from citrus fruit.

**Grease** To rub the surface of a dish, pan, or other cooking or baking utensil with a fat such as butter or vegetable shortening to keep food from sticking to it.

**Grind** To reduce an ingredient, such as nuts, to smaller particles, usually using a food grinder or blender.

**Honey** A natural sweetener "produced by bees" sold in comb form or, usually, as an extracted liquid. In some recipes, honey can be used as a substitute for sugar.

**Icing** A sugar-based mixture that is spread over the surface of a cookie. Icing is generally spread in a thinner layer than frosting, which is creamier. (See Frosting.)

**Knead** To use your hand(s) to work a mixture (such as a dough), using a "press, fold over, and press" motion to make it smooth.

**Lard** White pork fat that has been rendered down to a solid fat. Lard was used in many baked goods that now use butter or vegetable shortening in its place.

**Liqueur** A sweet alcoholic beverage, usually distilled from fruit and/or flavored with spices.

**Liquor** An alcoholic beverage such as rum, brandy, bourbon, or vodka.

**Madeira** A fortified wine from the island of Madeira; it resembles well-matured, full-bodied sherry.

**Maple Sugar** A sugar made by evaporating maple syrup.

**Margarine** A solid cooking fat made from vegetable oil.

**Marrons** The French word for chestnut. *Marrons glacées* are chestnuts preserved in syrup or candied.

**Marzipan** A sweetened almond paste often made into confections; it is also used as an ingredient in baking and sometimes is spread over a baked good, such as a cake, instead frosting. (See Almond Paste.)

**Melt** To liquefy by heating

**Meringue** A mixture of stiffly beaten egg whites and sugar.

**Mocha** A coffee flavoring; chocolate is often added.

**Molasses** A thick, dark syrup produced in the processing of sugar.

**Molded Cookies** Cookies formed into a particular shape by using a mold of some kind.

**Nuts** Edible seeds of various trees. (See page xxii.)

**Pastry Bag** A cone-shaped bag that can be fitted with metal tips, through which frosting and decorative icing can be pressed onto cookies or other baked goods. (See Pipe.)

**Patty Shell** An edible container made from puff pastry, used to hold creamed mixtures, fruit, or ice cream.

**Pipe** To force a mixture such as frosting through a pastry tube or the end of a pastry bag, to decorate cookies.

**Peel** The skin of a citrus fruit.

**Port Wine** A fortified wine from Portugal.

**Preheat** To heat an oven to a desired temperature in preparation for baking.

**Phyllo** Paper-thin pastry sheets used to make rich pastries and cookies.

**Powdered Sugar:** Sugar that is ground to a fine powder and mixed with a small amount of corn starch to keep it from caking. In many recipes confectioners' sugar

and powdered sugar are used interchangeably. The difference between the two is in how finely they are ground.

**Raw Sugar** Sugar that has not been processed.

**Reduce** To decrease the volume of a liquid by rapid boiling in an uncovered pan.

**Rice Flour** Flour made from ground rice, with a sweeter taste than wheat flour. In most cookie recipes, rice flour can be substituted for about one-quarter of the wheat flour.

**Roll** To roll dough out thin using a rolling pin (on a floured board) or similar utensil.

**Rolled Cookies** Cookies formed by the rolling out dough and cutting it into desired shapes.

**Rolled Oats** Oats that have been hulled, steamed, and flattened. Rolled oats add a moist, sweet, chewy texture to baked goods. When toasted, they add a crunchy texture.

**Rose Water** A liquid made from the extracted oil of rose petals. It can usually be purchased at many drugstores.

**Scald** To heat a liquid to just below the boiling point.

**Score** To cut or press shallow lines in the surface of a food for decoration or for easy division after baking.

**Sesame Seeds** Also called benne seeds, used as a flavorful garnish in cookies and breads.(See Spices and Herbs, page xxiv.)

**Shortening** A fat produced from bleached refined hydrogenated vegetable oil or animal fat. High-quality shortening is a solid fat that is a very good substitute for butter in baking.

**Sherry** A dry wine often used in cooking.

**Simmer** To heat a liquid to a low boil, so that a few bubbles come to the surface.

**Sliver** To cut or shred an ingredient into thin lengths.

**Stir** To blend ingredients with a spoon, using a circular motion.

**Sugar** A sweetener available in many forms; granulated sugar is most commonly used in cooking.

**Sultanas** Small green seedless raisins.

**Sweetened Condensed Milk** Processed milk that has a greater concentration of sugar because water has been removed and sugar added. The milk has the consistency of thick honey.

**Toast** To brown an ingredient in an oven or by means of direct heat.

**Vanilla Extract** A flavoring extracted from the vanilla bean (See page xxvi.)

**Vanilla Bean** The pod of a vanilla orchid plant.

**Vegetable Oil** A cooking oil extracted from corn.

**Vinegar** An acid liquid used for flavoring and preserving. It can be used to add an unusual subtle flavor to cookie doughs.

**Whip**  To beat rapidly with a wire whisk or electric mixer to incorporate air and thereby increase the volume of the mixture.

**Wheat Germ**  The nucleus of the wheat kernel, where there is a concentrated source of vitamins.

## NUTS

Most nuts are available in a variety of forms, including unshelled or shelled, blanched (peeled or skinned) or unblanched, chopped, halved, sliced, or slivered. Cashew nuts are unique in that they are not sold in the shell. Although walnuts, almonds, and pecans are the nuts most commonly used in baking, many other types can result in delicious cookies and baked goods—hazelnuts and hickory nuts, to name just two.

The most inexpensive way to purchase any nuts is in the shell. As a general rule of thumb, one pound of unshelled nuts will equal half a pound of shelled. However, for ease and convenience, many home bakers prefer to buy shelled nuts. Although nuts in the shell stay fresh for a long time, keeping them in the lower part of the refrigerator will prolong their shelf life. Shelled nuts turn rancid quickly and are best kept in airtight containers in the freezer.

The recipes in this book use sliced, slivered, chopped, and ground nuts as well as whole nuts. Chopped means that the nuts are in small corn kernel-size chunks. Ground is when the nut has been reduced to a very coarse, almost powder form.

**Almond**  The fruit of the almond tree can be purchased shelled or unshelled, blanched, or unblanched, slivered, sliced, and chopped. The shell is soft and easy to crack open. Unblanched almonds have a soft brown color; blanched nuts are a pale ivory color.

**Black Walnuts**  Black walnuts were once used extensively in baking recipes, but more widely available English walnuts have replaced them in popularity. Black Walnuts are still preferred by many cooks and bakers; if you come across them, you will want to try baking with these flavorful nuts.

**Brazil Nut**  Although brazil nuts were once available only during the Christmas holiday season, now they are available all year long. They are large nuts most effectively used ground or chopped in cookie recipes.

**Cashew**  This is one of the most popular eating nuts in the world. For baking purposes they are considered a soft nut.

**Chestnuts**  Chestnuts are available fresh in the winter and canned all year around. The best way to prepare fresh chestnuts for cookie recipes is to score them on the bottom and toast them in the oven to loosen their outer shells and skins.

**English Walnuts**  In the United States this is the most

popular nut for cooking purposes. (See Black Walnuts.)

**Filbert** (See Hazelnuts.)

**Hazelnuts** The hazelnut, also called filbert, is one of the most flavorful of all nuts. Hazelnuts are far more popular in Europe than in the United States, which is unfortunate in light of the nut's rich taste.

**Macadamia Nuts** The macadamia nut is one of the most expensive nuts in the world, partly, no doubt, because it takes up to five years before the macadamia tree can start to bear fruit. In addition, macadamia nut trees have never been successfully transplanted to mainland United States. Macadamia nuts have a rich, buttery flavor and are usually toasted in coconut oil.

**Peanut** This small slick nut (actually a legume), is the most popular eating nut in the United States. Half of the peanut crop is blended into peanut butter, but peanuts turn up in a variety of baked goods, including peanut butter cookies, a perennial favorite.

**Pecans** Many cooks and bakers prefer the pecan to any other nut; pecans are especially popular in the southern regions of the United States, where they grow profusely.

**Pine Nuts** Known as *piñon* in Spanish and *pignola* in Italian, the pine nut is usually considered more of an eating nut

than a baking nut, but it works very well in a variety of cookies because of its rich, full flavor.

**Pistachio Nuts** These nuts, when shelled and toasted work extremely well in cookies because of their complex flavor that melds so well with a variety of spices.

## FRUITS

Hundreds of cookie recipes that include fruit in various states—fresh, dried, or frozen.

Dried fruit should be rehydrated before use. The process of rehydration is simply nothing more than soaking the dried fruit in boiling water or another liquid.

**Apples** Although apples are available throughout the year, they are at their peak in the fall. Cored and sliced dried apples should usually be hydrated before they are used. Applesauce is added to many recipes both to make the cookies softer and to give them a fresh apple taste. Canned apples are not suitable for cookies.

**Apricots** Fresh apricots are generally available only in season, from May through July. But dried apricots are delicious. Canned apricots tend to be flavorless if used for baking.

**Bananas** Bananas are available every day of the year. There are two varieties: One is for eating and drying, the other, easily recognizable by

its dark skin color, is for cooking. The cooking banana is also smaller than the eating banana. Most home bakers use the eating variety for cooking. Dried banana chips are also available.

**Berries** Fresh berries including strawberries, blackberries, blueberries, boysenberries, raspberries, black raspberries, are available only in season. We are fortunate that they are always available in the form of jams and preserves which are used in many cookie recipes.

**Cherries** Fresh cherries are seldom used in cookie baking. They are seldom used as an additive in cookies. (See Glacé/Candied Cherries.)

**Dates** The fruit of the date palm tree has been used for centuries, as far back as ancient Egypt, as a means of sweetening dishes. Most of the recipes here call for pitted dates.

**Figs** It is surprising that so few cookie recipes use figs. Fig Newtons are one of this country's most popular cookies.

**Lemon Zest** Zest and juice of the lemon rind is seldom used in any state other than grated. This adds a pleasing lemon flavor to the cookies in which it is used.

**Orange Zest** Only the zest and the juice of the orange may be used in baking. The cookies using this zest may have a subtle or strong flavor, depending upon the amounts used.

**Peaches** Only dried peaches are appropriate for cookies; canned peaches do not hold up under the heat of cooking and become mushy. Fresh peaches may be sliced and layered in bar cookies. Peach puree can be used as a flavor in cookie recipes.

**Persimmons** A seasonal fruit with a sweet flavor, the persimmon really isn't edible until it is overripe. When the skin starts to turn brown and the pulp inside becomes almost mushy, it is ready to eat or use.

**Pineapple** Pineapples are readily available all year round, but for baking the canned fruit is most popular because of ease of preparation. It should be well drained before using. Candied pineapple is also good in cookies.

**Prunes** Dried prunes are used pitted, sliced, or diced in recipes.

### SPICES AND HERBS

**Allspice** These berries, the seeds of the allspice tree, are harvested and sun-dried until they are a deep reddish brown. They are made available whole and ground. Their flavor resembles a soft blend of cloves, cinnamon, and nutmeg (hence the name). Allspice is used to flavor cakes, pies, cookies, and breads. It is especially good in pastries made with fruit.

**Anise** Anise seeds, or aniseed, are greenish brown with a strong licorice flavor. They are available whole or crushed. Anise seeds are used extensively in cookies and fruit pies, especially in holiday specialties.

**Apple pie spice** This is a commercial blend of cinnamon, cloves, nutmeg, and some other sweet-type spices. It is used mainly for pies, but in baking, it can be substituted in any recipe that calls for cinnamon or nutmeg.

**Caraway seeds** Small greenish brown crescent-shaped seeds. Although caraway seeds are perhaps most associated with rye bread, they can be very flavorful in cookies and cakes. The seeds are always sold whole.

**Cardamom** A member of the ginger family, has a long history; its use has been documented as early as the fourth century B.C. It is available whole or ground. Its sweet flavor makes it a favorite spice in Danish pastries, and it is also used in cakes of all kinds and many cookies. Cardamom is the third most expensive spice in the world.

**Cinnamon** The bark of a laurel tree; it and its cousin cassia are the two oldest spices known. Both are available in reddish brown rolled sticks or ground. Its sweet pungent taste makes cinnamon one of our most popular spices, used in cakes, pies, cookies, breads,

puddings, and other baked goods.

**Cloves** Cloves are the dried bud of a tropical tree. They have a strong, pungent flavor. Cloves are available both whole and ground; the ground form is used in many cakes, cookies, pies, and fruit desserts; whole cloves are occasionally used in sweets, such as baklava.

**Coriander** The seed of the coriander, or cilantro plant; it is available whole or ground. The ground seeds are used in cookies, cakes, pies, candies, and other sweets.

**Cumin** An aromatic seed very similar to caraway seeds in flavor. It is available as seeds or ground.

**English spice** Commercial blend of several spices with a predominately cinnamon-allspice flavor. It can be used on its own or as a substitute in any baked good that calls for cinnamon, allspice, nutmeg, and cloves.

**Fennel seeds** These have a mild licorice flavor. They are used in breads and breakfast baked goods.

**Ginger** Fresh ginger, or ginger root, and the powdered, or dried spice have a hot sweet-spicy flavor. Ginger, both fresh and dried, is used in cakes, breads, cookies, and fruit desserts. Crystallized, or candied, ginger is preserved fresh ginger that has been rolled in sugar.

**Mace** The lacy outer membrane-like covering of the shell of the nutmeg. Its flavor is sweet, warm, and highly spicy. Mace is usually seen as a powder, but it is also available in flakes or blades.

**Mint** A perennial herb; peppermint and spearmint are the most popular varieties for flavorings. The dried leaves are available whole, crushed, and powdered.

**Nutmeg** The seed of the nutmeg tree. It has a sweet-hot taste and a pungent aroma. Available whole or ground, it is used in cakes, pies and cookies. (See Mace.)

**Poppy seeds** These have a sweet nut-like taste. The tiny black seeds are used extensively to garnish breads, rolls, and cookies.

**Sesame seeds** Known as benne seeds in the South, these are used to garnish breads, rolls, and cookies. When toasted, the seeds have a very nutty flavor.

**Vanilla bean** The seed capsule of the vanilla orchid. From this bean is derived the flavoring used to make vanilla extract. The bean itself is used in the preparation of vanilla sugar.

**Vanilla extract** A liquid derived from the vanilla bean and used extensively as a flavoring in baking and cooking. Synthetic vanillas are available for a lesser price.

## CHOCOLATE

For our purposes, cocoa powder, unsweetened chocolate, semisweet or bittersweet chocolate, chocolate syrup, and chocolate chips are the foundations of the world of the chocolate cookie.

Unsweetened chocolate means baker's-style chocolate. Baker's-style chocolate is bitter chocolate and is the base for most other chocolate products. It can be found in the supermarket in the baking section in 14- to 16-ounce packages. The chocolate is divided into small squares, and each square weighs one ounce.

Semisweet chocolate, sometimes called bittersweet, is packaged the same way, too, but there is a wide variety of imported bittersweet or semisweet chocolate available as well.

Cocoa is the powdered form of chocolate. For baking, use unsweetened cocoa powder, not the sweet cocoa for drinking.

Milk chocolate has long been a favorite of the candy-loving public. But milk chocolate can't be used interchangeably with other types of chocolate in most recipes.

White chocolate has gained in popularity in recent years. White chocolate is not actually chocolate, because it contains no chocolate liquor. It is cocoa butter with sugar and milk added.

Many of the recipes in this book call for melting chocolate. It isn't difficult if you follow a few separate rules. Chocolate should always be melted over low heat in an absolutely dry pan. *Dry* is the key word. When you are melting chocolate by itself, the slightest drop of liquid or moisture can cause the chocolate to seize, or to become stiff and lumpy. (If you are adding other ingredients, the general rule of thumb is one tablespoon of liquid to one ounce of chocolate. It is the minute amounts of liquid that cause the trouble.) *For this reason, the pan melting the chocolate in should never be covered* because condensation may form on the lid and drip into the chocolate. If chocolate should seize, you often can save it by stirring in one teaspoon per ounce of chocolate of vegetable shortening. (*Do not use butter or margarine.*)

Chocolate burns easily, so using a double boiler is recommended. If you don't have one, you can put the chocolate in a heatproof cup and place it in a saucepan partially filled with water, over very low heat. (Milk chocolate should be melted at a lower temperature than unsweetened or semisweet chocolate.) Then stir the chocolate occasionally, until it is smooth.

A microwave oven also works well for melting. Consult your owner's manual for instructions with your particular microwave.

## MISCELLANEOUS

**Candied Beads** *(Silver or Gold Balls)* Candied beads or balls have been around for many years. They are used more for decoration, especially for holiday cookies.

**Candied Citron** The citron is rarely available in the United States. At a time when oranges and lemons were not readily available, its peel was used in place of other members of the citrus family.

**Chocolate Candies** Usually the chocolate candies used in cookies are of the wafer type, such as mints or pralines.

**Chocolate Chips** In the early 1900s Ruth Wakefield, who worked at the The Tollhouse Inn in Massachusetts, chopped a baker's style bar of chocolate and added the pieces to a batch of cookie dough, making the first chocolate chip cookies. Because of that woman's inventiveness, a whole industry developed. In addition to semisweet chocolate chips, there are now butterscotch, peanut butter, and white chocolate used in baking.

**Glacé/Candied Cherries** This form of dried cherries sweetened with sugar are used diced up in cookie recipes, and as decorative toppings on cookies.

**Jelly Candies** Like other candies, they are used more for a decoration than for flavor. Jelly candies and gumdrops are used whole, or are chopped and added to the dough.

**Jimmies** These candies come in chocolate or rainbow colors, and are a great addition to many cookies.

**Sugar Crystals** These are sprinkled on the cookies after they have been formed and or baked. Like candy beads, they are added to a cookie strictly for decoration. They come colored or white.

## FLAVORINGS

Using liqueur or brandy in cookie recipes opens up a whole new world of flavoring possibilities, while keeping your costs at a minimum.

Each liqueur or brandy listed below is as economical as a small 1- or 2-ounce bottle of vanilla extract. If the products are kept well-corked or capped, there is little chance of them going bad before you have time to use them. Also, most of the imitation flavoring products have little or no alcohol, and have a better chance of going bad than the flavored liqueur. There is a world of flavoring out there in addition to those you see in the grocery store. (See Alternate Flavorings, page xxvii.)

| Liqueur/Brandy | Flavor |
|---|---|
| Abisante | anise and herb |
| Advokaat | eggnog |
| Ari | plum |
| Amaretto | apricot almond |
| Amaretto/Cognac | amaretto |
| Ambrosia Liqueur | caramel |
| Amer Picon | orange |
| Anisette | anise |
| Antioqueno | anise |
| Apry | apricot |
| Arak | rum |
| Ashanti Gold | chocolate |
| Averna Liqueur | herbal |
| Irish Cream | fresh cream |
| Baitz Island Creme | almond |
| | coconut |
| | chocolate |
| Barenjäger | honey |
| Benedictine | herbal |
| Blackberry Brandy | blackberry |
| Boggs Cranberry | cranberry |
| Bucca di Amore | anise |
| | herb |
| | spices |
| Cafe Brizard | coffee |
| Cafe orange | coffee & orange |
| Cafe Lolita | coffee |
| Campari | orange/caramel |
| | vanilla |
| Carmella | vanilla |
| Chambord Liqueur | raspberry |
| | fruit |
| | herb |
| | honey |
| CherriStock | cherry |
| Cherry Brandy | cherry |

| Liqueur/Brandy | Flavor |
|---|---|
| Choclair | chocolate/coconut |
| Cinnamon Schnapps | cinnamon |
| Club Raki | licorice |
| Coffee Brandy | coffee |
| Coffee Liqueur | coffee |
| Cranberria | cranberry |
| Conticream | chocolate cream |
| Crème de Almond | almond |
| Crème de Banana | banana |
| Crème de Cacao | chocolate |
| Crème de Cafe | coffee |
| Crème de Cassis | black currant |
| Crème de Framboise | raspberry |
| Crème de Menthe | peppermint |
| Crème de Prunella | plum |
| Crème de Strawberry | strawberry |
| Cuarenta Y Tres | vanilla |
| Droste Bittersweet | bittersweet chocolate |
| Fraise des Bois | wild strawberry |
| Ginger Brandy | ginger |
| Ginger Schnapps | ginger |
| Kümmel | caraway |
| Lemonier | lemon |
| Lemonique | tart lemon |
| Mandarinette | tangerines |
| Mandarino | tangy orange |
| | cherry |
| Marron Liqueur | chestnut |
| Midori | honeydew melon |
| Paso Fino Rum | rum |
| Peach Brandy | peach |
| Pear William | Anjou pear |
| Peppermint Schnapps | peppermint |
| Peter Herring | cherry |
| Praline Liqueur | vanilla & pecan |
| Spearmint Schnapps | spearmint |
| Straretto | strawberry |

# Pantry

These recipes are standard frostings, icings, fillings, and bar cookie crusts. They are referenced for use throughout the main cookie recipe text.

## FROSTINGS AND ICINGS

### RICH BUTTERCREAM
YIELD: 2 TO 2½ CUPS
½ cup butter, at room temperature
3½ cups powdered sugar
⅛ teaspoon salt
1 large egg yolk
About 1 tablespoon milk

In a large bowl, cream the butter. Beat in the powdered sugar. Beat in the salt and egg yolk. Add just enough milk to make a spreadable frosting. Flavor the buttercream with any of the following suggestions, or add a flavoring of your own choice. (Note: Buttercream frostings have a tendency to soften during hot weather. If this happens, beat in a little cornstarch to bring the mixture back to the desired consistency.)

For the following flavored buttercreams use the Rich Buttercream recipe with the added flavorings.

### VANILLA BUTTERCREAM
Add 1 teaspoon vanilla extract.

### ALMOND BUTTERCREAM
Add 1 teaspoon almond extract or Amaretto.

### ORANGE BUTTERCREAM
Add 1 teaspoon orange liqueur.

### LEMON BUTTERCREAM
Add 1 teaspoon lemon extract.

### RUM BUTTERCREAM
Add 1 teaspoon rum.

### BRANDY BUTTERCREAM
Add 1 teaspoon brandy or cognac.

### COCOA BUTTERCREAM
Add 1 teaspoon crème de cacao.

### RASPBERRY BUTTERCREAM
Add 1 teaspoon raspberry liqueur.

### COFFEE BUTTERCREAM
Add 1 teaspoon strong coffee.

### APRICOT BUTTERCREAM
Add 1 teaspoon apricot brandy.

### DECORATING BUTTERCREAM
YIELD: 4 TO 4½ CUPS
2 cups vegetable shortening
4 cups powdered sugar
1 to 2 large egg whites
Pinch of salt
Vanilla or other flavoring to taste

In a large bowl, cream the shortening. Gradually beat in the powdered sugar. Beat in the egg whites. Beat in the salt. Beat in the flavoring. Remember that a little flavoring goes a long way; think in terms of drops, not spoonfuls. (Note: Buttercream frostings have a tendency to soften during hot weather. If this happens, beat in a little cornstarch to bring the mixture back to the desired consistency.)

### CHOCOLATE FROSTING I
YIELD: 2 TO 2½ CUPS
5⅓ tablespoon butter, at room temperature
½ cup Dutch process unsweetened cocoa powder
Pinch of salt
3 tablespoons boiling water
1½ cups powdered sugar, or more if necessary

In a large bowl, cream the butter. Beat in the cocoa. Add the salt and boiling water, stirring until you have a smooth paste. Beat in the powdered sugar and beat until the frosting reaches a spreadable consistency. If it seems too thick, add a few drops of water; if it seems too thin, add a little more powdered sugar.

### CHOCOLATE FROSTING II
YIELD: 1 TO 1½ CUPS
1½ ounces unsweetened chocolate, chopped
1 tablespoon butter, at room temperature
¼ cup sour cream
½ teaspoon vanilla extract
1½ cups powdered sugar, or more if necessary

Melt the chocolate in a double boiler over low heat, stirring until smooth. Remove from the heat and beat in the butter and sour cream. Beat in the vanilla extract. Gradually beat in the powdered sugar and beat until the frosting reaches a spreadable consistency. If it seems too thick, add a few drops of water; if it seems too thin, add a little more powdered sugar.

### CHOCOLATE FROSTING III
YIELD: 1 TO 1¼ CUPS
1 cup (6 ounces) semisweet chocolate chips
2 teaspoons boiling water
2 tablespoons light corn syrup
2 teaspoons strong brewed coffee

Place the chocolate chips in a small bowl and pour the boiling water over them. Start beating and add the corn syrup and coffee. If it seems too thick, add a few drops of water; if it seems too thin, add a little more powdered sugar.

### DARK CHOCOLATE ICING
YIELD: 1 TO 1½ CUPS
6 ounces unsweetened chocolate, chopped
2 tablespoons butter, at room temperature
1 teaspoon vanilla extract
⅛ teaspoon salt
2 cups powdered sugar
⅓ cup milk

Melt the chocolate in the top of a double boiler over low heat, stirring until smooth. Remove from the heat and beat in the butter. Beat in the vanilla and salt. Gradually beat in the powdered sugar. Beat in just enough milk to make a spreadable frosting.

## VANILLA ICING I

YIELD: ABOUT ½ CUP

**½ cup powdered sugar**
**1 tablespoon water**

Put the powdered sugar in a small bowl. Beat in the water and continue beating until the icing reaches the desired consistency. If the icing is too thick, add more water; if it is too thin, add more powdered sugar.

## VANILLA ICING II

YIELD: 2 TO 2¼ CUPS

**3 cups powdered sugar**
**⅓ cup evaporated milk**
**1½ teaspoons vanilla extract**

Put 1 cup of the powdered sugar in a medium bowl and beat in the milk and vanilla extract. Gradually beat in the remaining 2 cups powdered sugar and continue beating until the icing reaches the desired consistency. If the icing is too thick, add more water; if it is too thin, add more powdered sugar.

## LEMON SUGAR ICING

YIELD: ABOUT ½ CUP

**½ cup powdered sugar**
**1 teaspoon fresh lemon juice**
**1 tablespoon water**

Put the powdered sugar in a small bowl. Beat in the lemon juice and water and continue beating until the icing reaches the desired consistency. If the icing is too thick add more water; if it is too thin add more powdered sugar.

**Baking notes:** For a tarter lemon taste, use lemon extract in place if the lemon juice.

## FILLINGS

## ALMOND CREAM FILLING

YIELD: 1¾ TO 2 CUPS

Combine 1½ cups heavy cream, 1 cup powdered sugar, and 1 cup finely ground almonds in a medium saucepan and bring to a boil, stirring frequently. Cook, stirring constantly, until the mixture has thickened and reduced to about 2 cups. Remove from the heat and stir in 2 tablespoons Amaretto.

## APPLE FILLING

YIELD: 2½ TO 3 CUPS

Peel, core, and thinly slice 5 apples. Place them in a large saucepan and add just enough water to cover. Bring to a boil and cook, stirring, occasionally, until the apples are very soft. Drain well and transfer to a medium bowl. Mash the apples with a wooden spoon or potato masher. Add ½ cup powdered sugar, 2 tablespoons Amaretto, 1 tablespoon fresh lemon juice, 1 tablespoon grated lemon zest, and ⅛ teaspoon ground nutmeg and stir until well blended.

## CHOCOLATE CHEESECAKE FILLING

YIELD: 3 TO 3½ CUPS

In a large bowl, combine 1 pound room-temperature cream cheese, ¾ cup unsweetened cocoa powder, and ½ cup granulated sugar and beat until smooth and creamy. Beat in 4 large eggs one at a time, beating well after each addition. Beat in 2 tablespoons chocolate syrup.

## COCONUT-PECAN FILLING

YIELD: 2½ TO 3 CUPS

Combine 1 cup evaporated milk, 3 large egg yolks, 1 cup granulated sugar, ½ cup vegetable shortening, and 1 teaspoon coconut flavoring in a large saucepan and cook over medium-low heat, stirring, until thick, 10 to 12 minutes. (Do not let the mixture boil.) Remove from the heat and stir in 1 cup flaked coconut and 1 cup chopped pecans. Let cool.

## LEMON FILLING

YIELD: 2 TO 2½ CUPS

In a large bowl, combine 4 large eggs and 2 cups granulated sugar and beat until thick and light-colored. Beat in ⅓ cup all-purpose flour, 6 tablespoons lemon juice concentrate, and 1 teaspoon grated lemon zest. (This filling is to be poured over a partially baked crust and then baked until set and firm to the touch.)

## PUMPKIN CHEESECAKE FILLING

YIELD: 3¼ TO 4 CUPS

In a large bowl, combine 11 ounces room-temperature cream cheese and ⅔ cups granulated sugar and beat until smooth and creamy. Beat in 16 ounces solid-pack pumpkin, 3 large eggs, 1½ teaspoons ground cinnamon, and 1 teaspoon vanilla extract (or another flavoring of your choice).

## VANILLA SUGAR

YIELD: 1½ TO 2 CUPS

Rinse a vanilla bean in cold water and dry thoroughly with paper towels. Put 1½ to 2 cups sugar in a pint jar, add the vanilla bean, and shake well. Let stand for a few days, shaking the jar occasionally, before using the flavored sugar. Replenish the jar as you use it.

## BAR COOKIE CRUSTS

Here are almost twenty-one ideas for bar cookie crusts. (These are to be spread or patted into the bottom of a baking pan and partially baked before a topping or filling is spread over the crust and baked until done.) But, in fact, these should provide you with ideas for dozens of crusts. Any of these combinations can be varied according to your personal taste. For example, in a recipe that calls for all-purpose flour, you could substitute whole wheat flour, rice flour, or even buckwheat flour for some (usually no more than about a quarter) of the white flour. Or use vegetable shortening in place of butter in a crust. Or replace granulated sugar with brown sugar or raw sugar. Use your favorite nuts in any nut crust, or your favorite cookies in a crumb crust. And of course you can also change the flavoring, substituting another extract for vanilla, adding a liqueur, and so forth.

Use your imagination, but do keep one guideline in mind. If you are changing the crust in a favorite recipe, be sure to replace it with a similar crust, one that "matches" the filling or topping as in the original recipe. A filling that is very runny before it is baked, for example, needs the right kind of crust to support the unbaked filling. A crust that takes a long time to bake will not be cooked if combined with a topping that takes only minutes to bake. Keep baking times in mind when you are experimenting. Have fun!

See Bar Cookies in the text for basic procedures for combining particular ingredients to make a crust.

**1**
1 cup all-purpose flour
½ cup powdered sugar
6 tablespoons butter
1 tablespoon heavy cream

**2**
3 cups all-purpose flour
1 cup granulated sugar
1 cup butter
4 large eggs, separated
2 large egg yolks
½ teaspoon salt

**3**
16 graham crackers, crushed
½ cup granulated sugar
¼ cup butter

**4**
1 cup all-purpose flour
¾ cup granulated sugar
½ cup butter
⅓ cup milk
1 large egg
¾ teaspoon Amaretto

**5**
1 cup all-purpose flour
½ cup butter
¼ teaspoon salt

**6**
24 gingersnaps, crushed
¼ cup powdered sugar
½ cup canola oil

**7**
2 cups all-purpose flour
¼ cup granulated sugar
½ cup butter
¼ cup walnuts, ground fine

**8**
1½ cups whole wheat flour
¾ cup butter
2 tablespoons granulated sugar

**9**
1¼ cups all-purpose flour
½ cup vegetable shortening
¼ teaspoon salt
3 tablespoons ice water

**10**
1 cup all-purpose flour
½ cup powdered sugar
½ cup butter
½ cup shredded coconut
¼ teaspoon salt

**11**
1½ cups all-purpose flour
⅔ cup granulated sugar
½ cup butter
3 large egg yolks
2 tablespoons milk

**12**
1⅓ cups all-purpose flour
½ cup packed light brown sugar
⅓ cup butter
½ teaspoon baking powder
½ cup almonds, chopped

**13**
2 cups all-purpose flour
3 tablespoons powdered sugar
2 large egg yolks
1 teaspoon instant coffee
   crystals
1 tablespoon water

**14**
1⅓ cups crushed gingersnaps
¼ cup packed light brown sugar
2 tablespoons butter
3½ ounces macadamia nuts,
   ground fine
1½ teaspoons crystallized ginger, chopped

## 15

1 cup all-purpose flour
¼ cup light brown sugar
6 tablespoons butter
½ cup pecans, chopped fine
¼ teaspoon salt

## 16

1⅓ cup all-purpose flour
½ cup packed light brown sugar
⅓ cup butter
½ teaspoon baking powder
¼ cup hazelnuts, ground fine

## 17

1 cup all-purpose flour
½ cup packed light brown sugar
½ cup butter
¼ teaspoon ground cloves
½ teaspoon ground ginger
¼ teaspoon ground nutmeg

## 18

1½ cups all-purpose flour
½ cup butter
¼ teaspoon salt
2½ tablespoons warm water

## 19

2 cups all-purpose flour
¼ cup granulated sugar
½ cup butter
½ cup walnuts, ground fine

## 20

2 cups all-purpose flour
2 cups packed light brown sugar
1 cup butter

## 21

1 cup all-purpose flour
¾ cup packed light brown sugar
⅓ cup butter
2 large egg yolks
1 cup shredded coconut

# RECIPES A TO Z

5½ cups all-purpose flour
1½ cups granulated sugar
1½ teaspoons baking powder
1½ cups vegetable shortening
3 large eggs
3 tablespoons milk, or more if
  needed
3 tablespoons caraway seeds
1½ teaspoons grated lemon zest

**1** Preheat the oven to 375 degrees.

**2** In a large bowl, combine the flour, sugar, and baking powder. Cut in the shortening until the mixture resembles coarse crumbs.

**3** In another bowl, beat the eggs, milk, caraway seeds, and lemon zest until well blended. Blend into the dry ingredients until smooth. If the dough seems too stiff, add a little more milk 1 teaspoon at a time.

**4** On a floured surface, roll out the dough ¼ inch thick. Using a 2-inch round cookie cutter, cut out cookies and place 1½ inches apart on ungreased baking sheets.

**5** Bake for 7 to 10 minutes, until the edges are lightly browned. Transfer to wire racks to cool.

**Baking notes:** Sweet creams or a lemon sugar frosting can be drizzled over the tops of these cookies, or they can be served plain at teatime with jam or preserves. For variation, this dough can be rolled out to a thickness of ⅛ inch and used to make sandwich cookies. The filling can be melted chocolate or a thick lemon custard. (See Pantry for recipes.)

# ABERNATHY BISCUITS

Rolled Cookies

YIELD: *2 to 3 dozen*
TOTAL TIME: *30 minutes*

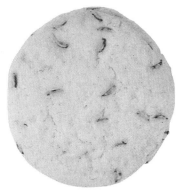

---

⅓ cup pitted dates, chopped fine
½ cup boiling water, or more to
  cover dates
1 cup all-purpose flour
¼ cup unsweetened cocoa powder
1 teaspoon baking powder
¾ cup vegetable shortening
¼ cup granulated sugar
1 teaspoon vanilla extract
2 cups cornflakes

**1** Preheat the oven to 350 degrees.

**2** Place the chopped dates in a small cup and cover with the boiling water for 10 to 15 minutes. Drain and discard the liquid.

**3** Combine the flour, cocoa, and baking powder.

**4** In a large bowl, cream the vegetable shortening and sugar until

light and fluffy. Stir in the dates. Beat in the vanilla extract. Gradually blend in the dry ingredients. Fold in the cornflakes.

**5** Break off walnut-sized pieces of the dough and roll into balls. Place 1½ inches apart on ungreased baking sheets.

**6** Bake for 12 to 15 minutes, or until firm to the touch. Transfer to wire racks to cool.

**Baking notes:** The balls can be rolled in finely chopped nuts before baking. They can also be dredged in powdered sugar after baking, but these are quite sweet, so taste one before you decide to roll them in sugar.

# AFGHANS

Formed Cookies

YIELD: *3 to 4 dozen*
TOTAL TIME: *30 minutes*

# ALL-BRAN COOKIES

Refrigerator Cookies

YIELD: *5 to 6 dozen*
TOTAL TIME: *30 minutes*

3 cups all-purpose flour
2 teaspoons baking powder
1 cup vegetable shortening
2 cups packed light brown sugar
1 large egg
1 cup All-Bran

**1** Combine the flour and baking powder.

**2** In a large bowl, cream the vegetable shortening and brown sugar until smooth. Beat in the egg. Fold in the All-Bran. Gradually blend in the dry ingredients.

**3** Roll the dough into a log 1½ inches in diameter. Wrap in waxed paper and chill until ready to bake.

**4** Preheat the oven to 375 degrees. Grease 2 baking sheets.

**5** Slice the log into ¼-inch-thick slices and place about 1 inch apart on the prepared baking sheets.

**6** Bake for 12 to 15 minutes, until the edges are lightly browned. Transfer to wire racks to cool.

**Baking notes:** Any type of bran cereal can be used in this recipe.

# ALMOND AWARDS

Bar Cookies

YIELD: *1 to 2 dozen*
TOTAL TIME: *50 minutes*

**CRUST**
1 cup all-purpose flour
½ teaspoon salt
½ cup vegetable shortening
½ cup granulated sugar
1 tablespoon grated lemon zest

**TOPPING**
½ cup vegetable shortening
½ cup granulated sugar
1 cup heavy cream
1 cup almonds, ground

**1** Preheat the oven to 375 degrees. Lightly grease an 11 by 7-inch baking pan.

**2** To make the crust, combine the flour and salt.

**3** In a large bowl, cream the shortening and sugar. Beat in the lemon zest. Gradually blend in the dry ingredients.

**4** Press the dough evenly over the bottom of the prepared baking pan. Bake for 12 minutes. Transfer pan to wire rack to cool slightly.

**5** Meanwhile, make the topping: Melt the shortening in a small saucepan. Stir in the sugar, cream, and almonds.

**6** Spread the almond topping over the warm crust. Bake for 20 minutes longer, or until firm to the touch.

**7** Cool in the pan on a wire rack before cutting into large or small bars.

# ALMOND BALLS

Formed Cookies

YIELD: *5 to 6 dozen*
TOTAL TIME: *35 minutes*

⅔ cup vegetable shortening
1 cup granulated sugar
2 large egg yolks
2 cups all-purpose flour
½ cup almonds, ground
Vegetable oil for deep-frying

**1** In a large bowl, cream the shortening and sugar until light and fluffy.

**2** In another bowl, beat the egg yolks until thick and light-colored. Beat the yolks into the shortening mixture.

**3** Gradually blend in the flour and ground almonds. The dough will be stiff. If it seems too dry, add a little water ½ teaspoon at a time.

**4** Break off walnut-sized pieces of the dough and roll into balls.

**5** In a deep-fryer or a deep heavy saucepan, heat the oil to 375 degrees. Fry the cookies, in batches, until golden brown. Drain on paper towels.

**Baking notes:** Be sure the oil is hot enough, or the cookies will absorb some of the oil. After the balls are cool, they can be sprinkled with powdered sugar or dipped in melted chocolate.

# ALMOND BARS I

Bar Cookies

YIELD: *2 to 3 dozen*
TOTAL TIME: *35 minutes*

½ cup all-purpose flour
¼ teaspoon baking powder
2 large eggs, separated
Pinch of salt
1 cup packed light brown sugar
1 teaspoon vanilla extract
⅓ cup butter, at room temperature
1 cup almonds, ground
Powdered sugar for dusting

1  Preheat the oven to 350 degrees. Lightly grease and flour a 9-inch square baking pan.

2  Combine the flour and baking powder.

3  In a large bowl, beat the egg whites with the salt until foamy. Gradually beat in the brown sugar. Beat in the vanilla extract. Blend in the flour mixture.

4  In another bowl, beat the egg yolks and butter until well blended.

5  Gradually fold the butter mixture into the egg-white mixture. Fold in the almonds.

6  Press the dough evenly into the prepared pan. Bake for 20 to 25 minutes, or until the top is a golden brown. Cool in the pan on a wire rack.

7  Dust with powdered sugar and cut into large or small bars.

**Baking notes:** If you like, drizzle white sugar icing over the top of these cookies in a crisscross pattern before cutting them into bars. For a festive look, use a colored icing and cut the bars into bite-sized pieces.

# ALMOND BARS II

Bar Cookies

YIELD: *1 to 2 dozen*
TOTAL TIME: *45 minutes*

2 large eggs
1 cup packed light brown sugar
1 ounce bittersweet chocolate, grated
½ teaspoon almond extract
¼ cup almonds, ground
1 tablespoon baking powder
¼ teaspoon ground cinnamon
2 cups all-purpose flour

1  Preheat the oven to 350 degrees. Lightly grease a 9-inch square baking pan.

2  In a large bowl, beat the eggs until thick and light-colored. Beat in the brown sugar. Beat in the chocolate and almond extract. Beat in the almonds, baking powder, and cinnamon. Gradually blend in the flour.

3  Spread the dough evenly into the prepared pan.

4  Bake for 28 to 30 minutes, or until the top is golden brown.

Cool in the pan on a rack before cutting into large or small bars.

**Baking notes:** For variation, spread half the dough in the bottom of a 8- or 9-inch square baking pan and bake for 8 to 10 minutes. While still warm, spread with 2 to 3 tablespoons of your favorite jam or preserves. Spread the remaining dough over the jam and bake for 12 to 15 minutes longer, or until the top is golden brown. Or prepare and bake the bars as directed. Meanwhile, beat 2 large egg whites with ¼ teaspoon salt until stiff but not dry. Fold in ¼ cup granulated sugar. While the cookies are still warm, spread the egg whites over the top. Sprinkle with ¼ cup ground almonds and bake for 8 to 10 minutes longer.

# ALMOND BARS III

Bar Cookies

YIELD: *1 to 2 dozen*
TOTAL TIME: *30 minutes*

**CRUST**
1 large egg yolk
1 teaspoon vanilla extract
1 cup vegetable shortening
½ cup granulated sugar
½ cup packed light brown sugar
2 cups all-purpose flour

**TOPPING**
9 ounces milk chocolate, chopped
½ cup almonds, chopped

**1** Preheat the oven to 350 degrees. Grease a 9-inch square baking pan.

**2** To make the crust, in a medium bowl, beat the egg yolk until thick and light-colored. Beat in the vanilla extract.

**3** In a large bowl, cream the vegetable shortening, granulated sugar, and brown sugar. Beat in the egg yolk. Gradually blend in the flour. The dough will be stiff.

**4** Press the dough evenly into the prepared pan. Bake for 18 to 20 minutes, or until the top is golden brown.

**5** Meanwhile, melt the chocolate in a double boiler over low heat, stirring until smooth. Remove from the heat.

**6** Spread the melted chocolate over the top of the warm cookies. Sprinkle with the almonds. Cool in the pan on a rack before cutting into large or small bars.

**Baking notes:** The chocolate can be baking chocolate, chocolate chips, or a candy bar. For variation, use white chocolate. For a stronger almond taste, use almond extract in place of the vanilla extract.

# ALMOND BARS IV

Bar Cookies

YIELD: *3 to 4 dozen*
TOTAL TIME: *45 minutes*

**CRUST**
1 cup all-purpose flour
½ cup powdered sugar
½ cup shredded coconut
¼ teaspoon salt
½ cup vegetable shortening

**TOPPING**
1 package white frosting mix
½ cup flaked coconut
½ cup almonds, chopped
½ teaspoon almond extract
½ cup semisweet chocolate chips

**1** Preheat the oven to 375 degrees.

**2** To make the crust, combine the flour, powdered sugar, coconut, and salt. Cut in the vegetable shortening until the mixture resembles coarse crumbs.

**3** Spread the mixture evenly in an ungreased 13 by 9-inch baking

pan. Bake for 12 minutes, until light-colored.

**4** Meanwhile, make the topping: Prepare the frosting mix according to the package directions. Stir in the coconut, almonds, and almond extract.

**5** Sprinkle the chocolate chips over the top of the warm cookies. Let sit for 1 to 2 minutes, or until melted, then spread the chocolate evenly over the cookies. Spread the frosting mixture over the chocolate.

**6** Cool in the pan on a rack before cutting into large or small bars.

**Baking notes:** You can use all shredded or all flaked coconut, but the two types together give more varied texture to the cookies.

**CRUST**
½ cup vegetable shortening
⅓ cup granulated sugar
3 large egg yolks
1½ cups all-purpose flour
2 tablespoons milk

**TOPPING**
3 large egg whites
1 cup granulated sugar
1½ cups almonds, chopped
Granulated sugar for sprinkling

**1** Preheat the oven to 350 degrees. Grease a 9-inch square baking pan.

**2** To make the crust, cream the vegetable shortening and sugar in a large bowl. Add the egg yolks one at a time, beating well after each addition. Gradually blend in the flour until a soft dough forms.

**3** On a floured surface, roll out the dough to a 9-inch square. Fit the dough into the prepared pan.

**4** To make the filling, beat the egg whites in a large bowl until stiff. Fold in the sugar, then fold in the almonds.

**5** Spread the filling over the pre-pared crust. Sprinkle a little sugar on top.

**6** Bake for 18 to 20 minutes, or until topping is lightly browned. Cool in the pan on a rack before cutting into large or small bars.

**Baking notes:** Grated chocolate can be sprinkled over the top of the bars after baking.

# ALMOND BARS V

Bar Cookies
YIELD: *1 to 2 dozen*
TOTAL TIME: *35 minutes*

---

**CRUST**
1⅓ cups all-purpose flour
½ teaspoon baking powder
⅓ cup butter, at room temperature
½ cup packed light brown sugar
¼ cup almonds, chopped

**TOPPING**
2 large eggs
¾ cup light corn syrup
1½ teaspoons almond extract
¼ cup packed light brown sugar
3 tablespoons all-purpose flour
½ teaspoon salt
¾ cup almonds, ground

**1** Preheat the oven to 350 degrees. Grease a 13 by 9-inch baking pan.

**2** To make the crust, combine the flour and baking powder.

**3** In a large bowl, cream the but-ter and brown sugar. Blend in the dry ingredients. Fold in the chopped almonds.

**4** Press the mixture evenly over the bottom of the prepared pan. Bake for 10 minutes.

**5** Meanwhile, make the topping: In a large bowl, beat the eggs until foamy and light-colored. Beat in the corn syrup and almond extract. Blend in the brown sugar, flour, and salt.

**6** Pour the topping mixture over the warm crust. Sprinkle the chopped almonds over the top.

**7** Bake for 30 minutes longer, or until a toothpick inserted in the center comes out clean. Cool in the pan on a rack before cutting into large or small bars.

**Baking notes:** These cookies are very rich.

# ALMOND BARS VI

Bar Cookies
YIELD: *2 dozen*
TOTAL TIME: *50 minutes*

# ALMOND BITS

Formed Cookies

YIELD: *6 dozen*
TOTAL TIME: *30 minutes*

2 cups all-purpose flour
1 teaspoon baking powder
¾ teaspoon ground cardamom
1 teaspoon ground cinnamon
½ teaspoon salt
½ cup vegetable shortening
½ cup granulated sugar
½ cup packed light brown sugar
1 large egg
1 teaspoon almond extract
60 whole blanched almonds

1  Preheat the oven to 350 degrees.

2  Combine the flour, baking powder, spices, and salt.

3  In a large bowl, cream the vegetable shortening and both sugars. Beat in the egg and vanilla extract. Gradually blend in the dry ingredients.

4  Divide the dough into 4 pieces. Roll each piece into a 15-inchlong rope. Cut each rope into 1-inch-long pieces.

5  Press an almond into each cookie, and place 1 inch apart on ungreased cookie sheets.

6  Bake for 12 to 14 minutes, until the edges are golden brown. Transfer to wire racks to cool.

# ALMOND BUTTERBALLS

Formed Cookies

YIELD: *3 to 4 dozen*
TOTAL TIME: *35 minutes*

1 cup (6 ounces) semisweet chocolate chips.
¾ cup butter, at room temperature
1 tablespoon milk
2 teaspoons almond extract
½ cup granulated sugar
½ teaspoon salt
½ cup almonds, ground
2 cups all-purpose flour
Powdered sugar for coating

1  Preheat the oven to 350 degrees.

2  Melt the chocolate chips in a double boiler over low heat, stirring until smooth. Remove from the heat and stir in the butter, milk, almond extract, sugar, and salt. Fold in the almonds. Gradually blend in the flour.

3  Break off walnut-sized pieces of dough and roll into balls. Roll the balls in powdered sugar and place 1 inch apart on ungreased baking sheets.

4  Bake for 12 to 15 minutes, or until firm to the touch. Let cool slightly.

5  Roll the cookies in the powdered sugar when cool.

**Baking notes:**  These cookies should be stored in a loosely covered container. To make *Walnut Butterballs*, substitute vanilla extract for the almond extract and walnuts for the almonds. For *Hazelnut Butterballs*, substitute hazelnut flavoring for the almond extract and hazelnuts for the almonds.

# ALMOND BUTTER COOKIES I

Rolled Cookies

YIELD: *2½ dozen*
TOTAL TIME: *45 minutes*

1¼ cups all-purpose flour
¼ cup granulated sugar
¾ cup butter
1 teaspoon almond extract
⅛ teaspoon salt
1 large egg white, lightly beaten

**TOPPING**
¼ cup granulated sugar
1 tablespoon finely ground toasted almonds
⅛ teaspoon ground cinnamon

1  In large bowl, beat together the flour, sugar, butter, almond extract, and salt. The dough will be crumbly. Cover and chill for at least 4 hours.

2  Preheat the oven to 350 degrees.

3  On a floured surface, roll out the dough to a 12 by 8-inch rectangle. Cut lengthwise into 1-inch-wide strips. Then cut each strip into 4 pieces and place 1 inch apart on ungreased baking sheets.

4  Brush the tops of the cookies with the beaten egg white. Let stand for 20 minutes.

5  To make the topping, combine all of the ingredients in a small bowl. Sprinkle evenly over the cookies.

6  Bake for 10 to 12 minutes, or until the cookies are very light brown. Transfer to wire racks to cool.

**Baking notes:**  For a different texture, coarsely grind the almonds for the topping. Sprinkle on the sugar and cinnamon, then sprinkle on the almonds.

# ALMOND BUTTER COOKIES II

Formed Cookies

YIELD: *4 to 6 dozen*
TOTAL TIME: *35 minutes*

2 cups all-purpose flour
1 teaspoon baking powder
1 cup butter, at room temperature
1 cup granulated sugar
2 large egg yolks
½ teaspoon lemon extract
¾ teaspoon almond extract
½ teaspoon vanilla extract
About 70 whole blanched almonds

1  Preheat the oven to 300 degrees.

2  Combine the flour and baking powder.

3  In a large bowl, cream the butter and sugar until light and fluffy. Beat in the egg yolks and the extracts. Blend in the dry ingredients.

4  Break off walnut-sized pieces of dough and roll into balls. Place 1½ inches apart on ungreased baking sheets.

5  Press an almond into the center of each cookie flattening them slightly. Bake for 15 to 20 minutes, until the cookies are golden brown. Transfer to wire racks to cool.

# ALMOND CAKES I

Drop Cookies

YIELD: *4 to 5 dozen*
TOTAL TIME: *30 minutes*

2 cups all-purpose flour
½ teaspoon baking powder
1 cup vegetable shortening
½ cup granulated sugar
2 teaspoons ground ginger
½ teaspoon almond extract
About 60 whole blanched almonds

1  Preheat the oven to 350 degrees.

2  Combine the flour and baking powder.

3  In a large bowl, cream the vegetable shortening and sugar. Beat in the ginger and almond extract. Gradually blend in the dry ingredients.

4  Drop the dough by teaspoonfuls onto ungreased baking sheets. Flatten each cookie slightly with the back of a spoon dipped in flour. Press an almond into the center of each cookie.

5  Bake for 12 to 15 minutes, until the cookies are a nice golden brown. Transfer to wire racks to cool.

**Baking notes:**  The ginger flavor will be more noticeable if the dough is refrigerated for 24 hours before baking. Melted almond bark or chocolate can be drizzled over the tops of the cooled cookies if desired.

# ALMOND CAKES II

Rolled Cookies

YIELD: *7 to 8 dozen*
TOTAL TIME: *30 minutes*

3 cups all-purpose flour
1½ teaspoons baking powder
5 large eggs
1½ cups packed light brown sugar
1 cup almonds, ground

**1** Preheat the oven to 350 degrees. Lightly grease 2 baking sheets.

**2** Combine the flour and baking powder.

**3** In a large bowl, beat the eggs until thick and light-colored. Beat in the brown sugar. Beat in the almonds. Gradually blend in the dry ingredients.

**4** On a floured surface, roll out the dough ¼ inch thick. Using cookie cutters, cut into shapes and place 1½ inches apart on the prepared baking sheets.

**5** Bake for 10 to 12 minutes, until the cookies are lightly colored and the edges are beginning to brown. Transfer to wire racks to cool.

# ALMOND CAKES III

Formed Cookies

YIELD: *5 to 6 dozen*
TOTAL TIME: *30 minutes*

2 large eggs
1 cup granulated sugar
½ teaspoon vanilla extract
1 cup almonds, ground
1 cup all-purpose flour

**1** Preheat the oven to 400 degrees. Lightly grease 2 baking sheets.

**2** In a large bowl, beat the eggs until thick and light-colored. Beat in the sugar and vanilla extract. Beat in the almonds. Gradually blend in the flour.

**3** Break off 1-inch pieces of dough and roll into balls. Place 2 inches apart on the prepared baking sheets.

**4** Bake for 8 to 10 minutes, or until a light golden color. Transfer to wire racks to cool.

**Baking notes:** The balls of dough can be flattened and a half a glacé cherry or a nut pressed into each one before baking. Or, the cookies can be dipped in melted chocolate after they have cooled.

# ALMOND CAKES IV

Formed Cookies

YIELD: *5 to 6 dozen*
TOTAL TIME: *40 minutes*
CHILLING TIME: *1 hour*

1 cup vegetable shortening
1 cup granulated sugar
3 large eggs
1 tablespoon water
¼ teaspoon almond extract
3 cups all-purpose flour
½ cup almonds, ground

**1** In a large bowl, cream the vegetable shortening, and sugar. Beat in the eggs. Beat in the water and almond extract. Gradually blend in the flour and almonds.

**2** Cover and chill for at least 1 hour.

**3** Preheat the oven to 350 degrees. Lightly grease 2 baking sheets.

**4** Break off 1-inch pieces of dough and roll into balls. Place 1½ inches apart on the prepared baking sheets.

**5** Bake for 15 to 20 minutes, until the edges of the cookies are golden brown. Transfer to wire racks to cool.

3 cups all-purpose flour
1½ teaspoons baking powder
5 large eggs
1½ cups packed light brown sugar
1 cup almonds, ground

**1** Preheat the oven to 350 degrees. Lightly grease 2 baking sheets.

**2** Combine the flour and baking powder.

**3** In a large bowl, beat the eggs until thick and light-colored. Beat in the brown sugar. Beat in the almonds. Gradually blend in the dry ingredients.

**4** On a lightly floured surface, roll out the dough ¼ inch thick. Using cookie cutters, cut into shapes and place 1½ inches apart on the prepared baking sheets.

**5** Bake for 10 to 12 minutes, until the edges are golden brown. Transfer to wire racks to cool.

# ALMOND CAKES V

Rolled Cookies

YIELD: *4 to 5 dozen*
TOTAL TIME: *30 minutes*

---

1½ cups vegetable shortening
1 cup granulated sugar
3 large egg yolks
1 teaspoon almond extract
4 cups all-purpose flour
1 large egg white, beaten
Granulated sugar for sprinkling

**1** Preheat the oven to 350 degrees.

**2** In large bowl, cream the vegetable shortening and sugar. Beat in the egg yolks one at a time, beating well after each addition. Beat in the almond extract. Gradually blend in the flour.

**3** On a floured surface, roll out the dough ⅛ inch thick. Cut into 1-inch squares and place 1 inch apart on ungreased baking sheets.

**4** Brush the tops of the cookies with the beaten egg white. Sprinkle with a little sugar.

**5** Bake for 12 to 15 minutes, until the edges are golden brown. Transfer to wire racks to cool.

**Baking notes:** For variation, combine 1 tablespoon granulated sugar, ½ teaspoon cinnamon, and 1 teaspoon finely chopped almonds and sprinkle on top of the squares before baking.

# ALMOND CAKES VI

Rolled Cookies

YIELD: *2 to 3 dozen*
TOTAL TIME: *30 minutes*

---

**CRUST**
½ cup butter
3 tablespoons powdered sugar
2 large egg yolks
1 teaspoon instant coffee granules
1 tablespoon warm water
2 cups all-purpose flour, or more if needed

**FILLING**
½ cup semisweet chocolate chips
2 large egg whites
Pinch of salt
¼ cup granulated sugar
¼ cup almonds, ground
¼ cup almonds, chopped

**1** Preheat the oven to 350 degrees. Lightly grease a 9-inch square baking pan.

**2** To make the crust, combine the butter, powdered sugar, egg yolks, coffee, and water in a large bowl and beat until smooth. Blend in the flour. The mixture should be crumbly. If necessary, add a little more flour.

**3** Press the mixture evenly over the bottom of the prepared pan. Bake for 20 minutes.

**4** Meanwhile, make the filling: Melt the chocolate chips in a double boiler over low heat, stirring until smooth. Let cool slightly.

**5** In a large bowl, beat the egg whites with the salt until frothy. Gradually beat in the sugar and beat until stiff peaks form. Fold in the melted chocolate. Fold in the almonds.

**6** Spread the filling over the hot crust. Sprinkle the chopped almonds over the top. Bake for 20 minutes longer, until topping is set. Cool in the pan on a rack before cutting into large or small bars.

# ALMOND-COFFEE DELIGHTS

Bar Cookies

YIELD: *1 to 3 dozen*
TOTAL TIME: *50 minutes*

**A**

# ALMOND COOKIES I

Drop Cookies

YIELD: *3 to 5 dozen*
TOTAL TIME: *30 minutes*

½ cup butter, at room temperature
½ cup granulated sugar
1 large egg
2 teaspoons Amaretto
½ cup almonds, ground
1¼ cups all-purpose flour

**1** Preheat the oven to 400 degrees.

**2** In a large bowl, cream the butter and sugar. Beat in the egg and Amaretto. Beat in the almonds. Gradually blend in the flour.

**3** Drop the dough by teaspoonfuls 1½ inches apart onto ungreased baking sheets.

**4** Bake for 5 to 7 minutes, until the cookies are light golden brown. Transfer to wire racks to cool.

# ALMOND COOKIES II

Refrigerator Cookies

YIELD: *4 to 5 dozen*
TOTAL TIME: *35 minutes*
CHILLING TIME: *1 hour*

½ cup vegetable shortening
½ cup butter, at room temperature
2½ cups all-purpose flour
1¼ cups granulated sugar
½ teaspoon baking soda
¼ teaspoon salt
1 large egg
½ teaspoon almond extract
½ cup almonds, ground
¼ cup ground almonds
4 ounces semisweet chocolate, chopped

**1** In a large bowl, cream the vegetable shortening and butter. Blend in 1 cup of the flour. Beat in the sugar, baking soda, and salt. Beat in the egg and almond extract. Gradually blend in the remaining 1½ cups flour and the ground almonds.

**2** Roll the dough into a 1-inch-thick log. Roll the log in the ground almonds. Wrap in waxed paper and chill for 1 hour.

**3** Preheat the oven to 350 degrees.

**4** Cut the dough into ¼-inch-thick slices and place 1 inch apart on ungreased baking sheets.

**5** Bake for 8 to 10 minutes, until the tops are very light golden brown. Transfer to wire racks to cool.

**6** Melt the chocolate in a double boiler over low heat, stirring until smooth. Dip half of each cookie in the melted chocolate. Let cool on wire racks lined with waxed paper.

# ALMOND COOKIES III

Refrigerator Cookies

YIELD: *3 to 4 dozen*
TOTAL TIME: *30 minutes*
CHILLING TIME: *4 hours*

1 cup all-purpose flour
½ cup granulated sugar
1 teaspoon baking powder
1 teaspoon salt
⅓ cup vegetable shortening
1 tablespoon milk
½ teaspoon almond extract
1 tablespoon Vanilla Sugar (see Pantry)

**1** Combine the flour, granulated sugar, baking powder, and salt in a large bowl. Cut in the vegetable shortening until the mixture resembles coarse crumbs. Stir in the milk and almond extract until a dough forms.

**2** Turn the dough out onto a work surface and shape into a loaf 12 inches long by 1½ inches wide by 1 inch high. Wrap in waxed paper and refrigerate for at least 4 hours.

**3** Preheat the oven to 350 degrees.

**4** Cut the loaf into ⅛-inch-thick slices and cut each slice on the diagonal into 2 triangles. Place the cookies 1¼ inch apart on ungreased baking sheets and sprinkle with the Vanilla Sugar.

**5** Bake for 10 to 12 minutes, or until the cookies just start to color. Transfer to a wire racks to cool.

**Baking notes:** Add a little ground cinnamon to the vanilla sugar for sprinkling if you like.

⅓ cup vegetable shortening
½ cup packed light brown sugar
1 cup almonds, ground
1 cup rice flour

**1** Preheat the oven to 350 degrees.

**2** In a large bowl, cream the vegetable shortening and brown sugar. Beat in ¾ cup of the almonds. Gradually blend in the rice flour.

**3** Break off walnut-sized pieces of dough and roll into balls. Roll the balls in the remaining ¼ cup almonds and place 1 inch apart on ungreased baking sheets. Flatten each cookie with the bottom of a glass dipped in flour.

**4** Bake for 10 to 12 minutes, until the edges of the cookies just start to color. Transfer to wire racks to cool.

**Baking notes:** If you find cookies made with all rice flour a little too grainy for your taste, try half rice flour and half all-purpose flour.

# ALMOND COOKIES IV

Formed Cookies

YIELD: *4 to 5 dozen*
TOTAL TIME: *30 minutes*

---

CRUST
1⅓ cups all-purpose flour
2 teaspoons baking powder
½ teaspoon salt
⅓ cup vegetable shortening
1 cup granulated sugar
2 large eggs
2 teaspoons almond extract
1 cup flaked coconut

TOPPING
1 tablespoon all-purpose flour
½ cup packed light brown sugar
1 large egg
¼ cup evaporated milk
½ cup almonds, chopped

**1** Preheat the oven to 350 degrees. Lightly grease a 9-inch square baking pan.

**2** To make the crust, combine the flour, baking powder and salt.

**3** In a large bowl, cream the vegetable shortening and sugar. Beat in the eggs and almond extract. Gradually blend in the flour mixture. Fold in the coconut.

**4** Press the mixture evenly over the bottom of the prepared pan.

**5** To make the topping, combine all the ingredients in a medium bowl and beat until well blended. Spread the topping evenly over the prepared crust.

**6** Bake for 35 to 40 minutes, until the topping has set. Let cool in the pan on a rack before cutting into large or small bars.

# ALMOND COOKIES V

Bar Cookies

YIELD: *2 to 3 dozen*
TOTAL TIME: *60 minutes*

---

1 cup butter, at room temperature
⅔ cup granulated sugar
3 large egg yolks
½ cup almonds, ground fine
½ teaspoon almond extract
½ teaspoon fresh lemon juice
2½ cups all-purpose flour

**1** Preheat the oven to 400 degrees.

**2** In a large bowl, cream the butter and sugar. Beat in the egg yolks. Beat in the almonds, then beat in the almond extract and lemon juice. Gradually blend in the flour.

**3** Place the dough in a cookie press or a pastry bag fitted with a star tip. Press or pipe out the dough onto ungreased baking sheets, spacing the cookies about 1 inch apart.

**4** Bake for 10 to 12 minutes, until lightly colored. Transfer to wire racks to cool.

# ALMOND COOKIES VI

Formed Cookies

YIELD: *2 to 3 dozen*
TOTAL TIME: *30 minutes*

# ALMOND COOKIES VII

Refrigerator Cookies

YIELD: *8 to 9 dozen*
TOTAL TIME: *30 minutes*
CHILLING TIME: *4 hours*

2 cups all-purpose flour
¾ cup almonds, ground fine
½ teaspoon ground cinnamon
½ teaspoon ground cloves
½ teaspoon ground nutmeg
½ cup vegetable shortening
½ cup granulated sugar
1 large egg
1 teaspoon almond extract
½ teaspoon grated lemon zest

**1** Combine the flour, almonds, and spices.

**2** In a large bowl, cream the vegetable shortening and sugar. Beat in the egg and almond extract. Beat in the lemon zest. Gradually blend in the dry ingredients.

**3** Divide the dough into 4 pieces. Roll each piece into a log about 6 inches long. Wrap in waxed paper and chill in the refrigerator for at least 4 hours, or overnight.

**4** Preheat the oven to 350 degrees. Lightly grease 2 baking sheets.

**5** Cut the dough into 1¼-inch-thick slices and place 1 inch apart on the prepared baking sheets.

**6** Bake for 6 to 8 minutes, or until the cookies are light golden brown. Transfer to wire racks to cool.

# ALMOND-CHERRY COOKIES

Rolled Cookies

YIELD: *4 to 5 dozen*
TOTAL TIME: *30 minutes*

½ cup vegetable shortening
1 cup granulated sugar
1 large egg yolk
½ teaspoon lemon extract
½ teaspoon almond extract
½ teaspoon grated orange zest
1¼ cups all-purpose flour
½ cup almonds, ground fine
25 to 30 glacé cherries, halved

**1** Preheat the oven to 350 degrees.

**2** In a large bowl, cream the vegetable shortening and sugar. Beat in the egg yolk, almond extract, and lemon extract. Beat in the orange zest. Gradually blend in the flour.

**3** On a floured surface, roll out the dough ¼ inch thick. Using cookie cutters, cut into shapes. Dredge the cookies in the ground almonds and place 1¼ inches apart on ungreased baking sheets.

**4** Press a glacé cherry half into the center of each cookie.

**5** Bake for 12 to 15 minutes, until the cookies are golden brown. Transfer to wire racks to cool.

**Baking notes:** For a different look, omit the ground almonds and sprinkle colored sugar crystals over the cookies as soon as they come from the oven.

1 cup vegetable shortening
1 cup granulated sugar
1 large egg, separated
1 large egg yolk
4 hard-boiled large egg yolks, crumbled
1 tablespoon grated lemon zest
3 cups all-purpose flour
¼ cup almonds, ground
Granulated sugar for sprinkling

1  Preheat the oven to 350 degrees.

2  In a large bowl, cream the vegetable shortening and sugar until smooth. Beat in the egg yolks. Beat in the hard boiled egg yolks one at a time, beating well after each addition. Beat in the lemon zest. Gradually blend in the flour.

3  In a medium bowl, beat the egg white until stiff but not dry.

4  Break off small pieces of dough and form into crescent shapes. Dip in the beaten egg white and place 1 inch apart on ungreased baking sheets. (See Baking notes).

5  Sprinkle the cookies with the almonds and sugar. Bake for 10 to 12 minutes, until lightly colored. Transfer to wire racks to cool

**Baking notes:**  If you prefer, place the cookies on the baking sheets and then brush with the beaten egg whites.

# ALMOND CRESCENTS I

Formed Cookies

YIELD: *2 to 4 dozen*
TOTAL TIME: *30 minutes*

---

1¼ cups all-purpose flour
½ teaspoon baking powder
¼ teaspoon salt
½ cup butter, at room temperature
½ cup powdered sugar
⅓ cup almonds, ground

1  Preheat the oven to 350 degrees.

2  Combine the flour, baking powder, and salt.

3  In a large bowl, cream the butter and powdered sugar. Gradually stir in the flour mixture. If the dough is very stiff, add a little water ½ tablespoon at a time. Fold in the almonds.

4  Break off small pieces of dough and form into crescent shapes. Place 1-inch apart on ungreased baking sheets.

5  Bake for 8 to 12 minutes, until lightly colored. Transfer to wire racks to cool.

**Baking notes:**  This dough may also be rolled out on a floured surface and cut into shapes with cookie cutters. Remember that a soft dough makes the most tender cookies, so don't use too much flour for rolling.

# ALMOND CRESCENTS II

Formed Cookies

YIELD: *2 to 3 dozen*
TOTAL TIME: *35 minutes*

# ALMOND CRISPS I

Refrigerator Cookies

YIELD: *3 to 4 dozen*
TOTAL TIME: *30 minutes*
CHILLING TIME: *4 hours*

1¾ cups all-purpose flour
1 teaspoon cream of tartar
⅛ teaspoon salt
½ cup vegetable shortening
¾ cup granulated sugar
2 large eggs, separated
½ teaspoon almond extract
1½ teaspoons baking soda
1½ teaspoons warm water
2 tablespoons milk
¼ cup almonds, ground
Granulated sugar for sprinkling

**1** Combine the flour, cream of tartar, and salt.

**2** In a large bowl, cream the vegetable shortening and sugar. Beat in the egg yolks and almond extract.

**3** Dissolve the baking soda in the warm water and add to the egg yolk mixture, beating until smooth. Add the milk, beating until smooth. Gradually blend the dry ingredients. Fold in the almonds.

**4** Roll the dough into a log about 2 inches in diameter. Wrap in waxed paper and chill for at least 4 hours.

**5** Preheat the oven to 375 degrees.

**6** Cut the dough into ⅛-inch-thick slices and place 2 inches apart on ungreased baking sheets.

**7** In a medium bowl, beat the egg whites until stiff but not dry. Brush the cookies with the beaten whites and sprinkle with sugar.

**8** Bake for 10 to 12 minutes, until lightly colored. Transfer to wire racks to cool.

**Baking notes:** For variation, roll the log of dough in additional ground almonds before chilling.

# ALMOND CRISPS II

Rolled Cookies

YIELD: *4 to 5 dozen*
TOTAL TIME: *35 minutes*
CHILLING TIME: *24 hours*

3 cups all-purpose flour
½ teaspoon baking powder
1 cup vegetable shortening
1 cup granulated sugar
1 large egg
2 tablespoons rum
½ cup almonds, ground
1 tablespoon grated lemon zest

TOPPING
¼ cup granulated sugar
½ teaspoon ground cinnamon

**1** Combine the flour and baking powder.

**2** In a large bowl, cream the vegetable shortening and sugar. Beat in the egg and rum. Stir in the almonds and lemon zest. Gradually blend in the dry ingredients.

**3** Cover the dough and chill for at least 24 hours.

**4** Preheat the oven to 325 degrees.

**5** Divide the dough into 4 pieces. Work with one piece at a time, keeping the remaining dough

refrigerated. On a lightly floured surface, roll out the dough ⅛ inch thick. Using cookie cutters, cut into shapes and place about 1¼ inches apart on ungreased baking sheets.

**6** Combine the sugar and cinnamon for the topping and sprinkle over the cookies.

**7** Bake for 10 to 12 minutes, until lightly colored. Transfer to wire racks to cool.

**Baking notes:** For a festive look, use colored sugar crystals in place of the granulated sugar for the topping.

1½ cups all-purpose flour
¼ teaspoon salt
½ cup vegetable shortening
⅓ cup packed light brown sugar
1 large egg
1 teaspoon almond extract
¼ teaspoon baking soda
½ teaspoon warm water
1½ cups almonds, ground

**1** Combine the flour and salt.

**2** In a large bowl, cream the vegetable shortening and brown sugar. Beat in the egg and almond extract.

**3** Dissolve the baking soda in the warm water and add to the egg mixture, beating until smooth. Gradually blend in the flour mixture.

**4** Form the dough into a log about 2 inches in diameter. Roll the log in the almonds. Wrap in waxed paper and chill for at least 8 hours.

**5** Preheat the oven to 350 degrees.

**6** Cut the dough into ¼-inch-thick slices and place about 1¼ inches apart on ungreased baking sheets.

**7** Bake for 12 to 15 minutes, until the cookies just start to color. Transfer to wire racks to cool.

**Baking notes:** The cookies may be frosted with an icing of your choice (see Pantry), or press an almond half into the center of each cookie.

# ALMOND CRISPS III

Refrigerator Cookies

YIELD: *3 to 4 dozen*
TOTAL TIME: *30 minutes*
CHILLING TIME: *8 hours*

---

4 cups all-purpose flour
2 teaspoons baking powder
1 cup vegetable oil
4 large eggs
1 cup granulated sugar
1 teaspoon almond extract
1 cup almonds, ground

**1** Preheat the oven to 350 degrees.

**2** Combine the flour and baking powder.

**3** In a large bowl, beat the oil, eggs, sugar, and almond extract until thick and light-colored. Gradually stir in the flour mixture and almonds.

**4** Divide the dough into 6 pieces. Shape each piece into a loaf about 12 inches long and 1 inch wide, and place on ungreased baking sheets.

**5** Bake for 30 minutes. Transfer the loaves to a cutting board and slice on the diagonal, ½ inch thick.

**6** Lay the slices on the baking sheets and bake for 15 minutes longer, or until dry. Transfer to wire racks to cool.

# ALMOND CRISPS IV

Formed Cookies

YIELD: *12 dozen*
TOTAL TIME: *55 minutes*

A

# ALMOND CROSTATA

Bar Cookies

YIELD: *3 to 4 dozen*
TOTAL TIME: *60 minutes*

**CRUST**
2½ cups all-purpose flour
2 teaspoons baking powder
¼ cup butter, at room temperature
¾ cup granulated sugar
2 large eggs
2 tablespoons vegetable shortening
2 teaspoons rum

**FILLING**
5 ounces semisweet chocolate, chopped
2 large eggs
5 tablespoons granulated sugar
2 teaspoons almond extract
2 cups slivered almonds
1 cup walnuts, chopped
5 tablespoons Amaretto

1 Preheat the oven to 350 degrees. Lightly grease a 13 by 9-inch baking pan.

2 To make the crust, combine the flour and baking powder.

3 In a large bowl, cream the butter and sugar. Beat in the eggs. Beat in the vegetable shortening and rum. Gradually blend in the flour mixture.

4 Divide the dough into 2 pieces, one twice as large as the other. On a floured surface, roll out the larger piece to a 13 by 9-inch rectangle. Fit the dough into the prepared pan.

5 To make the filling, melt the chocolate in a double boiler over low heat, stirring until smooth. Remove from the heat.

6 In a large bowl, lightly beat the eggs. Beat in the sugar. Beat in the melted chocolate and almond extract. Stir in the nuts.

7 Spread the filling evenly over the prepared crust.

8 Roll out the remaining dough to a ¼-inch-thick rectangle. Cut into ½-inch-wide strips and arrange in a lattice pattern over the filling.

9 Bake for 25 to 35 minutes, or until a the lattice strips are golden brown. Sprinkle the Amaretto over the hot cookies. Let cool slightly in the pan on a rack before cutting into large or small bars.

# ALMOND DREAMS

Drop Cookies

YIELD: *3 to 4 dozen*
TOTAL TIME: *45 minutes*

3½ cups granulated sugar
2 cups almonds, ground
5 large egg whites
1 teaspoon almond extract

1 Preheat the oven to 275 degrees. Line 2 baking sheets with parchment paper.

2 Combine the sugar and ground almonds.

3 In a large bowl, beat the egg whites until stiff but not dry. Fold in the almond extract. Gradually fold in the almond mixture.

4 Drop by teaspoonful 2 inches apart onto the prepared baking sheets.

5 Bake for 25 to 30 minutes, until just starting to color. Transfer to wire racks to cool.

**Baking notes:** Be sure to beat the egg whites to stiff peaks. Do not use waxed paper to line the baking sheets, or the cookies may stick to the paper.

²⁄₃ cup vegetable shortening
¾ cup powdered sugar
1¼ cups all-purpose flour
1 cup almonds, ground
2 large eggs, separated
Pinch of salt
½ teaspoon almond extract
Granulated sugar for sprinkling

1  In a large bowl, cream the vegetable shortening and powdered sugar. Gradually blend in the flour and almonds. Cover and chill for at least 8 hours.

2  Two hours before baking, remove the dough from the refrigerator.

3  Preheat the oven to 300 degrees.

4  In a large bowl, beat the egg whites with the salt until stiff but not dry. Fold in the almond extract.

5  In another bowl, beat the egg yolks until thick and light-colored and fold into the beaten whites.

6  On a floured surface, roll out the dough ¼ inch thick. Using a 2-inch round cookie cutter, cut out cookies and place 2 inches apart on ungreased baking sheets.

7  Brush the cookies with the egg mixture and sprinkle with granulated sugar.

8  Bake for 18 to 20 minutes, until golden brown. Transfer to wire racks to cool.

**Baking notes:**  This dough will keep for up to 2 weeks in the refrigerator, or several months in the freezer.

# ALMOND FLAKE NORMANDY

Rolled Cookies

YIELD: *5 to 6 dozen*
TOTAL TIME: *45 minutes*
CHILLING TIME: *8 hours*

---

2½ cups rolled oats
2 cups almonds, ground
½ cup whole wheat flour
1 cup canola oil
1 cup raw sugar
2 large eggs, beaten
¼ cup evaporated milk
1½ teaspoons almond extract

1  Preheat the oven to 350 degrees. Grease 2 baking sheets.

2  Combine the oats, almonds, and flour.

3  In a large bowl, beat the oil and sugar until smooth.

4  Beat the eggs into the oil mixture, then beat in the evaporated milk and almond extract. Blend in the dry ingredients.

5  Drop by teaspoonfuls 2 inches apart onto the prepared baking sheets. Flatten each cookie with the back of a spoon dipped in flour.

6  Bake for 7 to 10 minutes, until golden brown. Transfer to wire racks to cool.

# ALMOND-FLAVORED CRUNCHY COOKIES

Drop Cookies

YIELD: *2 to 4 dozen*
TOTAL TIME: *30 minutes*

# ALMOND-FRUIT COOKIES

Drop Cookies

YIELD: *1 to 2 dozen*
TOTAL TIME: *35 minutes*

3 cups rolled oats
1 cup all-purpose flour
1 cup soy flour
1 cup canola oil
1 cup packed dark brown sugar
2 large eggs
¼ cup skim milk
¼ teaspoon salt
1 cup dried apricots, chopped fine

1 Preheat the oven to 350 degrees. Grease 2 baking sheets.

2 Combine the oats, all-purpose flour, and soy flour.

3 In a large bowl, beat the oil and brown sugar until smooth. Beat in the eggs, milk, and salt. Gradually blend in the oat mixture. Stir in the apricots.

4 Drop the dough by tablespoonfuls 1½ inches apart onto the prepared baking sheets. Flatten each cookie with the bottom of a glass dipped in soy flour.

5 Bake for 10 to 12 minutes, until golden brown. Transfer to wire racks to cool.

**Baking notes:** Soy flour can be found in natural food stores and the natural food sections of large supermarkets.

# ALMOND-FRUIT WREATHS

Formed Cookies

YIELD: *2 dozen*
TOTAL TIME: *35 minutes*

1 cup vegetable shortening
¾ cup packed light brown sugar
2 large egg yolks
1 teaspoon almond extract
2½ cups all-purpose flour
¾ cup slivered almonds
½ cup dried candied fruit, chopped fine
1 large egg white
1 tablespoon light corn syrup
6 to 12 glacé cherries halved

1 Preheat the oven to 325 degrees.

2 In a large bowl, cream the vegetable shortening and brown sugar. Beat in the egg yolks and almond extract. Gradually blend in the flour. Fold in the almonds and candied fruit.

3 Pinch off walnut-sized pieces of dough and roll into pencil-thin ropes. Form the ropes into rings on ungreased baking sheets, placing them 1¼ inches apart, and pinch the ends together.

4 In a medium bowl, beat the egg white and corn syrup until smooth. Brush the rings with the mixture and place a glacé cherry half on each ring at the point where the ends meet.

5 Bake for 18 to 20 minutes, or until the cookies are lightly colored. Transfer to wire racks to cool.

**Baking notes:** For an even more festive variation, shape the cookies as directed and bake without the cherries. After the cookies have cooled, frost with a white icing and place the cherries on top.

2 cups granulated sugar
½ cup all-purpose flour
½ teaspoon baking powder
¼ teaspoon salt
4 large egg whites
2 cups almonds, ground fine
1 cup glacé cherries, chopped fine

**1** Preheat the oven to 325 degrees. Grease and lightly flour 2 baking sheets.

**2** In a large bowl, combine the sugar, flour, baking powder, salt, and egg whites. Fold in the almonds. Fold in the cherries.

**3** Drop the dough by spoonfuls 1½ inches apart onto the prepared baking sheets.

**4** Bake for 12 to 15 minutes, until lightly colored. Let cool slightly before transferring to wire racks to cool completely.

**Baking notes:** These cookies can be frosted if desired.

# ALMOND GEMS

Drop Cookies

YIELD: *2 to 4 dozen*
TOTAL TIME: *35 minutes*

---

2 small eggs
½ cup canola oil
1½ teaspoons almond extract
1 cup all-purpose flour
¾ cup granulated sugar
½ teaspoon baking powder
Pinch of salt

**1** Preheat the oven to 350 degrees. Grease a 9-inch square baking pan.

**2** In a large bowl, beat the eggs until thick and light-colored. Beat in the oil and almond extract. Blend in the flour, sugar, baking powder, and salt.

**3** Scrape the batter into the prepared pan. Bake for 18 to 20 minutes, or until firm to the touch.

**4** Let cool in the pan on a rack before cutting into large or small bars.

# ALMOND GÉNOISE

Bar Cookies

YIELD: *3 to 4 dozen*
TOTAL TIME: *30 minutes*

---

1½ cups rolled oats
1 cup whole wheat flour
¼ cup nonfat dry milk
¼ cup wheat germ
¼ teaspoon baking powder
½ teaspoon ground cinnamon
½ teaspoon salt
¾ cup vegetable shortening
1¼ cups raw sugar
1 large egg
¼ cup frozen lemon juice concentrate, thawed
1 cup sliced almonds
½ cup golden raisins

**1** Preheat the oven to 350 degrees.

**2** Combine the oats, flour, dry milk, wheat germ, baking powder, cinnamon, and salt.

**3** In a large bowl, cream the vegetable shortening and sugar. Beat in the egg and lemon juice concentrate. Gradually blend in the oat mixture. Fold in the almonds and raisins.

**4** Drop the batter by spoonfuls 1½ inches apart onto ungreased baking sheets. Flatten each cookie with the back of a spoon dipped in flour.

**5** Bake for 25 to 30 minutes, until the cookies are golden brown. Transfer to wire racks to cool.

**Baking notes:** If you like, sprinkle the cookies with sesame seeds before you flatten them.

# ALMOND HEALTH COOKIES

Drop Cookies

YIELD: *3 to 4 dozen*
TOTAL TIME: *40 minutes*

# ALMOND MACAROONS I

Formed Cookies

YIELD: *3 to 4 dozen*
TOTAL TIME: *40 minutes*

1 cup almond paste
2 large egg whites
Pinch of salt.
1 cup powdered sugar
Granulated sugar for sprinkling

1 Preheat the oven to 325 degrees. Line 2 baking sheets with parchment paper.

2 Crumble the almond paste into a large bowl and beat until smooth.

3 In another bowl, beat the egg whites with the salt until stiff and but not dry. Fold the beaten whites into the almond paste. Fold in the powdered sugar.

4 Place the dough in a pastry bag fitted with a large plain tip (see Baking notes). Pipe out 1-inch mounds onto the prepared baking sheets, spacing them 1 inch apart.

5 Sprinkle the cookies with granulated sugar. Bake for 20 to 25 minutes, until just starting to color. Transfer to wire racks to cool.

**Baking notes:** Don't use waxed paper or the cookies may stick or tear apart when you remove them; brown wrapping paper may be used instead of parchment. Slivered almonds and/or red and green glacé cherries can be used to decorate the cookies before baking. A pastry bag isn't essential; the dough may be dropped by spoonfuls onto the baking sheets. Store in an airtight container.

# ALMOND MACAROONS II

Formed Cookies

YIELD: *3 to 4 dozen*
TOTAL TIME: *30 minutes*
STANDING TIME: *8 hours*

1 cup almond paste
¾ cup granulated sugar
1 teaspoon grated lemon zest
3 large egg whites
½ cup powdered sugar

1 Line 2 baking sheets with parchment paper.

2 Crumble the almond paste into a medium bowl. Add the granulated sugar and lemon zest and beat until smooth. Add the egg whites and beat until a soft dough is formed.

3 Place the dough in a pastry bag fitted with a large pliant tip. Pipe out 1-inch mounds onto the prepared baking sheets, spacing the cookies about 1½ inches apart.

4 Sift the powdered sugar over the cookies, coating them heavily. Let stand for at least 8 and up to 24 hours, until the cookies form a crust.

5 Preheat the oven to 350 degrees.

6 Bake for 12 to 15 minutes, until firm to the touch. Spread a large kitchen towel on the countertop and slide the cookies, still on the parchment paper, onto the towel. Let cool before removing the cookies from the paper.

**Baking notes:** Don't use waxed paper or the cookies may stick or tear apart when you remove them; brown wrapping paper may be used instead of parchment. Slivered almonds and/or red and green glacé cherries can be used to decorate the cookies before baking. A pastry bag isn't essential; the dough may be dropped by spoonfuls onto the baking sheets. Store in an airtight container.

1 cup vegetable shortening
1 cup granulated sugar
2 large eggs
2 large egg yolks
2 cups all-purpose flour
½ cup almonds, ground
1 large egg white, beaten
3 tablespoons chopped almonds

**1** Preheat the oven to 375 degrees.

**2** In a large bowl, cream the vegetable shortening and sugar. Beat in the eggs and egg yolks. Blend in the flour and ground almonds.

**3** Break off small pieces of dough and roll each piece into a rope. Form ropes into pretzel shapes and place 1 inch apart on ungreased baking sheets.

**4** Brush the cookies with the beaten egg white and sprinkle with the chopped almonds.

**5** Bake for 10 to 12 minutes, or until golden brown. Transfer to wire racks to cool.

**Baking notes:** For decoration, drizzle colored icing over the pretzels, or dip them in melted chocolate when cool. The ropes can also be folded in half and twisted into braids, or they can be formed into circles.

# ALMOND PRETZELS

Formed Cookies

YIELD: *3 to 4 dozen*
TOTAL TIME: *45 minutes*

---

1 cup vegetable shortening
½ cup granulated sugar
1 large egg yolk
1 teaspoon almond extract
2 cups all-purpose flour
10 ounces milk chocolate (see Baking notes), chopped
½ cup almonds, sliced

**1** Preheat the oven to 350 degrees. Grease a 15 by 10-inch baking pan.

**2** In a large bowl, cream the vegetable shortening and sugar. Beat in the egg yolk and almond extract. Blend in the flour.

**3** Spread the dough evenly in the prepared pan. Bake for 18 to 20 minutes, until lightly colored.

**4** Meanwhile, melt the chocolate in a double boiler over low heat, stirring until smooth. Remove from the heat.

**5** Spread the melted chocolate over the top of the warm cookies. Sprinkle with the almonds. Let cool in the pan on a rack before cutting into large or small bars.

**Baking notes:** Do not use melted candy bars; use only baker's-style milk chocolate.

# ALMOND ROCA COOKIES

Bar Cookies

YIELD: *1 to 2 dozen*
TOTAL TIME: *35 minutes*

---

2 cups vegetable shortening
2½ cups packed light brown sugar
2 teaspoons almond extract
4½ cups all-purpose flour
1 cup almonds, ground

**1** Preheat the oven to 350 degrees.

**2** In a large bowl, cream the vegetable shortening and brown sugar. Beat in the almond extract. Gradually stir in the flour and almonds.

**3** Pinch off walnut-sized pieces of dough and roll into balls. Place 1 inch apart on ungreased baking sheets. Flatten each ball with the bottom of a glass dipped in flour.

**4** Bake for 10 to 15 minutes, until the edges start to color. Transfer to wire racks to cool.

# ALMOND SHORTBREAD I

Formed Cookies

YIELD: *4 to 5 dozen*
TOTAL TIME: *30 minutes*

# ALMOND SHORTBREAD II

Bar Cookies

YIELD: *4 to 6 dozen*
TOTAL TIME: *40 minutes*

½ cup butter, at room temperature
½ cup powdered sugar
2 cups all-purpose flour
½ cup almonds, ground

**1** Preheat the oven to 350 degrees.

**2** In a large bowl, cream the butter and powdered sugar. Blend in the flour and almonds. If the dough seems too dry, beat in a little water, ½ teaspoon at a time, until smooth.

**3** Spread the dough evenly in an ungreased 9-inch square baking pan. Prick all over with a fork. Using the back of a knife, score the dough into large or small bars.

**4** Bake for 28 to 30 minutes until very lightly colored. Let cool in the pan on a rack before cutting into bars.

**Baking notes:** This dough will keep for up to 2 weeks in the refrigerator or several months in the freezer. Half a teaspoon of almond extract can be substituted for the ground almonds. This recipe is a variation of classic Scotch shortbread; to obtain the traditional texture, substitute rice flour for half of the all-purpose flour.

# ALMOND SQUARES I

Bar Cookies

YIELD: *1 to 2 dozen*
TOTAL TIME: *50 minutes*

**CRUST**
1 cup all-purpose flour
¼ teaspoon salt
¼ cup vegetable shortening

**FILLING**
2 large eggs
¾ cup granulated sugar
1 teaspoon almond extract
2 tablespoons all-purpose flour
¼ teaspoon salt
2 cups shredded coconut
1 cup slivered almonds
Granulated sugar for sprinkling

**1** Preheat the oven to 350 degrees. Grease a 9-inch square baking pan.

**2** To make the crust, combine the flour and salt in a medium bowl. Cut in the shortening until the mixture resembles coarse crumbs.

**3** Press the mixture evenly over the bottom of the prepared pan. Bake for 15 minutes.

**4** Meanwhile, make the filling: Combine the eggs and sugar in a large bowl and beat until thick and light-colored. Beat in the almond extract. Stir in the flour and salt. Fold in the coconut and almonds.

**5** Spread the filling over the warm crust. Sprinkle lightly with sugar. Bake for 15 minutes longer, until the filling is set and it is lightly browned.

**6** Let cool in the pan on a rack before cutting into large or small bars.

1 cup vegetable shortening
1 cup granulated sugar
1 large egg, separated
½ teaspoon almond extract
¼ teaspoon salt
2 cups all-purpose flour
1½ cups sliced almonds

1 Preheat the oven to 325 degrees.

2 In a large bowl, cream the vegetable shortening and sugar. Beat in the egg yolk and almond extract. Beat in the salt. Gradually blend in the flour. The dough will be stiff.

3 Spread the dough evenly in an ungreased 9-inch baking pan.

4 In a medium bowl, beat the egg white until stiff but not dry. Spread evenly over the cookie dough. Sprinkle with the almonds.

5 Bake for 40 minutes, until the top is lightly colored. Let cool in the pan on a rack before cutting into large or small bars.

**Baking notes:** For variation, spread your favorite fruit preserves over the unbaked crust, then spread the beaten egg white over the fruit. Bake for 30 to 35 minutes.

# Almond Squares II

Bar Cookies

YIELD: *1 to 2 dozen*
TOTAL TIME: *60 minutes*

---

1¼ cups all-purpose flour
1½ teaspoons baking powder
¼ teaspoon salt
¼ cup vegetable shortening
¾ cup granulated sugar
1 large egg
2 tablespoons milk
½ teaspoon almond extract
1¼ cup almonds, chopped

1 Preheat the oven to 375 degrees. Grease a 9-inch square baking pan.

2 Combine the flour, baking powder, and salt.

3 In a large bowl, cream the vegetable shortening and sugar.

Beat in the egg, milk, and almond extract. Gradually blend in the dry ingredients. Fold in the almonds.

4 Spread the mixture evenly in the prepared pan.

5 Bake for 20 to 25 minutes, until the top is lightly colored. Cool in the pan on a rack before cutting into large or small bars.

# Almond Squares III

Bar Cookies

YIELD: *1 to 2 dozen*
TOTAL TIME: *35 minutes*

---

CRUST
2 cups all-purpose flour
¼ teaspoon salt
1 cup vegetable shortening
1 cup granulated sugar
1 large egg yolk
1 teaspoon almond extract

FILLING
1 large egg white
2 tablespoons granulated sugar
¼ teaspoon ground cinnamon
¼ cup almonds, ground

1 Preheat the oven to 350 degrees.

2 To make the crust, combine the flour and salt.

3 In a large bowl, cream the vegetable shortening and sugar. Beat

in the egg and almond extract. Blend in the flour mixture.

4 Spread the dough evenly over the bottom of an ungreased 13 by 9-inch baking pan.

5 To make the filling, beat the egg white in a medium bowl until frothy. Beat in the sugar and cinnamon until the whites hold stiff peaks. Fold in the almonds.

6 Spread the almond mixture evenly over the dough. Bake for 25 to 30 minutes, until the top is a golden color.

7 While the cookies are still warm, cut into 1½ by 1-inch strips. Transfer to wire racks to cool.

# Almond Strips I

Bar Cookies

YIELD: *6 dozen*
TOTAL TIME: *40 minutes*

# ALMOND STRIPS II

Rolled Cookies

YIELD: *3 to 4 dozen*
TOTAL TIME: *35 minutes*
CHILLING TIME: *4 hours*

3 cups all-purpose flour
1 teaspoon ground ginger
1 teaspoon salt
½ cup butter, at room temperature
½ cup packed dark brown sugar
½ cup molasses
1 teaspoon baking soda
¼ cup hot water
1½ cups almonds, chopped

**1** Combine the flour, ginger, and salt.

**2** In a large bowl, cream the butter and brown sugar. Beat in the molasses.

**3** Dissolve the baking soda in the hot water and add to the molasses mixture, beating until smooth. Gradually blend in the dry ingredients. Stir in the almonds. Cover and chill for at least 4 hours.

**4** Preheat the oven to 350 degrees. Grease 2 baking sheets.

**5** On a floured surface, roll out the dough ¼ inch thick. Cut into 3 by 1-inch strips and place 1 inch apart on the prepared baking sheets.

**6** Bake for 10 to 12 minutes, until lightly colored. Transfer to wire racks to cool.

**Baking notes:** See Hint 16 in Pantry for an easy way to measure molasses.

# ALMOND TEA COOKIES

Rolled Cookies

YIELD: *2 to 3 dozen*
TOTAL TIME: *35 minutes*

7 tablespoons butter, at room temperature
½ cup granulated sugar
¾ cup almonds, ground fine
Pinch of salt
1 teaspoon almond extract
3 cups all-purpose flour
Powdered sugar for dusting

**1** Preheat the oven to 350 degrees. Grease 2 baking sheets.

**2** In a large bowl, cream the butter and sugar until light and fluffy. Beat in the almonds and salt. Beat in the almond extract. Gradually blend in the flour.

**3** On a floured surface, roll out the dough ½ inch thick. Cut into 2 by ½-inch strips and place 1¼ inches apart on the prepared baking sheets.

**4** Bake for 15 to 20 minutes, until golden brown.

**5** Dust the warm cookies with powdered sugar. Transfer to wire racks to cool.

# ALMOND TULIP PASTRY CUPS

Drop Cookies

YIELD: *2 to 3 dozen*
TOTAL TIME: *60 minutes*

¼ cup vegetable shortening
½ cup powdered sugar
2 large egg whites
¾ teaspoon Amaretto
¼ cup all-purpose flour
⅓ cup almonds, ground fine

**1** Preheat the oven to 425 degrees.

**2** In a large bowl, cream the vegetable shortening and powdered sugar. Add the egg whites and Amaretto, beating until very smooth. Gradually blend in the flour. Fold in the almonds.

**3** Drop 1½ teaspoonfuls of the batter 5 inches apart onto ungreased baking sheets. With the back of a spoon, spread into 4- to 5-inch rounds.

**4** Bake for 5 to 6 minutes, or until the edges are lightly browned. Using a spatula, remove the cookies from the sheets and place each cookie over an upside-down cup or glass. (If they become too firm to shape, return briefly to the oven.) Let cool completely before removing.

**Baking notes:** These are very easy to overbake; watch them closely. The cups can be used to hold fresh fruit, custards, or mousses. Or make smaller cups and fill them with whipped cream and sprinkle with shaved chocolate. (Do not fill the cookies until just before serving.) In an airtight container, the cups will keep well in the freezer for up to 6 months.

½ cup almonds, ground fine
1 tablespoon milk, plus more if necessary
1 cup granulated sugar
4 large egg whites
Pinch of salt
Powdered sugar for sprinkling

1 Combine the almonds and milk in a blender and blend to a smooth paste. Transfer to a bowl and add the sugar. Stir in enough additional milk so the mixture is the consistency of corn syrup.

2 In a large bowl, beat the egg whites with the salt until stiff but not dry. Gradually fold about 2 tablespoons of the egg whites into the almond mixture. Then fold the mixture back into the egg whites.

3 Heat a griddle. Drop the batter by tablespoonfuls onto the hot griddle and cook, turning once, until golden brown on both sides.

4 While the cookies are still hot, roll each one up into a cylinder. Transfer to wire racks, sprinkle with powdered sugar, and let cool.

**Baking notes:** Chill the cylinders for 2 hours before filling. Using a pastry bag with a star tip, fill the rolls with whipped cream or a custard, such as pastry cream, and re-chill until ready to serve. Stored airtight, these unfilled cookies can be kept for up to 6 months in the freezer.

# ALMOND WAFER ROLLS

Drop Cookies

YIELD: *1 to 3 dozen*
TOTAL TIME: *60 minutes*
CHILLING TIME: *2 hours*

---

1½ cups all-purpose flour
1½ teaspoons baking powder
½ cup vegetable shortening
½ cup granulated sugar
2 large eggs
1 teaspoon almond extract
½ cup almonds, ground fine

1 Preheat the oven to 325 degrees.

2 Combine the flour and baking powder.

3 In a large bowl, cream the vegetable shortening and sugar. Beat in the eggs and almond extract. Gradually blend in the flour mixture and almonds. The dough will be stiff.

4 Shape the dough into a 13 by 2½-inch loaf and place on an ungreased baking sheet. Bake for 18 to 20 minutes, or until firm to the touch.

5 Transfer the loaf to a cutting board and cut into ½-inch-thick slices. Cut each slice diagonally in half and lay on ungreased baking sheets. Bake for 20 minutes longer, until dry.

6 Turn off the oven and leave the cookies in the oven, without opening the door, for 20 minutes longer. Transfer to wire racks to cool.

# ALMOND ZWIEBACK

Formed Cookies

YIELD: *4 to 5 dozen*
TOTAL TIME: *50 minutes*

---

2 cups all-purpose flour
½ teaspoon baking powder
½ teaspoon baking soda
¼ teaspoon salt
¾ cup vegetable shortening
1 cup packed light brown sugar
1 large egg
¼ cup fresh orange juice
1 tablespoon grated orange zest
1 cup (6 ounces) butterscotch chips
1 cup shredded coconut

1 Preheat the oven to 350 degrees. Grease a 13 by 9-inch baking pan.

2 Combine the flour, baking powder, baking soda, and salt.

3 In a large bowl, cream the vegetable shortening and brown sugar. Beat in the egg, orange juice, and zest. Gradually blend in the dry ingredients. Fold in the butterscotch chips and coconut.

4 Spread the batter evenly in the prepared pan.

5 Bake for 25 to 30 minutes, or until the top is a golden brown. Cool in the pan on a rack before cutting into large or small squares.

# AMBROSIA BARS

Bar Cookies

YIELD: *2 to 3 dozen*
TOTAL TIME: *35 minutes*

# AMERICAN OATMEAL CRISPS

Drop Cookies

YIELD: *2 to 3 dozen*
TOTAL TIME: *30 minutes*

1¼ cups all-purpose flour
½ teaspoon baking powder
½ teaspoon baking soda
½ teaspoon salt
1 cup vegetable shortening
¼ cup granulated sugar
1 cup packed light brown sugar
2 large eggs
¼ cup milk
1 teaspoon almond extract
3 cups rolled oats
1 cup (6 ounces) baking chips (see Baking notes)

**1** Preheat the oven to 350 degrees.

**2** Combine the flour, baking powder, baking soda, and salt.

**3** In a large bowl, cream the vegetable shortening and both sug-ars. Beat in the eggs. Beat in the milk and almond extract. Gradually blend in the dry ingredients. Fold in the oats and chips.

**4** Drop the dough by teaspoon-fuls about 1½ inches apart onto ungreased baking sheets.

**5** Bake for 10 to 12 minutes, until golden brown. Transfer to wire racks to cool.

**Baking notes:** The baking chips can be semisweet, milk chocolate, white chocolate, peanut butter or butterscotch. For a cookie the children will love, omit the baking chips and press 4 or 5 M & M's into the top of each cookie.

# AMERICAN SHORTBREAD

Rolled Cookies

YIELD: *8 dozen*
TOTAL TIME: *30 minutes*

2 cups (1 pound) butter, at room temperature
1¾ cups granulated sugar
6 large eggs
1 tablespoon caraway seeds
8 cups all-purpose flour

**1** Preheat the oven to 400 degrees.

**2** In a large bowl, cream the butter and sugar until light and fluffy.

**3** In another bowl, beat the eggs until thick and light-colored. Beat the eggs into the butter mixture. Stir in the caraway seeds. Gradually blend in the flour.

**4** On a floured surface, roll out the dough ¼ inch thick. Cut into 1-inch squares and place 1 inch apart on ungreased baking sheets.

**5** Bake for 12 to 15 minutes, until lightly colored. Transfer to wire racks to cool

**Baking notes:** For variation, substitute anise seeds for the caraway seeds. For variety, cut half of the cookies into squares and half into rounds with a cookie cutter.

# ANISE COOKIES I

Drop Cookies

YIELD: *2 to 3 dozen*
TOTAL TIME: *30 minutes*
CHILLING TIME: *8 hours*

2¼ cups all-purpose flour
½ teaspoon baking powder
¼ teaspoon salt
2 large eggs
1½ cups granulated sugar
2 teaspoons anise extract

**1** Combine the flour, baking powder, and salt.

**2** In a large bowl, beat the eggs until foamy. Beat in the sugar and anise extract. Gradually blend in the dry ingredients. Cover and chill for at least 8 hours, or overnight.

**3** Preheat the oven to 325 degrees. Grease 2 baking sheets.

**4** Drop the dough by spoonfuls 1½ inches apart onto the pre-pared baking sheets.

**5** Bake for 10 to 12 minutes, until lightly colored. Transfer to wire racks to cool.

**Baking notes:** For a more subtle flavor, substitute 2 teaspoons of anise seeds for the anise extract.

1¾ cups all-purpose flour
1½ teaspoons baking powder
1½ teaspoons anise seeds
½ teaspoon salt
½ cup vegetable shortening
1 cup granulated sugar
1 large egg
½ teaspoon vanilla extract

**1** Combine the flour, baking powder, anise seeds, and salt.

**2** In a large bowl, cream the vegetable shortening and sugar. Beat in the egg and vanilla extract. Gradually blend in the dry ingredients.

**3** Shape the dough into a log about 2 inches in diameter. Wrap in waxed paper and chill for at least 4 hours.

**4** Preheat the oven to 400 degrees. Grease 2 baking sheets.

**5** Cut the log into ¼-inch-thick slices and place 1 inch apart on the prepared baking sheets.

**6** Bake for 8 to 10 minutes, until lightly colored. Transfer to wire racks to cool.

# ANISE COOKIES II

Refrigerator Cookies

YIELD: *4 to 5 dozen*
TOTAL TIME: *30 minutes*
CHILLING TIME: *4 hours*

A

---

5 cups all-purpose flour
2 tablespoons baking powder
½ cup vegetable shortening
1¼ cups granulated sugar
6 large eggs
1 tablespoon plus 1 teaspoon anise extract
2 teaspoons vanilla extract

**1** Preheat the oven to 350 degrees. Grease 2 baking sheets.

**2** Combine the flour and baking powder.

**3** In a large bowl, cream the vegetable shortening and sugar. Beat in the eggs one at a time and both extracts. Gradually blend in the dry ingredients.

**4** Break off walnut-sized pieces of dough and roll into balls. Place 1½ inches apart on the prepared baking sheets. Flatten each ball with the bottom of a glass dipped in flour.

**5** Bake for 8 to 10 minutes, until lightly colored. Transfer to wire racks to cool.

# ANISE COOKIES III

Formed Cookies

YIELD: *6 to 7 dozen*
TOTAL TIME: *30 minutes*

---

4½ cups all-purpose flour
1 teaspoon baking powder
4 large eggs
3½ cups powdered sugar
1 teaspoon anise seeds
¼ teaspoon anise extract (optional)

**1** Combine the flour and baking powder.

**2** In a large bowl, beat the eggs and sugar until thick and light-colored. Beat in the anise seeds and the optional anise extract. Gradually blend in the dry ingredients. Cover and chill for at least 1 hour.

**3** On a lightly floured surface, roll out the dough ½ inch thick. Press down on the dough with a springerle rolling pin or mold to shape the cookies. Cut the cookies apart and place about 1 inch apart on ungreased baking sheets. Cover and let stand overnight.

**4** Preheat the oven to 350 degrees.

**5** Bake the cookies for 25 to 30 minutes, until firm to the touch. Transfer to wire racks to cool.

**6** Place the cookies in airtight containers and let age for at least 1 week before serving.

# ANISE COOKIES IV

Rolled Cookies

YIELD: *6 dozen*
TOTAL TIME: *45 minutes*
CHILLING TIME: *1 hour*
STANDING TIME: *8 hours*

# ANISE COOKIES V

Rolled Cookies

YIELD: *3 to 4 dozen*
TOTAL TIME: *35 minutes*
CHILLING TIME: *8 hours*

2 cups all-purpose flour
¼ teaspoon baking powder
⅛ teaspoon salt
½ cup vegetable shortening
¾ cups granulated sugar
1 large egg
¼ teaspoon baking soda
1 tablespoon warm water
¼ cup molasses
2 teaspoons anise seeds

**1** Combine the flour, baking powder, and salt.

**2** In a large bowl, cream the vegetable shortening and sugar. Beat in the egg.

**3** Dissolve the baking soda in the warm water and add to the egg mixture, beating until smooth. Beat in the molasses. Fold in the anise seeds. Gradually blend in the dry ingredients. Cover and chill for 8 hours.

**4** Preheat the oven to 350 degrees. Grease 2 baking sheets.

**5** On a floured surface, roll out the dough ¼ inch thick. Using cookie cutters, cut into shapes and place 1¼ inches apart on the prepared baking sheets.

**6** Bake for 6 to 8 minutes, until the edges are golden brown. Transfer to wire racks to cool.

**Baking notes:** For variation, cut out round cookies and place on the baking sheets. Press your thumb into the center of each one and put a bit of jam or preserves in the depression. You can also sprinkle the hot cookies with colored sugar crystals or granulated or powdered sugar.

# ANISE COOKIES VI

Drop Cookies

YIELD: *2 to 3 dozen*
TOTAL TIME: *30 minutes*
CHILLING TIME: *8 hours*

2¼ cups all-purpose flour
½ teaspoon baking powder
¼ teaspoon salt
2 large eggs
1½ cups granulated sugar
2 teaspoons anise extract

**1** Combine the flour, baking powder, and salt.

**2** In a large bowl, beat the eggs until thick and light-colored. Beat in the sugar, then beat in the anise extract. Gradually blend in the dry ingredients. Cover and chill for at least 8 hours.

**3** Preheat the oven to 325 degrees. Grease 2 baking sheets.

**4** Drop the dough by teaspoonfuls 1 inch apart onto the prepared baking sheets.

**5** Bake for 10 to 12 minutes, until lightly colored. Transfer to wire racks to cool.

# ANISE DROPS

Formed Cookies

YIELD: *2 to 3 dozen*
TOTAL TIME: *35 minutes*
CHILLING TIME: *30 minutes*

2 large egg whites
¼ teaspoon salt
½ teaspoon baking soda
1 tablespoon water
1½ cups packed dark brown sugar
2 teaspoons anise seeds
2¼ cups all-purpose flour

**1** In a large bowl, beat the egg whites with the salt until stiff but not dry.

**2** Dissolve the baking soda in the warm water and add to the egg whites. Fold in the brown sugar and anise seeds. Gradually blend in the flour. Cover and chill for at least 30 minutes.

**3** Preheat the oven to 350 degrees. Grease 2 baking sheets.

**4** Break off small pieces of dough and roll into balls. Place 1 inch apart on the prepared baking sheets.

**5** Bake for 10 to 12 minutes, or until firm to the touch. Transfer to wire racks to cool.

**Baking notes:** If you prefer, replace the anise seeds with ¼ teaspoon anise oil or ½ teaspoon anise extract.

2 cups all-purpose flour
1½ teaspoons baking powder
1¼ teaspoons baking soda
¼ teaspoon salt
2 large eggs
½ cup granulated sugar
1 teaspoon anise extract
1¼ teaspoons anise seeds

**1** Combine the flour, baking powder, baking soda, and salt.

**2** In a large bowl, beat the eggs and sugar until thick and light-colored. Beat in the anise extract and anise seeds. Gradually blend in the dry ingredients. Cover and chill for 2 hours.

**3** Preheat the oven to 350 degrees. Grease a baking sheet.

**4** Form the dough into two 12-inch-long logs and place side-by-side on the prepared baking sheet. Bake for 8 to 10 minutes, or until firm to the touch.

**5** Transfer the logs to the cutting board and slice each log diagonally into ½-inch-thick slices. Lay the slices on ungreased baking sheet and bake for 10 minutes longer, until dry. Transfer to wire racks to cool.

**6** When cool, drizzle with Vanilla Icing (see Pantry).

**Baking notes:** This is a classic European cookie, and the combination of the anise seeds and extract may be too strong for some tastes. The first time you make these, you might want to use only the seeds or the extract; then, if you find you really like the anise, use both the next time you make them.

# ANISEED BISCUITS

Formed Cookies

YIELD: *2 to 3 dozen*
TOTAL TIME: *35 minutes*
CHILLLING TIME: *2 hours*

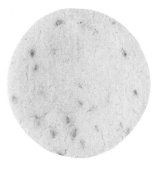

---

1¾ cups all-purpose flour
1½ teaspoons baking powder
¼ teaspoon salt
½ cup vegetable shortening
1 cup granulated sugar
1 large egg
½ teaspoon anise extract
1¾ teaspoons anise seeds

**1** Combine the flour, baking powder, and salt.

**2** In a large bowl, cream the vegetable shortening and sugar. Beat in the egg. Beat in the anise extract and anise seeds. Gradually blend in the dry ingredients.

**3** Roll the dough into a 2-inch-thick log. Wrap in waxed paper and chill for at least 4 hours.

**4** Preheat the oven to 400 degrees.

**5** Cut the dough into ¼-inch-thick slices and place 1 inch apart on ungreased baking sheets.

**6** Bake for 10 to 12 minutes, or until light golden. Transfer to wire racks to cool.

**Baking notes:** These cookies are strongly flavored with anise. For a more delicate flavor, use just the seeds or the extract. For variation, omit the anise extract and substitute caraway seeds for the anise seeds.

# ANISEED REFRIGERATOR COOKIES

Refrigerator Cookies

YIELD: *3 to 4 dozen*
TOTAL TIME: *40 minutes*
CHILLING TIME: *4 hours*

# Apple Bars I

Bar Cookies

Yield: *1 to 2 dozen*
Total time: *50 minutes*

¾ cup all-purpose flour
½ teaspoon baking powder
¼ teaspoon baking soda
½ teaspoon ground ginger
¼ teaspoon ground nutmeg
⅓ cup vegetable shortening
¾ cup granulated sugar
2 large eggs
1 cup diced, peeled apples

**Topping**
1½ teaspoons granulated sugar
½ teaspoon ground cinnamon

**1** Preheat the oven to 350 degrees.

**2** Combine the flour, baking powder, baking soda, ginger, and nutmeg.

**3** In a large bowl, cream the vegetable shortening and sugar. Beat in the eggs. Gradually blend in the dry ingredients. Fold in the apples.

**4** Spread the dough evenly in an ungreased 9-inch square baking pan.

**5** Combine the cinnamon and sugar for the topping. Sprinkle evenly over the dough.

**6** Bake for 25 to 30 minutes, or until firm to the touch. Let cool in the pan on a rack before cutting into large or small bars.

**Baking notes:** Add ½ cup raisins and/or ½ cup chopped nuts to the dough if desired. Drizzle white icing over the top as soon as the bars are baked. (See Pantry.)

# Apple Bars II

Bar Cookies

Yield: *2 to 3 dozen*
Total time: *60 minutes*

**Crust**
1 cup all-purpose flour
¼ cup granulated sugar
½ cup vegetable shortening

**Filling**
2 large eggs
⅓ cup water
½ teaspoon vanilla extract
⅓ cup all-purpose flour
1½ teaspoons light brown sugar
¼ cup almonds, ground fine
1 cup diced, peeled apples
Powdered sugar for sprinkling

**1** Preheat the oven to 350 degrees. Lightly grease an 8-inch square baking pan.

**2** To make the crust, combine the flour and sugar in a bowl. Cut in the vegetable shortening until the mixture resembles coarse crumbs.

**3** Press the mixture evenly into the bottom of the prepared pan. Bake for 25 minutes.

**4** Meanwhile, make the filling: In a large bowl, beat the eggs, water, and vanilla extract together. Gradually blend in the flour and brown sugar. Fold in the almonds and apples.

**5** Spread the apple mixture over the hot crust. Bake for about 25 minutes longer, or until the filling is set. Cool in the pan on a wire rack.

**6** Sprinkle powdered sugar over the cooled cookies and cut into large or small bars.

**Baking notes:** For variation, use pears instead of apples.

2 cups all-purpose flour
2 teaspoons baking powder
½ teaspoon ground nutmeg
½ teaspoon salt
2 teaspoons grated lemon zest
4 large eggs
2 cups granulated sugar
1½ cups diced, peeled apples
1 cup walnuts, chopped
Powdered sugar for sprinkling

1  Preheat the oven to 350 degrees. Grease a 13 by 9-inch baking pan.

2  Sift the flour, baking powder, nutmeg, and salt into a bowl. Add the lemon zest.

3  In a large bowl, beat the eggs and sugar until thick and light-colored. Gradually blend in the dry ingredients. Fold in the apples and nuts.

4  Spread the dough evenly in the prepared pan.

5  Bake for 15 to 20 minutes, until firm. Let cool in the pan on a wire rack.

6  Sprinkle powdered sugar over the cooled cookies and cut into large or small bars.

# APPLE BARS III

Bar Cookies

YIELD: *2 to 4 dozen*
TOTAL TIME: *35 minutes*

---

CRUST
½ cup vegetable shortening
1 cup all-purpose flour
¼ cup granulated sugar

FILLING
⅓ cup all-purpose flour
½ teaspoon baking powder
¼ teaspoon salt
2 large eggs
1 cup packed light brown sugar
⅓ cup brandy
3 large apples, peeled, cored, and diced
½ cup walnuts, chopped

1  Preheat the oven to 350 degrees.

2  To make the crust, combine the vegetable shortening, flour, and sugar in a bowl. Spread the mixture evenly over the bottom of an ungreased 9-inch square baking pan.

3  Bake for 15 minutes.

4  Meanwhile, make the filling: Combine the flour, baking powder, and salt.

5  In a large bowl, beat the eggs and brown sugar together until thick. Beat in the brandy. Gradually blend in the dry ingredients. Fold in the apples and walnuts.

6  Spread the filling over the hot crust. Bake for 30 minutes longer, or until the filling is set. Cool in the pan on a rack before cutting into large or small bars.

# APPLE BARS IV

Bar Cookies

YIELD: *3 to 4 dozen*
TOTAL TIME: *55 minutes*

# Apple Bars V

Bar Cookies

YIELD: *1 dozen*
TOTAL TIME: *60 minutes*

1 cup all-purpose flour
½ teaspoon baking powder
1 teaspoon ground cinnamon
¼ teaspoon salt
½ cup vegetable shortening
1 cup granulated sugar
1 large egg, beaten
½ teaspoon baking soda
1 tablespoon warm water
2 large apples, peeled, cored, and diced
½ cup walnuts, chopped

**TOPPING**
1 teaspoon ground cinnamon
½ teaspoon granulated sugar

1 Preheat the oven to 350 degrees.

2 Combine the flour, baking powder, cinnamon, and salt.

3 In a large bowl, cream the vegetable shortening and sugar. Beat in the egg.

4 Dissolve the baking soda in the warm water and add to the creamed mixture, beating well. Gradually blend in the dry ingredients. Fold in the apples and nuts.

5 Spread the dough evenly in an ungreased 13 by 9-inch baking pan. Combine the cinnamon and sugar for the topping and sprinkle evenly over the dough.

6 Bake for 40 to 45 minutes, or until a toothpick comes out clean. Cool in the pan on a rack before cutting into bars.

**Baking notes:** Raisins may be added to the dough if desired. These bars are delicious topped with a spoonful of ice cream or whipped cream.

# Apple-Bran Cookies

Drop Cookies

YIELD: *4 to 5 dozen*
TOTAL TIME: *35 minutes*

3 medium apples, peeled, cored, and diced
½ cup bran cereal
½ cup fresh lemon juice
1½ cups all-purpose flour
1 teaspoon baking powder
¾ teaspoon ground cinnamon
½ teaspoon salt
½ cup vegetable shortening
½ cup granulated sugar
½ cup packed light brown sugar
1 large egg
1 teaspoon vanilla extract
⅓ cup walnuts, chopped

1 Preheat the oven to 375 degrees. Grease 2 baking sheets.

2 Place the apples in a medium bowl and add boiling water to cover. Set aside.

3 Combine the bran cereal and lemon juice in a small bowl.

Combine the flour, baking powder, cinnamon, and salt.

4 In a large bowl, cream the vegetable shortening and both sugars. Beat in the egg and vanilla extract. Gradually blend in the dry ingredients. Fold in the bran cereal and walnuts.

5 Drain the apples and return them to the bowl. Mash with a fork and stir into the dough.

6 Drop the dough by spoonfuls 1½ inches apart onto the prepared baking sheets.

7 Bake for 10 to 12 minutes, until lightly colored. Transfer to wire racks to cool.

**Baking notes:** Raisins may be added if desired. For variation, use almonds or hazelnuts in place of the walnuts.

⅔ cup all-purpose flour
½ teaspoon baking powder
¼ teaspoon salt
½ cup vegetable shortening
½ cup apple butter
½ cup packed dark brown sugar
1 large egg
½ teaspoon baking soda
1 tablespoon warm water
1 cup rolled oats
1 cup flaked coconut (optional)

**1** Preheat the oven to 350 degrees. Grease a 13 by 9-inch baking pan.

**2** Combine the flour, baking powder and salt.

**3** In a large bowl, cream the vegetable shortening, apple butter, and brown sugar. Beat in the egg.

**4** Dissolve the baking soda in the warm water and add to the creamed mixture, beating until smooth. Gradually blend in the dry ingredients. Fold in the oats coconut.

**5** Spread the mixture evenly in the prepared pan.

**6** Bake for 15 to 20 minutes, or until lightly colored. Cool in the pan on a rack before cutting into large or small bars.

**Baking notes:** If you like chocolate, add chocolate chips to the dough and drizzle melted chocolate over the top of the cooled cookies.

# APPLE BUTTER-OATMEAL BARS

Bar Cookies

YIELD: *2 to 3 dozen*
TOTAL TIME: *30 minutes*

---

1 cup all-purpose flour
½ teaspoon baking powder
1 teaspoon ground cinnamon
½ teaspoon salt
½ cup vegetable shortening
½ cup packed light brown sugar
½ cup granulated sugar
1 large egg
1 teaspoon vanilla extract
½ teaspoon baking soda
1 teaspoon warm water
2 cups flaked coconut
½ cup rolled oats
½ cup diced, peeled apples

**1** Preheat the oven to 375 degrees. Grease 2 baking sheets.

**2** Combine the flour, baking powder, cinnamon, and salt.

**3** In a large bowl, cream the vegetable shortening and both sugars. Beat in the egg and vanilla extract.

**4** Dissolve the baking soda in the warm water and add to the egg mixture, beating until smooth. Gradually blend in the dry ingredients. Fold in the coconut, oats, and apples.

**5** Drop the dough by spoonfuls 1½ inches apart onto the prepared baking sheets.

**6** Bake for 10 to 12 minutes, or until golden brown. Transfer to wire racks to cool.

# APPLE-COCONUT DREAMS

Drop Cookies

YIELD: *4 to 5 dozen*
TOTAL TIME: *30 minutes*

# APPLE COOKIES

Drop Cookies

YIELD: *3 to 4 dozen*
TOTAL TIME: *35 minutes*

2 cups all-purpose flour
1 teaspoon baking powder
½ teaspoon ground nutmeg
1 teaspoon ground cinnamon
½ teaspoon ground cloves
½ teaspoon salt
½ cup butter, at room temperature
1½ cups packed light brown sugar
1 large egg
¼ cup fresh lemon juice
1 teaspoon vanilla extract
1 cup diced, peeled apples
1 cup walnuts, chopped
1 cup raisins

### GLAZE

1½ cups powdered sugar
1 tablespoon butter, at room temperature
2½ tablespoons evaporated milk
¼ teaspoon vanilla extract
Pinch of salt

**1** Preheat the oven to 400 degrees. Grease 2 baking sheets.

**2** Combine the flour, baking powder, spices, and salt.

**3** In a large bowl, cream the butter and brown sugar. Beat in the egg, lemon juice, and vanilla extract. Gradually blend in the dry ingredients. Fold in the apples, walnuts, and raisins.

**4** Drop the dough by teaspoonfuls 1½ inches apart onto the prepared baking sheets. Bake for 12 to 15 minutes, or until golden.

**5** Meanwhile, make the glaze: Combine all the ingredients in a small bowl and beat until smooth.

**6** Transfer the cookies to wire racks. Spread the glaze over the tops of the warm cookies, and let cool.

# APPLE DROPS

Drop Cookies

YIELD: *4 dozen*
TOTAL TIME: *30 minutes*

2 cups all-purpose flour
½ teaspoon baking powder
¼ teaspoon baking soda
½ teaspoon ground cinnamon
¼ teaspoon ground cloves
¼ teaspoon ground nutmeg
½ cup vegetable shortening
4 large eggs
¾ cup frozen apple juice concentrate, thawed

**1** Preheat the oven to 375 degrees. Grease 2 baking sheets.

**2** In a large bowl, combine the flour, baking powder, baking soda, and spices. Cut in the vegetable shortening until mixture to resembles fine crumbs.

**3** In a medium bowl, beat the eggs until thick and light-colored. Beat in the apple juice concentrate. Add the dry mixture and blend to make a smooth dough.

**4** Drop the dough by spoonfuls 1½-inches apart onto the prepared baking sheets.

**5** Bake for 6 to 8 minutes, or until golden brown. Transfer to wire racks to cool.

# APPLE-OATMEAL COOKIES I

Bar Cookies

YIELD: *1 to 2 dozen*
TOTAL TIME: *50 minutes*

½ cup vegetable shortening
1 cup packed light brown sugar
½ teaspoon baking soda
1 tablespoon warm water
2 large eggs
1 teaspoon vanilla extract
1 teaspoon ground cinnamon
¼ teaspoon salt
½ cup diced, peeled apples (about 1 apple)
1½ cups all-purpose flour
1 cup walnuts, ground
½ cup rolled oats

**1** Preheat the oven to 350 degrees. Grease an 8-inch square baking pan.

**2** In a large bowl, cream the vegetable shortening and brown sugar.

**3** Dissolve the baking soda in the warm water and add to the creamed mixture, beating until smooth.

**4** In another bowl, combine the eggs, vanilla extract, cinnamon, and salt. Fold in the apples. Stir into the creamed mixture. Gradually blend in the flour. Fold in the walnuts and oats.

**5** Spread the mixture evenly in the prepared pan.

**6** Bake for 30 to 35 minutes, until a toothpick comes out clean. Cool in the pan on a rack before cutting into large or small bars.

**Baking notes:** Raisins and/or shredded coconut may be added to the dough. For a different texture, substitute ½ cup apple butter for the chopped apples.

# APPLE-OATMEAL COOKIES II

Drop Cookies

YIELD: *3 to 4 dozen*
TOTAL TIME: *30 minutes*

1 cup all-purpose flour
1 teaspoon baking powder
1 teaspoon ground cinnamon
½ teaspoon ground nutmeg
½ teaspoon salt
½ cup vegetable shortening
¾ cup granulated sugar
2 each eggs
1 cup rolled oats
1 cup diced, peeled apples
1 cup walnuts, chopped

**1** Preheat the oven to 350 degrees. Grease 2 baking sheets.

**2** Combine the flour, baking powder, spices, and salt.

**3** In a large bowl, cream the vegetable shortening and sugar. Beat in the eggs. Gradually blend in the dry ingredients. Fold in the oats, apples, and walnuts.

**4** Drop the dough by spoonfuls 1½ inches apart onto the prepared baking sheets.

**5** Bake for 12 to 15 minutes, or until lightly colored. Transfer to wire racks to cool.

# APPLE-RAISIN BARS

Bar Cookies

YIELD: *2 to 3 dozen*
TOTAL TIME: *30 minutes*

1½ cups all-purpose flour
½ cup whole wheat flour
2 teaspoons baking powder
1 teaspoon baking soda
1 teaspoon ground cinnamon
1 teaspoon ground nutmeg
3 large eggs
½ cup unsweetened applesauce
½ cup unsweetened apple juice
¼ cup vegetable shortening
1 cup raisins
Ground cinnamon for sprinkling

1  Preheat the oven to 350 degrees. Grease an 8-inch square baking pan.

2  Combine both flours, the baking powder, baking soda, and spices.

3  In a large bowl, combine the eggs, applesauce, apple juice, and vegetable shortening and beat until well blended. Gradually blend in the dry ingredients. Fold in the raisins.

4  Spread the dough evenly in the prepared baking pan. Sprinkle a little cinnamon over the top.

5  Bake for 20 to 25 minutes, until a toothpick inserted in the center comes out clean. Cool in the pan on a rack before cutting into large or small bars.

# APPLE-RAISIN DROPS

Drop Cookies

YIELD: *3 to 4 dozen*
TOTAL TIME: *35 minutes*

2 cups all-purpose flour
1 teaspoon baking powder
1 teaspoon ground cinnamon
½ teaspoon ground nutmeg
¼ teaspoon ground cloves
½ teaspoon salt
½ cup vegetable shortening
1 cup packed light brown sugar
2 large eggs
¼ cup milk
1½ cups diced, peeled apples
1 cup golden raisins
½ cup walnuts, chopped

1  Preheat the oven to 350 degrees. Grease 2 baking sheets.

2  Combine the flour, baking powder, spices, and salt.

3  In a large bowl, cream the vegetable shortening and brown sugar. Beat in the eggs and milk. Gradually blend in the dry ingredients. Fold in the apples, raisins and walnuts.

4  Drop the dough by spoonfuls 1½ inches apart onto the prepared baking sheets.

5  Bake for 12 to 14 minutes, or until lightly colored. Transfer to wire racks to cool.

# APPLE-SPICE BARS

Bar Cookies

YIELD: *1 to 2 dozen*
TOTAL TIME: *55 minutes*

1½ cups all-purpose flour
½ teaspoon baking powder
½ teaspoon ground nutmeg
½ teaspoon ground ginger
¼ teaspoon salt
⅔ cup vegetable shortening
1½ cups granulated sugar
4 large eggs
½ teaspoon baking soda
1 tablespoon warm water
1 cup diced, peeled apples

TOPPING
¼ cup granulated sugar
1 teaspoon ground cinnamon

1  Preheat the oven to 350 degrees. Grease a 13 by 9-inch baking pan.

2  Combine the flour, baking powder, spices, and salt.

3  In a large bowl, cream the vegetable shortening and sugar. Beat in the eggs.

4  Dissolve the baking soda in the warm water and add to the egg mixture, beating until smooth. Gradually blend in the dry ingredients. Fold in the apples.

5  Spread the mixture evenly in the prepared pan. Combine the sugar and cinnamon for the topping and sprinkle evenly over the cookies.

6  Bake for 25 to 30 minutes, or until top is lightly browned. Cool in the pan on a rack before cutting into large or small bars.

2 ounces semisweet chocolate,
  chopped
1 cup all-purpose flour
1 teaspoon baking powder
½ teaspoon ground cinnamon
¼ teaspoon salt
½ cup vegetable shortening
1¼ cups granulated sugar
2 large eggs
1 teaspoon vanilla extract
½ cup unsweetened applesauce, at
  room temperature
½ cup walnuts, chopped

**1** Preheat the oven to 350
degrees. Grease a 13 by 9-inch
baking pan.

**2** Melt the chocolate in a double
boiler over low heat, stirring
until smooth. Let cool.

**3** Combine the flour, baking
powder, cinnamon, and salt.

**4** In a large bowl, cream the vegetable shortening and sugar. Beat
in the eggs one at a time.

**5** In a medium bowl, combine
the applesauce, melted chocolate,
and vanilla extract. Add to the
egg mixture, beating until
smooth. Gradually blend in the
dry ingredients. Fold in the nuts.

**6** Spread the mixture evenly in
the prepared pan.

**7** Bake for 20 to 25 minutes, or
until a toothpick inserted in the
center comes out clean. Cool in
the pan on a rack before cutting
into large or small bars.

**Baking notes:** For variation, substitute almond extract for the
vanilla extract and almonds,
chopped for the walnuts.

# Applesauce Brownies

Bar Cookies

Yield: *1 to 2 dozen*
Total time: *40 minutes*

---

1 cup golden raisins
About ⅓ cup brandy
1 package spice cake mix
½ cup canola oil
½ cup unsweetened applesauce
1 large egg

**1** Preheat the oven to 350
degrees.

**2** Place the raisins in a small
bowl and add enough brandy to
just cover. Set aside to plump for
10 minutes.

**3** Prepare the cake mix according
to the package directions, adding
the oil, applesauce, and egg.
Drain the raisins and fold them
into the dough.

**4** Drop the dough by spoonfuls 2
inches apart onto ungreased baking sheets.

**5** Bake for 12 to 15 minutes, or
until golden. Transfer to wire
racks to cool.

# Applesauce Cookies I

Drop Cookies

Yield: *5 to 6 dozen*
Total time: *35 minutes*
Plumping time: *10 minutes*

# APPLESAUCE COOKIES II

Drop Cookies

YIELD: *2 to 3 dozen*
TOTAL TIME: *35 minutes*

2 tablespoons vegetable shortening
½ cup granulated sugar
1 large egg
½ cup unsweetened applesauce
1 cup packaged biscuit mix
1½ teaspoons caraway seeds
1 teaspoon grated lemon zest

**1** Preheat the oven to 375 degrees. Generously grease 2 baking sheets.

**2** In a large bowl, cream the vegetable shortening and sugar. Beat in the egg. Beat in the applesauce. Gradually blend in the biscuit mix. Fold in the caraway seeds and lemon zest.

**3** Drop the dough by spoonfuls 1½ inches apart onto the prepared baking sheets.

**4** Bake for 8 to 10 minutes, or until golden brown. Transfer to wire racks to cool.

# APPLESAUCE COOKIES III

Drop Cookies

YIELD: *1 to 2 dozen*
TOTAL TIME: *35 minutes*

1 cup all-purpose flour
1 teaspoon baking soda
1 teaspoon ground allspice
½ teaspoon salt
1 cup vegetable shortening
1½ cups packed light brown sugar
2 large eggs
1 teaspoon vanilla extract
½ cup unsweetened applesauce
1 cup cornflakes

**1** Preheat the oven to 350 degrees.

**2** Combine the flour, baking soda, allspice, and salt.

**3** In a large bowl, cream the vegetable shortening and brown sugar. Beat in the eggs and vanilla extract. Beat in the applesauce. Gradually blend in the dry ingredients. Fold in the cornflakes.

**4** Drop the dough by spoonfuls 1½ inches apart onto ungreased baking sheets.

**5** Bake for 12 to 14 minutes, until a golden brown. Transfer to wire racks to cool.

**Baking notes:** Almost any type of not-too-sweet breakfast cereal can be used. Add ½ cup wheat germ if you like; nuts and raisins are also good additions.

# APPLESAUCE COOKIES IV

Drop Cookies

YIELD: *3 to 4 dozen*
TOTAL TIME: *35 minutes*

2½ cups all-purpose flour
½ teaspoon ground cinnamon
½ teaspoon ground cloves
½ teaspoon ground nutmeg
½ teaspoon salt
½ cup vegetable shortening
1 cup granulated sugar
1 large egg
1 teaspoon baking soda
1 tablespoon warm water
1 cup unsweetened applesauce
1 cup walnuts, chopped
½ cup raisins

**1** Preheat the oven to 350 degrees. Grease 2 baking sheets.

**2** Combine the flour, spices and salt.

**3** In a large bowl, cream the vegetable shortening and sugar. Beat in the egg.

**4** Dissolve the baking soda in the warm water and add to the creamed mixture, beating until smooth. Beat in the applesauce. Gradually blend in the dry ingredients. Fold in the walnuts and raisins.

**5** Drop the dough by spoonfuls 1½ inches apart onto the prepared baking sheets.

**6** Bake for 15 to 20 minutes, or until lightly colored. Transfer to wire racks to cool.

2 cups all-purpose flour
1 teaspoon ground cinnamon
½ teaspoon ground cardamom
Pinch of salt
¾ cup vegetable shortening
1 cup granulated sugar
2 teaspoons baking soda
1 tablespoon warm water
2 large eggs
2 cups unsweetened applesauce
1 cup pitted dates, chopped
1 cup walnuts, chopped

**1** Preheat the oven to 350 degrees. Grease a 13 by 9-inch baking pan.

**2** Combine the flour, cinnamon, cardamom, and salt.

**3** In a large bowl, cream the vegetable shortening and sugar.

**4** Dissolve the baking soda in the warm water and add to the creamed mixture, beating until

smooth. Beat in the eggs. Beat in the applesauce. Gradually blend in the dry ingredients. Fold in the dates and walnuts.

**5** Spread the mixture evenly in the prepared pan.

**6** Bake for 25 to 30 minutes, or until golden brown on top. Cool in the pan on a rack before cutting into large or small bars.

**Baking notes:** For a decorative touch, frost these with Vanilla Icing (see Pantry), and drizzle Dark Chocolate Icing (see Pantry) over the top.

# APPLESAUCE DATE BARS

Bar Cookies

YIELD: *2 to 3 dozen*
TOTAL TIME: *45 minutes*

---

1 cup raisins
About ⅓ cup brandy
1 cup walnuts, chopped
2 cups all-purpose flour
1 teaspoon ground cinnamon
½ teaspoon ground nutmeg
¼ teaspoon ground cloves
½ teaspoon salt
½ cup vegetable shortening
1 cup granulated sugar
1 large egg
1 teaspoon baking soda
1 tablespoon warm water
1 cup unsweetened applesauce

**1** Combine the raisins and enough brandy to cover in a small bowl. Set aside to plump for 1 hour.

**2** Preheat the oven to 350 degrees. Grease 2 baking sheets.

**3** Drain the raisins and return to the bowl. Add the walnuts. Combine the flour, spices, and salt.

**4** In a large bowl, cream the vegetable shortening and sugar. Beat in the egg.

**5** In a small bowl, dissolve the baking soda in the warm water. Stir in the applesauce. Add to the egg mixture, beating until smooth. Gradually blend in the dry ingredients. Fold in the raisins and walnuts.

**6** Drop the dough by spoonfuls 1½ inches apart onto the prepared baking sheets

**7** Bake for 12 to 15 minutes, until lightly colored. Transfer to wire racks to cool.

**Baking notes:** For a decorative touch, drizzle Vanilla Icing (see Pantry) over the baked cookies.

# APPLESAUCE-NUT-RAISIN COOKIES

Drop Cookies

YIELD: *2 to 3 dozen*
TOTAL TIME: *35 minutes*

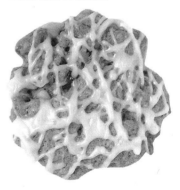

# APPLESAUCE-SPICE COOKIES

Drop Cookies

YIELD: *2 to 3 dozen*
TOTAL TIME: *30 minutes*

**2 cups all-purpose flour**
**1 teaspoon baking powder**
**½ teaspoon ground cinnamon**
**¼ teaspoon ground cloves**
**½ cup vegetable shortening**
**1 cup granulated sugar**
**1 large egg**
**1 teaspoon baking powder**
**1 tablespoon warm water**
**1 cup unsweetened applesauce**

**1** Preheat the oven to 350 degrees. Grease 2 baking sheets.

**2** Combine the flour, baking powder, cinnamon, cloves, and salt.

**3** In a large bowl, cream the vegetable shortening and sugar. Beat in the egg.

**4** Dissolve the baking soda in the warm water and add to the egg mixture, beating until smooth.

Beat in the applesauce. Gradually blend in the dry ingredients.

**5** Drop the dough by spoonfuls 1½ inches apart onto the prepared baking sheets.

**6** Bake for 10 to 15 minutes, until the cookies are light golden. Transfer to wire racks to cool.

# APPLE STRIPS

Bar Cookies

YIELD: *3 to 4 dozen*
TOTAL TIME: *45 minutes*
CHILLING TIME: *2 hours*

**CRUST**
**2 cups all-purpose flour**
**¼ cup granulated sugar**
**¾ cup vegetable shortening**
**3 tablespoons sour cream**
**½ teaspoon grated lemon zest**

**FILLING**
**5 medium apples, peeled, cored and sliced thin**
**½ cup granulated sugar**
**1 tablespoon raisins**
**1 large egg yolk, beaten**
**Powdered sugar for sprinkling**

**1** To make the crust, combine the flour and sugar in a bowl. Cut in the vegetable shortening until the mixture resembles coarse crumbs. Stir in the sour cream and lemon zest.

**2** Divide the dough in half. Wrap in waxed paper and let chill for 2 hours.

**3** Preheat the oven to 325 degrees.

**4** On a lightly floured surface, roll out half of the dough to a 9-inch square. Fit the dough into an ungreased 9-inch square baking pan.

**5** To make filling, layer the apples evenly over the crust. Sprinkle the sugar and the raisins on top.

**6** Roll out the remaining dough to a 9-inch square. Cut into 1-inch-wide strips and arrange in a lattice pattern over the filling. Brush the lattice strips with the beaten egg yolk.

**7** Bake for 18 to 20 minutes, or until the crust is golden brown. Sprinkle powdered sugar over the warm cookies, and cut into 2 by 1-inch strips.

**Baking notes:** Shredded coconut may be added to the crust for a different flavor and texture.

1¾ cups all-purpose flour
½ cup almonds, ground fine
½ teaspoon salt
¾ cup vegetable shortening
¾ cup powdered sugar
½ teaspoon almond extract

**FILLING**
One 12-ounce jar apricot preserves
½ cup glacé cherries, diced
1½ teaspoons brandy

**1** Preheat the oven to 350 degrees.

**2** Combine the flour, almonds, and salt.

**3** In a large bowl, cream the vegetable shortening and powdered sugar. Beat in the almond extract. Gradually blend in the dry ingredients.

**4** Set aside 1 cup of the almond mixture for the topping. Spread the remaining mixture evenly over the bottom of an ungreased 13 by 9-inch baking pan.

**5** To make the filling, combine the apricot preserves, cherries, and brandy in a small bowl, and stir until well blended. Spread the filling evenly over the almond mixture. Crumble the reserved almond mixture over the filling.

**6** Bake for 30 to 35 minutes, until the edges are dark golden brown. Cut into large or small bars while still warm, and cool in the pan on a rack.

# APRICOT BARS I

Bar Cookies

YIELD: *2 to 3 dozen*
TOTAL TIME: *45 minutes*

---

2 cups all-purpose flour
2 teaspoons baking powder
½ teaspoon ground nutmeg
½ teaspoon salt
2 teaspoons grated orange zest
4 large eggs
2 cups granulated sugar
1½ cups dried apricots, diced
1 cup walnuts, chopped
Powdered sugar for sprinkling

**1** Preheat the oven to 350 degrees. Grease a 13 by 9-inch baking pan.

**2** Sift the flour, baking powder, nutmeg, and salt into a bowl. Stir in the orange zest.

**3** In a large bowl, beat the eggs and sugar until thick and light-colored. Gradually blend in the dry ingredients. Fold in the apricots and walnuts.

**4** Spread the batter evenly in the prepared pan. Bake for 15 to 20 minutes, until the top is golden, and a toothpick inserted into the center comes out clean.

**5** Cool in the pan on a rack before cutting into large or small bars. Sprinkle with powdered sugar.

# APRICOT BARS II

Bar Cookies

YIELD: *2 to 4 dozen*
TOTAL TIME: *40 minutes*

# APRICOT BARS III

Bar Cookies

YIELD: *3 to 4 dozen*
TOTAL TIME: *60 minutes*

**FILLING**
**1 cup dried apricots**
**⅓ cup all purpose flour**
**½ teaspoon baking powder**
**¼ teaspoon salt**
**2 large eggs**
**1 cup packed light brown sugar**
**⅓ cup apricot liqueur**
**½ cup almonds, chopped**

**CRUST**
**1 cup all-purpose flour**
**¼ cup granulated sugar**
**½ cup vegetable shortening**

**1** Preheat the oven to 350 degrees. Grease a 9-inch square baking pan.

**2** Put the apricots in a small saucepan and add just enough water to cover. Bring to a boil and cook until very soft, about 10 minutes. Drain and let cool, then chop very fine. Set aside.

**3** To make the crust, combine the flour and sugar in a bowl. Cut in the vegetable shortening until the mixture resembles coarse crumbs.

**4** Press the mixture evenly into the bottom of the prepared pan. Bake for 15 minutes.

**5** Meanwhile, make the filling: combine the flour, baking powder, and salt.

**6** In a medium bowl, beat the eggs and brown sugar until thick and well blended. Beat in the liqueur. Gradually blend in the dry ingredients. Fold in the chopped apricots and almonds.

**7** Spread the filling over the warm crust. Bake for 30 minutes longer, until filling is set, or until firm to the touch.

**8** Cool in the pan on a rack before cutting into large or small bars.

# APRICOT BARS IV

Bar Cookies

YIELD: *2 to 3 dozen*
TOTAL TIME: *75 minutes*

**FILLING**
**⅔ cup dried apricots**
**⅓ cup all-purpose flour**
**½ teaspoon baking powder**
**¼ teaspoon salt**
**½ cup walnuts, chopped**
**1½ cups packed light brown sugar**
**2 large eggs**
**½ teaspoon vanilla extract**

**CRUST**
**1 cup all-purpose flour**
**¼ cup granulated sugar**
**½ cup vegetable shortening**
**Powdered sugar for sprinkling**

**1** Preheat the oven to 350 degrees. Lightly grease an 8-inch square baking pan.

**2** Combine the apricots and ⅓ cup water in a small saucepan. Cover and bring to a boil over medium heat. Cook for 15 minutes, or until soft. Drain and let cool, then chop fine. Set aside.

**3** To make the crust, combine the flour and sugar in a bowl. Cut in the vegetable shortening until the mixture resembles coarse crumbs.

**4** Press the mixture evenly into the bottom of the prepared pan. Bake for 25 minutes.

**5** Meanwhile, make the filling: Combine the flour, baking powder, and salt. Add the walnuts and apricots.

**6** In a medium bowl, beat the brown sugar, eggs, and vanilla extract together until thick. Gradually blend in the dry ingredients.

**7** Spread the apricot mixture evenly over the warm crust. Bake for 25 minutes longer, until filling is set.

**8** Cool in the pan on a rack before cutting into large or small bars. Sprinkle with powdered sugar.

1 cup dried apricots, diced
½ cup bran cereal
½ cup fresh orange juice
1½ cups all-purpose flour
1 teaspoon baking powder
¾ teaspoon ground cinnamon
½ teaspoon salt
½ cup vegetable shortening
½ cup granulated sugar
½ cup packed light brown sugar
1 large egg
1 teaspoon vanilla extract
⅓ cup walnuts, chopped

1 Preheat the oven to 375 degrees. Grease 2 baking sheets.

2 Place the apricots in a small bowl and add boiling water to cover. Set aside.

3 Combine the bran cereal and orange juice in a small bowl. Combine the flour, baking powder, cinnamon, and salt.

4 In a large bowl, cream the vegetable shortening and both sugars. Beat in the egg and vanilla extract. Gradually blend in the dry ingredients. Fold in the bran cereal with the orange juice. Fold in the walnuts.

5 Drain the apricots and fold them into the dough.

6 Drop the dough by spoonfuls 1½ inches apart onto the prepared baking sheets.

7 Bake for 8 to 10 minutes, until golden brown. Transfer to wire racks to cool.

**Baking notes:** Raisins may be added if desired; plump them by adding them to the soaking apricots.

# APRICOT-BRAN COOKIES

Drop Cookies

YIELD: *4 to 5 dozen*
TOTAL TIME: *30 minutes*

¼ cup vegetable shortening
¼ cup packed light brown sugar
2 large eggs
¼ cup warm water
1 package yellow cake mix
1 cup dried apricots, diced
½ cup maraschino cherries, drained and chopped
Powdered sugar for sprinkling

1 Preheat the oven to 350 degrees. Grease a 15½ by 10½-inch baking pan.

2 In a large bowl, cream the vegetable shortening and brown sugar. Beat in the eggs and warm water. Beat in half the cake mix. Stir in the apricots and cherries.

3 Spread the mixture evenly in the prepared pan. Sprinkle the remaining mix over the top.

4 Bake for 20 to 25 minutes until firm to the touch.

5 Cool in the pan on a rack. Sprinkle with powdered sugar and cut into small or large bars.

# APRICOT-CHERRY BARS

Bar Cookies

YIELD: *2 to 3 dozen*
TOTAL TIME: *40 minutes*

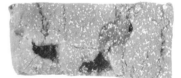

# APRICOT-CHOCOLATE SPRITZ COOKIES

Formed Cookies

YIELD: *3 to 4 dozen*
TOTAL TIME: *35 minutes*

2 ounces bittersweet chocolate, chopped
2¼ cups all-purpose flour
¼ teaspoon salt
¾ cup vegetable shortening
½ cup granulated sugar
1 large egg
1 teaspoon almond extract
½ cup apricot preserves

TOPPING
½ cup almonds, chopped
2 tablespoons granulated sugar

**1** Preheat the oven to 400 degrees.

**2** Melt the chocolate in a double boiler over a low heat, stirring until smooth. Let cool.

**3** Combine the flour and salt.

**4** In a large bowl, cream the vegetable shortening and sugar. Beat in the egg, melted chocolate, and almond extract. Gradually blend in the dry ingredients.

**5** Place the dough in a cookie press or a pastry bag fitted with a ribbon tip. Press or pipe out four 12½-inch-long stips on an ungreased baking sheet. Spread a thin layer of apricot preserves over each strip, and press or pipe out another strip of dough on top.

**6** To make the topping, combine the almonds and sugar in a small bowl. Sprinkle evenly over the top of the ribbon sandwiches. Cut each sandwich into 5 pieces.

**7** Bake for 10 to 12 minutes, until golden. Transfer to wire racks to cool.

**Baking notes:** Almost any type of fruit preserves can be used in these cookies.

# APRICOT CRESCENTS

Rolled Cookies

YIELD: *3 dozen*
TOTAL TIME: *40 minutes*
CHILLING TIME: *4 hours*

2 cups all-purpose flour
1 teaspoon granulated sugar
Pinch of salt
1 cup vegetable shortening
1 cup sour cream
1 large egg
½ cup apricot preserves
½ cup walnuts, chopped
Powdered sugar for dusting

**1** Combine the flour, sugar, and salt in a bowl. Cut in the vegetable shortening until the mixture resembles coarse crumbs. With a fork stir in the sour cream and egg until a stiff dough forms. Cover and chill for at least 4 hours, or overnight.

**2** Preheat the oven to 350 degrees. Grease 2 baking sheets.

**3** Divide the dough into 3 pieces. On a floured surface, roll out

each piece to an 11-inch round. Spread one-third of the apricot preserves evenly over each round, and sprinkle each round with one-third of the walnuts.

**4** Cut each round into 12 wedges. Starting at the wide end, roll up each wedge. Place seam side down on the prepared baking sheets, placing the cookies about 1 inch apart and curving the ends to form crescent shapes.

**5** Bake for 25 to 30 minutes, until lightly colored. Dust the warm cookies with powdered sugar and transfer to wire racks to cool.

**FILLING**
½ cup dried apricots
½ cup granulated sugar
½ cup pecans, ground

**CRUST**
1 cups all-purpose flour
1 cup rolled oats
⅔ cup packed light brown sugar
¼ teaspoon salt
½ teaspoon vegetable shortening

**1** Preheat the oven to 350 degrees. Grease an 8-inch square baking pan.

**2** To make the filling, place the apricots in a bowl and add boiling water to cover. Let soak for 15 minutes.

**3** Drain the apricots and dice very fine. Place in a bowl, add the sugar and pecans, and toss to mix.

**4** To make the crust, combine the flour, oats, baking powder, brown sugar, and salt in a bowl.

Cut in the vegetable shortening until the mixture resembles coarse crumbs.

**5** Spread two-thirds of the crust mixture evenly over the bottom of the prepared pan. Spread the apricot filling over the crust. Sprinkle the remaining crust mixture over the filling, and press down lightly.

**6** Bake for 20 to 35 minutes, until firm to the touch. Cool in the pan on a rack before cutting into large or small bars.

# APRICOT-FILLED COOKIES

Bar Cookies
YIELD: *2 to 3 dozen*
TOTAL TIME: *55 minutes*

---

1 cup dried apricots, diced
1½ cups all-purpose flour
1 teaspoon baking powder
¼ teaspoon salt
½ cup vegetable shortening
1 cup granulated sugar
½ cup packed light brown sugar
2 large eggs
½ cup buttermilk
¼ teaspoon grated orange zest
1 teaspoon baking soda
1 tablespoon warm water
1 cup pecans, chopped
Powdered sugar for sprinkling

**1** Preheat the oven to 350 degrees. Grease a 10-inch square baking pan.

**2** Place the apricots in a small bowl and add boiling water to cover. Set aside and let soften for 10 minutes.

**3** Combine the flour, baking powder, and salt.

**4** In a large bowl, cream the vegetable shortening, granulated sugar, and brown sugar. Beat in the eggs and buttermilk. Beat in the orange zest.

**5** Dissolve the baking soda in the warm water and add to the buttermilk mixture, beating until smooth. Gradually blend in the dry ingredients.

**6** Drain the apricots and fold into the dough. Fold in the nuts.

**7** Spread the dough evenly in the prepared pan. Bake for 20 to 25 minutes, until the top is golden.

**8** Cool in the pan on a rack. Sprinkle with powdered sugar and cut into large or small bars.

# APRICOT-PECAN GEMS

Bar Cookies
YIELD: *1 to 3 dozen*
TOTAL TIME: *40 minutes*

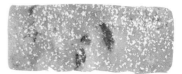

# APRICOT-SPICE COOKIES

Drop Cookies

YIELD: *2 to 3 dozen*
TOTAL TIME: *35 minutes*
CHILLING TIME: *1 hour*

1 cup dried apricots
2 cups all-purpose flour
1 teaspoon baking powder
1 teaspoon ground allspice
½ teaspoon ground cinnamon
½ teaspoon salt
½ cup vegetable shortening
1 cup granulated sugar
1 teaspoon baking soda
1 tablespoon warm water
1 large egg
1 cup golden raisins
1 cup pecans, chopped

1 Put the apricots through a food grinder, or grind them in a food processor or blender.

2 Combine the flour, baking powder, spices, and salt.

3 In a large bowl, cream the vegetable shortening and sugar.

4 Dissolve the baking soda in the warm water and add to the creamed mixture, beating until smooth. Beat in the egg. Gradually blend in the dry ingredients. Fold in the apricots, raisins, and pecans. Cover and chill for at least 1 hour.

5 Preheat the oven to 375 degrees. Grease 2 baking sheets.

6 Drop the dough by spoonfuls 1½ inches apart onto the prepared baking sheets.

7 Bake for 18 to 20 minutes, until browned on top. Transfer to wire racks to cool.

# APRICOT SQUARES

Bar Cookies

YIELD: *2 to 3 dozen*
TOTAL TIME: *45 minutes*

2 cups all-purpose flour
¼ teaspoon salt
¾ cup vegetable shortening
1 cup granulated sugar
1 large egg
¼ teaspoon salt
1 teaspoon vanilla extract
1½ cups shredded coconut
½ cup walnuts, chopped
One 10-ounce jar apricot preserves

1 Preheat the oven to 350 degrees.

2 Combine the flour and salt.

3 In a large bowl, cream the vegetable shortening and sugar. Beat in the egg and vanilla extract. Gradually blend in the dry ingredients. Fold in the coconut and walnuts.

4 Press three-quarters of the mixture evenly into the bottom of an ungreased 13 by 9-inch baking pan. Spread the apricot preserves over the mixture. Crumble the remaining coconut mixture over the preserves.

5 Bake for 25 to 30 minutes, until firm to the touch and lightly browned. Cool in the pan on a rack before cutting into large or small bars.

**CRUST**

2 cups all-purpose flour
¼ cup granulated sugar
¾ cup vegetable shortening
3 tablespoons sour cream
½ teaspoon grated lemon zest

**FILLING**

1½ cups dried apricots, sliced
½ cup granulated sguar
1 tablespoon raisins
1 large egg yolk, beaten
Powdered sugar for sprinkling

**1** To make the crust, combine the flour and sugar in a bowl. Cut in the vegetable shortening until the mixture resembles coarse crumbs. Stir in the sour cream and lemon zest until a stiff dough forms.

**2** Divide the dough in half. Wrap in waxed paper and chill for 2 hours.

**3** Place the apricots in a small bowl and add boiling water to cover. Let soak for 30 minutes.

**4** Preheat the oven to 325 degrees. Grease a 9-inch square baking pan.

**5** On a floured surface, roll out half the dough to a 9-inch square. Fit the dough into the prepared pan.

**6** Drain the apricots well. Layer the apricots on the crust and sprinkle with the sugar. Sprinkle the raisins on top.

**7** Roll out the remaining dough to a 9-inch square. Cut into 1-inch-wide strips and arrange in a lattice pattern on top of the apricot filling. Brush the lattice strips with the beaten egg yolk.

**8** Bake for 18 to 20 minutes, until firm to the touch and crust is golden.

**9** Dust the warm cookies with powdered sugar, and cut into strips.

**Baking notes:** Shredded coconut may be added for flavor and texture.

# APRICOT STRIPS

Bar Cookies

YIELD: *3 to 4 dozen*
TOTAL TIME: *40 minutes*
SOAKING TIME: *30 minutes*
CHILLING TIME: *2 hours*

---

**FILLING**

¾ cup dried apricots, diced
⅓ cup all-purpose flour
½ teaspoon baking powder
¼ teaspoon salt
2 large eggs
1 cup packed light brown sugar
½ teaspoon vanilla extract
½ cup walnuts, chopped

**CRUST**

1 cup all-purpose flour
¼ cup granulated sugar
½ cup vegetable shortening

**1** Preheat the oven to 325 degrees.

**2** Place the apricots in a small saucepan and add just enough water to cover. Bring to a boil, reduce the heat, and simmer for 10 minutes, or until soft. Drain and let cool.

**3** To make the crust, combine the flour and sugar in a medium

bowl. Cut in the vegetable shrotening until the mixture resembles coarse crumbs.

**4** Press the mixture evenly into the bottom of an ungreased 9-inch square baking pan. Bake for 25 minutes.

**5** Meanwhile, make the filling: Combine the flour, baking powder, and salt.

**6** In a large bowl, beat the eggs and brown sugar until thick. Beat in the vanilla extact. Gradually blend in the dry ingredients. Fold in the apricots and walnuts.

**7** Spread the filling evenly over the warm crust. Bake for 35 minutes longer, until the filling is set.

**8** Cool in the pan on a rack before cutting into large or small bars.

# APRICOT-WALNUT BARS

Bar Cookies

YIELD: *2 to 3 dozen*
TOTAL TIME: *70 minutes*

# ARROWROOT BISCUITS

Drop Cookies

YIELD: *3 to 4 dozen*
TOTAL TIME: *30 minutes*

1½ cups all-purpose flour
½ cup arrowroot flour
¼ cup vegetable shortening
½ cup granulated sugar
2 large eggs
Granulated sugar for sprinkling

1 Preheat the oven to 350 degrees.

2 Sift together the all-purpose flour and arrowroot flour.

3 In a large bowl, cream the vegetable shortening and sugar until light and fluffy.

4 In another bowl, beat the eggs until thick and light-colored. Beat the eggs into the shortening. Fold in the flours.

5 Drop the dough by spoonfuls 1½ inches apart onto ungreased baking sheets.

6 Bake for 12 to 15 minutes, until lightly colored. Sprinkle the warm cookies with sugar and transfer to wire racks to cool.

**Baking notes:** Finely ground nuts, such as walnuts or almonds, can be added to the dough.

---

# ARROWROOT CAKES

Bar Cookies

YIELD: *1 to 3 dozen*
TOTAL TIME: *45 minutes*

2 cups arrowroot flour
2 cups all-purpose flour
1 cup vegetable shortening
½ cup powdered sugar
½ teaspoon almond extract
6 large egg whites
Granulated sugar for sprinkling

1 Preheat the oven to 350 degrees. Grease a 9-inch baking pan.

2 Combine the arrowroot flour and all-purpose flour

3 In a large bowl beat the vegetable shortening and powdered sugar together until light and fluffy. Beat in the almond extract. Gradually blend in the flours.

4 In a large bowl, beat the egg whites until stiff but not dry. Fold the whites into the arrowroot mixture.

5 Spread the mixture evenly in the prepared pan. Bake for 25 to 30 minutes, until dry to the touch.

6 Sprinkle the hot cookies with sugar. Cool in the pan on a rack before cutting into large or small bars.

**Baking notes:** Finely ground nuts, such as walnuts or almonds, can be added to the dough.

---

# ARROWROOT WAFERS

Rolled Cookies

YIELD: *3 to 4 dozen*
TOTAL TIME: *30 minutes*
CHILLING TIME: *4 hours*

1 cup all-purpose flour
½ cup arrowroot flour
¼ teaspoon baking powder
2 tablespoons butter, at room temperature
⅓ cup granulated sugar
2 large eggs
½ teaspoon vanilla extract

1 Sift together the all-purpose flour, arrowroot flour, and baking powder.

2 In a large bowl, cream the butter and sugar. Beat in the eggs one at a time. Beat in the vanilla extract. Gradually blend in the dry ingredients. The dough will be very sticky. Cover and chill for at least 4 hours.

3 Preheat the oven to 350 degrees. Grease 2 baking sheets.

4 On a floured surface, roll out the dough ⅛ inch thick. Using a 2½-inch round cutter, cut into rounds and place 1 inch apart on the prepared baking sheets.

5 Bake for 12 to 15 minutes, until the edges just start to color. Transfer to wire racks to cool.

**Baking notes:** This dough is very difficult to work with; it must be kept well chilled. Keep the work surface and rolling pin well floured, and dip the cookie cutter in flour before you cut out each cookie. The scraps must be rechilled before they can be rerolled.

3 cups all-purpose flour
1 teaspoon baking powder
1 cup vegetable shortening
1½ cups granulated sugar
3 large eggs
1 teaspoon vanilla extract
1 teaspoon baking soda
2 tablespoons hot water
1 cup walnuts, chopped
1 cup raisins

1  Preheat the oven to 325 degrees. Grease 2 baking sheets.

2  Combine the flour and baking powder.

3  In a large bowl, cream the vegetable shortening and sugar until light and fluffy.

4  In another bowl, beat the eggs until thick and light-colored. Beat the eggs into the shortening mixture. Beat in the vanilla extract.

5  Dissolve the baking soda in the hot water and add to the egg mixture, beating until smooth. Gradually blend in the dry ingredients. Fold in the walnuts and raisins.

6  Drop the dough by spoonfuls 1½ inches apart onto the prepared baking sheets.

7  Bake for 10 to 12 minutes, until lightly colored. Transfer to wire racks to cool.

**Baking notes:** According to my father, this recipe is of Swedish origin.

# AUNT LIZZIE'S COOKIES

Drop Cookies

YIELD: *5 to 6 dozen*
TOTAL TIME: *30 minutes*

---

1 cup vegetable shortening
⅔ cup granulated sugar
2 teaspoons vanilla extract
2½ cups all-purpose flour
¼ cup walnuts, chopped
Powdered sugar for rolling

1  In a large bowl, cream the vegetable shortening and sugar. Beat in the vanilla extract. Gradually blend in the flour and nuts. Cover and chill for at least 4 hours.

2  Preheat the oven to 325 degrees.

3  Break off small pieces of the dough and form into crescent shapes, curving the ends. Place 1 inch apart on ungreased baking sheets.

4  Bake for 15 to 20 minutes, until the edges are a light brown. Transfer to wire racks to cool slightly.

5  Roll the warm cookies in powdered sugar to coat. Let cool on the racks.

**Baking notes:**  To make hazelnut crescents, an elegant variation, substitute hazelnut extract for the vanilla extract and chopped hazelnuts for the walnuts.

# AUSTRIAN WALNUT CRESCENTS

Formed Cookies

YIELD: *4 to 6 dozen*
TOTAL TIME: *40 minutes*
CHILLING TIME: *4 hours*

# BACK BAY COOKIES

Drop Cookies

YIELD: *2 to 3 dozen*
TOTAL TIME: *30 minutes*

2 cups all-purpose flour
¾ teaspoon baking soda
1 teaspoon ground cinnamon
¼ teaspoon salt
⅔ cup butter, at room temperature
1 cup granulated sugar
2 large eggs
⅔ cup golden raisins
½ cup chestnuts, chopped

**1** Preheat the oven to 350 degrees. Grease 2 baking sheets.

**2** Combine the flour, baking soda, cinnamon, and salt.

**3** In a large bowl, cream the butter and sugar. Beat in the eggs. Gradually blend in the dry ingredients. Fold in the raisins and chestnuts.

**4** Drop the dough by spoonfuls 1½ inches apart onto the prepared baking sheets.

**5** Bake for 10 to 12 minutes, until lightly colored. Transfer to wire racks to cool.

**Baking notes:** These cookies have a long history, dating back to revolutionary days; this is an updated version.

# BACKPACKERS' BARS

Bar Cookies

YIELD: *1 to 3 dozen*
TOTAL TIME: *45 minutes*

CRUST
½ cup vegetable shortening
¾ cup packed light brown sugar
¾ cup all-purpose flour
½ cup rolled oats
¼ cup toasted wheat germ
1 tablespoon grated orange zest

FILLING
2 large eggs
¼ cup packed light brown sugar
½ cup shredded coconut
⅔ cup slivered almonds

**1** Preheat the oven to 350 degrees.

**2** To make the crust, cream the vegetable shortening and brown sugar in a large bowl. Blend in the flour, oats, wheat germ, orange zest. The mixture will be dry.

**3** Press the crust mixture evenly over the bottom of an ungreased 8-inch square baking pan.

**4** To make the filling, combine the eggs and brown sugar in a

medium bowl and beat until well blended. Stir in the coconut.

**5** Spread the filling over the crust. Sprinkle the almonds over the top.

**6** Bake for 30 to 35 minutes, until firm to the touch. Cool in the pan on a rack before cutting into large or small bars.

**Baking notes:** To enhance the flavor of these bars, add ¼ teaspoon almond extract to the filling. Raisins may also be added if desired.

## CRUST

⅓ cup vegetable shortening
⅓ cup packed light brown sugar
1 cup all-purpose flour
½ cup walnuts, chopped

## FILLING

7 ounces cream cheese, at room
    temperature
¼ cup granulated sugar
1 large egg
2 tablespoons milk
1 tablespoon fresh lemon juice
½ teaspoon vanilla extract

**1** Preheat the oven to 350 degrees.

**2** To make the crust, cream the vegetable shortening and brown sugar in a large bowl. Gradually blend in the flour. Stir in the walnuts. The mixture will be crumbly.

**3** Reserve 1 cup of the crust mixture, and press the remaining mixture evenly into the bottom of an 8-inch square baking pan. Bake for 15 minutes.

**4** Meanwhile, make the filling: In a large bowl, beat the cream cheese and sugar. Beat in the egg, milk, lemon juice, and vanilla extract until well blended.

**5** Spread the filling over the warm crust. Sprinkle with the reserved crust mixture. Bake for 25 minutes longer, or until firm to the touch.

**6** Cool in the pan on a rack before cutting into large or small bars.

**Baking notes:** For variation, substitute almonds for the walnuts and almond extract for the vanilla extract.

# BAKED CHEESECAKE BARS I

Bar Cookies

YIELD: *1 to 3 dozen*
TOTAL TIME: *50 minutes*

## CRUST

1 cup all-purpose flour
⅓ cup packed light brown sugar
⅓ cup vegetable shortening

## FILLING

2 large eggs
1 pound cream cheese, at room
    temperature
½ cup granulated sugar
2 tablespoons fresh lemon juice
1 tablespoon marsala

**1** Preheat the oven to 350 degrees.

**2** To make the crust, combine the flour and brown sugar in a bowl. Cut in the vegetable shortening until the mixture resembles coarse crumbs.

**3** Press the mixture evenly into the bottom of a 9-inch square baking pan. Bake for 15 minutes.

**4** Meanwhile, make the filling: In a large bowl, beat the eggs until thick and light-colored. Beat in the cream cheese and sugar until smooth. Beat in the lemon juice and marsala.

**5** Spread the filling evenly over the warm crust. Bake for 20 minutes longer, or until firm to the touch.

**6** Cool in the pan on a rack before cutting into large or small bars.

**Baking notes:** A teaspoon of almond extract can be used in place of the marsala.

# BAKED CHEESECAKE BARS II

Bar Cookies

YIELD: *1 to 2 dozen*
TOTAL TIME: *40 minutes*

# BAKLAVA

Bar Cookies

YIELD: *1 to 4 dozen*
TOTAL TIME: *75 minutes*

1 pound unsalted butter (see Baking note)
½ pound phyllo dough, thawed if frozen
2 cups pecans, chopped
1 to 2 tablespoons whole cloves
⅓ cup granulated sugar
3 cups water
1 cinnamon stick
1 cup honey

1 Preheat the oven to 450 degrees.

2 Melt the butter in a small saucepan.

3 Pour 2 tablespoons of the butter into the bottom of a 13 by 9-inch baking pan. Layer 3 sheets of phyllo dough in the pan, trimming them to fit. Sprinkle about 2 tablespoons of the pecans over the phyllo. Top with 3 more sheets of phyllo and sprinkle with pecans. Continue layering until the pan is three-quarters full. (Do not sprinkle nuts over the top sheet.)

4 Using a sharp knife, score the phyllo to form diamonds. Press a clove into the pointed ends of each diamond. Gradually pour the remaining melted butter over the pastry.

5 Bake for 45 to 50 minutes, until the phyllo is golden brown.

6 Meanwhile, combine the sugar, water, and cinnamon stick in a medium saucepan and bring to a boil, stirring until the sugar dissolves. Lower the heat and simmer for 10 minutes. Add the honey and simmer for 2 minutes longer. Remove from the heat and remove and discard the cinnamon stick.

7 Pour the honey mixture over the hot baklava. Cool in the pan on a rack before cutting into diamonds.

**Baking notes:** You must use unsalted (sweet) butter for this recipe. Phyllo, or filo, dough is also known as strudel leaves. It can be purchased in specialty stores and many supermarkets. If you like honey, you will like baklava.

# BANANA BARS

Bar Cookies

YIELD: *1 to 2 dozen*
TOTAL TIME: *40 minutes*

1½ cups all-purpose flour
1½ teaspoons baking powder
½ teaspoon salt
¼ cup vegetable shortening
1 cup packed light brown sugar
2 to 3 bananas, mashed
½ teaspoon pineapple juice
½ teaspoon vanilla extract
½ cup walnuts, chopped

TOPPING
⅓ cup powdered sugar
1 teaspoon ground cinnamon

1 Preheat the oven to 350 degrees. Grease a 13 by 9-inch baking pan.

2 Combine the flour, baking powder, and salt.

3 In a large bowl, cream the vegetable shortening and brown sugar. Beat in the bananas, pineapple juice, and vanilla extract. Gradually blend in the dry ingredients. Fold in the nuts.

4 Spread the batter evenly in the prepared pan. Bake for 30 to 35 minutes, until firm to the touch.

5 Combine the powdered sugar and cinnamon for the topping, and sprinkle over the warm cookies. Cut into large or small bars and cool in pans on wire racks.

¾ cup all-purpose flour
1 cup bran flakes
½ teaspoon baking powder
¼ teaspoon baking soda
¼ teaspoon salt
⅓ cup vegetable shortening
⅓ cup granulated sugar
1 large egg
½ cup mashed bananas
½ teaspoon ground cinnamon
⅛ teaspoon ground allspice
⅛ teaspoon ground cloves
¼ cup walnuts, chopped fine

**1** Preheat the oven to 375 degrees.

**2** Combine the flour, bran flakes, baking powder, baking soda, and salt.

**3** In a large bowl, cream the vegetable shortening and sugar. Beat in the egg and bananas. Beat in the spices. Gradually blend in the dry ingredients. Fold in the nuts.

**4** Drop the dough by spoonfuls 1½ inches apart onto ungreased baking sheets.

**5** Bake for 10 to 12 minutes, until golden brown. Transfer to wire racks to cool.

**Baking notes:** For even more flavor, add ⅓ cup semisweet chocolate chips to the dough. If you live in the Northeast, you may be familiar with a product called English Spice; ¾ teaspoon English Spice can replace the cinnamon, allspice, and cloves in this recipe.

# BANANA-BRAN COOKIES

Drop Cookies

YIELD: *1 to 2 dozen*
TOTAL TIME: *35 minutes*

---

2 cups all-purpose flour
2 teaspoons baking powder
½ teaspoon salt
¾ cup vegetable shortening
1 cup granulated sugar
¼ cup packed light brown sugar
1 large egg
1 teaspoon vanilla extract
1 cup mashed bananas
1 cup (6 ounces) semisweet chocolate chips

**1** Preheat the oven to 350 degrees. Grease a 13 by 9-inch baking pan.

**2** Combine the flour, baking powder, and salt.

**3** In a large bowl, cream the vegetable shortening and both sugars. Beat in the egg and vanilla extract. Beat in the bananas.

Gradually blend in the dry ingredients. Fold in the chocolate chips.

**4** Spread the mixture evenly in the prepared pan.

**5** Bake for 25 to 30 minutes, until golden brown on top. Cool in the pan on a rack before cutting into large or small bars.

**Baking notes:** A packaged banana cream frosting goes very well with these bars.

# BANANA-CHIP BARS I

Bar Cookies

YIELD: *1 to 2 dozen*
TOTAL TIME: *40 minutes*

# BANANA-CHIP BARS II

Bar Cookies

YIELD: *1 to 2 dozen*
TOTAL TIME: *45 minutes*

1¾ cups all-purpose flour
1½ teaspoons baking powder
¼ teaspoon salt
6 tablespoons vegetable shortening
1 cup packed light brown sugar
1 large egg
½ teaspoon vanilla extract
3 to 4 large bananas, mashed
1 cup (6 ounces) semisweet chocolate chips

1 Preheat the oven to 350 degrees.
2 Combine the flour, baking powder, and salt.
3 In a large bowl, cream the vegetable shortening and brown sugar. Beat in the egg and vanilla extract. Beat in the bananas. Gradually blend in the dry ingredients. Fold in the chocolate chips.

4 Spread the mixture evenly in an ungreased 8-inch square baking pan.
5 Bake for 30 to 35 minutes, until the top is lightly colored. Cool in the pan on a rack before cutting into large or small bars.

**Baking notes:** Although this recipe calls for semisweet chocolate chips, any type of chip can be used: Try butterscotch, peanut butter chips, or white chocolate, or a combination. Raisins can be substituted for the chips, or add them too. These bars are good served warm with a spoonful of whipped cream on top; you can rewarm them in a microwave oven.

# BANANA-COCONUT BARS

Bar Cookies

YIELD: *2 to 3 dozen*
TOTAL TIME: *30 minutes*

1¾ cups all-purpose flour
2 teaspoons baking powder
1 teaspoon baking soda
⅓ cup vegetable shortening
2 to 3 medium bananas, mashed
1 large egg
½ cup milk
¼ teaspoon fresh lemon juice
1½ cups flaked coconut

1 Preheat the oven to 350 degrees. Grease a 13 by 9-inch baking pan.
2 Combine the flour, baking powder, and baking soda.
3 In a large bowl, beat the vegetable shortening and bananas until smooth. Beat in the egg,

milk, and lemon juice. Gradually blend in the dry ingredients. Fold in 1 cup of the coconut.

4 Spread the mixture evenly in the prepared pan. Sprinkle the remaining ½ cup coconut over the top.
5 Bake for 15 to 20 minutes, until the top is lightly colored, and a toothpick inserted into the center comes out clean. Cool in the pan on a rack before cutting into large or small bars.

# BANANA COOKIES

Drop Cookies

YIELD: *3 to 4 dozen*
TOTAL TIME: *35 minutes*

1 cup all-purpose flour
1 cup whole wheat flour
1 teaspoon baking powder
½ teaspoon ground allspice
1 teaspoon salt
¾ cup vegetable shortening
1 cup granulated sugar
1 large egg
2 to 3 large bananas, mashed
1 cup sesame seeds, toasted

1 Preheat the oven to 350 degrees. Grease 2 baking sheets.
2 Combine both flours, the baking powder, allspice, and salt.
3 In a large bowl, cream the vegetables shortening and sugar.

Beat in the egg. Beat in the bananas. Gradually blend in the dry ingredients. Fold in the sesame seeds.

4 Drop the dough by spoonfuls 1½ inches apart onto the prepared baking sheets.
5 Bake for 8 to 10 minutes, until lightly colored. Transfer to wire racks to cool.

**Baking notes:** For a chewier cookie, bake for only 6 to 8 minutes. This cookie is of Southeast Asian origin; if you are not fond of sesame seeds, add only ½ cup to the dough.

1 cup dates, pitted and chopped fine
1 teaspoon lemon extract
⅓ cup canola oil
2 to 3 bananas, mashed
1 tablespoon brandy
2 cups rolled oats
½ cup pecans, chopped

**1** Preheat the oven to 350 degrees.

**2** Combine the dates and lemon extract in a medium saucepan and add just enough water to cover. Bring to a simmer over medium-low heat and cook until all the liquid has evaporated.

**3** Remove from the heat and stir in the oil with a wooden spoon.

Beat in the bananas. Beat in the brandy. Gradually blend in the oats. Fold in the pecans.

**4** Drop the dough by spoonfuls 1½ inches apart onto ungreased baking sheets.

**5** Bake for 20 to 25 minutes, until lightly colored. Transfer to wire racks to cool.

# BANANA-DATE COOKIES

Drop Cookies

Yield: *2 to 3 dozen*
Total time: *30 minutes*

---

1½ cups all-purpose flour
1 cup granulated sugar
½ teaspoon baking soda
¾ teaspoon ground cinnamon
¼ teaspoon ground nutmeg
1 teaspoon salt
¾ cup vegetable shortening
1 large egg
2 to 3 large bananas, mashed
1¾ cup rolled oats
2 cups (12 ounces) semisweet chocolate chips

**1** Preheat the oven to 400 degrees.

**2** Sift the flour, sugar, baking soda, cinnamon, nutmeg, and salt into a large bowl. Cut in the vegetable shortening. Stir in the egg and bananas until smooth.

Fold in the oats and chocolate chips.

**3** Drop the dough by spoonfuls 1½ inches apart onto ungreased baking sheets.

**4** Bake for 12 to 15 minutes, until lightly colored. Transfer to wire racks to cool.

**Baking notes:** Raisins may be added to the dough. The chips can be of any type: semisweet or milk chocolate, butterscotch, or peanut butter.

# BANANA DROPS

Drop Cookies

Yield: *3 to 4 dozen*
Total time: *35 minutes*

---

2¼ cups all-purpose flour
2 teaspoons baking powder
½ teaspoon salt
⅓ cup vegetable shortening
1 cup granulated sugar
2 large eggs
½ teaspoon vanilla extract
¼ teaspoon lemon extract
2 to 3 large bananas, mashed
½ cup walnuts, ground fine

**1** Preheat the oven to 350 degrees. Grease 2 baking sheets.

**2** Combine the flour, baking powder, and salt.

**3** In a large bowl, cream the vegetable shortening and sugar. Beat

in the eggs, vanilla extract, and lemon extract. Beat in the bananas and ground walnuts. Gradually blend in the dry ingredients.

**4** Drop the dough by spoonfuls 1½ inches apart onto the prepared baking sheets.

**5** Bake for 12 to 15 minute, until lightly colored. Transfer to wire racks to cool.

# BANANA-NUT DROPS

Drop Cookies

Yield: *3 to 4 dozen*
Total time: *35 minutes*

# Banana-Oatmeal Cookies I

Drop Cookies
Yield: *3 to 5 dozen*
Total time: *30 minutes*

1½ cups all-purpose flour
½ teaspoon baking soda
¾ teaspoon ground cinnamon
¼ teaspoon ground nutmeg
¼ teaspoon salt
¾ cup vegetable shortening
1 cup granulated sugar
1 large egg
2 to 3 large bananas, mashed
1¾ cups rolled oats
½ cup almonds, chopped fine

**1** Preheat the oven to 400 degrees.

**2** Combine the flour, baking soda, cinnamon, nutmeg, and salt.

**3** In a large bowl, cream the vegetable shortening and sugar. Beat in the egg and bananas. Gradually blend in the dry ingredients. Fold in the oats and almonds.

**4** Drop the dough by spoonfuls 1½ inches apart onto ungreased baking sheets.

**5** Bake for 12 to 15 minutes, until lightly colored. Transfer to wire racks to cool.

# Banana-Oatmeal Cookies II

Drop Cookies
Yield: *1 to 2 dozen*
Total time: *35 minutes*

1½ cups all-purpose flour
¾ teaspoon ground cinnamon
¼ teaspoon ground nutmeg
¾ cup vegetable shortening
1 cup granulated sugar
1 large egg
½ cup mashed bananas
½ teaspoon baking soda
1 tablespoon warm water
1 teaspoon fresh lemon juice
1½ cup rolled oats

**1** Preheat the oven to 350 degrees. Grease 2 baking sheets.

**2** Combine the flour, cinnamon, and nutmeg.

**3** In a large bowl, cream the vegetable shortening and sugar. Beat in the egg and bananas.

**4** Dissolve the baking soda in the warm water and add to the banana mixture, beating until smooth. Beat in the lemon juice. Gradually blend in the dry ingredients. Fold in the oats.

**5** Drop the dough by spoonfuls 1½ inches apart onto the prepared baking sheets.

**6** Bake for 10 to 12 minutes, until golden brown. Transfer to wire racks to cool.

**Baking notes:** Raisins are good in this recipe.

# Bannocks

Rolled Cookies
Yield: *4–6*
Total time: *35 minutes*

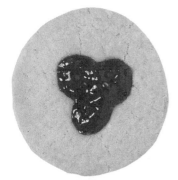

1¼ cups rolled oats
¾ cup all-purpose flour
1 tablespoon granulated sugar
1 tablespoon baking powder
½ teaspoon salt
5 tablespoons vegetable shortening
2 to 3 tablespoons water, or more as needed

**1** Preheat the oven to 350 degrees.

**2** Combine the rolled oats, flour, sugar, baking powder, and salt in a bowl. Using your fingertips, work in the vegetable shortening until the mixture resembles coarse crumbs. Add just enough water to form the mixture into a smooth dough.

**3** On a floured surface, roll out the dough ½ inch thick. Using a butter plate as a guide, cut out 6-inch circles and place 1 inch apart on ungreased baking sheets.

**4** Bake for 18 to 20 minutes, until the Bannocks are slightly colored and firm to the touch. Transfer to wire racks to cool.

**Baking notes:** This is a very old Scottish recipe. Bannocks are usually served with jam or jelly.

1 cup all-purpose flour
1 cup almonds, ground fine
1 teaspoon baking powder
3 large eggs, separated
1 cup granulated sugar
1 large egg white
⅛ teaspoon salt

**1** Preheat the oven to 350 degrees. Grease a 13 by 9-inch baking pan.

**2** Combine the flour, almonds, and baking powder.

**3** In a large bowl, beat the egg yolks and sugar until thick and light-colored. Gradually blend in the dry ingredients.

**4** In another bowl, beat the egg whites with the salt until stiff but not dry. Fold the beaten whites into the egg yolk mixture.

**5** Spread the mixture evenly in the prepared pan.

**6** Bake for 20 to 25 minutes, until the cookies form a crust and are lightly colored on top. Cool in the pan on a rack before cutting into large or small bars.

**Baking notes:** These cookies can be flavored in a variety of ways: Add 1 teaspoon vanilla or almond extract, or your favorite extract. Add ¼ teaspoon raspberry flavoring or ¼ cup of chocolate syrup. Omit the almonds and add raisins, or add flaked coconut. Use your imagination.

# BASIC BARS

Bar Cookies

YIELD: *1 to 2 dozen*
TOTAL TIME: *35 minutes*

---

3 cups all-purpose flour
2 cups unsweetened cocoa powder
1 tablespoon baking powder
2 teaspoons salt
3½ cups vegetable shortening (see Baking notes)
5 cups granulated sugar

**1** Combine the flour, cocoa powder, baking powder, and salt.

**2** In a large bowl, cream the vegetable shortening and sugar. Gradually blend in the dry ingredients. Store in an airtight container until ready to use.

**3** Preheat the oven to 350 degrees. Grease a 9-inch baking pan.

**4** To make the cookies: add 2 beaten eggs and 1 teaspoon vanilla extract to 2¾ cups of the Basic Brownie Mix. Beat thoroughly.

**5** Spread the mixture evenly in a prepared baking pan.

**6** Bake for 25 to 30 minutes, or until a toothpick inserted in the cookie is removed clean. Cool in the pan on a rack before cutting into large or small bars.

**Baking notes:** This mix will make enough to make 5 recipes. The vegetable shortening must be of the type that does not need refrigeration. Optional "add-ins" may include walnuts, peanuts, or almonds, mint flavoring, semisweet chocolate chips, white chocolate chips, peanut butter chips, or butterscotch chips, etc.

# BASIC BROWNIE MIX

Bar Cookies

YIELD: *14 cups*
TOTAL TIME: *40 minutes*

# BASIC DROP COOKIES

Drop Cookies

YIELD: *3 to 4 dozen*
TOTAL TIME: *30 minutes*

1½ cups all-purpose flour
1½ teaspoons baking powder
¼ teaspoon salt
6 tablespoons vegetable shortening
¾ cup granulated sugar
1 large egg
2 tablespoons milk
½ teaspoon vanilla extract

**1** Preheat the oven to 375 degrees. Grease 2 baking sheets.

**2** Combine the flour, baking powder, and salt.

**3** In a large bowl, cream the vegetable shortening and sugar. Beat in the egg. Beat in the milk and vanilla extract. Gradually blend in the dry ingredients.

**4** Drop the dough by spoonfuls 1½ inches apart onto the prepared baking sheets.

**5** Bake for 10 to 12 minutes, until the edges start to color. Transfer to wire racks to cool

**Baking notes:** This basic recipe is the starting point for endless variations: Add nuts, raisins, coconut, chocolate chips, peanut butter, peanut butter chips, and/or candied citrus peel. Add cinnamon and/or nutmeg, or spices, as you like.

# BASIC FILLED COOKIES

Rolled Cookies

YIELD: *5 to 6 dozen*
TOTAL TIME: *40 minutes*

4¾ cups all-purpose flour
¼ teaspoon salt
¾ cup vegetable shortening
1½ cups granulated sugar
2 large eggs
2 teaspoons vanilla extract
½ teaspoon baking soda
1 tablespoon warm water
¾ cup sour cream
1½ cups filling, such as jams or
    preserves

**1** Preheat the oven to 400 degrees. Grease 2 baking sheets.

**2** Combine the flour and salt.

**3** In a large bowl, cream the vegetable shortening and sugar. Beat in the eggs and vanilla extract.

**4** Dissolve the baking soda in the warm water and add to the egg mixture, beating until smooth. Beat in the sour cream. Gradually blend in the dry ingredients.

**5** On a floured surface, roll out the dough ¼ inch thick. Using a round cookie cutter, cut out an even number of cookies.

**6** Place ½ teaspoonful of the filling in the center of half the cookies, and top each one with another cookie. Pinch the edges to seal and place 1½ inches apart on the prepared baking sheets.

**7** Bake for 10 to 12 minutes, until golden brown in color. Transfer to wire racks to cool.

**Baking notes:** You can cut out these cookies in almost any shape you like; just be sure to have equal numbers of matching "tops" and "bottoms." If you make round cookies, you can cut out holes in the center of the tops before baking so the filling will show through.

½ cup plus 2 tablespoons vegetable shortening
2 tablespoons unsweetened cocoa powder
1 cup granulated sugar
2 large eggs
1 teaspoon vanilla extract
½ cup all-purpose flour

**1** Preheat the oven to 350 degrees. Grease a 9-inch square baking pan.

**2** Combine the vegetable shortening and cocoa in the top of a double boiler and heat over low heat, stirring occasionally, until the shortening is melted.

**3** Remove from the heat and stir in the sugar. Stir in the eggs and

vanilla extract until well blended. Stir in the flour.

**4** Spread the mixture evenly in the prepared pan.

**5** Bake for 18 to 20 minutes, until a toothpick inserted in the center comes out clean. Cool in the pan on a rack before cutting into large or small bars.

**Baking notes:** When cool, these can be spread with chocolate glaze and sprinkled with chopped walnuts before being cut into bars.

# BASIC FUDGE BROWNIES

Bar Cookies

YIELD: *1 to 2 dozen*
TOTAL TIME: *30 minutes*

---

¼ cup honey
¾ cup hot water
¾ cup granulated sugar
4 cups all-purpose flour
1½ tablespoons vegetable shortening

**1** In a small bowl, combine the honey and ¼ cup of the hot water. In another small bowl, combine the sugar and the remaining ½ cup hot water. Cover both mixtures and let sit overnight.

**2** Preheat the oven to 375 degrees. Grease 2 baking sheets.

**3** Place the flour in a large bowl. Cut in the vegetable shortening until the mixture resembles

coarse crumbs. Stir in the honey and sugar mixtures until smooth.

**4** On a floured surface, roll out the dough ¼ inch thick. Using a 2-inch round cutter, cut out rounds and place 1 inch apart on the prepared baking sheets.

**5** Bake for 12 to 14 minutes, until lightly colored. Transfer to wire racks to cool

**Baking notes:** If you don't particularly like honey, you can substitute light corn syrup.

# BATH BUNS

Rolled Cookies

YIELD: *2 to 3 dozen*
TOTAL TIME: *30 minutes*

---

3 cups all-purpose flour
1 teaspoon baking soda
1 teaspoon ground cinnamon
1 teaspoon ground cloves
½ teaspoon salt
½ cup vegetable shortening
1 cup packed light brown sugar
1 large egg
½ cup lukewarm water
½ cup dark molasses
1 cup raisins

**1** Preheat the oven to 350 degrees. Grease 2 baking sheets

**2** Combine the flour, baking soda, spices, and salt.

**3** In a large bowl, cream the vegetable shortening and brown

sugar. Beat in the egg. Beat in the warm water and molasses. Gradually blend in the dry ingredients. Fold in the raisins.

**4** Drop the dough by spoonfuls 1½ inches apart onto the prepared baking sheets.

**5** Bake for 10 to 12 minutes, until lightly colored. Transfer to wire racks to cool.

# BAYOU HERMITS

Drop Cookies

YIELD: *5 to 6 dozen*
TOTAL TIME: *20 minutes*

# BEAUMONT INN COOKIES

Drop Cookies

YIELD: *2 to 3 dozen*
TOTAL TIME: *30 minutes*

2½ cups all-purpose flour
1 teaspoon baking powder
2 tablespoons butter, at room
    temperature
1 cup granulated sugar
1 large egg
½ cup milk

**1** Preheat the oven to 425 degrees. Grease 2 baking sheets.

**2** Combine the flour and baking powder.

**3** In a large bowl, cream the butter and sugar. Beat in the egg and milk. Gradually blend in the dry ingredients.

**4** Drop the dough by spoonfuls 1½ inches apart onto the prepared baking sheets.

**5** Bake for 12 to 15 minutes, until golden brown. Transfer to wire racks to cool.

**Baking notes:** The Beaumont Inn is located in Harrodsburg, Kentucky. These cookies can be decorated with raisins, slivered nuts, or glacé cherries before baking.

# BEAUMONT INN DROP COOKIES

Drop Cookies

YIELD: *3 to 4 dozen*
TOTAL TIME: *30 minutes*

2 cups all-purpose flour
2 teaspoons baking powder
½ teaspoon salt
½ cup butter, at room temperature
2 cups packed light brown sugar
2 large eggs
2 tablespoons heavy cream
1 cup pecans, chopped
1 cup golden raisins, chopped
1 cup glacé cherries, chopped

**1** Preheat the oven to 325 degrees. Grease 2 baking sheets.

**2** Combine the flour, baking powder, and salt.

**3** In a large bowl, cream the butter and brown sugar. Beat in the eggs and cream. Gradually blend in the dry ingredients. Fold in the pecans, raisins, and cherries.

**4** Drop the dough by spoonfuls 1½ inches apart onto the prepared baking sheets.

**5** Bake for 15 to 20 minutes, until lightly colored. Transfer to wire racks to cool.

# BEAUMONT INN TEA CAKES

Rolled Cookies

YIELD: *6 to 7 dozen*
TOTAL TIME: *30 minutes*

4 cups all-purpose flour
2 teaspoons baking powder
3 tablespoons butter, at room
    temperature
1½ cups granulated sugar
2 large eggs
½ cup milk
1 teaspoon orange extract
1 teaspoon lemon extract
1 teaspoon vanilla extract

**1** Preheat the oven to 350 degrees.

**2** Combine the flour and baking powder.

**3** In a large bowl, cream the butter and sugar. Beat in the eggs. Beat in the milk, then beat in all the extracts. Gradually blend in the dry ingredients.

**4** On a floured surface, roll out the dough ¼ inch thick. Using cookie cutters, cut into shapes and place 1½ inches apart on ungreased baking sheets.

**5** Bake for 10 to 12 minutes, until lightly colored. Transfer to wire racks to cool.

1⅔ cups all-purpose flour
1½ teaspoons baking powder
½ teaspoon salt
⅔ cup vegetable shortening
1 cup packed light brown sugar
2 large eggs
1 teaspoon almond extract
½ cup walnuts, chopped
½ teaspoon ground cinnamon
Red and green sugar crystals for
  sprinkling

**1** Preheat the oven to 375 degrees.

**2** Combine the flour, baking powder, and salt.

**3** In a large bowl, cream the vegetable shortening and brown sugar. Beat in the eggs and almond extract. Gradually blend in the dry ingredients.

**4** Spread the mixture evenly in an ungreased 13 by 9-inch baking pan. Sprinkle the walnuts and cinnamon over the top. Sprinkle with the colored sugar.

**5** Bake for 10 to 12 minutes, until lightly colored. Cut into large or small bars while still warm and cool in the pan on a wire rack.

**Baking notes:** Use your favorite nuts in these cookies. A tablespoon or so of chopped candied fruit added to the dough will make the cookies even more festive.

# BELGIAN CHRISTMAS COOKIES

Bar Cookies

YIELD: *1 to 2 dozen*
TOTAL TIME: *25 minutes*

---

1¼ cups all-purpose flour
¼ teaspoon baking powder
¼ teaspoon salt
¾ cup butter, at room temperature
1½ cups packed light brown sugar
2 large eggs
1 teaspoon vanilla extract
½ cup sesame seeds, toasted

**1** Preheat the oven to 350 degrees. Grease 2 baking sheets.

**2** Combine the flour, baking powder, and salt.

**3** In a large bowl, cream the butter and sugar. Beat in the eggs and vanilla extract. Gradually blend in the dry ingredients. Fold in the sesame seeds.

**4** Drop the dough by spoonfuls 1½ inches apart onto the prepared baking sheets.

**5** Bake for 10 to 12 minutes, until lightly colored. Transfer to wire racks to cool.

**Baking notes:** These cookies are an old Southern favorite. Sesame seeds are called "Benne seeds" in the South.

# BENNE (SESAME SEED) COOKIES

Drop Cookies

YIELD: *3 to 4 dozen*
TOTAL TIME: *30 minutes*

**B**

# BENNE (SESAME SEED) ICEBOX COOKIES

Refrigerator Cookies

YIELD: *3 to 4 dozen*
TOTAL TIME: *30 minutes*
CHILLING TIME: *8 hours*

2 cups all-purpose flour
¼ teaspoon salt
½ cup butter, at room temperature
1 cup granulated sugar
1 large egg
¼ cup milk
7½ tablespoons sesame seeds, toasted

1 Combine the flour and salt.

2 In a large bowl, cream the butter and sugar. Beat in the egg and milk. Gradually blend in the dry ingredients. Fold in the sesame seeds.

3 Form the dough into a 1-inch-thick log. Wrap in waxed paper and chill for at least 8 hours.

4 Preheat the oven to 375 degrees. Grease 2 baking sheets.

5 Slice the log into ¼-inch-thick slices and place 1½ inches apart on the prepared baking sheets.

6 Bake for 10 to 12 minutes, until lightly colored. Transfer to wire racks to cool.

# BERLIN GARLANDS

Rolled Cookies

YIELD: *4 to 5 dozen*
TOTAL TIME: *35 minutes*
CHILLING TIME: *8 hours*

2 large egg yolks
2 hard-boiled large eggs, coarsely chopped
1½ cups powdered sugar
¾ cup butter, at room temperature
2 cups all-purpose flour
2 large egg whites
Powdered sugar for sprinkling

1 In a large bowl, combine the egg yolks and hard-boiled eggs and beat until thick and light-colored. Beat in the sugar. Beat in the butter. Gradually blend in the flour. Cover and chill for 8 hours.

2 Preheat the oven to 350 degrees. Grease 2 baking sheets.

3 On a floured surface, roll out the dough ½ inch thick. Cut into pencil-thin strips 6 to 8 inches long.

4 For each cookie, braid 3 strips together, shape into a circle and pinch the ends to seal. Place the cookies 1 inch apart on the prepared baking sheets.

5 In a large bowl, beat the egg whites until they hold stiff peaks. Brush the cookies with the beaten egg whites and sprinkle with powdered sugar.

6 Bake for 12 to 15 minutes, until lightly colored. Transfer to wire racks to cool.

**Baking notes:** It is important to allow the batter to sit for 8 hours or overnight. The strips should be about the size of a pencil. I also like to combine finely chopped hazelnuts with the powdered sugar for sprinkling.

**TOPPING**
½ cup vegetable shortening
¼ cup granulated sugar
2 tablespoons honey
2 tablespoons milk
2 tablespoons almond extract
1 cup almonds, ground fine

**CRUST**
1¾ cups all-purpose flour
2 teaspoons baking powder
¼ teaspoon salt
½ cup vegetable shortening
½ cup granulated sugar
1 large egg
1 teaspoon vanilla extract

**1** Preheat the oven to 350 degrees.

**2** To make the topping, combine all the ingredients in a medium saucepan and bring to a rolling boil. Stir to dissolve the sugar. Remove from the heat and let cool.

**3** To make the crust, combine the flour, baking powder, and salt.

**4** In a large bowl, cream the vegetable shortening and sugar. Beat in the egg and vanilla extract. Gradually blend in the dry ingredients.

**5** Press the mixture evenly into the bottom of 13 by 9-inch baking pan. Pour the topping mixture over the crust.

**6** Bake for 55 to 60 minutes, until the top is lightly colored. Cool in the pan on a wire rack before cutting into bars (see Baking notes).

**Baking notes:** Several older versions of this recipe call for buttermilk or soured milk in place of the whole milk. One recipe uses hazelnuts instead of almonds and schnapps in place of the almond extract. These are traditionally cut into squares or triangles.

# BIENENSTICH

Bar Cookies

YIELD: *5 to 7 dozen*
TOTAL TIME: *75 minutes*

---

**CRUST**
1 cup all-purpose flour
½ cup powdered sugar
6 tablespoons butter, at room temperature
1 tablespoon heavy cream

**TOPPING**
4 large eggs
1¼ cups powdered sugar
6 tablespoons fresh orange juice
2 tablespoons fresh lemon juice
3 tablespoons grated orange zest

**1** Preheat the oven to 350 degrees. Grease a 13 by 9-inch baking pan.

**2** To make the crust, combine the flour and powdered sugar in a bowl. Cut in the butter until the mixture resembles coarse crumbs. Blend in the cream.

**3** Press the mixture evenly into the bottom of the prepared pan. Bake for 20 minutes.

**4** Meanwhile, make the topping: In a large bowl, beat the eggs until thick and light-colored. Beat in the powdered sugar. Beat in the orange juice and lemon juice. Fold in the orange zest.

**5** Pour the topping mixture over the warm crust. Bake for 25 to 30 minutes longer, until the topping is set.

**6** Cool in the pan on a rack before cutting into large or small bars.

**Baking notes:** These can be garnished with thin slices of sweet oranges.

# BIG ORANGE BARS

Bar Cookies

YIELD: *1 to 3 dozen*
TOTAL TIME: *60 minutes*

# BILLY GOATS

Drop Cookies

YIELD: *5 to 6 dozen*
TOTAL TIME: *30 minutes*

4 cups all-purpose flour
1 tablespoon plus 1 teaspoon baking powder
1 teaspoon ground allspice
1 cup walnuts, chopped
½ teaspoon salt
1 cup vegetable shortening
2 cups granulated sugar
4 large eggs
1 teaspoon vanilla extract
1 teaspoon baking soda
1 tablespoon warm water
1 cup sour cream
1½ cups dates, pitted and chopped

**1** Preheat the oven to 350 degrees. Grease 2 baking sheets.

**2** Combine the flour, baking powder, allspice, and salt.

**3** In a large bowl, cream the vegetable shortening and sugar. Beat in the eggs one at a time. Beat in the vanilla extract.

**4** Dissolve the baking soda in the warm water and add to the egg mixture, beating until smooth. Beat in the sour cream. Gradually blend in the dry ingredients. Fold in the dates and walnuts.

**5** Drop the dough by spoonfuls 1½ inches apart onto the prepared baking sheets.

**6** Bake for 12 to 15 minutes, until golden. Transfer to wire racks to cool.

**Baking notes:** Raisins may be substituted for the dates; plump them in warm water before using. For a slightly different flavor, ground nutmeg may be used in place of the allspice.

# BIRD'S NEST COOKIES

Formed Cookies

YIELD: *3 to 4 dozen*
TOTAL TIME: *35 minutes*

2 cups all-purpose flour
¼ teaspoon salt
1 cup vegetable shortening
½ cup granulated sugar
1 large egg, separated
1 large egg yolk
1½ teaspoons vanilla extract
1 cup walnuts, chopped
Chocolate kisses for garnish

**1** Preheat the oven to 375 degrees.

**2** Combine the flour and salt.

**3** In a large bowl, cream the vegetable shortening and sugar. Beat in the egg yolks and vanilla extract. Gradually blend in the dry ingredients.

**4** In a shallow bowl, beat the egg white until frothy. Spread the walnuts on waxed paper.

**5** Break off 1-inch pieces of dough and roll into balls. Dip the balls in the egg white to coat, then roll in the walnuts and place 1 inch apart on ungreased baking sheets.

**6** With your finger, make a small depression in the center of each cookie. Bake for 12 to 15 minutes, until lightly colored.

**7** Press an upside-down chocolate kiss into the center of each hot cookie, and transfer to wire racks to cool.

## BISCOTTI I

Rolled Cookies

YIELD: *3 to 4 dozen*
TOTAL TIME: *30 minutes*

2 cups all-purpose flour
½ cup granulated sugar
½ teaspoon baking powder
6 tablespoons vegetable shortening
4 large eggs
½ cup walnuts, chopped

1  Preheat the oven to 350 degrees. Grease 2 baking sheets.

2  In a medium bowl, combine the flour, sugar, and baking powder. Cut in the vegetable shortening until the mixture resembles coarse crumbs.

3  In a large bowl, beat the eggs until thick and light-colored.

Gradually beat the eggs into the flour mixture. Fold in the walnuts.

4  On a floured surface, roll out the dough ¼ inch thick. Using a cookie cutter, cut into shapes and place 1½ inches apart on the prepared baking sheets.

5  Bake for 12 to 14 minutes, until lightly colored. Transfer to wire racks to cool.

## BISCOTTI II

Formed Cookies

YIELD: *4 dozen*
TOTAL TIME: *45 minutes*

1½ cups whole wheat flour
1 cup toasted hazelnuts, grated
2 teaspoons baking powder
½ cup butter, at room temperature
6 tablespoons honey
2 large eggs

1  Preheat the oven to 350 degrees. Grease a baking sheet.

2  Combine the flour, hazelnuts, and baking powder.

3  In a large bowl, beat the butter and honey until smooth. Beat in the eggs one at a time, beating well after each addition. Gradually blend in the dry ingredients.

4  Divide the dough in half. On the prepared baking sheet, form each half into a log about 12 inches long and 2 inches wide, spacing them about 2 inches apart.

5  Bake for 14 to 16 minutes, until golden brown. Transfer the logs to the cutting board and cut on the diagonal into ½-inch-thick slices. Lay the slices on ungreased baking sheets and bake for 10 to 12 minutes longer, until dry.

6  Transfer to wire racks to cool. Store in a tightly sealed container and let age for a few days before serving.

**Baking notes:**  These simple cookies are traditionally served after a meal, dipped in coffee or wine.

## BISHOP'S PEPPER COOKIES

Rolled Cookies

YIELD: *3 to 4 dozen*
TOTAL TIME: *30 minutes*
CHILLING TIME: *4 hours*

2½ cups all-purpose flour
¼ cup almonds, ground fine
½ teaspoon baking soda
1 teaspoon ground cinnamon
1 teaspoon ground ginger
½ teaspoon ground allspice
½ teaspoon salt
1 cup vegetable shortening
1 cup granulated sugar
½ cup corn syrup
1 large egg

1  Combine the flour, almonds, baking soda, spices, and salt.

2  In a large bowl, cream the vegetable shortening and sugar. Beat in the corn syrup. Beat in the egg. Gradually blend in the dry ingredients. Cover and chill for at least 4 hours.

3  Preheat the oven to 350 degrees.

4  On a floured surface, roll out the dough ¼ inch thick. Using cookie cutters, cut out shapes and place 1½ inches apart on ungreased baking sheets.

5  Bake for 8 to 10 minutes, until lightly colored. Transfer to wire racks to cool.

**Baking notes:**  These cookies are traditionally decorated with Royal Icing (see Pantry) piped in various designs over the top.

**B**

# BITTERSWEET BROWNIES

Bar Cookies

YIELD: *1 to 3 dozen*
TOTAL TIME: *35 minutes*

2 ounces unsweetened chocolate, chopped
½ cup all-purpose flour
1 teaspoon baking soda
¼ teaspoon salt
½ cup vegetable shortening
¾ cup granulated sugar
2 large eggs
1 teaspoon vanilla extract
1½ cups pecans, chopped

**1** Preheat the oven to 350 degrees. Grease a 9-inch square baking pan.

**2** Melt the chocolate in a double boiler over low heat, stirring until smooth. Remove from the heat.

**3** Combine the flour, baking powder, and salt.

**4** In a large bowl, cream the vegetable shortening and sugar. Beat in the eggs and vanilla extract. Beat in the melted chocolate. Gradually blend in the dry ingredients. Stir in the pecans.

**5** Spread the mixture evenly in the prepared pan.

**6** Bake for 20 to 25 minutes, until a toothpick inserted in the center comes out clean. Cool in the pan on a rack.

**7** Frost with chocolate frosting and cut into large or small bars.

# BLACKBERRY COOKIES

Drop Cookies

YIELD: *4 to 5 dozen*
TOTAL TIME: *30 minutes*
CHILLING TIME: *4 hours*

2 cups all-purpose flour
2 teaspoons baking powder
½ teaspoon salt
½ cup vegetable shortening
1 cup granulated sugar
1 large egg
¼ cup milk
1½ teaspoons grated lemon zest
1 cup blackberry puree, unstrained

**1** Combine the flour, baking powder, and salt.

**2** In a large bowl, cream the vegetable shortening and sugar. Beat in the egg and milk. Beat in the lemon zest. Gradually blend in the dry ingredients. Fold in the blackberry puree. Cover and chill for at least 4 hours.

**3** Preheat the oven to 375 degrees.

**4** Drop the dough by spoonfuls 1½ inches apart onto ungreased baking sheets.

**5** Bake for 12 to 15 minutes, until lightly colored. Transfer to wire racks to cool.

**Baking notes:** You can make these with fresh blackberries instead of the puree. Rinse and thoroughly dry fresh berries. Add the berries to the flour mixture, tossing them gently to coat thoroughly.

**CRUST**
¾ cup vegetable shortening
¼ cup granulated sugar
2 large egg yolks
1½ cups all-purpose flour

**TOPPING**
2 large egg whites
½ cup granulated sugar
1 cup almonds, chopped
1 cup blackberry puree, unstrained
1 cup shaved fresh coconut (see Baking notes)

**1** Preheat the oven to 350 degrees.

**2** To make the crust, in a large bowl, cream the vegetable shortening and sugar. Beat in the egg yolks. Gradually blend in the flour.

**3** Spread the mixture evenly in the bottom of an ungreased 13 by 9-inch baking pan. Bake for 15 minutes.

**4** Meanwhile, make the topping: In a medium bowl, beat the egg whites into stiff peaks. Beat in the sugar. Fold in the nuts.

**5** Spread the blackberry puree over the warm crust. Sprinkle with the coconut. Spread the meringue evenly over the top.

**6** Bake for 20 to 25 minutes longer, until the topping is set. Cool in the pan on a rack before cutting into large or small bars.

**Baking notes:** The blackberry puree can be fresh, canned, frozen, preserved, or a compote. If you do not have fresh coconut available packaged flaked coconut can be used. These cookies can be made with almost any type of berry. If desired, add ¼ teaspoon almond extract to the crust for subtle flavor.

# BLACKBERRY MERINGUE BARS

Bar Cookies

YIELD: *3 to 4 dozen*
TOTAL TIME: *45 minutes*

---

2½ cups all-purpose flour
1 teaspoon baking powder
1 teaspoon salt
¾ cup vegetable shortening
1¼ cups granulated sugar
2 large eggs
1 teaspoon anise extract
Sugar Glaze (see Pantry)
Licorice gumdrops for garnish

**1** Preheat the oven to 350 degrees.

**2** Combine the flour, baking powder and salt.

**3** In a large bowl, cream the vegetable shortening and sugar. Beat in the eggs and anise extract. Gradually blend in the dry ingredients.

**4** Divide the dough into 2 pieces, one slightly larger than the other. On a floured surface, roll out the larger piece ⅛ inch thick. Using a scalloped 2-inch round cutter, cut out rounds and place 1½ inches apart on ungreased baking sheets. Roll out the remaining dough. Using a 1¼-inch plain round cutter, cut out rounds and place 1½ inches apart on ungreased baking sheets. (You should have an equal number of cookies of each size.)

**5** Bake for 5 to 7 minutes, until lightly colored. Transfer to wire racks to cool

**6** Brush the centers of the scalloped cookies with the sugar glaze and place a plain cookie on top of each one. Brush the center of each plain cookie with glaze, and set a gumdrop on top.

**Baking notes:** The variations on this cookie are almost endless: Cut the cookies into different shapes with your favorite cookie cutters and use gumdrops of all colors and flavors to decorate them.

# BLACK EYED SUSANS

Rolled Cookies

YIELD: *3 to 4 dozen*
TOTAL TIME: *30 minutes*

# BLACK WALNUT COOKIES I

Rolled Cookies

YIELD: *4 to 5 dozen*

TOTAL TIME: *30 minutes*

CHILLING TIME: *3 hours*

3 cups all-purpose flour
1 teaspoon baking powder
½ teaspoon salt
1 cup vegetable shortening
1½ cups granulated sugar
3 large eggs
1 cup milk
1 cup black walnuts, chopped

**1** Combine the flour, baking powder, and salt.

**2** In a large bowl, cream the vegetable shortening and sugar. Beat in the eggs one at a time. Beat in the milk. Gradually blend in the dry ingredients. Stir in the nuts. Cover and chill for at least 3 hours.

**3** Preheat the oven to 350 degrees.

**4** On a floured surface, roll out the dough ¼ inch thick. Using cookie cutters, cut into shapes and place 1½ inches apart on ungreased baking sheets.

**5** Bake for 15 to 18 minutes, until golden brown. Transfer to wire racks to cool.

**Baking notes:** Black walnuts have a stronger flavor than other walnuts. They are available in specialty food markets, but if you can't get them substitute regular walnuts.

# BLACK WALNUT COOKIES II

Drop Cookies

YIELD: *5 to 6 dozen*

TOTAL TIME: *30 minutes*

½ cup all-purpose flour
½ teaspoon baking powder
¼ teaspoon salt
4 large eggs
2 cups packed light brown sugar
1½ cups black walnuts, chopped

**1** Preheat the oven to 375 degrees. Grease 2 baking sheets.

**2** Combine the flour, baking powder, and salt.

**3** In a large bowl, beat the eggs and brown sugar until thick and light-colored. Gradually blend in the dry ingredients. Stir in the walnuts.

**4** Drop the dough by spoonfuls 1½ inches apart onto the prepared baking sheets.

**5** Bake for 10 to 12 minutes, until lightly colored. Transfer to wire racks to cool.

2⅔ cups all-purpose flour
2 teaspoons baking powder
¼ teaspoon salt
¾ cup butter, at room temperature
1½ cups packed light brown sugar
2 large eggs
1 teaspoon vanilla extract
1½ cups black walnuts, chopped

1  Combine the flour, baking powder, and salt.

2  In a large bowl, cream the butter and brown sugar. Beat in the eggs and vanilla extract. Gradually blend in the dry ingredients. Fold in the walnuts. Cover and refrigerate just until firm enough to shape, about 30 minutes.

3  Divide the dough into 3 pieces. Form each piece into a log about 8 inches long. Wrap in waxed paper and chill for at least 24 hours.

4  Preheat the oven to 375 degrees. Grease 2 baking sheets.

5  Slice the logs into ¼-inch-thick slices and place 1 inch apart on the prepared baking sheets.

6  Bake for 8 to 10 minutes, until lightly colored. Transfer to wire racks to cool.

# BLACK WALNUT REFRIGERATOR COOKIES

Refrigerator Cookies

YIELD: *8 to 9 dozen*
TOTAL TIME: *30 minutes*
CHILLING TIME: *24 hours*

---

CRUST
1 cup vegetable shortening
1 cup granulated sugar
2 large eggs, separated
3 cups flour
½ teaspoon salt

TOPPING
2 large egg whites
½ cup almonds, ground fine
¾ teaspoon ground cinnamon
¼ teaspoon granulated sugar

1  Preheat the oven to 350 degrees.

2  To make the crust, cream the vegetable shortening and sugar in a large bowl. Combine flour and salt and add. Beat in the egg yolks.

3  In another bowl, beat the egg whites with the salt until they hold stiff peaks. Fold the egg whites into the egg yolk mixture. Gradually fold in the flour.

4  Press the mixture evenly into the bottom of an ungreased 8-inch square baking pan.

5  To make the topping: In a medium bowl, beat the egg whites until stiff but not dry. Fold in the ground almonds, then fold in the cinnamon and sugar.

6  Spread the topping evenly over the prepared crust.

7  Bake for 25 to 30 minutes, until firm to the touch. Cool in the pan on a rack before cutting into large or small bars.

# BLITZKUCHEN

Bar Cookies

YIELD: *1 to 2 dozen*
TOTAL TIME: *45 minutes*

---

½ cup butter, at room temperature
2 cups packed light brown sugar
4 large eggs
2 teaspoons almond extract
2½ cups all-purpose flour
2 teaspoons baking powder
1½ cups almonds, chopped
1½ cups (9 ounces) semisweet chocolate chips

1  Preheat the oven to 375 degrees.

2  In a large bowl, cream the butter and brown sugar. Beat in the eggs and almond extract. Gradually blend in the flour and baking powder. Stir in the almonds and chocolate chips.

3  Spread the batter evenly in an ungreased 13 by 9-inch baking pan.

4  Bake for 15 to 20 minutes, until a toothpick inserted in the center comes out clean. Cut into large or small bars while still warm and cool in the pan on a rack.

# BLOND BROWNIES I

Bar Cookies

YIELD: *1 to 2 dozen*
TOTAL TIME: *30 minutes*

# BLOND BROWNIES II

Bar Cookies

YIELD: *1 to 3 dozen*
TOTAL TIME: *30 minutes*

2⅔ cups all-purpose flour
2½ teaspoons baking powder
½ teaspoon salt
⅔ cup vegetable shortening
2 cups packed light brown sugar
3 large eggs
1 teaspoon vanilla extract
1 cup (6 ounces) semisweet choco-
    late chips

**1** Preheat the oven to 375
degrees. Grease a 9-inch square
baking pan.

**2** Combine the flour, baking
powder, and salt.

**3** Melt the vegetable shortening
in a medium saucepan. Stir in the
brown sugar and cook over low
heat for 10 minutes. Remove
from the heat.

**4** Add the eggs one at a time
beating well after each addition.

Beat in the vanilla extract. Gradually blend in the dry ingredients.
Stir in the chocolate chips.

**5** Spread the batter evenly in the
prepared pan.

**6** Bake for 12 to 15 minutes, until
a toothpick inserted in the center
comes out clean. Cool in the pan
on a rack before cutting into large
or small bars.

**Baking notes:** A creamy chocolate frosting flavored with 1 or 2
drops of mint extract goes very
well with these bars. Using an 8-
inch square baking pan will produce a thicker, cake-type
brownie; a 13 by 9-inch baking
pan will produce a thinner,
chewier brownie.

# BLUEBERRY BARS I

Bar Cookies

YIELD: *3 to 4 dozen*
TOTAL TIME: *30 minutes*

CRUST
½ cup granulated sugar
16 graham crackers, crushed
¼ cup vegetable shortening

FILLING
2 large eggs
8 ounces cream cheese, at room
    temperature
½ cup granulated sugar
½ teaspoon almond extract

TOPPING
12 ounces blueberries
2 tablespoons cornstarch
½ cup water
1 teaspoon fresh lemon juice

**1** Preheat the oven to 350
degrees. Lightly grease a 13 by 9-
inch baking pan.

**2** To make the crust, combine the
sugar and vegetable shortening
in a medium bowl. Add the graham crackers and work the mixture with your fingertips until
crumbly. Press the mixture
evenly into the prepared baking
pan.

**3** To make the filling, combine
the eggs, cream cheese, sugar,

and almond extract in a bowl and
beat until smooth. Spread evenly
over the crust.

**4** Bake for 15 to 18 minutes, until
firm to the touch. Cool in the pan
on a wire rack.

**5** Meanwhile, make the topping:
Heat the blueberries on top of a
double boiler over medium heat.
Add cornstarch, water, and
lemon juice. Continue cooking
over medium heat until the mixture is about as thick as mayon-
naise. Remove from the heat and
let cool.

**6** Spread the blueberry mixture
over the top of the cooled cookies. Refrigerate for 15 to 20 minutes before cutting into large or
small bars.

**Baking notes:** Vanilla wafers
may be substituted for the graham crackers. To serve, place a
dab of whipped cream on each
bar and sprinkle with finely
ground almonds.

**B**

## BLUEBERRY BARS II

Bar Cookies

YIELD: *1 to 2 dozen*

TOTAL TIME: *1 hour and 10 minutes*

**CRUST**

1 cup all-purpose flour
1¼ teaspoons baking powder
½ cup vegetable shortening
¾ cup granulated sugar
1 large egg
¾ teaspoon almond extract
⅓ cup milk
1½ cups fresh blueberries, cleaned

**TOPPING**

2 large eggs
8 ounces cream cheese, at room
    temperature
⅓ cup powdered sugar
1 teaspoon almond extract

**1** Preheat the oven to 350 degrees. Lightly grease a 9-inch square baking pan.

**2** To make the crust, combine the flour and baking powder.

**3** In a large bowl, cream the vegetable shortening and sugar. Beat in the egg and almond extract. Beat in the milk. Gradually blend in the dry ingredients.

**4** Spread the mixture evenly in the prepared baking pan.

**5** Sprinkle the blueberries over the crust in the pan.

**6** To make the topping, in a medium bowl, beat the eggs and cream cheese until smooth. Beat in the powdered sugar and almond extract. Spread this mixture over the blueberries.

**7** Bake for 55 to 60 minutes, or until firm to the touch. Cool in the pan on a wire rack before cutting into large or small bars.

---

## BLUEBERRY COOKIES

Drop Cookies

YIELD: *4 to 5 dozen*

TOTAL TIME: *30 minutes*

CHILLING TIME: *4 hours*

2 cups all-purpose flour
2 teaspoons baking powder
½ teaspoon salt
½ cup vegetable shortening
1 cup granulated sugar
1 large egg
¼ cup milk
1 teaspoon almond extract
1½ teaspoons grated lemon zest
1 cup blueberries

**1** Combine the flour, baking powder, and salt.

**2** In a large bowl, cream the vegetable shortening and sugar. Beat in the egg. Beat in the milk, almond extract, and lemon zest. Gradually blend in the dry ingredients. Fold in the blueberries.

**3** Cover and chill for at least 4 hours.

**4** Preheat the oven to 375 degrees.

**5** Drop the dough by spoonfuls about 1 inch apart onto ungreased baking sheets.

**6** Bake for 12 to 15 minutes, until lightly colored. Transfer to wire racks to cool

**Baking notes:** Canned or frozen blueberries can be used, but fresh give the best results.

---

## BLUSHING COOKIES

Rolled Cookies

YIELD: *2 to 3 dozen*

TOTAL TIME: *30 minutes*

2 cups all-purpose flour
1 cup walnuts, chopped fine
¼ teaspoon ground cinnamon
½ cup vegetable shortening
¾ cup powdered sugar
Red jimmies for sprinkling

**1** Preheat the oven to 400 degrees.

**2** Combine the flour, walnuts, and cinnamon.

**3** In a large bowl, cream the vegetable shortening and powdered sugar until light and fluffy. Gradually blend in the dry ingredients.

**4** On a floured surface, roll out the dough ¼ inch thick. Using cookie cutter, cut into shapes and place on ungreased baking sheets. Sprinkle the rainbow jimmies over the tops of the cookies.

**5** Bake for 8 to 10 minutes, until lightly colored. Transfer to wire racks to cool.

# BOHEMIAN BUTTER COOKIES

Rolled Cookies

YIELD: *4 to 5 dozen*
TOTAL TIME: *40 minutes*
CHILLING TIME: *30 minutes*

3½ cups all-purpose flour
¼ teaspoon salt
1 cup butter, at room temperature
¾ cup granulated sugar
2 large egg yolks
2 hard-boiled large egg yolks, chopped
½ teaspoon fresh lemon juice
¼ teaspoon fresh grated lemon zest

**1** Combine the flour and salt.

**2** In a large bowl, cream the butter and sugar.

**3** In a small bowl, beat the raw egg yolks and hard-boiled egg yolks together. Beat in the lemon juice and zest. Beat this into the butter mixture. Gradually blend in the dry ingredients.

**4** Divide the dough into 3 pieces. Wrap in waxed paper and chill until firm enough to roll.

**5** Preheat the oven to 375 degrees. Lightly grease 2 baking sheets.

**6** On a floured surface, roll out the dough to a thickness of ¼ inch. Cut into shapes with cookie cutters and place 1 inch apart on the prepared baking sheets.

**7** Bake for 8 to 10 minutes, until lightly colored. Transfer to wire racks to cool.

# BOHEMIAN COOKIES

Formed Cookies

YIELD: *4 to 5 dozen*
TOTAL TIME: *60 minutes*

1¼ cups all-purpose flour
1 cup hazelnuts, chopped fine
Pinch of salt
1 cup vegetable shortening
1¼ cups powdered sugar
¾ cup milk
1 teaspoon vanilla extract

**1** Preheat the oven to 300 degrees.

**2** Combine the flour, hazelnuts, and salt.

**3** In a large bowl, cream the vegetable shortening and powdered sugar. Beat in the milk and vanilla extract. Gradually blend in the dry ingredients.

**4** Break off small pieces of dough and form into balls. Place each ball 1 inch apart on ungreased baking sheets.

**5** Bake for 35 to 40 minutes, or until lightly colored. Transfer to wire racks to cool.

# BOILED COOKIES

Drop Cookies

YIELD: *1 to 2 dozen*
TOTAL TIME: *30 minutes*
CHILLING TIME: *20 minutes*

½ cup peanut butter
2 tablespoons vanilla extract
5 tablespoons cocoa powder
3 cups rolled oats

**TOPPING**
2 cups granulated sugar
½ cup milk
½ teaspoon vegetable shortening

**1** Line 2 baking sheets with waxed paper.

**2** In a large bowl, beat the peanut butter and vanilla extract until smooth. Gradually blend in the cocoa. Fold in the oats.

**3** Drop the dough by spoonfuls onto the waxed paper-lined bak-ing sheets. Cover with waxed paper and chill for 20 minutes.

**4** Meanwhile, prepare the topping: In a small saucepan, combine the sugar, milk, and vegetable shortening. Stir to dissolve the sugar. Bring to a boil over medium heat and boil for one minute. Remove from the heat. Place a spoonful of the warm topping on each cookie. Chill for 20 minutes, then wrap individually in waxed paper.

**Baking notes:** While these are simply good cookies, they are a high-energy bar for hikers and backpackers.

1½ cups all-purpose flour
½ teaspoon salt
½ cup vegetable shortening
½ cups powdered sugar
2 tablespoons heavy cream
2 teaspoons vanilla extract
36 candied glacé cherries

**1** Preheat the oven to 350 degrees.

**2** Combine the flour and salt.

**3** In a large bowl, cream the vegetable shortening and powdered sugar. Beat in the cream and vanilla extract. Gradually blend in the dry ingredients.

**4** Break off pieces of dough and flatten each one on a floured surface into a round about 3 to 4 inches in diameter. Place a candied cherry in the center of each round and wrap the dough up around the cherry. Pinch to seal. Place 1 inch apart on ungreased baking sheets.

**5** Bake for 8 to 10 minutes, until the dough is set (see Baking notes). Transfer to wire racks to cool.

**Baking notes:** It is important not to overbake these cookies; bake only until the dough is set. Do not let it color at all. To decorate, dip the top of each ball into sugar icing or melted chocolate. To completely coat the cookies with chocolate, place the cookies one at a time on a bamboo skewer and dip in melted chocolate. Hold the skewer at an angle so cookie does not slip off it. For an unusual variation, add 3 tablespoons of unsweetened cocoa powder to the dough, and dip the tops of the baked bonbons in melted white chocolate.

# BONBONS
Formed Cookies

YIELD: *3 dozen*
TOTAL TIME: *40 minutes*

⅓ cup large egg whites (3 to 4)
1 cup powdered sugar
2 cup hazelnuts, ground
1 teaspoon grated lemon zest
¾ cup ground cinnamon
Powdered sugar for rolling
Strawberry preserves

**1** Line 2 baking sheets with parchment paper.

**2** In a large bowl, start beating the egg whites and gradually add the powdered sugar, then beat to very stiff peaks. Beat for about 5 minutes.

**3** Measure out ⅓ cup of the mixture and set aside. Fold the hazelnuts, lemon zest, and ground cinnamon into the remaining mixture.

**4** Line a work surface with parchment paper and sprinkle liberally with powdered sugar.

Roll out the dough to ¼ inch thick. Sprinkle the dough with powdered sugar and cut with a 2-inch star cutter. Sprinkle each star with powdered sugar and place on the prepared baking sheets. Place a ⅛ dessert teaspoon of strawberry preserves in the center of each star and place a dab of the reserved egg mixture on the strawberry preserves. Set aside for 1½ hours.

**5** Preheat the oven to 375 degrees.

**6** Bake for 7 to 10 minutes, until firm to the touch. Cool on the baking sheets on wire racks before removing from the parchment paper.

# BORDER COOKIES
Rolled Cookies

YIELD: *2 to 4 dozen*
TOTAL TIME: *40 minutes*
SITTING TIME: *90 minutes*

# BOURBON BALLS

Formed Cookies

YIELD: *3 to 5 dozen*
TOTAL TIME: *30 minutes*

2½ cups crushed vanilla wafers
1 cup walnuts, ground fine
¾ cup semisweet chocolate chips
½ cup granulated sugar
2 tablespoons corn syrup
½ cup bourbon
Powdered sugar for rolling

**1** Combine the vanilla wafers and walnuts.

**2** Melt the chocolate chips in a double boiler over low heat, stirring until smooth. Stir in the sugar and corn syrup. Remove from the heat and stir in the bourbon. Add the vanilla wafer mixture all at once and blend to form a thick dough.

**3** Break off pieces of dough and form into balls. Roll each ball in powdered sugar. Store in an airtight container until ready to serve.

**Baking notes:** Almost any type of whiskey can be substituted for the bourbon. Obviously, these cookies are not for children.

# BOURBON CHEWS

Drop Cookies

YIELD: *3 to 4 dozen*
TOTAL TIME: *30 minutes*

1 cup all-purpose flour
1 teaspoon ground ginger
½ teaspoon salt
½ cup molasses
¼ cup vegetable shortening
2 tablespoons bourbon
½ cup packed light brown sugar
¼ cup walnuts, chopped

**1** Preheat the oven to 325 degrees. Lightly grease 2 baking sheets.

**2** Combine the flour, ginger, and salt together.

**3** In a small saucepan combine the molasses and vegetable shortening and heat over low heat, stirring until smooth. Remove

from the heat and add the bourbon. Beat in the brown sugar. Gradually blend in the dry ingredients. Fold in the walnuts.

**4** Drop the dough by spoonfuls onto the prepared baking sheets.

**5** Bake for 10 to 12 minutes, until lightly colored. Transfer to wire racks to cool.

# BOW COOKIES

Rolled Cookies

YIELD: *4 to 5 dozen*
TOTAL TIME: *30 minutes*

3 large eggs
3 tablespoons granulated sugar
¼ teaspoon salt
1 tablespoon vanilla extract
3 cups all-purpose flour
Vegetable oil for deep-frying
Powdered sugar for sprinkling

**1** In a large bowl, beat the eggs until thick and light-colored. Beat in the sugar and salt. Beat in the vanilla extract. Gradually blend in the flour.

**2** On a floured surface, roll out the dough ⅛ inch thick. Cut into strips 6 inches by 1½ inches. Make a ¾-inch-long slit down the center of each strip and pull one

end of the strip through the slit to form a bow tie.

**3** In a deep-fryer or deep heavy pot, heat the oil to 375 degrees. Fry the cookies, in batches, until golden brown. Drain on a wire rack lined with paper towels, then sprinkle with powdered sugar.

**Baking notes:** Colored sugar crystals can be used to create colored bows for the holidays. For a distinctive look, use a pastry wheel to cut the strips.

2 cups all-purpose flour
2 teaspoons baking powder
½ teaspoon salt
½ cup vegetable shortening
1 cup granulated sugar
1 large egg
¼ cup milk
1½ teaspoons grated lemon zest
1 cup boysenberries, crushed and
   strained to remove the seeds

**1** Combine the flour, baking powder and salt.

**2** In a large bowl, cream the vegetable shortening and sugar. Beat in the egg. Beat in the milk and lemon zest. Gradually blend in the dry ingredients. Blend in the boysenberries. Cover and chill for at least 4 hours.

**3** Preheat the oven to 375 degrees.

**4** Drop the dough by spoonfuls about 1 inch apart onto ungreased baking sheets.

**5** Bake for 12 to 15 minutes, until golden. Transfer to wire racks to cool.

# BOYSENBERRY COOKIES

Drop Cookies

YIELD: *4 to 5 dozen*
TOTAL TIME: *30 minutes*
CHILLING TIME: *4 hours*

---

**CRUST**
¾ cup vegetable shortening
¼ cup granulated sugar
2 large eggs yolks
1½ cups all-purpose flour

**TOPPING**
2 large egg whites
¾ cup granulated sugar
1 cup hazelnuts, chopped
1 cup shredded coconut
1 cup boysenberry puree

**1** Preheat the oven to 350 degrees.

**2** To make the crust, cream the vegetable shortening and sugar in a large bowl. Beat in the egg yolks. Gradually blend in the flour to make a crumbly dough.

**3** Spread the dough evenly over the bottom of a 13 by 9-inch baking pan. Bake for 15 minutes.

**4** Meanwhile, make the topping: In a large bowl, beat the egg whites until foamy. Gradually beat in the sugar. Beat to stiff peaks. Fold in the hazelnuts and coconut.

**5** Spread the boysenberry puree over the warm crust. Spread the meringue evenly over the puree. Bake for 20 to 25 minutes longer, or until the topping is firm.

**6** Cool in the pan on a wire rack before cutting into large or small bars.

# BOYSENBERRY MERINGUE BARS

Bar Cookies

YIELD: *1 to 4 dozen*
TOTAL TIME: *30 minutes*

B

# BRANDIED BREAKFAST COOKIES

Drop Cookies

YIELD: *4 to 5 dozen*
TOTAL TIME: *30 minutes*

1½ cups all-purpose flour
1½ teaspoons baking soda
¼ teaspoon salt
2 cups cornflakes, crushed
½ cup vegetable shortening
1 cup packed light brown sugar
2 large eggs
¼ cup strong brewed coffee
1 teaspoon brandy

**1** Preheat the oven to 400 degrees. Lightly grease 2 baking sheets.

**2** Combine the flour, baking soda, and salt. Spread the crushed cornflakes on a large plate.

**3** In a large bowl, cream the vegetable shortening and brown sugar. Beat in the eggs one at a time, beating well after each

addition. Beat in the coffee and brandy. Gradually blend in the dry ingredients.

**4** Drop the dough by spoonfuls, a few at a time, onto the cornflakes. Roll each one in the cornflakes until well coated and place 1½ inches apart on the prepared baking sheets.

**5** Bake for 10 to 12 minutes, until golden. Transfer to wire racks to cool.

---

# BRANDY ALEXANDER BROWNIES

Bar Cookies

YIELD: *2 to 3 dozen*
TOTAL TIME: *35 minutes*

⅔ cup all-purpose flour
1 tablespoon unsweetened cocoa powder
½ teaspoon baking powder
¼ teaspoon salt
½ cup vegetable shortening
¾ cup granulated sugar
2 large eggs
2 tablespoons crème de cacao
2 tablespoons brandy

**1** Preheat the oven to 350 degrees. Grease a 9-inch square baking pan.

**2** Combine the flour, cocoa powder, baking powder, and salt.

**3** In a large bowl, cream the vegetable shortening and sugar. Beat in the eggs. Beat in the crème de cacao and brandy. Gradually blend in the dry ingredients.

**4** Spread the dough evenly in the prepared baking pan.

**5** Bake for 20 to 25 minutes, until the top is lightly colored. Cool in the pan on a wire rack before cutting into large or small bars.

---

# BRANDY BALLS

Formed Cookies

YIELD: *3 to 4 dozen*
TOTAL TIME: *30 minutes*

1 pound vanilla wafers, crushed fine
½ cup honey
⅓ cup brandy
⅓ cup light rum
1½ cups chopped nuts
Powdered sugar for rolling

**1** In a large bowl, combine the vanilla wafers, honey, brandy, rum, and walnuts and stir to form a stiff, sticky dough.

**2** Break off walnut-sized pieces of dough and roll into balls. Roll each ball in powdered sugar. Store in an airtight container.

**Baking notes:** These cookies are not for children.

1 cup all-purpose flour
½ teaspoon ground ginger
½ teaspoon ground nutmeg
6 tablespoons vegetable shortening
½ cup packed light brown sugar
¼ cup molasses
1 tablespoon brandy

**1** Preheat the oven to 350 degrees.

**2** Combine the flour, ginger, and nutmeg.

**3** In a large bowl cream the vegetable shortening and brown sugar. Beat in the molasses and brandy. Gradually blend in the dry ingredients.

**4** Drop the dough by spoonfuls 2 inches apart onto ungreased baking sheets.

**5** Bake for 5 to 6 minutes, or until lightly colored. As soon as the cookies cool enough so you can handle them, lift them one at a time from the baking sheet roll up around a metal cone. If cookies harden before you are able to form them, re-heat them for 30 second in a hot oven. Cool on wire racks before using.

**Baking notes:** You need metal cone forms to shape the cookies; they are available in cookware shops. These cones can be filled with many types of dessert topping or ice cream. If you use ice cream, place the cones in the freezer for at least 30 minutes before you fill them.

# BRANDY CONES

Drop Cookies

YIELD: *5 to 6 dozen*
TOTAL TIME: *30 minutes*

---

1 cup vegetable shortening
½ cup granulated sugar
1 tablespoon brandy
¼ cup unsweetened cocoa powder
3 cups all-purpose flour

**1** Preheat the oven to 350 degrees.

**2** In large bowl, cream the vegetable shortening and sugar. Beat in the brandy. Blend in the cocoa powder. Gradually blend in the flour.

**3** Place the dough in a cookie press or a pastry bag fitted with a plain round tip. Press or pipe the dough onto ungreased baking sheets, spacing the cookies 1½ inches apart.

**4** Bake for 8 to 10 minutes, until light golden. Transfer to wire racks to cool.

**Baking notes:** These cookies are usually formed using a plain round tip, but you can experiment with other shapes. This dough keeps well in the rerigerator; it also freezes well. It can also be rolled out ¼ inch thick and cut into shapes with cookie cutters. For variation, use candied fruit to decorate the cookies.

# BRANDY COOKIES I

Formed Cookies

YIELD: *1 to 3 dozen*
TOTAL TIME: *30 minutes*

# BRANDY COOKIES II

Formed Cookies

YIELD: *4 to 5 dozen*
TOTAL TIME: *30 minutes*

1 cup vegetable shortening
¾ cup granulated sugar
3 tablespoons brandy
3 cups all-purpose flour

**1** Preheat the oven to 350 degrees.

**2** In a large bowl, cream the vegetable shortening and sugar. Beat in the brandy. Gradually blend in the flour.

**3** Break off pieces of dough and roll into pencil-thin ropes 8 inches long. For each cookie, twist 2 ropes together and then form into a ring. Moisten the ends lightly with water and pinch to seal, and place the rings 1 inch apart on ungreased baking sheets.

**4** Bake for 12 to 15 minutes, until golden brown. Transfer to wire racks to cool.

**Baking notes:** These can be sprinkled with sugar crystals when cookies are warm or drizzled with icing or melted chocolate.

# BRANDY SNAPS

Drop Cookies

YIELD: *1 to 3 dozen*
TOTAL TIME: *30 minutes*

1 cup vegetable shortening
1 cup granulated sugar
1 large egg
½ teaspoon baking soda
¾ cup dark corn syrup
½ cup brandy
1½ teaspoons red wine vinegar
3 cups all-purpose flour

**GLAZE**
1 tablespoon powdered sugar
¼ teaspoon brandy

**1** Preheat the oven to 350 degrees.

**2** In a large bowl, cream the vegetable shortening and sugar. Beat in the egg. Beat in the baking soda. Beat in the corn syrup, brandy, and vinegar. Gradually blend in the flour.

**3** Drop the dough by spoonfuls 1½ inches apart onto ungreased baking sheets.

**4** To make the topping, dissolve the powdered sugar in the brandy. Lightly brush the cookies with the glaze.

**5** Bake for 10 to 12 minutes, until lightly colored. Transfer to wire racks to cool.

# BRASLER BRÜNSLI

Rolled Cookies

YIELD: *1 to 3 dozen*
TOTAL TIME: *30 minutes*
CHILLING TIME: *2 hours*

2½ cups granulated sugar
1¼ cups almonds, ground fine
4½ tablespoons unsweetened cocoa powder
1 teaspoon ground cinnamon
1 tablespoon kirsch
4 large egg whites
Granulated sugar for rolling

**1** Combine the sugar, almonds, cocoa powder, and cinnamon in a large bowl. Drizzle the kirsch over the top.

**2** In another large bowl, beat the egg whites until stiff and dry. Gradually fold the egg whites into the dry ingredients. Cover and chill for 2 hours.

**3** Preheat the oven to 300 degrees. Line 2 baking sheets with parchment paper.

**4** Sprinkle a work surface with granulated sugar. Roll out the dough ¼ inch thick. Using a 1¼-inch round cookie cutter, cut out the cookies and place 1½ inches apart on the prepared baking sheets.

**5** Bake for 12 to 15 minutes, until firm to the touch. Cool on the baking sheets on wire racks before removing the cookies from the parchment.

**Baking notes:** The secret of these cookies is in the handling. Work as quickly as possible when cutting the chilled dough. Dusting your hands with sugar as you work also helps.

2 cups all-purpose flour
1 teaspoon baking powder
½ cup vegetable shortening
1 cup granulated sugar
1 large egg
1 tablespoon heavy cream
2 tablespoons poppy seeds

TOPPING
1 tablespoon granulated sugar
½ teaspoon ground cinnamon

**1** Combine the flour and baking powder.

**2** In a lage bowl, cream the vegetable shortening and sugar. Beat in the egg and heavy cream. Gradually blend in the dry ingredients.

**3** Divide the dough in half. Knead the poppy seeds into half the dough. Wrap the dough in waxed paper and chill for at least 1 hour.

**4** Preheat the oven to 400 degrees.

**5** On a floured surface, roll out the poppy seed dough as thin as possible. Using a knife or a pastry wheel, cut the dough into 2 by 1-inch rectangles and place ½ inch apart on ungreased baking sheets. Combine the sugar and cinnamon for the topping and sprinkle over the cookies. Roll out the remaining dough and, using a 2-inch round cookie cutter, cut into circles.

**6** Bake for 10 to 12 minutes, until lightly colored. Transfer to wire racks to cool.

# BRATISLAVIAN THINS

Rolled Cookies

YIELD: *1 to 2 dozen*
TOTAL TIME: *30 minutes*
CHILLING TIME: *1 hour*

---

4 cups all-purpose flour
1 teaspoon baking soda
1 teaspoon ground cinnamon
1 teaspoon ground cloves
½ teaspoon salt
⅔ cup honey
1 cup sugar
½ cup butter
1 large egg
⅓ cup warm water
⅔ cup hazelnuts, chopped
½ cup candied citron, chopped

**1** Combine the flour, baking soda, cinnamon, cloves, and salt.

**2** Combine the honey, sugar, and butter in a saucepan and bring to a boil. Cook for 5 minutes. Remove from the heat and let cool slightly.

**3** Beat the egg and water into the honey mixture. Gradually blend in the dry ingredients. Stir in the nuts and candied citron.

**4** Form into a ball and wrap in waxed paper and chill for 4 days.

**5** Preheat the oven to 350 degrees. Grease 2 baking sheets.

**6** On a floured surface, roll out the dough to a thickness of ¼ inch. Using cookie cutters, cut into shapes and place 1½ inches apart on the prepared baking sheets.

**7** Bake for 15 to 18 minutes, or until lightly colored. Transfer to wire racks to cool.

**Baking notes:** By tradition, these cookie are iced with colored sugar icing.

# BRAUNE LEBKÜCHEN

Rolled Cookies

YIELD: *3 to 4 dozen*
TOTAL TIME: *30 minutes*
CHILLING TIME: *4 days*

# BRAZIL-NUT BALLS

Formed Cookies

YIELD: *6 to 8 dozen*
TOTAL TIME: *30 minutes*

2 cups all-purpose flour
½ teaspoon salt
¾ cup vegetable shortening
½ cup granulated sugar
1 large egg
2 cups brazil nuts, ground fine
Powdered sugar for rolling

1  Preheat the oven to 350 degrees.

2  Combine the flour and salt.

3  In a large bowl, cream the vegetable shortening and sugar. Beat in the egg. Gradually blend in the dry ingredients. Stir in the nuts.

4  Break off walnut-sized pieces of dough and form into balls.

Roll in powered sugar and place 1 inch apart on ungreased baking sheets.

5  Bake for 15 to 20 minutes, until firm to the touch. Roll the hot cookies in powdered sugar and place on wire racks to cool. When cool roll in powdered sugar again.

# BRAZIL-NUT BARS

Bar Cookies

YIELD: *1 to 2 dozen*
TOTAL TIME: *40 minutes*

CRUST
½ cup vegetable shortening
1 cup all-purpose flour
¼ teaspoon salt

TOPPING
2 large eggs
¾ cup packed light brown sugar
1½ cups brazil nuts, ground fine
¼ teaspoon salt
½ cup flaked coconut
1 teaspoon vanilla extract
2 tablespoons all-purpose flour
Frosting to decorate

1  Preheat the oven to 375 degrees. Lightly grease a 9-inch square baking pan.

2  To make the crust, cream the vegetable shortening in a large bowl. Blend in the flour and salt.

3  Press the mixture evenly into the bottom of the prepared baking pan. Bake for 15 minutes.

4  Meanwhile make the topping: In a large bowl, beat the eggs and brown sugar together until thick. Beat in the brazil nuts and salt. Beat in the coconut, vanilla extract, and flour.

5  Spread this mixture evenly over the warm crust. Bake for 15 minutes longer, until firm to the touch.

6  Cool in the pan on a rack and top with frosting before cutting into large or small bars. (See Pantry).

# BRAZIL-NUT COOKIES I

Drop Cookies

YIELD: *2 to 3 dozen*
TOTAL TIME: *30 minutes*

2 ounces bittersweet chocolate, chopped
½ cup vegetable shortening
1 cup granulated sugar
1 large egg
1 teaspoon vanilla extract
¾ cup all-purpose flour
½ cup brazil nuts, chopped fine

1  Preheat the oven to 325 degrees. Lightly grease 2 baking sheets.

2  Melt the chocolate in the top of a double boiler over low heat, stirring until smooth. Remove from the heat.

3  In a large bowl, cream the vegetable shortening and sugar. Beat in the egg and vanilla extract.

Beat in the melted chocolate. Gradually blend in the flour. Stir in the brazil nuts.

4  Drop the dough by spoonfuls 1½ inches apart onto the prepared baking sheets. Flatten the cookies with the bottom of a glass dipped in flour.

5  Bake for 12 to 15 minutes, until lightly colored. Transfer to wire racks to cool.

**Baking notes:** For a special look, decorate the cookies with a chocolate buttercream frosting and top with slivered brazil nuts. (See Pantry).

1¾ cups all-purpose flour
½ teaspoon salt
1 cup vegetable shortening
1 cup granulated sugar
1 large egg
1 teaspoon vanilla extract
1 cup brazil nuts, sliced thin
About 1½ cups whole brazil nuts

1 Combine the flour and salt.

2 In a large bowl, cream the vegetable shortening and sugar. Beat in the egg. Beat in the vanilla extract. Gradually blend in the dry ingredients. Fold in the sliced nuts. Cover and chill for at least 4 hours.

3 Preheat the oven to 375 degrees. Lightly grease 2 baking sheets.

4 Drop the dough by tablespoonfuls 1½ inches apart onto the prepared baking sheets. Press a whole brazil nut into each cookie.

5 Bake for 10 to 12 minutes, until golden brown. Transfer to wire racks to cool.

## BRAZIL-NUT COOKIES II

Drop Cookies

YIELD: *2 to 3 dozen*
TOTAL TIME: *30 minutes*
CHILLING TIME: *4 hours*

1 cup all-purpose flour
¼ cup brazil nuts, chopped fine
¼ teaspoon salt
½ cup vegetable shortening
⅓ cup granulated sugar
2 large egg yolks
3 tablespoons fresh orange juice
½ teaspoon grated lemon zest
Powdered sugar for sprinkling

1 Preheat the oven to 400 degrees.

2 Combine the flour, brazil nuts, and salt.

3 In a large bowl, cream the vegetable shortening and sugar. Beat in the egg yolks and orange juice. Beat in the lemon zest. Gradually blend in the dry ingredients.

4 Drop the dough by spoonfuls 1½ inches apart onto ungreased baking sheets.

5 Bake for 10 to 12 minutes, until lightly colored. Sprinkle with powdered sugar and transfer to wire racks to cool.

## BRAZIL-NUT COOKIES III

Drop Cookies

YIELD: *5 dozen*
TOTAL TIME: *30 minutes*

4½ cups all-purpose flour
1 cup brazil nuts, ground fine
2 cups vegetable shortening
2½ cups packed light brown sugar
2 teaspoons dark rum

1 Preheat the oven to 350 degrees.

2 Combine the flour and brazil nuts.

3 In a large bowl, cream the vegetable shortening and brown sugar until light and fluffy. Beat in the rum. Gradually fold in the dry ingredients.

4 Pinch off pieces of dough and form into small balls. Place on ungreased baking sheets and flatten the cookies with the bottom of a glass dipped in flour.

5 Bake for 10 to 15 minutes, until just starting to color. Transfer to wire racks to cool.

## BRAZIL-NUT SHORTBREAD

Formed Cookies

YIELD: *6 to 8 dozen*
TOTAL TIME: *30 minutes*

## BRAZIL-NUT STRIPS

Rolled Cookies

YIELD: *3 to 4 dozen*
TOTAL TIME: *35 minutes*
CHILLING TIME: *4 hours*

3 cups all-purpose flour
1 teaspoon ground ginger
¼ teaspoon ground nutmeg
½ teaspoon salt
½ cup butter, at room temperature
½ cup packed dark brown sugar
½ cup molasses
1 teaspoon baking soda
¼ cup hot water
1¾ cups brazil nuts, chopped fine

**1** Combine the flour, spices, and salt.

**2** In a large bowl, cream the butter and brown sugar. Beat in the molasses.

**3** Dissolve the baking soda in the hot water and beat into the molasses mixture. Gradually blend in the dry ingredients. Fold in the nuts. Cover and chill for at least 4 hours.

**4** Preheat the oven to 350 degrees. Lightly grease 2 baking sheets.

**5** On a floured surface, roll out the dough to a thickness of ¼ inch. With a sharp knife or a pastry wheel, cut into 3 by 1-inch strips. Place 1 inch apart on the prepared baking sheets.

**6** Bake for 10 to 12 minutes, until lightly colored. Transfer to wire racks to cool.

## BREAKFAST COOKIES

Drop Cookies

YIELD: *4 to 5 dozen*
TOTAL TIME: *30 minutes*

1¼ cups all-purpose flour
1 teaspoon baking powder
⅔ cup granulated sugar
½ cup vegetable shortening
1 large egg
2 tablespoons frozen orange juice concentrate, thawed
1 tablespoon grated orange zest
½ cup Grape-Nuts
1 tablespoon bacon bits (See Baking notes)

**1** Preheat the oven to 350 degrees.

**2** Combine the flour, baking powder, and sugar.

**3** In a large bowl, beat the vegetable shortening, egg, orange juice, and orange zest until thick.

Gradually blend in the dry ingredients. Blend in the Grape-Nuts and bacon bits.

**4** Drop the dough by spoonfuls 1½ inches apart onto ungreased baking sheets.

**5** Bake for 10 to 12 minutes, until lightly colored. Transfer to wire racks to cool.

**Baking notes:** The bacon bits can be real or artificial. Soy bacon bits are actually better suited for these cookies, because they don't add fat to the dough.

## BROWN-AND-WHITE BROWNIES

Bar Cookies

YIELD: *2 to 3 dozen*
TOTAL TIME: *30 minutes*

1 tablespoon vegetable shortening
¼ cup granulated sugar
1 large egg
¾ cup milk
½ teaspoon vanilla extract
2 cups packaged cookie mix
⅓ cup chocolate syrup
1 cup (6 ounces) white chocolate chips
½ cup (3 ounces) semisweet chocolate chips

**1** Preheat the oven to 375 degrees. Lightly grease a 9-inch square baking pan.

**2** In a large bowl, cream the vegetable shortening and sugar. Beat in the egg. Beat in the milk and vanilla extract. Gradually blend in the cookie mix. Transfer half the batter to another bowl.

**3** For the brown layer, beat the chocolate syrup into half the batter. Stir in the white chocolate chips. Spread this mixture evenly in the prepared baking pan.

**4** For the white layer, stir the semisweet chocolate chips into the remaining batter. Spread evenly over the dark layer.

**5** Bake for 12 to 15 minutes, or until a toothpick inserted into the center comes out clean. Cool in the pan on a wire rack before cutting into large or small bars.

1¾ cups all-purpose flour
¼ teaspoon salt
¾ cup vegetable shortening
½ cup granulated sugar
1 large egg
1 teaspoon vanilla extract
7 ounces milk chocolate, chopped

**1** Combine the flour and salt.

**2** In a large bowl, cream the vegetable shortening and sugar. Beat in the egg. Beat in the vanilla extract. Gradually blend in the dry ingredients. Cover and chill for 1 hour.

**3** Preheat the oven to 400 degrees.

**4** Melt the milk chocolate in the top half of a double boiler over a low heat, stirring until smooth. Remove from the heat; keep warm over hot water.

**5** Break off small pieces of the dough and roll into balls. Place 1½ inches apart on ungreased baking sheets. Press your finger into the center of each ball to make a slight indentation.

**6** Bake for 8 to 10 minutes, until lightly colored. Spoon a little of the melted milk chocolate into the center of each hot cookie and transfer to wire racks to cool.

**Baking notes:** This dough can be frozen for up to a month. You can also shape the dough into balls and freeze until ready to bake; let stand for two hours at room temperature. Then bake according to the instructions above. Fill the centers of the cookies with jam or jelly instead of the milk chocolate. Or add 2 tablespoons unsweetened cocoa powder to the dough, and fill the baked cookies with melted white chocolate.

# Brown-Eyed Susans

Formed Cookies

YIELD: *4 to 5 dozen*
TOTAL TIME: *30 minutes*
CHILLING TIME: *1 hour*

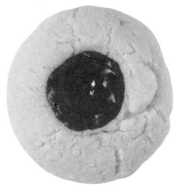

---

4 ounces unsweetened chocolate, chopped
¾ cup vegetable shortening
2 cups granulated sugar
1 teaspoon vanilla extract
3 large eggs
1 cup all-purpose flour
1 cup walnuts, chopped fine

**1** Preheat the oven to 350 degrees. Lightly grease a 13 by 9-inch baking pan.

**2** In a large saucepan, melt the unsweetened chocolate and vegetable shortening over low heat, stirring until smooth. Remove from the heat and beat in the sugar and vanilla extract. Beat in the eggs. Gradually blend in the flour. Fold in the walnuts. Spread the batter evenly in the prepared baking pan.

**3** Bake for 35 to 40 minutes, until a toothpick inserted into the center comes out clean. Cool in the pan on a wire rack before cutting into large or small bars.

# Brownies I

Bar Cookies

YIELD: *1 to 2 dozen*
TOTAL TIME: *50 minutes*

# BROWNIES II

Bar Cookies

YIELD: *1 to 2 dozen*
TOTAL TIME: *35 minutes*

½ cup all-purpose flour
½ teaspoon salt
¼ cup vegetable shortening
2 ounces semisweet chocolate, chopped
1 cup granulated sugar
1 teaspoon vanilla extract
2 large eggs
1 cup raisins (optional)
1 cup miniature marshmallows (optional)

**1** Preheat the oven to 325 degrees. Lightly grease an 8-inch square baking pan.

**2** Combine the flour and salt.

**3** In a double boiler, melt the vegetable shortening and chocolate over low heat, stirring until smooth. Remove from the heat and beat in the sugar and vanilla extract. Beat in the eggs. Gradually blend in the dry ingredients. Fold in the optional raisins and marshmallows. Spread the batter evenly in the prepared baking pan.

**4** Bake for 20 to 25 minutes, until a toothpick inserted in the center comes out clean. Cut into large or small squares while still warm and cool in the pan on a wire rack.

# BROWNIES III

Bar Cookies

YIELD: *1 to 2 dozen*
TOTAL TIME: *35 minutes*

2 large eggs
1 cup granulated sugar
½ cup vegetable shortening
2 ounces bittersweet chocolate, chopped
½ cup semisweet chocolate chips
½ teaspoon vanilla extract
1 cup all-purpose flour
½ cup almonds, chopped
1 cup miniature marshmallows

**1** Preheat the oven to 350 degrees. Lightly grease a 9-inch square baking pan.

**2** In a medium bowl, beat the eggs until thick and light-colored. Beat in the sugar.

**3** Melt the vegetable shortening, bittersweet chocolate, semisweet chocolate, and vanilla extract in the top of a double boiler over low heat, stirring until smooth. Remove from the heat and add the egg mixture in a thin steady stream, beating constantly. Gradually blend in the flour. Fold in the almonds and marshmallows. Spread the batter evenly in the prepared baking pan.

**4** Bake for 25 to 30 minutes, until a toothpick inserted in the center comes out clean. Cut into large or small squares while still warm and cool in the pan on a wire rack.

**Baking notes:** For variation, substitute white chocolate chips for the marshmallows. If desired, frost the cooled brownies with an icing of your choice (see Icings and Frostings, in Pantry).

1 cup granulated sugar
1 cup vegetable shortening
4 large eggs
1 cup chocolate syrup
1 cup all-purpose flour

TOPPING
⅓ cup milk
½ cup semisweet chocolate chips
½ cup walnuts, chopped

**1** Preheat the oven to 350 degrees.

**2** In a large bowl, cream the granulated sugar and vegetable shortening. Beat in the eggs and chocolate syrup. Gradually blend in the flour.

**3** Spread the batter evenly in an ungreased 9-inch square baking pan. Bake for 25 to 30 minutes, until a toothpick inserted in the center comes out clean.

**4** Meanwhile, prepare the topping: In a saucepan, bring the milk to a boil, and boil for 1 minute. Remove from the heat and add the chocolate chips and walnuts. Let cool.

**5** Spread the topping over the brownies. Cool in the pan on a wire rack before cutting into large or small bars.

**Baking notes:** Shredded coconut can be sprinkled over the still-warm topping.

# BROWNIES IV

Bar Cookies

YIELD: *1 to 2 dozen*
TOTAL TIME: *35 minutes*

½ cup vegetable shortening
1 cup granulated sugar
4 large eggs
1 cup chocolate syrup
Pinch of salt
1 cup all-purpose flour
1 cup walnuts, chopped
1 cup miniature marshmallows
   (optional)

**1** Preheat the oven to 350 degrees.

**2** In a large bowl, cream the vegetable shortening and sugar. Beat in the eggs one at a time. Beat in the chocolate syrup. Beat in the salt. Gradually blend in the flour. Fold in the walnuts and the optional marshmallows. Spread the mixture evenly in an ungreased 9-inch square baking pan.

**3** Bake for 35 to 40 minutes, until a toothpick inserted in the center comes out clean. Cool in the pan on a wire rack before cutting into large or small bars.

# BROWNIES V

Bar Cookies

YIELD: *1 to 2 dozen*
TOTAL TIME: *50 minutes*

¾ cup all-purpose flour
½ teaspoon baking powder
½ teaspoon salt
2 ounces unsweetened chocolate,
   chopped
⅓ cup unsalted butter
1 cup granulated sugar
1 teaspoon vanilla extract
2 large eggs
½ cup walnuts, chopped

**1** Preheat the oven to 350 degrees. Lightly grease a 9-inch square baking pan.

**2** Combine the flour, baking powder, and salt.

**3** In a large saucepan, melt the chocolate and butter over low heat, stirring until smooth. Remove from the heat and beat in the sugar and vanilla extract. Beat in the eggs. Gradually blend in the dry ingredients. Stir in the walnuts. Spread the batter evenly in the prepared baking pan.

**4** Bake for 30 to 35 minutes, until a toothpick inserted in the center comes out clean. Cool in the pan on a wire rack before cutting into large or small bars.

# BROWNIES VI

Bar Cookies

YIELD: *1 to 2 dozen*
TOTAL TIME: *40 minutes*

# BROWNIES VII

Bar Cookies

YIELD: *1 to 2 dozen*
TOTAL TIME: *40 minutes*

½ cup vegetable shortening
¼ cup unsweetened cocoa powder
1 teaspoon vanilla extract (optional)
4 large eggs
1 cup packed light brown sugar
1 cup all-purpose flour
1 cup miniature marshmallows
½ cup walnuts, chopped

**1** Preheat the oven to 350 degrees. Lightly grease a 9-inch square baking pan.

**2** Melt the vegetable shortening in a medium saucepan. Stir in the cocoa powder and vanilla extract until well blended. Remove from the heat.

**3** In a large bowl, beat the eggs and brown sugar until thick and light-colored. Beat in the chocolate mixture in a steady stream. Gradually blend in the flour. Fold in the marshmallows and walnuts. Spread the batter evenly in the prepared baking pan.

**4** Bake for 25 to 30 minutes, until a toothpick inserted in the center comes out clean. Cool in the pan on a wire rack before cutting into large or small bars.

# BROWNIES VIII

Bar Cookies

YIELD: *1 to 2 dozen*
TOTAL TIME: *30 minutes*

¼ cup unbleached flour
¼ cup soy flour
½ cup walnuts, ground fine
2 tablespoons unsweetened cocoa powder
½ teaspoon salt
1 large egg, separated
½ cup canola oil
1 cup packed light brown sugar

**1** Preheat the oven to 350 degrees. Lightly grease a 9-inch square baking pan.

**2** Combine the two flours, the walnuts, the cocoa powder, and salt.

**3** In a small bowl, beat the egg white until stiff but not dry.

**4** In a large bowl, beat the canola oil and brown sugar together. Beat in the egg yolk. Gradually blend in the dry ingredients. Fold in the beaten egg white. Spread the mixture evenly in the prepared baking pan.

**5** Bake for 18 to 20 minutes, until firm to the touch. Cool in the pan on a wire rack before cutting into large or small bars.

# BROWNIES (SUGARLESS)

Bar Cookies

YIELD: *1 to 2 dozen*
TOTAL TIME: *30 minutes*

2 ounces unsweetened chocolate, chopped
¾ cup all-purpose flour
1 teaspoon baking powder
½ cup unsalted butter, at room temperature
3 tablespoons nonnutritive sweetener (see Baking notes)
2 large eggs
½ teaspoon vanilla extract
½ cup walnuts, chopped fine

**1** Preheat the oven to 350 degrees. Lightly grease an 8-inch square baking pan.

**2** Melt the chocolate in a double boiler over low heat, stirring until smooth. Remove from the heat.

**3** Combine the flour and baking powder.

**4** In a large bowl, cream the butter and sweetener. Beat in the melted chocolate. Beat in the eggs and vanilla. Gradually blend in the dry ingredients. Fold in the walnuts. Spread the batter evenly in the prepared baking pan.

**5** Bake for 25 to 30 minutes, until firm to the touch. Cool in the pan on a wire rack before cutting into large or small squares.

**Baking notes:** Although created for diabetics, these brownies will appeal to anyone on a sugar-restricted diet. There are several nonnutritive sweeteners on the market.

4 cups all-purpose flour
¼ teaspoon baking soda
1 teaspoon ground cinnamon
½ teaspoon ground cloves
¼ teaspoon ground ginger
¼ teaspoon salt
1 cup vegetable shortening
1 cup packed light brown sugar
1½ cups molasses, warmed
½ teaspoon red wine vinegar

**1** Combine the flour, baking soda, spices, and salt.

**2** In a large bowl, cream the vegetable shortening and brown sugar. Beat in the molasses and vinegar. Gradually blend in the dry ingredients. Cover and chill for at least 2 hours.

**3** Preheat the oven to 350 degrees.

**4** On a floured surface, roll out the dough to a thickness of ¼ inch. Using cookie cutters, cut into shapes and place the cookies 1½ inches apart on ungreased baking sheets.

**5** Bake for 10 to 12 minutes, until firm to the touch. Transfer to wire racks to cool.

# Brown Moravian

Rolled Cookies

YIELD: *2 to 3 dozen*
TOTAL TIME: *30 minutes*
CHILLING TIME: *2 hours*

---

2½ cups all-purpose flour
¼ teaspoon salt
½ cup dark corn syrup
½ cup molasses
¼ cup vegetable shortening
½ cup packed light brown sugar
½ teaspoon baking soda
1½ teaspoons ground ginger
1½ teaspoons ground cinnamon
¼ teaspoon ground cloves

**1** Combine the flour and salt.

**2** In a double boiler, combine the corn syrup, molasses, and vegetable shortening and heat. Stir until well blended. Remove from the heat, and beat in the brown sugar, baking soda, and spices. Gradually blend in the flour mixture.

**3** Wrap the dough in waxed paper and chill for at least 2 hours.

**4** Preheat the oven to 375 degrees. Lightly grease 2 baking sheets.

**5** On a floured surface, roll out the dough ¼ inch thick. Using cookie cutters, cut into shapes and place 1½ inches apart on the prepared baking sheets.

**6** Bake for 7 to 10 minutes, until lightly colored. Transfer to wire racks to cool.

# Brown Sugar Christmas Cookies

Rolled Cookies

YIELD: *4 to 5 dozen*
TOTAL TIME: *30 minutes*
CHILLING TIME: *2 hours*

# BROWN SUGAR COCOA BROWNIES

Bar Cookies

YIELD: *1 to 2 dozen*
TOTAL TIME: *30 minutes*

½ cup all-purpose flour
1 teaspoon baking powder
½ cup unsweetened cocoa powder
¼ teaspoon salt
3 large eggs
1¼ cups packed light brown sugar
1 teaspoon vanilla extract
1 cup walnuts, chopped fine

**1** Preheat the oven to 325 degrees. Lightly grease a 9-inch square baking pan.

**2** Combine the flour, baking powder, cocoa powder, and salt.

**3** In a large bowl, beat the eggs and brown sugar. Beat in the vanilla extract until thick. Gradually blend in the dry ingredients. Fold in the walnuts. Spread this mixture evenly in the prepared baking pan.

**4** Bake for 20 to 25 minutes, until a toothpick inserted in the center comes out clean. Cut into large or small bars and cool in the pan on a wire rack.

# BROWN SUGAR COOKIES I

Rolled Cookies

YIELD: *3 to 5 dozen*
TOTAL TIME: *30 minutes*
CHILLING TIME: *4 hours*

2 cups all-purpose flour
1½ teaspoons baking powder
¼ teaspoon salt
½ cup butter, at room temperature
½ cup packed light brown sugar
1 large egg
1 tablespoon heavy cream
1½ teaspoons vanilla extract

**1** Combine the flour, baking powder, and salt.

**2** In a large bowl, cream the butter and brown sugar. Beat in the egg. Beat in the heavy cream and vanilla extract. Gradually blend in the dry ingredients. The dough will be stiff. If it seems too dry, add a little water, ½ teaspoon at a time. Cover and chill for 4 hours.

**3** Preheat the oven to 375 degrees.

**4** On a floured surface, roll out the dough to a thickness of ⅛ inch. With cookie cutters, cut into shapes and place 1½ inches apart on ungreased baking sheets.

**5** Bake for 8 to 10 minutes, until lightly browned around the edges. Transfer to wire racks to cool.

**Baking Notes:** Store these cookies in an airtight container.

5 cups all-purpose flour
1 teaspoon baking soda.
½ teaspoon salt
1 cup vegetable shortening
2 cups packed light brown sugar
3 large eggs
¼ cup milk
1 tablespoon dark rum

**1** Preheat the oven to 350 degrees. Lightly grease 2 baking sheets

**2** Combine the flour, baking soda, and salt.

**3** In a large bowl, cream the vegetable shortening and brown sugar. Beat in the eggs. Beat in the milk and rum. Gradually blend in the dry ingredients.

**4** Drop the dough by spoonfuls 1½ inches apart onto the prepared baking sheets.

**5** Bake for 10 to 12 minutes, until firm to the touch. Transfer to wire racks to cool.

# BROWN SUGAR COOKIES II

Drop Cookies

YIELD: *6 to 8 dozen*
TOTAL TIME: *30 minutes*

---

2 cups all-purpose flour
½ cup walnuts, ground fine
2 teaspoons baking powder
¼ teaspoon baking soda
1 teaspoon ground cinnamon
½ teaspoon ground cloves
½ teaspoon salt
⅔ cup vegetable shortening
1½ cups packed light brown sugar
2 large eggs
2 tablespoons sour milk
1 tablespoon grated orange zest
1 cup raisins (optional)

**1** Preheat the oven to 350 degrees.

**2** Combine the flour, walnuts, baking powder, baking soda, spices, and salt.

**3** In a large bowl, cream the vegetable shortening and brown sugar. Beat in the eggs and milk. Beat in the orange zest. Gradually blend in the dry ingredients. Fold in the optional raisins.

**4** Drop the dough by spoonfuls 1½ inches apart onto ungreased baking sheets.

**5** Bake for 12 to 15 minutes, until just firm to the touch. Transfer to wire racks to cool.

# BROWN SUGAR COOKIES III

Drop Cookies

YIELD: *2 to 3 dozen*
TOTAL TIME: *30 minutes*

# Brown Sugar Refrigerator Cookies

Refrigerator Cookies

YIELD: *8 to 9 dozen*
TOTAL TIME: *30 minutes*
CHILLING TIME: *8 hours*

3½ cups all-purpose flour
½ teaspoon baking soda
½ teaspoon salt
1 cup vegetable shortening
2 cups packed light brown sugar
3 large eggs
1 teaspoon vanilla extract
½ cup walnuts, chopped

**1** Combine the flour, baking soda, and salt.

**2** In a large bowl, cream the vegetable shortening and brown sugar. Beat in the eggs. Beat in the vanilla. Gradually blend in the dry ingredients. Fold in the walnuts.

**3** Divide the dough in thirds. Form each piece into a log 8 about inches long. Wrap in

waxed paper and chill for 8 hours or overnight.

**4** Preheat the oven to 375 degrees.

**5** Slice the log into ¼-inch-thick-slices and place 1 inch apart on ungreased baking sheets.

**6** Bake for 7 to 10 minutes, until lightly colored. Transfer to wire racks to cool.

---

# Brown Sugar Sand Tarts

Rolled Cookies

YIELD: *3 to 5 dozen*
TOTAL TIME: *30 minutes*
CHILLING TIME: *2 hours*

¾ cup all-purpose flour
¼ teaspoon baking powder
¼ teaspoon salt
¼ cup butter, at room temperature
⅓ cup packed light brown sugar
1 large egg
½ teaspoon vanilla extract
Light brown sugar for sprinkling

**1** Combine the flour, baking powder, and salt.

**2** In a large bowl, cream the butter and brown sugar. Beat in the egg. Beat in the vanilla extract. Gradually blend in the dry ingredients. Cover and chill for 2 hours.

**3** Preheat the oven to 375 degrees. Lightly grease 2 baking sheets.

**4** On a floured surface, roll out the dough to a thickness of ⅛ inch. With cookie cutters, cut into shapes and place 1 inch apart on the prepared baking sheets. Sprinkle with brown sugar and lightly press the sugar into the cookie.

**5** Bake for 8 to 10 minutes, until firmto the touch. Transfer to wire racks to cool.

---

# Brown Sugar Shortbread

Rolled Cookies

YIELD: *6 to 8 dozen*
TOTAL TIME: *30 minutes*
CHILING TIME: *12 hours*

1 cup vegetable shortening
1¼ cups packed light brown sugar
1 teaspoon vanilla extract
2½ cups all-purpose flour

**1** In a large bowl, cream the vegetable shortening and brown sugar. Blend in the vanilla extract. Gradually blend in the flour. Cover and chill for at least 12 hours.

**2** Preheat the oven to 375 degrees.

**3** On a floured surface, roll out the dough ¼ inch thick. With cookie cutters, cut into shapes and place 1 inches apart on ungreased baking sheets.

**4** Bake for 12 to 15 minutes, until lightly browned around the edges. Transfer to wire racks to cool.

**Baking notes:** For added flavor and texture, substitute ¼ cup rice flour for ¼ cup of the all-purpose flour.

2¼ cups all-purpose flour
¼ cup hazelnuts, ground fine
¼ teaspoon salt
1 cup butter, at room temperature
⅓ cup packed light brown sugar
¼ cup granulated sugar
1 large egg yolk
½ teaspoon hazelnut extract

**1** Preheat the oven to 350 degrees.

**2** Combine the flour, hazelnuts, and salt.

**3** In a large bowl, cream the butter and both sugars. Beat in the egg yolk. Beat in the hazelnut extract. Gradually blend in the dry ingredients.

**4** Place the dough in a cookie press or a pastry bag with a ribbon tip. Press or pipe 2½-inch-long strips onto ungreased baking sheets, spacing the cookies 1 inch apart.

**5** Bake for 8 to 10 minutes, until lightly browned. Transfer to wire racks to cool.

**Baking notes:** This recipe must be made with butter; do not substitute vegetable shortening. To decorate, dip one end of each cookie in melted semisweet chocolate.

# BROWN SUGAR SPRITZ COOKIES

Formed Cookies

YIELD: *4 to 6 dozen*
TOTAL TIME: *30 minutes*

---

2⅓ cups all-purpose flour
1 cup hazelnuts, ground fine
¾ teaspoon baking soda
½ teaspoon ground cloves
¼ teaspoon salt
⅔ cup vegetable shortening
¾ cup granulated sugar
½ cup plain yogurt
2 teaspoons orange extract
Powdered sugar for rolling

**1** Combine the flour, hazelnuts, baking soda, cloves, and salt.

**2** In a large bowl, cream the vegetable shortening and sugar. Beat in the yogurt and orange extract. Gradually blend in the dry ingredients. Cover and chill 24 hours.

**3** Preheat the oven to 350 degrees. Lightly grease 2 baking sheets.

**4** Break off walnut-sized pieces of dough and roll into balls. Place 1 inch apart on the prepared baking sheets.

**5** Bake for 15 to 20 minutes, until lightly browned. Roll in powdered sugar and transfer to wire racks to cool.

**6** After the balls have cooled, roll them again in powdered sugar.

# BULGARIAN COOKIES

Formed Cookies

YIELD: *4 to 6 dozen*
TOTAL TIME: *30 minutes*
CHILLING TIME: *24 hours*

---

1 cup all-purpose flour
1 teaspoon baking soda
½ cup vegetable shortening
¼ cup honey
¼ cup granulated sugar
1 large egg yolk
Granulated sugar for rolling

**1** Preheat the oven to 350 degrees.

**2** Combine the flour and baking soda.

**3** In a medium saucepan, melt the vegetable shortening with the honey, stirring until smooth. Remove from the heat and beat in the sugar and egg yolk. Gradually blend in the dry ingredients.

**4** Break off small pieces of dough and roll into balls. Roll each ball in granulated sugar and place 1½ inches apart on ungreased baking sheets.

**5** Bake for 10 to 12 minutes, until firm to the touch. Transfer to wire racks to cool.

# BULGARIAN HONEY COOKIES

Formed Cookies

YIELD: *2 to 4 dozen*
TOTAL TIME: *30 minutes*

**B**

# BUTTER-ALMOND STRIPS

Rolled Cookies

YIELD: *5 to 6 dozen*
TOTAL TIME: *35 minutes*
CHILLING TIME: *1 hour*

2 cups all-purpose flour
¼ teaspoon salt
¾ cup butter, at room temperature
¼ cup granulated sugar
½ teaspoon almond extract

**TOPPING**
2 tablespoons granulated sugar
¼ teaspoon ground cinnamon
½ cup almonds, ground fine
1 large egg white, slightly beaten

**1** Combine the flour and salt.

**2** In large bowl, cream the butter and sugar. Beat in the almond extract. Gradually blend in the dry ingredients. Cover and chill for 1 hour.

**3** Preheat the oven to 350 degrees. Lightly grease 2 baking sheets.

**4** To prepare the topping, combine the sugar, cinnamon, and almonds.

**5** On a floured surface, roll out the dough to a thickness of ⅛ inch. Cut into 2 by 1-inch strips and place 1 inch apart on the prepared baking sheets. Brush the cookies with the beaten egg white and sprinkle lightly with the topping.

**6** Bake for 8 to 10 minutes, until lightly colored. Transfer to wire racks to cool.

---

# BUTTERBALLS

Formed Cookies

YIELD: *3 to 4 dozen*
TOTAL TIME: *30 minutes*

1 cup butter, at room temperature
½ cup powdered sugar
2 cups all-purpose flour
1½ cups shredded coconut
Powdered sugar for rolling

**1** Preheat the oven to 350 degrees.

**2** In a large bowl, cream the butter and powdered sugar. Gradually blend in the flour. Fold in the coconut.

**3** Break off walnut-sized pieces of dough and roll into balls. Roll in powdered sugar and place 1

inch apart on ungreased baking sheets.

**4** Bake for 18 to 20 minutes, until lightly colored. Roll in powdered sugar again and transfer to wire racks to cool.

---

# BUTTER COOKIES I

Rolled Cookies

YIELD: *2 to 3 dozen*
TOTAL TIME: *30 minutes*
CHILLING TIME: *12 hours*

1 cup butter, at room temperature
½ cup granulated sugar
1 large egg yolk
½ teaspoon almond extract
2⅓ cups all-purpose flour
½ cup almonds, ground fine
1 large egg white, lightly beaten
Jam or preserves for filling

**1** In a large bowl, cream the butter and sugar. Beat in the egg yolk. Beat in the almond extract. Gradually blend in the flour. Cover and chill for 12 hours.

**2** Preheat the oven to 350 degrees.

**3** On a floured surface, roll out the dough to a thickness of ¼ inch. Using a 2-inch round cookie cutter, cut into circles. Using a ½-inch round cookie cutter, cut out

the centers of one half of the cookies. Place the cookies 1½ inches apart on ungreased baking sheets. Brush the cut-out cookies with beaten egg white and sprinkle the ground almonds over the top.

**4** Bake for 8 to 10 minutes, until lightly colored. Transfer to wire racks to cool.

**5** Spread a layer of jam or preserves over the plain cookies and top with the cut-out cookies.

**Baking notes:** Jelly does not usually make a good filling for cookies because it is too thin. Use any small cookie cutter to make the center cut-out: angels, dogs, cats, Santa's, etc.

1 cup butter
4 cups all-purpose flour
3 large eggs
2 cups granulated sugar

**1** Preheat the oven to 350 degrees.

**2** Melt the butter in a large saucepan. Remove from heat and add 2 cups of the flour all at once. Beat in the eggs one at a time. Beat in the sugar. Gradually blend in the remaining flour.

**3** On a floured surface, roll out the dough to a thickness of ¼ inch. Using cookie cutters, cut into shapes and place the cookies 1½ inches apart on ungreased baking sheets.

**4** Bake for 12 to 15 minutes, until lightly colored. Transfer to wire racks to cool.

**Baking notes:** For a different texture, substitute ½ cup rice flour for ½ cup of the all-purpose flour.

# BUTTER COOKIES II

Rolled Cookies

YIELD: *6 to 8 dozen*
TOTAL TIME: *30 minutes*

---

2 cups butter, at room temperature
1 cup powdered sugar
2 large eggs
4 cups all-purpose flour

**1** Preheat the oven to 350 degrees.

**2** In a large bowl, cream the butter and powdered sugar. Beat in the eggs one at a time. Gradually blend in the flour.

**3** On a floured surface, roll out the dough to a thickness of ¼ inch. With a 1½-inch round cookie cutter, cut out circles and place them 1 inch apart on ungreased baking sheets.

**4** Bake for 12 to 15 minutes, until lightly colored. Transfer to wire racks to cool.

# BUTTER COOKIES III

Rolled Cookies

YIELD: *6 to 10 dozen*
TOTAL TIME: *30 minutes*

---

2 cups all-purpose flour
½ teaspoon salt
¾ cup butter, at room temperature
½ cup granulated sugar
1 large egg
2 tablespoons fresh orange juice
½ teaspoon almond extract

**1** Preheat the oven to 350 degrees. Lightly grease 2 baking sheets.

**2** Combine the flour and salt.

**3** In a large bowl, cream the butter and sugar. Beat in the egg. Beat in the orange juice and almond extract. Gradually blend in the dry ingredients.

**4** Place the dough in a cookie press or a pastry bag fitted with a large star tip. Press or pipe out cookies 1½ inches apart on the prepared baking sheets.

**5** Bake for 7 to 10 minutes, until lightly colored. Transfer to wire racks to a cool.

# BUTTER COOKIES IV

Formed Cookies

YIELD: *4 to 5 dozen*
TOTAL TIME: *30 minutes*

**B**

# BUTTER COOKIES V

Rolled Cookies

YIELD: *4 to 5 dozen*
TOTAL TIME: *30 minutes*

4 cups all-purpose flour
1 teaspoon ground cinnamon
1 teaspoon ground ginger
¼ teaspoon salt
1 cup butter, at room temperature
1½ cups packed light brown sugar
2 large eggs
1 tablespoon grated lemon zest

**1** Preheat the oven to 350 degrees.

**2** Combine the flour, spices, and salt.

**3** In a large bowl, cream the butter and sugar. Beat in the eggs one at a time. Beat in the lemon zest. Gradually blend in the dry ingredients.

**4** On a floured surface, roll out the dough ¼ inch thick. Using cookie cutters, cut into shapes and place 1½ inches apart on ungreased baking sheets.

**5** Bake for 12 to 15 minutes, until lightly colored. Transfer to wire racks to cool.

# BUTTER COOKIES VI

Rolled Cookies

YIELD: *4 to 5 dozen*
TOTAL TIME: *30 minutes*

1½ cups butter, at room temperature
½ cup packed light brown sugar
6 hard-boiled large egg yolks, chopped
½ teaspoon almond extract
4 cups all-purpose flour

**1** Preheat the oven to 350 degrees.

**2** In a large bowl, cream the butter and brown sugar. Beat in the egg yolks. Beat in the almond extract. Gradually blend in the flour.

**3** On a floured surface, roll out the dough ¼ thick. With cookie cutters, cut into shapes and place 1½ inches apart on ungreased baking sheets.

**4** Bake for 10 to 12 minutes, until lightly colored. Transfer to wire racks to cool.

**Baking notes:** Traditionally, these cookies are cut into rings. Cut out 2-inch circles and cut out the centers with a ½-inch round cutter.

# BUTTER COOKIES VII

Formed Cookies

YIELD: *2 to 3 dozen*
TOTAL TIME: *30 minutes*

3 cups all-purpose flour
1 teaspoon baking powder
1 cup butter, at room temperature
½ cup granulated sugar
½ cup powdered sugar
2 large eggs

**1** Preheat the oven to 350 degrees.

**2** Combine the flour and baking powder.

**3** In a large bowl, cream the butter and both sugars. Beat in the eggs. Gradually blend in the dry ingredients.

**4** Place the dough in a cookie press or a pastry bag fitted with a plain ½ inch tip. Press or pipe out small rings of dough onto ungreased baking sheets, spacing them about 1 inch apart.

**5** Bake for 12 to 15 minutes, until lightly colored. Transfer to wire racks to cool.

2¼ cups all-purpose flour (see Baking notes)
1 teaspoon cream of tartar
½ teaspoon baking soda
1 cup butter, at room temperature
1 cup granulated sugar
2 large eggs
½ teaspoon vanilla extract
½ teaspoon fresh lemon juice
Glacé cherry halves for decoration (optional)

**1** Combine the flour, cream of tartar, and baking soda.

**2** In a large bowl, cream the butter and sugar. Beat in the eggs. Beat in the vanilla extract and lemon juice. Gradually blend in the dry ingredients. Cover and chill for 4 hours.

**3** Preheat the oven to 375 degrees. Lightly grease 2 baking sheets.

**4** On a floured surface, roll out the dough to a thickness of ⅛ inch. Using cookie cutters, cut into shapes and place 1½ inches apart on the prepared baking sheets. If desired, press a glacé cherry half in the center of each cookie.

**5** Bake for 8 to 10 minutes, until lightly colored. Transfer to wire racks to cool.

**Baking notes:** For a crisper cookie, use ¼ cup less flour.

# BUTTER COOKIES VIII

Rolled Cookies

YIELD: *3 to 5 dozen*
TOTAL TIME: *30 minutes*
CHILLING TIME: *4 hours*

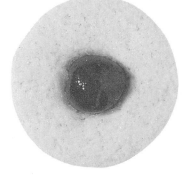

2½ cups rolled oats
2 teaspoons baking powder
½ teaspoon salt
2 tablespoons butter, at room temperature
1 cup granulated sugar
2 large eggs
1 teaspoon almond extract

**1** Preheat the oven to 375 degrees. Lightly grease 2 baking sheets.

**2** Combine the oats, baking powder, and salt.

**3** In a large bowl, cream the butter and sugar. Beat in the eggs. Beat in the almond extract. Gradually blend in the dry ingredients.

**4** Drop the dough by spoonfuls 1½ inches apart onto the prepared baking sheets.

**5** Bake for 10 to 12 minutes, until lightly browned. Transfer to wire racks to cool.

# BUTTER CRISPS

Drop Cookies

YIELD: *3 to 4 dozen*
TOTAL TIME: *30 minutes*

**B**

# BUTTERMILK BROWNIES

Bar Cookies

YIELD: *1 to 2 dozen*
TOTAL TIME: *30 minutes*

2 cups all-purpose flour
1¾ cups granulated sugar
¼ cup packed light brown sugar
½ teaspoon salt
1 cup vegetable shortening
⅓ cup unsweetened cocoa powder
1 cup water
1 teaspoon baking soda
1 tablespoon warm water
2 large eggs
½ cup buttermilk
1 teaspoon vanilla extract

**1** Preheat the oven to 375 degrees. Lightly grease a 13 by 9-inch baking pan.

**2** Combine the flour, both sugars, and salt.

**3** In a large saucepan, combine the vegetable shortening, cocoa powder, and the 1 cup water, stir until smooth and bring to a boil over high heat. Remove from the heat.

**4** Dissolve the baking soda in the warm water and beat into the cocoa mixture. Beat in the eggs. Beat in the buttermilk and vanilla extract. Gradually blend in the dry ingredients. Pour the batter into the prepared baking pan.

**5** Bake for 18 to 20 minutes, or until a toothpick inserted in the center comes out clean. Cool in the pan on a wire rack before cutting into large or small bars.

# BUTTERMILK COOKIES

Rolled Cookies

YIELD: *3 to 4 dozen*
TOTAL TIME: *30 minutes*
CHILLING TIME: *8 hours*

3½ cups all-purpose flour
1 teaspoon baking soda
1 teaspoon ground nutmeg
⅛ teaspoon salt
1 cup vegetable shortening
1 cup granulated sugar
1 large egg
½ cup buttermilk

**1** Combine the flour, baking soda, nutmeg, and salt.

**2** In a large bowl, cream the vegetable shortening and sugar. Beat in the egg. Beat in the buttermilk. Gradually blend in the dry ingredients. Cover and chill for 8 hours or overnight.

**3** Preheat the oven to 350 degrees.

**4** On a floured surface, roll out the dough to a thickness of ¼ inch. Using cookie cutters, cut into shapes and place 1½ inches apart on ungreased baking sheets.

**5** Bake for 10 to 12 minutes, until lightly colored. Transfer to wire racks to cool.

½ cup vegetable shortening
¼ cup granulated sugar
1 large egg
1 teaspoon vanilla extract
1 tablespoon fresh lemon juice
2 tablespoons grated orange zest
1 tablespoon grated lemon zest
1 cup all-purpose flour
1 egg white
½ cup brazil nuts, chopped
Candied cherries for garnish

**1** In a large bowl, cream the vegetable shortening and sugar. Beat in the egg. Beat in the vanilla extract and lemon juice. Beat in the orange and lemon zest. Gradually blend in the flour. Cover and chill for 4 hours.

**2** Preheat the oven to 350 degrees.

**3** In a small bowl, beat the egg white until stiff but not dry. Spread the chopped nuts on a plate.

**4** Break off small pieces of dough and form into balls. Roll each ball in the beaten egg white, then in the brazil nuts, and place 1½ inches apart on ungreased baking sheets. Press a candied cherry into the center of each ball.

**5** Bake for 12 to 15 minutes, or until golden brown. Transfer to wire racks to cool.

# BUTTERNUT DROPS

Formed Cookies

YIELD: *4 to 6 dozen*
TOTAL TIME: *30 minutes*
CHILLING TIME: *4 hours*

---

1½ cups all-purpose flour
1 cup almonds, ground fine
¼ teaspoon salt
¾ cup vegetable shortening
½ cup powdered sugar
1 cup hard butterscotch candies, crushed
Granulated sugar

**1** Preheat the oven to 325 degrees.

**2** Combine the flour, almonds, salt.

**3** In a large bowl, cream the vegetable shortening and powdered sugar. Gradually blend in the dry ingredients. Fold in the crushed candy.

**4** Break off small pieces of the dough and roll into balls. Place the balls 1½ inches apart on ungreased baking sheets. Dip the bottom of a glass in granulated sugar and flatten each cookie.

**5** Bake for 12 to 15 minutes, or until lightly colored. Transfer to wire racks to cool.

**Baking notes:** If you like, place a pecan half in the center of each cookie before baking.

# BUTTERNUTS

Formed Cookies

YIELD: *7 to 8 dozen*
TOTAL TIME: *30 minutes*

---

2 cups all-purpose flour
½ teaspoon salt
1 cup butter, at room temperature
⅔ cup packed light brown sugar
1 large egg
About 1½ cups pecan halves

**1** Combine the flour and salt.

**2** In a large bowl, cream the butter and brown sugar. Beat in the egg. Gradually blend in the dry ingredients. Cover and chill for at least 1 hour.

**3** Preheat the oven to 375 degrees.

**4** Break off walnut-sized pieces of dough and roll into balls. Place 1½ inches apart on ungreased baking sheets. Flatten the balls with the bottom of a glass dipped in flour and press a pecan into the center of each cookie.

**5** Bake for 10 to 12 minutes, until lightly colored. Transfer to wire racks to cool.

# BUTTER PECAN DROP COOKIES

Drop Cookies

YIELD: *3 to 4 dozen*
TOTAL TIME: *30 minutes*
CHILLING TIME: *1 hour*

# BUTTERSCOTCH BARS I

Bar Cookies

YIELD: *2 to 3 dozen*
TOTAL TIME: *40 minutes*

**2 cups all-purpose flour**
**2 teaspoons baking powder**
**½ cup vegetable shortening**
**2 cups packed light brown sugar**
**2 large eggs**
**1 teaspoon vanilla extract**
**1 cup shredded coconut**
**1 cup walnuts, chopped**

**1** Preheat the oven to 350 degrees. Lightly grease a 13 by 9-inch baking pan.

**2** Combine the flour and baking powder.

**3** In a large bowl, cream the vegetable shortening and brown sugar. Beat in the eggs. Beat in the vanilla extract. Gradually blend in the dry ingredients. Fold in the coconut and walnuts.

Spread the mixture evenly in the prepared baking pan.

**4** Bake for 20 to 25 minutes, until a toothpick inserted into the center comes out clean. Cut into large or small bars and cool in the pan on a wire rack.

# BUTTERSCOTCH BARS II

Bar Cookies

YIELD: *2 to 3 dozen*
TOTAL TIME: *45 minutes*

**1⅓ cups all-purpose flour**
**2 teaspoons baking powder**
**1 teaspoon salt**
**1 cup almonds, ground**
**½ cup vegetable oil**
**2 cups packed light brown sugar**
**2 large eggs**
**1 teaspoon vanilla extract**
**1 cup flaked coconut**

**TOPPING**
**2 tablespoons vegetable shortening**
**¾ cup packed light brown sugar**
**¼ cup light corn syrup**
**3 tablespoons heavy cream**
**1 teaspoon vanilla extract**

**1** Preheat the oven to 350 degrees. Lightly grease a 9-inch square baking pan.

**2** Combine the flour, baking powder, salt, and almonds.

**3** In a large bowl, cream the vegetable oil and brown sugar. Beat in the eggs. Beat in the vanilla extract. Gradually blend in the dry ingredients. Stir in the coconut. Spread the batter evenly in the prepared baking pan.

**4** To make the topping, cream the vegetable shortening and brown sugar in a small bowl. Beat in the corn syrup, cream, and vanilla extract. Spread the topping over the batter.

**5** Bake for 25 to 30 minutes, until a toothpick inserted in the center comes out clean. Cool in the pan on a wire rack before cutting into large or small bars.

⅔ cup all-purpose flour
½ cup walnuts, ground fine
1 teaspoon baking powder
¼ teaspoon salt
¼ cup vegetable shortening
1 cup packed light brown sugar
1 large egg
1 teaspoon vanilla extract

**1** Preheat the oven to 350 degrees. Lightly grease an 8-inch square baking pan.

**2** Combine the flour, walnuts, baking powder, and salt.

**3** In a large bowl, cream the vegetable shortening and sugar. Beat in the egg. Beat in the vanilla extract. Gradually blend in the dry ingredients. Spread the

dough evenly in the prepared baking pan.

**4** Bake for 20 to 25 minutes, or until a toothpick inserted in the center comes out clean. Cut into large or small bars and cool in the pan on a wire rack.

## BUTTERSCOTCH BROWNIES I

Bar Cookies

YIELD: *1 to 2 dozen*
TOTAL TIME: *35 minutes*

1½ cups all-purpose flour
2 teaspoons baking powder
¼ teaspoon salt
⅔ cup vegetable shortening
2 cups packed light brown sugar
2 large eggs
1 teaspoon almond extract
1 cup almonds, chopped
¼ cup sliced almonds

**1** Preheat the oven to 350 degrees. Lightly grease a 9-inch square baking pan.

**2** Combine the flour, baking powder, and salt.

**3** In a large bowl, cream the vegetable shortening and brown sugar. Beat in the eggs. Beat in the almond extract. Gradually

blend in the dry ingredients. Stir in the chopped almonds.

**4** Spread the batter evenly in the prepared baking pan. Sprinkle the sliced almonds over the top and press down lightly.

**5** Bake for 30 to 35 minutes, until firm and a toothpick inserted in the center comes out clean. Cool in the pan on a wire rack before cutting into large or small bars.

## BUTTERSCOTCH BROWNIES II

Bar Cookies

YIELD: *2 to 3 dozen*
TOTAL TIME: *45 minutes*

1½ cups all-purpose flour
1 teaspoon baking powder
½ teaspoon salt
⅔ cup butter, at room temperature
⅔ cups packed dark brown sugar
⅔ cup dark corn syrup
2 large eggs
1 teaspoon hazelnut extract
1 cup hazelnuts, chopped

**1** Preheat the oven to 325 degrees. Lightly grease a 9-inch square baking pan.

**2** Combine the flour, baking powder, and salt.

**3** In a large bowl, cream the butter and brown sugar. Beat in the corn syrup. Beat in the eggs and hazelnut extract. Gradually blend

in the dry ingredients. Stir in the hazelnuts. Scrape the mixture into the prepared baking pan.

**4** Bake for 20 to 25 minutes, until firm to the touch. Cool in the pan on a wire rack before cutting into large or small bars.

## BUTTERSCOTCH BROWNIES III

Bar Cookies

YIELD: *1 to 2 dozen*
TOTAL TIME: *30 minutes*

# Butterscotch Brownies IV

Bar Cookies

YIELD: *2 to 3 dozen*
TOTAL TIME: *35 minutes*

½ cup vegetable shortening
1½ cups packed light brown sugar
1 large egg
1 teaspoon almond extract
1 cup all-purpose flour
½ cup slivered almonds

**1** Preheat the oven to 325 degrees. Lightly grease an 8-inch square baking pan.

**2** In a large bowl, cream the vegetable shortening and brown sugar. Beat in the egg and almond extract. Gradually blend in the flour.

**3** Spread the batter evenly into the prepared baking pan. Sprinkle the slivered almonds over the top.

**4** Bake for 25 to 30 minutes, until firm to the touch. Cool in the pan on a wire rack before cutting into large or small bars.

# Butterscotch Cheesecake Bars

Bar Cookies

YIELD: *1 to 2 dozen*
TOTAL TIME: *30 minutes*

**CRUST**
¾ cup butterscotch chips
⅓ cup butter, at room temperature
2 cups graham cracker crumbs
1 cup walnuts, ground fine

**FILLING**
8 ounces cream cheese, at room temperature
One 14-ounce can sweetened condensed milk
1 large egg
1 teaspoon vanilla extract

**1** Preheat the oven to 350 degrees. Lightly grease a 13 by 9-inch baking pan.

**2** To make the crust, melt the butterscotch chips and butter in a medium saucepan, stirring until smooth. Remove from the heat and blend in the graham cracker crumbs and walnuts. Spread half of this mixture evenly into the bottom of the prepared baking pan.

**3** To make the filling, beat the cream cheese and condensed milk together in a small bowl. Beat in the egg and vanilla extract. Pour this mixture over the crust.

**4** Spread the remaining crust mixture over the filling.

**5** Bake for 25 to 30 minutes, until a knife inserted into the center comes out clean. Cool in the pan on a wire rack before cutting into large or small bars.

2 cups all-purpose flour
2 teaspoons baking powder
¼ teaspoon salt
½ cup vegetable shortening
2 cups packed light brown sugar
2 large eggs
½ teaspoon vanilla extract
1⅓ cups sliced almonds

**1** Preheat the oven to 350 degrees. Lightly grease a 9-inch square baking pan.

**2** Combine the flour, baking powder, and salt.

**3** In a large bowl, cream the vegetable shortening and sugar. Beat in the eggs. Beat in the vanilla extract. Gradually blend in the dry ingredients.

**4** Spread the mixture evenly in the prepared baking pan. Sprinkle the almonds over the top and press down gently.

**5** Bake for 20 to 25 minutes, until firm to the touch. Cool in the pan on a wire rack before cutting into large or small bars.

# BUTTERSCOTCH CHEWS

Bar Cookies

YIELD: *1 to 2 dozen*
TOTAL TIME: *35 minutes*

---

**BUTTERSCOTCH DOUGH**
1½ cups all-purpose flour
½ teaspoon baking soda
¼ teaspoon salt
½ cup butter, at room temperature
1 cup packed light brown sugar
1 large egg
1 teaspoon vanilla extract

**CHOCOLATE DOUGH**
1 cup all-purpose flour
½ cup rice flour
1 tablespoon unsweetened cocoa powder
½ teaspoon baking soda
¼ teaspoon salt
½ cup vegetable shortening
1 cup granulated sugar
1 large egg
1 teaspoon vanilla extract

**1** To make the butterscotch dough, combine the flour, baking soda, and salt.

**2** In a large bowl, cream the butter and brown sugar. Beat in the egg and vanilla extract. Gradually blend in the dry ingredients. Divide the dough in half. Wrap each half in waxed paper and chill for 2 hours.

**3** Meanwhile, make the chocolate dough: Combine the flour, rice flour, cocoa powder, baking soda, and salt.

**4** In a large bowl, cream the vegetable shortening and sugar. Beat in the egg and vanilla extract. Gradually blend in the dry ingredients. Divide the dough in half. Wrap each half in waxed paper and chill for 2 hours.

**5** On a floured surface, roll out half the butterscotch dough to a 10 by 8-inch rectangle. Roll out half the chocolate dough to the same size. Brush the top of the butterscotch dough lightly with water and place the chocolate square on top. Starting at a long end, roll up jelly-roll fashion, and pinch the seam to seal. Wrap in waxed paper and chill for 24 hours. Repeat with the remaining dough.

**6** Preheat the oven to 375 degrees. Lightly grease 2 baking sheets.

**7** Slice the rolls into ¼-inch-thick-slices and place 1½ inches apart on the prepared baking sheets.

**8** Bake for 8 to 10 minutes, until lightly browned. Transfer to wire racks to cool.

# BUTTERSCOTCH CHOCOLATE PINWHEELS

Refrigerator Cookies

YIELD: *4 to 6 dozen*
TOTAL TIME: *30 minutes*
CHILLING TIME: *26 hours*

# BUTTERSCOTCH COOKIES I

Drop Cookies

YIELD: *3 to 5 dozen*
TOTAL TIME: *30 minutes*

2 cups all-purpose flour
½ teaspoon baking soda
½ teaspoon salt
¾ cup vegetable shortening
1 cup packed light brown sugar
2 large eggs
1 cup (6 ounces) rolled oats
½ cup almonds, chopped
1 cup butterscotch chips

**1** Preheat the oven to 350 degrees. Lightly grease 2 baking sheets.

**2** Combine the flour, baking soda, and salt.

**3** In a large bowl, cream the vegetable shortening and brown sugar. Beat in the eggs. Gradually blend in the dry ingredients. Fold in the oats and almonds. Fold in the butterscotch chips.

**4** Drop the dough by spoonfuls 2 inches apart onto the prepared baking sheets.

**5** Bake for 10 to 12 minutes, until lightly browned. Transfer to wire racks to cool.

# BUTTERSCOTCH COOKIES II

Refrigerator Cookies

YIELD: *2 to 3 dozen*
TOTAL TIME: *30 minutes*
CHILLING TIME: *8 hours*

3½ cups all-purpose flour
1 teaspoon baking powder
¼ teaspoon salt
½ cup butter, at room temperature
2 cups packed light brown sugar
2 large eggs

**1** Combine the flour, baking powder, and salt.

**2** In a large bowl, cream the butter and brown sugar. Beat in the eggs. Gradually blend in the dry ingredients.

**3** Divide the dough in half. Form each half into a log 2 inches in diameter. Wrap in waxed paper and chill for 8 hours or overnight.

**4** Preheat the oven to 375 degrees.

**5** Slice the logs into ¼-inch-thick slices and place 1½ inches apart on ungreased baking sheets.

**6** Bake for 12 to 15 minutes, or until lightly colored. Transfer to wire racks to cool.

# BUTTERSCOTCH COOKIES III

Formed Cookies

YIELD: *4 to 5 dozen*
TOTAL TIME: *30 minutes*
CHILLING TIME: *8 hours*

5½ cups all-purpose flour
½ teaspoon baking soda
¾ cup vegetable shortening
2½ cups packed light brown sugar
2½ cups molasses
1 cup grated coconut

**1** Combine the flour and baking soda.

**2** In a large bowl, cream the vegetable shortening and brown sugar. Beat in the molasses. Gradually blend in the dry ingredients. Fold in the coconut. Cover and chill for 8 hours or overnight.

**3** Preheat the oven to 350 degrees. Lightly grease 2 baking sheets.

**4** Break off small pieces of the dough and roll into balls. Place the balls 1½ inches apart on the prepared baking sheets. Flatten each ball with the bottom of a glass dipped in flour.

**5** Bake for 12 to 15 minutes, until lightly colored. Transfer to wire racks to cool.

1 cup (6 ounces) butterscotch chips
½ cup peanut butter
3 cups cornflakes (see Baking notes)

**1** Line 2 baking sheets with waxed paper.

**2** Combine the butterscotch chips and peanut butter in the top of a double boiler and heat over medium heat, stirring, until the butterscotch chips are melted and the mixture is smooth. Remove from the heat, add the cornflakes and stir until well coated.

**3** Drop by spoonfuls onto the prepared baking sheets and chill until set.

**Baking notes:** Almost any type of sweetened cereal can be used in this recipe.

# BUTTERSCOTCH DROPS

Drop Cookies

YIELD: *2 to 3 dozen*
TOTAL TIME: *30 minutes*

1½ cups all-purpose flour
1 teaspoon baking soda
1 cup vegetable shortening
¾ cup packed light brown sugar
¾ cup granulated sugar
2 large eggs
1 teaspoon vanilla extract
2 cups rolled oats
½ cup walnuts, chopped
2 cups (12 ounces) butterscotch chips

**1** Preheat the oven to 375 degrees. Lightly grease 2 baking sheets.

**2** Combine the flour and baking soda.

**3** In a large bowl, cream the vegetable shortening and the two sugars. Beat in the eggs. Beat in the vanilla extract. Gradually blend in the dry ingredients. Fold in the rolled oats and walnuts. Fold in the butterscotch chips.

**4** Drop the dough by spoonfuls 1½ inches apart onto the prepared baking sheets.

**5** Bake for 10 to 12 minutes, until lightly colored. Transfer to wire racks to cool.

**Baking notes:** For an unusual variation, use crushed butterscotch candy in place of the butterscotch chips.

# BUTTERSCOTCH-OATMEAL COOKIES

Drop Cookies

YIELD: *3 to 4 dozen*
TOTAL TIME: *30 minutes*

# BUTTERSCOTCH REFRIGERATOR COOKIES

Refrigerator Cookies

YIELD: *2 to 3 dozen*
TOTAL TIME: *30 minutes*
CHILLING TIME: *8 hours*

1 cup all-purpose flour
1 package butterscotch pudding mix
½ teaspoon baking powder
¼ teaspoon salt
¼ cup butter, at room temperature
2 tablespoons light brown sugar
1 large egg
¼ teaspoon vanilla extract

**1** Combine the flour, butterscotch pudding mix, baking powder and salt.

**2** In a large bowl, cream the butter and brown sugar. Beat in the egg. Beat in the vanilla extract. Gradually blend in the dry ingredients.

**3** Form the dough into a log 2 inches in diameter. Wrap in waxed paper and chill for 8 hours or overnight.

**4** Preheat the oven to 375 degrees. Lightly grease 2 baking sheets.

**5** Slice the log into ⅛-inch-thick slices and place 1 inch apart on the prepared baking sheets.

**6** Bake for 8 to 10 minutes, until firm. Transfer to wire racks to cool.

# BUTTERSCOTCH SHORTBREAD

Bar Cookies

YIELD: *1 to 2 dozen*
TOTAL TIME: *30 minutes*

1/2 cup butter, at room temperature
½ cup packed light brown sugar
1 large egg
2 cups all-purpose flour

**1** Preheat the oven to 350 degrees.

**2** In a large bowl, cream the butter and brown sugar. Beat in the egg. Gradually blend in the flour.

**3** Spread the dough evenly in an ungreased 9-inch square baking pan. Score the bars, using with the back of a knife.

**4** Bake for 15 to 20 minutes, until firm to the touch. Cut into bars and cool in the pan on a rack.

# BUTTERSCOTCH SLICES

Refrigerator Cookies

YIELD: *8 to 10 dozen*
TOTAL TIME: *30 minutes*
CHILLING TIME: *8 hours*

3¼ cups all-purpose flour
¾ teaspoon baking soda
½ teaspoon salt
1 cup vegetable shortening
1½ cups packed light brown sugar
2 large eggs
½ teaspoon vanilla extract
1 cup raisins, chopped
1 cup walnuts, ground fine

**1** Combine the flour, baking soda, and salt.

**2** In a large bowl, cream the vegetable shortening and brown sugar. Beat in the eggs. Beat in the vanilla. Gradually blend in the dry ingredients. Fold in the raisins and walnuts.

**3** Divide the dough in half. Form each half into a log 1½ inches in diameter and wrap in waxed paper. Chill for 8 hours or overnight.

**4** Preheat the oven to 400 degrees.

**5** Slice the logs into ⅛-inch-thick slices and place 1 inch apart on ungreased baking sheets.

**6** Bake for 8 to 10 minutes, until lightly colored. Transfer to wire racks to cool.

1¼ cups all-purpose flour
1 teaspoon baking powder
¼ teaspoon salt
½ cup vegetable shortening
½ cup peanut butter
1½ cups packed light brown sugar
2 large eggs
1 teaspoon vanilla extract

**1** Preheat the oven to 350 degrees. Lightly grease a 9-inch square baking pan.

**2** Combine the flour, baking powder, and salt.

**3** In medium saucepan, combine the vegetable shortening, peanut butter, and brown sugar and heat over medium heat, stirring, until the shortening melts and the

sugar dissolves. Remove from the heat and let cool slightly.

**4** Beat the eggs into the peanut butter mixture. Beat in the vanilla extract. Gradually blend in the dry ingredients.

**5** Spread the mixture evenly in the prepared baking pan.

**6** Bake for 25 to 30 minutes, or until a toothpick inserted in the center comes out clean. Cool in the pan on a wire rack before cutting into large or small bars.

# BUTTERSCOTCH SQUARES

Bar Cookies
YIELD: *1 to 2 dozen*
TOTAL TIME: *40 minutes*

---

¾ cup all-purpose flour
¾ cup whole wheat flour
1 cup wheat germ
1 teaspoon baking soda
1 teaspoon ground cinnamon
½ teaspoon salt
1 cup vegetable shortening
1⅓ cup packed dark brown sugar
1 large egg
1 teaspoon almond extract
2 cups rolled oats

**1** Preheat the oven to 375 degrees. Lightly grease 2 baking sheets.

**2** Combine the two flours, the wheat germ, baking soda, cinnamon, and salt.

**3** In a large bowl, cream the vegetable shortening and brown sugar. Beat in the egg and

almond extract. Gradually blend in the dry ingredients. If the mixture seems a little dry, add a little water 1 teaspoon at a time. Fold in the oats.

**4** Drop the dough by spoonfuls 1½ inches apart onto the prepared baking sheets.

**5** Bake for 7 to 9 minutes, until lightly colored. Transfer to wire racks to cool.

# BUTTERSCOTCH-WHEAT GERM COOKIES

Drop Cookies
YIELD: *6 to 7 dozen*
TOTAL TIME: *30 minutes*

---

3 cups all-purpose flour
½ teaspoon baking soda
½ teaspoon salt
⅔ cup butter, at room temperature
½ cup granulated sugar
2 large eggs
1 teaspoon almond extract

**1** Preheat the oven to 400 degrees.

**2** Combine the flour, baking soda, and salt.

**3** In a large bowl, cream the butter and sugar. Beat in the eggs. Beat in the almond extract. Gradually blend in the dry ingredients.

**4** Place the dough in a cookie press or a pastry bag fitted with a ribbon tip. Press or pipe out 3½-inch-long strips onto ungreased baking sheets, spacing them 1 inch apart.

**5** Bake for 10 to 12 minutes, until lightly colored. Transfer to wire racks to cool.

# BUTTER STICKS I

Formed Cookies
YIELD: *2 to 3 dozen*
TOTAL TIME: *30 minutes*

# BUTTER STICKS II

Rolled Cookies

YIELD: *varies*
TOTAL TIME: *30 minutes*

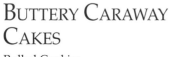

3 large egg yolks
1 cup butter, at room temperature
¼ cup granulated sugar
½ teaspoon almond extract
2½ cups all-purpose flour
1 large egg white, lightly beaten
Ground cinnamon for sprinkling

**1** Preheat the oven to 350 degrees.

**2** In a small bowl, beat the egg yolks until thick and light-colored.

**3** In a large bowl, cream the butter and sugar. Beat in the almond extract. Beat in the egg yolks. Gradually blend in the flour.

**4** On a floured surface, roll out the dough into a large square ¼ inch thick. Brush the dough with the beaten egg white and sprinkle with cinnamon. Cut into 4 by ½-inch strips and place 1 inch apart on ungreased baking sheets.

**5** Bake for 8 to 10 minutes, until lightly colored. Transfer to wire racks to cool.

# BUTTERY CARAWAY CAKES

Rolled Cookies

YIELD: *3 to 4 dozen*
TOTAL TIME: *30 minutes*
CHILLING TIME: *2 to 4 hours*

3 cups all-purpose flour
½ teaspoon baking soda
¾ teaspoon ground mace
1½ cups butter, at room temperature
3 cups powdered sugar
4 large eggs
¼ cup sherry
½ teaspoon caraway seeds

**1** Combine the flour, baking soda, and mace.

**2** In a large bowl, cream the butter and sugar. Beat in the eggs. Beat in the sherry. Gradually blend in the dry ingredients. Fold in the caraway seeds. Cover and chill for 2 to 4 hours, until firm enough to roll.

**3** Preheat the oven to 350 degrees. Lightly grease 2 baking sheets.

**4** On a floured surface, roll out the dough to a thickness of ¼ inch. Using cookie cutters, cut
into shapes and place 1½ inches apart on the prepared baking sheets.

**5** Bake for 10 to 12 minutes, until lightly colored. Transfer to wire racks to cool.

**Baking notes:** These make very good Christmas cookies. For variation, anise seeds can be substituted for the caraway seeds. Other sweet wines can be used in place of the sherry.

1 cup all-purpose flour
1 teaspoon baking powder
⅛ teaspoon salt
3 large large egg whites
¾ cup granulated sugar
1 teaspoon vanilla extract

**FILLING**
½ cup heavy cream
2 tablespoons granulated sugar

**1** Preheat the oven to 400 degrees. Lightly grease 2 baking sheets.

**2** Combine the flour, baking powder, and salt.

**3** In a large bowl, beat the egg whites until stiff but not dry. Beat in the sugar and vanilla extract. Gradually fold in the dry ingredients. Beat for 2 minutes.

**4** Drop the dough by spoonfuls onto the prepared baking sheets.

**5** Bake for 8 to 10 minutes, until golden. While the cookies are still hot, roll each one into a cone shape and place seam side down on wire racks to cool.

**6** To prepare the filling, in a small bowl beat the heavy cream with the sugar until it holds soft peaks. Just before serving, fill the cones with the whipped cream

**Baking notes:** For variation, add diced fresh fruit to the whipped cream before filling the cones.

# CALLA LILIES

Drop Cookies

YIELD: *2 to 3 dozen*
TOTAL TIME: *30 minutes*

---

2 cups all-purpose flour
1 teaspoon baking soda
1 teaspoon salt
1 cup vegetable shortening
1 cup granulated sugar
1 cup packed light brown sugar
2 large eggs
1 teaspoon vanilla extract
2 cups rolled oats
1 cup shredded coconut
1 cup gumdrops, diced
Powdered sugar for rolling

**1** Preheat the oven to 350 degrees. Lightly grease 2 baking sheets.

**2** Combine the flour, baking soda and salt.

**3** In a large bowl, cream the vegetable shortening and two sugars. Beat in the eggs one at a time. Beat in the vanilla extract. Gradually blend in the dry ingredients. Fold in the oats, coconut, and gumdrops.

**4** Pinch off small pieces of the dough and form into balls. Place 1 inch apart on the prepared baking sheets.

**5** Bake for 10 to 12 minutes, until firm to the touch. Transfer to wire racks to cool.

**6** When the cookies are cool, roll them in powdered sugar.

**Baking notes:** For flat cookies, place the balls 1½ inches apart on the baking sheets and flatten them with the bottom of a glass dipped in flour.

# CANDY GUMDROP COOKIES

Formed Cookies

YIELD: *2 to 3 dozen*
TOTAL TIME: *30 minutes*

# CARAMEL BARS

Bar Cookies

YIELD: *1 to 2 dozen*
TOTAL TIME: *45 minutes*

One 14-ounce package caramels (light or dark)
⅔ cup evaporated milk
¾ cup vegetable shortening.
1 package German chocolate cake mix
1 cup peanuts, chopped
1 cup (6 ounces) semisweet chocolate chips

**1** Preheat the oven to 350 degrees. Lightly grease a 9-inch square baking pan.

**2** In the top of a double boiler, melt the caramel candy with ⅓ cup of the evaporated milk, stirring until smooth. Remove from the heat.

**3** In a large bowl, combine the vegetable shortening and cake mix and beat until smooth. Beat in the milk and stir in the peanuts. The mixture will be crumbly.

**4** Press half of the cake mixture into the prepared baking pan. Bake for 8 minutes.

**5** Sprinkle the chocolate chips over the warm dough. Spread the caramel mixture over the chocolate chips and spread the remaining cake mixture over the caramel layer.

**6** Bake for 18 to 20 minutes longer, until firm to the touch. Cool in the pan on a wire rack before cutting into large or small bars.

# CARAMEL COOKIES

Refrigerator Cookies

YIELD: *4 to 5 dozen*
TOTAL TIME: *30 minutes*
CHILLING TIME: *4 hours*

3 cups all-purpose flour
1 teaspoon cream of tartar
½ teaspoon baking soda
¼ teaspoon ground nutmeg
1 cup canola oil
2 cups packed light brown sugar
2 large eggs
1 teaspoon vanilla extract

**1** Combine the flour, cream of tartar, baking soda, and nutmeg.

**2** In a large bowl, beat the canola oil and brown sugar together. Beat in the eggs. Beat in the vanilla extract. Gradually blend in the dry ingredients.

**3** Form the dough into a log 1½ inches in diameter. Wrap in waxed paper and chill for 4 hours.

**4** Preheat the oven to 375 degrees. Lightly grease 2 baking sheets.

**5** Slice the log into ¼-inch-thick slices and place 1 inch apart on the prepared baking sheets.

**6** Bake for 8 to 10 minutes, until lightly colored. Transfer to wire racks to cool.

**CARAMEL**
½ cup granulated sugar
½ cup boiling water

**COOKIES**
2¼ cups all-purpose flour
2 teaspoons baking powder
¼ teaspoon salt
½ cup vegetable shortening
1¼ cups granulated sugar
2 large eggs
1 teaspoon vanilla extract
½ cup walnuts, chopped

**TOPPING**
1 tablespoon butter or margarine, at room temperature
1 cup powdered sugar
About 1 tablespoon milk

**1** Preheat the oven to 375 degrees. Lightly grease a 13 by 9-inch baking pan.

**2** To make the caramel, put the sugar in a heavy saucepan and cook over low heat, stirring constantly, until the sugar melts. Continue cooking, without stirring, until a golden brown caramel. Immediately remove from the heat and slowly stir in the boiling water. Return to low heat and stir until any lumps of caramel have dissolved. Bring to a boil, and boil until reduced to ⅓ cup. Set aside.

**3** To make the cookies, combine the flour, baking powder, and salt.

**4** In a large saucepan, melt the vegetable shortening. Beat in the sugar. Remove from the heat and beat in the eggs one at a time. Beat in the vanilla extract. Beat in 3 tablespoons of the caramel. Gradually blend in the dry ingredients. Fold in the walnuts.

**5** Spread the mixture evenly in the prepared baking pan. Bake for 15 to 18 minutes, or until the top is golden-colored.

**6** Meanwhile, make the topping: In a medium bowl, cream the butter and powdered sugar. Beat in the remaining caramel. Beat in just enough enough milk to make the mixture spreadable.

**7** Spread the topping over the warm cookies. Cool in the pan on a wire rack before cutting into large or small bars.

# CARAMEL SUGAR SQUARES

Bar Cookies

YIELD: *2 to 3 dozen*
TOTAL TIME: *45 minutes*

---

¾ cup all-purpose flour
¼ cup whole wheat flour
½ teaspoon baking powder
¼ cup butter, at room temperature
½ cup mashed bananas
1 large egg
1 cup rolled oats
1 cup carob chips

**1** Preheat the oven to 350 degrees. Lightly grease 2 baking sheets.

**2** Combine the two flours and baking powder.

**3** In a large bowl, beat the butter and bananas together. Beat in the egg. Gradually blend in the dry ingredients. Fold in the oats and carob chips.

**4** Drop the dough by spoonfuls 1½ inches apart onto the prepared baking sheets.

**5** Bake for 8 to 10 minutes, until lightly colored. Transfer to wire racks to cool.

# CAROB CHIP BANANA COOKIES

Drop Cookies

YIELD: *3 to 4 dozen*
TOTAL TIME: *30 minutes*

# Carob Chip Oatmeal Cookies

Drop Cookies

YIELD: *2 to 3 dozen*
TOTAL TIME: *30 minutes*

2½ cup all-purpose flour
1 tablespoon baking soda
¼ teaspoon salt
1 cup vegetable shortening
¼ cup honey
2 large eggs
2 cups rolled oats
¾ cup carob chips
1 cup golden raisins
1 cup walnuts, chopped

**1** Preheat the oven to 350 degrees. Lightly grease 2 baking sheets.

**2** Combine the flour, baking soda, and salt.

**3** In a large saucepan, melt the vegetable shortening with the honey, stirring until smooth. Remove from the heat and beat in the eggs one at a time. Gradually blend in the dry ingredients. Fold in the oats, carob chips, raisins, and walnuts.

**4** Drop the dough by spoonfuls 1½ inches apart onto the prepared baking sheets.

**5** Bake for 12 to 15 minutes, until golden brown. Transfer to wire racks to cool.

# Carob Drop Cookies

Drop Cookies

YIELD: *3 to 4 dozen*
TOTAL TIME: *35 minutes*

1 cup carob chips
1 cup rolled oats
1 cup almonds, chopped fine
1 cup unsweetened flaked coconut

**1** Line 2 baking sheets with waxed paper.

**2** In the top of a double boiler, melt the carob chips, stirring until smooth. Blend in the oats, almonds, and coconut.

**3** Drop the mixture by spoonfuls 1 inch apart onto the prepared baking sheets.

**4** Chill until the cookies are firm.

# Carrot Coconut Bars

Bar Cookies

YIELD: *1 to 3 dozen*
TOTAL TIME: *45 minutes*

1¼ cups all-purpose flour
1 teaspoon baking powder
1 teaspoon ground cardamom
¼ teaspoon ground nutmeg
¼ teaspoon salt
½ cup vegetable shortening
1 cup granulated sugar
2 large eggs
¾ cup grated carrots
2 tablespoons Amaretto
1 tablespoon orange liqueur
¾ cup shredded coconut
¾ cup almonds, chopped

**1** Preheat the oven to 375 degrees. Grease a 13 by 9-inch baking pan.

**2** Combine the flour, baking powder, spices, and salt.

**3** In a large bowl, cream the vegetable shortening and sugar. Beat in the eggs. Beat in the carrots. Beat in the Amaretto and orange liqueur. Gradually blend in the dry ingredients. Fold in the coconut and almonds. Spread the batter evenly in the prepared baking pan.

**4** Bake for 20 to 25 minutes, until golden brown on top. Cool in the pan on a wire rack before cutting into large or small bars.

1 cup all-purpose flour
1 cup whole wheat flour
1 cup almonds, chopped fine
2 teaspoons baking powder
¼ teaspoon baking soda
¼ teaspoon salt
½ cup vegetable shortening
½ cup packed light brown sugar
1 large egg
1 teaspoon fresh lemon juice
½ teaspoon almond extract
1 cup finely grated carrots
1 cup golden raisins

**1** Combine the two flours, almonds, baking powder, baking soda, and salt.

**2** In a large bowl, cream the vegetable shortening and brown sugar. Beat in the egg. Beat in the lemon juice and almond extract. Beat in the carrots. Gradually blend in the dry ingredients. Fold in the raisins. Cover and chill for 4 hours.

**3** Preheat the oven to 375 degrees. Lightly grease 2 baking sheets.

**4** Drop the dough by spoonfuls 1½ inches apart onto the prepared baking sheets.

**5** Bake for 10 to 12 minutes, until golden brown. Transfer to wire racks to cool.

# Carrot Cookies I

Drop Cookies

Yield: *4 to 6 dozen*
Total time: *35 minutes*
Chilling time: *4 hours*

2 cups all-purpose flour
½ cup almonds, ground fine
1 teaspoon baking powder
½ teaspoon baking soda
1 teaspoon ground cinnamon
¼ teaspoon ground nutmeg
¼ teaspoon ground cloves
¼ teaspoon salt
⅔ cup vegetable shortening
1 cup packed light brown sugar
2 large eggs
½ cup buttermilk
1 teaspoon almond extract
1 cup carrots, grated
1 cup rolled oats

**1** Preheat the oven to 400 degrees. Lightly grease 2 baking sheets.

**2** Combine the flour, almonds, baking powder, baking soda, spices, and salt.

**3** In a large bowl, cream the vegetable shortening and brown sugar. Beat in the eggs. Beat in the buttermilk and almond extract. Beat in the carrots. Gradually blend in the dry ingredients. Fold in the oats.

**4** Drop the dough by spoonfuls 1½ inches apart onto the prepared baking sheets.

**5** Bake for 12 to 15 minutes, until lightly browned. Transfer to wire racks to cool.

# Carrot Cookies II

Drop Cookies

Yield: *4 to 6 dozen*
Total time: *30 minutes*

2 cups all-purpose flour
2 teaspoons baking powder
½ teaspoon ground cinnamon
¼ teaspoon ground ginger
¼ teaspoon ground allspice
¼ teaspoon salt
½ cup vegetable shortening
1 cup granulated sugar
1 large egg
½ teaspoon vanilla extract
1 tablespoon grated lemon zest
1 cup mashed, cooked carrots (2 to 3 carrots)

**1** Preheat the oven to 350 degrees. Lightly grease 2 baking sheets.

**2** Combine the flour, baking powder, spices, and salt.

**3** In a large bowl, cream the vegetable shortening and sugar. Beat in the egg and vanilla extract. Beat in the lemon zest. Beat in the carrots. Gradually blend in the dry ingredients.

**4** Drop the dough by spoonfuls 1½ inches apart onto the prepared baking sheets.

**5** Bake for 12 to 15 minutes, until golden brown. Cool on the baking sheets on wire racks.

# Carrot Cookies III

Drop Cookies

Yield: *4 to 5 dozen*
Total time: *35 minutes*

# Carrot-Molasses Cookies

Drop Cookies

YIELD: *3 to 4 dozen*
TOTAL TIME: *30 minutes*

1½ cups all-purpose flour
½ cup soy flour
2 tablespoons active dry yeast (optional)
½ teaspoon ground cinnamon
½ teaspoon ground nutmeg
½ cup molasses
2 tablespoons canola oil
½ cup mashed, cooked carrots (about 1 to 2 carrots)
1 cup pecans, chopped
½ cup dates, pitted and chopped

1 Preheat the oven to 350 degrees. Lightly grease 2 baking sheets.

2 Combine the two flours, optional yeast, and spices.

3 In a saucepan, heat the molasses and canola oil until warm. Remove from the heat and beat in the carrots. Gradually blend in the dry ingredients. If the dough seems dry, stir in a little water 1 teaspoon at a time. Fold in the pecans and dates.

4 Drop by the dough by spoonfuls 1½ inches apart onto the prepared baking sheets.

5 Bake for 12 to 15 minutes, until golden brown. Transfer to wire racks to cool.

# Cashew Bars

Bar Cookies

YIELD: *2 to 3 dozen*
TOTAL TIME: *30 minutes*

2 cups all-purpose flour
1 cup cashews, ground fine
2 teaspoons baking powder
1 teaspoon baking soda
1 teaspoon ground nutmeg
½ cup vegetable shortening
3 large eggs
½ cup mashed bananas
½ cup cashews, chopped

1 Preheat the oven to 350 degrees. Lightly grease a 13 by 9-inch baking pan.

2 Combine the flour, ground cashews, baking powder, baking soda, and nutmeg.

3 In a large bowl, beat the vegetable shortening and eggs together. Beat in the bananas. Gradually blend in the dry ingredients.

4 Spread the mixture evenly in the prepared baking pan. Sprinkle the chopped cashews over the batter and press down gently.

5 Bake for 18 to 20 minutes, or until a toothpick inserted in the center comes out clean. Cool in the pan on a wire rack before cutting into large or small bars.

# Cashew-Caramel Cookies

Bar Cookies

YIELD: *1 to 2 dozen*
TOTAL TIME: *35 minutes*

¾ cup all-purpose flour
½ teaspoon baking powder
¼ teaspoon salt
2 large eggs
½ cup granulated sugar
2 tablespoons light brown sugar
½ cup cashews, chopped

TOPPING
2 tablespoons butter
1 tablespoon evaporated milk
2 tablespoons light brown sugar
½ cup cashews, chopped

1 Preheat the oven to 350 degrees. Lightly grease a 9-inch square baking pan.

2 Combine the flour, baking powder, and salt.

3 In a large bowl, beat the eggs, and both sugars together until thick. Add the cashews. Gradually blend in the dry ingredients.

4 Spread the dough evenly in the prepared baking pan. Bake for 25 minutes.

5 Meanwhile, make the topping in a saucepan: Combine all the ingredients and cook, stirring, until smooth. Remove from the heat.

6 Preheat the boiler.

7 Spread the topping over the warm cookies and place under the broiler for 1 minute, or until the topping starts to bubble. Cut into large or small bars while still warm, and cool in the pan on a rack.

⅓ cup all-purpose flour
⅓ cup rice flour
2 cups cashews, ground fine
¼ teaspoon baking soda
4 large eggs
1 tablespoon rum
Chopped cashews for topping

**1** Preheat the oven to 350 degrees. Lightly grease 2 baking sheets.

**2** Combine the two flours, the ground cashews, and baking soda.

**3** In a large bowl, beat the eggs until light and foamy. Beat in the rum. Gradually blend in the dry ingredients.

**4** Drop the cookies by spoonfuls 1½ inches apart onto the prepared baking sheets and sprinkle chopped cashews on top of the cookies.

**5** Bake for 5 to 8 minutes, until lightly colored. Transfer to wire racks to cool.

# CASHEW COOKIES

Drop Cookies

YIELD: *3 to 5 dozen*
TOTAL TIME: *30 minutes*

---

6 cups rolled oats
1 cup shredded coconuts
1 cup wheat germ
1 cup golden raisins
½ cup sunflower seeds, shelled
¼ cup sesame seeds, toasted
1 teaspoon ground allspice
1 cup honey
¾ cup canola oil
⅓ cup water
1½ teaspoons vanilla extract

**1** Preheat the oven to 350 degrees. Lightly grease a 13 by 9-inch baking pan.

**2** In a large bowl, combine the oats, coconut, wheat germ, raisins, sunflower seeds, sesame seeds, and allspice.

**3** In a medium saucepan, combine the honey, oil, water, and vanilla extract and heat until warm.

**4** Pour over the dry ingredients and blend thoroughly. Spread the mixture evenly in the prepared baking pan.

**5** Bake for 30 to 40 minutes, until firm and no longer sticking. Cut into large or small bars while still warm, and cool in the pan on a wire rack.

# CASHEW GRANOLA BARS

Bar Cookies

YIELD: *3 to 4 dozen*
TOTAL TIME: *45 minutes*

---

4½ cups all-purpose flour
1 cup cashews, ground fine
2 cups vegetable shortening
2½ cups packed light brown sugar

**1** Preheat the oven to 350 degrees.

**2** Combine the flour and cashews.

**3** In a large bowl, cream the vegetable shortening and brown sugar. Gradually blend in the dry ingredients.

**4** Pinch off small pieces of dough and roll into a balls. Place 1 inch apart on ungreased baking sheets. Flatten the balls with the bottom of a glass dipped in flour.

**5** Bake for 10 to 15 minutes, until lightly colored. Transfer to wire racks to cool.

# CASHEW SHORTBREAD

Formed Cookies

YIELD: *4 to 5 dozen*
TOTAL TIME: *30 minutes*

# CEREAL FLAKE MACAROONS

Drop Cookies

YIELD: *4 to 5 dozen*
TOTAL TIME: *40 minutes*

3 large egg whites
½ teaspoon salt
1½ cups granulated sugar
¼ teaspoon vanilla extract
3 cups cereal flakes
1½ cups shredded coconut

**1** Preheat the oven to 325 degrees. Lightly grease 2 baking sheets.

**2** In a large bowl, beat the egg whites until they just hold their shape. Beat in the salt. Gradually beat in the sugar and continue beating until the until the whites hold stiff peaks. Beat in the vanilla extract. Gradually fold in the cereal and coconut.

**3** Drop the mixture by spoonfuls 1½ inches apart onto the prepared baking sheets.

**4** Bake for 15 to 20 minutes, until the cookies start to just color. Transfer to wire racks to cool.

# CEREAL REFRIGERATOR COOKIES

Refrigerator Cookies

YIELD: *4 to 5 dozen*
TOTAL TIME: *30 minutes*
CHILLING TIME: *4 hours*

3 cups all-purpose flour
2 teaspoons baking powder
¼ teaspoon salt
1 cup vegetable shortening
2 cups packed light brown sugar
2 large eggs
1 cup All-Bran
1 cup Grape Nuts

**1** Combine the flour, baking powder, and salt.

**2** In a large bowl, cream the vegetable shortening and brown sugar. Beat in the eggs. Gradually blend in the dry ingredients. Fold in the two cereals.

**3** Form the dough into a log 2 inches in diameter. Wrap in waxed paper and chill for 4 hours.

**4** Preheat the oven to 375 degrees.

**5** Cut the log into ¼-inch-thick slices and place 1 inch apart on ungreased baking sheets.

**6** Bake for 12 to 15 minutes, until lightly colored. Transfer to wire racks to cool.

1 ounce bittersweet chocolate,
  chopped
2½ cups all-purpose flour
¾ teaspoon baking powder
½ teaspoon salt
¾ cup butter, at room temperature
1 cup granulated sugar
2 large eggs
1 teaspoon vanilla extract

**1** Melt the chocolate in a double boiler over low heat, stirring until smooth. Remove from the heat.

**2** Combine the flour, baking powder, and salt.

**3** In a large bowl, cream the butter and sugar. Beat in the eggs. Beat in the vanilla extract. Gradually blend in the dry ingredients.

**4** Transfer half the dough to another bowl. Blend the melted chocolate into half the dough. Divide each half in half again and form each piece into a square log 6 to 8 inches long.

**5** Press half of the chocolate dough evenly into the bottom of an 8 by 4-inch loaf pan. Place half of the plain dough on top of the chocolate dough and press down. Cover with waxed paper and refrigerate for 30 minutes, or until firm.

**6** Place the remaining chocolate dough on top of the chilled dough, pressing down gently; and place the remaining plain dough on top, pressing down on it. Cover with waxed paper and refrigerate for 8 hours or overnight.

**7** Preheat the oven to 400 degrees.

**8** Remove the dough from the loaf pan and cut it into ¼-inch-thick slices. Place 1 inch apart on ungreased baking sheets.

**9** Bake for 8 to 10 minutes, until lightly colored. Transfer to wire racks to cool.

**Baking notes:** This recipe dates from the 1930s. These cookies can also be formed by just placing the four logs together, wrapping them, and chilling them overnight. Lightly brush the dough with water to help the logs stick together.

# CHECKERBOARD COOKIES

Formed Cookies

YIELD: *5 to 6 dozen*
TOTAL TIME: *45 minutes*
CHILLING TIME: *8 hours*

C

---

2 cups all-purpose flour
1 teaspoon paprika
½ teaspoon salt
¼ teaspoon cayenne pepper
¾ cup butter, at room temperature
1½ cups grated Cheddar cheese
Granulated sugar for sprinkling
  (optional)

**1** Preheat the oven to 400 degrees.

**2** Combine the flour, paprika, salt, and cayenne pepper.

**3** In a large bowl, cream the butter. Beat in the dry ingredients. Blend in the Cheddar cheese.

**4** On a floured surface, roll out the dough to a thickness of ⅛ inch. With cookie cutters, cut into shapes and place 1 inch apart on ungreased baking sheets.

**5** Bake for 4 to 6 minutes, until lightly colored. Sprinkle with optional granulated sugar and transfer to wire racks to cool.

**Baking notes:** You can substitute Swiss cheese or Colby for the Cheddar. For a different flavor, use onion powder in place of the cayenne pepper.

# CHEDDAR DREAMS

Rolled Cookies

YIELD: *5 to 6 dozen*
TOTAL TIME: *45 minutes*

# CHEESECAKE COOKIES

Bar Cookies

YIELD: *1 to 3 dozen*
TOTAL TIME: *40 minutes*

**CRUST**
½ **cup canola oil**
¼ **cup powdered sugar**
24 **gingersnaps, crushed**

**FILLING**
1 **pound cream cheese, at room temperature**
½ **cup granulated sugar**
2 **large eggs**
1 **tablespoon fresh lemon juice**
1 **tablespoon marsala**
1 **tablespoon honey**
¼ **teaspoon ground allspice**

1 Preheat the oven to 375 degrees.

2 To make the crust, beat the canola oil and powdered sugar together in a large bowl. Gradually work in the crushed gingersnaps.

3 Press the mixture evenly into an ungreased 9-inch square baking pan.

4 Bake for about 6 minutes.

5 Meanwhile, make the filling: In a large bowl, beat the cream cheese and sugar until creamy. Beat in the eggs. Beat in the lemon juice, marsala, honey, and allspice.

6 Spread the filling over the hot crust. Bake for 12 to 15 minutes longer, until set. Cool in the pan on a wire rack before cutting into large or small bars.

**Baking notes:** For dessert, serve cut into large bars with sliced strawberries and whipped cream.

# CHERRY-ALMOND KOLACKY

Rolled Cookies

YIELD: *3 to 4 dozen*
TOTAL TIME: *35 minutes*
CHILLING TIME: *4 hours*

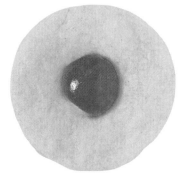

⅔ **cup butter, at room temperature**
¼ **cup rice flour**
½ **teaspoon Amaretto**
1 **tablespoon plus 1 teaspoon orange liqueur**
10 **ounces cream cheese, at room temperature**
2 **cups all-purpose flour**
Approximately 1 **cup glacé cherries, cut in half**

1 In a large bowl, beat the butter and rice flour until smooth. Beat in the Amaretto and 1 teaspoon of the orange liqueur. Beat in the cream cheese. Gradually blend in the all-purpose flour. Cover and chill for 4 hours.

2 Meanwhile, combine the cherries 1 cup warm water, and the remaining 1 tablespoon orange liqueur in a small bowl. Set aside and let plump for at least 1 hour.

3 Preheat the oven to 350 degrees.

4 Drain the cherries, discarding the liquid.

5 On a floured surface, roll out the dough to a thickness of ¼ inch. Using a 2- to 2½-inch round cookie cutter, cut into rounds and place 1 inch apart on ungreased baking sheets. Press a cherry half into the center of each cookie.

6 Bake for 10 to 15 minutes, until the edges are lighly colored. Transfer to wire racks to cool.

**Baking notes:** Use a combination of both red and green cherries if you like.

**CRUST**
1 cup all-purpose flour
¼ teaspoon salt
½ cup vegetable shortening
⅓ cup powdered sugar

**TOPPING**
3 ounces cream cheese
½ cup crumbled almond paste
1 large egg
½ cup red maraschino cherries, chopped

**1** Preheat the oven to 350 degrees.

**2** Combine the flour and salt.

**3** To make the crust, cream the vegetable shortening and powdered sugar in a large bowl,. Gradually blend in the dry ingredients. The mixture will be crumbly.

**4** Press the mixture evenly into the bottom of an ungreased 9-inch square baking pan. Bake for 15 minutes.

**5** Meanwhile, make the topping: In a large bowl, beat the cream cheese and almond paste until smooth and creamy. Beat in the egg. Fold in the maraschino cherries.

**6** Spread the topping over the warm crust. Bake for 15 minutes longer, until set. Cool in the pan on a wire rack before cutting into large or small bars.

# CHERRY-ALMOND SQUARES

Bar Cookies

YIELD: *1 to 2 dozen*
TOTAL TIME: *45 minutes*

---

2 cups all-purpose flour
1 tablespoon granulated sugar
¼ teaspoon salt
1 cup vegetable shortening
1 cup sour cream
1 large egg

**TOPPING**
½ cup cherry preserves
½ cup almonds, chopped
Powdered sugar for dusting

**1** In a large bowl, combine the flour, sugar, and salt. Cut in the vegetable shortening.

**2** In a medium bowl, beat the sour cream and the egg until well-blended. Blend into the flour mixture. Divide the dough into 3 pieces, wrap in waxed paper and chill for 4 hours.

**3** Preheat the oven to 350 degrees. Lightly grease 2 baking sheets.

**4** On a floured surface, roll out one piece of dough into an 11-inch round. Brush the dough with one-third of the cherry preserves and sprinkle with one-third of the almonds. Cut the round into 8 wedges. Starting at the wide end, roll up each piece, curve the ends to form crescents, and place, seam side down, 1½ inches apart on the prepared baking sheets. Repeat with the remaining dough.

**5** Bake for 18 to 20 minutes, until lightly colored. Dust with powdered sugar and transfer to wire racks to cool.

# CHERRY CRESCENTS

Rolled Cookies

YIELD: *2 to 3 dozen*
TOTAL TIME: *40 minutes*
CHILLING TIME: *4 hours*

# CHERRY-NUT CLOVERS

Formed Cookies

YIELD: *2 to 3 dozen*
TOTAL TIME: *40 minutes*
CHILLING TIME: *4 hours*

3 large eggs, separated
1½ cups powdered sugar
2 cups almonds, chopped
1 cup glacé cherries, cut in half
Powdered sugar for dusting

**1** In a large bowl, beat the egg yolks and sugar together until thick and light. Stir in the almonds.

**2** In a medium bowl, beat the egg whites until stiff but not dry. Fold the whites into the yolks. Cover and chill for 4 hours.

**3** Preheat the oven to 300 degrees. Line 2 baking sheets with parchment paper.

**4** Dust your hands with powdered sugar. Pinching off pieces about the size of an olive, roll into balls. Place the balls in groups of 3, touching each other, 1 inch apart on the prepared baking sheets. Press a half-cherry, round side up, into the center of each threesome.

**5** Bake for 28 to 30 minutes, or until the edges start to color. Transfer to wire racks to cool.

**Baking notes:** If the dough seems thin, add more powdered sugar a tablespoonful at a time.

# CHERRY SQUARES

Bar Cookies

YIELD: *2 to 3 dozen*
TOTAL TIME: *45 minutes*

2 cups all-purpose flour
¼ teaspoon salt
¾ cup vegetable shortening
1 cup granulated sugar
1 large egg
1 teaspoon vanilla extract
1½ cups shredded coconut
One 10-ounce jar cherry preserves

**1** Preheat the oven to 350 degrees. Lightly grease a 13 by 9-inch baking pan.

**2** Combine the flour and salt.

**3** In a large bowl, cream the vegetable shortening and sugar. Beat in the egg. Beat in the vanilla extract. Gradually blend in the dry ingredients. Fold in the coconut.

**4** Press three-quarters of the dough evenly into the prepared baking pan. Spread the cherry preserves over the dough. Crumble the remaining dough over the preserves.

**5** Bake for 25 to 30 minutes, until firm and lightly colored on top. Cool in the pan on a wire rack before cutting into large or small bars.

## CRUST

2 cups all-purpose flour
¼ cup granulated sugar
1½ tablespoons grated lemon zest
¾ cup vegetable shortening
3 tablespoons sour cream
½ teaspoon almond extract

## FILLING

1½ cups canned cherries, pitted &
   sliced
1 tablespoon raisins
¼ cup granulated sugar
1 large egg yolk, beaten
Powdered sugar for dusting

**1** To make the crust, combine the flour, sugar, and lemon zest in a large bowl. Cut in the vegetable shortening. Stir in the sour cream and almond extract.

**2** Divide the dough in half. Wrap in waxed paper and set aside at room temperature for 2 hours.

**3** Drain the cherries and reserve for at least one hour.

**4** Preheat the oven to 325 degrees. Lightly grease a 9-inch square baking pan.

**5** On a floured surface, roll out half the dough to a 9-inch square. Fit it into the prepared baking pan. Layer the sliced cherries over the dough. Sprinkle the raisins and then the sugar over the top.

**6** Roll out the remaining dough to a 9-inch square. Cut into 1-inch strips. Arrange the strips over filling in a lattice pattern. Brush the strips with the egg yolk.

**7** Bake for 18 to 20 minutes, until the lattice strips start to color. Dust the top with powdered sugar and cool in the pan on a wire rack before cutting into large or small strips.

**Baking notes:** Shredded coconut is a good addition to these bars. The cherries may be sliced, diced, or crushed.

# CHERRY STRIPS

Bar Cookies

YIELD: *3 to 5 dozen*
TOTAL TIME: *35 minutes*
CHILLING TIME: *2 hours*

---

1 cup all-purpose flour
½ teaspoon baking powder
1 tablespoon ground cinnamon
¼ teaspoon salt
1 cup vegetable shortening
1 cup granulated sugar
2 large egg yolks

## TOPPING

2 large egg whites
1½ teaspoons powdered sugar
1 cup pecans, chopped

**1** Preheat the oven to 300 degrees.

**2** Combine the flour, baking powder, cinnamon, and salt.

**3** In a large bowl, cream the vegetable shortening and sugar. Beat in the large egg yolks. Gradually blend in the dry ingredients. Spread the dough evenly into a 13 by 9-inch square baking pan.

**4** To make the topping, beat the large egg whites in a medium bowl, until stiff and frothy. Fold in the powdered sugar. Spread the topping over the dough. Sprinkle the chopped pecans over the top.

**5** Bake for 40 to 45 minutes, or until the topping is lightly colored. Cool in the pan on a wire rack before cutting into large or small bars.

# CHEWY PECAN BARS

Bar Cookies

YIELD: *1 to 2 dozen*
TOTAL TIME: *60 minutes*

# CHIPPERS

Drop Cookies

YIELD: *4 to 5 dozen*
TOTAL TIME: *30 minutes*

1¼ cups all-purpose flour
½ teaspoon baking soda
¼ teaspoon salt
⅓ cup butter, at room temperature
½ cup packed light brown sugar
1 large egg
1 teaspoon vanilla extract
1 cup (6 ounces) semisweet chocolate chips
½ cup walnuts, chopped fine

**1** Preheat the oven to 375 degrees. Lightly grease 2 baking sheets.

**2** Combine the flour, baking soda, and salt.

**3** In a large bowl, cream the butter and brown sugar. Beat in the egg and vanilla extract. Gradu- ally blend in the dry ingredients. Fold in the chocolate chips and walnuts.

**4** Drop the dough by spoonful 2 inches apart onto the prepared baking sheets

**5** Bake for 10 to 12 minutes, or until lightly colored. Transfer to wire racks to cool.

# CHOCOLATE BONBONS

Drop Cookies

YIELD: *3 to 5 dozen*
TOTAL TIME: *40 minutes*

½ cup all-purpose flour
¼ teaspoon salt
2 tablespoons butter, at room temperature
½ cup granulated sugar
1 large egg
2 tablespoons evaporated milk
1 teaspoon vanilla extract
⅓ cup unsweetened cocoa powder
1¼ cups walnuts, ground fine

**1** Preheat the oven to 350 degrees. Lightly grease 2 baking sheets.

**2** Combine the flour and salt.

**3** In a large bowl, cream the butter and sugar. Beat in the egg. Beat in the milk and vanilla extract. Stir in the cocoa powder. Gradually blend in the dry ingredients.

**4** Drop the dough by spoonfuls 1 inch apart onto the prepared baking sheets.

**5** Bake for 10 to 12 minutes, until lightly colored. Roll the warm cookies in the ground walnuts before transferring to wire racks to cool.

**Baking notes (Alternate method): 1.** Combine all the ingredients except the walnuts in the top of a double boiler and cook over high heat, stirring for 15 minutes, or until the mixture is very stiff. **2.** Drop by spoonfuls onto wax paper-lined baking sheets. Sprinkle with half the chopped nuts. **3.** Let cool slightly roll, then roll in the remaining chopped nuts.

½ cup vegetable shortening
2 ounces bittersweet chocolate, chopped
2 large eggs
1 cup granulated sugar
½ teaspoon almond extract
½ cup all-purpose flour
1 cup slivered almonds

**1** Preheat the oven to 350
d̶ ̶ ̶ ̶ ̶L̶ightly grease an 11 by

and almond extract. Blend in the flour.

**3** Spread the dough evenly in the prepared baking pan. Sprinkle the slivered almonds over the top

**4** Bake for 35 to 40 minutes, until firm to the touch. Cool in the pan on a wire rack before cutting into large or small bars.

# CHOCOLATE CHEWS

Bar Cookies

YIELD: *2 to 3 dozen*
TOTAL TIME: *50 minutes*

owl, cream the veg-
____ing and brown
_____ the eggs. Beat in
_____ vanilla extract.
_____end in the dry ingre-
_____ in the chocolate

_____e dough evenly in the
_____aking pan.
_____25 to 30 minutes, or
_____n brown on top. Cool
_____on a wire rack before
_____o large or small bars.

_____tes: For an unusual
_____substitute white crème
_____e for the vanilla extract.

# CHOCOLATE CHIP BAR COOKIES

Bar Cookies

YIELD: *2 to 3 dozen*
TOTAL TIME: *45 minutes*

_____venly into the prepared
_____an.
_____or 18 to 20 minutes, or
_____lden brown on top. Cool
_____an on a wire rack before
_____into large or small bars.

_____**notes:** These can be
_____in a 13 by 9-inch baking
_____ut the texture of the cook-
_____ll be drier so bake for a
_____r time.

# CHOCOLATE CHIP BARS

Bar Cookies

YIELD: *3 to 4 dozen*
TOTAL TIME: *45 minutes*

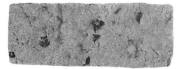

# CHOCOLATE CHIP COOKIES I

Drop Cookies

YIELD: *6 to 7 dozen*
TOTAL TIME: *30 minutes*

2¼ cups all-purpose flour
1 teaspoon baking soda
1 package vanilla-flavored instant
   pudding
1 cup vegetable shortening
¼ cup granulated sugar
¾ cup packed light brown sugar
2 large eggs
1 teaspoon vanilla extract
1½ cups (9 ounces) semisweet
   chocolate chips
1 cup walnuts, chopped fine

**1** Preheat the oven to 375
degrees.

**2** Combine the flour, baking
soda, and vanilla pudding

**3** In a large bowl, cream the vegetable shortening and the two

sugars. Beat in the eggs. Beat in
the vanilla extract. Gradually
blend in the dry ingredients. Fold
in the chocolate chips and
walnuts.

**4** Drop the dough by spoonfuls
1½ inches apart onto ungreased
baking sheets.

**5** Bake for 8 to 10 minutes, until
lightly colored. Transfer to wire
racks to cool.

**Baking notes:** For chocolate
chocolate chip cookies, use a
chocolate instant pudding in
place of the vanilla pudding.

---

# CHOCOLATE CHIP COOKIES II

Formed Cookies

YIELD: *3 to 5 dozen*
TOTAL TIME: *30 minutes*

½ cup butter, at room temperature
1 large egg, beaten
1 teaspoon vanilla extract
2 cups Basic Drop Cookie Mix (see
   p. 58)
½ cup semisweet chocolate chips

**1** Preheat the oven to 350
degrees. Lightly grease 2 baking
sheets.

**2** In a large bowl, beat the butter, egg, and vanilla extract
together. Gradually blend in the
cookie mix. Fold in the chocolate
chips.

**3** Pinch off walnut-sized pieces
of dough and roll into balls.
Place 2 inches apart on the prepared baking sheets.

**4** Bake for 10 to 14 minutes, until

firm to the touch. Cool on the
pans for 1 minute before transferring to wire racks to cool
completely.

**Baking notes:** This dough can be
used to make drop cookies. Bake
for 8 to 10 minutes.

---

# CHOCOLATE CHIP COOKIES III

Drop Cookies

YIELD: *3 to 5 dozen*
TOTAL TIME: *30 minutes*
CHILLING TIME: *1 hour*

2 cups all-purpose flour
1 teaspoon baking soda
½ teaspoon salt
1 cup vegetable shortening
½ cup granulated sugar
¾ cup packed light brown sugar
1 large egg
2½ teaspoons white crème de
   menthe
1⅓ cups (8 ounces) semisweet
   chocolate chips

**1** Combine the flour, baking
soda, and salt.

**2** In a large bowl, cream the vegetable shortening and the two
sugars. Beat in the egg and crème
de menthe. Gradually blend in
the dry ingredients. Fold in the

chocolate chips. Cover and
refrigerate for 1 hour.

**3** Preheat the oven to 350
degrees. Lightly grease 2 baking
sheets.

**4** Drop the dough by spoonfuls
1½ inches apart onto the prepared baking sheets.

**5** Bake for 10 to 12 minutes, until
lightly colored. Transfer to wire
racks to cool.

4 cups powdered sugar
1 cup cream cheese, at room temperature
¼ teaspoon ground nutmeg
¼ teaspoon ground cardamom
1 tablespoon evaporated milk
1 teaspoon Amaretto
1 cup miniature semisweet chocolate chips
1 cup almonds, chopped

**1** In a large bowl, beat together the powdered sugar and cream cheese until smooth. Beat in the spices, milk and Amaretto. Stir in the chocolate chips.
**2** Pinch off walnut-sized pieces of the mixture and roll into small balls. Roll the balls in the

almonds. Store in the refrigerator in an airtight container.

**Baking notes:** Other miniature candies can be substituted for the chocolate chips.

# CHOCOLATE CHIP EGGNOG BALLS

Formed Cookies

YIELD: *6 to 8 dozen*
TOTAL TIME: *30 minutes*

½ cup all-purpose flour
½ teaspoon baking powder
¼ teaspoon salt
1 large egg
½ cup granulated sugar
1 teaspoon butter, melted
2 teaspoons hot water
⅔ cup walnuts, chopped fine
½ cup almonds, chopped fine
1 cup (6 ounces) semisweet chocolate chips

**1** Preheat the oven to 325 degrees. Lightly grease an 8-inch square baking pan.
**2** Combine the flour, baking powder, and salt.
**3** In a large bowl, beat the egg until thick and light-colored. Beat

in the sugar. Beat in the butter and and hot water. Beat in the nuts. Gradually blend in the dry ingredients. Fold in the chocolate chips.
**4** Spread the batter evenly into the prepared baking pan. Bake for 25 to 30 minutes, or until lightly colored on top. Cool in the pan on a wire rack before cutting into large or small bars.

# CHOCOLATE CHIP NUT BARS

Bar Cookies

YIELD: *2 to 3 dozen*
TOTAL TIME: *45 minutes*

1 cup semisweet chocolate chips
½ cup peanut butter
½ cup peanuts, chopped (optional)
4 cups cocoa krispies

**1** Lightly grease a 9-inch square baking pan.
**2** Melt the chocolate chips with the peanut butter in a saucepan over a low heat, stirring until smooth. Blend in the optional peanuts. Gradually blend in the krispies, stirring until well coated.
**3** Spread the mixture out evenly in the prepared pan. Let cool in the pan on a wire rack until the mixture hardens slightly.

**4** Cut into 2 by 1-inch bars. Roll each bar between your hands to form logs. Wrap individually in waxed paper and store tightly covered.

**Baking notes:** This is a great cookie for children to make with your help. Let them form the logs.

# CHOCOLATE CHIP PEANUT LOGS

Formed Cookies

YIELD: *2 to 3 dozen*
TOTAL TIME: *30 minutes*

# Chocolate Chip Squares

Bar Cookies

YIELD: *3 to 5 dozen*
TOTAL TIME: *30 minutes*

**CRUST**
2¼ cups all-purpose flour
1 teaspoon baking soda
½ teaspoon salt
1 cup canola oil
½ cup granulated sugar
¾ cup packed light brown sugar
1 large egg
2½ teaspoons white crème de menthe
1⅓ cups (8 ounces) semisweet chocolate chips

**TOPPING**
½ cup (3 ounces) semisweet chocolate chips

**1** Preheat the oven to 350 degrees. Lightly grease a 13 by 9-inch baking pan.

**2** Combine the flour, baking soda, and salt.

**3** In a large bowl, beat the canola oil and the two sugars. Beat in the egg. Beat in the crème de menthe. Gradually blend in the dry ingredients. Fold in the chocolate chips.

**4** Spread the dough evenly in the prepared pan. Bake for 15 to 20 minutes, until the top is golden brown.

**5** For the topping, spread the chocolate chips over the hot cookies. With a spatula, spread the melted chocolate chips evenly over the top. Cool in the pan on a wire rack before cutting into large or small bars.

# Chocolate-Coconut Bars

Bar Cookies

YIELD: *1 to 2 dozen*
TOTAL TIME: *40 minutes*

1½ cups crushed graham crackers
One 14-ounce can sweetened condensed milk
1½ cups flaked coconut
½ cup semisweet chocolate chips

**1** Preheat the oven to 350 degrees. Grease a 9-inch square baking pan.

**2** In a large bowl, combine all the ingredients, stirring until well blended. Press the mixture evenly into the prepared baking pan.

**3** Bake for 30 minutes until set. Cool in the pan on a wire rack before cutting into large or small bars.

1½ cups all-purpose flour
1½ teaspoons baking powder
¼ teaspoon salt
6 tablespoons butter, at room temperature
¾ cup plus 2 tablespoons granulated sugar
1 large egg
2 tablespoons milk
½ teaspoon vanilla extract
1 ounce bittersweet chocolate, chopped
1 teaspoon grated orange zest
¼ cup pecans, chopped
⅔ cup shredded coconut

**1** Preheat the oven to 375 degrees. Lightly grease two 8-inch square baking pans.

**2** Combine the flour, baking powder, and salt.

**3** In a large bowl, cream the butter and sugar. Beat in the egg. Beat in the milk and vanilla extract. Gradually blend in the dry ingredients. Divide the dough in half and transfer half to another bowl.

**4** Melt the chocolate in a double boiler over low heat, stirring until smooth. Remove from the heat and work into half the dough.

**5** On a floured surface, roll out the chocolate dough to an 8-inch square Fit it into one of the prepared baking pans and sprinkle with 1 tablespoon of the sugar and half the orange zest.

**6** Bake 10 to 15 minutes, until firm to the touch. Cool in the pan on a wire rack before cutting into 2 by 1-inch strips.

**7** Meanwhile, blend the pecans and coconut into the remaining dough. Roll out the dough, fit it into the second baking pan, and sprinkle with the remaining 1 tablespoon of sugar and remaining orange zest.

**8** Bake as directed, cool, and cut into strips.

# CHOCOLATE-COCONUT TEA STRIPS

Bar Cookies

YIELD: *3 to 4 dozen*
TOTAL TIME: *35 minutes*

---

1½ cups all-purpose flour
½ cup unsweetened cocoa powder
1½ teaspoons baking powder
¼ teaspoon salt
½ cup butter, at room temperature
1 cup packed light brown sugar
1 large egg
½ cup milk
1 tablespoon heavy cream
1 teaspoon vanilla extract
¾ cup walnuts, chopped
Granulated sugar for sprinkling

**1** Preheat the oven to 400 degrees.

**2** Combine the flour, cocoa, baking powder, and salt.

**3** In a large bowl, cream the butter and brown sugar. Beat in the egg. Beat in the milk, cream, and vanilla extract. Gradually blend in the dry ingredients. Fold in the walnuts.

**4** On a floured surface, roll out the dough to a thickness of ¼ inch. Using a 1½-inch round cookie cutter, cut into circles and place 1½ inches apart on ungreased baking sheets.

**5** Bake for 10 to 12 minutes, or until firm to the touch. Sprinkle the warm cookies with granulated sugar and transfer to wire racks to cool.

# CHOCOLATE COOKIES

Rolled Cookies

YIELD: *4 to 5 dozen*
TOTAL TIME: *40 minutes*

# CHOCOLATE CRINKLES

Formed Cookies

YIELD: *3 to 4 dozen*
TOTAL TIME: *30 minutes*

2 cups all-purpose flour
2 teaspoons baking powder
3 ounces semisweet chocolate, chopped
½ cup canola oil
1½ cups granulated sugar
2 large eggs
¼ cup milk
1 teaspoon vanilla extract
Powdered sugar for rolling

**1** Preheat the oven to 350 degrees. Lightly grease 2 baking sheets.

**2** Combine the flour and baking powder.

**3** Melt the chocolate in a double boiler over low heat, stirring until smooth. Remove from the heat.

**4** In a large bowl, beat the canola oil and sugar until well blended. Beat in the eggs one at a time, beating well after each addition. Beat in the chocolate. Beat in the milk and vanilla extract. Gradually blend in the dry ingredients.

**5** Pinch off walnut-sized pieces of dough and roll into balls. Roll in powdered sugar and place 1½ inches apart on the prepared baking sheets.

**6** Bake for 12 to 15 minutes, or until firm to the touch. Roll in powdered sugar while still warm and transfer to wire racks to cool.

# CHOCOLATE DE LA HARINA DE AVENA BROWNIES

Bar Cookies

YIELD: *2 to 3 dozen*
TOTAL TIME: *35 minutes*

3 ounces bittersweet chocolate, chopped
1 cup all-purpose flour
1 cup almonds, chopped fine
½ teaspoon salt
⅔ cup vegetable shortening
1 cup packed light brown sugar
½ cup granulated sugar
4 large eggs
2 teaspoons vanilla extract
1 cup rolled oats

**1** Preheat the oven to 325 degrees. Lightly grease a 13 by 9-inch baking pan.

**2** Melt the chocolate in a double boiler over low heat, stirring until smooth. Remove from the heat.

**3** Combine the flour, almonds, and salt.

**4** In a large bowl, cream the vegetable shortening and the two sugars. Beat in the eggs. Beat in the vanilla extract, then the melted chocolate. Gradually blend in the dry ingredients. Fold in the oats.

**5** Spread the dough evenly in the prepared baking pan. Bake for 25 to 30 minutes, or until a toothpick inserted into the center comes out clean but not dry; do not overbake. Cool in the pan on a wire rack before cutting into large or small bars.

**Baking notes:** Add 1 cup of raisins to the dough if desired. These are traditional Mexican cookies.

# CHOCOLATE DELIGHT BARS

Bar Cookies

YIELD: *1 to 2 dozen*
TOTAL TIME: *40 minutes*

**CRUST**
½ cup butter, at room temperature
3 tablespoons powdered sugar
2 large yolks
1 teaspoon instant coffee crystals
1 tablespoon warm water
2 cups all-purpose flour

**TOPPING**
½ cup semisweet chocolate chips
2 large egg whites
¼ cup granulated sugar
¼ cup almonds, ground fine
¼ cup almonds, chopped

**1** Preheat the oven to 350 degrees. Lightly grease a 9-inch square baking pan.

**2** In a large bowl, combine the butter, powdered sugar, egg yolks, coffee crystals, and water and beat until well blended.

Gradually blend in the flour. The mixture will be crumbly.

**3** Press the mixture evenly into the bottom of the prepared baking pan. Bake for 20 minutes.

**4** Meanwhile, melt the chocolate in the top of a double boiler, stirring until smooth. Remove from the heat.

**5** In a medium bowl, beat the egg whites until foamy. Gradually beat in the sugar and beat until the whites hold stiff peaks. In a steady stream, beat in the melted chocolate. Fold in the ground almonds.

**6** Spread the topping over the warm crust. Sprinkle with the chopped almonds and bake for 20 minutes longer, until set.

# CHOCOLATE DROP COOKIES I

Drop Cookies

YIELD: *3 to 4 dozen*
TOTAL TIME: *30 minutes*

½ cup butter
3 ounces unsweetened chocolate, chopped
1 large egg, beaten
¼ cup water
1 teaspoon almond extract
2 cups Basic Cookie Mix (see Pantry)

**1** Preheat the oven to 350 degrees. Lightly grease 2 baking sheets.

**2** Melt the butter and chocolate in the top of a double boiler over low heat, stirring until smooth. Remove from the heat and beat in the egg. Beat in the water and almond extract. Gradually blend in the cookie mix.

**3** Drop the dough by spoonfuls 1½ inches apart onto the prepared baking sheets.

**4** Bake for 10 to 12 minutes, until firm to the touch. Transfer to wire racks to cool.

# CHOCOLATE DROP COOKIES II

Drop Cookies

YIELD: *4 to 5 dozen*
TOTAL TIME: *20 minutes*

½ cup butter
½ cup peanut butter
½ cup unsweetened cocoa powder
½ cup evaporated milk
2 cups powdered sugar
2½ cups rolled oats

**1** Line 2 baking sheets with waxed paper.

**2** In a large saucepan, combine the butter, peanut butter, and cocoa and bring to a boil, stirring until the butter melts. Remove from the heat. Beat in the milk. Gradually beat in the powdered sugar. Gradually blend in the rolled oats.

**3** Drop the dough by spoonfuls onto the prepared baking sheet. Let cool.

# Chocolate Drop Cookies III

Drop Cookies

YIELD: *2 to 3 dozen*
TOTAL TIME: *30 minutes*

2 ounces semisweet chocolate, chopped
2 cups all-purpose flour
½ teaspoon baking soda
½ cup almonds, ground fine
½ teaspoon salt
½ cup vegetable shortening
½ cup granulated sugar
½ cup packed light brown sugar
1 large egg
1 teaspoon vanilla extract
¾ cup buttermilk

1 Preheat the oven to 400 degrees. Lightly grease 2 baking sheets.

2 Melt the chocolate in a double boiler over low heat, stirring until smooth.

3 Combine the flour, almonds, baking soda, and salt.

4 In a large bowl, cream the vegetable shortening and the two sugars. Beat in the egg. Beat in the vanilla extract. Beat in the buttermilk and melted chocolate. Gradually blend in the dry ingredients.

5 Drop the dough by spoonfuls 1½ inches apart onto the prepared baking sheets.

6 Bake for 8 to 10 minutes, until firm to the touch. Transfer to wire racks to cool.

---

# Chocolate-Filled Pinwheels

Refrigerator Cookies

YIELD: *4 to 5 dozen*
TOTAL TIME: *45 minutes*
CHILLING TIME: *2 hours and overnight*

2 cups all-purpose flour
1 teaspoon baking powder
½ teaspoon salt
¾ cup vegetable shortening
1 cup granulated sugar
1 large egg
1 tablespoon vanilla extract

FILLING
1 cup (6 ounces) semisweet chocolate chips
2 tablespoons butter
1 cup walnuts, ground fine
½ tablespoon vanilla extract

1 Combine the flour, baking powder, and salt.

2 Cream the vegetable shortening and sugar in a large bowl. Beat in the egg. Beat in the vanilla extract. Gradually blend in the dry ingredients. Measure out ⅔ cup of the dough and set aside. Cover the remaining dough and chill for 2 hours.

3 To make the filling, melt the chocolate and butter in the top of a double boiler over low heat, strring until smooth. Remove from the heat and stir in the walnuts and vanilla extract. Blend in the reserved dough.

4 On a floured surface, roll out the chilled dough to a 16 by 12-inch rectangle. Spread the chocolate mixture over the dough to within ¼ inch of the edges. Starting on a long side, roll the dough up jelly-roll fashion. Pinch the seam to seal. Cut in half to make two 8-inch logs. Wrap in waxed paper and chill overnight.

5 Preheat the oven to 350 degrees.

6 Slice the logs into ¼-inch-thick slices and place 1½ inches apart on ungreased baking sheets.

7 Bake for 10 to 12 minutes, until lightly colored. Transfer to wire racks to cool.

**Baking notes:** To decorate, drizzle melted white or dark chocolate over the top of the cooled cookies.

1 cup all-purpose flour
6 tablespoons unsweetened cocoa
  powder
½ teaspoon baking soda
½ teaspoon salt
1½ cups vegetable shortening
1½ cups granulated sugar
1 large egg
¼ cup water
1 teaspoon vanilla extract
3 cups rolled oats
¾ cup semisweet chocolate chips

**1** Preheat the oven to 350 degrees. Lightly grease 2 baking sheets.

**2** Combine the flour, cocoa powder, baking soda, and salt.

**3** In a large bowl, cream the vegetable shortening and sugar. Beat in the egg. Beat in the water and vanilla extract. Gradually blend in the dry ingredients. Fold in the oats and chocolate chips.

**4** Drop the dough by tablespoonfuls 2 inches apart onto the prepared baking sheets.

**5** Bake for 12 to 15 minutes, until lightly colored. Transfer to wire racks to cool.

# CHOCOLATE JUMBO COOKIES

Drop Cookies

YIELD: *2 to 4 dozen*
TOTAL TIME: *30 minutes*

---

1 ounce unsweetened chocolate,
  chopped
4 large egg whites
¼ teaspoon salt
¼ teaspoon cream of tartar
1 cup granulated sugar
¼ teaspoon almond extract

**1** Preheat the oven to 250 degrees. Line 2 baking sheets with parchment paper.

**2** Melt the chocolate in a double boiler over low heat, stirring until smooth. Remove from the heat.

**3** In a large bowl, beat the egg whites until foamy. Beat in the salt and cream of tartar. Beat in the sugar and almond extract and continue beating until whites form stiff peaks. Fold in the melted chocolate.

**4** Drop the mixture by spoonfuls 1 inch apart onto the prepared baking sheets.

**5** Bake for 35 to 40 minutes, until firm to the touch. Transfer to wire racks to cool

**Baking notes:** For crisper kisses, turn the oven off and let the cookies cool completely in the oven. (Do not open the door.)

# CHOCOLATE KISSES

Drop Cookies

YIELD: *2 to 3 dozen*
TOTAL TIME: *50–55 minutes*

# CHOCOLATE HAZELNUT COOKIES

Drop Cookies

YIELD: *3 to 4 dozen*
TOTAL TIME: *30 minutes*

**2 ounces unsweetened chocolate, chopped**
**¾ cup all-purpose flour**
**¼ teaspoon salt**
**¾ cup hazelnuts, ground**
**½ cup vegetable shortening**
**1 cup granulated sugar**
**1 large egg**
**1 teaspoon vanilla extract**
**Powdered sugar**

**1** Preheat the oven to 325 degrees. Lightly grease 2 baking sheets.

**2** Melt the chocolate in a double boiler over low heat, stirring until smooth. Remove from the heat.

**3** Combine the flour and salt.

**4** In a large bowl, cream the vegetable shortening and sugar. Beat in the melted chocolate. Beat in the egg and vanilla extract. Gradually blend in the dry ingredients.

**5** Drop the dough by spoonfuls 1½ inches apart onto the prepared baking sheets. Flatten the cookies with the back of a spoon dipped in powdered sugar.

**6** Bake for 12 to 15 minutes, until firm to the touch. Transfer to wire racks to cool.

# CHOCOLATE-LEMON DESSERT COOKIES

Drop Cookies

YIELD: *3 to 4 dozen*
TOTAL TIME: *45 minutes*

**2 tablespoons packaged lemon dessert**
**3 tablespoons cold water**
**1 ounce semisweet chocolate, grated**
**One 14-ounce can sweetened condensed milk**
**1½ cups shredded coconut**
**1 teaspoon vanilla extract**

**1** Preheat the oven to 350 degrees. Lightly grease 2 baking sheets.

**2** In a saucepan, stir the lemon dessert, cold water, and chocolate over low heat until smooth. Stir in the condensed milk. Cook for 3 minutes, stirring constantly. Remove from the heat and stir in the coconut. Stir in the vanilla extract.

**3** Drop the dough by spoonfuls onto the prepared baking sheets.

**4** Bake for 10 to 12 minutes, until lightly colored and firm to the touch. Transfer to wire racks to cool.

## CRUST

2½ cups all-purpose flour
1 teaspoon baking soda
1 teaspoon salt
1 cup vegetable shortening
2 cups packed light brown sugar
2 large eggs
2 teaspoons vanilla extract
3 cups rolled oats

## FILLING

2 cups (12 ounces) semisweet chocolate chips
2 tablespoons butter
One 14-ounce can sweetened condensed milk
2 teaspoons vanilla extract
1 cup walnuts, chopped

**1** Preheat the oven to 350 degrees.

**2** To make the crust, combine the flour, baking soda, and salt.

**3** In a large bowl, cream the vegetable shortening and brown sugar. Beat in the eggs and vanilla. Gradually blend in the dry ingredients. Fold in the rolled oats.

**4** Press two-thirds of the crust mixture evenly into an ungreased 13 by 9-inch baking pan.

**5** To prepare the filling, melt the chocolate chips and butter in a double boiler over low heat, stirring until smooth. Remove from the heat and stir in the condensed milk and vanilla extract. Fold in the nuts.

**6** Spread the filling evenly over the crust in the baking pan. Press the remaining crust mixture on top of the filling.

**7** Bake for 25 to 30 minutes, until firm to the touch. Cool in the pan on a wire rack before cutting into large or small bars.

# CHOCOLATE OATMEAL BARS

Bar Cookies

YIELD: *3 to 4 dozen*
TOTAL TIME: *45 minutes*

---

2 ounces bittersweet chocolate, chopped
1 cup all-purpose flour
½ teaspoon baking soda
½ cup vegetable shortening
1 cup granulated sugar
1 large egg
1½ teaspoons Amaretto
1 cup rolled oats
½ cup pecans, chopped
Granulated sugar

**1** Preheat the oven to 350 degrees. Lightly grease 2 baking sheets.

**2** Melt the chocolate in a double boiler over low heat, stirring until smooth. Remove from the heat.

**3** Combine the flour and baking soda.

**4** In a large bowl, cream the vegetable shortening and sugar. Beat in the egg. Beat in the Amaretto.

Stir in the melted chocolate. Gradually blend in the dry ingredients. Fold in the oats and pecans.

**5** Pinch off walnut-sized pieces of dough and roll into balls. Place 1½ inches apart on the prepared baking sheets. Flatten the balls with the bottom of a glass dipped in sugar.

**6** Bake for 10 to 12 minutes, until lightly colored. Transfer to wire racks to cool.

# CHOCOLATE OATMEAL COOKIES

Formed Cookies

YIELD: *3 to 4 dozen*
TOTAL TIME: *30 minutes*

# CHOCOLATE PECAN COOKIES

Drop Cookies

YIELD: *4 to 5 dozen*
TOTAL TIME: *35 minutes*
CHILLING TIME: *2 hours*

1 ounce bittersweet chocolate, chopped
¾ cup all-purpose flour
¼ teaspoon salt
½ cup vegetable shortening
1 cup raw sugar
2 large eggs
1 teaspoon rum flavoring
¾ cup pecans, chopped fine

**1** Melt the chocolate in a double boiler over low heat, stirring until smooth. Remove from the heat.

**2** Combine the flour and salt.

**3** In a large bowl, cream the vegetable shortening and sugar. Beat in the eggs one at a time, beating vigorously after each addition. Beat in the rum flavoring. Gradually blend in the dry ingredients. Fold in the pecans. Cover and chill in the refrigerator for 2 hours.

**4** Preheat the oven to 350 degrees. Lightly grease 2 baking sheets.

**5** Drop the dough by spoonfuls 1½ inches apart onto the prepared baking sheets.

**6** Bake for 12 to 15 minutes, until firm to the touch. Transfer to wire racks to cool.

# CHOCOLATE PUDDING BROWNIES

Bar Cookies

YIELD: *1 to 2 dozen*
TOTAL TIME: *45 minutes*

½ cup all-purpose flour
One 4-ounce package chocolate pudding mix
½ teaspoon baking powder
¼ teaspoon salt
6 tablespoons vegetable shortening
⅔ cup granulated sugar
2 large eggs
¼ cup milk
1 teaspoon vanilla extract
½ cup walnuts, chopped
Powdered sugar for sprinkling

**1** Preheat the oven to 350 degrees. Lightly grease a 9-inch square baking pan.

**2** Combine the flour, chocolate pudding mix, baking powder, and salt.

**3** In a large bowl, cream the vegetable shortening and sugar. Beat in the eggs. Beat in the milk and vanilla extract. Gradually blend in the dry ingredients. Fold in the walnuts. Spread the mixture evenly in the prepared baking pan.

**4** Bake for 25 to 30 minutes, until a toothpick inserted in the center comes out clean. Cool in the pan on a wire rack.

**5** Place a paper doily on top of the cooled cookies and sprinkle with powdered sugar. Remove the doily and cut into large or small bars.

# CHOCOLATE RAISIN DROPS

Drop Cookies

YIELD: *2 to 4 dozen*
TOTAL TIME: *30 minutes*

1 cup all-purpose flour
½ cup walnuts, ground fine
½ teaspoon baking soda
¼ teaspoon salt
½ cup vegetable shortening
½ cup granulated sugar
¼ cup packed light brown sugar
1 large egg
½ teaspoon vanilla extract
¾ cup chocolate-covered raisins

**1** Preheat the oven to 350 degrees. Lightly grease 2 baking sheets.

**2** Combine the flour, walnuts, baking soda, and salt.

**3** In a large bowl, cream the vegetable shortening and the two sugars. Beat in the egg. Beat in the vanilla extract. Gradually blend in the dry ingredients. Fold in the raisins.

**4** Drop the dough by spoonfuls 1½ inches apart onto the prepared baking sheets.

**5** Bake for 12 to 15 minutes, until lightly colored. Transfer to wire racks to cool.

2 cups all-purpose flour
½ teaspoon baking soda
½ teaspoon salt
½ cup vegetable shortening
1 cup packed dark brown sugar
1 large egg
2 tablespoons chocolate syrup
2 teaspoons vanilla extract

**1** Combine the flour, baking soda, and salt.

**2** In a large bowl, cream the vegetable shortening and brown sugar. Beat in the large egg. Beat in the chocolate syrup and vanilla extract. Gradually blend in the dry ingredients.

**3** Form the dough into a log 2 inches in diameter. Wrap in waxed paper and chill for 4 hours.

**4** Preheat the oven to 400 degrees.

**5** Cut the log into ¼-inch-thick slices and place 1 inch apart on ungreased baking sheets.

**6** Bake for 8 to 10 minutes, or until lightly colored. Transfer to wire racks to cool

**Baking notes:** For variation, roll the log in chopped nuts before chilling it. This dough can be frozen for up to 3 months.

# CHOCOLATE REFRIGERATOR COOKIES I

Refrigerator Cookies

YIELD: *5 to 6 dozen*
TOTAL TIME: *30 minutes*
CHILLING TIME: *4 hours*

3 ounces bittersweet chocolate, chopped
3 cups all-purpose flour
1 tablespoon baking powder
½ teaspoon salt
1 cup vegetable shortening
1 cup granulated sugar
1 large egg
2 teaspoons crème de cacao

**1** Melt the chocolate in a double boiler over low heat, stirring until smooth. Remove from the heat.

**2** Combine the flour, baking powder, and salt.

**3** In a large bowl, cream the vegetable shortening and sugar. Beat in the egg. Beat in the melted chocolate and crème de cacao. Gradually blend in the dry ingredients.

**4** Divide the dough in half. Form each piece into a log 2 inches in diameter. Wrap in waxed paper and chill for 4 hours.

**5** Preheat the oven to 350 degrees.

**6** Cut the logs into ⅛-inch-thick slices. Place 1 inch apart on ungreased baking sheets.

**7** Bake for 10 to 12 minutes, until firm to the thouch and dry. Transfer to wire racks to cool.

# CHOCOLATE REFRIGERATOR COOKIES II

Refrigerator Cookies

YIELD: *7 to 8 dozen*
TOTAL TIME: *40 minutes*
CHILLING TIME: *4 hours*

# CHOCOLATE RUM BALLS

Formed Cookies

YIELD: *2 to 3 dozen*

TOTAL TIME: *30 minutes*

SITTING TIME: *1 hour*

**1½ cups crushed chocolate wafer cookies**
**½ cup powdered sugar**
**½ cup walnuts, ground fine**
**¼ cup light corn syrup**
**3 tablespoons rum**
**Powdered sugar for rolling**

**1** In a large bowl, combine the crushed cookies, powdered sugar, and walnuts.

**2** In a small saucepan, heat the light corn syrup and rum until warm. Add the dry ingredients and blend thoroughly.

**3** Pinch off walnut-sized pieces of dough and roll into balls. Roll in powdered sugar and place on wire racks.

**4** Let sit for 1 hour.

**5** Roll the balls in powdered sugar a second time. Store in an airtight container.

# CHOCOLATE SANDWICHES

Rolled Cookies

YIELD: *3 to 4 dozen*

TOTAL TIME: *45 minutes*

**1¼ cups all-purpose flour**
**1 cup walnuts, ground fine**
**½ teaspoon salt**
**⅔ cup vegetable shortening**
**1 cup granulated sugar**
**1 teaspoon vanilla extract**
**¾ cup semisweet chocolate chips**

**1** Preheat the oven to 400 degrees. Lightly grease 2 baking sheets.

**2** Combine the flour, walnuts, and salt.

**3** In a large bowl, cream the vegetable shortening and sugar. Beat in the vanilla. Gradually blend in the dry ingredients.

**4** On a floured surface, roll out the dough to a thickness of ⅛ inch. Using a 2-inch fluted round cookie cutter, cut the dough into rounds and place 1 inch apart on the prepared baking sheets.

**5** Bake for 8 to 10 minutes, until firm to the touch. Transfer to wire racks to cool.

**6** Melt the chocolate in a double boiler over low heat, stirring until smooth. Spread a thin layer of chocolate on the bottom half of the cookies and top with the remaining cookies to form sandwich cookies.

**Baking notes:** These cookies tend to be dry. This can be remedied by using Chocolate Butter Cream for the filling (see Pantry).

2 ounces semisweet chocolate,
  chopped
2⅔ cups all-purpose flour
2 teaspoons cream of tartar
1 teaspoon baking soda
¼ teaspoon salt
1 cup vegetable shortening
1¼ cups granulated sugar
2 large eggs
½ teaspoon vanilla extract
Granulated sugar for rolling

**1** Melt the chocolate in a double boiler over low heat, stirring until smooth. Remove from the heat.

**2** Combine the flour, cream of tartar, baking soda, and salt.

**3** In a large bowl, cream the vegetable shortening and sugar. Beat in the eggs. Beat in the melted chocolate and vanilla extract. Gradually blend in the dry ingredients. Cover and chill for 2 hours.

**4** Preheat the oven to 400 degrees.

**5** Pinch off walnut-sized pieces and roll into balls. Roll in granulated sugar and place 1½ inches apart on ungreased baking sheets.

**6** Bake for 8 to 10 minutes, until firm to the touch. Transfer to wire racks to cool.

# CHOCOLATE SPARKLES

Formed Cookies

YIELD: *5 to 6 dozen*
TOTAL TIME: *30 minutes*
CHILLING TIME: *2 hours*

2 ounces bittersweet chocolate,
  chopped
3 cups all-purpose flour
1 cup walnuts, ground fine
1 teaspoon baking soda
1 teaspoon ground cinnamon
1 teaspoon ground allspice
½ teaspoon ground cloves
½ cup butter, at room temperature
1½ cups granulated sugar
2 large eggs
⅔ cup sour cream
1 cup raisins

**1** Preheat the oven to 350 degrees.

**2** Melt the chocolate in a double boiler over low heat, stirring until smooth. Remove from the heat.

**3** Combine the flour, walnuts, baking soda, and spices.

**4** In a large bowl, cream the butter and sugar. Beat in the eggs one at a time, beating vigorously after each addition. Beat in the sour cream and melted chocolate. Gradually blend in the dry ingredients. Fold in the raisins.

**5** Drop the dough by spoonfuls 1½ inches apart onto ungreased baking sheets.

**6** Bake for 18 to 20 minutes, until firm. Transfer to wire racks to cool.

# CHOCOLATE SPICE DROPS

Drop Cookies

YIELD: *6 to 7 dozen*
TOTAL TIME: *30 minutes*

2 ounces semisweet chocolate,
  chopped
1½ cups all-purpose flour
½ teaspoon baking soda
¼ teaspoon salt
½ cup vegetable shortening
1 cup packed light brown sugar
1 large egg
1 teaspoon vanilla extract
½ cup shredded coconut
½ cup walnuts, chopped

**1** Preheat the oven to 350 degrees. Lightly grease a 13 by 9-inch baking pan.

**2** Melt the chocolate in a double boiler over low heat, stirring until smooth. Remove from the heat.

**3** Combine the flour, baking soda, and salt.

**4** In a large bowl, cream the vegetable shortening and brown sugar. Beat in the egg. Beat in the melted chocolate and vanilla extract. Gradually blend in the dry ingredients.

**5** Spread the batter evenly in the prepared baking pan. Sprinkle the coconut and walnuts over the top.

**6** Bake for 10 to 12 minutes, until firm to the touch. Cool in the pan on a wire rack before cutting into large or small bars.

# CHOCOLATE SQUARES

Bar Cookies

YIELD: *1 to 3 dozen*
TOTAL TIME: *30 minutes*

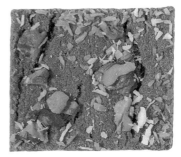

# CHOCOLATE STICKS

Formed Cookies

YIELD: *2 to 3 dozen*
TOTAL TIME: *30 minutes*

3 ounces unsweetened chocolate, chopped
3 cups all-purpose flour
½ teaspoon baking soda
½ teaspoon salt
⅔ cup butter, at room temperature
½ cups granulated sugar
2 large eggs
1 teaspoon almond extract

**1** Preheat the oven to 400 degrees.

**2** Melt the chocolate in a double boiler over low heat, stirring until smooth. Remove from the heat.

**3** Combine the flour, baking soda, and salt.

**4** In a large bowl, cream the butter and sugar. Beat in the melted chocolate. Beat in the eggs. Beat in the almond extract. Gradually blend in the dry ingredients.

**5** Fill a cookie press or a pastry bag fitted with a medium plain tip with the dough. Press or pipe out 3½ inch by ½-inch-wide strips onto ungreased baking sheets, spacing them 1 inch apart.

**6** Bake for 10 to 12 minutes, or until firm to the touch. Transfer to wire racks to cool.

# CHOCOLATE SUGAR COOKIES

Rolled Cookies

YIELD: *5 to 6 dozen*
TOTAL TIME: *30 minutes*
CHILLING TIME: *2 hours*

3¾ cups all-purpose flour
1½ teaspoons baking powder
½ teaspoon salt
1 cup vegetable shortening
1½ cups granulated sugar
2 large eggs
¼ cup chocolate syrup
2 teaspoons vanilla extract
Granulated sugar for sprinkling

**1** Combine the flour, baking powder, and salt.

**2** In a large bowl, cream the vegetable shortening and sugar. Beat in the eggs. Beat in the chocolate syrup and vanilla extract. Gradually blend in the dry ingredients. Cover and chill for 2 hours.

**3** Preheat the oven to 375 degrees. Lightly grease 2 baking sheets.

**4** On a floured surface, roll out the dough to a thickness of ⅛ inch. Using a 2-inch round cookie cutter, cut the dough rounds and place 1½ inches apart on the prepared baking sheets. Lightly brush the cookies with water and sprinkle with granulated sugar.

**5** Bake for 8 to 9 minutes, until firm to the touch. Transfer to wire racks to cool.

**Baking notes:** This dough can also be used for refrigerator cookies. Form the dough into a log 2 inches in diameter, wrap in waxed paper, and chill overnight. Slice into ¼-inch slices and bake as directed.

2 cups all-purpose flour
½ teaspoon baking powder
¼ teaspoon ground cinnamon
½ cup vegetable shortening
1¾ cups powdered sugar
2 large eggs
1 teaspoon fresh lemon juice
Vanilla Icing (see Pantry)

**1** Combine the flour, baking powder, and cinnamon.

**2** In a large bowl, cream the vegetable shortening and powdered sugar. Beat in the eggs one at a time, beating vigorously after each addition. Beat in the lemon juice. Gradually blend in the dry ingredients. Cover and chill for 8 hours.

**3** Preheat the oven to 350 degrees. Lightly grease 2 baking sheets.

**4** On a floured surface, roll out the dough to a thickness of ⅛ inch. Using a bell-shaped cookie cutter, cut out cookies and place 1½ inches apart on the prepared baking sheets.

**5** Bake for 8 to 10 minutes, until firm to the touch. Transfer to wire racks to cool.

**6** Decorate the cookies with the icing (see Baking notes).

**Baking notes:** There are many different ways to decorate these cookies. You can frost them with the vanilla icing and then pipe lines of colored icing across the bells. Or press small candies or colored sprinkles into the white icing. Or don't ice them at all—simply sprinkle the cookies with colored sugar crystals or powdered sugar. And of course you can cut the dough into different shapes to make Christmas stars or trees or angels. If you want to use these as Christmas ornaments, cut paper straws into ½-inch lengths and press a piece of straw through the top of each cookie before baking. You can decorate both sides of the cookie ornaments: Frost one side of the cookies and let dry completely before decorating the other side.

# CHRISTMAS BELLS

Rolled Cookies

YIELD: *3 to 4 dozen*
TOTAL TIME: *30 minutes*
CHILLING TIME: *8 hours*

---

2 cups all-purpose flour
2 teaspoons baking powder
½ teaspoon ground cinnamon
½ teaspoon ground cloves
½ teaspoon salt
1 cup butter, at room temperature
1 cup granulated sugar
4 large eggs
¼ cup Amaretto
4 cups pecans, chopped fine
1½ cups red and green glacé cherries, chopped
1½ cups red and green candied pineapple pieces

**1** Combine the flour, baking powder, spices, and salt.

**2** In a large bowl, cream the butter and sugar. Beat in the eggs. Beat in the Amaretto. Gradually blend in the dry ingredients. Fold in the pecans. Fold in the glacé cherries and pineapple. Cover and chill for 8 hours.

**3** Preheat the oven to 350 degrees.

**4** Drop the dough by spoonfuls 1½ inches apart on ungreased baking sheets.

**5** Bake for 12 to 15 minutes, until lightly colored. Transfer to wire racks to cool.

**Baking notes:** If desired, decorate these cookies with Vanilla Icing (see Pantry).

# CHRISTMAS COOKIES I

Drop Cookies

YIELD: *1 to 2 dozen*
TOTAL TIME: *30 minutes*
CHILLING TIME: *8 hours*

# CHRISTMAS COOKIES II

Formed Cookies

YIELD: *5 to 6 dozen*
TOTAL TIME: *30 minutes*
CHILLLING TIME: *8 hours*

2 cups all-purpose flour
1 teaspoon baking soda
¼ teaspoon salt
½ cup vegetable shortening
⅔ cup packed light brown sugar
1 large egg
¼ cup cider vinegar
1½ teaspoons rum
½ cup flaked coconut
½ cup candied citrus peel, chopped fine
½ cup red and green glacé cherries
1 large egg white, beaten
¼ cup slivered almonds for the topping

**1** Combine the flour, baking soda, and salt.

**2** In a large bowl, cream the vegetable shortening and sugar. Beat in the egg. Beat in the vinegar and rum. Gradually blend in the dry ingredients. Fold in the coconut, candied citrus peel, and glacé cherries. Cover and chill for 8 hours or overnight.

**3** Preheat the oven to 350 degrees. Lightly grease 2 baking sheets.

**4** Working with one quarter of the dough at a time, pinch off walnut-sized pieces of dough and roll into balls. Place 2 inches apart on the prepared baking sheets. Flatten each ball with the bottom of a glass dipped in flour, then brush the cookies with the beaten egg white and sprinkle with the slivered almonds.

**5** Bake for 8 to 10 minutes, until lightly colored. Transfer to wire racks to cool.

# CHRISTMAS COOKIES III

Rolled Cookies

YIELD: *3 to 5 dozen*
TOTAL TIME: *30 minutes*
CHILLING TIME: *2 hours*

1½ cups all-purpose flour
¼ teaspoon ground cinnamon
½ teaspoon grated orange zest
¼ teaspoon grated lemon zest
6 tablespoons butter, at room temperature
¼ cup granulated sugar
1 large egg
2 tablespoons canola oil
1½ teaspoons white port
Powdered sugar for sprinkling

**1** Combine the flour, cinnamon, and orange and lemon zest.

**2** In a large bowl, cream the butter and sugar. Beat in the egg. Beat in the oil and wine. Gradually blend in the dry ingredients. Cover and chill 2 for hours.

**3** Preheat the oven to 350 degrees. Lightly grease 2 baking sheets.

**4** On a floured surface, roll out the dough to a thickness of ¼ inch. Using cookie cutters, cut into shapes and place 1½ inches apart on the prepared baking sheets.

**5** Bake for 12 to 15 minutes, until lightly colored. Transfer to wire racks to cool.

**6** When cool, sprinkle the cookies with powdered sugar.

2½ cups all-purpose flour
2 teaspoons baking powder
1 teaspoon ground cinnamon
1 cup butter, at room temperature
1 cup granulated sugar
2 large eggs
1 teaspoon almond extract
½ cup almonds, chopped
1 large egg white, beaten

**1** Preheat the oven to 375 degrees. Lightly grease 2 baking sheets.

**2** Combine the flour, baking powder, almonds, and cinnamon.

**3** In a large bowl, cream the butter and sugar. Beat in the eggs. Beat in the almond extract. Gradually blend in the dry ingredients. Fold in the almonds.

**4** On a floured surface, roll out the dough to a thickness of ¼ inch. Using cookie cutter, cut into shapes. Place 1½ inches apart on the prepared baking sheets and brush with the beaten egg white.

**5** Bake for 10 to 12 minutes, until lightly colored. Transfer to wire racks to cool.

# CHRISTMAS COOKIES IV

Rolled Cookies

YIELD: *4 to 5 dozen*
TOTAL TIME: *40 minutes*

---

4½ cups unbleached all-purpose flour
1 cup nonfat dry milk
¾ teaspoon ground ginger
¾ teaspoon ground cinnamon
¼ teaspoon ground mace
¼ teaspoon ground allspice
¼ teaspoon ground nutmeg
¼ teaspoon ground cloves
1 cup molasses
½ cup canola oil
Colored sugar crystals for sprinkling

**1** Combine the flour, milk, and spices.

**2** In a large saucepan, heat the molasses and canola oil until warm. Remove from the heat and gradually blend into the dry ingredients. The dough will be stiff. Wrap the dough in waxed paper and chill for 4 hours.

**3** Preheat the oven to 375 degrees. Lightly grease 2 baking sheets.

**4** On a floured surface, roll out the dough to a thickness of ¼. Using cookie cutters, cut into shapes and place 1½ inches apart on the prepared baking sheets. Sprinkle colored sugar crystals over the cookies.

**5** Bake for 6 to 8 minutes, until lightly colored. Transfer to wire racks to cool.

**Baking notes:** These cookies should be stored in airtight containers for at least 2 weeks to age before serving. They keep very well.

# CHRISTMAS COOKIES V

Rolled Cookies

YIELD: *4 to 5 dozen*
TOTAL TIME: *40 minutes*
CHILLING TIME: *4 hours*

C

# CHRISTMAS EVE COOKIES

Formed Cookies

YIELD: *2 to 4 dozen*
TOTAL TIME: *30 minutes*

2½ cups whole wheat flour
1½ tablespoons brewer's yeast
¾ cup nonfat dry milk
1 teaspoon salt
1 tablespoon honey
¼ cup water

1  Preheat the oven to 400 degrees. Lightly grease 2 baking sheets.

2  Combine the flour, yeast, dry milk, and salt.

3  In a saucepan, warm the honey and water. Remove from the heat. Gradually blend in the dry ingredients. Form the dough into a log ½ inch square. Cut the log into ½ inch strips and cut the strips into ½ inch cubes. Place the cubes 1 inch apart on the pre-pared baking sheets.

4  Bake for 8 to 10 minutes, until lightly colored. Transfer to wire racks to cool.

# CHRISTMAS ORNAMENT COOKIES

Rolled Cookies

YIELD: *varies according to size of cookie cutter*
TOTAL TIME *30 minutes*
CHILLING TIME: *4 hours*

3½ cups all-purpose flour
1 teaspoon baking powder
½ teaspoon salt
1 cup vegetable shortening
1½ cups granulated sugar
2 large eggs
2 teaspoons vanilla extract
Paper drinking straws, cut into
  1-inch lengths (optional)

1  Combine the flour, baking powder, and salt.

2  In a large bowl, cream the vegetable shortening and sugar. Beat in the eggs. Beat in the vanilla extract. Gradually blend in the dry ingredients. Cover and chill for 4 hours.

3  Preheat the oven to 400 degrees. Lightly grease 2 baking sheets.

4  On a floured surface, roll out the dough ⅛ inch thick. Using cookie cutters, cut into shapes. Place 1½ inches apart on the pre-pared baking sheets and press a piece of drinking straw through the top of each cookie.

5  Bake for 8 to 10 minutes, until lightly colored. Transfer to wire racks and let cool before removing the straws. Decorate with the colored icing if desired.

**Baking notes:** If you are looking for cookies to use as an ornament and are not interested in eating them afterwards, see the recipe for nonedible cookies (see Pantry).

4 cups all-purpose flour
1¼ teaspoons baking powder
1½ cups butter, at room temperature
½ cup granulated sugar
1 large egg
1 cup light cream
4 drops green food coloring
1 large egg white, beaten
Glacé cherries, halved, for decoration
Sugar crystals for sprinkling

**1** Combine the flour and baking powder.

**2** In a large bowl, cream the butter and sugar. Beat in the egg and cream. Beat in the food coloring. Gradually blend in the dry ingredients. Cover and chill for 4 hours.

**3** Preheat the oven to 400 degrees. Lightly grease 2 baking sheets.

**4** Pinch off pieces of the dough and roll each one into a pencil-thin rope about 8 inches long. To shape each wreath, twist 2 ropes together and form into a ring, pinching the ends together. Place 1 inch apart on the prepared baking sheets. Brush with the beaten egg white and sprinkle with sugar crystals. Press half a glacé cherry into each wreath at the point where the ropes join.

**5** Bake for 18 to 20 minutes, until the cookies start to color. Transfer to wire racks to cool.

# CHRISTMAS WREATHS I

Formed Cookies

YIELD: *3 to 4 dozen*
TOTAL TIME: *30 minutes*
CHILLING TIME: *4 hours*

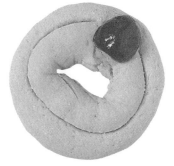

---

1 cup vegetable shortening
½ cup granulated sugar
1 large egg
1 teaspoon vanilla extract
2½ tablespoons all-purpose flour
1⅓ cups almonds, ground fine
¼ cup maple syrup
Red and green glacé cherries, halved

**1** Preheat the oven to 350 degrees. Lightly grease 2 baking sheets.

**2** In a large bowl, cream the vegetable shortening and sugar. Beat in the egg and vanilla extract. Gradually blend in the flour. Transfer one-third of the dough to a medium ball.

**3** Fill a cookie press or a pastry bag fitted with a small star tip with the remaining dough and press or pipe out small rings onto the prepared baking sheets, spacing them 1 inch apart.

**4** Add the almonds and maple syrup to the reserved cookie dough and blend well. Place ¼ to ½ teaspoon of this filling in the center of each ring, and place a half cherry at the point where the ends of each ring join.

**5** Bake for 10 to 12 minutes, until lightly colored. Transfer to wire racks to cool.

# CHRISTMAS WREATHS II

Formed Cookies

YIELD: *3 to 4 dozen*
TOTAL TIME: *30 minutes*

# CHRISTMAS WREATHS III

Formed Cookies

YIELD: *2 dozen*
TOTAL TIME: *30 minutes*
CHILLING TIME: *1 hour*

6 tablespoons vegetable shortening
32 marshmallows
½ teaspoon vanilla extract
½ teaspoon almond extract
½ teaspoon green food coloring
4 cups cornflakes
Red cinnamon candies for
    decoration

1  Line 2 baking sheets with waxed paper.

2  In a double boiler, melt the vegetable shortening and marshmallows over low heat, stirring until smooth. Remove from the heat and beat in the vanilla extract, almond extract, and food coloring. Gradually blend in the cornflakes.

3  Return the double boiler to the heat. Lightly oil your hands to make working with the mixture easier.

4  Drop the mixture by tablespoonfuls 1½ inches apart onto the prepared baking sheets. With your fingers, form each mound into a wreath. Sprinkle with a few red cinnamon candies. Let cool for 15 minutes, then chill for 1 hour to firm.

**Baking notes:**  These are great cookies to make with your kids. Prepare the cornflake mixture and let the children form the wreath.

# CHUNKY CHOCOLATE BROWNIES

Bar Cookies

YIELD: *1 to 2 dozen*
TOTAL TIME: *30 minutes*

½ cup plus 2 tablespoons vegetable
    shortening
¼ cup unsweetened cocoa powder
1 cup granulated sugar
2 large eggs
1 teaspoon vanilla extract
⅔ cup all-purpose flour
2½ ounces milk chocolate, cut into
    small chunks
2½ ounces white chocolate, cut into
    small chunks
¾ cup chocolate glaze
12 to 24 walnut halves for decoration

1  Preheat the oven to 350 degrees. Lightly grease a 9-inch square baking pan.

2  In the top of a double boiler, melt the vegetable shortening with the cocoa powder, stirring until smooth. Remove from the

heat and beat in the sugar. Beat in the eggs and vanilla extract. Gradually blend in the flour. Fold in the milk and white chocolate chunks. Spread the mixture evenly in the prepared baking pan.

3  Bake for 18 to 20 minutes until firm to the touch.

4  Spread the chocolate glaze over the top. Cut into large or small bars, then place a walnut in the center of each. Cool in the pan on a wire rack.

# CINNAMON BALLS

Formed Cookies

YIELD: *3 to 4 dozen*
TOTAL TIME: *30 minutes*

3 cups all-purpose flour
2 teaspoons baking powder
¼ teaspoon salt
1 cup vegetable shortening
1⅓ cups granulated sugar
2 large eggs
1 teaspoon vanilla extract

CINNAMON SUGAR
3 tablespoons granulated sugar
2 teaspoons ground cinnamon

1  Preheat the oven to 350 degrees. Lightly grease 2 baking sheets.

2  Combine the flour, baking powder, and salt.

3  In a large bowl, cream the vegetable shortening and sugar. Beat in the eggs and vanilla extract. Gradually blend in the dry ingredients.

4  Combine the sugar and cinnamon in a shallow dish.

5  Pinch off 1-inch pieces of dough and roll into balls. Roll in the cinnamon sugar and place 1½ inches apart on the prepared baking sheets.

6  Bake for 10 to 14 minutes, until lightly colored. Transfer to wire racks to cool.

4½ cups all-purpose flour
1 teaspoon baking soda
2 teaspoons ground ginger
1 teaspoon salt
¾ cup vegetable shortening
¾ cup granulated sugar
1 large egg
1 cup molasses, warmed

FILLING
1 tablespoon butter, at room
  temperature
1 cup powdered sugar
½ teaspoon ground cinnamon
1 tablespoon boiling water

**1** Preheat the oven to 350
degrees. Lightly grease 2 baking
sheets.

**2** Combine the flour, baking
soda, ginger, and salt.

**3** In a large bowl, cream the vegetable shortening and sugar. Beat
in the egg. Beat in the molasses.
Gradually blend in the dry
ingredients.

**4** On a floured surface, roll out
the dough to a thickness of ⅛
inch. Using a 2-inch round cookie
cutter, cut out an even numbers
of cookies. Using a 1-inch fancy
cookie cutter, cut out the centers
of half the rounds. Place the
rounds 1½ inches apart on the
prepared baking sheets.

**5** Bake for 10 to 12 minutes, until
lightly colored. Transfer to wire
racks to cool.

**6** To make the filling, cream the
butter and sugar together in a
medium bowl. Beat in the cinnamon. Beat in the boiling water.

**7** To assemble the sandwiches,
spread ½ teaspoon of the filling
across the bottom of each plain
cookie. Top with the cut-out
cookies and press together
gently.

# CINNAMON-CREAM MOLASSES COOKIES

Rolled Cookies

YIELD: *3 to 4 dozen*
TOTAL TIME: *40 minutes*

---

1¼ cups all-purpose flour
1 teaspoon baking soda
¼ teaspoon salt
½ cup vegetable shortening
1 cup granulated sugar
1 large egg
1 teaspoon almond extract
½ cup almonds, chopped fine
2 teaspoons ground cinnamon

**1** Preheat the oven to 375
degrees. Lightly grease 2 baking
sheets.

**2** Combine the flour, baking
soda, and salt.

**3** In a large bowl, cream the vegetable shortening and sugar. Beat
in the egg. Beat in the almond
extract. Gradually blend in the
dry ingredients.

**4** Combine the almonds and cinnamon in a shallow dish.

**5** Pinch off walnut-sized pieces
of dough and roll into balls. Roll
in the almond mixture and place
1½ inches apart on the prepared
baking sheets.

**6** Bake for 10 to 12 minutes, until
lightly colored. Transfer to wire
racks to cool.

# CINNAMON CRISPS

Formed Cookies

YIELD: *3 to 4 dozen*
TOTAL TIME: *30 minutes*

# CINNAMON DIAMONDS

Bar Cookies

YIELD: *3 to 4 dozen*
TOTAL TIME: *30 minutes*

2 cups all-purpose flour
1½ teaspoons ground cinnamon
1 cup vegetable shortening
1 cup packed light brown sugar
1 large egg, separated
1 teaspoon vanilla extract
¾ cup walnuts, chopped
Glacé cherries, halved (optional)

**1** Preheat the oven to 350 degrees. Lightly grease a 13 by 9-inch baking pan.

**2** Combine the flour and cinnamon.

**3** In a large bowl, cream the vegetable shortening and brown sugar. Beat in the egg yolk and vanilla extract. Gradually blend in the dry ingredients.

**4** Spread the dough into the prepared baking pan.

**5** Beat the egg white until foamy. Brush over the top of the crust and sprinkle with the chopped nuts.

**6** Bake for 18 to 20 minutes, until lightly colored on top. Cut lengthwise into strips, then cut each strip on the diagonal to form diamonds. If desired, place a glacé cherry half in the center of each diamond. Cool in the pan on a wire rack.

# CINNAMON-GINGER WAFERS

Formed Cookies

YIELD: *3 to 5 dozen*
TOTAL TIME: *30 minutes*
CHILLING TIME: *4 hours*

2 cups all-purpose flour
¼ teaspoon baking powder
1¼ teaspoons ground ginger
1¼ teaspoons ground cinnamon
6 tablespoons molasses
⅓ cup granulated sugar
1 large egg yolk

**1** Combine the flour, baking powder, and spices.

**2** In a double boiler, heat the molasses and sugar, stirring until the sugar is dissolved. Remove from the heat and beat in the egg yolk. Gradually blend in the dry ingredients. Transfer to a bowl, cover, and refrigerate for 4 hours.

**3** Preheat the oven to 400 degrees. Lightly grease 2 baking sheets.

**4** Dust your hands with flour. Pinch off ½-inch pieces of dough and roll into balls. Place 1 inch apart on the prepared baking sheets. With the back of a spoon dipped in flour, flatten each cookie into a wafer-thin round.

**5** Bake for 3 to 4 minutes, just until the edges begin to color. Carefully transfer to wire racks to cool.

**Baking notes:** The secret of making these cookies is in the handling. They burn easily, so watch carefully. And they are so thin that they break easily after they are baked.

# CINNAMON STICKS

Formed Cookies

YIELD: *2 to 3 dozen*
TOTAL TIME: *30 minutes*

3 cups all-purpose flour
½ teaspoon baking soda
½ teaspoon salt
⅔ cup butter, at room temperature
½ cups granulated sugar
2 large eggs
1 teaspoon almond extract

**1** Preheat the oven to 400 degrees.

**2** Combine the flour, baking soda, and salt.

**3** In a large bowl, cream the butter and sugar. Beat in the eggs and almond extract. Gradually blend in the dry ingredients.

**4** Place the dough in a cookie press or a pastry bag fitted with a medium plain tip and press or pipe out 3½ inch by ¼-inch-thick strips onto ungreased baking sheets, spacing them 1 inch apart.

**5** Bake for 10 to 12 minutes, until lightly colored. Cool for 1 minute on the baking sheets before transferring to wire racks to cool completely.

2½ cups all-purpose flour
2 teaspoons baking powder
1 teaspoon baking soda
½ teaspoon ground cinnamon
¼ teaspoon ground cloves
¼ cup vegetable shortening
2 large eggs
1½ cups grapefruit juice
1 teaspoon orange extract
1 cup cranberries, chopped
1 cup walnuts, chopped

**TOPPING**
¾ cup flaked coconut
¾ cup crushed pineapple, drained

**1** Preheat the oven to 350 degrees. Lightly grease a 13 by 9-inch baking pan.

**2** Combine the flour, baking powder, baking soda, and spices.

**3** In a large bowl, beat the vegetable shortening, eggs, grapefruit juice, and orange extract.

Gradually blend in the dry ingredients. Fold in the cranberries and walnuts.

**4** Spread the mixture evenly in the prepared baking pan. Sprinkle the coconut and pineapple over the top.

**5** Bake for 20 to 25 minutes, until firm to the touch. Cool in the pan on a wire rack before cutting into large or small bars.

# CITRUS BARS I

Bar Cookies

YIELD: *2 to 3 dozen*
TOTAL TIME: *45 minutes*

---

**CRUST**
2 cups all-purpose flour
¼ cup walnuts, ground fine
½ teaspoon baking powder
¼ cup granulated sugar
¼ cup rolled oats
½ cup vegetable shortening

**TOPPING**
4 large eggs
2 cups granulated sugar
¼ cup fresh lemon juice
1 teaspoon grated lemon zest
¼ cup all-purpose flour

**1** Preheat the oven to 350 degrees. Lightly grease a 13 by 9-inch baking pan.

**2** To make the crust, combine the flour, walnuts, baking powder, sugar, and oats in a large bowl. Cut in the shortening. Press the mixture evenly into the prepared baking pan.

**3** Bake for 30 minutes.

**4** Meanwhile, in a medium bowl, beat the eggs until thick and light-colored. Beat in the sugar. Beat in the lemon juice and lemon zest. Beat in the flour.

**5** Pour the topping over the hot crust. Bake for 20 minutes longer, or until a toothpick inserted into the center comes out clean. Cool in the pan on a wire rack before cutting into large or small bars.

**Baking notes:** Substitute orange, grapefruit, or other citrus juice and zest for the lemon.

# CITRUS BARS II

Bar Cookies

YIELD: *1 to 3 dozen*
TOTAL TIME: *60 minutes*

# COCOA BROWNIES

Bar Cookies

YIELD: *2 to 3 dozen*
TOTAL TIME: *45 minutes*

½ cup all-purpose flour
½ cup unsweetened cocoa powder
1 teaspoon baking powder
Pinch of salt
3 large eggs
1¼ cups packed light brown sugar
1 teaspoon vanilla extract
1 cup walnuts, chopped

**1** Preheat the oven to 325 degrees. Lightly grease a 9-inch square baking pan.

**2** Combine the flour, cocoa, baking powder, and salt.

**3** In a large bowl, beat the eggs and brown sugar together until thick. Beat in the vanilla extract.

Gradually blend in the dry ingredients.

**4** Spread the mixture evenly into the prepared baking pan. Sprinkle the walnuts over the top.

**5** Bake for 20 to 25 minutes, until a toothpick inserted in the center comes out clean. Cool in the pan on a wire rack before cutting into large or small bars.

# COCOA DROP COOKIES

Drop Cookies

YIELD: *4 to 5 dozen*
TOTAL TIME: *40 minutes*

2 cups all-purpose flour
2 teaspoons baking powder
¼ teaspoon salt
6 tablespoons butter, at room temperature
1 cup granulated sugar
3 tablespoons unsweetened cocoa powder
3 large eggs
1 tablespoon milk
2 teaspoons vanilla extract
Walnut halves for decoration

**1** Preheat the oven to 375 degrees. Lightly grease 2 baking sheets.

**2** Combine the flour, baking powder, and salt.

**3** In a large bowl, cream the butter and sugar. Beat in the cocoa.

Beat in the eggs, milk, and vanilla extract.

**4** Drop the dough by spoonfuls 1½ inches apart onto the prepared baking sheets. Press a walnut half into the center of each cookie.

**5** Bake for 10 to 12 minutes, until firm to the touch. Transfer to wire racks to cool.

# COCOA INDIANS

Bar Cookies

YIELD: *1 to 2 dozen*
TOTAL TIME: *35 minutes*

1 cup all-purpose flour
¼ cup unsweetened cocoa powder
¼ teaspoon baking powder
¼ teaspoon salt
½ cup vegetable shortening
1 cup granulated sugar
2 large eggs
¼ cup milk
1 teaspoon vanilla extract
⅔ cup raisins

**1** Preheat the oven to 400 degrees. Lightly grease a 13 by 9 inch baking pan.

**2** Combine the flour, cocoa, baking powder, and salt.

**3** In a large bowl, cream the vegetable shortening and sugar. Beat

in the eggs. Beat in the milk and vanilla extract. Gradually blend in the dry ingredients. Fold in the raisins

**4** Spread the mixture evenly in the prepared baking pan.

**5** Bake for 20 to 25 minutes, until a toothpick inserted inserted in the center comes out clean. Cool slightly in the pan before cutting into large or small bars.

# Cocoa Molasses Bars

Bar Cookies

YIELD: *1 to 4 dozen*
TOTAL TIME: *35–40 minutes*

2 cups all-purpose flour
¼ cup unsweetened cocoa powder
1 teaspoon baking powder
1 teaspoon ground cinnamon
1 teaspoon ground allspice
½ teaspoon ground nutmeg
½ teaspoon salt
3 large eggs
2 cups packed dark brown sugar
¼ cup molasses
2 tablespoons rum
1 teaspoon vanilla extract
1½ cups pecans, chopped

**1** Preheat the oven to 325 degrees. Lightly grease a 13 by 9-inch baking pan.

**2** Combine the flour, cocoa, baking powder, spices, and salt.

**3** In a large bowl, beat the eggs until thick and light-colored. Beat in the brown sugar. Beat in the molasses, rum, and vanilla extract. Gradually blend in the dry ingredients. Fold in the pecans. Spread the batter evenly in the prepared baking pan.

**4** Bake for 25 to 30 minutes, until the top looks dry and a toothpick inserted into the center comes out clean. Cool in the pan on a wire rack before cutting into large or small bars.

# Cocoa Pecan Cookies

Drop Cookies

YIELD: *3 to 4 dozen*
TOTAL TIME: *30 minutes.*

¾ cup all-purpose flour
2 tablespoons unsweetened cocoa powder
½ teaspoon salt
½ cup butter, at room temperature
1 cup granulated sugar
2 large eggs
1 tablespoon crème de cacao
1 cup pecans, chopped

**1** Preheat the oven to 350 degrees. Lightly grease 2 baking sheets.

**2** Combine the flour, cocoa, and salt.

**3** In a large bowl, cream the butter and sugar. Beat in the eggs. Beat in the crème de cacao. Gradually blend in the dry ingredients. Fold in the pecans.

**4** Drop the dough by spoonfuls 1½ inches apart onto the prepared baking sheets.

**5** Bake for 12 to 15 minutes, until lightly colored. Transfer to wire racks to cool.

# Coconut Balls I

Drop Cookies

YIELD: *2 to 3 dozen*
TOTAL TIME: *30 minutes*

2 cups grated fresh (or packaged) coconut
3 tablespoons marsala
3 tablespoons Amaretto
2 large egg whites
Powdered sugar

**1** Preheat the oven to 350 degrees. Generously grease 2 baking sheets.

**2** In a medium bowl, combine the coconut, marsala and Amaretto.

**3** In a large bowl, beat the egg whites until they hold stiff peaks. Fold in the coconut mixture.

**4** Using a spoon dipped in powdered sugar, drop the dough by spoonfuls 1½ inches apart onto the prepared baking sheets.

**5** Bake for 18 to 20 minutes, until lightly colored. Transfer to wire racks to cool

# COCONUT BALLS II

Formed Cookies

YIELD: *5 to 6 dozen*
TOTAL TIME: *30 minutes*
CHILLING TIME: *4 hours*

2 cups powdered sugar
¾ cup mashed potatoes
4 cups shredded coconut
1 tablespoon Amaretto

**TOPPING**
1 package chocolate frosting mix
3 tablespoons water
2 tablespoons butter
2 tablespoons corn syrup

**1** In a large bowl, blend together the sugar, mashed potatoes, coconut, and Amaretto. Cover and chill for 4 hours.

**2** In the top of a double boiler, combine all the topping ingredients and heat, stirring, until butter melts and mixture is smooth. Remove from the heat.

**3** Line 2 baking sheets with waxed paper

**4** Pinch off large walnut-sized pieces of the coconut mixture. Dip in the topping and place on the prepared baking sheets. Chill in the refrigerator for at least 2 hours.

**Baking notes:** The mashed potatoes in this recipe are used to form a paste base, similar to using flour and eggs as binding components.

# COCONUT BARS I

Bar Cookies

YIELD: *1 to 2 dozen*
TOTAL TIME: *30 minutes*

2 cups all-purpose flour
1½ teaspoons baking soda
¾ cup vegetable shortening
½ cup packed light brown sugar
1 cup unsweetened applesauce
½ teaspoon vanilla extract
2 cups flaked coconut
½ cup shredded coconut

**1** Preheat the oven to 350 degrees. Lightly grease a 13 by 9-inch baking pan.

**2** Combine the flour and baking soda.

**3** In a large bowl, cream the vegetable shortening and brown sugar. Beat in the applesauce and

vanilla extract. Fold in the flaked coconut.

**4** Spread the dough evenly in the prepared baking pan. Sprinkle the shredded coconut on top.

**5** Bake for 18 to 20 minutes, until the top is lightly colored. Cool in the pan on a wire rack before cutting into large or small bars.

**Baking notes:** For an added touch, drizzle White Sugar Icing over the top before cutting into bars (see Pantry).

# COCONUT BARS II

Bar Cookies

YIELD: *2 dozen*
TOTAL TIME: *40 minutes*

7 tablespoons vegetable shortening, melted
1 cup dried bread crumbs
1 cup shredded coconut
1 cup (6 ounces) butterscotch chips
1 cup (6 ounces) semisweet chocolate chips
1 cup nuts, chopped
One 14-ounce can sweetened condensed milk

**1** Preheat the oven to 350 degrees.

**2** Pour the melted vegetable shortening into a 9-inch square baking pan. Sprinkle the bread crumbs evenly in the pan. Sprinkle the coconut, butterscotch chips, chocolate chips, and nuts

evenly over the bread crumbs. Drizzle the condensed milk over the top.

**3** Bake for 25 to 30 minutes, until firm to the touch. Cool in the pan on a wire rack before cutting into small bars.

¾ cup all-purpose flour
½ teaspoon baking powder
¼ teaspoon salt
½ cup vegetable shortening
1 cup granulated sugar
2 large eggs
1½ tablespoons chocolate syrup
1 teaspoon vanilla extract
1 cup grated fresh (or packaged) coconut

**1** Preheat the oven to 400 degrees. Lightly grease a 9-inch square baking pan.

**2** Combine the flour, baking powder, and salt.

**3** In a large bowl, cream the vegetable shortening and sugar. Beat in the eggs. Beat in the chocolate syrup and vanilla extract. Gradually blend in the dry ingredients.

Fold in the coconut. Spread the mixture evenly in the prepared baking pan.

**4** Bake for 30 to 35 minutes, until a toothpick inserted in the center comes out clean. Cool in the pan on a wire rack before cutting into large or small bars.

# COCONUT BROWNIES

Bar Cookies

YIELD: *1 to 2 dozen*
TOTAL TIME: *45 minutes*

---

2 cups all-purpose flour
½ teaspoon salt
1 cup butter, at room temperature
½ cup powdered sugar
2 teaspoons vanilla extract
1 cup flaked coconut
Powdered sugar for rolling

**1** Combine the flour and salt.

**2** In a large bowl, cream the butter and powdered sugar. Beat in the vanilla extract. Gradually blend in the dry ingredients. Fold in the coconut. Cover and chill for 4 hours.

**3** Preheat the oven to 350 degrees.

**4** Pinch off walnut-sized pieces of dough and roll into balls. Place each ball 1 inch apart on ungreased baking sheets.

**5** Bake for 10 to 12 minutes, until lightly colored. Transfer to wire racks to cool.

**6** Just before serving, roll the balls in powdered sugar.

# COCONUT BUTTERBALLS

Formed Cookies

YIELD: *3 to 4 dozen*
TOTAL TIME: *30 minutes*
CHILLING TIME: *4 hours*

# COCONUT-CARAMEL BARS

Bar Cookies

YIELD: *1 to 2 dozen*
TOTAL TIME: *55 minutes*

**CRUST**
½ cup vegetable shortening
½ cup powdered sugar
1 cup all-purpose flour

**TOPPING**
One 14-ounce can sweetened condensed milk
1 cup (6 ounces) butterscotch chips
1 cup flaked coconut
1 teaspoon vanilla extract

1  Preheat the oven to 350 degrees. Lightly grease a 9-inch square baking pan.

2  To make the crust, cream the vegetable shortening and powdered sugar in a medium bowl. Gradually work in the flour. Press the mixture evenly into the prepared baking pan.

3  Bake for 14 minutes.

4  Meanwhile, make the topping: In a large bowl, combine the condensed milk, butterscotch chips, coconut, and vanilla extract and stir until well blended.

5  Pour the topping mixture over the hot crust. Bake for 25 to 30 minutes longer, until a toothpick inserted in the center comes out clean. Cool in the pan on a wire rack before cutting into large or small bars.

# COCONUT CHEWIES

Bar Cookies

YIELD: *1 to 2 dozen*
TOTAL TIME: *35 minutes*

2 cups all-purpose flour
1 teaspoon baking powder
½ teaspoon salt
⅔ cup vegetable shortening
2 cups packed light brown sugar
3 large eggs
1 teaspoon vanilla extract
1½ cups (9 ounces) semisweet chocolate chips
¾ cup walnuts, chopped
½ cup shredded coconut

1  Preheat the oven to 350 degrees. Lightly grease a 9-inch square baking pan.

2  Combine the flour, baking powder, and salt.

3  In a large bowl, cream the vegetable shortening and brown sugar. Beat in the eggs. Beat in the vanilla extract. Gradually blend in the dry ingredients. Fold in the chocolate chips, walnuts, and coconut. Spread the mixture evenly in the prepared baking pan.

4  Bake for 20 to 25 minutes, until firm to the touch. Cool in the pan on a wire rack before cutting into large or small bars.

# COCONUT CHEWS I

Bar Cookies

YIELD: *2 to 3 dozen*
TOTAL TIME: *45 minutes*

**CRUST**
¾ teaspoon vegetable shortening
3 tablespoons granulated sugar
1½ cups whole wheat flour

**TOPPING**
2 large eggs
1 cup almonds, chopped
1 cup flaked coconut

1  Preheat the oven to 375 degrees. Lightly grease a 13 by 9-inch baking pan.

2  To make the crust, cream the vegetable shortening and sugar in a medium bowl. Gradually blend in the flour. Press the mixture evenly into the bottom of the prepared baking pan.

3  Bake for 15 minutes.

4  Meanwhile, prepare the topping: In a large bowl, beat the eggs with the almonds and coconut.

5  Spread the topping over the hot crust and bake for 20 minutes longer, until set. Cool in the pan on a wire rack before cutting into large or small bars.

1 package white cake mix
½ cup butter, chilled
½ cup milk
1 cup caramel topping (storebought)
¼ cup all-purpose flour
1 cup flaked coconut

1 Preheat the oven to 350 degrees.

2 Put the cake mix in a large bowl and cut in the butter until the mixture resembles coarse crumbs. Stir in the milk. Reserve 1 cup of this mixture. Press the remaining mixture into an ungreased 13 by 9-inch baking pan.

3 Bake for 10 minutes.

4 Meanwhile, combine the caramel topping and flour in a double boiler and cook, stirring constantly. Remove from the heat.

5 Sprinkle the coconut over the warm crust and bake for 5 minutes, until toasted.

6 Sprinkle the reserved crust mixture over the coconut. Drizzle the caramel topping over the top and bake for 20 minutes longer.

7 Cut into large or small bars while still warm and remove the bars to wire racks to cool.

# COCONUT CHEWS II

Bar Cookies

YIELD: *2 to 3 dozen*
TOTAL TIME: *45 minutes*

---

3½ cups all-purpose flour
1 teaspoon baking soda
2 cups vegetable shortening
2 cups granulated sugar
2 large eggs
1 tablespoon almond extract
4 cups shredded coconut
1 large egg white, beaten

1 Combine the flour and baking soda.

2 In a large bowl, cream the vegetable shortening and sugar. Beat in the eggs. Beat in the almond extract. Blend in 3 cups of the coconut. Gradually blend in the dry ingredients.

3 Form the dough into a 1½-inch-thick log. Brush the log with the beaten egg white and roll in the remaining 1 cup coconut.

Wrap in waxed paper and chill for 4 hours.

4 Preheat the oven to 325 degrees.

5 Cut the log into ¼-inch-thick slices and place 1 inch apart on ungreased baking sheets.

6 Bake for 12 to 15 minutes, until lightly colored. Transfer to wire racks to cool.

# COCONUT CLASSICS

Refrigerator Cookies

YIELD: *5 to 6 dozen*
TOTAL TIME: *40 minutes*
CHILLING TIME: *4 hours*

# COCONUT COOKIES I

Refrigerator Cookies

YIELD: *5 to 6 dozen*
TOTAL TIME: *45 minutes*
CHILLING TIME: *8 hours*

2 cups all-purpose flour
½ teaspoon baking soda
1 cup vegetable shortening
1 cup granulated sugar
1 large egg
½ teaspoon almond extract
3½ cups shredded coconut
1 large egg yolk
1 tablespoon milk
About 1 cup whole blanched
    almonds

**1** Combine the flour and baking soda.

**2** In a large bowl, cream the vegetable shortening and sugar. Beat in the egg and almond extract. Fold in 2 cups of the coconut. Gradually blend in the dry ingredients.

**3** Divide the dough into thirds. Form each piece into logs 1½ inches in diameter. Roll the logs in the remaining 1½ cups coconut, pressing gently so it adheres. Wrap in waxed paper and chill for 8 hours or overnight.

**4** Preheat the oven to 350 degrees.

**5** In a small bowl, beat the egg yolk and milk together for an egg glaze.

**6** Cut the logs into ¼-inch-thick slices and place 1 inch apart on ungreased baking sheets. Brush the cookies with the egg glaze and press an almond into the center of each cookie.

**7** Bake for 12 to 15 minutes, until lightly colored. Transfer to wire racks to cool.

# COCONUT COOKIES II

Rolled Cookies

YIELD: *4 to 5 dozen*
TOTAL TIME: *30 minutes*
CHILLING TIME: *3 hours*

1½ cups all-purpose flour
1 cup cornstarch
1 teaspoon baking powder
¼ teaspoon salt
1 cup vegetable shortening
1 cup granulated sugar
1 large egg
1 teaspoon almond extract
1 teaspoon grated orange zest
1⅓ cups shredded coconut

**1** Combine the flour, cornstarch, baking powder, and salt.

**2** In a large bowl, cream the vegetable shortening and sugar. Beat in the egg and almond extract. Beat in the orange zest. Gradually blend in the dry ingredients. Fold in the coconut. Cover and chill for 3 hours.

**3** Preheat the oven to 350 degrees. Lightly grease 2 baking sheets.

**4** On a floured surface, roll out the dough to a thickness of ¼ inch. Using a 2-inch round cookie cutter, cut out rounds and place 1 inch apart on the prepared baking sheets.

**5** Bake for 8 to 10 minutes, until lightly colored. Transfer to wire racks to cool.

1½ cups all-purpose flour
1 teaspoon baking powder
¼ teaspoon baking soda
¼ teaspoon salt
½ cup vegetable shortening
1 cup packed light brown sugar
1 large egg
⅓ cup milk
1½ teaspoon vanilla extract
1½ cups cornflakes
1 cup shredded coconut

**1** Preheat the oven to 350 degrees. Grease 2 baking sheets.

**2** Combine the flour, baking powder, baking soda, and salt.

**3** In a large bowl, cream the vegetable shortening and brown sugar. Beat in the egg, milk, and vanilla. Gradually blend in the dry ingredients. Fold in the cornflakes and coconut.

**4** Drop the dough by spoonfuls 2 inches apart onto the prepared baking sheets.

**5** Bake for 12 to 15 minutes, until lightly colored. Transfer to wire racks to cool.

# COCONUT-CORNFLAKE COOKIES

Drop Cookies

YIELD: *3 to 4 dozen*
TOTAL TIME: *35 minutes*

---

2 tablespoons vegetable shortening
½ cup granulated sugar
1 large egg
2 tablespoons heavy cream
¼ teaspoon rum
1 cup packaged biscuit mix
⅔ cup grated fresh (or packaged) coconut

**1** Preheat the oven to 375 degrees. Lightly grease 2 baking sheets.

**2** In a large bowl, beat the vegetable shortening, sugar, egg, heavy cream, and rum. Gradually blend in the biscuit mix and coconut.

**3** Drop the dough by spoonfuls 1½ inches apart onto the prepared baking sheets.

**4** Bake for 8 to 10 minutes, until lightly colored. Transfer to wire racks to cool.

# COCONUT DISCS

Drop Cookies

YIELD: *5 to 6 dozen*
TOTAL TIME: *35 minutes*

---

1 cup all-purpose flour
⅓ cup granulated sugar
¾ teaspoon baking powder
2 ounces semisweet chocolate, coarsely chopped
¼ cup vegetable shortening
1½ cups flaked coconut

**1** Preheat the oven to 350 degrees.

**2** Combine the flour, sugar, and baking powder.

**3** In a double boiler, melt the chocolate and vegetable shortening over low heat, stirring until smooth. Remove from the heat. Blend in the dry ingredients. Fold in the coconut.

**4** Pinch off walnut-sized pieces of dough and roll into balls. Place 1 inch apart on ungreased baking sheets.

**5** Bake for 20 to 30 minutes, until firm to the touch. Transfer to wire racks to cool.

# COCONUT DREAMS

Formed Cookies

YIELD: *2 to 4 dozen*
TOTAL TIME: *45 minutes*

# COCONUT DROMEDARIES

Rolled Cookies

YIELD: *3 to 4 dozen*
TOTAL TIME: *35 minutes*
CHILLING TIME: *4 hours*

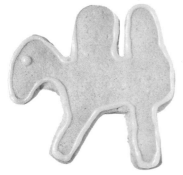

**5 cups all-purpose flour**
**1 teaspoon baking powder**
**1 cup vegetable shortening**
**1 cup granulated sugar**
**3 large eggs**
**3 tablespoons milk**
**2 teaspoons almond extract**
**1 cup shredded coconut**

**1** Combine the flour and baking powder.

**2** In a large bowl, cream the vegetable shortening and sugar. Beat in the eggs. Beat in the milk and almond extract. Gradually blend in the dry ingredients. Fold in the coconut. Cover and chill for 4 hours.

**3** Preheat the oven to 350 degrees.

**4** On a floured surface, roll out the dough to a thickness of ¼ inch. Using a camel-shaped cookie cutter, cut out the cookies and place the cookies 1 inch apart on ungreased baking sheets.

**5** Bake for 12 to 15 minutes, until golden brown. Transfer to wire racks to cool.

**Baking notes:** To decorate these camel cookies, spread a thin layer of chocolate icing over the cookies and sprinkle with finely ground nuts.

# COCONUT DROP COOKIES I

Drop Cookies

YIELD: *3 to 4 dozen*
TOTAL TIME: *30 minutes*

**2 cups all-purpose flour**
**2 teaspoons baking powder**
**⅔ cup vegetable shortening**
**1 cup packed light brown sugar**
**2 large eggs**
**2 tablespoons milk**
**1 teaspoon almond extract**
**2 cups flaked coconut**

**1** Preheat the oven to 350 degrees. Lightly grease 2 baking sheets.

**2** Combine the flour and baking powder.

**3** In a large bowl, combine the vegetable shortening, brown sugar, eggs, milk, and almond extract and beat until smooth.

Gradually blend in the dry ingredients. Fold in the coconut.

**4** Drop the dough by spoonfuls 1½ inches apart onto the prepared baking sheets.

**5** Bake for 12 to 15 minutes, until lightly colored. Transfer to wire racks to cool.

# COCONUT DROP COOKIES II

Drop Cookies

YIELD: *2 to 4 dozen*
TOTAL TIME: *30 minutes*

**1½ cups flaked coconut**
**One 14-ounce can sweetened condensed milk**
**1 teaspoon vanilla extract**
**⅛ teaspoon salt**

**1** Preheat the oven to 250 degrees. Lightly grease 2 baking sheets.

**2** In a large bowl, combine all of the ingredients and stir until well blended.

**3** Drop the dough by spoonfuls 1 inch apart onto the prepared baking sheets.

**4** Bake for 20 to 25 minutes, or until firm to the touch and dry. Transfer to wire racks to cool. (If

the cookies fall apart when you remove them from the baking sheet, return to the oven and bake for a few minutes longer.)

4 large egg whites
2 cups granulated sugar
½ teaspoon fresh lemon juice
¼ teaspoon almond extract
1½ cups shredded coconut

**1** Line 2 baking sheets with parchment paper.

**2** In a large bowl, beat the egg whites until they hold stiff picks. Blend in the sugar. Fold in the lemon juice and almond extract. Fold in the coconut.

**3** Drop the dough by spoonfuls 1 inch apart onto the prepared baking sheets. Set aside for 30 minutes at room temperature.

**4** Preheat the oven to 250 degrees.

**5** Just before baking, pinch the cookies so they come to a point, like a pyramid shape.

**6** Bake for 35 to 40 minutes, until lightly colored. Transfer to wire racks to cool.

**Baking notes:** If all the cookies don't fit on 2 baking sheets, place on additional sheets of parchment (cut to fit pans) to dry.

# COCONUT GEMS

Drop Cookies

YIELD: *4 to 6 dozen*
TOTAL TIME: *60 minutes*

---

1 cup all-purpose flour
½ cup rolled oats
½ teaspoon baking powder
½ teaspoon baking soda
½ teaspoon salt
2 cups flaked coconut
1 cup finely chopped apples (2 apples)
½ cup butter, at room temperature
½ cup granulated sugar
½ cup packed light brown sugar
1 large egg
1 teaspoon almond extract

**1** Preheat the oven to 375 degrees. Lightly grease 2 baking sheets.

**2** Combine the flour, oats, baking powder, baking soda, and salt. Combine the coconut and apples in a medium bowl and toss to mix.

**3** In a large bowl, cream the butter and the two sugars. Beat in the egg. Beat in the almond extract. Gradually blend in the dry ingredients. Fold in the apples and coconut.

**4** Drop the dough by spoonfuls 1½ inches apart onto the prepared baking sheets.

**5** Bake for 8 to 10 minutes, until lightly colored. Transfer to wire racks to cool.

# COCONUT HOMESTEADS

Drop Cookies

YIELD: *3 to 4 dozen*
TOTAL TIME: *30 minutes*

# Coconut-Jam Squares

Bar Cookies

YIELD: *2 to 3 dozen*
TOTAL TIME: *60 minutes*

**CRUST**
1¼ cups all-purpose flour
¼ teaspoon salt
½ cup vegetable shortening
3 tablespoons ice water

**FILLING**
2 large eggs
½ cup powdered sugar
2⅔ cup flaked coconut
⅓ cup raspberry preserves

**1** Preheat the oven to 425 degrees. Lightly grease a 9-inch square baking pan.

**2** To make the crust, combine the flour and salt in a large bowl. Cut in the vegetable shortening until the mixture resembles coarse crumbs. Press the mixture evenly into the bottom of the prepared baking pan, and sprinkle the water over the top.

**3** Bake for 20 minutes.

**4** Meanwhile, make the topping: In a large bowl, beat the eggs and sugar until thick and light-colored. Gently fold in the coconut.

**5** Spread the raspberry preserves over the warm baked crust. Spread the filling over the preserves.

**6** Reduce the oven temperature to 375 degrees and bake for 20 to 25 minutes longer, or until firm to the touch. Cool in the pan on a wire rack before cutting into large or small bars.

# Coconut Kisses

Drop Cookies

YIELD: *2 to 3 dozen*
TOTAL TIME: *55 minutes*

4 large egg whites
¼ teaspoon cream of tartar
¼ teaspoon salt
1 cup granulated sugar
¼ teaspoon almond extract
1½ cups flaked coconut

**1** Preheat the oven to 250 degrees. Line 2 baking sheets with parchment paper.

**2** In a large bowl, beat the egg whites until foamy. Beat in the cream of tartar and salt. Beat in the sugar a tablespoon at a time. Beat in the almond extract and beat until the whites hold stiff peaks. Gently fold in the coconut.

**3** Drop the mixture by spoonfuls 1½ inches apart onto the prepared baking sheets.

**4** Bake for 35 to 45 minutes, until firm to the touch. Transfer to wire racks to cool.

**Baking notes:** For crisper kisses, when the cookies are done, turn the oven off and let the cookies cool completely in the oven.

# Coconut Macaroons I

Drop Cookies

YIELD: *2 to 3 dozen*
TOTAL TIME: *40 minutes*

½ cup shredded coconut
2 teaspoons cornstarch
⅛ teaspoon salt
3 large egg whites
1 cup granulated sugar
1 teaspoon vanilla extract

**1** Preheat the oven to 275 degrees. Line 2 baking sheets with parchment paper.

**2** Combine the coconut, cornstarch, and salt in a medium bowl and toss to mix.

**3** In a large bowl, beat the egg whites until stiff but not dry. Fold in the sugar and vanilla extract. Gradually fold in the coconut mixture.

**4** Drop the dough by spoonfuls 1½ inches apart onto the prepared baking sheets.

**5** Bake for 28 to 30 minutes, until lightly colored. Transfer to wire racks to cool.

1 large egg white
⅓ cup sweetened condensed milk
1 teaspoon vanilla extract
1½ cups shredded coconut

**1** Preheat the oven to 300 degrees. Line 2 baking sheets with parchment paper.

**2** In a large bowl, beat the egg white until stiff but not dry. Gently blend in the condensed milk and vanilla extract. Fold in the coconut.

**3** Drop the mixture by teaspoonfuls 1½ inch apart onto the prepared baking sheets.

**4** Bake for 20 to 30 minutes, until lightly colored. Let cool completely on the baking sheets.

# COCONUT MACAROONS II

Drop Cookies

YIELD: *2 to 3 dozen*
TOTAL TIME: *45 minutes*

---

2½ cups shredded coconut
1 cup granulated sugar
1 tablespoon cornstarch
6 large egg whites
¼ teaspoon almond extract
About 1½ cups candied cherries, halved

**1** Preheat the oven to 350 degrees. Line 2 baking sheets with parchment paper.

**2** Combine the coconut, sugar, and cornstarch in a medium bowl and toss to mix.

**3** Combine the egg whites and almond extract in the top of a double boiler. Add the coconut mixture and cook, stirring for about 20 minutes until thickened (a candy thermometer will register about 148 degrees). Remove from the heat and let cool for 5 minutes.

**4** Place the mixture in a cookie press or a pastry bag fitted with a large star tip and press or pipe out rounds 1½ inches apart onto the prepared baking sheets. Press a half-cherry into the center of each cookie.

**5** Bake for 18 to 20 minutes, or until lightly colored. Transfer to wire racks to cool.

# COCONUT MACAROONS DELUXE

Formed Cookies

YIELD: *5 to 6 dozen*
TOTAL TIME: *50 minutes*

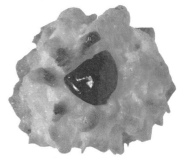

# Coconut Macaroons (Low-Calorie)

Drop Cookies

YIELD: *3 to 4 dozen*
TOTAL TIME: *30 minutes*

2 tablespoons all-purpose flour
¼ teaspoon baking powder
2 large egg whites
Pinch of cream of tartar
Pinch of salt
2 cups shredded coconut

1  Preheat the oven to 350 degrees. Line 2 baking sheets with parchment paper.
2  Combine the flour and baking powder.
3  In a large bowl, beat the egg whites until foamy. Beat in the cream of tartar and salt and beat until the mixture holds its shape. Gradually blend in the dry ingredients. Fold in the coconut.
4  Drop the dough by level teaspoonfuls 1 inch apart onto the prepared baking sheets.

5  Bake for 12 to 15 minutes, until lightly colored. Transfer to wire racks to cool.

# Coconut-Oatmeal Cookies

Drop Cookies

YIELD: *5 to 6 dozen*
TOTAL TIME: *35 minutes.*

¾ cup all-purpose flour
½ teaspoon baking powder
½ teaspoon baking soda
½ teaspoon salt
¼ cup vegetable shortening
½ cup granulated sugar
½ cup packed light brown sugar
1 large egg
1 tablespoon Amaretto
1 cup rolled oats
1 cup shredded coconut
½ cup almonds, chopped

1  Preheat the oven to 350 degrees. Lightly grease 2 baking sheets.
2  Combine the flour, baking powder, baking soda, and salt.
3  In a large bowl, beat the vegetable shortening, granulated sugar, brown sugar, egg, and Amaretto. Gradually blend in the dry ingredients. Fold in the oatmeal, coconut, almonds. The dough will be stiff.

4  Pinch off large walnut-sized pieces of dough and roll into balls. Place 3 inches apart on the prepared baking sheets.
5  Bake for 10 to 12 minutes, until lightly colored. Transfer to wire racks to cool.

**Baking notes:** Be sure to leave ample space between the cookies on the baking sheets. They spread more than most cookies.

# COCONUT-OATMEAL CRISPS

Drop Cookies

YIELD: *5 to 6 dozen*
TOTAL TIME: *30 minutes*

1¼ cups all-purpose flour
½ teaspoon baking powder
½ teaspoon baking soda
½ teaspoon salt
1 cup vegetable shortening
1 cup packed light brown sugar
½ cup granulated sugar
2 large eggs
¼ cup milk
1 teaspoon vanilla extract
3 cups rolled oats
¾ cups shredded coconut

1 Preheat the oven to 350 degrees.

2 Combine the flour, baking powder, baking soda, and salt.

3 In a large bowl, cream the vegetable shortening and both sugars. Beat in the eggs. Beat in the milk and vanilla extract. Gradually blend in the dry ingredients. Fold in the oats and coconut.

4 Drop the dough by spoonfuls 1½ inches apart onto ungreased baking sheets.

5 Bake for 8 to 11 minutes, until lightly colored. Transfer to wire racks to cool.

# COCONUT-PINEAPPLE SQUARES

Bar Cookies

YIELD: *1 to 3 dozen*
TOTAL TIME: *30 minutes*

2½ cups all-purpose flour
2 teaspoons baking powder
1 teaspoon baking soda
1 teaspoon ground cinnamon
½ cup vegetable shortening
3 large eggs
1 cup pineapple juice
2 cups flaked coconut
One 20-ounce can crushed pineapple, drained
½ cup shredded coconut

1 Preheat the oven to 350 degrees. Lightly grease a 13 by 9-inch baking pan.

2 Combine the flour, baking powder, baking soda, and cinnamon.

3 In a large bowl, beat the vegetable shortening, eggs, and pineapple juice. Gradually blend in the dry ingredients. Fold in the flaked coconut and pineapple.

4 Spread the mixture evenly in the prepared baking pan.

5 Bake for 15 minutes. Sprinkle the shredded coconut over the top and bake for 10 to 15 minutes longer, until coconut is lightly colored. Cool in the pan on a wire rack before cutting into large or small bars.

# COCONUT SANDWICHES

Rolled Cookies

YIELD: *2 to 3 dozen*
TOTAL TIME: *30 minutes*
CHILLING TIME: *2 hours*

¾ cup vegetable shortening
½ cup granulated sugar
1 large egg yolk
½ teaspoon vanilla extract
2 cups all-purpose flour
1⅓ cups flaked coconut
¾ to 1 cup Butter Cream Filling (see Pantry)

1 In a large bowl, cream the vegetable shortening and sugar. Beat in the egg yolk. Beat in the vanilla extract. Gradually blend in the flour. Fold in the coconut. Cover and chill for 2 hours.

2 Preheat the oven to 350 degrees. Lightly grease 2 baking sheets.

3 On a floured surface, roll out the dough to a thickness of ¼ inch. Using a 1½-inch round cookie cutter, cut out an even number of cookies and place 1 inch apart on the prepared baking sheets.

4 Bake for 8 to 10 minutes, or until lightly colored. Transfer to wire racks to cool.

5 To sandwich the cookies, spread a thin layer of the filling over the bottom of half the cookies. Place the remaining cookies on top and press together gently.

# Coconut Sugar Cookies

Rolled Cookies

YIELD: *5 to 6 dozen*
TOTAL TIME: *30 minutes*
CHILLING TIME: *2 hours*

3¾ cups all-purpose flour
1¼ cups coconut, ground fine
1½ teaspoons baking powder
½ teaspoon salt
1 cup vegetable shortening
1½ cups granulated sugar
2 large eggs
1 teaspoon coconut extract
Granulated sugar for sprinkling

**1** Combine the flour, coconut, baking powder, and salt.

**2** In a large bowl, cream the vegetable shortening and sugar. Beat in the eggs one at a time. Beat in the coconut extract. Gradually blend in the dry ingredients. Cover and chill for 2 hours.

**3** Preheat the oven to 375 degrees. Lightly grease 2 baking sheets.

**4** On a floured surface, roll out the dough to a thickness of ⅛ inch. Using a 2-inch round cookie cutter, cut into rounds and place 1½ inches apart on the prepared baking sheets. Lightly brush the cookies with water and sprinkle with granulated sugar.

**5** Bake for 8 to 10 minutes, until lightly colored. Transfer to wire racks to cool.

**Baking notes:** The secret of these cookies is to grind the coconut as fine as possible. You can also form this dough into a log 2 inches in diameter, wrap in waxed paper, and chill for 4 hours. Slice into ¼-inch-thick slices and bake as directed. Ground coconut is sold in specialty stores. It looks like heavy granules of coconut. If you can't find ground coconut then buy unsweetened coconut and grind it in a food processor.

# Coconut Wafers

Drop Cookies

YIELD: *4 to 5 dozen*
TOTAL TIME: *30 minutes*

4 cups all-purpose flour
½ teaspoon baking soda
½ cup vegetable shortening
2 cups granulated sugar
5 large eggs, separated
1 cup sour milk (see Baking notes)
2 teaspoons rose water
1 cup flaked coconut

**1** Preheat the oven to 350 degrees.

**2** Combine the flour and baking soda.

**3** In a large bowl, cream the vegetable shortening and sugar. Beat in the egg yolks. Beat in the milk and rose water. Gradually blend in the dry ingredients. Fold in the coconut.

**4** In another large bowl, beat the egg whites until stiff but not dry. Fold the whites into the coconut mixture.

**5** Drop the dough by spoonfuls 1½ inches apart onto ungreased baking sheets.

**6** Bake for 12 to 15 minutes, until lightly colored. Transfer to wire racks to cool.

**Baking notes:** To sour the milk, add 1 teaspoon of lemon juice or cider vinegar to 1 cup of milk, and stir.

1¾ cups all-purpose flour
2 teaspoons baking powder
¼ teaspoon ground cinnamon
⅛ teaspoon salt
2 ounces bittersweet chocolate,
    chopped
¾ cup butter
1 tablespoon brewed coffee
½ teaspoon vanilla extract
1 large egg
1 cup granulated sugar
Granulated sugar for sprinkling

**1** Preheat the oven to 350 degrees. Lightly grease 2 baking sheets.

**2** Combine the flour, baking powder, cinnamon, and salt.

**3** Melt the chocolate and butter in a double boiler over low heat, stirring until smooth. Remove from the heat and beat in the cof-fee and vanilla extract. Beat in the egg. Beat in the sugar. Gradually blend in the dry ingredients.

**4** On a floured surface, roll out the dough to a thickness of ¼ inch. Using a 1½-inch scalloped round cookie cutter, cut out cookies and place the rounds 1½ inches apart on the prepared baking sheets. Sprinkle with granulated sugar.

**5** Bake for 8 to 10 minutes, until lightly colored. Transfer to wire racks to cool.

# COFFEE-CHOCOLATE KRINGLES

Rolled Cookies

YIELD: *4 to 5 dozen*
TOTAL TIME: *40 minutes*

---

5 cups all-purpose flour
1 tablespoon baking soda
2 teaspoons ground ginger
1 teaspoon salt
1 cup vegetable shortening
2 cups granulated sugar
1 large egg
1 cup molasses
2 tablespoons brewed coffee
½ teaspoon vanilla extract

**1** Combine the flour, baking soda, ginger, and salt.

**2** In a large bowl, cream the vegetable shortening and sugar. Beat in the egg. Beat in the molasses, coffee, and vanilla extract. Gradually blend in the dry ingredients. Cover and chill for 3 hours.

**3** Preheat the oven to 350 degrees. Lightly grease 2 baking sheets.

**4** On a floured surface, roll out the dough to a thickness of ⅜ inch. Using cookie cutters, cut into shapes and place the cookies 1½ inches apart on the prepared baking sheets.

**5** Bake for 12 to 15 minutes, until lightly colored. Transfer to wire racks to cool.

# COFFEE COOKIES I

Rolled Cookies

YIELD: *6 to 7 dozen*
TOTAL TIME: *30 minutes*
CHILLING TIME: *3 hours*

---

3 cups all-purpose flour
1 teaspoon baking soda
1 teaspoon ground cinnamon
½ teaspoon salt
1 cup vegetable shortening
2 cups packed dark brown sugar
2 large eggs
1 cup strong brewed coffee
1 cup raisins

**1** Preheat the oven to 350 degrees. Lightly grease 2 baking sheets.

**2** Combine the flour, baking soda, cinnamon, and salt.

**3** In a large bowl, cream the vegetable shortening and brown sugar. Beat in the eggs one at a time. Beat in the coffee. Gradually blend in the dry ingredients. Stir in the raisins.

**4** Drop the dough by spoonfuls 1½ inches apart onto the prepared baking sheets.

**5** Bake for 10 to 12 minutes, until lightly colored. Transfer to wire racks to cool.

# COFFEE COOKIES II

Drop Cookies

YIELD: *3 to 4 dozen*
TOTAL TIME: *30 minutes*

# COFFEE-FLAVORED BROWNIES

Bar Cookies

YIELD: *1 to 2 dozen*
TOTAL TIME: *35 minutes*

¾ cup all-purpose flour
½ teaspoon baking powder
2 tablespoons instant coffee crystals
¼ teaspoon salt
2 ounces unsweetened chocolate, chopped
⅓ cup vegetable shortening
2 large eggs
1 teaspoon vanilla extract
1 cup granulated sugar
½ cup walnuts, chopped

1  Preheat the oven to 375 degrees. Lightly grease an 8-inch square baking pan.

2  Combine the flour, baking powder, coffee crystals, and salt.

3  In the top of a double boiler, melt the chocolate and shortening over low heat, stirring until smooth. Remove from the heat.

4  In a large bowl, beat the eggs until thick and light-colored. Gradually beat in the chocolate mixture and vanilla extract. Beat in the sugar. Gradually blend in the dry ingredients. Stir in the walnuts.

5  Spread the batter evenly in the prepared baking pans.

6  Bake for 20 to 25 minutes, until a toothpick inserted in the center comes out clean. Cool in the pan on a wire rack before cutting into large or small bars.

# COFFEE-FLAVORED MOLASSES COOKIES

Drop Cookies

YIELD: *3 to 5 dozen*
TOTAL TIME: *35 minutes*

4½ cups all-purpose flour
2 teaspoons ground ginger
2 teaspoons ground cinnamon
1 cup vegetable shortening
1 cup granulated sugar
1 large egg
1 tablespoon plus 1 teaspoon baking soda
¼ cup hot water
1 cup molasses, warmed
¾ cup strong brewed coffee

1  Preheat the oven to 375 degrees. Lightly grease 2 baking sheets.

2  Combine the flour, ginger, and cinnamon.

3  In a large bowl, cream the vegetable shortening and sugar. Beat in the egg.

4  Dissolve the baking soda in the hot water and add to the egg mixture, beating until smooth. Beat in the molasses and coffee. Gradually blend in the dry ingredients.

5  Drop the dough by spoonfuls 1½ inches apart onto the prepared baking sheets.

6  Bake for 8 to 10 minutes, until just starting to color. Transfer to a wire rack to cool.

# COFFEE KISSES

Drop Cookies

YIELD: *2 to 3 dozen*
TOTAL TIME: *60 minutes*

1 tablespoon plus 1 teaspoon instant coffee powder
1 tablespoon boiling water
4 large egg whites
¼ teaspoon cream of tartar
¼ teaspoon salt
1 cups granulated sugar
1 teaspoon crème de cacao

1  Preheat the oven to 250 degrees. Line 2 baking sheets with parchment paper.

2  In a cup, dissolve the coffee powder in the boiling water. Let cool.

3  In a large bowl, beat the egg whites until foamy. Beat in the cream of tartar and salt. Beat in the sugar 1 tablespoon at a time. Beat in the crème de cacao and beat until the whites form stiff peaks. Fold in the coffee.

4  Drop the dough by spoonfuls 1 inch apart onto the prepared baking sheets.

5  Bake for 35 to 40 minutes, until firm to the touch. Cool completely on the baking sheets on wire racks.

2 large egg whites
1 teaspoon salt
1⅓ cups granulated sugar
⅓ cup hazelnuts, chopped
2 teaspoons brewed coffee
½ teaspoon vanilla extract
1 tablespoon finely ground
   hazelnuts

**1** Preheat the oven to 400 degrees. Line 2 baking sheets with parchment paper.

**2** In a large bowl, beat the egg whites until foamy. Beat in the salt. Gradually beat in the sugar and beat until the whites form stiff peaks. Fold in the chopped hazelnuts. Fold in the coffee and vanilla extract.

**3** Drop the dough by spoonfuls 1½ inches apart onto the prepared baking sheets. Sprinkle with the ground hazelnuts.

**4** Bake for 8 to 10 minutes, until firm to the touch. Transfer the pans to wire racks to cool.

# COFFEE MERINGUES

Drop Cookies

YIELD: *3 to 4 dozen*
TOTAL TIME: *30 minutes*

---

3½ cups all-purpose flour
1 teaspoon baking soda
2 teaspoons pumpkin pie spice
½ teaspoon salt
½ cup vegetable shortening
2 cups packed light brown sugar
2 large eggs
1¾ cups solid-pack pumpkin
½ cup brewed coffee
½ cup raisins
½ cup hazelnuts, chopped

**1** Preheat the oven to 400 degrees.

**2** Combine the flour, baking soda, pumpkin pie spice, and salt.

**3** In a large bowl, cream the vegetable shortening and brown sugar. Beat in the eggs one at a time. Beat in the pumpkin and coffee. Gradually blend in the dry ingredients. Fold in the raisins and hazelnuts.

**4** Drop the dough by spoonfuls 1½ inches apart onto ungreased baking sheets.

**5** Bake for 10 to 12 minutes, until golden brown. Transfer to wire racks to cool.

# COFFEE-PUMPKIN COOKIES

Drop Cookies

YIELD: *5 to 6 dozen*
TOTAL TIME: *30 minutes*

# COFFEE SQUARES

Bar Cookies

YIELD: *2 to 3 dozen*
TOTAL TIME: *35 minutes*

1½ cups all-purpose flour
1 teaspoon baking powder
¼ teaspoon baking soda
½ teaspoon ground cardamom
¼ teaspoon salt
½ cup milk
2 teaspoons instant coffee crystals
¼ cup vegetable shortening
1 cup granulated sugar
1 cup powdered sugar
1 large egg
1 cup almonds, chopped
1 recipe for Vanilla Icing (see Pantry)

1 Preheat the oven to 350 degrees. Lightly grease a 13 by 9-inch baking pan.

2 Combine the flour, baking powder, baking soda, cardamom, and salt.

3 Combine milk and coffee crystals in a saucepan and heat, stirring, until the coffee dissolves. Remove from the heat.

4 In a large bowl, cream the vegetable shortening and both sugars. Beat in the egg. Beat in the coffee. Gradually blend in the dry ingredients. Fold in the almonds.

5 Spread the dough evenly in the prepared baking pan.

6 Bake for 18 to 20 minutes, until a toothpick inserted in the center comes out clean. Cool in the pan on a wire rack.

7 Frost the cooled cookies with the icing and cut into large or small bars.

# COLUMBIA DROP COOKIES

Drop Cookies

YIELD: *3 to 5 dozen*
TOTAL TIME: *30 minutes*

1½ cups all-purpose flour
½ teaspoon baking soda
1 teaspoon ground cinnamon
½ teaspoon ground cloves
½ teaspoon ground allspice
⅛ teaspoon salt
½ cup butter, at room temperature
¾ cup packed light brown sugar
2 large eggs
¼ cup Amaretto
1 cup almonds, chopped
1 cup raisins

1 Preheat the oven to 375 degrees. Lightly grease 2 baking sheets.

2 Combine the flour, baking soda, spices, and salt.

3 In a large bowl, cream the butter and brown sugar. Beat in the eggs. Beat in the Amaretto. Gradually blend in the dry ingredients. Fold in the almonds and raisins.

4 Drop the dough by spoonfuls 1½ inches apart onto the prepared baking sheets.

5 Bake for 10 to 12 minutes, until lightly colored. Transfer to wire racks to cool.

3 cups all-purpose flour
1 cup almonds, ground fine
¼ teaspoon salt
1 cup butter, at room temperature
1 cup granulated sugar
2 large eggs
2 large egg yolks
2 tablespoons milk
1 teaspoon lemon zest, grated

**1** Combine the flour, almonds, and salt.

**2** In a large bowl, cream the butter and sugar. Beat in the whole eggs and 1 egg yolk. Beat in the milk and lemon zest. Gradually blend in the dry ingredients. Cover and chill for 4 hours.

**3** Preheat the oven to 375 degrees. Lightly grease 2 baking sheets.

**4** In a small bowl, beat the remaining egg yolk.

**5** On a floured surface, roll out the dough to a thickness of ⅛ inch. Using cookie cutters, cut into shapes and place 1½ inches apart on the prepared baking sheets. Brush the tops of the cookies with the beaten egg yolk.

**6** Bake for 8 to 10 minutes, until golden brown. Transfer to wire racks to cool.

# CONTINENTAL BISCUITS

Rolled Cookies

YIELD: *5 to 6 dozen*
TOTAL TIME: *45 minutes*
CHILLING TIME: *4 hours*

---

2 cups all-purpose flour
½ teaspoon salt
1 cup vegetable shortening
1 cup granulated sugar
½ teaspoon vanilla extract
1 cup (6 ounces) semisweet chocolate chips
1 cup peanuts, unsalted

**1** Preheat the oven to 350 degrees. Lightly grease a 15 by 10-inch baking pan.

**2** Combine the flour and salt.

**3** In a large bowl, cream the vegetable shortening and sugar. Beat in the vanilla extract. Gradually blend in the dry ingredients. Fold in the chocolate chips.

**4** Spread the dough evenly in the prepared baking pan (it will make a very thin layer). Sprinkle the peanuts over the top and press them gently into the dough.

**5** Bake for 20 to 25 minutes, until the top is lightly colored. Cool in the pan on a wire rack before breaking into large or small pieces.

**Baking notes:** The secret of this cookie is that it should be very thin.

# COOKIE-BRITTLE COOKIES

Bar Cookies

YIELD: *2 to 4 dozen*
TOTAL TIME: *35 minutes*

# COOKIE FACES

Rolled Cookies

YIELD: *2 to 3 dozen*
TOTAL TIME: *35 minutes*

**3½ cups all-purpose flour**
**2 teaspoons baking powder**
**1 teaspoon ground cinnamon**
**1 teaspoon salt**
**1⅓ cups vegetable shortening**
**¾ cup granulated sugar**
**¾ cup packed light brown sugar**
**2 large eggs**
**2 teaspoons vanilla extract**
**Popsicle sticks**

**1** Preheat the oven to 350 degrees. Lightly grease 2 baking sheets.

**2** Combine the flour, baking powder, cinnamon, and salt.

**3** In a large bowl, cream the vegetable shortening and the two sugars. Beat in the eggs one at a time. Beat in the vanilla extract. Gradually blend in the dry ingredients.

**4** On a floured surface, roll out the dough to a thickness of ⅜ inch. Using cookie cutter, cut into 3- or 4-inch rounds or ovals. Use the scraps of dough to make the cookie faces (see Baking notes).

Place 1 inch apart on the prepared baking sheets. Insert a popsicle stick into each cookie.

**5** Bake for 12 to 15 minutes, until firm to the touch. Transfer to wire racks to cool.

**Baking notes:** These are cookies to make with kids. To create the faces, pinch the center of each dough circle or oval to form the nose. Make an indentation on either side of the nose for the eyes. Roll small bits of dough into very thin ropes for the eyebrows. Roll more tiny pieces of dough into balls for the eyes. Roll small bits of dough to form the lips. Roll out another small piece of dough and cut into ears. (The dough used for the eyebrows, eyes, and lips can be colored using food coloring.)

# COOKIE PIZZA

Formed Cookies

YIELD: *4 dozen*
TOTAL TIME: *30 minutes*

**CRUST**
**¾ cup all-purpose flour**
**½ teaspoon baking powder**
**½ teaspoon baking soda**
**Pinch of salt**
**½ cup vegetable shortening**
**¾ cup packed light brown sugar**
**1 large egg**
**1 teaspoon vanilla extract**
**1 cup rolled oats**
**½ cup flaked coconut**

**TOPPING**
**1 cup (6 ounces) semisweet choco-
late chips**
**1 cup walnuts, chopped**
**½ cup M&Ms**

**1** Preheat the oven to 350 degrees. Lightly grease a 14 to 15-inch pizza pan.

**2** Combine the flour, baking powder, baking soda, and salt.

**3** In a large bowl, cream the vegetable shortening and brown sugar. Beat in the egg and vanilla.

Gradually blend in the dry ingredients. Fold in the oats and coconut.

**4** Press the dough evenly into the prepared pan. Sprinkle the chocolate chips and walnuts evenly over the top.

**5** Bake for 12 to 15 minutes, until lightly colored. Sprinkle the M&Ms over the hot cookies. Cool in the pan on a wire rack for a few minutes before cutting into wedges.

2½ cups all-purpose flour
¼ teaspoon baking soda
½ teaspoon salt
1 cup vegetable shortening
½ cup powdered sugar
2 tablespoons evaporated milk
1 teaspoon vanilla extract
1 teaspoon almond extract
About 1 cup jam, preserves, or soft-
    ened cream cheese

**1** Preheat the oven to 350 degrees.

**2** Combine the flour, baking soda, and salt.

**3** In a large bowl, cream the vegetable shortening and powdered sugar. Beat in the milk and vanilla and almond extracts. Gradually blend in the dry ingredients.

**4** On a floured surface, roll out the dough to a thickness of ¼ inch. Using a 1½-inch round cookie cutter, cut out an even number of cookies. Using a small star or diamond cookie cutter, cut out the centers of half of the cookies. Place the cookies 1 inch apart on ungreased baking sheets.

**5** Bake for 12 to 15 minutes, until lightly colored. Transfer to wire racks to cool.

**6** Spread a thin layer of filling over the bottom of each solid cookie, top with a cut-out cookie, and gently press together.

# Cookie Sandwiches

Rolled Cookies

YIELD: *1 to 3 dozen*
TOTAL TIME: *30 minutes*

---

2 cups crushed cookie crumbs (see
    Baking notes)
2 cups (12 ounces) semisweet choco-
    late chips
¾ cup shredded coconut
One 14-ounce can sweetened con-
    densed milk
½ cup walnuts, ground fine

**1** Preheat the oven to 325 degrees. Lightly grease a 13 by 9-inch baking pan.

**2** In a large bowl, combine all of the ingredients and knead together into a dough by hand. Press the mixture evenly into the prepared baking pan.

**3** Bake for 8 to 10 minutes, until firm to the touch. Cut into large or small bars, then cool in the pan on a wire rack.

**Baking notes:** The crushed cookies can be almost any type, such as wafers, Oreos, etc.

# Cookie Squares

Bar Cookies

YIELD: *1 to 2 dozen*
TOTAL TIME: *20 minutes*

# COOKIE TWISTS

Formed Cookies

YIELD: *2 to 4 dozen*
TOTAL TIME: *45 minutes*

½ cup vegetable shortening
¾ cup granulated sugar
6 large egg yolks
1 tablespoon sherry
1 tablespoon grated orange zest
3 cups all-purpose flour
1 large egg white, beaten

1  Preheat the oven to 350 degrees.

2  In a large bowl, cream the vegetable shortening and sugar. Beat in the egg yolks. Beat in the sherry and orange zest. Gradually blend in the flour.

3  Pinch off small pieces of dough and roll into ¼-inch-thick ropes. Fold each rope in half and twist.

Place 1½ inches apart on ungreased baking sheets. Brush the cookies with the beaten egg white.

4  Bake for 12 to 15 minutes, until lightly colored. Transfer to wire racks to cool.

**Baking notes:**  This recipe is similar to an old recipe for cookies called biscochos, except they are made without sugar, and sesame seeds are sprinkled on top of the twists.

# CORNFLAKE COOKIES I

Formed Cookies

YIELD: *4 to 6 dozen*
TOTAL TIME: *30 minutes*

2 cups all-purpose flour
2 teaspoons baking powder
1 cup butter, at room temperature
1 cup granulated sugar
1 cup packed light brown sugar
2 large eggs
1 tablespoon Amaretto
2 cups cornflakes
1 cup flaked coconut
Powdered sugar for sprinkling

1  Preheat the oven to 375 degrees.

2  Combine the flour and baking powder.

3  In a large bowl, cream the butter and two sugars. Beat in the eggs. Beat in the Amaretto. Gradually blend in the dry ingredients. Fold in the cornflakes and coconut.

4  Pinch off walnut-sized pieces of dough and roll into balls. Place 1½ inches apart on ungreased baking sheets.

5  Bake for 10 to 12 minutes, until lightly colored. Transfer to wire racks to cool, then sprinkle with powdered sugar.

# CORNFLAKE COOKIES II

Drop Cookies

YIELD: *5 to 6 dozen*
TOTAL TIME: *30 minutes*

2 cups all-purpose flour
½ teaspoon baking powder
½ teaspoon baking soda
½ teaspoon salt
1 cup vegetable shortening
1 cup granulated sugar
1 cup packed light brown sugar
2 large eggs
½ teaspoon vanilla extract
1 cup cornflakes
1 cup rolled oats
1 cup shredded coconut
½ cup walnuts, chopped

1  Preheat the oven to 350 degrees.

2  Combine the flour, baking powder, baking soda, and salt.

3  In a large bowl, cream the vegetable shortening and two sugars. Beat in the eggs. Beat in the vanilla extract. Gradually blend in the dry ingredients. Stir in the cornflakes, oats, coconut, and walnuts. The dough will be stiff, so knead it together.

4  Drop the dough by spoonfuls 1½ inches apart onto ungreased baking sheets.

5  Bake for 10 to 12 minutes, until lightly colored. Transfer to wire racks to cool.

2⅔ cups all-purpose flour
1 cup yellow cornmeal
1 teaspoon baking powder
1 teaspoon ground nutmeg
¼ teaspoon salt
1 cup vegetable shortening
1½ cups granulated sugar
2 large eggs
1 teaspoon fresh lemon juice
½ cup raisins, chopped fine

**1** Preheat the oven to 400 degrees. Lightly grease 2 baking sheets.

**2** Combine the flour, cornmeal, baking powder, nutmeg, and salt.

**3** In a large bowl, cream the vegetable shortening and sugar. Beat in the eggs one at a time. Beat in the lemon juice. Gradually blend in the dry ingredients. Fold in the raisins.

**4** Drop the dough by spoonfuls 1½ inches apart onto the prepared baking sheets.

**5** Bake for 8 to 10 minutes, until lightly colored. Transfer to wire racks to cool.

# CORNMEAL COOKIES

Drop Cookies

YIELD: *5 to 7 dozen*
TOTAL TIME: *30 minutes*

---

1½ cups graham cracker crumbs
One 14-ounce can sweetened condensed milk
¾ cup semisweet chocolate chips
½ cup chopped nuts, such as walnuts or pecans
½ cup shredded coconut

**1** Preheat the oven to 350 degrees. Lightly grease a 9-inch square baking pan.

**2** In a large bowl, combine all of the ingredients and stir to make a soft dough. Spread the dough evenly in the prepared baking pan.

**3** Bake for 25 to 30 minutes, until a toothpick inserted in the center comes out clean. Cool in the pan on a wire rack before cutting into large or small bars.

# CRACKER BROWNIES I

Bar Cookies

YIELD: *1 to 2 dozen*
TOTAL TIME: *35 minutes*

C

# CRACKER BROWNIES II

Bar Cookies

YIELD: *1 to 2 dozen*
TOTAL TIME: *45 minutes*

¾ cup vegetable shortening
1 cup granulated sugar
2 large eggs
1 teaspoon vanilla extract
2½ cups crushed honey graham crackers
2 cups miniature marshmallows
¼ cup peanuts, ground fine

**TOPPING**
1 cup (6 ounces) semisweet chocolate chips
¼ cup peanut butter

1 Lightly grease a 9-inch square baking pan.

2 In the top of a double boiler, melt the vegetable shortening with the sugar. Stir to dissolve the sugar. Remove from the heat and beat in the eggs one at a time. Beat in the vanilla. Return to the heat and cook, stirring, until the mixture thickens. Remove from the heat and stir in the graham crackers, marshmallows, and peanuts.

3 Spread the mixture evenly in the prepared baking pan. Refrigerate until thoroughly chilled.

4 To make the topping, melt the chocolate chips with the peanut butter in a double boiler over low heat, stirring constantly. Spread this mixture evenly over the top of the graham cracker mixture. Refrigerate until the topping is set, then and cut into large or small bars.

# CRACKLE BROWNIES

Bar Cookies

YIELD: *1 to 2 dozen*
TOTAL TIME: *45 minutes*

1 cup (6 ounces) semisweet chocolate chips
1 cup all-purpose flour
½ teaspoon baking powder
⅓ cup vegetable shortening
¾ cup granulated sugar
2 large eggs
1 teaspoon vanilla extract
¾ cup rice krispies

**TOPPING**
½ cup (3 ounces) semisweet chocolate chips
¼ cup rice krispies

1 Preheat the oven to 350 degrees. Lightly grease an 8-inch square baking pan.

2 Melt the chocolate chips in a double boiler over low heat, stirring until smooth. Remove from the heat.

3 Combine the flour and baking powder.

4 In a large bowl, cream the vegetable shortening and sugar. Beat in the eggs and vanilla extract. Beat in the melted chocolate. Gradually blend in the dry ingredients. Fold in the rice krispies. Spread the mixture evenly in the prepared baking pan.

5 Bake for 20 to 25 minutes, until a toothpick inserted in the center comes out clean.

6 For the topping, sprinkle the chocolate chips over the top of the warm brownies. Let sit for 1 to 2 minutes, until the chocolate melts, then spread the chocolate evenly over the brownies. Sprinkle the rice krispies over the top. Cool in the pan on a wire rack before cutting into large or small bars.

1½ cups all-purpose flour
1 cup almonds, ground fine
1½ teaspoons baking powder
¼ teaspoon salt
2 large eggs
1 cup granulated sugar
2 teaspoons fresh lemon juice
1 cup jellied cranberry sauce,
    chopped fine

**1** Preheat the oven to 350 degrees. Lightly grease a 13 by 9-inch baking pan.

**2** Combine the flour, almonds, baking powder, and salt.

**3** In a large bowl, beat the eggs, sugar, and lemon juice. Beat in the cranberry sauce. Gradually blend in the dry ingredients. Spread the dough evenly in the prepared baking pan.

**4** Bake for 25 to 30 minutes, until the top is lightly colored and firm to the touch. Cut into large or small bars and cool in the pan on a wire rack.

# CRANBERRY BARS

Bar Cookies

YIELD: *1 to 2 dozen*
TOTAL TIME: *45 minutes*

---

1½ cups all-purpose flour
½ teaspoon baking powder
¼ teaspoon salt
½ cup vegetable shortening
¾ cup powdered sugar
3 tablespoons milk
1 teaspoon Amaretto
¾ cup cranberries, fresh or dried,
    chopped fine (see Baking notes)
½ cup flaked coconut

**1** Combine the flour, baking powder, and salt.

**2** In a large bowl, cream the vegetable shortening and powdered sugar. Beat in the milk and Amaretto. Gradually blend in the dry ingredients. Fold in the cranberries.

**3** Divide the dough in half. Form each half into a log 1½ inches in diameter. Roll in coconut. Wrap in waxed paper and chill for 8 hours.

**4** Preheat the oven to 375 degrees.

**5** Cut the logs into ¼-inch-thick slices and place each slice 1 inch apart on ungreased baking sheets.

**6** Bake for 12 to 15 minutes, until lightly colored. Transfer to wire racks to cool.

**Baking notes:** If using dried cranberries, cover cranberries with boiling water and plump for 10 minutes before chopping.

# CRANBERRY COOKIES

Refrigerator Cookies

YIELD: *3 to 4 dozen*
TOTAL TIME: *45 minutes*
CHILLING TIME: *8 hours*

# CRANBERRY ORANGE BARS

Bar Cookies

YIELD: *1 to 2 dozen*
TOTAL TIME: *45 minutes*

**1½ cups all-purpose flour**
**1 teaspoon baking powder**
**½ teaspoon salt**
**6 tablespoons vegetable shortening**
**¾ cup granulated sugar**
**2 large eggs**
**1 cup cranberries, chopped fine**
**¾ cup orange marmalade**

**TOPPING**
**2 tablespoons butter, at room temperature**
**1 cup powdered sugar**
**¼ cup pecans, ground fine**
**1 tablespoon milk**
**2 tablespoons diced cranberries**

**1** Preheat the oven to 350 degrees. Lightly grease a 13 by 9-inch baking pan.

**2** Combine the flour, baking powder, and salt.

**3** In a large bowl, cream the vegetable shortening and sugar. Beat in the eggs. Beat in the cranberries and marmalade. Gradually blend in the dry ingredients. Spread the dough evenly into the prepared baking pan.

**4** Bake for 25 to 30 minutes, until firm to the touch.

**5** Meanwhile, make the topping: In a medium bowl, cream the butter and powdered sugar. Beat in the pecans. Beat in the milk.

**6** Spread the topping evenly over the hot cookies. Sprinkle the diced cranberries on top. Cool in the pan on a wire rack before cutting into large or small bars.

**Baking notes:** Refrigerate these bars once they have cooled. Serve them with whipped cream.

---

# CREAM CHEESE BROWNIES

Bar Cookies

YIELD: *2 to 3 dozen*
TOTAL TIME: *50 minutes*

**½ cup all-purpose flour**
**½ teaspoon baking powder**
**¼ teaspoon salt**
**⅓ cup semisweet chocolate chips**
**5 tablespoons vegetable shortening**
**1 cup granulated sugar**
**3 ounces cream cheese, at room temperature**
**3 large eggs**
**2 teaspoons vanilla extract**
**½ teaspoon almond extract**
**½ cup almonds, chopped**

**1** Preheat the oven to 350 degrees. Lightly grease a 9-inch square baking pan.

**2** Combine the flour, baking powder, and salt.

**3** In the top of a double boiler, melt the chocolate chips and vegetable shortening, stirring until smooth. Transfer to a large bowl.

**4** Add the sugar to the chocolate mixture and beat until smooth. Beat in the cream cheese. Beat in the eggs, beating well after each addition. Beat in the vanilla and almond extracts. Gradually blend in the dry ingredients. Fold in the almonds. Scrape the batter into the prepared baking pan.

**5** Bake for 35 to 40 minutes, until a toothpick inserted in the center comes out clean. Cool in the pan on a wire rack before cutting into large or small bars.

1¼ cups all-purpose flour
¼ cup pecans, ground fine
¼ teaspoon salt
½ cup vegetable shortening
4 ounces cream cheese, at room
  temperature
½ cup granulated sugar
1 teaspoon almond extract
½ cup colored sugar crystals
About 1 cup whole blanched
  almonds

1 Combine the flour, pecans, and salt.

2 In a large bowl, beat the vegetable shortening, cream cheese and sugar together until smooth. Beat in the almond extract. Gradually blend in the dry ingredients.

3 Divide the dough in half. Form each half into a log 2 inches in diameter. Wrap in waxed paper and chill for 8 hours or overnight.

4 Preheat the oven to 325 degrees.

5 Cut the logs into ¼-inch-thick slices and place 1½ inches apart on ungreased baking sheets. Sprinkle the cookies with colored sugar crystals and press a whole almond into the center of each one.

6 Bake for 12 to 15 minutes, until lightly colored. Transfer to wire racks to cool.

**Baking notes:** For variation, reduce the almond extract to ½ teaspoon and add 3 drops of raspberry flavoring.

# CREAM CHEESE CHRISTMAS COOKIES

Refrigerator Cookies

YIELD: *3 to 4 dozen*
TOTAL TIME: *30 minutes*
CHILLING TIME: *8 hours*

---

2½ cups all-purpose flour
¼ teaspoon salt
1 cup vegetable shortening
3 ounces cream cheese, at room
  temperature
1 cup granulated sugar
1 tablespoon milk
1 tablespoon grated lemon zest

1 Preheat the oven to 350 degrees.

2 Combine the flour and salt.

3 In a large bowl, beat the vegetable shortening, cream cheese, and sugar until smooth. Beat in the milk. Beat in the lemon zest. Gradually blend in the dry ingredients.

4 Drop the dough by spoonfuls 1½ inches apart onto ungreased baking sheets.

5 Bake for 12 to 15 minutes, until lightly colored. Cool on the baking sheets on wire racks.

**Baking notes:** For added flavor place a chocolate chip into the center of each cookie after it has been dropped onto the baking tray.

# CREAM CHEESE COOKIES

Drop Cookies

YIELD: *4 to 5 dozen*
TOTAL TIME: *35 minutes*

# CREAM CHEESE CUSHIONS

Rolled Cookies

YIELD: *2 to 3 dozen*
TOTAL TIME: *30 minutes*
CHILLING TIME: *2 hours*

**2 cups all-purpose flour**
**1 cup rolled oats**
**½ teaspoon salt**
**1 cup vegetable shortening**
**8 ounces cream cheese, at room temperature**
**1 teaspoon almond extract**
**About ⅓ cup cherry preserves**

**1** Combine the flour, oats, and salt.

**2** In a large bowl, beat the vegetable shortening and cream cheese until smooth. Beat in the almond extract. Gradually blend in the dry ingredients. Cover and chill for 2 hours.

**3** Preheat the oven to 425 degrees. Lightly grease 2 baking sheets.

**4** On a floured surface, roll out the dough to a thickness of ½ inch. Using a cookie cutter, cut out squares or rounds and place 1½ inches apart on the prepared baking sheets. Place ½ teaspoon cherry preserves in the center of each cookie and fold the dough over to form a triangle or half-moon. Press the edges together to seal.

**5** Bake for 10 to 12 minutes, until lightly colored. Transfer to wire racks to cool.

**Baking notes:** These cookies are baked in a hot oven; keep an eye on them while they bake.

# CREAM CHEESE REFRIGERATOR COOKIES

Refrigerator Cookies

YIELD: *2 to 3 dozen*
TOTAL TIME: *30 minutes.*
CHILLING TIME: *4 hours*

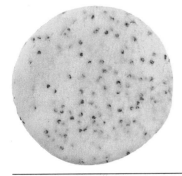

**1 cup all-purpose flour**
**3 tablespoons poppy seeds**
**¼ teaspoon salt**
**4 ounces cream cheese, at room temperature**
**⅓ cup canola oil**
**¼ cup honey, warmed**

**1** Combine the flour, poppy seeds, and salt.

**2** In a large bowl, beat the cream cheese, oil, and honey until well blended and smooth. Gradually blend in the dry ingredients. Shape the dough into a log 2½ inches in diameter. Wrap in waxed paper and chill for 4 hours.

**3** Preheat the oven to 400 degrees. Lightly grease 2 baking sheets.

**4** Cut the log into ¼-inch-thick slices and place 1 inch apart on the prepared baking sheets.

**5** Bake for 6 to 8 minutes, or until lightly browned. Transfer to wire racks to cool.

1½ cups all-purpose flour
½ teaspoon salt
½ cup vegetable shortening
3 ounces cream cheese
⅓ cup granulated sugar
1 large egg yolk
1½ teaspoons orange extract

**1** Preheat the oven to 375 degrees. Lightly grease 2 baking sheets.

**2** Combine the flour and salt.

**3** In a large bowl, beat the vegetable shortening, cream cheese, and sugar until smooth. Beat in the egg yolk and orange extract. Gradually blend in the dry ingredients.

**4** Place the dough in a cookie press or a pastry bag fitted with a ribbon tip and press or pipe out 3-inch-long strips, spacing them on the prepared baking sheets 1 inch apart.

**5** Bake for 8 to 10 minutes, until lightly colored. Transfer to wire racks to cool.

# CREAM CHEESE SPRITZ COOKIES

Formed Cookies

YIELD: *2 to 3 dozen*
TOTAL TIME: *30 minutes*

---

2 cups all-purpose flour
¼ teaspoon salt
1 cup vegetable shortening
8 ounces cream cheese, at room temperature
½ cup powdered sugar
About ¼ cup raspberry preserves
Powdered sugar for sprinkling

**1** Combine the flour and salt.

**2** In a large bowl, beat the vegetable shortening, cream cheese, and powdered sugar until smooth. Gradually blend in the dry ingredients. Divide the dough in half. Wrap each half in waxed paper and chill for 8 hours.

**3** Preheat the oven to 375 degrees.

**4** On a floured surface, roll out one-half of the dough to a rectangle approximately 10 inches by 11½ inches. Trim the edges of the dough and cut lengthwise into 4 strips. Cut each strip into 5 squares. Place ¼ teaspoon raspberry preserves in the center of each square and fold the dough over to form a triangle. Press the edges together to seal and place 1 inch apart on ungreased baking sheets. Repeat with the other half of the dough.

**5** Bake for 10 to 12 minutes, until lightly colored. Sprinkle with powdered sugar and transfer to wire racks to cool.

**Baking notes:** Use fluted pastry cutter to cut the dough into decorative shapes if you like.

# CREAM CHEESE TASTIES

Rolled Cookies

YIELD: *3½ dozen*
TOTAL TIME: *40 minutes*
CHILLING TIME: *8 hours*

# CREAM WAFERS

Rolled Cookies

YIELD: *3 to 4 dozen*
TOTAL TIME: *30 minutes*
CHILLING TIME: *4 hours*

2 cups all-purpose flour
1 cup butter
⅓ cup heavy cream
Granulated sugar for sprinkling

**FILLING**
¼ cup vegetable shortening
¾ cup powdered sugar
1 large egg yolk
1 teaspoon almond extract

**1** Put the flour in a large bowl. Cut in the butter until the mixture resembles coarse crumbs. Stir in the heavy cream. Divide the dough into thirds. Wrap in waxed paper and chill for 4 hours.

**2** Preheat the oven to 375 degrees.

**3** On a floured surface, roll out the dough to a thickness of ⅛ inch. Using a 2-inch round cookie cutter, cut out cookies and place each round 1 inch apart on ungreased baking sheets. Sprinkle the cookies with granulated sugar and prick the surface of each cookie several times with a fork.

**4** Bake for 8 to 10 minutes, until lightly colored. Transfer to wire racks to cool.

**5** Meanwhile, make the filling: In a medium bowl, cream the vegetable shortening and powdered sugar. Beat in the egg yolk and almond extract. Cover and refrigerate until ready to use.

**6** To assemble, spread the filling over the bottom of half the cooled cookies. Top with the remaining cookies and press together gently.

**Baking notes:** For a richer flavor, cream cheese can be used in place of the vegetable shortening in the filling.

# CREAMY JUMBLE COOKIES

Drop Cookies

YIELD: *3 to 4 dozen*
TOTAL TIME: *30 minutes*

2¾ cup all-purpose flour
½ teaspoon baking soda
¼ teaspoon salt
½ cup vegetable shortening
1 cup packed light brown sugar
2 large eggs
1 teaspoon Amaretto
½ cup shredded coconut
¼ cup raisins, chopped
¼ cup semisweet chocolate chips

**1** Preheat the oven to 375 degrees. Lightly grease 2 baking sheets.

**2** Combine the flour, baking soda, and salt.

**3** In a large bowl, cream the vegetable shortening and brown sugar. Beat in the eggs one at a time. Beat in the Amaretto. Gradually blend in the dry ingredients. Fold in the coconut, raisins, and chocolate chips.

**4** Drop the dough by spoonfuls 1½ inches apart onto the prepared baking sheets.

**5** Bake for 8 to 10 minutes, until lightly colored. Transfer to wire racks to cool.

½ cup plus 2 tablespoons vegetable shortening
¼ cup unsweetened cocoa powder
1 cup granulated sugar
2 large eggs
½ teaspoon crème de menthe
⅔ cup all-purpose flour
Green crème de menthe icing (see Pantry)
Walnut halves

**1** Preheat the oven to 350 degrees. Lightly grease a 9-inch square baking pan.

**2** Melt the vegetable shortening in a large saucepan. Beat in the cocoa powder. Remove from the heat and beat in the sugar. Beat in the eggs and crème de menthe. Gradually blend in the flour.

Spread the batter evenly in the prepared baking pan.

**3** Bake for 18 to 20 minutes, until a toothpick inserted into the center comes out clean. Cool in the pan on a wire rack.

**4** Spread the icing over the top of the brownies and cut into large or small bars. Place a walnut half in the center of each brownie. Chill for about at least 1 hour before removing from the pan.

# CRÈME DE MENTHE BROWNIES

Bar Cookies

YIELD: *1 to 2 dozen*
TOTAL TIME: *40 minutes*
CHILLING TIME: *1 hour*

---

2½ cups all-purpose flour
2 teaspoons baking soda
1 teaspoon ground cinnamon
1 teaspoon ground ginger
½ teaspoon ground cloves
½ teaspoon salt
¾ cup vegetable shortening
1 cup packed light brown sugar
1 large egg
¼ cup molasses
Granulated sugar for coating

**1** Combine the flour, baking soda, spices, and salt.

**2** In a large bowl, cream the vegetable shortening and brown sugar. Beat in the egg. Beat in the molasses. Gradually blend in the

dry ingredients. Cover and chill for 2 hours.

**3** Preheat the oven to 375 degrees. Lightly grease 2 baking sheets.

**4** Pinch off 1½-inch pieces of dough and roll into balls. Dip half of each ball in granulated sugar and place the balls sugar side up 2½ inches apart on the prepared baking sheets. Sprinkle each cookie with 1 or 2 drops of cold water.

**5** Bake for 12 to 15 minutes, until lightly colored. Transfer to wire racks to cool.

# CRINKLES

Formed Cookies

YIELD: *4 to 6 dozen*
TOTAL TIME: *30 minutes*
CHILLING TIME: *2 hours*

---

2 cups all-purpose flour
½ teaspoon baking soda
¼ teaspoon salt
1 cup butter, at room temperature
1 cup granulated sugar
1 large egg

**1** Combine the flour, baking soda, and salt.

**2** In a large bowl, cream the butter and sugar. Beat in the egg. Gradually blend in the dry ingredients.

**3** Divide the dough in half. Form each half into a log 1½ inches in diameter. Wrap in waxed paper and chill for 4 hours.

**4** Preheat the oven to 400 degrees. Lightly grease 2 baking sheets.

**5** Cut the logs into ¼-inch-thick slices and place 1 inch apart on the prepared baking sheets.

**6** Bake for 8 to 10 minutes, until lightly colored. Transfer to wire racks to cool.

# CRISP BUTTER COOKIES

Refrigerator Cookies

YIELD: *3 to 4 dozen*
TOTAL TIME: *30 minutes*
CHILLING TIME: *4 hours*

# CRISP COOKIES

Rolled Cookies

YIELD: *3 to 4 dozen*
TOTAL TIME: *30 minutes*
CHILLING TIME: *4 hours*

1¾ cup all-purpose flour
⅓ cup wheat germ
1 teaspoon baking soda
½ teaspoon ground allspice
½ cup vegetable shortening
½ cup dark corn syrup
Granulated sugar for sprinkling

**1** Combine the flour, wheat germ, baking soda, and allspice.

**2** In a large bowl, beat the vegetable shortening and corn syrup until smooth. Gradually blend in the dry ingredients. Cover and chill for 4 hours.

**3** Preheat the oven to 350 degrees. Lightly grease 2 baking sheets.

**4** On a floured surface, roll out the dough to a thickness of ⅛ inch. Using cookie cutters, cut into shapes and place 1 inch apart on the prepared baking sheets. Sprinkle the cookies with granulated sugar.

**5** Bake for 8 to 10 minutes, or until lightly colored. Transfer to wire racks to cool.

# CRISP LEMON COOKIES

Rolled Cookies

YIELD: *7 to 10 dozen*
TOTAL TIME: *35 minutes*
CHILLING TIME: *4 hours*

4 cups all-purpose flour
1 teaspoon baking powder
1 cup butter, at room temperature
2 cups granulated sugar
2 large eggs
1 teaspoon lemon extract
Granulated sugar for spinkling

**1** Combine the flour and baking powder.

**2** In a large bowl, cream the butter and sugar. Beat in the eggs. Beat in the lemon extract. Gradually blend in the dry ingredients. Cover and chill for 4 hours.

**3** Preheat the oven to 375 degrees. Lightly grease 2 baking sheets.

**4** On a floured surface, roll the dough out to a thickness of ⅛ inch. Using cookie cutters, cut into shapes and place 1 inch apart on the prepared baking sheets. Sprinkle the cookies with granulated sugar.

**5** Bake for 10 to 12 minutes, until lightly colored. Transfer to wire racks to cool.

**Baking notes:** For a different look, sprinkle some of the cookies with colored crystals.

# CRISP MOLASSES COOKIES

Rolled Cookies

YIELD: *3 to 4 dozen*
TOTAL TIME: *30 minutes*

1¾ cups all-purpose flour
¼ teaspoon salt
2 tablespoons vegetable shortening
2 tablespoons granulated sugar
½ cup molasses
¾ teaspoon baking soda
3 tablespoons warm water

**1** Preheat the oven to 350 degrees. Lightly grease 2 baking sheets.

**2** Combine the flour and salt.

**3** In a large bowl, cream the vegetable shortening and sugar. Beat in the molasses.

**4** Dissolve the baking soda in the hot water and add to the molasses mixture, beating until smooth. Gradually blend in the dry ingredients.

**5** On a floured surface, roll out the dough to a thickness of ¼ inch. Using a 2-inch round cookie cutter, cut into rounds and place 1 inch apart on the prepared baking sheets.

**6** Bake for 8 to 10 minutes, until lightly colored and firm to the touch. Transfer to wire racks to cool.

5 cups all-purpose flour
1 tablespoon plus 1 teaspoon cream of tartar
2 teaspoons baking soda
1 teaspoon salt
2 cups vegetable shortening
2 cups granulated sugar
4 large eggs
2 teaspoons vanilla extract
Granulated sugar

**1** Combine the flour, cream of tartar, baking soda, and salt.

**2** In a large bowl, cream the vegetable shortening and sugar. Beat in the eggs. Beat in the vanilla extract. Gradually blend in the dry ingredients. Cover and chill for 8 hours or overnight.

**3** Preheat the oven to 375 degrees. Lightly grease 2 baking sheets.

**4** Pinch off walnut-sized pieces of dough and roll into balls. Place the balls 1½ inches apart on the prepared baking sheets. Dip the bottom of a glass in water and then in granulated sugar, and press to flatten each ball to a thickness of ¼ inch.

**5** Bake for 8 to 10 minutes, until lightly colored. Transfer to wire racks to cool.

# CRISP SUGAR COOKIES

Formed Cookies

YIELD: *5 to 6 dozen*
TOTAL TIME: *30 minutes*
CHILLING TIME: *8 hours*

---

2½ cups cookie crumbs (see Baking notes)
1 cup (6 ounce) semisweet chocolate chips
1 cup walnuts, chopped
1 teaspoon rum extract
One 14-ounce can sweetened condensed milk

**1** Preheat the oven to 350 degrees. Grease a 9-inch square baking pan.

**2** In a large bowl, combine the cookie crumbs, chocolate chips, walnuts, and rum extract and toss to mix. Press the mixture evenly into the prepared baking pan. Drizzle the condensed milk over the top.

**3** Bake for 15 to 20 minutes, until lightly browned on top. Cool in the pan on a wire rack before cutting into large or small bars.

**Baking notes:** You can use graham crackers, chocolate cream-filled sandwich cookies, or even toasted bread crumbs. For variety, substitute bittersweet chocolate chips or milk chocolate chips for the semisweet chips. Hazelnuts or almonds can be used in place of the walnuts.

# CRUMB COOKIES I

Bar Cookies

YIELD: *1 to 3 dozen*
TOTAL TIME: *30 minutes*

# CRUMB COOKIES II

### Rolled Cookies

YIELD: *3 to 4 dozen*
TOTAL TIME: *35 minutes*
CHILLING TIME: *4 hours*

1 cup all-purpose flour
1 teaspoon baking powder
½ teaspoon baking soda
½ teaspoon ground cinnamon
¼ teaspoon ground cloves
⅔ cup vegetable shortening
1 cup packed light brown sugar
2 large eggs
½ cup molasses
2½ cups bread crumbs
Milk for glazing

**1** Combine the flour, baking powder, baking soda, and spices.

**2** In a large bowl, cream the vegetable shortening and brown sugar. Beat in the eggs one at a time. Beat in the molasses. Gradually blend in the dry ingredients. Fold in the bread crumbs. Cover and chill for 4 hours.

**3** Preheat the oven to 350 degrees. Lightly grease 2 baking sheets.

**4** On a floured surface, roll out the dough to a thickness of ¼ inch. Using a 2-inch round cookie cutter, cut into rounds and place 1½ inches apart on the prepared baking sheets. Lightly brush the tops of the cookies with milk.

**5** Bake for 6 to 8 minutes, until lightly colored. Transfer to wire racks to cool.

# CRUNCH DROPS

### Drop Cookies

YIELD: *3 to 4 dozen*
TOTAL TIME: *30 minutes*

1½ cups all-purpose flour
½ teaspoon baking soda
1 teaspoon ground cinnamon
½ teaspoon salt
½ cup vegetable shortening
½ cup granulated sugar
1 large egg
½ cup dark corn syrup
¼ cup milk
½ cup golden raisins
½ cup walnuts, chopped
4 squares shredded wheat, crumbled

**1** Preheat the oven to 375 degrees. Lightly grease 2 baking sheets.

**2** Combine the flour, baking soda, cinnamon, and salt.

**3** In a large bowl, cream the vegetable shortening and sugar. Beat in the egg. Beat in the corn syrup and milk. Gradually blend in the dry ingredients. Fold in the raisins, walnuts, and shredded wheat.

**4** Drop the dough by spoonful 1½ inches apart onto the prepared baking sheets.

**5** Bake for 12 to 15 minutes, until lightly colored. Transfer to wire racks to cool.

**Baking notes:** You can use any stone-ground wheat biscuits or crackers to make these cookies; do not use soda crackers—they will soak up too much liquid.

2 cups all-purpose flour
1 teaspoon baking soda
1 teaspoon salt
1 cup vegetable shortening
½ cup granulated sugar
1 cup packed light brown sugar
2 large eggs
2 tablespoons milk
1 teaspoon vanilla extract
1 cup hard butterscotch candies, crushed

**1** Preheat the oven to 375 degrees.

**2** Combine the flour, baking soda, and salt.

**3** In a large bowl, cream the vegetable shortening and two sugars. Beat in the eggs. Beat in the milk and vanilla extract. Gradu-ally blend in the dry ingredients. Fold in the candies.

**4** Drop the dough by spoonfuls 1½ inches apart onto ungreased baking sheets.

**5** Bake for 10 to 12 minutes, until lightly colored. Transfer to wire racks to cool.

**Baking notes:** You can also use this dough to make formed cook-ies: Chill the dough for at least 4 hours. Pull off walnut-sized chunks of dough and roll them into balls. Place the balls 1½ inches apart on ungreased bak-ing sheets and bake as directed.

# CRUNCHY BUTTERSCOTCH COOKIES

Drop Cookies

YIELD: *3 to 4 dozen*
TOTAL TIME: *30 minutes*

---

2 cups (12 ounces) semisweet choco-late chips
¾ cup chunky peanut butter
3 cups Cheerios

**1** Grease an 8-inch square baking pan.

**2** In the top of a double boiler, melt the chocolate chips with the peanut butter, stirring until smooth. Remove from the heat and gradually blend in the cereal.

**3** Spread the dough evenly in the prepared baking pan. Refrigerate until thoroughly chilled, then cut into large or small bars.

# CRUNCHY CHOCOLATE BARS

Bar Cookies

YIELD: *1 to 2 dozen*
TOTAL TIME: *30 minutes*

---

1 cup whole wheat flour
½ cup pecans, ground fine
½ cup canola oil
¼ cup honey
1 teaspoon grated lemon zest
2 cups dates, finely chopped
¼ cup water
½ cup shredded coconut

**1** Preheat the oven to 400 degrees.

**2** Combine the flour and pecans.

**3** In a large bowl, beat the oil and honey together. Beat in the lemon zest. Gradually blend in the dry ingredients. Press the mixture evenly into an ungreased 9-inch square baking pan.

**4** Bake for 15 minutes.

**5** Meanwhile, combine the dates and water in a saucepan and cook until the mixture turns very soft. Transfer to a large bowl.

**6** Add the warm dough to the dates, add the coconut, and mix thoroughly. Dust your hands with flour and form the mixture into a 2-inch log. Wrap in waxed paper and chill for 1 week.

**7** Cut the log into ¼-inch-thick slices and enjoy.

# CRUNCHY COOKIES

Refrigerator Cookies

YIELD: *2 to 3 dozen*
TOTAL TIME: *30 minutes*
CHILLING TIME: *1 week*

**C**

# CUCCIDATI

Formed Cookies

YIELD: *11 to 12 dozen*
TOTAL TIME: *1 hour*
CHILLING TIME: *2 hours*

FILLING

8 cups chopped finely, peeled tart
    apples
1¾ cup chopped figs
1¾ cup dates, pitted and chopped
½ cup lemon juice
⅓ cup packed light brown sugar
1 cup almonds, chopped
5 cups all-purpose flour
2 teaspoons baking powder
1 teaspoon baking soda
½ teaspoon salt
1 cup butter, at room temperature
1 cup granulated sugar
2 large eggs
1 cup sour cream
2 teaspoons almond extract
Powdered sugar for sprinkling

**1** To make the filling combine
the apples, figs, dates, lemon
juice, and brown sugar in a large
saucepan and cook, stirring, until
most of the liquid is evaporated.
Remove from the heat and let
cool.

**2** Stir the almonds into the filling
and refrigerate for 1 hour.

**3** Combine the flour, baking
powder, baking soda, and salt.

**4** In a large bowl, cream the butter and sugar. Beat in the eggs.
Beat in the sour cream and
almond extract. Gradually blend
in the dry ingredients. Divide the
dough into 8 equal pieces. Wrap
in waxed paper and chill for 1
hour.

**5** Preheat the oven to 375
degrees. Lightly grease 2 baking
sheets.

**6** On a floured surface, roll out
one piece of dough to a 10 by 5-
inch rectangle. Spoon ¾ cup of
the filling down the center of the
dough. Fold the sides over the
filling and pinch the seam to seal.
Pinch together and place the roll
seam side down a prepared baking trays. Repeat with the
remaining dough and filling.

**7** Bake for 25 to 30 minutes, until
golden brown. Sprinkle with
powdered sugar and let cool on
the baking sheets on wire racks,
then cut into ½-inch-thick slices.

# CURRANT BARS

Bar Cookies

YIELD: *2 to 4 dozen*
TOTAL TIME: *35 minutes*

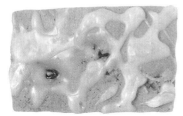

3 cups all-purpose flour
½ teaspoon baking scda
½ teaspoon ground cinnamon
¼ teaspoon ground cloves
½ teaspoon salt
1 cup vegetable shortening
¾ cup granulated sugar
¾ cup packed light brown sugar
2 large eggs, slightly beaten
⅓ cup orange juice
1 cup currants
1 cup flaked coconut

TOPPING
¾ cup powdered sugar
1 tablespoon plus 1 teaspoon fresh
    orange juice
1 teaspoon finely shredded orange
    zest

**1** Preheat the oven to 350
degrees. Lightly grease 2 baking
sheets.

**2** Combine the flour, baking
soda, spices, and salt.

**3** Melt the vegetable shortening
in a large saucepan. Remove

from the heat and beat in the two
sugars. Beat in the eggs one at a
time. Beat in the orange juice.
Gradually blend in the dry ingredients. Fold in the currants and
coconut. Spread the mixture
evenly in the prepared baking
pan.

**4** Bake for 20 to 25 minutes, until
light colored on top.

**5** Meanwhile, in a small bowl
combine all of the ingredients for
the topping and stir until
smooth.

**6** Spread the topping over the
warm cookies. Cool in the pan on
a wire rack before cutting into
large or small bars.

1 cup all-purpose flour
1 teaspoon baking powder
¼ teaspoon salt
2 large eggs
1 cup granulated sugar
1 teaspoon fresh lemon juice
¾ cup golden raisins
¾ cup currants

**1** Preheat the oven to 350 degrees. Lightly grease a 13 by 9-inch square baking pan.

**2** Combine the flour, baking powder, and salt.

**3** In a large bowl, beat the eggs and sugar until thick and light-colored. Beat in the lemon juice. Gradually blend in the dry ingredients. Fold in the raisins and currants. Spread the batter evenly in the prepared baking pan.

**4** Bake for 20 to 25 minutes, until a toothpick inserted in the center come out clean. Cool in the pan on a wire rack before cutting into large or small bars.

# CURRANT-RAISIN BARS

Bar Cookies

YIELD: *1 to 2 dozen*
TOTAL TIME: *35 minutes*

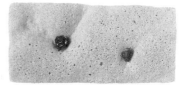

---

2½ cups all-purpose flour
1¼ teaspoons baking powder
⅛ teaspoon salt
¼ cup canola oil
¾ cup powdered sugar
1 large egg
¼ cup milk
1 teaspoon vanilla extract
1 teaspoon grated lemon zest
Vanilla Icing (see Pantry)

**1** Combine the flour, baking powder, and salt.

**2** In a large bowl, beat the oil and sugar. Beat in the egg. Beat in the milk and vanilla extract. Beat in the lemon zest. Gradually blend in the dry ingredients. Cover and chill for 6 hours.

**3** Preheat the oven to 350 degrees.

**4** On a floured surface, roll out the dough to a thickness of ⅛ inch. Using cookie cutters, cut into shapes and place 1½ inches apart on ungreased baking sheets.

**5** Bake for 6 to 8 minutes, until lightly colored. Transfer to wire racks to cool before decorating with the icing.

# CUT-OUT HANUKKAH COOKIES

Rolled Cookies

YIELD: *3 to 4 dozen*
TOTAL TIME: *30 minutes*
CHILLING TIME: *6 hours*

C

# CZECHOSLOVAKIAN CHRISTMAS COOKIES

Rolled Cookies

YIELD: *10 to 12 dozen*
TOTAL TIME: *40 minutes*
CHILLING TIME: *1 week*

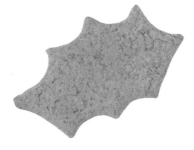

3¾ cup all-purpose flour
½ teaspoon baking soda
1 teaspoon ground cinnamon
¾ teaspoon ground ginger
½ teaspoon ground cloves
¼ teaspoon ground allspice
¼ teaspoon ground nutmeg
¼ teaspoon salt
½ cup butter, at room temperature
⅓ cup packed dark brown sugar
1 cup molasses, warmed

**1** Combine the flour, baking soda, spices, and salt.

**2** In a large bowl, cream the butter and brown sugar. Beat in the molasses. Gradually blend in the dry ingredients. If the mixture seems dry, add warm water 1 teaspoonful at a time. Shape the dough into a disk, wrap in waxed paper, and refrigerate for 1 week.

**3** Three hours before ready to bake, remove the dough from the refrigerator.

**4** Preheat the oven to 375 degrees. Lightly grease 2 baking sheets.

**5** On a floured surface, roll out the dough to a thickness of ¼ inch. Using cookie cutters, cut into shapes and place 1 inch apart on the prepared baking sheets.

**6** Bake for 7 to 10 minutes, until lightly colored. Transfer to wire racks to cool. Store in airtight containers.

# CZECHOSLOVAKIAN COOKIES

Rolled Cookies

YIELD: *4 to 6 dozen*
TOTAL TIME: *30 minutes*
CHILLING TIME: *4 hours*

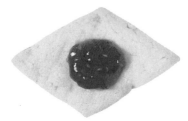

1 cup vegetable shortening
1 cup granulated sugar
2 large eggs
1 teaspoon vanilla extract
2½ cups all-purpose flour
1 cup hazelnuts, chopped fine
About ¼ cup strawberry jam

**1** In a large bowl, cream the vegetable shortening and sugar. Beat in the eggs. Beat in the vanilla. Gradually blend in the flour. Blend in the hazelnuts. Cover and chill for 4 hours.

**2** Preheat the oven to 325 degrees.

**3** On a floured surface, roll out the dough to a thickness of ¼ inch. Using cookie cutters, cut into shapes and place 1 inch apart on ungreased baking sheets. Place ¼ teaspoon of strawberry jam in the center of each cookie.

**4** Bake for 8 to 12 minutes, until lightly colored. Transfer to wire racks to cool.

**Baking notes:** This is a very basic recipe that lends itself to many variations; substitute your favorite nuts for the hazelnuts and use a variety of fruit jams and preserves to fill the centers of the cookies.

2½ cups all-purpose flour
¾ teaspoon baking powder
¼ teaspoon salt
1 cup vegetable shortening
⅔ cup granulated sugar
1 large egg
Food coloring

**1** Preheat the oven to 325 degrees.

**2** Combine the flour, baking powder, and salt.

**3** In a large bowl, cream the vegetable shortening and sugar. Beat in the egg. Gradually blend in the dry ingredients.

**4** Transfer one-third of the dough to a medium bowl and another third to another bowl. Work a few drops of different-colored food coloring into each third.

**5** Drop the dough by spoonfuls onto ungreased baking sheets.

**6** Bake for 12 to 15 minutes, until lightly colored. Transfer to wire racks to cool.

**Baking notes:** This dough may be formed into logs, chilled and sliced, molded in a cookie mold, or pressed out through a cookie press or pastry bag.

# DAINTIES

Drop Cookies

YIELD: *4 to 5 dozen*
TOTAL TIME: *30 minutes*

---

**CRUST**
2½ cups all-purpose flour
1 teaspoon salt
1 large egg yolk
⅓ cup plus 2 teaspoons milk
1 cup vegetable shortening
¾ cup granulated sugar
1 cup cornflakes
8 cups peeled, sliced apples

**FILLING**
1 cup powdered sugar
1 teaspoon ground cinnamon
1 large egg white, beaten
Powdered sugar for sprinkling

**1** Preheat the oven to 375 degrees. Lightly grease a 15 by 10-inch baking pan.

**2** To make the crust, combine the flour and salt.

**3** Place the egg yolk in a measuring cup, and add enough milk to measure a ⅔ cup.

**4** In a large bowl, cream the vegetable shortening and sugar. Beat in the egg yolk and milk. Gradually blend in the dry ingredients.

**5** Divide the dough in half. On a floured surface, roll out half of the dough to a 16 by 11-inch rec-

tangle and fit it into the prepared baking pan.

**6** Spread the cornflakes on top of the dough and arrange the apple on top of the cornflakes. Combine the powdered sugar and cinnamon and sprinkle over the apples.

**7** Roll out the remaining dough to a 16 by 11-inch rectangle and place it on top of the filling. Pinch the edges of the dough together to seal. Cut 2 or 3 slits in the top for steam to escape. Brush the top with the beaten egg whites.

**8** Bake for 45 to 50 minutes, until the crust is golden brown. Sprinkle with powdered sugar and cool in the pan on a wire rack before cutting into large or small bars.

# DANISH APPLE BARS

Bar Cookies

YIELD: *3 to 4 dozen*
TOTAL TIME: *60 minutes*

# DANISH APRICOT BARS

Bar Cookies

YIELD: *3 to 4 dozen*
TOTAL TIME: *60 minutes*

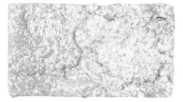

**CRUST**
2½ cups all-purpose flour
1 teaspoon salt
1 cup butter, at room temperature
¾ cup packed light brown sugar
1 large egg yolk
1 tablespoon plus ½ teaspoon sour milk

**FILLING**
1 cup rolled oats
1½ tablespoons butter, at room temperature
8 cups thinly sliced apricots
1 cup granulated sugar
1 teaspoon ground allspice
1 large egg white, beaten
Granulated sugar for sprinkling

**1** Preheat the oven to 375 degrees. Lightly grease a 15 by 10-inch baking pan.

**2** To make the crust, combine the flour and salt.

**3** In a large bowl, cream the butter and brown sugar. Beat in the egg yolk and sour milk. Gradually blend in the dry ingredients.

**4** Divide the dough in half. On a floured surface, roll out half of the dough to a 6 by 11-inch rectangle and fit it into the prepared baking pan.

**5** Spread the oats on top of the dough and dot with butter. Arrange the apricot slices on top of the oats. Combine the sugar and allspice and sprinkle over the apricots.

**6** Roll out the remaining dough to a 16 by 11-inch rectangle and place it on top of the filling. Pinch the edges of the dough to seal. Cut 2 or 3 slits in the top for steam to escape. Brush the top with the beaten egg white and sprinkle with granulated sugar.

**7** Bake for 45 to 50 minutes, until the crust is golden brown. Cool in the pan on a wire rack before cutting into large or small bars.

---

# DANISH GYPSY COOKIES

Rolled Cookies

YIELD: *3 to 4 dozen*
TOTAL TIME: *30 minutes*

2½ cups all-purpose flour
1⅓ cups cookie crumbs
1 teaspoon baking soda
1 teaspoon ground cinnamon
½ cup vegetable shortening
¾ cup granulated sugar
1 large egg
1 teaspoon vanilla extract
Granulated sugar for rolling

**1** Preheat the oven to 350 degrees.

**2** Combine the flour, cookie crumbs, baking soda, and cinnamon.

**3** In a large bowl, cream the vegetable shortening and sugar. Beat in the egg. Beat in the vanilla extract. Gradually blend in the dry ingredients.

**4** On a floured surface, roll out the dough to a thickness of ½ inch. Cut into strips 1½ inches long and ½ inch wide. Roll the strips into logs between your palms, roll in granulated sugar, and place 1 inch apart on ungreased baking sheets.

**5** Bake for 10 to 12 minutes, until lightly colored. Transfer to wire racks to cool.

1¾ cups all-purpose flour
¾ cup rolled oats
1½ teaspoons baking powder
½ cup butter, at room temperature
½ cup granulated sugar
1 large egg
1½ tablespoons water

**1** Combine the flour, oats, and baking powder.

**2** In a large bowl, cream the butter and sugar. Beat in the egg and water. Gradually blend in the dry ingredients. Cover and chill for 2 hours.

**3** Preheat the oven to 375 degrees. Lightly grease 2 baking sheets.

**4** On a floured surface, roll out the dough to a thickness of ⅛ inch. Using a 3-inch round cookie cutter, cut into rounds and place

1½ inches apart on the prepared baking sheets. Prick each cookie several times with the tines of a fork.

**5** Bake for 8 to 10 minutes, or until golden brown. Transfer to wire racks to cool.

# DANISH OATMEAL BISCUITS

Rolled Cookies

YIELD: *2 to 3 dozen*
TOTAL TIME: *30 minutes*
CHILLING TIME: *2 hours*

---

**CRUST**
2½ cups all-purpose flour
1 teaspoon salt
1 cup butter, at room temperature
¾ cup powdered sugar
1 large egg yolk
2 ounces cream cheese, at room temperature

**FILLING**
1 cup wheat flake cereal, crushed
8 cups dices dried peaches
1 cup loosely packed light brown sugar
1 teaspoon ground allspice
1 large egg white, beaten
Granulated sugar for sprinkling

**1** Preheat the oven to 375 degrees. Lightly grease a 15 by 10-inch baking pan.

**2** To make the crust, combine the flour and salt.

**3** In a large bowl, cream the butter and powdered sugar. Beat in the egg yolk. Beat in the cream cheese. Gradually blend in the dry ingredients.

**4** Divide the dough in half. On a floured surface, roll out half of the dough to a 16 by 11-inch rectangle and fit it into the prepared baking pan.

**5** Spread the cereal on top of the dough and layer the peaches on top of the cereal. Combine the brown sugar and allspice and sprinkle over the peaches.

**6** Roll out the remaining dough to a 16 by 11-inch rectangle and place it on top of the filling. Pinch the edges of the dough to seal. Cut 2 or 3 slits in the top for steam to escape. Brush the top with the beaten egg white and sprinkle with granulated sugar.

**7** Bake for 45 to 50 minutes, until the crust is golden brown. Cool in the pan on a wire rack before cutting into large or small bars.

# DANISH PEACH BARS

Bar Cookies

YIELD: *1 to 2 dozen*
TOTAL TIME: *60 minutes*

# DARK SECRETS

Bar Cookies

YIELD: *6 to 7 dozen*
TOTAL TIME: *35 minutes*

5 cups all-purpose flour
1 teaspoon baking powder
¼ teaspoon salt
2 tablespoons vegetable shortening
¾ cup granulated sugar
¼ cup packed light brown sugar
3 large eggs
1 teaspoon rum
1 cup dates, pitted and chopped
1 cup pecans, chopped
Powdered sugar for rolling

1  Preheat the oven to 350 degrees. Lightly grease a 15 by 10-inch baking pan.

2  Combine the flour, baking powder, and salt.

3  In a large bowl, cream the vegetable shortening and two sug-ars. Beat in the eggs one at a time. Beat in the rum. Gradually blend in the dry ingredients. Fold in the dates and pecans. Spread the dough evenly in the prepared baking pan.

4  Bake for 15 to 20 minutes, until just lightly colored; do not over-bake. Cool slightly in the pan on a wire rack.

5  Cut the warm cookies into 2 by 1-inch strips and roll them in powdered sugar.

# DATE BALLS

Formed Cookies

YIELD: *4 to 5 dozen*
TOTAL TIME: *30 minutes*

1¼ cups all-purpose flour
Pinch of salt
½ cup vegetable shortening
⅓ cup powdered sugar
1 tablespoon water
1 teaspoon vanilla extract
⅔ cup dates, pitted and chopped
½ cup walnuts, chopped
Powdered sugar for rolling

1  Preheat the oven to 300 degrees.

2  Combine the flour and salt.

3  In a large bowl, cream the vegetable shortening and powdered sugar. Beat in the water and vanilla extract. Gradually blend in the dry ingredients. Fold in the dates and walnuts.

4  Pinch off 1-inch pieces of dough and roll into balls. Place 1 inch apart on the ungreased baking sheets.

5  Bake for 18 to 20 minutes, or just until the cookies start to color slightly. Roll in powdered sugar and transfer to wire racks to cool.

# DATE BARS I

Bar Cookies

YIELD: *1 to 2 dozen*
TOTAL TIME: *35 minutes*

½ cup all-purpose flour
½ teaspoon baking powder
Pinch of salt
⅔ cup sweetened condensed milk
½ teaspoon vanilla extract
½ cup dates, pitted and chopped
¼ cup walnuts, chopped

1  Preheat the oven to 375 degrees. Lightly grease a 9-inch square baking pan.

2  Combine the flour, baking powder, and salt.

3  In a medium bowl, beat the condensed milk and vanilla extract together. Gradually blend in the dry ingredients. Stir in the dates and walnuts. Spread the mixture evenly in the prepared baking pan.

4  Bake for 18 to 20 minutes, until lightly colored on top. Cool in the pan on a wire rack before cutting into large or small bars.

1 cup all purpose flour
2 teaspoons baking powder
¼ teaspoon salt
4 large eggs, separated
1½ cups granulated sugar
¼ cup milk
1 teaspoon vanilla extract
1 cup bran
1½ cups dates, pitted and chopped
1 cup walnuts, chopped
Powdered sugar for sprinkling

1 Preheat the oven to 350 degrees. Lightly grease an 8-inch square baking pan.

2 Combine the flour, baking powder, and salt.

3 In a large bowl, beat the egg yolks and sugar until thick. Beat in the milk and vanilla extract. Gradually blend in the dry ingredients. Fold in the bran flakes, dates, and walnuts.

4 In a large bowl, beat the egg whites until stiff but not dry. Fold the whites into the date mixture. Spread the batter evenly in the prepared baking pan.

5 Bake for 15 to 20 minutes, until the top is lightly colored. Cool in the pan on a wire rack.

6 Cut the cookies into 1-inch strips and sprinkle with powdered sugar.

# DATE BARS II

Bar Cookies

Yield: *1 to 2 dozen*
Total time: *30 minutes*

---

1 cup whole wheat flour
½ cup soy flour
¼ teaspoon salt
2 large eggs, separated
1 cup packed light brown sugar
¼ cup boiling water
1 teaspoon vanilla extract
1 cup dates, pitted and chopped
1 cup walnuts, chopped

1 Preheat the oven to 350 degrees. Lightly grease a 13 by 9-inch baking pan.

2 Combine the flour, soy flour, and salt.

3 In a large bowl, beat the egg yolks until thick and light-colored. Beat in the brown sugar and water. Beat in the vanilla extract. Gradually blend in the dry ingredients. Fold in the dates and walnuts.

4 In a large bowl, beat the egg whites until stiff but not dry. Fold the whites into the date mixture. Spread the batter evenly in the prepared baking pan.

5 Bake for 30 to 35 minutes, until lightly colored on top. Cool in the pan on a wire rack before cutting into large or small bars.

# DATE BARS III

Bar Cookies

Yield: *2 to 3 dozen*
Total time: *45 minutes*

---

½ cup all-purpose flour
¼ teaspoon baking powder
¼ teaspoon salt
2 ounces bittersweet chocolate, chopped
½ cup vegetable shortening
1 cup granulated sugar
2 large eggs
1 teaspoon vanilla extract
1 cup walnuts, chopped
⅔ cup dates, pitted and chopped

1 Preheat the oven to 325 degrees. Lightly grease a 9-inch square baking pan.

2 Combine the flour, baking powder, and salt.

3 In the top of a double boiler, melt the chocolate and vegetable shortening, stirring until smooth. Remove from the heat and beat in the sugar. Beat in the eggs one at a time. Beat in the vanilla extract. Gradually blend in the dry ingredients. Stir in the walnuts and dates. Spread the mixture evenly in the prepared baking pan.

4 Bake for 20 to 25 minutes, or until a toothpick inserted in the center comes out clean. Cool in the pan on a wire rack before cutting into large or small bars.

# DATE BROWNIES I

Bar Cookies

Yield: *1 to 3 dozen*
Total time: *35 minutes*

# DATE BROWNIES II

Bar Cookies

YIELD: *1 to 2 dozen*
TOTAL TIME: *60 minutes*

**CRUST**
2 ounces semisweet chocolate, chopped
1¾ cups all-purpose flour
1 teaspoon baking powder
½ teaspoon salt
¾ cup vegetable shortening
1 cup packed light brown sugar
2 each large eggs
1 teaspoon vanilla extract
⅓ cup walnuts, chopped

**FILLING**
¾ cup dates, pitted and chopped fine
½ cup water
¼ cup granulated sugar
¼ teaspoon vanilla extract

**1** Preheat the oven to 350 degrees. Lightly grease a 9-inch square baking pan.

**2** In the top of a double boiler, melt the chocolate over low heat, stirring until smooth. Remove from the heat.

**3** Combine the flour, baking powder, and salt.

**4** In a large bowl, cream the vegetable shortening and brown sugar. Beat in the eggs one at a time. Beat in the vanilla extract. Beat in the melted chocolate. Gradually blend in the dry ingredients. Fold in the walnuts.

**5** Spread half of the mixture evenly in the prepared baking pan.

**6** To make the filling, combine the dates, water, and sugar in a saucepan and cook over low heat, stirring until thick, 3 to 5 minutes. Remove from the heat and stir in the vanilla extract.

**7** Spoon the filling over the crust in the baking pan. Spread the remaining crust mixture over the date filling.

**8** Bake for 35 to 40 minutes, until lightly colored on top and firm to the touch. Cool in the pan on a wire rack before cutting into large or small bars.

# DATE DROPS I

Drop Cookies

YIELD: *4 to 5 dozen*
TOTAL TIME: *30 minutes*

1½ cups all-purpose flour
1 teaspoon baking powder
1 teaspoon ground cinnamon
½ teaspoon ground cloves
¼ teaspoon salt
½ cup vegetable shortening
1 cup granulated sugar
2 large eggs
1½ cups dates, pitted and chopped
1 cup walnuts, chopped

**1** Preheat the oven to 350 degrees.

**2** Combine the flour, baking powder, spices, and salt.

**3** In a large bowl, cream the vegetable shortening and sugar. Beat in the eggs one at a time. Gradually blend in the dry ingredients. Fold in the dates and walnuts.

**4** Drop the dough by spoonfuls 1½ inches apart onto ungreased baking sheets.

**5** Bake for 12 to 15 minutes, until lightly colored. Transfer to wire racks to cool.

**Baking notes:** These cookies are delicious iced with a Rum Buttercream (see Pantry).

1¼ cups all-purpose flour
½ teaspoon baking powder
½ teaspoon baking soda
¼ teaspoon salt
¼ cup vegetable shortening
¾ cup packed light brown sugar
1 large egg
½ cup sour cream
1 pound dates, pitted and chopped
About ½ cup walnuts
Vanilla Icing (see Pantry)

**1** Preheat the oven to 400 degrees. Lightly grease 2 baking sheets.

**2** Combine the flour, baking powder, baking soda, and salt.

**3** In a large bowl, cream the vegetable shortening and brown sugar. Beat in the egg and sour cream. Gradually blend in the dry ingredients. Fold in the dates.

**4** Drop the dough by spoonfuls 1½ inches apart onto the prepared baking sheets. Press a walnut into the center of each cookie.

**5** Bake for 8 to 10 minutes, until lightly colored. Transfer to wire racks to cool.

**6** Fill a pastry bag fitted with a small plain tip with the icing and pipe a ring of icing around each walnut.

**Baking notes:** In an old version of this recipe, whole pitted dates are stuffed with walnut halves and placed on baking sheets, then the dough is dropped on top of the dates.

# DATE DROPS II

Drop Cookies

<small>YIELD: *1 to 2 dozen*</small>
<small>TOTAL TIME: *40 minutes*</small>

---

3 cups all-purpose flour
½ teaspoon baking soda
¼ teaspoon salt
1 cup vegetable shortening
½ cup granulated sugar
½ cup packed light brown sugar
1 large egg
1 teaspoon vanilla extract

FILLING
2 cups dates, pitted and chopped
⅓ cup granulated sugar
½ cup water
2 tablespoons fresh lemon juice
¼ teaspoon salt
1 large egg, beaten
Granulated sugar for sprinkling

**1** Combine the flour, baking soda, and salt.

**2** In a large bowl, cream the vegetable shortening and two sugars. Beat in the egg. Beat in the vanilla extract. Gradually blend in the dry ingredients. Divide the dough in half. Wrap each half in waxed paper and chill for 4 hours.

**3** To make the filling, combine the dates, sugar, water, lemon juice, and salt in a saucepan and cook, stirring until very thick. Remove from the heat.

**4** Preheat the oven to 350 degrees.

**5** On a floured surface, roll out the dough to a thickness of ⅛ inch. Using a 2½-inch round cookie cutter, cut out an equal number of cookies. Place half the rounds 1½ inches apart on ungreased baking sheets. Brush lightly with water and place a level tablespoonful of filling in the center of each round. Place the remaining rounds on top, and crimp the edges with a fork to seal. Make 2 slits in the top of each round and brush the tops with the beaten egg. Sprinkle with granulated sugar.

**6** Bake for 10 to 12 minutes, until lightly colored. Transfer to wire racks to cool

# DATE-FILLED COOKIES

Rolled Cookies

<small>YIELD: *2 to 3 dozen*</small>
<small>TOTAL TIME: *45 minutes*</small>
<small>CHILLING TIME: *4 hours*</small>

# DATE FINGERS

Rolled Cookies

YIELD: *1 to 2 dozen*
TOTAL TIME: *50 minutes*
RESTING TIME: *24 hours*

**FILLING**
2 tablespoons vegetable shortening
3 tablespoons granulated sugar
½ teaspoon ground ginger
½ teaspoon ground cinnamon
⅔ cup currants
⅔ cup dates, pitted and chopped

**CRUST**
2 cups all-purpose flour
1 teaspoon salt
¾ cups vegetable shortening
3 to 4 tablespoons ice water
1 large egg, beaten
2 tablespoons powdered sugar

**1** To make the filling, melt the shortening in a large saucepan. Stir in the sugar, ginger, cinnamon, currants, and dates and bring to a boil. Transfer to a bowl, cover, and set aside undisturbed for 24 hours.

**2** Preheat the oven to 350 degrees. Lightly grease a 15 by 9-inch baking sheet.

**3** To make the crust, combine the flour and salt in a large bowl. Cut in the vegetable shortening until the mixture resembles coarse crumbs. Stir in just enough water to make a soft pliable dough.

**4** Divide the dough in half. On a floured surface, roll out half of the dough to a 15 by 10-inch rectangle. Fit it into the prepared baking sheet. Spread the filling over the dough, leaving a ½-inch border all around the edges.

**5** Roll out the remaining dough to a 15 by 10-inch rectangle. Lightly brush the edges of the dough in the baking pan with water and lay the second sheet of dough over the filling. Crimp the edges with a fork to seal. Prick the dough with a fork. Brush with the beaten egg and sprinkle with the powdered sugar.

**6** Bake for 25 to 30 minutes, until the crust is lightly colored. Cool on the baking sheet on a wire rack before cutting into finger-sized pieces.

**Baking notes:** This dough and filling can also be used to make 2- or 3-inch round cookies. Drizzle Vanilla Icing (see Pantry) over the tops of the filled cookies.

# DATE-GRANOLA SQUARES

Bar Cookies

YIELD: *1 to 3 dozen*
TOTAL TIME: *35 minutes*

2½ cups all purpose flour
2 teaspoons baking powder
½ teaspoon baking soda
1 teaspoon ground cinnamon
½ teaspoon ground nutmeg
¼ teaspoon ground ginger
¼ teaspoon salt
½ cup canola oil
2 large eggs
1½ cup pear juice
1 cup unsweetened granola (see Baking notes)
1 cup dates, pitted and chopped

**TOPPING**
½ cup dates, pitted and chopped very fine
½ cup unsweetened granola

**1** Preheat the oven to 350 degrees. Lightly grease a 13 by 9-inch baking pan.

**2** Combine the flour, baking powder, baking soda, spices, and salt.

**3** In a large bowl, beat the canola oil and eggs together. Beat in the pear juice. Gradually blend in the dry ingredients. Stir in the granola and dates. Spread the mixture evenly in the prepared baking pan.

**4** To make the topping, combine the dates and granola in a small bowl and toss to mix. Sprinkle evenly over the top of the granola mixture.

**5** Bake for 25 to 30 minutes, until firm to the touch. Cool in the pan on a wire rack before cutting into large or small bars.

**Baking notes:** If you wish to make your own granola, combine equal amounts of rolled oats, chopped nuts, flaked coconut, sesame seeds, chopped sunflower seeds, and chopped dried fruit, such as banana chips and/or raisins.

## DATE-HONEY FINGERS

Bar Cookies

YIELD: *4 to 5 dozen*
TOTAL TIME: *40 minutes*

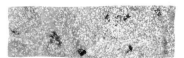

¾ cup all purpose flour
½ teaspoon baking powder
Pinch of salt
¼ cup butter, at room temperature
5 tablespoons honey
2 large eggs
⅔ cup dates, pitted and chopped
½ cup walnuts, chopped fine
Powdered sugar for sprinkling

**1** Preheat the oven to 375 degrees. Lightly grease an 8-inch square baking pan.

**2** Combine the flour, baking powder, and salt.

**3** In a large bowl, beat the butter and honey until smooth. Beat in the eggs. Gradually blend in the dry ingredients. Fold in the dates and walnuts. Spread the dough evenly in the prepared baking pan.

**4** Bake for 25 to 30 minutes, until firm to the touch. Cool in the pan on a wire rack.

**5** Sprinkle the cookies with powdered sugar and cut into finger-sized bars.

## DATE LOGS

Bar Cookies

YIELD: *3 to 4 dozen*
TOTAL TIME: *50 minutes*

1 cup all-purpose flour
½ teaspoon baking powder
3 large egg whites
Pinch of salt
1 cup granulated sugar
⅔ cup dates, pitted and chopped
½ cup walnuts, chopped fine
Powdered sugar for sprinkling

**1** Preheat the oven to 350 degrees. Lightly grease a 9-inch square baking pan.

**2** Combine the flour and baking powder.

**3** In a large bowl, beat the egg whites with the salt and sugar until stiff but not dry. Gradually fold in the dry ingredients. Fold in the dates and walnuts. Spread the mixture evenly in the prepared baking pan.

**4** Bake for 20 to 30 minutes, until firm to the touch. Cool in the pan on a wire rack just until cool enough to handle.

**5** Cut the cookies into finger-sized lengths and roll between the palms of your hands to form logs. Roll each log in powdered sugar and cool completely on the racks.

## DATE MACAROONS

Drop Cookies

YIELD: *4 to 5 dozen*
TOTAL TIME: *40 minutes*

2 large egg whites
⅛ teaspoon salt
⅔ cup powdered sugar
1 teaspoon vanilla extract
1 cup dates, pitted and chopped fine
½ cup shredded coconut

**1** Preheat the oven to 325 degrees. Lightly grease 2 baking sheets.

**2** In a large bowl, beat the egg whites with the salt until stiff but not dry. Fold in the powdered sugar. Fold in the vanilla extract. Fold in the dates and coconut.

**3** Drop the dough by spoonfuls 1½ inches apart onto the prepared baking sheets.

**4** Bake for 8 to 10 minutes, until lightly colored. Transfer to wire racks to cool.

# DATE NEWTONS

Formed Cookies

YIELD: *3 to 4 dozen*
TOTAL TIME: *50 minutes*
CHILLING TIME: *24 hours*

1¼ cups all-purpose flour
1 cup whole wheat flour
¼ cup wheat germ
¼ teaspoon baking soda
¼ teaspoon salt
½ cup vegetable shortening
½ cup granulated sugar
½ cup packed light brown sugar
2 large eggs
½ teaspoon vanilla extract

FILLING
⅓ cup granulated sugar
½ cup water
2 tablespoons fresh lemon juice
2 teaspoons grated lemon zest
2 cups dates, pitted and chopped
½ cup walnuts, chopped

**1** Combine the two flours, the wheat germ, baking soda, and salt.

**2** In a large bowl, cream the vegetable shortening and two sugars. Beat in the eggs. Beat in the vanilla extract. Gradually blend in the dry ingredients. Cover and chill for 24 hours.

**3** To make the filling, combine all of the ingredients in a saucepan and bring to a boil. Cook until the mixture is very thick. Remove from the heat, and set aside to cool.

**4** Lightly grease 2 baking sheets.

**5** Divide the dough in half and keep one half chilled while you work with the other. On a floured surface, roll out the dough to a 15 by 9-inch rectangle. Trim the edges and cut each into 3 strips lengthwise. Using half of the date filling, spoon the mixture down the center of three strips, spreading it to the very ends. Lightly moisten the long sides of each strip. Fold them over until they meet in the center and pinch to seal them. Gently turn each roll seam side down and cut into thirds. Place 1 inch apart on one of the prepared baking sheets, cover with a cloth, and chill for 1 hour. Repeat with the remaining dough and filling.

**6** Preheat the oven to 350 degrees.

**7** Bake the cookies for 15 to 20 minutes, until lightly colored. Cool on the baking sheet on a wire rack before cutting into "traditional" Newton-sized bars.

**Baking notes:** These cookies can be difficult to make. One of the secrets of success is to make sure the edges of the long strips are perfectly straight and even. Another is to cook the filling until very thick.

# DATE-NUT BARS

Bar Cookies

YIELD: *1 to 2 dozen*
TOTAL TIME: *45 minutes*

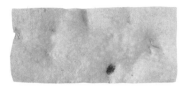

¾ cup all-purpose flour
½ teaspoon baking powder
½ teaspoon salt
2 large eggs
1 cup packed light brown sugar
1 cup dates, pitted and sliced
    crosswise
½ cup brazil nuts

**1** Preheat the oven to 350 degrees. Lightly grease a 9-inch square baking pan.

**2** Combine the flour, dates, baking powder, and salt.

**3** In a large bowl, beat the eggs until they are thick and light-colored. Beat in the brown sugar. Gradually blend in the dry ingredients. Fold in the dates and nuts. Spread the mixture evenly in the prepared baking pan.

**4** Bake for 25 to 30 minutes, or until the top is a light brown. Cool in the pan on a wire rack, then cut into 2 by 1-inch-wide strips.

**Baking notes:** The cookies may be rolled in powdered sugar before serving.

1¼ cups toasted rice cereal
1 cup dates, pitted and chopped fine
1 cup pecans, chopped
½ cup butter
¼ cup granulated sugar
¼ cup packed light brown sugar
1 large egg
1 cup shredded coconut

**1** Combine the cereal, dates, and pecans in a large bowl.

**2** Combine the butter and two sugars in the top of a double boiler and cook over low heat, stirring, until the butter melts and the sugar dissolves. Beat in the egg and cook for 20 minutes, stirring occasionally, until very thick. Do not allow the mixture to boil.

**3** Pour the hot sugar mixture over the date mixture and stir to coat well. Let cool slightly.

**4** Pinch off pieces of dough and form into 2 by 1-inch strips. Roll the strips in the shredded coconut and let cool.

# DATE-NUT FINGERS

Formed Cookies

YIELD: *4 to 5 dozen*
TOTAL TIME: *50 minutes*

---

FILLING
2 cups dates, pitted and chopped
1 cup water
2 tablespoons granulated sugar

CRUST
1 cup all-purpose flour
½ cup packed light brown sugar
1 cup rolled oats
⅓ cup vegetable shortening

**1** Preheat the oven to 400 degrees. Lightly grease a 9-inch square baking pan.

**2** To make the filling, combine the dates, water, and sugar in a saucepan and bring to a simmer. Cook, stirring constantly, for 7 to 10 minutes, until the mixture thickens. Let cool slightly. Pour the filling over the crust. Spread the remaining half of the crust mixture on top and press down slightly.

**3** To make the crust, combine the flour, brown sugar, and oats in a large bowl. Cut in the vegetable shortening until a dough forms.

**4** Press half of the mixture into the bottom of the prepared baking pan.

**5** Bake for 45 to 50 minutes, until lightly colored on top. Cool in the pan on a wire rack before cutting into large or small bars.

# DATE-OATMEAL BARS

Bar Cookies

YIELD: *1 to 3 dozen*
TOTAL TIME: *65 minutes*

---

¾ cup all-purpose flour
½ teaspoon baking powder
¼ teaspoon salt
3 each large eggs
1 cup granulated sugar
2 tablespoons fresh orange juice
¼ cup grated orange zest
1 cup dates, pitted and chopped
1 cup pecans, chopped
Granulated sugar for rolling

**1** Preheat the oven to 350 degrees. Lightly grease a 9-inch square baking pan.

**2** Combine the flour, baking powder, and salt.

**3** In a large bowl, beat the eggs until thick and light-colored. Beat in the sugar, orange juice, and orange zest. Gradually blend in the dry ingredients. Fold in the dates and pecans. Spread the dough evenly in the prepared baking pan.

**4** Bake for 20 to 25 minutes, until lightly colored on top. Cool in the pan on a wire rack before cutting into small squares. Roll each square in granulated sugar.

# DATE-PECAN CHEWS

Bar Cookies

YIELD: *4 to 5 dozen*
TOTAL TIME: *50 minutes*

D

# DATE PINWHEELS

Rolled Cookies

YIELD: *4 to 5 dozen*
TOTAL TIME: *45 minutes*
CHILLING TIME: *Crust: 4 hours*
            *Roll: 24 hours*

2⅓ cups all-purpose flour
½ teaspoon baking powder
¼ teaspoon baking soda
¼ teaspoon ground cinnamon
¼ teaspoon salt
½ cup vegetable shortening
1 cup packed light brown sugar
2 large eggs
½ teaspoon vanilla extract

**FILLING**
1½ cups dates, pitted and chopped
    fine
⅓ cup water
⅓ cup granulated sugar
½ cup walnuts, ground fine
½ teaspoon vanilla extract

**1** Combine the flour, baking powder, baking soda, cinnamon, and salt.

**2** In a large bowl, cream the vegetable shortening and brown sugar. Beat in the eggs. Beat in the vanilla extract. Gradually blend in the dry ingredients. Cover and chill for 4 hours.

**3** To make the filling, combine the dates, water, and sugar in a saucepan and bring to a boil. Reduce the heat and cook, stirring, until very thick. Remove

from the heat and stir in the walnuts and vanilla.

**4** On a floured surface, roll out the dough to a ¼-inch-thick rectangle. Spread the date filling evenly over the dough, leaving a ¼-inch border all around the edges. Starting on a long side, roll up the dough jelly-roll fashion and pinch the seam to seal. Cut the roll in half, wrap in waxed paper, and chill for 24 hours.

**5** Preheat the oven to 350 degrees. Lightly grease 2 baking sheets.

**6** Cut the rolls into ¼-inch-thick slices and place 1 inch apart on the prepared baking sheets.

**7** Bake for 8 to 10 minutes, until lightly colored. Transfer to wire racks to cool.

# DATE SQUARES I

Bar Cookies

YIELD: *1 to 4 dozen*
TOTAL TIME: *40 minutes*

**FILLING**
1 pound dates, pitted and chopped
½ cup packed light brown sugar
1 cup water

**CRUST**
2 cups all-purpose flour
3 cups oats
1 cup packed light brown sugar
1 teaspoon baking powder
½ teaspoon salt
1 cup vegetable shortening

**1** Preheat the oven to 350 degrees. Lightly grease a 9-inch square baking pan.

**2** To make the filling, combine the dates, brown sugar, and water in a saucepan and bring to a boil. Cook, stirring constantly for 10 minutes. Remove from the heat.

**3** To make the crust, combine the flour, oats, brown sugar, baking powder, and salt in a large bowl. Cut in the vegetable shortening

until the mixture resembles coarse crumbs.

**4** Press half the crust evenly into the prepared baking pan. Spread the date mixture over the top and crumble the remaining crust mixture over the top.

**5** Bake for 20 to 25 minutes, until lightly colored on top. Cool in the pan on a wire rack before cutting into large or small squares.

## FILLING
2 cups dates, pitted and chopped
½ cup fresh orange juice
¼ cup water

## CRUST
1½ cups all-purpose flour
¾ teaspoon baking soda
¼ teaspoon salt
¾ cup vegetable shortening
⅔ cup packed light brown sugar
⅛ teaspoon almond extract
1¼ cup oats
½ cup pecans, chopped

1  Preheat the oven to 400 degrees. Lightly grease a 9-inch square baking pan.

2  To make the filling, combine the dates, orange juice, and water in a saucepan and bring to a boil. Cook, stirring, for 15 minutes or until very thick. Remove from the heat.

3  To make the crust, combine the flour, baking soda, and salt.

4  In a large bowl, cream the vegetable shortening and brown sugar. Beat in the almond extract. Gradually blend in the dry ingredients. Stir in the oats and pecans.

5  Press half of the crust mixture into the prepared baking pan. Spread the date filling over the top of the crust. Spread the remaining crust mixture over the filling and press lightly.

6  Bake for 20 to 25 minutes, until lightly colored on top. Cool in the pan on a wire rack before cutting into large or small bars.

# DATE SQUARES II

Bar Cookies

YIELD: *1 to 2 dozen*
TOTAL TIME: *50 minutes*

---

1⅓ cups all-purpose flour
¼ teaspoon salt
⅓ cup vegetable shortening
8 ounces cream cheese, at room temperature
2 tablespoons water

## FILLING
1 cup dates, pitted and chopped
½ cup packed light brown sugar
¼ cup water

1  Combine the flour and salt.

2  In a large bowl, beat the vegetable shortening and cream cheese until smooth. Gradually blend in the dry ingredients. Blend in enough water to make a soft dough. Cover and chill for 8 hours.

3  To make the filling, combine the dates, brown sugar, and water in a sauce and bring to a boil. Cook, stirring, until the mixture thickens. Remove from the heat.

4  Preheat the oven to 375 degrees. Lightly grease 2 baking sheets.

5  On a floured surface, roll out the dough to a thickness of ¼ inch. Using a 3-inch round cookie cutter, cut out rounds and place 1 inch apart on the prepared baking sheets. Place 1½ teaspoonfuls of the date filling in the center of each round. Fold the dough over to make half-moons and press down to seal the edges.

6  Bake for 8 to 10 minutes, until lightly browned. Transfer to wire racks to cool.

# DATE TURNOVERS

Rolled Cookies

YIELD: *1 to 2 dozen*
TOTAL TIME: *45 minutes*
CHILLING TIME: *8 hours*

# Decorative Cookies

**D**

Rolled Cookies

YIELD: *4 to 5 dozen*

TOTAL TIME: *50 minutes*

3¾ cups all purpose flour
1½ teaspoons baking powder
1 teaspoon salt
1 cup vegetable shortening
2 cups granulated sugar
2 large eggs
2 teaspoons vanilla extract

**1** Preheat the oven to 375 degrees. Lightly grease 2 baking sheets.

**2** Combine the flour, baking powder, and salt.

**3** In a large bowl, cream the vegetable shortening and sugar. Beat in the eggs. Beat in the vanilla extract. Gradually blend in the dry ingredients.

**4** On a floured surface, roll out the dough to a thickness of ¼ inch. Using cookie cutters, cut into shapes and place 1½ inches apart on the prepared baking sheets.

**5** Bake for 8 to 10 minutes, or until lightly colored. Transfer to wire racks to cool.

**Baking notes:** These cookies are sweeter than most rolled cookies. To decorate them, spread a frosting over them or pipe designs onto them (see Icings and Frostings, in Pantry). You can also use a wide variety of small candies or jimmies to decorate them. If you want to hang these cookies for tree ornaments, press a ½-inch length of a paper drinking straw through the top of each cookie before baking; let the cookies cool before removing the straws.

# Decorator Cookies (Nonedible)

Rolled Cookies

YIELD: *varies*

TOTAL TIME: *30 minutes.*

2 cups all-purpose flour
1 cup salt
1 cup water

**1** Preheat the oven to 350 degrees.

**2** In a large bowl, combine all of the ingredients and stir until a smooth dough forms.

**3** On a floured surface, roll out the dough to a thickness of about ¼ inch. Using cookie cutters, cut into desired shape and place 1 inch apart on ungreased baking sheets.

**4** Bake for 8 to 10 minutes, or until the cookies are a light brown. Transfer to wire racks to cool, before varnishing them.

**5** When cool, use a spray varnish to coat the cookies to preserve them.

**Baking notes:** Make a batch of this dough to amuse the kids on rainy days. They can mold it like clay into different shapes, which then can be baked and saved. Food coloring can be added to make different-colored doughs, or the baked shapes can be painted. You can even make small cookies, overbake them, and turn them into refrigerator magnets.

# DELICIOUS FUDGE BROWNIES

Bar Cookies

YIELD: *1 to 2 dozen*
TOTAL TIME: *45 minutes*

1⅓ cups all-purpose flour
¾ cup unsweetened cocoa powder
¼ teaspoon salt
⅔ cup vegetable oil
2 cups granulated sugar
2 large eggs
1 teaspoon vanilla extract
½ cup walnuts, chopped

**1** Preheat the oven to 350 degrees. Lightly grease a 13 by 9-inch baking pan.

**2** Combine the flour, cocoa powder, and salt.

**3** In a large bowl, beat the vegetable oil and sugar. Beat in the eggs one at a time. Beat in the vanilla extract. Gradually blend in the dry ingredients. Fold in the walnuts. Spread the mixture evenly in the prepared baking pan.

**4** Bake for 25 to 30 minutes, or until a toothpick inserted in the center comes out clean. Cool in the pan on a wire rack before cutting into large or small bars.

**Baking notes:** For a more decorative appearance, sprinkle the walnuts on top of the batter before baking.

# DESERT MERINGUES

Drop Cookies

YIELD: *1 to 2 dozen*
TOTAL TIME: *35 minutes*

3 large egg whites
¼ teaspoon salt
¾ cup granulated sugar
¼ teaspoon almond extract
¾ cup almonds, chopped
¾ cup dates, pitted and chopped

**1** Preheat the oven to 250 degrees. Line 2 baking sheets with parchment paper.

**2** In a large bowl, beat the egg whites and salt until foamy. Gradually beat in the sugar and beat until stiff but not dry. Fold in the almond extract. Fold in the almonds and dates.

**3** Drop the dough by spoonfuls about 1½ inches apart onto the prepared baking sheets.

**4** Bake for 25 to 30 minutes, until firm to the touch and just starting to color. Transfer to wire racks to cool.

# DESERT MYSTERIES

Rolled Cookies

YIELD: *2 to 3 dozen*
TOTAL TIME: *40 minutes*

FILLING
1 tablespoon vegetable shortening
1 cup packed light brown sugar
1 large egg
1 teaspoon vanilla extract
¼ cup walnuts, chopped
1 cup dates, pitted and chopped
1 cup vegetable shortening
2 cups packed light brown sugar
4 large eggs
4 cups whole wheat flour

**1** Preheat the oven to 350 degrees. Lightly grease 2 baking sheets.

**2** To make the filling, cream the vegetable shortening and brown sugar in a medium bowl. Beat in the egg and vanilla extract. Stir in the walnuts and dates.

**3** To make the crust, cream the vegetable shortening and brown sugar in a large bowl. Beat in the eggs. Gradually blend in the flour.

**4** On a floured surface, roll out the dough into a 15 by 15-inch square to a thickness of ¼ inch. Using a knife, cut into 3-inch squares. Drop a teaspoonful of the filling into the center of each square. Working quickly, bring up the 4 corners of each square over the filling and pinch together to form a little bag. Place 1 inch apart on the prepared baking sheet.

**5** Bake for 12 to 15 minutes, until lightly colored. Transfer to wire racks to cool.

**Baking notes:** Let these cookies cool completely before eating them, or the filling will still be hot.

# DIGESTIVE BISCUITS

Rolled Cookies

YIELD: *2 to 3 dozen*
TOTAL TIME: *35 minutes*

1½ cups all-purpose flour
¼ cup rolled oats
¼ cup granulated sugar
2 tablespoons baking powder
¼ teaspoon salt
3 tablespoons butter
2 tablespoons milk

**1** Preheat the oven to 400 degrees. Lightly grease 2 baking sheets.

**2** In a large bowl, combine the flour, oats, sugar, baking powder, and salt. Cut in the butter until the mixture resembles coarse crumbs. Add just enough milk to make a firm dough.

**3** Transfer the dough to a floured surface and knead until smooth. Roll it out to a thickness of ⅛ inch. Using a fork, prick all over. Using a 1½-inch round cookie cutter, cut into rounds and place 1 inch apart on the prepared baking sheets.

**4** Bake for 12 to 15 minutes, or until the crust is golden brown. Transfer to wire racks to cool.

**Baking notes:** This recipe dates back to Victorian England. The cookies are intended to be quite bland; add ½ teaspoon vanilla extract before adding milk if you desire.

# DO-EVERYTHING COOKIES

Drop Cookies

YIELD: *5 to 6 dozen*
TOTAL TIME: *30 minutes*
CHILLING TIME: *3 hours*

3 cups all-purpose flour
¾ teaspoon baking powder
¼ teaspoon salt
4 large eggs
1½ cups granulated sugar
2½ teaspoons caraway seeds
  (optional)

**1** Combine the flour, baking powder, and salt.

**2** In a large bowl, beat the eggs and sugar until thick and light-colored. Gradually blend in the dry ingredients. Stir in the optional caraway seeds. Cover and chill for 3 hours.

**3** Preheat the oven to 350 degrees. Lightly grease 2 baking sheets.

**4** Drop the dough by spoonfuls 1½ onto the prepared baking sheets

**5** Bake for 10 to 12 minutes, until very lightly colored; do not allow to brown. Cool on the baking sheets on wire racks.

**Baking notes:** This basic recipe can be used to make just about any type of cookie you might want. The caraway seeds are one option; finely ground walnuts or other nuts, or 1 teaspoon of your favorite flavoring or extract can be added. Chopped peel or zest may be worked into the dough. Chocolate chips or other types of baking drops can be incorporated. Use your imagination.

## DOUBLE PEANUT-FLAVORED COOKIES

Formed Cookies

YIELD: *5 to 6 dozen*
TOTAL TIME: *30 minutes*

2¼ cups all-purpose flour
2 teaspoons baking soda
1 cup vegetable shortening
1 cup granulated sugar
1 cup packed light brown sugar
1 cup peanut butter
2 large eggs
1 teaspoon vanilla extract
1 cup unsalted peanuts, chopped

**1** Preheat the oven to 350 degrees.

**2** Combine the flour and baking soda.

**3** In a large bowl, cream the vegetable shortening and two sugars. Beat in the peanut butter. Beat in the eggs and vanilla extract. Gradually blend in the dry ingredients. Fold in the peanuts.

**4** Pinch off walnut-sized pieces of dough and roll into small balls. Place each 1½ inches apart on ungreased baking sheets and flatten each ball with the bottom of a glass dipped in flour.

**5** Bake for 8 to 10 minutes, until lightly colored. Transfer to wire racks to cool.

## DREAM BARS

Bar Cookies

YIELD: *1 to 2 dozen*
TOTAL TIME: *50 minutes*

**CRUST**
1 cup all-purpose flour
3 tablespoons powdered sugar
½ cup vegetable shortening

**TOPPING**
2 tablespoons all-purpose flour
¼ teaspoon baking powder
⅛ teaspoon salt
1½ cups packed light brown sugar
2 large eggs
1½ teaspoons vanilla extract
¾ cup walnuts, chopped
½ cups flaked coconut

**1** Preheat the oven to 350 degrees. Lightly grease a 9-inch square baking pan.

**2** To make the crust, combine the flour and powdered sugar in a small bowl. Cut in the vegetable shortening until the dough resembles coarse crumbs. Press the mixture into the prepared baking pan.

**3** Bake for 15 minutes.

**4** Meanwhile, make the topping: Combine the flour, baking powder, and salt.

**5** In a medium bowl, beat the brown sugar and eggs together until thick. Beat in the vanilla extract. Gradually blend in the dry ingredients. Stir in the walnuts and coconut.

**6** Spread the topping over the warm crust and bake for 25 to 30 minutes longer, or until firm to the touch. Cool in the pan on a wire rack before cutting into large or small bars.

## DREAMS END

Formed Cookies

YIELD: *3 to 4 dozen*
TOTAL TIME: *30 minutes*

2½ cups all-purpose flour
½ teaspoon baking soda
½ teaspoon cream of tartar
1 cup butter, at room temperature
1 cup powdered sugar
2 teaspoons raspberry brandy

**1** Preheat the oven to 325 degrees. Lightly grease 2 baking sheets.

**2** Combine the flour, baking soda, and cream of tartar.

**3** In a large bowl, cream the butter and powdered sugar. Beat in the brandy. Gradually blend in the dry ingredients. The dough will be very stiff; if it seems too dry, add water a teaspoonful at a time.

**4** Pinch off pieces of the dough about the size of large olives and roll into balls. Place 1 inch apart on the prepared baking sheets.

**5** Bake for 8 to 10 minutes, or until lightly colored. Transfer to wire racks to cool.

# DREAMY SQUARES

Bar Cookies

YIELD: *2 to 3 dozen*
TOTAL TIME: *55 minutes*

**CRUST**
1 cup all-purpose flour
1½ teaspoons baking powder
¼ teaspoon salt
½ cup butter, at room temperature
1¼ cups packed light brown sugar
2 large eggs

**TOPPING**
2 tablespoons all-purpose flour
2 tablespoons powdered sugar
2 tablespoons butter, at room
   temperature
1 cup walnuts, chopped
1 cup shredded coconut

**1** Preheat the oven to 350 degrees. Lightly grease an 8-inch square baking pan.

**2** To make the crust, combine the flour, baking powder, and salt.

**3** In a large bowl, cream the butter and brown sugar. Beat in the eggs. Gradually blend in the dry ingredients. Spread the dough evenly into the prepared baking pan.

**4** Bake for 25 minutes.

**5** Meanwhile, make the topping: In a small bowl, combine the flour and powdered sugar. Cut in the butter. Blend in the walnuts and coconut.

**6** Spread the topping evenly over the warm crust. Bake for 20 to 30 minutes longer, or until lightly browned on the top. Cool in the pan on a wire rack before cutting into large or small bars.

---

# DROP COOKIES I

Drop Cookies

YIELD: *5 to 6 dozen*
TOTAL TIME: *35 minutes*

3 cups all-purpose flour
½ teaspoon salt
8 large eggs
2 cups granulated sugar

**1** Preheat the oven to 350 degrees. Lightly grease 2 baking sheets.

**2** Combine the flour and salt.

**3** In a large bowl, beat the eggs and sugar. Gradually blend in the dry ingredients.

**4** Drop the dough by spoonfuls 1½ inches apart onto the prepared baking sheets.

**5** Bake for 10 to 12 minutes, until lightly colored. Transfer to wire racks to cool.

**Baking notes:** This recipe dates back to the early 1800s. The original recipe calls for 8 large eggs, but try using 6 medium eggs instead.

---

# DROP COOKIES II

Drop Cookies

YIELD: *5 to 6 dozen*
TOTAL TIME: *30 minutes*
CHILLING TIME: *2 hours*

2 cups all-purpose flour
3 tablespoons unsweetened cocoa
   powder
2 teaspoons baking powder
¼ teaspoon salt
6 tablespoons butter, at room
   temperature
1 cup granulated sugar
3 large eggs
1 tablespoon milk
2 teaspoons vanilla extract

**1** Combine the flour, cocoa powder, baking powder, and salt.

**2** In a large bowl, cream the butter and sugar. Beat in the eggs one at a time. Beat in the milk and vanilla extract. Gradually blend in the dry ingredients. Cover and chill for 2 hours.

**3** Preheat the oven to 375 degrees. Lightly grease 2 baking sheets.

**4** Drop the dough by spoonfuls 2 inches apart onto the prepared baking sheets.

**5** Bake for 10 to 12 minutes, until lightly colored. Transfer to wire racks to cool.

**Baking notes:** One-half cup of packed light brown sugar can be substituted for the granulated sugar.

2 large eggs
1 large egg yolk
1 cup powdered sugar
2 cups all-purpose flour

**1** Preheat the oven to 350 degrees. Lightly grease 2 baking sheets.

**2** In a large bowl, beat the eggs, egg yolks, and powdered sugar until thick and light-colored. Gradually blend in the flour.

**3** Drop the dough by spoonfuls onto the prepared baking sheets.

**4** Bake for 10 to 12 minutes, until lightly colored. Transfer to wire racks to cool.

# DROP COOKIES III

Drop Cookies

YIELD: *3 to 4 dozen*
TOTAL TIME: *30 minutes*

2 cups all-purpose flour
1 teaspoon baking powder
½ teaspoon baking soda
1 teaspoon ground cinnamon
1 teaspoon ground nutmeg
¼ teaspoon ground cloves
Pinch of salt
½ cup butter, at room temperature
¾ cup packed light brown sugar
1 large egg
¼ cup milk
1 teaspoon vanilla extract
½ cup golden raisins
¼ cup candied citron, chopped fine (optional)

**1** Combine the flour, baking powder, baking soda, spices, and salt.

**2** In a large bowl, cream the butter and brown sugar. Beat in the egg. Beat in the milk and vanilla. Gradually blend in the dry ingredients. Fold in the raisins and candied citron. Cover and chill for 8 hours.

**3** Preheat the oven to 375 degrees. Lightly grease 2 baking sheets.

**4** Drop the dough by spoonfuls 1½ inches apart onto the prepared baking sheets.

**5** Bake for 10 to 12 minutes, until lightly colored. Transfer to wire racks to cool.

**Baking notes:** Substitute ¼ cup chopped nuts or ½ cup chopped glacé cherries for the candied citron.

# DROP COOKIES IV

Drop Cookies

YIELD: *5 to 6 dozen*
TOTAL TIME: *30 minutes*
CHILLING TIME: *8 hours*

3 cups all-purpose flour
1 tablespoon baking powder
¼ teaspoon salt
⅔ cup butter, at room temperature
1½ cups granulated sugar
2 large eggs
¼ cup fresh orange juice
1 tablespoon water
½ teaspoon almond extract
1 tablespoon grated orange zest
1 cup raisins, chopped

**1** Preheat the oven to 375 degrees. Lightly grease 2 baking sheets.

**2** Combine the flour, baking powder, and salt.

**3** In a large bowl, cream the butter and sugar. Beat in the eggs one at a time. Beat in orange juice, water, and almond extract. Beat in the orange zest. Gradually blend in the dry ingredients. Fold in the raisins.

**4** Drop the dough by spoonfuls 1½ inches apart onto the prepared baking sheets.

**5** Bake for 10 to 12 minutes, until lightly colored. Transfer to wire racks to cool.

# DROP COOKIES V

Drop Cookies

YIELD: *3 to 4 dozen*
TOTAL TIME: *30 minutes*

**D**

# DUIMPJES

Drop Cookies

YIELD: *3 to 4 dozen*
TOTAL TIME: *30 minutes*

2½ cups all-purpose flour
2 teaspoons baking powder
1 teaspoon anise seeds
¼ teaspoon salt
½ cup butter, at room temperature
¾ cups granulated sugar
1 cup milk
½ cup almonds, chopped

**1** Preheat the oven to 400 degrees. Lightly grease 2 baking sheets.

**2** Combine the flour, baking powder, anise, and salt.

**3** In a large bowl, cream the butter and sugar. Beat in the milk.

Gradually blend in the dry ingredients. Fold in the almonds.

**4** Drop the dough by spoonfuls 1½ inches apart onto the prepared baking sheets.

**5** Bake for 10 to 12 minutes, or until lightly colored. Transfer to wire racks to cool.

---

# DUTCH-CRUNCH APPLESAUCE BARS

Bar Cookies

YIELD: *1 to 2 dozen*
TOTAL TIME: *40 minutes*

2 cups all-purpose flour
1 teaspoon baking soda
1 teaspoon ground cinnamon
½ teaspoon ground nutmeg
¼ teaspoon salt
1 cup granulated sugar
1 cup unsweetened applesauce
1 teaspoon vanilla extract
½ cup walnuts, chopped

**TOPPING**
2 tablespoons butter, at room temperature
¼ cup granulated sugar
⅔ cup crushed breakfast cereal (such as cornflakes)

**1** Preheat the oven to 350 degrees. Lightly grease a 13 by 9-inch baking pan.

**2** Combine the flour, baking soda, spices, and salt.

**3** In a large bowl, beat the sugar, applesauce, and vanilla extract. Gradually blend in the dry ingredients. Stir in the walnuts. Spread the mixture evenly in the prepared baking pan.

**4** To make the topping cream the butter and sugar in a small bowl. Gradually blend in the cereal. Spread this over the dough.

**5** Bake for 20 to 30 minutes, until lightly browned on top. Cool in the pan on a wire rack before cutting into large or small bars.

---

# DUTCH SOUR CREAM COOKIES

Refrigerator Cookies

YIELD: *3 to 4 dozen*
TOTAL TIME: *40 minutes*
CHILLING TIME: *8 hours*

3 cups all-purpose flour
¼ teaspoon baking soda
½ cup vegetable shortening
1 cup granulated sugar
1 large egg
½ teaspoon vanilla extract
½ teaspoon lemon extract
¼ cup sour cream

**1** Combine the flour and baking soda.

**2** In a large bowl, cream the vegetable shortening and sugar. Beat in the egg, vanilla and lemon extracts. Beat in the sour cream. Gradually blend in the dry ingredients.

**3** Shape the dough into a log 2 inches in diameter. Wrap in

waxed paper and chill for 8 hours.

**4** Preheat the oven to 375 degrees. Lightly grease 2 baking sheets.

**5** Cut the log into ¼-inch-thick slices, and place 1 inch apart on the prepared baking sheets.

**6** Bake for 10 to 12 minutes, until lightly colored. Transfer to wire racks to cool.

1 cup all-purpose flour
3 tablespoons almonds, ground
¼ teaspoon baking powder
½ teaspoon ground cinnamon
¼ teaspoon ground cloves
¼ teaspoon ground ginger
¼ teaspoon ground nutmeg
¼ teaspoon salt
5 tablespoons vegetable shortening
⅓ cup packed light brown sugar
1 tablespoon milk
2 tablespoons chopped candied citrus peel

1 Combine the flour, almonds, baking powder, spices, and salt.

2 In a large bowl, cream the shortening and brown sugar. Beat in the milk. Gradually blend in the dry ingredients. Fold in the citrus peel.

3 Transfer the dough to a floured surface and knead until smooth. Wrap in waxed paper and chill for 8 hours.

4 Preheat the oven to 350 degrees. Lightly grease 2 baking sheets.

5 On a floured surface, roll out the dough to a thickness of ¼ inch. Using cookie cutters, cut into shapes and place 1 inch apart on the prepared baking sheets.

6 Bake for 18 to 20 minutes, until firm to the touch. Transfer to wire racks to cool.

**Baking notes:** This dough may also be used with a speculaas mold to form cookies.

# DUTCH SPICE COOKIES

Rolled Cookies

YIELD: *4 to 5 dozen*
TOTAL TIME: *30 minutes*
CHILLING TIME: *8 hours*

---

4 cups all-purpose flour
1 cup packed light brown sugar
1 teaspoon baking powder
1 teaspoon ground cinnamon
½ teaspoon ground cloves
1 cup candied citrus peel, chopped fine
1 cup milk
1 cup molasses
Powdered sugar for sprinkling

1 Preheat the oven to 300 degrees. Lightly grease a 9-inch square baking pan.

2 In a large bowl, combine the flour, brown sugar, baking powder, spices, and candied peel. Gradually stir in the milk and molasses. Spread the dough evenly in the prepared baking pan.

3 Bake for 1½ to 2 hours, or until firm and the top looks dry. Place a paper doily on top of the hot cookies and sprinkle with sugar. Let cool on a rack before cutting into large or small bars.

# DUTCH TEA CAKES

Bar Cookies

YIELD: *3 to 4 dozen*
TOTAL TIME: *2 hours*

---

2¾ cups all-purpose flour
¼ teaspoon baking soda
2 teaspoons ground cinnamon
½ teaspoon ground nutmeg
¼ teaspoon salt
1 cup vegetable shortening
1 cup packed light brown sugar
¼ cup sour cream
½ cup walnuts, chopped

1 Combine the flour, baking soda, spices, and salt.

2 In a large bowl, cream the vegetable shortening and brown sugar. Beat in the sour cream. Gradually blend in the dry ingredients. Fold in the walnuts.

3 Divide the dough in half. Form each half into a log 2 inches in diameter. Wrap in waxed paper and chill for 8 hours.

4 Preheat the oven to 375 degrees.

5 Cut the logs into ⅛-inch-thick slices, and place 1½ inches apart on ungreased baking sheets.

6 Bake for 8 to 10 minutes, until lightly colored. Transfer to wire racks to cool.

# DUTCH WAFERS

Refrigerator Cookies

YIELD: *4 to 5 dozen*
TOTAL TIME: *30 minutes*
CHILLING TIME: *8 hours*

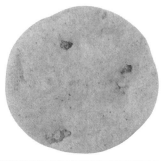

# EASY BUTTERSCOTCH DROP COOKIES

Drop Cookies

YIELD: *3 to 4 dozen*
TOTAL TIME: *30 minutes*

**2 cups all-purpose flour**
**2 teaspoons baking powder**
**½ teaspoon salt**
**⅔ cup canola oil**
**1 cup packed dark brown sugar**
**2 large eggs**
**2 teaspoons vanilla extract**
**1 teaspoon sugar**
**½ teaspoon cinnamon**

**1** Preheat the oven to 350 degrees.

**2** Combine the flour, baking powder, and salt.

**3** In a large bowl, beat the oil and brown sugar. Beat in the eggs one at a time. Beat in the vanilla extract. Gradually blend in the dry ingredients.

**4** Combine sugar and cinnamon in a small bowl.

**5** Drop the dough by spoonfuls 1½ inches apart onto ungreased baking sheets. Flatten each cookie with the bottom of a glass dipped in canola oil and then in the cinnamon sugar.

**6** Bake for 12 to 15 minutes, until lightly colored. Transfer to wire racks to cool.

# EASY FUDGE COOKIES

Refrigerator Cookies

YIELD: *6 to 7 dozen*
TOTAL TIME: *35 minutes*
CHILLING TIME: *8 hours*

**2 ounces semisweet chocolate, chopped**
**4⅓ cups all-purpose flour**
**1 teaspoon baking powder**
**½ teaspoon baking soda**
**¼ teaspoon salt**
**1 cup vegetable shortening**
**1 cup packed light brown sugar**
**1 cup granulated sugar**
**2 large eggs**
**⅓ cup milk**
**1 teaspoon vanilla extract**
**½ cup walnuts, chopped (optional)**

**1** Melt the chocolate in a double boiler over low heat, stirring until smooth. Remove from the heat.

**2** Combine the flour, baking powder, baking soda, and salt.

**3** In a large bowl, cream the vegetable shortening and two sugars. Beat in the eggs one at a time. Beat in the milk and vanilla extract. Beat in the melted chocolate. Gradually blend in the dry ingredients. Fold in the walnuts.

**4** Divide the dough in half. Form each half into a 2-inch-thick logs. Wrap in waxed paper and chill for 8 hours or overnight.

**5** Preheat the oven to 375 degrees.

**6** Cut the logs into ⅛-inch-thick slices and place 1 inch apart on ungreased baking sheets.

**7** Bake for 12 to 15 minutes, until lightly colored. Transfer to wire racks to cool.

1½ cups all-purpose flour
1 teaspoon salt
¾ cup vegetable shortening
3 tablespoons water

FILLING
1 tablespoon butter, at room
   temperature
½ cup granulated sugar
½ teaspoon ground cinnamon
¼ teaspoon ground nutmeg
1 tablespoon grated lemon zest
⅔ cup currants
1 large egg, beaten

**1** In a large bowl, combine the
flour and salt. Cut in the vegetable shortening until the mixture resembles coarse crumbs.
Stir in just enough water to make
a soft dough. Cover and chill
for 4 hours.

**2** Preheat the oven to 350
degrees. Lightly grease 2 baking
sheets.

**3** To make the filling, cream the
butter and sugar in a small bowl.
Beat in the cinnamon and nutmeg. Beat in the lemon zest. Fold
in the currants.

**4** On a floured surface, roll out
the dough to a thickness of ¼
inch. Using a 2½-cookie cutter,
cut out an even number of
rounds. Place half the rounds 1
inch apart on the prepared baking sheets and drop 1 teaspoonful of the filling in the center of
each one. Place the remaining
rounds on top and crimp the
edges with a fork to seal. Brush
the tops with the beaten egg.

**5** Bake for 18 to 20 minutes, until
golden brown. Transfer to wire
racks to cool.

**Baking notes:** This same recipe
can be used to make miniature
turnovers. Use only one round
per cookie; place the filling in the
center and fold over the dough to
form a half-moon. Crimp the
edges to seal and bake.

# ECCLES CAKES

Rolled Cookies

YIELD: *1 to 2 dozen*
TOTAL TIME: *35 minutes*
CHILLING TIME: *4 hours*

---

4 cups all-purpose flour
1 teaspoon baking soda
½ teaspoon salt
¾ cups butter, at room temperature
2 cups packed dark brown sugar
3 large eggs
1 teaspoon vanilla extract

**1** Preheat the oven to 350
degrees. Lightly grease 2 baking
sheets.

**2** Combine the flour, baking
soda, and salt.

**3** In a large bowl, cream the butter and brown sugar. Beat in the
eggs one at a time. Beat in the
vanilla extract. Gradually blend
in the dry ingredients.

**4** On a floured surface, roll out
the dough to a thickness of ¼
inch. Using cookie cutters, cut
into shapes and place 1½ inches
apart on the prepared baking
sheets.

**5** Bake for 10 to 12 minutes, until
lightly colored. Transfer to wire
racks to cool

**Baking notes:** This recipe, said
to be a specialty of Edenton,
North Carolina, dates back to the
late 1700s. The cookies are traditionally cut out with a fluted
cutter.

# EDENTON TEA
# PARTY BISCUITS

Rolled Cookies

YIELD: *4 to 5 dozen*
TOTAL TIME: *30 minutes*

# EDINBURGH SQUARES

Bar Cookies

YIELD: *1 to 2 dozen*
TOTAL TIME: *40 minutes*

**CRUST**
½ cup vegetable shortening
¼ cup granulated sugar
2 large egg yolks
1½ cups all-purpose flour

**TOPPING**
1 egg white
⅛ teaspoon cream of tartar
1½ ounces chocolate, shaved
¼ cup granulated sugar
1½ tablespoons jam or preserves
¾ cup almonds, ground

**1** Preheat the oven to 350 degrees. Lightly grease a 9-inch square baking pan.

**2** To make the crust, cream the vegetable shortening and sugar in a large bowl. Beat in the egg yolks. Gradually blend in the flour. Spread the dough evenly into the bottom of the prepared baking pan.

**3** To make the topping, in a medium bowl, beat the egg white with the cream of tartar until stiff but not dry. Fold in the chocolate and sugar.

**4** Spread the jam over the crust. Spread the topping over the jam and sprinkle the almonds over the top.

**5** Bake for 18 to 20 minutes, until firm to the touch. Cool in the pan on a wire rack before cutting into large or small bars.

# ENGLISH SNAPS

Rolled Cookies

YIELD: *5 to 6 dozen*
TOTAL TIME: *30 minutes*

3 cups all-purpose flour
1½ teaspoons baking soda
1 teaspoon ground cinnamon
¼ teaspoon ground allspice
¼ teaspoon ground cloves
1 cup vegetable shortening
1 cup granulated sugar
1 large egg
¾ cup corn syrup
1½ teaspoons cider vinegar

**1** Preheat the oven to 350 degrees. Lightly grease 2 baking sheets.

**2** Combine the flour, baking soda, and spices.

**3** In a large bowl, cream the vegetable shortening and sugar. Beat in the egg. Beat in the corn syrup and cider vinegar. Gradually blend in the dry ingredients.

**4** On a floured surface, roll out the dough to a thickness of ¼ inch. Using a 1½-inch round cookie cutter, cut the dough into rounds and place 1½ inches apart on the prepared baking sheets.

**5** Bake for 8 to 12 minutes, until firm to the touch. Transfer to wire racks to cool.

**Baking notes:** The vinegar adds a great very faintly sour taste that really enhances these cookies. You may want to try a teaspoon or so as flavoring in other spice recipes.

4¼ cups all-purpose flour
¼ teaspoon baking soda
¼ teaspoon ground nutmeg
½ cup vegetable shortening
1½ cups granulated sugar
2 large eggs
½ cup heavy cream

**1** Preheat the oven to 350 degrees. Lightly grease 2 baking sheets.

**2** Combine the flour, baking soda, and nutmeg.

**3** In a large bowl, cream the vegetable shortening and sugar. Beat in the eggs one at a time. Beat in the cream. Gradually blend in the dry ingredients.

**4** On a floured surface, roll out the dough to a thickness of ⅛ inch. Using a 1½- to 2-inch round cookie cutter, cut into rounds and place 1 inch apart on the prepared baking sheets.

**5** Bake for 12 to 15 minutes, until lightly colored. Transfer to wire racks to cool.

**Baking notes:** Other spices, such as cinnamon, cloves, or allspice, can be substituted for the nutmeg. If you use ground cloves, reduce the amount by half.

# ENGLISH TEA BISCUITS

Rolled Cookies

YIELD: *3 to 4 dozen*
TOTAL TIME: *30 minutes*

---

1 cup vegetable shortening
1 cup granulated sugar
4 large eggs
1 cup all-purpose flour
1½ cup currants
Powdered sugar for sprinkling

**1** Preheat the oven to 350 degrees. Lightly grease a 13 by 9-inch baking pan.

**2** In a large bowl, cream the vegetable shortening and sugar. Beat in the eggs one at a time. Gradually blend in the flour. Fold in the currants. Spread the dough evenly in the prepared baking pan.

**3** Bake for 25 to 30 minutes, until lightly colored on top. Cool in the pan on a wire rack.

**4** Sprinkle with powdered sugar and cut into large or small bars.

**Baking notes:** One cup raisins, chopped fine, can be substituted for the currants.

# ENGLISH TEA CAKES I

Bar Cookies

YIELD: *1 to 3 dozen*
TOTAL TIME: *40 minutes*

# ENGLISH TEA CAKES II

Formed Cookies

YIELD: *3 to 4 dozen*

TOTAL TIME: *50 minutes*

CHILLING TIME: *4 hours*

1¾ cups all-purpose flour
1½ teaspoons baking powder
¼ teaspoon salt
½ cup butter, at room temperature
¾ cup granulated sugar
1 large egg
2 tablespoons milk
½ cup candied citron, chopped fine
½ cup currants
1 large egg white
Granulated sugar for coating

1  Combine the flour, baking powder and salt.

2  In a large bowl, cream the butter and sugar. Beat in the egg and milk. Gradually blend in the dry ingredients. Fold in the candied citron and currants. Cover and chill for 4 hours.

3  Preheat the oven to 400 degrees. Lightly grease 2 baking sheets.

4  In a small bowl, beat the egg white until foamy.

5  Pinch off walnut-sized pieces of dough and roll into balls. Dip half of each ball in the beaten egg white and then in granulated sugar and place the balls, sugar side up, 1½ inches apart on the prepared baking sheets.

6  Bake for 12 to 15 minutes, until lightly colored. Transfer to wire racks to cool.

# ENGLISH TEA COOKIES

Refrigerator Cookies

YIELD: *2 to 4 dozen*

TOTAL TIME: *35 minutes*

CHILLING TIME: *4 hours*

2¼ cups all-purpose flour
½ teaspoon salt
½ cup butter, at room temperature
½ cup granulated sugar
2 large egg yolks
2 tablespoons fresh lemon juice
1 tablespoon grated lemon zest
⅔ cup shredded coconut

1  Combine the flour and salt.

2  In a large bowl, cream the butter and sugar. Beat in the egg yolks. Beat in the lemon juice and zest. Gradually blend in the dry ingredients. Fold in the coconut. Form the dough into a log 2½ inches in diameter. Wrap in waxed paper and chill for 4 hours.

3  Preheat the oven to 350 degrees. Lightly grease 2 baking sheets.

4  Cut the log into ⅛-inch-thick slices and place 1 inch apart on the prepared baking sheets.

5  Bake for 12 to 15 minutes, until lightly colored. Transfer to wire racks to cool.

**Baking notes:** To make a more elegant version of these cookies, dip half of each cooled cookie in melted chocolate. Place on wire racks to allow the chocolate to set.

# ENGLISH TOFFEE BARS

Bar Cookies

YIELD: *1 to 2 dozen*

TOTAL TIME: *75 minutes*

2 cups all-purpose flour
1 teaspoon ground cinnamon
1 cup vegetable shortening
1 cup packed light brown sugar
1 large egg yolk
1 cup black or regular walnuts, chopped

1  Preheat the oven to 275 degrees. Lightly grease a 9-inch square baking pan.

2  Combine the flour and cinnamon.

3  In a large bowl, cream the vegetable shortening and brown sugar. Beat in the egg yolk. Gradually blend in the dry ingredients. Fold in the walnuts. Spread the mixture evenly in the prepared baking pan.

4  Bake for 55 to 60 minutes, until firm to the touch. Cool in the pan on a wire rack before cutting into large or small bars.

5 cups all-purpose flour
2 teaspoons baking powder
1 teaspoon baking soda
1 cup vegetable shortening
2 cups granulated sugar
2 large eggs
1 cup milk
1 teaspoon vanilla extract

**1** Preheat the oven to 350 degrees. Lightly grease 2 baking sheets.

**2** Combine the flour, baking powder, and baking soda.

**3** In a large bowl, cream the vegetable shortening and sugar. Beat in the eggs one at a time. Beat in the milk and vanilla extract. Gradually blend in the dry ingredients.

**4** Drop the dough by spoonfuls 1½ inches apart onto the prepared baking sheets.

**5** Bake for 8 to 10 minutes, until lightly colored. Transfer to wire racks to cool.

# Fat City Sugar Cookies

Drop Cookies

YIELD: *6 to 8 dozen*
TOTAL TIME: *30 minutes*

---

3½ cups all-purpose flour
½ teaspoon ground cardamom
¼ teaspoon salt
¼ cup vegetable shortening
¾ cup granulated sugar
6 large egg yolks
¾ cup heavy cream
1 tablespoon brandy
½ teaspoon lemon extract
Vegetable oil for deep-frying
Powdered sugar for sprinkling

**1** Combine the flour, cardamom, and salt.

**2** In a large bowl, cream the vegetable shortening and sugar. Beat in the egg yolks. Beat in the cream. Beat in the brandy and lemon extract. Gradually blend in the dry ingredients.

**3** In a deep-fryer or deep heavy pot, heat the oil until very hot but not smoking.

**4** Meanwhile, on a floured surface, roll out the dough to a thickness of ¼ inch. Using a diamond-shaped cookie cutter, cut out cookies. Using a sharp knife, cut a slit across the center of each diamond and pull one of the long ends through the slit.

**5** Deep-fry the diamonds until golden brown. Drain on paper towels on wire racks. Sprinkle with powdered sugar.

# Fattigman

Rolled Cookies

YIELD: *5 to 6 dozen*
TOTAL TIME: *35 minutes*

# FAVORITE OATMEAL COOKIES

Drop Cookies

YIELD: *4 to 6 dozen*
TOTAL TIME: *40 minutes*

2½ cups all-purpose flour
2 teaspoons baking powder
¼ teaspoon baking soda
1 teaspoon ground cinnamon
¼ teaspoon salt
¾ cup vegetable shortening
1 cup packed light brown sugar
1 large egg
1 teaspoon vanilla extract
1 cup whole oats
¼ cup golden raisins

**1** Preheat the oven to 375 degrees. Lightly grease 2 baking sheets.

**2** Combine the flour, baking powder, baking soda, cinnamon, and salt.

**3** In a large bowl, cream the vegetable shortening and brown sugar. Beat in the egg and vanilla extract. Gradually blend in the dry ingredients. Stir in the oats. Fold in the raisins.

**4** Drop the dough by spoonfuls 1½ inches apart onto the prepared baking sheets.

**5** Bake for 18 to 20 minutes, until lightly colored. Transfer to wire racks to cool.

# FENNEL COOKIES

Formed Cookies

YIELD: *5 to 6 dozen*
TOTAL TIME: *30 minutes*

2½ cups all-purpose flour
½ teaspoon baking powder
1 teaspoon fennel seeds
1 cup vegetable shortening
½ cup granulated sugar
1 large egg
1 teaspoon vanilla extract

**1** Preheat the oven to 350 degrees.

**2** Combine the flour, baking powder, and fennel seeds.

**3** In a large bowl, cream the vegetable shortening and sugar. Beat in the egg. Beat in the vanilla extract. Gradually blend in the dry ingredients

**4** Place dough in a cookie press or a pastry bag fitted with a large star tip and press or pipe out the dough in small mounds onto ungreased baking sheets, spacing them 1 inch apart.

**5** Bake for 10 to 12 minutes, until lightly colored. Transfer to wire racks to cool.

# FIG DROPS

Drop Cookies

YIELD: *4 to 5 dozen*
TOTAL TIME: *30 minutes*

1 cup canola oil
1½ cups packed dark brown sugar
3 each large eggs
1 tablespoon water
1 teaspoon vanilla extract
1½ cups whole wheat flour
1 cup soy flour
2 cups ripe figs, chopped fine
1 cup walnuts, chopped fine
   (optional)

**1** Preheat the oven to 350 degrees. Lightly grease 2 baking sheets

**2** In a large bowl, beat the oil and brown sugar. Beat in the eggs one at a time. Beat in the water and vanilla extract.

Gradually blend in the two flours. Fold in the figs and the optional walnuts.

**3** Drop the dough by spoonfuls 1½ inches apart onto the prepared baking sheets.

**4** Bake for 10 to 12 minutes, until lightly colored. Transfer to wire racks to cool.

4¾ cups all-purpose flour
½ teaspoon baking soda
¼ teaspoon salt
¾ cup vegetable shortening
1½ cups granulated sugar
2 large eggs
¾ cup sour cream
2 teaspoons vanilla extract

**FILLING**
¾ cup water
½ cup granulated sugar
2 tablespoons fresh lemon juice
2 cups dried figs, chopped, fine
¼ teaspoon ground ginger
½ teaspoon ground cinnamon
2 teaspoons grated lemon zest

**1** Combine the flour, baking soda, and salt.

**2** In a large bowl, cream the vegetable shortening and sugar. Beat in the eggs one at a time. Beat in the sour cream and vanilla extract. Gradually blend in the dry ingredients. Cover and chill for 4 hours.

**3** To make the filling, combine all the ingredients in a saucepan and bring to a simmer. Cook, stirring until the mixture is very thick. Remove from the heat.

**4** Preheat the oven to 400 degrees. Lightly grease 2 baking sheets.

**5** On a floured surface, roll out the dough to a thickenss of ⅛ inch. Using a 2-inch round cookie cutter, cut the dough into rounds. Place half the rounds 1 inch apart on the prepared baking sheets. Place a spoonful of the fig filling in the center of the rounds and place the remaining rounds on the top. Crimp the edges with a fork to seal.

**6** Bake for 10 to 12 minutes, until lightly colored. Transfer to wire racks to cool.

# FIG-FILLED COOKIES

Rolled Cookies

YIELD: *4 to 6 dozen*
TOTAL TIME: *30 minutes*
CHILLING TIME: *4 hours*

---

2 cups all-purpose flour
2 cups Cheddar cheese, grated fine
½ teaspoon salt
½ cup vegetable shortening
¼ cup milk

**FILLING**
¾ cup raspberry jam
2 tablespoons light brown sugar
2 teaspoons ground cinnamon
¼ teaspoon salt
1½ cups walnuts, chopped fine

**1** In a large bowl, combine the flour, cheese, and salt. Cut in the vegetable shotening until the mixture resembles coarse crumbs. Stir in the milk. Cover and chill in the refrigerator for at least 2 hours.

**2** Preheat the oven to 400 degrees. Lightly grease 2 baking sheets.

**3** To make the filling, combine the jam, brown sugar, cinnamon, and salt in a small bowl and stir to blend. Stir in the walnuts.

**4** On a floured surface, roll out the dough to a thickness of ⅛ inch. Using a 1½-inch round cookie cutter, cut out an even number of cookies. Place a spoonful of the filling in the center of half the cookie. Place the remaining cookies on top and seal the edges. Place 1 inch apart on the prepared baking sheets.

**5** Bake for 12 to 15 minutes, until lightly colored. Transfer to wire racks to cool

# FILLED CHEESE COOKIES

Rolled Cookies

YIELD: *3 to 5 dozen*
TOTAL TIME: *30 minutes*
CHILLING TIME: *2 hours*

# FINNISH BRIDAL COOKIES I

Rolled Cookies

YIELD: *3 to 4 dozen*
TOTAL TIME: *30 minutes*

1 cup vegetable shortening
½ cup Vanilla Sugar (see Pantry)
¾ cup all-purpose flour
1 large egg white
About ¼ cup jam or preserves of
   your choice for filling

**1** Preheat the oven to 375 degrees. Lightly grease 2 baking sheets.

**2** In a large bowl, cream the vegetable shortening and vanilla sugar. Gradually blend in the flour.

**3** In a small bowl, beat the egg white until stiff but not dry. Fold the egg white into the dough.

**4** On a floured surface, roll the dough out to a thickness of ¼ inch. Using a 1½-inch round cookie cutter, cut out an even number of rounds and place 1 inch apart on the prepared baking sheets.

**5** Bake for 8 to 10 minutes, until lightly colored. Transfer to wire racks to cool.

**6** To assemble, spread ½ teaspoon of the jam or preserves over the bottom of half the cookies, top with the remaining cookies and gently press together.

# FINNISH BRIDAL COOKIES II

Formed Cookies

YIELD: *4 to 6 dozen*
TOTAL TIME: *35 minutes*

2½ cups all-purpose flour
¼ teaspoon salt
1 cup vegetable shortening
½ cup granulated sugar
1 large egg yolk
1 teaspoon vanilla extract
½ teaspoon grated lemon zest
Jam or preserves
½ cup Vanilla Icing (see Pantry)

**1** Preheat the oven to 350 degrees. Lightly grease 2 baking sheets.

**2** Combine the flour and salt.

**3** In a large bowl, cream the vegetable shortening and sugar. Beat in the egg yolk and vanilla extract. Beat in the lemon zest. Gradually blend in the dry ingredients.

**4** Divide the dough in half. Shape each piece into a 16-inch-long log and place the logs 1 inch apart on the prepared baking sheets. With the back of a knife, cut a ½-inch-deep slit down the length of each log.

**5** Bake for 10 minutes. Spoon the jam or preserves into the slit in each log and bake for 8 to 10 minutes longer, until lightly colored.

**6** Drizzle the icing over the tops of the logs and cut the logs on a 45-degree angle into 1-inch slices.

## FINNISH COFFEE STRIPS

Rolled Cookies

YIELD: *5 to 6 dozen*
TOTAL TIME: *35 minutes*
CHILLING TIME: *1 hour*

2½ cups unbleached flour
3 tablespoons bitter almonds, grated fine (see Baking notes)
Pinch of salt
1 cup butter, at room temperature
2 tablespoons granulated sugar
1 large egg, beaten
½ cup almonds, chopped fine

**1** Combine the flour, grated almonds, and salt.

**2** In a large bowl, cream the butter and sugar. Gradually blend in the dry ingredients. Cover and chill in for 1 hour.

**3** Preheat the oven to 375 degrees. Lightly grease 2 baking sheets.

**4** On a floured surface, roll out the dough to a thickness of ¾ inch. Using a sharp knife or a pastry wheel, cut the dough into strips 2 inches long. Brush with the beaten egg, and dredge in the chopped almonds, and place 1½ inches apart on the prepared baking sheets.

**5** Bake for 8 to 10 minutes, until lightly colored. Tansfer to wire racks to cool.

**Baking notes:** Bitter almonds can be found in specialty stores, but if you can't find them substitute hazelnuts.

## FINNISH COOKIES

Rolled Cookies

YIELD: *4 to 5 dozen*
TOTAL TIME: *35 mintues*

2¼ cup all-purpose flour
2 teaspoons unsweetened cocoa powder
¾ cup vegetable shortening
1 cup powdered sugar
¾ cup vanilla extract

**1** Preheat the oven to 350 degrees. Lightly grease 2 baking sheets.

**2** Combine the flour and cocoa powder.

**3** In a large bowl, cream the vegetable shortening and powdered sugar. Beat in the vanilla extract. Gradually blend in the dry ingredients.

**4** On a floured surface, roll out the dough to a thickness of ¼ inch. Using cookie cutters, cut out cookies and place them 1 inch apart on the prepared baking sheets.

**5** Bake for 12 to 15 minutes, until lightly colored. Transfer to wire racks to cool.

## FINNISH RYE COOKIES

Rolled Cookies

YIELD: *2 to 3 dozen*
TOTAL TIME: *30 minutes*

½ cup vegetable shortening
6 tablespoons granulated sugar
2 cups all-purpose flour
1 cup rye flour

**1** Preheat the oven to 400 degrees. Lightly grease 2 baking sheets.

**2** In a large bowl, cream the vegetable shortening and sugar. Gradually blend in the two flours.

**3** Turn the dough out on a floured surface and knead to a soft dough. Roll out the dough to a thickness of about ¼ inch. Using a 3-inch round cookie cutter, cut out rounds. Using a 1-inch cutter, cut out the centers of the rounds. Place 1 inch apart on the prepared baking sheets and prick the cookies all over with a fork.

**4** Bake for 5 to 7 minutes, until lightly colored. Transfer to wire racks to cool.

**Baking notes:** A very old version of this recipe calls for ¼ cup of honey in place of the granulated sugar; the honey dough is slightly easier to work with.

**F**

# First Lady Cookies

Rolled Cookies

YIELD: *5 to 6 dozen*
TOTAL TIME: *30 minutes*

4 cups all-purpose flour
1 cup butter
2 cups granulated sugar
3 large eggs

**1** Preheat the oven to 350 degrees. Lightly grease 2 baking sheets.

**2** Put the flour in a large bowl.

**3** Melt the butter. Add the hot butter to the flour in a steady stream, beating constantly. Beat in the sugar. Beat in the eggs.

**4** On a floured surface, roll out the dough to a thickness of ¼ inch. Using a 1½-inch round cutter, cut out the cookies and place 1 inch apart on the prepared baking sheets. Prick each cookie twice with the tines of a fork.

**5** Bake for 12 to 15 minutes, until lightly colored. Transfer to wire racks to cool.

**Baking notes:** This is a very old recipe, dating from the time of the Revolutionary War. If you wish, add a little vanilla extract or another extract, or a spice such as cinnamon.

# Florentines

Drop Cookies

YIELD: *2 to 4 dozen*
TOTAL TIME: *30 minutes*

¾ cup almonds, ground fine
¼ cup all-purpose flour
¼ cup butter
⅓ cup granulated sugar
5 tablespoons heavy cream
½ cup grated orange zest

TOPPING
4 ounces semisweet chocolate, chopped
3 tablespoons butter

**1** Preheat the oven to 375 degrees. Lightly grease and flour 2 baking sheets.

**2** Combine the almonds and flour.

**3** Combine the butter, sugar, and cream in a saucepan and bring to a boil. Remove from the heat and gradually blend in the dry ingredients. Stir in the orange zest. The mixture will be very thin.

**4** Drop the batter by tablespoonfuls 3 inches apart onto the prepared baking sheets. With the back of a spoon dipped in flour, spread the batter into 2- inch rounds.

**5** Bake for 12 to 15 minutes, until the edges start to brown (the cen-

ters may still look bubbly). Cool on the baking sheets on wire racks.

**6** For the topping, melt the chocolate and butter in the top of a double boiler, stirring until smooth. Remove from the heat.

**7** Place the cooled cookies upside down on the wire racks. Using a pastry brush, paint a thin layer of the melted chocolate over the bottom of each one. Let cool until the chocolate sets.

1 large egg
¼ cup granulated sugar
2 tablespoons canola oil
2 tablespoons water
¼ cup cornstarch

**1** In a medium bowl, beat the egg and sugar until thick and light-colored. Beat in the canola oil.

**2** Transfer 1 teaspoon of the egg mixture to a small bowl, add the water and cornstarch, and stir until smooth. Blend the cornstarch mixture into the egg mixture.

**3** Preheat a griddle or cast-iron frying pan.

**4** Drop the batter by tablespoonfuls onto the hot griddle and use the back of the spoon to spread the batter into 3½- to 4-inch circles. Cook for 5 to 8 minutes, until the cookies are golden. Remove from the griddle and fold in half over a pencil or wooden dowel to form into the fortune cookie shape.

# Fortune Cookies

Drop Cookies

YIELD: *3 to 4 dozen*
TOTAL TIME: *35 minutes*

---

5½ cups all-purpose flour
2 teaspoons baking powder
1 cup vegetable shortening
1 teaspoon salt
2 cups granulated sugar
3 large eggs
6 tablespoons milk
2 teaspoons vanilla extract

**1** Combine the flour, baking powder, and salt.

**2** In a large bowl, cream the vegetables shortening and sugar. Beat in the eggs one at a time. Beat in the milk and vanilla extract. Gradually blend in the dry ingredients. Divide the dough into quarters. Wrap each quarter in waxed paper and chill for 4 hours.

**3** Preheat the oven to 350 degrees. Lightly grease 2 baking sheets.

**4** On a floured surface roll out the dough to a thickness of ¼ inch. Cut into shapes and place 1½ inches apart on the prepared baking sheets.

**5** Bake for 12 to 15 minutes, until lightly colored. Transfer to wire racks to cool.

**Baking notes:** The dough keeps well in the refrigerator for a week or so and in the freezer for up to 6 months. Here are just a few of the many variations that can be created from this basic recipe:

CINNAMON COOKIES: Sprinkle the cookies with a mixture of ground cinnamon and granulated sugar before baking.

CARAWAY SEED COOKIES: Add caraway seeds to the dough.

COCONUT COOKIES: add 1 cup of shredded or flaked coconut to the dough.

JELLY COOKIES: Cut the dough into rounds, bake, and cool. Dab 1 teaspoon of jelly on top of half the cookies and sandwich with the remaining cookies.

LEMON COOKIES: Substitute lemon extract for the vanilla extract.

SPICE COOKIES: Add 1 teaspoon ground cinnamon, ½ teaspoon ground nutmeg, and ¼ teaspoon ground cloves to the dough. Sprinkle the hot cookies with granulated sugar.

# Foundation Base

Rolled Cookies

YIELD: *6 to 8 dozen*
TOTAL TIME: *40 minutes*
CHILLING TIME: *4 hours*

# FRENCH MERINGUE COOKIES

Drop Cookies

*Yield: 3 to 4 dozen*
*Total time: 70 minutes*

2 cups granulated sugar
1 cup water
6 large egg whites
¼ teaspoon cream of tartar
¼ teaspoon salt
1 teaspoon vanilla extract

**1** Preheat the oven to 250 degrees. Line 2 baking sheets with parchment paper.

**2** Combine the sugar and water in a heavy saucepan and bring to a boil, stirring to dissolve the sugar. Brush down the sides of the pan with a pastry brush and boil until the syrup registers 238 degrees on a candy thermometer. Immediately remove from the heat.

**3** Meanwhile, in a large bowl beat the egg whites until frothy. Beat in the cream of tartar and salt.

**4** Slowly pour the sugar syrup, into the egg whites, beating con-

stantly. Beat in the vanilla extract and beat until the mixture is cool.

**5** Place the dough in a pastry bag fitted with a star tip and pipe out mounds 1 inch apart onto the prepared baking sheets (or drop the batter by spoonfuls onto the sheets).

**6** Bake for 40 to 45 minutes, until lightly colored. Cool on the baking sheets on wire racks.

**Baking notes:** Finely ground almonds may be sprinkled over the meringues before baking.

# FRESH PLUM BARS

Bar Cookies

*Yield: 1 to 3 dozen*
*Total time: 55 minutes*

**CRUST**
1½ cups all-purpose flour
¼ teaspoon salt
½ cup vegetable shortening
¼ cup granulated sugar
1 large egg yolk
4 cups pitted plums, sliced
½ cup powdered sugar

**FILLING**
8 ounces cream cheese, at room temperature
¾ cup sour cream
3 large eggs
¾ cup powdered sugar
½ teaspoon grated lemon zest
1 teaspoon almond extract
1 teaspoon ground cinnamon
¼ teaspoon ground cloves

**1** Preheat the oven to 350 degrees. Lightly grease a 9-inch square baking pan.

**2** To make the crust, combine the flour and salt.

**3** In a large bowl, cream the vegetable shortening and sugar. Beat in the egg yolk. Gradually blend in the dry ingredients. Spread the dough evenly in the prepared baking pan.

**4** Arrange the sliced plums on top of the dough. Sprinkle the powdered sugar over the plums. Bake for 15 minutes.

**5** Meanwhile, make the filling: In a large bowl, combine the cream cheese, sour cream, eggs, powdered sugar, lemon zest, almond extract, and spices and beat until smooth.

**6** Spread the topping evenly over the hot crust. Bake for 30 to 35 minutes longer, or until firm to the touch. Cool in the pan on a wire rack before cutting into large or small bars, then refrigerate until ready to serve.

**Baking notes:** These bars should be served well chilled, with a dab of whipped cream on top.

2 large eggs
¼ cup granulated sugar
2½ tablespoons vegetable
  shortening
2½ tablespoons brandy
2 teaspoons anise seeds
¼ teaspoon salt
2 cups all-purpose flour
Vegetable oil for deep-frying
Powdered sugar for sprinkling

**1** In a large bowl, beat the eggs and sugar together until thick and light-colored. Beat in the vegetable shortening. Beat in the brandy, anise seeds, and salt. Gradually blend in the flour.

**2** Turn the dough out onto a floured surface and knead until smooth. Divide the dough in half, wrap in waxed paper and chill for at least 2 hours.

**3** In a deep-fryer or deep heavy pot, heat the oil to 360 degrees.

**4** Meanwhile, roll out the dough: Work with only half the dough at a time, keeping the remaining dough in the refrigerator. On a floured surface, roll out the dough to a 15 by 12-inch rectangle. Using a pastry wheel, cut the dough into 6 by 1-inch strips. Carefully tie a knot in the center of each strip. Repeat with the remaining dough.

**5** Deep-fry the knots until golden brown. Drain on paper towels on wire racks. When the cookies are cool, sprinkle heavily with powdered sugar.

# FRIED COOKIES

Rolled Cookies

YIELD: *6 to 7 dozen*
TOTAL TIME: *35 minutes*
CHILLING TIME: *at least 2 hours*

---

1¾ cups all-purpose flour
2 teaspoons baking soda
¼ teaspoon salt
½ cup vegetable shortening
1 cup granulated sugar
½ cup peanut butter
1 large egg
1 teaspoon vanilla extract
½ teaspoon grated lemon zest

**1** Combine the flour, baking soda, and salt.

**2** In a large bowl, cream the vegetable shortening and sugar. Beat in the peanut butter. Beat in the egg and vanilla extract. Beat in the lemon zest. Gradually blend in the dry ingredients.

**3** Form the dough into a log 2 inches in diameter. Wrap in waxed paper and chill for 8 hours or overnight.

**4** Preheat the oven to 350 degrees.

**5** Cut the log into ¼-inch-thick slices and place 1 inch apart on ungreased baking sheets. With the tines of a fork, press a criss-cross pattern into the top of each cookie.

**6** Bake for 7 to 10 minutes, until lightly browned. Transfer to wire racks to cool.

**Baking notes:** For a "peanuttier" flavor, the log can be rolled in chopped peanuts before chilling.

# FRIGGIES

Refrigerator Cookies

YIELD: *4 to 5 dozen*
TOTAL TIME: *30 minutes*
CHILLING TIME: *8 hours*

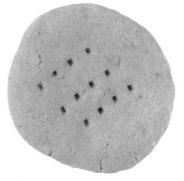

# FROSTED CHOCOLATE DROPS

Drop Cookies

YIELD: *3 to 4 dozen*
TOTAL TIME: *30 minutes*

1¾ cups all-purpose flour
½ teaspoon baking soda
½ teaspoon salt
2 ounces unsweetened chocolate, chopped
½ cup vegetable shortening
¾ cups granulated sugar
1 large egg
½ cup evaporated milk
1 teaspoon vanilla extract
½ cup walnuts, chopped
Chocolate Icing (see Pantry)

1 Preheat the oven to 375 degrees. Lightly grease 2 baking sheets.

2 Combine the flour, baking soda, and salt.

3 In the top of a double boiler, melt the chocolate and vegetable shortening, stirring until smooth.

Remove from the heat and beat in the sugar. Beat in the egg. Beat in the milk and vanilla extract. Gradually blend in the dry ingredients. Fold in the chopped walnuts.

4 Drop the dough by spoonfuls 1½ inches apart onto the prepared baking sheets.

5 Bake for 12 to 15 minutes, until firm to the touch. Transfer to wire racks to cool.

6 Frost the cookies with the chocolate icing.

# FROSTED GINGER CREAMS

Bar Cookies

YIELD: *8 to 9 dozen*
TOTAL TIME: *30 minutes*

3½ cups all-purpose flour
2 teaspoons baking soda
1 teaspoon ground ginger
1 teaspoon ground cinnamon
½ teaspoon salt
1 cup vegetable shortening
½ cup granulated sugar
2 large egg yolks
1 cup molasses, warmed
½ cup milk
1 cup raisins
White Sugar Icing (see Pantry)

1 Preheat the oven to 350 degrees. Lightly grease a 15 by 10-inch baking pan.

2 Combine the flour, baking soda, ginger, cinnamon, and salt.

3 In a large bowl, cream the vegetable shortening and sugar. Beat in the egg yolks. Beat in the molasses and milk. Gradually blend in the dry ingredients. Fold

in the raisins. Spread the mixture evenly in the prepared baking pan.

4 Bake for 12 to 15 minutes, until lightly colored. Cool in the pan on a wire rack.

5 Frost the cookies with the sugar glaze and cut into 2 by 1½-inch bars.

3 cups all-purpose flour
1 teaspoon baking soda
½ teaspoon ground cinnamon
¼ teaspoon ground nutmeg
¼ teaspoon ground cloves
¼ teaspoon ground ginger
½ teaspoon salt
¾ cup vegetable shortening
1 cup granulated sugar
¼ cup white port
1 cup evaporated milk
½ cup finely chopped candied citron
¼ cup finely chopped candied pineapple
¼ cup finely chopped candied cherries
¼ cup finely chopped candied orange peel
1 tablespoon grated lemon zest
½ cup walnuts, chopped

**1** Combine the flour, baking soda, spices, and salt.

**2** In a large bowl, cream the vegetable shortening and sugar. Beat in the port. Beat in the milk. Gradually blend in the dry ingredients. Fold in the candied fruit and lemon zest. Stir in the wal-

nuts. Cover and chill for 8 hours or overnight.

**3** Preheat the oven to 350 degrees.

**4** Spread the dough evenly in an ungreased 13 by 9-inch baking pan. Bake for 25 to 30 minutes, until golden on top.

**5** Cool in the pan on a wire rack before cutting into large or small bars.

**Baking notes:** These are good frosted with Rum Buttercream (see Pantry). Store these bars tightly covered.

# Fruit Bars I

Bar Cookies

Yield: *1 to 4 dozen*
Total time: *45 minutes*
Chilling time: *8 hours*

---

4 cups all-purpose flour
1 teaspoon ground cinnamon
1 teaspoon ground ginger
½ cup molasses
½ cup boiling water
1 teaspoon baking soda
1 cup vegetable shortening
1½ cups granulated sugar
3 large eggs
1 cup raisins
1 cup currants
1 cup walnuts, chopped

**1** Combine the flour, cinnamon, and ginger.

**2** Combine the molasses and boiling water in a small bowl. Add the baking soda and stir to dissolve.

**3** In a large bowl, cream the vegetable shortening and sugar. Beat in the eggs one at a time. Beat in the molasses mixture. Gradually blend in the dry ingredients. Fold

in the raisins, currants, and walnuts. Cover and chill for 2 hours.

**4** Preheat the oven to 350 degrees. Lightly grease a 13 by 9-inch baking pan.

**5** Spread the dough evenly in the prepared baking pan.

**6** Bake for 15 to 30 minutes, until lightly colored on top. Cool in the pan on a wire rack.

**7** Frost the cookies with the Buttercream Frosting (see Pantry) and cut into large or small bars.

# Fruit Bars II

Bar Cookies

Yield: *1 to 3 dozen*
Total time: *45 minutes*
Chilling time: *2 hours*

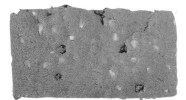

# FRUITCAKE COOKIES

Bar Cookies

YIELD: *1 to 3 dozen*
TOTAL TIME: *45 minutes*

1 cup all-purpose flour
½ teaspoon baking powder
6 tablespoons vegetable shortening
½ cup granulated sugar
2 large eggs
¼ cup fresh orange juice
1 cup mixed candied fruit
1 cup raisins
½ cup dates, pitted and chopped (optional)
½ cup walnuts, chopped

**1** Preheat the oven to 350 degrees. Lightly grease a 9-inch square baking pan.

**2** Combine the flour and baking powder.

**3** In a large bowl, cream the vegetable shortening and sugar. Beat in the eggs. Beat in the orange juice. Gradually blend in the dry ingredients. Fold in the candied fruit, raisins, the optional dates, and walnuts. Spread the dough evenly into the prepared baking pan.

**4** Bake for 30 to 35 minutes, until lightly colored on top. Cool in the pan on a wire rack before cutting into large or small bars.

**Baking notes:** These bars are like miniature holiday fruitcakes. Add a little ground cinnamon or ground nutmeg, or both, just to emphasize the fruitcake flavor.

# FRUIT CHEWIES

Bar Cookies

YIELD: *1 to 3 dozen*
TOTAL TIME: *40 minutes*

FILLING
1¾ cups dried apricots, chopped
1 cup dates, pitted and chopped
1¾ cups water
¼ teaspoon fresh lemon juice
2 cups all-purpose flour
1 teaspoon baking soda
¼ teaspoon salt
¾ cup vegetable shortening
¾ cup packed dark brown sugar
¼ cup molasses
1 teaspoon vanilla extract
2 cup rolled oats

**1** To make the filling, combine the apricots, dates, water, and lemon juice in a blender and blend to a puree. Transfer to a bowl and refrigerate until cold.

**2** Preheat the oven to 350 degrees. Lightly grease a 13 by 9-inch baking pan.

**3** Combine the flour, baking soda, and salt.

**4** In a large bowl, cream the vegetable shortening and brown sugar. Beat in the molasses and vanilla extract. Gradually blend in the dry ingredients. Fold in the oats.

**5** Press half of the dough evenly into the bottom of the prepared baking pan, packing it down.

**6** Spread the chilled filling over the dough, leaving a ½-inch border all around the edges. Spread the remaining dough evenly on top of the fruit.

**7** Bake for 20 to 25 minutes, until lightly colored on top. Cool in the pan on a wire rack before cutting into large or small bars.

2 cups all-purpose flour
1 teaspoon baking powder
½ teaspoon baking soda
2 teaspoons ground allspice
¼ teaspoon salt
1 cup granulated sugar
⅓ cup vegetable oil
2 large eggs
2 cups raisins
⅓ cup almonds, chopped

**1** Preheat the oven to 375 degrees. Lightly grease 2 baking sheets.

**2** Combine the flour, baking powder, baking soda, allspice, and salt.

**3** In a large bowl, beat the sugar and vegetable oil. Beat in the eggs. Gradually blend in the dry ingredients. Stir in the raisins and almonds.

**4** Drop the dough by spoonfuls 1½ inches apart onto the prepared baking sheets.

**5** Bake for 10 to 12 minutes, until lightly colored and firm to the touch. Transfer to wire racks to cool.

# FRUIT COOKIES I

Drop Cookies

YIELD: *5 to 6 dozen*
TOTAL TIME: *30 minutes*

---

3 cups all-purpose flour
½ teaspoon baking soda
1 teaspoon baking powder
½ teaspoon ground nutmeg
¼ teaspoon ground cloves
½ teaspoon ground cinnamon
2 cups packed light brown sugar
4 large eggs
½ cup candied citron, choppped
½ cup walnuts, chopped

**1** Preheat the oven to 350 degrees. Lightly grease 2 baking sheets.

**2** Combine the flour, baking soda, baking powder, and spices.

**3** In a large bowl, beat the brown sugar and eggs until thick. Grad-ually blend in the dry ingredients. Fold in the candied citron and walnuts.

**4** Drop the dough by spoonfuls 1½ inches apart onto the prepared baking sheets.

**5** Bake for 20 to 30 minutes, until lightly colored. Transfer to wire racks to cool.

**Baking notes:** These cookies are good with lemon- or orange-flavored frosting.

# FRUIT COOKIES II

Drop Cookies

YIELD: *4 to 5 dozen*
TOTAL TIME: *45 minutes*

---

4½ cups all-purpose flour
1 teaspoon baking soda
1 teaspoon ground cinnamon
1 teaspoon ground allspice
¼ teaspoon ground cloves
¼ teaspoon ground nutmeg
1 cup vegetable shortening
1½ cups packed light brown sugar
1½ cups molasses
2½ teaspoons milk
1 cup raisins
1 cup currants

**1** Preheat the oven to 350 degrees.

**2** Combine the flour, baking soda, and spices.

**3** In a large bowl, cream the vegetable shortening and brown sugar. Beat in the molasses and milk. Gradually blend in the dry ingredients. Stir in the raisins and currants.

**4** On a floured surface, roll out the dough to a thickness of ¼ inch. Using round cookie cutters, cut out cookies and place 1½ inches apart on ungreased baking sheets.

**5** Bake for 12 to 15 minutes, or until lightly colored. Transfer to wire racks to cool.

# FRUIT COOKIES III

Rolled Cookies

YIELD: *4 to 6 dozen*
TOTAL TIME: *30 minutes*

# FRUIT COOKIES IV

Drop Cookies

YIELD: *4 to 5 dozen*
TOTAL TIME: *30 minutes*

**2½ cups all-purpose flour**
**1 teaspoon baking soda**
**1 teaspoon baking powder**
**1 teaspoon ground mace**
**½ teaspoon ground cloves**
**2 teaspoons ground cinnamon**
**1 cup vegetable shortening**
**2 cups packed light brown sugar**
**3 large eggs**
**2 cups raisins**
**1 cup walnuts, chopped**

**1** Preheat the oven to 350 degrees.

**2** Combine the flour, baking soda, baking powder, and spices.

**3** In a large bowl, cream the vegetable shortening and brown sugar. Beat in the eggs one at a time. Gradually blend in the dry ingredients. Fold in the raisins and walnuts.

**4** Drop the dough by spoonfuls 1½ inches apart onto ungreased baking sheets.

**5** Bake for 12 to 15 minutes, until lightly colored. Transfer to wire racks to cool.

# FRUIT COOKIES V

Drop Cookies

YIELD: *4 to 5 dozen*
TOTAL TIME: *30 minutes*

**2½ cups unbleached all-purpose flour**
**½ teaspoon ground cinnamon**
**¼ teaspoon salt**
**½ cup canola oil**
**¼ cup honey**
**1 large egg, beaten**
**¼ cup unsweetened applesauce, or more as needed**
**¼ cup peaches, stewed and mashed (see Baking notes)**
**1 cup rolled oats**
**1 cup raisins, chopped**
**¼ cup canned crushed pineapple, drained**

**1** Preheat the oven to 400 degrees. Lightly grease 2 baking sheets.

**2** Combine the flour, cinnamon, and salt.

**3** In a small saucepan, heat the canola oil and honey just until warm. Transfer to a large bowl and beat in the egg. Beat in the applesauce and peaches. Gradually blend in the dry ingredients. Fold in the oats, raisins, and pineapple. If the dough seems too dry, add more applesauce 1 teaspoon at a time.

**4** Drop the dough by spoonfuls 1½ inches apart onto the prepared baking sheets.

**5** Bake for 15 to 20 minutes, until lightly colored. Tranfer to wire racks to cool.

**Baking notes:** To prepare peaches: Peel, pit, and slice 1 large or 2 medium peaches. Place the slices in a small saucepan, and add enough water to cover. Sprinkle with 2 teaspoons granulated sugar and stir. Bring to a boil, then reduce heat and cook until peaches are softened. Remove from the heat and mash. Let cool before using.

5 cups all-purpose flour
1 teaspoon baking soda
¼ teaspoon ground nutmeg
1 teaspoon ground cinnamon
1½ cups vegetable shortening
2 cups packed light brown sugar
3 large eggs
1 cup sour cream
2 cups raisins

1 Preheat the oven to 350 degrees.

2 Combine the flour, baking soda, nutmeg, and cinnamon.

3 In a large bowl, cream the vegetable shortening and brown sugar. Beat in the eggs one at a time. Beat in the sour cream. Gradually blend in the dry ingredients. Fold in the raisins.

4 On a floured surface, roll out the dough to a thickness of ¼ inch. Using cookie cutters, cut into shapes and place 1 inch apart on ungreased baking sheets.

5 Bake for 12 to 15 minutes, until lightly colored. Transfer to wire racks to cool.

# FRUIT COOKIES VI

Rolled Cookies

YIELD: *7 to 8 dozen*
TOTAL TIME: *30 minutes*

---

4 cups all-purpose flour
1 teaspoon baking powder
1 teaspoon baking soda
1½ cups vegetable shortening
1 cup packed light brown sugar
2 large eggs
1 cup raisins
1 cup walnuts, chopped
1 cup candied citron, chopped
1 cup pitted prunes, chopped
½ cup flaked coconut
Granulated sugar for sprinkling
Almonds, ground fine

1 Preheat the oven to 350 degrees. Lightly grease 2 baking sheets.

2 Combine the flour, baking powder, and baking soda.

3 In a large bowl, cream the vegetable shortening and brown sugar. Beat in the eggs. Gradually blend in the dry ingredients. Fold in the raisins, walnuts, candied citron, prunes, and coconut.

4 On a floured surface, roll out the dough to a thickness of ⅛ inch. Using cookie cutters, cut into shapes and place 1 inch apart on the prepared baking sheets.

5 Bake for 12 to 15 minutes, until lightly colored. Sprinkle with granulated sugar and the ground almonds and transfer to wire racks to cool.

# FRUIT COOKIES VII

Rolled Cookies

YIELD: *5 to 6 dozen*
TOTAL TIME: *40 minutes*

---

1¾ cups all-purpose flour
½ teaspoon ground cinnamon
½ cup vegetable shortening
½ cup granulated sugar
1 large egg
½ teaspoon vanilla extract
¼ cup heavy cream

1 Combine the flour and cinnamon.

2 In a large bowl, cream the vegetable shortening and sugar. Beat in the egg. Beat in the vanilla extract and heavy cream. Gradually blend in the dry ingredients. Cover and chill for 8 hours or overnight.

3 Preheat the oven to 375 degrees.

4 On a floured surface, roll out the dough to a thickness of ¼ inch. Using a 3-inch round cookie cutter, cut out an even number of rounds and place 1 inch apart on ungreased baking sheets.

5 Bake for 12 to 15 minutes, until lightly colored. Transfer to wire racks to cool.

6 In a small bowl, whip the cream until it holds stiff peaks.

7 To assemble, spread a thin layer of whipped cream over the bottom of one cookie, place another cookie on top and gently press together. Repeat with the remaining cookies and cream.

**Baking notes:** A sweet custard filling can be used in place of the whipped cream.

# FRUIT DREAMS

Rolled Cookies

YIELD: *3 to 4 dozen*
TOTAL TIME: *35 minutes*
CHILLING TIME: *8 hours*

# FRUIT DROPS I

Drop Cookies

YIELD: *2 to 3 dozen*
TOTAL TIME: *30 minutes*

1 cup cornflakes, crushed
2 cups shredded coconut
½ teaspoon salt
1 cup sweetened condensed milk
1 cup dates, pitted and chopped fine
1 cup pitted prunes, chopped fine
1 cup figs, chopped fine
1 cup golden raisins, chopped fine
1 cup currants

**1** Preheat the oven to 350 degrees. Lightly grease 2 baking sheets.

**2** In a large bowl, combine the cornflakes, coconut, and salt. Stir in the condensed milk. Stir in all the fruit and blend thoroughly.

**3** Drop the mixture by spoonfuls 1 inch apart onto the prepared baking sheets.

**4** Bake for 12 to 15 minutes, until golden colored. Transfer to wire racks to cool.

**Baking notes:** If you like, drizzle melted chocolate or vanilla icing over the top of the cooled cookies.

# FRUIT DROPS II

Drop Cookies

YIELD: *2 to 3 dozen*
TOTAL TIME: *30 minutes*

¼ cup all-purpose flour
1¼ cups soy flour
¼ teaspoon salt
¼ cup packed dark brown sugar
2 hard-boiled large egg yolks, chopped
½ cup heavy cream
¼ cup water
¾ teaspoon almond extract
2 large egg whites
1 cup dates, pitted and chopped fine
1 cup golden raisins, chopped fine

**1** Preheat the oven to 350 degrees. Lightly grease 2 baking sheets.

**2** Combine the flour, soy flour, and salt.

**3** In a large bowl, beat the brown sugar, egg yolks, cream, water, and almond extract.

**4** In a medium bowl, beat the egg whites until stiff but not dry. Fold the whites into the egg yolk mixture. Gradually blend in the dry ingredients. Fold in the dates and raisins.

**5** Drop the dough by spoonfuls 1½ inches apart onto the prepared baking sheets.

**6** Bake for 10 to 12 minutes, until lightly colored. Transfer to wire racks to cool.

# FRUIT-FILLED OATCAKES

Bar Cookies

YIELD: *1 to 3 dozen*
TOTAL TIME: *45 minutes*

1½ cups all-purpose flour
1½ cups rolled oats
½ teaspoon baking soda
½ teaspoon salt
½ cup vegetable shortening
1 cup packed light brown sugar
Fruit filling (your choice of jam or preserves)

**1** Preheat the oven to 350 degrees. Lightly grease a 13 by 9-inch baking pan.

**2** Cream the flour, rolled oats, baking soda, and salt.

**3** In a large bowl, cream the vegetable shortening and brown sugar. Gradually blend in the dry ingredients.

**4** Spread half of the dough evenly into the prepared pan.

Spread the fruit filling over the dough and press the remaining dough over the top of the fruit.

**5** Bake for 20 to 25 minutes, until lightly colored on top. Cool in the pan on a wire rack before cutting into large or small bars.

**Baking notes:** You can dress up these bars with a drizzle of white or lemon frosting (see Pantry).

## CRUST

2 cups all-purpose flour
1 teaspoon salt
⅔ cup vegetable shortening
¼ cup water

## FILLING

3 medium apples, cored and
   chopped
1½ cups golden raisins
1 cup currants
½ cup granulated sugar
Pinch of ground nutmeg
1 tablespoon fresh lemon juice
1 large egg, beaten
Granulated sugar for sprinkling

1  To make the crust, combine the flour and salt in a large bowl. Cut in the vegetable shortening. Add just enough water to make a smooth dough. Divide the dough in half. Wrap in waxed paper and chill for 1 hour.

2  Preheat the oven to 350 degrees. Lightly grease a baking sheet.

3  To make the filling, combine the apples, raisins, currants, sugar, and nutmeg in a medium bowl. Add the lemon juice and toss to blend.

4  On a floured surface, roll out half of the dough to a 15 by 10-inch rectangle and fit it into the prepared baking sheet. Spread the filling evenly over the dough, leaving a ½-inch border all around the edges.

5  Roll out the remaining dough to a 15 by 10-inch rectangle. Moisten the edges of the dough in the baking pan. Lay the rolled-out dough on top and press the edges to seal. Using a fork, prick the surface of the top crust a few times. Brush with the beaten egg and sprinkle with granulated sugar.

6  Bake for 30 to 35 minutes, until the crust is lightly colored. Cool in the pan on a wire rack before cutting into finger-shaped bars.

# FRUIT FINGERS

Rolled Cookies

YIELD: *4 to 6 dozen*
TOTAL TIME: *50 minutes*
CHILLING TIME: *1 hour*

---

## CRUST

¾ cup vegetable shortening
¼ cup granulated sugar
2 large egg yolks
1½ cups all-purpose flour

## TOPPING

2 large egg whites, beaten
½ cup granulated sugar
1 cup almonds, chopped

## FILLING

1 cup raspberry puree (see Baking
   notes)
1 cup flaked coconut

1  Preheat the oven to 350 degrees. Lightly grease a 13 by 9-inch baking pan.

2  To make the crust, cream the vegetable shortening and sugar in a medium bowl. Beat in the egg yolks. Gradually blend in the flour. Press the dough evenly into the prepared baking pan.

3  Bake for 15 minutes.

4  Meanwhile, make the topping: In a medium bowl, beat the egg whites until foamy. Fold in the sugar and almonds.

5  Spread the raspberry puree over the hot crust. Sprinkle the coconut over the puree. Spread the topping over the coconut.

6  Bake for 20 to 25 minutes longer until the topping is set and lightly colored. Cool in a pan on a wire rack before cutting into large or small bars.

**Baking notes:** To make raspberry puree, place drained, frozen raspberries in a blender and puree.

# FRUIT MERINGUE BARS

Bar Cookies

YIELD: *1 to 4 dozen*
TOTAL TIME: *45 minutes*

# FRUIT SQUARES

Bar Cookies

YIELD: *1 to 3 dozen*
TOTAL TIME: *45 minutes*

1 cup all-purpose flour
1 teaspoon baking powder
½ teaspoon salt
2 large eggs
1 cup packed light brown sugar
2 teaspoons vanilla extract
1 cup mixed candied fruit, chopped fine
1 cup raisins, chopped

**1** Preheat the oven to 350 degrees.

**2** Combine the flour, baking powder, and salt.

**3** In a large bowl, beat the eggs with the brown sugar until thick and light-colored. Beat in the vanilla extract. Gradually blend in the dry ingredients. Stir in the candied fruit and raisins. Spread the dough evenly in an ungreased 8-inch square baking pan.

**4** Bake for 30 to 35 minutes, until lightly colored on top. Cool in the pan on a wire rack before cutting into large or small bars.

**Baking notes:** Lemon Sugar Icing goes very well with these bars (see Pantry).

# FUDGE BROWNIES I

Bar Cookies

YIELD: *1 to 2 dozen*
TOTAL TIME: *45 minutes*

½ cup vegetable shortening
2 ounces semisweet chocolate, chopped
2 cups granulated sugar
4 large egg yolks
1¼ teaspoons vanilla extract
1 cup all-purpose flour
1 cup walnuts, chopped

**1** Preheat the oven to 325 degrees. Lightly grease a 9-inch square baking pan.

**2** In the top of a double boiler, melt the vegetable shortening and chocolate, stirring until smooth. Remove from the heat and beat in the sugar. Beat in the egg yolks one at a time. Beat in the vanilla extract. Gradually blend in the flour. Fold in the nuts. Spread the batter evenly in the prepared baking pan.

**3** Bake for 25 to 30 minutes, until a toothpick inserted in the center comes out clean. Cool in the pan on a wire rack before cutting into large or small bars.

**Baking notes:** Frost before cutting into bars if you wish (see Pantry).

# FUDGE BROWNIES II

Bar Cookies

YIELD: *1 to 2 dozen*
TOTAL TIME: *45 minutes*

1⅓ cups all-purpose flour
¾ cup unsweetened, cocoa powder
¼ teaspoon salt
⅔ cup vegetable oil
2 cups granulated sugar
2 large eggs
1 teaspoon almond extract
½ cup almonds, chopped

**1** Preheat the oven to 350 degrees. Lightly grease a 13 by 9-inch square baking pan.

**2** Combine the flour, cocoa powder, and salt.

**3** In a large bowl, beat the vegetable oil and sugar together. Beat in the eggs one at a time. Beat in the almond extract. Gradually blend in the dry ingredi-ents. Stir in the almonds. Spread the mixture evenly into the pre-pared baking pan.

**4** Bake for 25 to 30 minutes, until a toothpick inserted into the cen-ter comes out clean. Cool in the pan on a wire rack before cutting into large or small bars.

**Baking notes:** Frost before cut-ting if you wish (see Pantry).

## FUDGE BROWNIES III

Bar Cookies

YIELD: *1 to 2 dozen*
TOTAL TIME: *45 minutes*

¾ cup all-purpose flour
½ teaspoon baking powder
½ teaspoon salt
6 ounces bittersweet chocolate, chopped
⅓ cup vegetable shortening
1 cup granulated sugar
2 large eggs
½ cup walnuts, chopped

**1** Preheat the oven to 350 degrees. Lightly grease a 9-inch square baking pan.

**2** Combine the flour, baking powder, and salt.

**3** In the top of a double boiler, melt the chocolate and vegetable shortening, stirring until smooth. Remove from the heat and beat in the sugar. Beat in the eggs one at a time. Gradually blend in the dry ingredients. Fold in the walnuts.

**4** Spread the batter evenly in the prepared pan.

**5** Bake for 30 to 35 minutes, until a toothpick inserted in the center comes out clean. Cool in the pan on a wire rack before cutting into large or small bars.

**Baking notes:** Frost before cutting into bars if you like (see Pantry).

## FUDGIES I

Drop Cookies

YIELD: *4 to 6 dozen*
TOTAL TIME: *30 minutes*

2 cups all-purpose flour
½ cup unsweetened cocoa powder
½ teaspoon baking soda
¼ teaspoon salt
¼ cup vegetable shortening
½ cup granulated sugar
1 large egg
½ cup buttermilk
½ cup molasses
1 teaspoon vanilla extract
¾ cup walnuts, chopped

**1** Preheat the oven to 350 degrees. Lightly grease 2 baking sheets.

**2** Combine the flour, cocoa powder, baking soda, and salt.

**3** In a large bowl, cream the vegetable shortening and sugar. Beat in the egg. Beat in the buttermilk and molasses. Beat in the vanilla extract. Gradually blend in the dry ingredients. Fold in the walnuts.

**4** Drop the dough by spoonfuls 1½ inches apart onto the prepared baking sheets.

**5** Bake for 12 to 15 minutes, until firm to the touch. Transfer to wire racks to cool.

**Baking notes:** Sour milk can be used in place of the buttermilk.

## FUDGIES II

Bar Cookies

YIELD: *1 to 2 dozen*
TOTAL TIME: *45 mintues*

1⅓ cups all-purpose flour
1 teaspoon baking powder
½ teaspoon salt
3 ounces unsweetened chocolate, chopped
⅔ cup vegetable shortening
2 cups granulated sugar
4 large eggs
2 teaspoons vanilla extract
1 cup walnuts, chopped

**1** Preheat the oven to 350 degrees. Lightly grease and flour a 9-inch square baking pan.

**2** Combine the flour, baking powder, and salt.

**3** In the top of a double boiler, melt the chocolate and vegetable shortening, stirring until smooth. Remove from the heat and beat in the sugar. Beat in the eggs one at a time. Beat in the vanilla extract. Gradually blend in the dry ingredients. Stir in the walnuts.

**4** Spread the batter evenly in the prepared baking pan.

**5** Bake for 30 to 35 minutes, or until a toothpick inserted in the center comes out clean. Cool in the pan on a wire rack before cutting into large or small bars.

**Baking notes:** Cut into large bars and serve as a dessert with a dab of whipped cream on top.

# GALAKTOBOUIRIKO

Formed Cookies

YIELD: *3 to 4 dozen*
TOTAL TIME: *45 minutes*

**CUSTARD**
¾ **cup rice flour**
½ **teaspoon ground cinnamon**
½ **teaspoon grated orange zest**
¼ **cup milk**
1½ **cups granulated sugar**
1 **cup vegetable shortening**
8 **large eggs, separated**

½ **pound butter, melted**
1 **pound phyllo dough, thawed if frozen**
1½ **cups water**
¾ **cup granulated sugar**
**Grated zest of 1 orange**

**1** To make the custard, combine the rice flour, cinnamon, and orange zest.

**2** In a large bowl, beat the milk and 1 cup of sugar. Beat in the dry ingredients. Add the vegetable shortening. Place the mixture in the top of a double boiler, and slow heat until the mixture thickens. Remove from the heat and cool.

**3** Beat the egg yolks with ½ cup of sugar.

**4** In a medium bowl, beat the egg whites stiff but not dry.

**5** Combine and gently blend together the beaten egg whites, the egg yolks, and cooled custard mix.

**6** Preheat the oven to 350 degrees. Lightly grease a 13 by 9-inch baking pan.

**7** Fit one phyllo sheet in the bottom of the prepared baking sheet. Using a pastry brush, brush a thin coat of custard on the phyllo. Lay a second sheet of phyllo on top of the custard and brush it with a layer of custard. Repeat the process until all of the custard is used up. Brush the last sheet with water, sprinkle with granulated sugar and the grated orange zest.

**8** Bake for 15 to 25 minutes, until lightly colored. Cool in the pan on a wire rack before cutting into large or small bars.

# GALETTE BRETONNE

Rolled Cookies

YIELD: *3 to 4 dozen*
TOTAL TIME: *45 minutes*
CHILLING TIME: *4 hours*

4 **cups all-purpose flour**
½ **cup rice flour**
1 **cup hazelnuts, ground fine**
1 **tablespoon baking powder**
½ **cup plus 2 tablespoons butter, at room temperature**
2¼ **cups powdered sugar**
3 **large eggs**
1½ **teaspoons dry sherry**
¼ **cup mixed candied fruit, chopped very fine**

**1** Combine the two flours, hazelnuts, and baking powder.

**2** In a large bowl, cream the butter and powdered sugar. Beat in the eggs one at a time. Beat in the sherry. Gradually blend in the dry ingredients. Fold in the candied fruit.

**3** Turn the dough out onto a floured surface and knead until well blended. Wrap in waxed paper and chill for 4 hours.

**4** Preheat the oven to 350 degrees. Lightly grease 2 baking sheets.

**5** On a floured surface, roll out the dough to a thickness of ¾ inch. Using a small plate as a guide, cut into rounds about 6 inches in diameter. Place 1 inch apart on the prepared baking sheets and score the rounds into wedges.

**6** Bake for 18 to 20 minutes, until lightly colored. Transfer to wire racks to cool slightly before cutting the wedges along the scored lines.

**Baking notes:** In some versions of this recipe, rounds are pricked with a fork to create a diamond pattern. In others, split hazelnuts are pressed into the center of each wedge before baking.

1 cup whole wheat flour
1½ cups rolled oats
½ cup wheat germ
1 teaspoon baking soda
1 teaspoon ground cinnamon
½ teaspoon salt
1 cup vegetable shortening
½ cup granulated sugar
1 cup packed light brown sugar
2 large eggs
1 teaspoon vanilla extract
1 cup walnuts, chopped
Granulated sugar

1 Preheat the oven to 350 degrees. Lightly grease 2 baking sheets.

2 Combine the flour, oats, wheat germ, baking soda, cinnamon, and salt.

3 In a large bowl, cream the vegetable shortening and two sugars. Beat in the eggs. Beat in the vanilla extract. Gradually blend in the dry ingredients. Fold in the walnuts.

4 Pinch off walnut-sized pieces of dough and roll into balls. Place 1 inch apart on the prepared baking sheets. Flatten each ball with the bottom of a glass dipped in water and then in granulated sugar.

5 Bake for 8 to 10 minutes, until lightly colored. Transfer to wire racks to cool.

# GALLETAS DE LA HARINA DE AVENA

Formed Cookies

YIELD: *3 to 4 dozen*
TOTAL TIME: *30 minutes*

---

2¼ cups all-purpose flour
½ teaspoon salt
1 cup butter, chilled
¼ cup ice water

FILLING
8 ounces almond paste
2 tablespoons granulated sugar
1 large egg
⅓ cup almonds, ground fine
Powdered sugar for dredging

1 Combine the flour and salt in a large bowl. Cut in the butter. Add just enough ice water to form a stiff dough. Divide the dough into thirds. Flatten each piece into a disk, wrap in waxed paper, and chill for 2 hours.

2 To make the filling, crumble the almond paste into a medium bowl. Add the sugar and egg and beat until smooth. Beat in the almonds.

3 Divide the mixture into thirds. On a floured surface, roll each piece into a 16-inch-long rope. Cut each rope into 16 pieces.

4 Preheat the oven to 350 degrees. Lightly grease 2 baking sheets.

5 On a floured surface, roll out one piece of dough to a 12 inch square. Trim the edges and cut into 3-inch squares. Place a piece of the almond filling across one corner and roll up jelly-roll fashion. Pinch to seal the seam. Repeat with the remaining squares and place 1 inch apart on the prepared baking sheets, curving the ends of each cookie into the shape of a crescent. Repeat with the remaining dough and filling.

6 Bake for 12 to 15 minutes, until lightly colored. Transfer to wire racks to cool, then dredge in powdered sugar.

# GAZELLE HORNS

Formed Cookies

YIELD: *2 to 3 dozen*
TOTAL TIME: *45 minutes*
CHILLING TIME: *2 hours*

# GERMAN ALMOND WAFERS

Formed Cookies

YIELD: *2 to 3 dozen*
TOTAL TIME: *30 minutes*
CHILLING TIME: *4 hours*

1⅔ cups all-purpose flour
2 teaspoons baking powder
½ cup vegetable shortening
1 cup granulated sugar
1 large egg
1 teaspoon vanilla extract

**TOPPING**
⅔ cup heavy cream
2 teaspoons granulated sugar
1 cup sliced almonds

**1** Combine the flour and baking powder.

**2** In a large bowl, cream the vegetable shortening and sugar. Beat in the egg. Beat in the vanilla extract. Gradually blend in the dry ingredients. Cover and chill for 4 hours.

**3** To prepare the topping, combine the cream and sugar in a saucepan. Remove from the heat and add the almonds.

**4** Preheat the oven to 350 degrees. Lightly grease 2 baking sheets.

**5** Pinch off walnut-sized pieces of dough and roll into balls. Place 1½ inches apart on the prepared baking sheets. Using the bottom of a glass dipped in flour, flatten each ball to a thickness of ¼ inch. Spread a teaspoon of the topping over each cookie.

**6** Bake for 10 to 14 minutes, until lightly colored. Transfer to wire racks to cool.

# GERMAN BONBONS

Formed Cookies

YIELD: *4 to 6 dozen*
TOTAL TIME: *45 minutes*
CHILLING TIME: *1 hour*

3 large egg whites
2 cups powdered sugar
1 pound hazelnuts, toasted and ground
Powdered sugar for shaping
6 ounces semisweet chocolate

**1** Preheat the oven to 350 degrees. Line 2 baking sheets with waxed paper.

**2** Combine the eggs, sugar, and hazelnuts in a food processor or blender, and process to a paste.

**3** Dust your hands with powdered sugar. Pinch off 1-inch pieces of dough and roll into balls. Place 1 inch apart on the prepared baking sheets.

**4** Bake for 10 to 12 minutes, until firm to the touch. Transfer to wire racks to cool.

**5** Melt the chocolate in the top of a double boiler over low heat, stirring until smooth. Remove from the heat and keep warm over hot water.

**6** One at a time, insert a bamboo skewer into each ball and dip in the melted chocolate. Let the excess drip off and chill for at least 1 hour on wire racks

**Baking notes:** If the hazelnut dough seems too dry, add additional egg whites, one at a time. If it seems too wet, add more ground hazelnuts. Substitute almonds, brazil nuts, or even chestnuts for the hazelnuts.

½ cup all-purpose flour
½ cup walnuts, ground
½ teaspoon baking powder
¼ teaspoon salt
5 tablespoons vegetable shortening
4 tablespoons semisweet chocolate
3 ounces cream cheese, at room temperature
1 cup granulated sugar
3 large eggs
½ teaspoon almond extract

**1** Preheat the oven to 350 degrees. Lightly grease a 9-inch square baking pan.

**2** Combine the flour, walnuts, baking powder, and salt.

**3** In the top of a double boiler, melt 3 tablespoons of the vegetable shortening and the chocolate, stirring until smooth. Remove from the heat and beat in the remaining 2 tablespoons shortening and the cream cheese. Beat in the sugar. Beat in the eggs and almond extract. Gradually blend in the dry ingredients. Spread the batter evenly in the prepared baking pan.

**4** Bake for 12 to 15 minutes, or until a toothpick inserted in the center comes out clean. Cool in the pan on a wire rack before cutting into large or small bars.

**Baking notes:** Frost these with chocolate icing to make them even more indulgent.

# GERMAN BROWNIES

Bar Cookies

YIELD: *1 to 2 dozen*
TOTAL TIME: *45 minutes*

---

¾ cup vegetable shortening
1½ cups powdered sugar
2 large egg yolks
2 hard-boiled large eggs, chopped
2 cups all-purpose flour
2 large egg whites, beaten
Powdered sugar for sprinkling

**1** In a large bowl, cream the vegetable shortening and powdered-sugar. Beat in the egg yolks and hard-boiled eggs. Gradually blend in the flour. Cover and chill for 8 hours or overnight.

**2** Preheat the oven to 350 degrees. Lightly grease 2 baking sheets.

**3** On a floured surface, roll out the dough to a thickness of ¼ inch. Cut into pencil-thin strips 6 to 8 inches long. For each cookie, braid 3 of the strips together, form into a wreath shape, and pinch the ends to seal. Place the cookies 1 inch apart on the prepared baking sheets. Brush with

the beaten egg whites and sprinkle with powdered sugar.

**4** Bake for 12 to 15 minutes, until lightly colored. Transfer to wire racks to cool.

**Baking notes:** Finely chopped hazelnuts can be mixed with the powdered sugar for sprinkling.

# GERMAN CHRISTMAS COOKIES I

Rolled Cookies

YIELD: *4 to 5 dozen*
TOTAL TIME: *35 minutes*
CHILLING TIME: *8 hours*

# GERMAN CHRISTMAS COOKIES II

Rolled Cookies

YIELD: *4 to 5 dozen*
TOTAL TIME: *35 minutes*

2 cups all-purpose flour
Pinch of pimento powder
Pinch of ground coriander
Pinch of ground anise
Pinch of salt
1 cup vegetable shortening
1 cup granulated sugar
2 large eggs
1 teaspoon fresh lemon juice
2 tablespoons grated lemon zest

**1** Preheat the oven to 350 degrees.

**2** Combine the flour, pimento powder, coriander, anise, and salt.

**3** In a large bowl, cream the vegetable shortening and sugar. Beat in the eggs one at a time. Beat in the lemon juice and lemon zest. Gradually blend in the dry ingredients.

**4** On a floured surface, roll out the dough out to a thickness of ¼ inch. Using cookie cutters, cut into shapes and place 1 inch apart on ungreased baking sheets.

**5** Bake for 12 to 15 minutes, until lightly colored. Transfer to wire racks to cool.

**Baking notes:** Ice and decorate the cookies if desired.

# GERMAN GEBACK COOKIES

Formed Cookies

YIELD: *3 to 4 dozen*
TOTAL TIME: *30 minutes*
CHILLING TIME: *4 hours*

½ cup butter, at room temperature
⅔ cup granulated sugar
4 each large egg yolks
½ teaspoon grated lemon zest
2 cups all-purpose flour
1 each large egg white

**1** In a large bowl, cream the butter and sugar. Beat in the egg yolks. Beat in the lemon zest. Gradually blend in the flour. Divide the dough into 4 pieces. Wrap in waxed paper and chill for 4 hours.

**2** Preheat the oven to 350 degrees. Lightly grease 2 baking sheets.

**3** Work with one piece of dough at a time, keeping the remainder in the refrigerator. On a floured surface, roll out the dough to a thickness of ¼ inch. With a sharp knife, cut into strips 4 inches long and ¾ inches wide. Shape each strip into an S-shape and place 1 inch apart on the prepared baking sheets. Brush the tops of the cookies with the beaten egg white.

**4** Bake for 8 to 10 minutes, until lightly colored. Transfer to wire racks to cool.

**Baking notes:** These cookies are often sprinkled with white or colored sugar crystals before baking. An alternate method of shaping the cookies is to use a cookie press or a pastry bag fitted with a ribbon tip and to press or pipe out S-shapes onto the baking sheets.

**CRUST**
1¾ cups all-purpose flour
¼ cup granulated sugar
1 cup almonds, ground fine
2 teaspoons baking powder
¼ teaspoon salt
½ cup vegetable shortening

**TOPPING**
½ cup vegetable shortening
½ cup granulated sugar
1 large egg
2 tablespoons honey
2 tablespoons milk
1 teaspoon vanilla extract
2 tablespoons almond extract

**1** Preheat the oven to 350 degrees.

**2** To make the crust, combine the flour, sugar, almonds, baking powder, and salt in a large bowl. Cut inthe vegetable shortening until the mixture resembles coarse crumbs. Press the mixture evenly into an ungreased 9-inch square baking pan.

**3** To make the topping, combine the vegetable shortening, sugar, egg, honey, and milk in a saucepan and bring to a boil. Remove from the heat and stir in the almond and vanilla extracts. Let cool slightly.

**4** Pour the topping over the crust. Bake for 55 to 60 minutes, until lightly colored on top and firm to the touch. Cool in the pan on a wire rack before cutting into large or small bars.

**Baking notes:** Older versions of this recipe call for buttermilk or sour milk in place of the whole milk. Others use hazelnuts instead of almonds and schnapps instead of the almond extract. These are traditionally cut into squares or triangles.

# GERMAN HONEY COOKIES

Bar Cookies

YIELD: *5 to 7 dozen*
TOTAL TIME: *75 minutes*

---

3¾ cups all-purpose flour
1 teaspoon baking powder
1 teaspoon ground cinnamon
½ teaspoon ground cloves
½ teaspoon ground cardamom
¼ teaspoon ground ginger
3 tablespoons butter, at room
   temperature
1 cup powdered sugar
1½ cups dark molasses, warmed
½ cup walnuts, chopped fine
½ cup candied citrus peel, chopped
**Rum Buttercream (see Pantry)**

**1** Preheat the oven to 350 degrees. Lightly grease a 13 by 9-inch baking pan.

**2** Combine the flour, baking powder, and spices.

**3** In a large bowl, cream the butter and powdered sugar. Beat in the molasses. Gradually blend in the dry ingredients. Fold in the walnuts and candied peel. Spread the dough evenly in the prepared baking pan.

**4** Bake for 20 to 25 minutes, until lightly colored. Cool in the pan on a wire rack.

**5** Frost the cooled cookies with the buttercream and cut into large or small bars.

# GERMAN MOLASSES COOKIES I

Bar Cookies

YIELD: *2 to 3 dozen*
TOTAL TIME: *40 minutes*

# German Molasses Cookies II

Rolled Cookies

YIELD: *3 to 4 dozen*
TOTAL TIME: *35 minutes*
CHILLING TIME: *2 days*

4 cups all-purpose flour
1 teaspoon baking soda
2 teaspoons ground ginger
1 teaspoon ground cinnamon
½ teaspoon ground cloves
1 cup vegetable shortening
¾ cup packed light brown sugar
1¼ cups molasses

**1** Combine the flour, baking soda, and spices.

**2** In a medium saucepan, melt the vegetable shortening with the brown sugar and molasses, stirring to dissolve the sugars. Remove from the heat and gradually blend in the dry ingredients.

**3** Transfer the dough to a floured surface and knead until smooth. Wrap in waxed paper and chill for at least 2 days.

**4** Preheat the oven to 350 degrees.

**5** On a floured surface, roll out the dough to a thickness of ⅛ inch. Using a 3-inch round cookie cutter, cut out cookies and place 1 inch apart on ungreased baking sheets.

**6** Bake for 7 to 10 minutes, until lightly colored. Transfer to wire racks to cool.

# German Puff Pastry Cookies

Rolled Cookies

YIELD: *1 to 3 dozen*
TOTAL TIME: *40 minutes*
CHILLING TIME: *2 hours*

1 cup mashed potatoes, chilled
1 teaspoon vanilla extract
2 cups all-purpose flour, chilled
¼ cup powdered sugar, chilled
1 cup vegetable shortening

**1** Put the mashed potatoes in a medium bowl. Add the vanilla extract and blend well.

**2** Combine the flour and sugar in a large bowl. Cut in the vegetable shortening. Stir in the mashed potatoes. Cover and chill for at least 2 hours.

**3** Preheat the oven to 400 degrees. Lightly grease 2 baking sheets.

**4** On a floured surface, roll out the dough to a thickness of ¼ inch. Using a 1¾-inch round cookie cutter, cut into rounds. Using a ¾-inch cutter, cut out the centers of two-thirds of the rounds. Place the plain rounds 1½ inches apart on the prepared baking sheets and brush the edges with water. Place a cut-out round on top of each one, brush with water, and top with the remaining cut-out rounds.

**5** Bake for 15 to 18 minutes. Transfer to wire racks to cool.

**Baking notes:** Fill these patty shells with fresh fruit or fruit compote and top with whipped cream. Or make two-layer patty shells, and fill with a lemon custard.

4 cups all-purpose flour
2 cups walnuts, ground
2 teaspoons baking powder
¼ teaspoon paprika
¼ teaspoon freshly ground black pepper
¼ teaspoon ground ginger
¼ teaspoon ground cloves
¼ teaspoon ground coriander
¼ teaspoon anise seeds
1½ cups vegetable shortening
1 cup granulated sugar
1 large egg

**1** Combine the flour, walnuts, baking powder, and spices.

**2** In a large bowl, cream the vegetable shortening with the sugar until light and fluffy. Beat in the egg. Gradually blend in the dry ingredients. Cover and chill for 8 hours.

**3** Preheat the oven to 350 degrees.

**4** On a floured surface, roll out the dough to a thickness of ¼ inch. Using a 2-inch round cookie cutter, cut into rounds and place 1½ inches apart on ungreased baking sheets.

**5** Bake for 15 to 18 minutes, until lightly colored. Transfer to wire racks to cool.

**Baking notes:** If desired, drizzle melted chocolate over the cooled cookies.

# GERMAN SPICE COOKIES

Rolled Cookies

YIELD: *2 to 4 dozen*
TOTAL TIME: *35 minutes*
CHILLING TIME: *8 hours*

---

4 large egg whites
1 cup powdered sugar
2 cup hazelnuts, ground
1 teaspoon grated lemon zest
2 teaspoons ground cinnamon
Powdered sugar for rolling
About 3 tablespoons strawberry preserves

**1** Preheat the oven to 375 degrees. Line 2 baking sheets with parchment paper.

**2** In a large bowl, beat the egg whites until foamy and they hold soft peaks, add powdered sugar, and beat until stiff and glossy. Measure out ⅓ cup of beaten whites and set aside. Gradually fold the hazelnuts into the remaining whites. Fold in the lemon zest and cinnamon.

**3** Line a work surface with parchment paper and liberally sprinkle it with powdered sugar. Roll out the dough to a thickness of ¼ inch. Sprinkle the dough with powdered sugar. Using a 2-inch star cookie cutter, cut out

cookies. Sprinkle each star with powdered sugar and place 1½ inches apart on the prepared baking sheets. Place ¼ teaspoon of strawberry preserves in the center of each star. Using the spoon, spread the juice from the preserves out to the tips of each star. Place a tiny dab of the reserved egg mixture on top of the preserves. Set aside at room temperature for 1 to 2 hours.

**4** Bake for 8 to 10 minutes, until firm to the touch. Cool on the baking sheets on wire racks.

# GERMAN-SWISS HOLIDAY COOKIES

Rolled Cookies

YIELD: *2 to 4 dozen*
TOTAL TIME: *40 minutes*
RESTING TIME: *1 to 2 hours*

# GINGER BARS

Bar Cookies

YIELD: *1 to 4 dozen*
TOTAL TIME: *35 minutes*

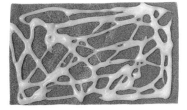

1½ cups all-purpose flour
½ teaspoon ground cinnamon
½ teaspoon ground ginger
½ teaspoon ground nutmeg
½ teaspoon salt
½ teaspoon baking soda
½ cup hot water
½ cup butter, at room temperature
½ cup packed light brown sugar
2 large eggs
½ cup molasses
Vanilla Icing (see Pantry)

1  Preheat the oven to 350 degrees. Lightly grease a 13 by 9-inch baking pan.

2  Combine the flour, spices, and salt.

3  In a small bowl, dissolve the baking soda in the hot water. Stir in the molasses.

4  In a large bowl, cream the butter and brown sugar. Beat in the eggs. Beat in the molasses mix-ture. Gradually blend in the dry ingredients. Spread the dough evenly in the prepared baking pan.

5  Bake for 18 to 20 minutes, or until a toothpick inserted in the center comes out clean.

6  Frost the warm cookies with icing. Let cool before cutting into large or smalls.

# GINGERBREAD COOKIES I

Rolled Cookies

YIELD: *8 to 10 dozen*
TOTAL TIME: *35 minutes*
CHILLING TIME: *24 hours*

6½ cups all-purpose flour
1 teaspoon ground ginger
1 teaspoon ground cinnamon
¼ teaspoon ground cloves
2 teaspoons salt
1 cup vegetable shortening
1 cup packed light brown sugar
2 teaspoons baking soda
½ teaspoon warm water
1½ cups molasses

1  Combine the flour, spices, and salt.

2  In a large bowl, cream the vegetable shortening and brown sugar.

3  Dissolve the baking soda in the warm water and add to the creamed mixture, beating until smooth. Beat in the molasses. Gradually blend in the dry ingredients. Cover and chill for 24 hours.

4  Preheat the oven to 350 degrees. Lightly grease 2 baking sheets.

5  On a floured surface, roll out the dough to a thickness of ¼ inch. Using a 1¾-inch round cookie cutter, cut out cookies and place 1½ inches apart on the pre-pared baking sheets.

6  Bake for 10 to 12 minutes, until dry-looking and firm to the touch. Transfer to wire racks to cool.

**Baking notes:**  This dough can be used for making gingerbread houses or gingerbread men (see Pantry); it can also be pressed into large cookie molds and baked.

4 cups all-purpose flour
½ teaspoon ground ginger
½ teaspoon salt
½ cup vegetable shortening
½ cup packed light brown sugar
½ cup molasses, warmed
¼ teaspoon baking soda
1½ teaspoons warm water

**1** Combine the flour, ginger, and salt.

**2** In a large bowl, cream the vegetable shortening and brown sugar. Beat in the molasses.

**3** Dissolve the baking soda in the warm water and add to the molasses mixture, beating until smooth. Gradually blend in the dry ingredients. Cover and chill for at least 4 hours.

**4** Preheat the oven to 350 degrees. Lightly grease 2 baking sheets.

**5** On a floured surface, roll out the dough to a thickness of ½ inch. Using a 2 inch-round cookie cutter, cut into rounds and place 1 inch apart on the prepared baking sheets.

**6** Bake for 10 to 12 minutes, until dry-looking and firm to the touch. Transfer to wire racks to cool.

**Baking notes:** This dough can also be used to make large gingerbread men.

# GINGERBREAD COOKIES II

Rolled Cookies

YIELD: *3 to 5 dozen*
TOTAL TIME: *35 minutes*
CHILLING TIME: *4 hours*

---

6 cups all-purpose flour
1 tablespoon ground cinnamon
1 tablespoon ground ginger
1 tablespoon ground cinnamon
⅔ cup vegetable shortening
1¾ cups packed light brown sugar
2 eggs
1 cup sour cream
1 teaspoon vanilla extract

**1** Combine the flour and spices.

**2** In a large bowl, cream the vegetable shortening and brown sugar. Beat in the eggs. Beat in the sour cream. Beat in the vanilla extract. Gradually blend in the dry ingredients. Cover and chill for at least 4 hours.

**3** Preheat the oven to 350 degrees. Lightly grease 2 baking sheets.

**4** On a floured surface, roll out the dough to a thickness of ½ inch. Using cookie cutters, cut into shapes and place 1 inch apart on the prepared baking sheets.

**5** Bake for 10 to 12 minutes, until dry-looking and firm to the touch. Transfer to wire racks to cool.

**Baking notes:** This dough is sturdy enough to be used for gingerbread houses.

# GINGERBREAD COOKIES III

Rolled Cookies

YIELD: *3 to 4 dozen*
TOTAL TIME: *35 minutes*
CHILLING TIME: *4 hours*

# GINGERBREAD MEN

Rolled Cookies

YIELD: *3 to 5 dozen*
TOTAL TIME: *35 minutes*
CHILLING TIME: *24 hours*

3½ cups all-purpose flour
1½ teaspoons ground ginger
1½ teaspoons ground cinnamon
¼ teaspoon salt
½ cup vegetable shortening
½ cup granulated sugar
1 large egg
1 cup molasses, warmed
1 teaspoon baking soda
1½ teaspoons warm water
Raisins for decorations

1 Combine the flour, spices, and salt.

2 In a large bowl, cream the vegetable shortening and sugar. Beat in the egg. Beat in the molasses.

3 Dissolve the baking soda in the warm water and add the molasses to the mixture, beating until smooth. Gradually blend in the dry ingredients. Cover and chill for 24 hours.

4 Preheat the oven to 350 degrees. Lightly grease 2 baking sheets.

5 On a floured surface, roll out the dough to a thickness of ¼ inch. Using cookie cutters, cut out gingerbread men and place 1½ inches apart on the prepared baking sheets. Use raisins to make eyes, noses, and 2 to 3 buttons on the belly.

6 Bake for 10 to 12 minutes, until dry-looking and firm to the touch. Transfer to wire racks to cool.

**Baking notes:** You can make these cookies a little thicker if you like, and decorate the cooled cookies using Royal Icing (see Pantry).

# GINGER BUTTER TREATS

Rolled Cookies

YIELD: *2 to 4 dozen*
TOTAL TIME: *35 minutes*

4 cups all-purpose flour
1 tablespoon ground ginger
1 teaspoon ground cinnamon
½ teaspoon salt
1 cup butter, at room temperature
1¼ cups packed light brown sugar
2 large eggs
½ teaspoon grated lemon zest

1 Preheat the oven to 350 degrees. Lightly grease 2 baking sheets.

2 Combine the flour, ginger, cinnamon, and salt.

3 In a large bowl, cream the butter and brown sugar. Beat in the eggs. Beat in the lemon zest. Gradually blend in the dry ingredients.

4 On a flour surface, roll out the dough to a thickness of ¼ inch. Using a 2-inch round cookie cutter, cut out cookies and place 1 inch apart on the prepared baking sheets.

5 Bake for 12 to 15 minutes, until lightly colored. Transfer to wire racks to cool.

1½ cups all-purpose flour
½ teaspoon baking soda
¾ teaspoon ground ginger
¼ teaspoon salt
1 cup vegetable shortening
½ cup granulated sugar
2 large eggs
½ tablespoon molasses

**1** Preheat the oven to 350 degrees. Lightly grease 2 baking sheets.

**2** Combine the flour, baking soda, ginger, and salt.

**3** In a large bowl, cream the vegetable shortening and sugar. Beat in the eggs. Beat in the molasses. Gradually blend in the dry ingredients.

**4** Wrap the dough in waxed paper and chill for 8 hours or overnight.

**5** On a flour surface, roll out the dough to a thickness of ¼ inch. Using a 1½-inch cookie cutter, cut out cookies and place 1 inch apart on the prepared baking sheets.

**6** Bake for 12 to 15 minutes, until firm to the touch. Transfer to wire racks to cool.

**Baking notes:** The flavor of the ground ginger will be stronger if the dough is refrigerated for at least 1 hour before baking.

# GINGER COOKIES I

Rolled Cookies

YIELD: *3 to 4 dozen*
TOTAL TIME: *30 minutes*
CHILLING TIME: *8 hours*

---

4 cups all-purpose flour
⅓ cup hazelnuts, ground
1 tablespoon ground ginger
1 teaspoon ground cinnamon
1 teaspoon ground cardamom
½ teaspoon ground mace
1½ cups vegetable shortening
2 cups molasses
1 cup powdered sugar
2 large eggs
½ cup candied citron, chopped
½ cup candied orange peel, chopped

**1** Combine the flour, hazelnuts, and spices.

**2** In a medium saucepan, melt the vegetable shortening with the molasses. Remove from the heat and beat in the powdered sugar. Transfer to a large bowl and let cool slightly.

**3** One at a time, beat the eggs into the molasses mixture. Beat in the candied citron and orange peel. Gradually blend in all of the dry ingredients. Cover and chill overnight.

**4** Preheat the oven to 350 degrees. Lightly grease 2 baking sheets.

**5** On a floured surface, roll out the dough to a thickness of ¼ inch. Using a 1½-inch cookie cutter, cut out the cookies and place 1 inch apart on the prepared baking sheets.

**6** Bake for 12 to 15 minutes, until lightly colored. Transfer to wire racks to cool.

# GINGER COOKIES II

Rolled Cookies

YIELD: *5 to 6 dozen*
TOTAL TIME: *35 minutes*
CHILLING TIME: *24 hours*

# GINGER COOKIES III

Rolled Cookies

YIELD: *3 to 6 dozen*
TOTAL TIME: *35 minutes*
CHILLING TIME: *4 hours*

3 cups all-purpose flour
1½ teaspoons ground ginger
¼ teaspoon ground cloves
¼ teaspoon salt
¼ cup vegetable shortening
¼ cup molasses
½ cup granulated sugar

**1** Combine the flour, ginger, cloves, and salt.

**2** In a large saucepan, melt the vegetable shortening with the molasses. Remove from the heat and beat in the sugar. Gradually blend in the dry ingredients. Transfer the dough to a large bowl, cover, and chill for 4 hours.

**3** Preheat the oven to 350 degrees. Lightly grease 2 baking sheets.

**4** On a floured surface, roll out the dough to a thickness of ¼ inch. Using a 1½-inch cookie cutter, cut into rounds and place 1 inch apart on the prepared baking sheets.

**5** Bake for 12 to 15 minutes, until lightly colored. Transfer to wire racks to cool.

**Baking notes:** This dough can be rolled out without chilling, but the ginger flavor is stronger when the dough is chilled.

---

# GINGER COOKIES IV

Rolled Cookies

YIELD: *3 to 6 dozen*
TOTAL TIME: *35 minutes*
CHILLING TIME: *4 hours*

2½ cups all-purpose flour
¾ teaspoon baking soda
1½ teaspoons ground ginger
½ teaspoon ground cinnamon
½ cup vegetable shortening
1 cup molasses
½ cup sour cream
⅓ cup granulated sugar
1 large egg

**1** Combine the flour, baking soda, ginger, and cinnamon.

**2** In a large saucepan, melt the vegetable shortening with the molasses. Beat in the sour cream. Remove from the heat and beat in the sugar. Beat in the egg. Gradually blend in the dry ingredients. Transfer the dough to a

bowl, cover, and chill for at least 4 hours.

**3** Preheat the oven to 350 degrees. Lightly grease 2 baking sheets.

**4** On a floured surface, roll out the dough to a thickness of ¼ inch. Using a 1½-inch cookie cutter, cut out cookies and place 1 inch apart on the prepared baking sheets.

**5** Bake for 10 to 12 minutes, until lightly colored. Transfer to wire racks to cool.

---

# GINGER COOKIES V

Rolled Cookies

YIELD: *3 to 4 dozen*
TOTAL TIME: *35 minutes*
CHILLING TIME: *24 hours*

⅔ cup vegetable shortening
⅓ cup packed light brown sugar
2 tablespoons dark corn syrup
2 teaspoons ground cinnamon
2 teaspoons ground cloves
2 teaspoons ground ginger
2 teaspoons baking soda
¼ cup warm water
2½ cups all-purpose flour

**1** Melt the vegetable shortening in a large saucepan. Remove from the heat and beat in the sugar, corn syrup, and spices.

**2** Dissolve the baking soda in the warm water and add to corn syrup mixture, beating until

smooth. Gradually blend in the flour. Transfer the dough to a bowl, cover, and chill for at least 24 hours.

**3** Preheat the oven to 325 degrees. Lightly grease 2 baking sheets.

**4** On a floured surface, roll out the dough as thin as possible. Using a 2½-inch cookie cutter, cut out cookies and place 1 inch apart on baking sheets.

**5** Bake for 8 to 10 minutes, until lightly colored. Transfer to wire racks to cool.

3½ cups all-purpose flour
2 teaspoons baking soda
1 teaspoon ground ginger
1 teaspoon ground cinnamon
½ teaspoon salt
1 cup vegetable shortening
1 cup molasses
½ cup granulated sugar
2 large egg yolks
½ cup milk
1 cup raisins

**1** Preheat the oven to 350 degrees. Grease a 15 by 10-inch baking pan.

**2** Combine the flour, baking soda, spices, and salt.

**3** In a large saucepan, melt the vegetable shortening with the molasses. Remove from the heat and beat in the sugar. Beat in the egg yolks. Beat in the milk. Gradually blend in the dry ingredients. Stir in the raisins. Spread the batter evenly in the prepared baking pan.

**4** Bake for 12 to 15 minutes, until lightly colored. Cool in the pan on a wire rack before cutting into large or small squares.

# GINGER CREAMS

Bar Cookies

YIELD: *8 to 9 dozen*
TOTAL TIME: *25 minutes*

---

2 cups all-purpose flour
2 teaspoons baking soda
1 teaspoon ground cinnamon
1 teaspoon ground ginger
¼ teaspoon salt
1 cup granulated sugar
⅔ cup canola oil
1 large egg
¼ cup molasses, warmed
Granulated sugar for rolling

**1** Preheat the oven to 350 degrees.

**2** Combine the flour, baking soda, spices, and salt.

**3** In a large bowl, beat the sugar and oil together. Beat in the egg. Beat in the molasses. Gradually blend in the dry ingredients.

**4** Pinch off walnut-sized pieces of dough and roll into balls. Roll in granulated sugar until well coated and place the balls 3 inches apart on ungreased baking sheets.

**5** Bake for 12 to 15 minutes, until lightly colored. Transfer to wire racks to cool.

**Baking notes:** The dough can also be dropped by spoonfuls into a bowl of sugar and then rolled into balls.

# GINGER CRINKLES

Formed Cookies

YIELD: *4 to 5 dozen*
TOTAL TIME: *40 minutes*

---

1 tablespoon baking soda
5 tablespoons warm water
1½ cups molasses
4 cups all-purpose flour
1½ teaspoons ground ginger
1 teaspoon ground cinnamon
1 teaspoon salt
¾ cup vegetable shortening

**1** In a small bowl, dissolve the baking soda in the warm water. Stir in the molasses.

**2** In a large bowl, combine the flour, spices, and salt. Cut in the vegetable shortening. Beat in the molasses mixture. Divide the dough into quarters. Wrap in waxed paper and chill for 24 hours.

**3** Preheat the oven to 350 degrees. Lightly grease 2 baking sheets.

**4** Roll out one-quarter of the dough at a time, keeping the remaining dough chilled. On a floured surface, roll out the dough to a thickness of ¼ inch. Using a 1¼-inch round cookie cutter, cut out the cookies and place the cookie 1 inch apart on the prepared baking sheets.

**5** Bake for 10 to 12 minutes, until lightly colored. Transfer to wire racks to cool.

**Baking notes:** These cookies can be frosted if desired.

# GINGERS

Rolled Cookies

YIELD: *4 to 5 dozen*
TOTAL TIME: *30 minutes*
CHILLING TIME: *24 hours*

# GINGER SHORTBREAD

Bar Cookies

YIELD: *3 dozen*
TOTAL TIME: *45 minutes*
CHILLING TIME: *4 hours*

1½ cups all-purpose flour
1 teaspoon ground ginger
¼ teaspoon salt
½ cup vegetable shortening
½ cup granulated sugar
1 tablespoon heavy cream

**1** Combine the flour, ginger, and salt.

**2** In a large bowl, cream the vegetable shortening and sugar. Beat in the cream. Gradually blend in the dry ingredients. Cover and chill for 4 hours.

**3** Preheat the oven to 350 degrees. Lightly grease a 9-inch square baking pan.

**4** On a floured surface, roll out the dough to a 9-inch square. Fit it into the prepared baking pan and prick it all over with the tines of a fork.

**5** Bake for 20 to 25 minutes, until lightly colored. Cool in the pan on a wire rack, then cut into 2 by 1-inch bars.

---

# GINGERSNAPS I

Rolled Cookies

YIELD: *2 to 3 dozen*
TOTAL TIME: *30 minutes*
CHILLING TIME: *4 hours*

3 cups all-purpose flour
1 teaspoon baking powder
1 teaspoon ground ginger
1 teaspoon ground cinnamon
½ teaspoon salt
½ cup granulated sugar
¾ cup vegetable shortening
½ cup heavy cream
¼ cup light corn syrup

**1** Combine the flour, baking powder, spices, and salt.

**2** In a large bowl, cream the sugar and vegetable shortening. Beat in the cream and corn syrup. Gradually blend in the dry ingredients. Cover and chill for 4 hours.

**3** Preheat the oven to 350 degrees. Lightly grease 2 baking sheets.

**4** On a floured surface, roll out the dough to a thickness of ¼ inch. Using a 3-inch round cookie cutter, cut into rounds and place 1 inch apart on the prepared baking sheets.

**5** Bake for 10 to 12 minutes, until lightly colored. Transfer to wire racks to cool.

**Baking notes:** If you like spicy gingersnaps, you can add up to 1 tablespoon ground ginger to the dough.

---

# GINGERSNAPS II

Rolled Cookies

YIELD: *3 to 4 dozen*
TOTAL TIME: *35 minutes*
CHILLING TIME: *4 hours*

3 cups all-purpose flour
½ teaspoon ground ginger
½ teaspoon ground cloves
½ teaspoon salt
½ cup vegetable shortening
½ cup granulated sugar
½ cup molasses, warmed
½ teaspoon baking soda
¼ cup warm water

**1** Combine the flour, spices, and salt.

**2** In a large bowl, cream the vegetable shortening and sugar. Beat in the molasses.

**3** Dissolve the baking soda in the warm water, and add to the molasses mixture, beating until smooth. Gradually blend in the dry ingredients. Cover and chill for 4 hours.

**4** Preheat the oven to 350 degrees. Lightly grease 2 baking sheets.

**5** On a floured surface, roll out the dough to a thickness of ¼ inch. Using a 1½-inch round cookie cutter, cut out cookies and place 1 inch apart on the prepared baking sheets.

**6** Bake for 10 to 12 minutes, until firm to the touch. Transfer to wire racks to cool.

3 cups all-purpose flour
1 tablespoon ground ginger
1 teaspoon salt
¾ cup vegetable shortening
½ cup granulated sugar
1 cup molasses, warmed

**1** Combine the flour, ginger, and salt.

**2** In a large bowl, cream the vegetable shortening and sugar. Beat in the molasses. Gradually blend in the dry ingredients. Cover and chill for 4 hours.

**3** Preheat the oven to 350 degrees. Lightly grease 2 baking sheets.

**4** On a floured surface, roll out the dough to a thickness of ¼ inch. Using a 1¾-inch round cookie cutter, cut into rounds and place 1 inch apart on the prepared baking sheets.

**5** Bake for 10 to 12 minutes, until lightly colored and firm to the touch. Transfer to wire racks to cool.

# GINGERSNAPS III

Rolled Cookies

YIELD: *3 to 4 dozen*
TOTAL TIME: *35 minutes*
CHILLING TIME: *4 hours*

---

2¼ cups all-purpose flour
1 teaspoon ground ginger
1 teaspoon ground cinnamon
1 teaspoon ground cloves
1 teaspoon salt
¾ cup vegetable shortening
1 cup packed light brown sugar
1 large egg
¼ cup molasses
Granulated sugar for rolling

**1** Preheat the oven to 375 degrees. Lightly grease 2 baking sheets.

**2** Combine the flour, spices, and salt.

**3** In a large bowl, cream the vegetable shortening and brown sugar. Beat in the egg. Beat in the molasses. Gradually blend in the dry ingredients.

**4** Pinch off walnut-sized pieces of dough and roll into balls. Roll in granulated sugar, and place 2 inches apart on the prepared baking sheets.

**5** Bake for 10 to 12 minutes, until lightly colored. Transfer to wire racks to cool.

# GINGERSNAPS IV

Formed Cookies

YIELD: *3 to 4 dozen*
TOTAL TIME: *35 minutes*

---

1 cup all-purpose flour
3 cups rolled oats
2 teaspoons baking powder
½ teaspoon salt
1 cup butter, melted
¼ cup boiling water
1 cup packed dark brown sugar
1 teaspoon vanilla extract

**1** Combine the flour, oats, baking powder, and salt.

**2** In a large bowl, whisk the melted butter and boiling water. Beat in the brown sugar. Beat in the vanilla extract. Gradually blend in the dry ingredients. Form the dough into a log 2 inches in diameter. Wrap in waxed paper and chill for at least 4 hours.

**3** Preheat the oven to 350 degrees. Lightly grease 2 baking sheets.

**4** Cut the log into ¼-inch-thick slices and place 1 inch apart on the prepared baking sheets.

**5** Bake for 10 to 12 minutes, until lightly colored. Transfer to wire racks to cool.

**Baking notes:** The longer you bake these cookies, the crisper they will be.

# GLENDA'S FAVORITE COOKIES

Refrigerator Cookies

YIELD: *7 to 8 dozen*
TOTAL TIME: *30 minutes*
CHILLING TIME: *4 hours*

# GOLDEN HONEY COOKIES

Drop Cookies

YIELD: *5 to 6 dozen*
TOTAL TIME: *30 minutes*

3 cups whole wheat flour
1 cup all-purpose flour
2 teaspoons baking soda
½ teaspoon salt
1 cup honey, warmed
½ cup vegetable shortening
3 large eggs
1 cup walnuts, chopped fine
1 cup golden raisins, plumped in
  brandy

**1** Preheat the oven to 400 degrees. Lightly grease 2 baking sheets.

**2** Combine the two flours, the baking soda, and salt.

**3** In a large bowl, beat the honey and vegetable shortening until smooth. Beat in the eggs one at a time. Gradually blend in the dry ingredients. Fold in the walnuts and raisins.

**4** Drop the dough by spoonfuls 1½ inches apart onto the prepared baking sheets. Flatten each cookie using the bottom of a glass dipped in flour.

**5** Bake for 8 to 10 minutes, until lightly colored. Transfer to wire racks to cool.

# GOOD-FOR-YOU PEANUT BUTTER COOKIES

Formed Cookies

YIELD: *3 to 4 dozen*
TOTAL TIME: *30 minutes*

1 cup whipped vegetable shortening
1 cup packed light brown sugar
½ cup peanut butter
3 large egg whites
2 cups all-purpose flour

**1** Preheat the oven to 375 degrees. Lightly grease 2 baking sheets.

**2** In a large bowl, cream the vegetable shortening and brown sugar. Beat in the peanut butter. Beat in the egg whites. Gradually blend in the flour.

**3** Pinch off 1-inch pieces of dough and roll into balls. Place the balls 1½ inches apart on the prepared baking sheets. Using the tines of a fork, flatten the balls to ¼ inch thick.

**4** Bake for 8 to 10 minutes, until lightly colored. Transfer to wire racks to cool.

# GRAHAM CRACKER BROWNIES I

Bar Cookies

YIELD: *1 to 2 dozen*
TOTAL TIME: *35 minutes*

1½ cups graham cracker crumbs
¾ cup semisweet chocolate chips
½ cup almonds, chopped
½ cup shredded coconut
One 14-ounce can sweetened condensed milk

**1** Preheat the oven to 350 degrees. Lightly grease a 9-inch square baking pan.

**2** In a large bowl, combine all of the ingredients and blend well. Spread the mixture evenly in the prepared baking pan.

**3** Bake for 20 to 25 minutes, until firm to the touch. Cool in the pan on a wire rack before cutting into large or small bars.

¾ cup vegetable shortening
¼ cup peanut butter
1 cup granulated sugar
2 large eggs
2½ cups graham crackers crumbs
2 cups miniature marshmallows
1 teaspoon vanilla extract

**TOPPING**
1 cup (6 ounces) semisweet chocolate chips
¼ cup peanuts, ground fine

**1** Lightly grease a 9-inch square
baking pan.

**2** In the top of a double boiler,
melt the vegetable shortening
with the peanut butter. Beat in
the sugar. Remove from the heat
and beat in the eggs one at a
time. Return to the heat and
cook, stirring, until the mixture
thickens. Remove from the heat
and stir in the graham crackers,
marshmallows, and vanilla
extract.

**3** Spread the mixture evenly into
the prepared baking pan. Chill
for 2 hours.

**4** To make the topping, melt the
chocolate chips in a double boiler
over low heat, stirring until
smooth. Remove from the heat
and stir in the ground peanuts.

**5** Spread the topping evenly
over the chilled brownies. Chill
for 1 hour before cutting into
large or small bars.

# GRAHAM CRACKER BROWNIES II

Bar Cookies

YIELD: *1 to 2 dozen*
TOTAL TIME: *25 minutes*
CHILLING TIME: *2 hours*

---

1½ cups granulated sugar
1½ cups vegetable shortening
3 tablespoons corn syrup
½ teaspoon vanilla extract
3 cups prunes, pitted and chopped
3½ cup graham cracker crumbs
Powdered sugar for sprinkling

**1** Lightly grease a 13 by 9-inch
baking pan.

**2** In a large saucepan, combine
the sugar, vegetable shortening,
corn syrup, and vanilla extract
and cook until the sugar dissolves. Remove from the heat
and stir in the chopped prunes.
Gradually blend in the graham
cracker crumbs.

**3** Spread the mixture evenly in
the prepared baking pan. Chill
for 2 hours.

**4** Sprinkle with powdered sugar
and cut into large or small bars.

**Baking notes:** These bars can be
made with dates or raisins
instead of prunes.

# GRAHAM CRACKER PRUNE BARS

Bar Cookies

YIELD: *1 to 2 dozen*
TOTAL TIME: *30 minutes*
CHILLING TIME: *2 hours*

# GRAHAM CRACKERS

Rolled Cookies

YIELD: *varies according to individual scoring size*

TOTAL TIME: *35 minutes*

3 cups whole wheat flour
½ teaspoon baking soda
½ teaspoon salt
½ cup canola oil
½ cup packed light brown sugar
1 large egg
¼ cup honey
¼ cup evaporated milk
1 teaspoon fresh lemon juice
1 teaspoon vanilla extract

**1** Preheat the oven to 375 degrees. Lightly grease 2 baking sheets.

**2** Combine the flour, baking soda, and salt.

**3** In a large bowl, beat the oil and brown sugar. Beat in the egg, honey, and milk. Beat in the lemon juice. Beat in the vanilla extract. Gradually blend in the dry ingredients.

**4** Divide the dough in half. Place one piece on each baking sheet and roll out to a thickness of ⅛ inch. Using a pastry cutter, lightly score the dough into 2-inch squares.

**5** Bake for 8 to 10 minutes, until lightly browned. Cool on the baking sheets on wire racks, then cut into squares along the scored lines.

**Baking notes:** If you don't like the taste of honey, you can substitute molasses.

# GRANDMA'S REFRIGERATOR COOKIES

Refrigerator Cookies

YIELD: *4 to 5 dozen*

TOTAL TIME: *35 minutes*

CHILLING TIME: *4 hours*

1 ounce semisweet chocolate, chopped
2 cups all-purpose flour
½ teaspoon baking soda
¼ teaspoon salt
1 cup butter, at room temperature
½ cup granulated sugar
½ cup packed light brown sugar
1 large egg
½ teaspoon vanilla extract
¼ cup raisins, chopped
¼ cup pecans, chopped
¼ cup shredded coconut
½ teaspoon ground nutmeg
½ teaspoon ground cinnamon

**1** Melt the chocolate in a double boiler over low heat, stirring until smooth. Remove from the heat.

**2** Combine the flour, baking soda, and salt.

**3** In a large bowl, cream the butter and two sugars. Beat in the egg. Beat in the vanilla extract. Gradually blend in the dry ingredients.

**4** Divide the dough into 6 equal parts. Add the melted chocolate to one piece and blend well. Shape the dough into a log and wrap in waxed paper. Add the chopped raisins to the second piece, the chopped pecans to the third, the shredded coconut to the fourth, the nutmeg to the fifth, and the ground cinnamon to the sixth piece, blending well. Shape each separate dough into a log and wrap in waxed paper. Chill for 4 hours.

**5** Preheat the oven to 375 degrees.

**6** Cut the logs into ⅛-inch-thick slices and place 1 inch apart on ungreased baking sheets.

**7** Bake for 10 to 12 minutes, until lightly colored. Transfer to wire racks to cool.

**Baking notes:** When adding the various flavoring ingredients, be sure to blend thoroughly.

## GRANNY'S COOKIES

Rolled Cookies
YIELD: *7 to 8 dozen*
TOTAL TIME: *40 minutes*

4 cups all-purpose flour
1 tablespoon baking powder
¼ teaspoon ground nutmeg
¾ cup vegetable shortening
2 cups granulated sugar
2 large eggs
¼ cup milk
1 teaspoon vanilla extract

**1** Preheat the oven to 400 degrees. Lightly grease 2 baking sheets.

**2** Combine the flour, baking powder, and nutmeg.

**3** In a large bowl, cream the vegetable shortening and sugar. Beat in the eggs one at a time. Beat in the milk and vanilla extract.

Gradually blend in the dry ingredients.

**4** On a floured surface, roll out the dough to a thickness of ¼ inch. Using cookie cutters, cut into shapes and place 1½ inches apart into the prepared baking sheets.

**5** Bake for 10 to 12 minutes, until lightly colored. Transfer to wire racks to cool.

**Baking notes:** To decorate these cookies, sprinkle with colored sugar crystals or place a raisin or walnut half in the center of each one before baking.

## GRANOLA BARS I

Bar Cookies
YIELD: *3 to 4 dozen*
TOTAL TIME: *50 minutes*

6 cups rolled oats
1 cup shredded coconut
1 cup wheat germ
1 cup golden raisins
½ cup sunflower seeds
¼ cup sesame seeds, toasted
1 teaspoon ground allspice
1 cup honey
¾ cup canola oil
⅓ cup water
1½ teaspoons vanilla extract

**1** Preheat the oven to 350 degrees. Lightly grease a 13 by 9-inch baking pan.

**2** Combine the oats, coconut, wheat germ, raisins, sunflower seeds, sesame seeds, and allspice in a large bowl.

**3** In a saucepan, combine the honey, oil, and water and heat. Remove from the heat and stir in the vanilla extract. Add to the dry ingredients and stir to coat well. Spread the mixture evenly in the prepared baking pan.

**4** Bake for 30 to 40 minutes, until firm to the touch and no longer sticky. Transfer to wire racks to cool before cutting into large or small bars.

**5** To store, wrap the bars individually in waxed paper.

## GRANOLA BARS II

Bar Cookies
YIELD: *1 to 3 dozen*
TOTAL TIME: *40 minutes*

¾ cup all-purpose flour
¾ cup whole wheat flour
½ cup walnuts, ground
2 teaspoons baking powder
¾ teaspoon salt
½ cup vegetable shortening
1¾ cups packed light brown sugar
2 large eggs
1 teaspoon vanilla extract
1½ cups granola

**1** Preheat the oven to 350 degrees. Lightly grease a 9-inch square baking pan.

**2** Combine the two flours, the walnuts, baking powder, and salt.

**3** In a large bowl, cream the vegetable shortening and brown

sugar. Beat in the eggs one at a time. Beat in the vanilla extract. Gradually blend in the dry ingredients. Fold in the granola. Spread the mixture evenly in the prepared baking pan.

**4** Bake for 20 to 25 minutes, until firm to the touch. Cool in the pan on a wire rack before cutting into large or small bars.

**5** Wrap each bar in waxed paper and store in an airtight container.

**Baking notes:** Dried fruit can be added to this dough. Soak the fruit in boiling water for 10 minutes, drain well, and chop fine. Add with the dry ingredients.

# GRANOLA COOKIES I

Drop Cookies

YIELD: *3 to 5 dozen*
TOTAL TIME: *30 minutes.*

2 cups all-purpose flour
½ teaspoon baking powder
1 teaspoon ground cinnamon
½ teaspoon ground nutmeg
2 cups granola
2 tablespoons canola oil
2 large eggs
1 cup unsweetened applesauce
2 tablespoons frozen apple juice
   concentrate, thawed

**1** Preheat the oven to 350 degrees. Lightly grease 2 baking sheets.

**2** Combine the flour, baking powder, and spices.

**3** In a large bowl, beat the canola oil and eggs together. Beat in the applesauce and apple juice.

Gradually blend in the dry ingredients. Stir in the granola.

**4** Drop the mixture by spoonfuls 1½ inches apart onto the prepared baking sheets.

**5** Bake for 8 to 10 minutes, until lightly colored and firm to the touch. Transfer to wire racks to cool.

# GRANOLA COOKIES II

Drop Cookies

YIELD: *2 to 4 dozen*
TOTAL TIME: *30 minutes*

1 cup whole wheat flour
½ cup rice flour
½ cup soy flour
½ teaspoon salt
1 cup honey
1 cup canola oil
2 large eggs
1 teaspoon almond extract
2½ cups granola
1 cup almonds, chopped fine

**1** Preheat the oven to 300 degrees. Lightly grease 2 baking sheets.

**2** Combine the three flours and the salt.

**3** In a large saucepan, heat the honey and oil just until warm. Remove from the heat and beat

in the eggs one at a time. Beat in the almond extract. Gradually blend in the dry ingredients. Stir in the granola and almonds.

**4** Drop the dough by spoonfuls 1½ inches apart onto the prepared baking sheets.

**5** Bake for 18 to 20 minutes, until lightly colored. Transfer to wire racks to cool.

**Baking notes:** For a cookie with real crunch, bake these until they are golden brown.

# GRANOLA COOKIES III

Drop Cookies

YIELD: *3 to 4 dozen*
TOTAL TIME: *40 minutes*

1½ cups all-purpose flour
¼ cup wheat germ
½ teaspoon baking powder
½ teaspoon baking soda
¼ teaspoon salt
½ cup vegetable shortening
1 cup granulated sugar
½ cup packed light brown sugar
1 large egg
¼ cup milk
1 teaspoon almond extract
1½ cups (9 ounces) semisweet
   chocolate chips
1 cup rolled oats
1 cup almonds, chopped
¾ cup golden raisins

**1** Preheat the oven to 350 degrees. Lightly grease 2 baking sheets.

**2** Combine the flour, wheat germ, baking powder, baking soda, and salt.

**3** In a large bowl, cream the vegetable shortening and two sugars. Beat in the egg. Beat in the milk and almond extract. Gradually blend in the dry ingredients. Fold in the chocolate chips, oats, almonds, and raisins.

**4** Drop the dough by spoonfuls 1½ inches apart onto the prepared baking sheets.

**5** Bake for 8 to 10 minutes, or until lightly colored. Transfer to wire racks to cool.

**CRUST**
1½ cups all-purpose flour
½ teaspoon baking soda
½ teaspoon salt
¾ cup vegetable shortening
1 cup granulated sugar

**TOPPING**
1½ cups dried apricots, chopped fine
½ cup dates, pitted and chopped
½ cup grape jelly
¼ cup fresh orange juice
½ cup walnuts, grounds
1½ cups rolled oats

**1** Preheat the oven to 350 degrees. Lightly grease a 13 by 9-inch baking pan.

**2** To make the crust, combine the flour, baking soda, and salt.

**3** In a large bowl, cream the vegetable shortening and sugar. Gradually blend in the dry ingredients. Spread the mixture evenly in the prepared baking pan.

**4** Bake for 20 minutes.

**5** Meanwhile, make the topping: In a saucepan, combine the apricots, dates, grape jelly, orange juice, and walnuts and cook until soft. Remove from the heat.

**6** Spread the topping over the hot crust. Sprinkle the oats evenly over the top and press down lightly.

**7** Bake for 10 minutes longer, or until lightly colored. Transfer to wire racks to cool before cutting into large or small bars.

# GRAPE BARS

Bar Cookies

YIELD: *1 to 3 dozen*
TOTAL TIME: *45 minutes*

---

2 cups all-purpose flour
1 teaspoon baking soda
1 teaspoon ground cinnamon
½ teaspoon salt
¾ cup vegetable shortening
1½ cups packed light brown sugar
2 large eggs
3 tablespoons fresh grapefruit juice
3 tablespoons grated grapefruit zest

**1** Preheat the oven to 350 degrees. Lightly grease a 9-inch square baking pan.

**2** Combine the flour, baking soda, cinnamon, and salt.

**3** In a large bowl, cream the vegetable shortening and brown sugar. Beat in the eggs. Beat in the grapefruit juice and zest. Gradually blend in the dry ingredients. Spread the batter evenly into the prepared baking pan.

**4** Bake for 25 to 30 minutes, until lightly colored on top. Cool in the pan on a wire rack before cutting into large or small bars.

**Baking notes:** You can substitute lemon or orange juice and zest for the grapefruit ingredients. An orange or lemon icing would go very well with these bars.

# GRAPEFRUIT BARS

Bar Cookies

YIELD: *1 to 3 dozen*
TOTAL TIME: *35 minutes*

---

5 cups all-purpose flour
1 tablespoon baking powder
2 cups vegetable shortening
2 cups powdered sugar
5 large eggs
3 tablespoons anisette liqueur

**1** Preheat the oven to 350 degrees. Lightly grease 2 baking sheets.

**2** Combine the flour and baking powder.

**3** In a large bowl, cream the vegetable shortening and powdered sugar. Beat in the eggs one at a time. Beat in the anisette. Gradually blend in the dry ingredients. Transfer the dough to a floured surface and knead until smooth.

**4** Pinch off small pieces of dough and form into shapes such as circles, pretzels, "S", bows, etc. Place 1½ inches apart on the prepared baking sheets.

**5** Bake for 12 to 15 minutes, until lightly colored. Transfer to wire racks to cool.

# GREEK ANISETTE COOKIES

Formed Cookies

YIELD: *3 to 4 dozen*
TOTAL TIME: *45 minutes*

# GREEK BUTTERBALLS

Formed Cookies

YIELD: *3 to 4 dozen*
TOTAL TIME: *40 minutes*

3 cups all-purpose flour
¼ teaspoon baking soda
¾ cup walnuts, ground
1 cup butter (see Baking notes)
1 tablespoon granulated sugar
1½ teaspoons brandy
1 teaspoon almond extract
1 teaspoon vegetable oil
½ teaspoon fresh lemon juice
1 large egg yolk
Powdered sugar for rolling

**1** Preheat the oven to 350 degrees. Lightly grease 2 baking sheets.

**2** Combine the flour, baking soda, and nuts.

**3** Melt the butter in a medium saucepan. Transfer to a large bowl and let cool. Beat the sugar into the melted butter. Beat in the brandy, almond extract, vegetable oil and lemon juice. Beat in the egg yolk. Gradually blend in the dry ingredients.

**4** Pinch off small pieces of dough and roll into balls. Place 1 inch apart on the prepared baking sheets.

**5** Bake for 12 to 15 minutes, until firm to the touch. Roll in powdered sugar and place on wire racks to cool, then roll in powdered sugar a second time.

**Baking notes:** These cookies must be made with unsalted butter.

# GREEK CLOUD COOKIES

Formed Cookies

YIELD: *5 dozen*
TOTAL TIME: *30 minutes*
CHILLING TIME: *4 hours*

2 cups (1 pound) butter, at room temperature
¾ cup powdered sugar
1 large egg yolk
2 tablespoons brandy
4½ cups all-purpose flour
About 60 whole cloves
Powdered sugar for rolling

**1** In a large bowl, cream the butter and powdered sugar. Beat in the egg yolk. Beat in the brandy. Gradually blend in the flour. Cover and chill for 4 hours.

**2** Preheat the oven to 350 degrees. Lightly grease 2 baking sheets.

**3** Pinch off 1½-inch pieces of dough and roll into balls. Place 1 inch apart on the prepared baking sheets and press a clove into the top of each ball.

**4** Bake for 12 to 15 minutes, until lightly colored. Remove the cloves, roll the balls in powdered sugar, and transfer to wire racks to cool.

**Baking notes:** The cloves add a subtle spicy flavor to the cookies.

2⅓ cups all-purpose flour
1 teaspoon baking powder
¼ teaspoon salt
½ cup vegetable shortening
½ cup granulated sugar
2 large egg yolks
3 tablespoons heavy cream
1 large egg yolk beaten with 1 tablespoon heavy cream
3 tablespoons sesame seeds

**1** Preheat the oven to 350 degrees.

**2** Combine the flour, baking powder, and salt.

**3** In a large bowl, cream the vegetable shortening and sugar. Beat in the egg yolks. Beat in the cream. Gradually blend in the dry ingredients.

**4** Pinch off walnut-sized pieces of the dough and form into 7-inch ropes. Fold each rope in half and twist to form a braid, leaving an open loop at the top. Place the twists 1 inch apart on ungreased baking sheets.

**5** Brush the twists with the beaten egg yolk and sprinkle with the sesame seeds.

**6** Bake for 12 to 14 minutes, until golden brown. Transfer to wire racks to cool.

# Greek Sesame Cookies

Formed Cookies

YIELD: *3 dozen*
TOTAL TIME: *45 minutes*

3½ cups all-purpose flour
½ teaspoon baking powder
½ teaspoon baking soda
1 cup vegetable shortening
¾ cup granulated sugar
2 large egg yolks
¼ teaspoon brandy
⅛ teaspoon rose water
½ cup almonds, ground

**1** Combine the flour, baking powder, and baking soda.

**2** In a large bowl, cream the vegetable shortening and sugar. Beat in the egg yolks. Beat in the brandy and rose water. Gradually blend in the dry ingredients. Cover and chill for 4 hours.

**3** Preheat the oven to 325 degrees.

**4** On a floured surface, roll out the dough to a thickness of ¼ inch. Using a 1½-inch round cookie cutter, cut out cookies. Dredge in the ground almonds and place 1 inch apart on ungreased baking sheets.

**5** Bake for 25 to 30 minutes, until lightly colored. Transfer to wire racks to cool.

# Greek Shortbread

Rolled Cookies

YIELD: *3 to 4 dozen*
TOTAL TIME: *45 minutes*
CHILLING TIME: *4 hours*

6 tablespoons vegetable shortening
32 marshmallows
½ teaspoon vanilla extract
½ teaspoon almond extract
½ teaspoon green food coloring
4 cups cornflakes, crushed
Red cinnamon candy

**1** Line 2 baking sheets with waxed paper.

**2** In the top of a double boiler, melt the vegetable shortening with the marshmallows. Add the vanilla and almond extracts. Stir in the food coloring. Remove from the heat and stir in the corn-flakes. Replace over bottom half of double boiler to keep warm.

**3** Drop the mix by tablespoonful 2 inches apart onto the prepared baking sheets. With well-oiled hands, form the batter into wreath shapes. Decorate with cinnamon candy and chill until set.

**Baking notes:** These are great cookies to let kids play with. You mix them and let the children form them. To give a more festive taste, use a few drops of peppermint in place of the vanilla and almond extracts.

# Green Wreaths

Formed Cookies

YIELD: *2 to 3 dozen*
TOTAL TIME: *30 minutes*

# GUMDROP BARS

Bar Cookies

YIELD: *2 to 3 dozen*
TOTAL TIME: *35 minutes*

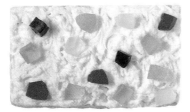

**2 cups all-purpose flour**
**1 teaspoon ground cinnamon**
**¼ teaspoon salt**
**3 large eggs**
**2 cups packed light brown sugar**
**¼ cup evaporated milk**
**1 cup walnuts, chopped fine**
**1 cup gumdrops, chopped**

**1** Preheat the oven to 325 degrees. Lightly grease a 9-inch square baking pan.

**2** Combine the flour, cinnamon, and salt.

**3** In a large bowl, beat the eggs until thick and light-colored. Beat in the brown sugar. Beat in the milk. Gradually blend in the dry ingredients. Stir in the walnuts and gumdrops. Spread the dough evenly in the prepared baking pan.

**4** Bake for 30 to 35 minutes, until lightly colored on top. Transfer to wire racks to cool.

**Baking notes:** For a whimsical look, frost the bars with Vanilla Icing and decorate with sliced gumdrops.

# GUMDROP COOKIES I

Formed Cookies

YIELD: *5 to 6 dozen*
TOTAL TIME: *45 minutes*

**1 cup all-purpose flour**
**¼ teaspoon salt**
**½ cup vegetable shortening**
**¼ cup packed light brown sugar**
**1 large egg yolk**
**1½ teaspoon vanilla extract**
**2 cups gumdrops, chopped**
**Gumdrops for decorating**

**1** Preheat the oven to 350 degrees.

**2** Combine the flour and salt.

**3** In a large bowl, cream the vegetable shortening and brown sugar. Beat in the egg yolk. Beat in the vanilla extract. Gradually blend in the dry ingredients. Fold in the gumdrops.

**4** Pinch off walnut-sized pieces of dough and roll into balls. Place 1½ inches apart on ungreased baking sheets.

**5** Bake for 5 minutes. Press a whole gumdrop into the center of each ball and bake for 8 to 10 minutes longer, until lightly colored. Transfer to wire racks to cool.

2 cups all-purpose flour
1 teaspoon baking soda
1 teaspoon salt
1 cup vegetable shortening
1 cup granulated sugar
1 cup packed light brown sugar
2 large eggs
1 teaspoon vanilla extract
2 cups rolled oats
1 cup shredded coconut
1 cup miniature gumdrops (see Baking notes)
Powdered sugar for rolling

**1** Preheat the oven to 350 degrees. Lightly grease 2 baking sheets.

**2** Combine the flour, baking soda, and salt.

**3** In a large bowl, cream the vegetable shortening and two sugars. Beat in the eggs one at a time. Beat in the vanilla extract. Gradually blend in the dry ingredients. Fold in the oats, coconut, and gumdrops.

**4** Pinch off walnut-sized pieces of dough and roll into balls. Place 1½ inches apart on the prepared baking sheets.

**5** Bake for 10 to 12 minutes, until lightly colored. Transfer to wire racks to cool.

**6** Roll the cooled cookies in powdered sugar.

**Baking notes:** If you can't find miniature gumdrops, chop enough regular gumdrops to make 1 cup.

# GUMDROP COOKIES II

Formed Cookies

YIELD: *2 to 3 dozen*
TOTAL TIME: *30 minutes*

¾ cup all-purpose flour
½ teaspoon baking powder
¼ teaspoon baking soda
¼ teaspoon salt
½ cup vegetable shortening
½ cup packed light brown sugar
½ cup granulated sugar
1 large egg
½ teaspoon lemon extract
¾ cup rolled oats
½ cup flaked coconut
½ cup small gumdrops, cut into quarters

**1** Preheat the oven to 375 degrees.

**2** Combine the flour, baking powder, baking soda, and salt.

**3** In a large bowl, cream the vegetable shortening and two sugars. Beat in the egg. Beat in the lemon extract. Gradually blend

in the dry ingredients. Fold in the oats, coconut, and gumdrops.

**4** Drop the dough by spoonfuls 1½ inches apart onto ungreased baking sheets.

**5** Bake for 10 to 12 minutes, until lightly colored. Transfer to wire racks to cool.

# GUMDROP COOKIES III

Drop Cookies

YIELD: *3 to 4 dozen*
TOTAL TIME: *35 minutes*

# HALLOWEEN COOKIES

Drop Cookies

YIELD: *3 to 4 dozen*
TOTAL TIME: *50 minutes*

1 cup all-purpose flour
¼ teaspoon baking soda
¼ teaspoon salt
½ cup vegetable shortening
1 tablespoon granulated sugar
1 large egg
⅓ cup molasses, warmed
¼ cup buttermilk
¼ cup powdered sugar
A few drops of milk
Food coloring
Popsicle sticks

1 Preheat the oven to 375 degrees. Lightly grease 2 baking sheets.

2 Combine the flour, baking soda, and salt.

3 In a large bowl, cream the vegetable shortening and sugar. Beat in the egg. Beat in the molasses and buttermilk. Gradually blend in the dry ingredients.

4 Drop the dough by spoonfuls 1½ inches apart onto the prepared baking sheets. Insert a popsicle stick into each cookie.

5 Bake for 12 to 15 minutes, until lightly colored. Transfer to wire racks to cool.

6 To decorate the cookies, put the powdered sugar in a small bowl and stir in enough milk to make a spreadable icing. Tint the icing with orange food coloring and spread the icing over the cookies. Or tint the icing another color, place it into a pastry bag fitted with a small plain tip, and pipe eyes, a nose, and a mouth on each cookie.

# HAMAN'S POCKETS (HAMANTASHEN)

Rolled Cookies

YIELD: *2 to 3 dozen*
TOTAL TIME: *30 minutes*

2 cups all-purpose flour
1 teaspoon baking powder
Pinch of salt
⅓ cup granulated sugar
2 large eggs
1 teaspoon vanilla extract
One 10-ounce jar apricot butter (see Baking notes)
1 large egg white, beaten
Granulated sugar for sprinkling

1 Preheat the oven to 350 degrees. Lightly grease 2 baking sheets.

2 Combine the flour, baking powder, and salt.

3 In a large bowl, beat the sugar and eggs until thick and light-colored. Beat in the vanilla extract. Gradually blend in the dry ingredients.

4 On a floured surface, roll out the dough to a large square the thickness of ¼ inch. Using a sharp knife, cut into 2-inch squares. Place the squares 1 inch apart on the prepared baking sheets. Place a dab of apricot butter in the center of each square and fold the corners into the center like an envelope. Brush with the beaten egg white and sprinkle granulated sugar over the top.

5 Bake for 12 to 15 minutes, until lightly colored. Transfer to wire racks to cool.

**Baking notes:** If you can't find apricot butter, you can make your own by combining pureed dried apricots and softened unsalted butter (in a proportion of 3 parts apricot to 2 parts butter).

¾ cup all-purpose flour
½ cup hazelnuts, ground
⅛ teaspoon baking powder
⅛ teaspoon ground cinnamon
⅛ teaspoon ground nutmeg
⅛ teaspoon ground cloves
¼ teaspoon salt
6 tablespoons vegetable shortening
½ cup powdered sugar
1 teaspoon grated lemon zest

**1** Preheat the oven to 375 degrees.

**2** Combine the flour, hazelnuts, baking powder, spices, and salt.

**3** In a large bowl, cream the vegetable shortening and powdered sugar. Beat in the lemon zest. Gradually blend in the dry ingre-dients. Press the dough evenly into an ungreased 9-inch square baking pan.

**4** Bake for 18 to 20 minutes, until the top is golden and firm to the touch. Cool in the pan on a wire rack before cutting into large or small bars.

# HAZELNUT BARS I

Bar Cookies

YIELD: *1 to 2 dozen*
TOTAL TIME: *30 minutes*

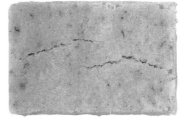

**CRUST**
1⅓ cups all-purpose flour
½ cup baking powder
⅓ cup vegetable shortening
½ cup packed light brown sugar
¼ cup hazelnuts, chopped

**TOPPING**
2 large eggs
¼ cup packed light brown sugar
½ teaspoon salt
¾ cup light corn syrup
1½ teaspoons rum
3 tablespoons all-purpose flour
¾ cup hazelnuts, ground fine

**1** Preheat the oven to 350 degrees. Grease a 13 by 9-inch baking pan.

**2** To make the crust, combine the flour and baking powder.

**3** In a large bowl, cream the vegetable shortening and brown sugar. Gradually blend in the dry ingredients. Stir in the hazelnuts. Press the mixture evenly into the prepared baking pan.

**4** Bake for 10 minutes.

**5** Meanwhile, make the topping: In a medium bowl, beat the eggs until thick and light-colored. Beat in the brown sugar. Beat in the corn syrup and rum. Gradually blend in the flour and salt.

**6** Spread the topping over the warm crust and sprinkle the hazelnuts on the top. Bake for 25 to 30 minutes longer, or until firm to the touch. Cool in the pan on a wire rack before cutting into large or small bars.

# HAZELNUT BARS II

Bar Cookies

YIELD: *1 to 2 dozen*
TOTAL TIME: *45 minutes*

# HAZELNUT COOKIES I

Refrigerator Cookies

YIELD: *4 to 5 dozen*
TOTAL TIME: *30 minutes*
CHILLING TIME: *2 hours*

¾ cup all-purpose flour
½ teaspoon baking soda
½ teaspoon ground cinnamon
½ cup vegetable shortening
½ cup granulated sugar
⅓ cup hazelnuts, chopped

TOPPING
½ cup all-purpose flour
1 tablespoon granulated sugar
4 tablespoons butter

1  Combine the flour, baking soda, and cinnamon.

2  In a large bowl, cream the vegetable shortening and sugar. Gradually blend in the dry ingredients. Fold in the hazelnuts. Form the dough into a log 1¼ inches in diameter. Wrap in waxed paper and chill for 2 hours.

3  Preheat the oven to 350 degrees.

4  To make the topping, put the flour and sugar in a small bowl and cut in the butter. Put the mixture in a pastry bag fitted with a star tip.

5  Cut the log into ¼-inch-thick slices and place 1 inch apart on ungreased baking sheets. Pipe a strip of the topping over each slice.

6  Bake for 12 to 15 minutes, until lightly colored. Transfer to wire racks to cool.

# HAZELNUT COOKIES II

Refrigerator Cookies

YIELD: *4 to 5 dozen*
TOTAL TIME: *30 minutes*
CHILLING TIME: *48 hours*

2½ cups all-purpose flour
½ teaspoon baking soda
¼ teaspoon salt
½ cup vegetable shortening
½ cup butter, at room temperature
1¼ cup packed light brown sugar
1 each large egg
¼ teaspoon vanilla extract
½ cup hazelnuts, chopped fine
3 ounces semisweet chocolate, melted

1  Combine 1½ cups of the flour, the baking soda, and salt.

2  In a large bowl, beat the vegetable shortening, butter, and the remaining 1 cup of flour until smooth. Beat in the brown sugar. Beat in the egg. Beat in the vanilla extract. Gradually blend in the dry ingredients. Fold in ¼ cup of the hazelnuts.

3  Divide the dough into 2 logs 1 inch in diameter and roll in the remaining ¼ cup hazelnuts. Wrap in waxed paper and chill in the refrigerator for 48 hours.

4  Preheat the oven to 350 degrees.

5  Slice the logs into ¼-inch-thick slices and place 1 inch apart on ungreased baking sheets.

6  Bake for 8 to 10 minutes, until lightly colored. Transfer to wire racks to cool.

7  Dip half of each cookie into the melted chocolate and let cool until set.

# HAZELNUT CRESCENTS I

Formed Cookies

YIELD: *2 to 3 dozen*
TOTAL TIME: *40 minutes*

¾ cup butter, at room temperature
½ cup granulated sugar
½ teaspoon almond extract
½ teaspoon vanilla extract
2 cups all-purpose flour
½ cup hazelnuts, chopped fine
Powdered sugar for rolling

**1** Preheat the oven to 300 degrees.

**2** In a large bowl, cream the butter and sugar. Beat in the almond and vanilla extracts. Gradually blend in the flour. Fold in the hazelnuts. The dough will be stiff.

**3** Pinch off walnut-sized pieces of dough and form each one into a crescent shape. Place 1½ inches apart on ungreased baking sheets.

**4** Bake for 15 to 20 minutes, until lightly colored. Roll in powdered sugar and transfer to wire racks to cool.

# HAZELNUT CRESCENTS II

Formed Cookies

YIELD: *2 to 3 dozen*
TOTAL TIME: *30 minutes*

1¼ cups all-purpose flour
½ teaspoon baking powder
¼ teaspoon salt
½ cup vegetable shortening
½ cup powdered sugar
⅓ cup hazelnuts, chopped

**1** Preheat the oven to 350 degrees.

**2** Combine the flour, baking powder, and salt.

**3** In a large bowl, cream the vegetable shortening and powdered sugar. Gradually blend in the dry ingredients. Fold in the hazelnuts.

**4** Pinch off walnut-sized pieces of the dough and form into crescent shapes. Place 1 inch apart on ungreased baking sheets.

**5** Bake for 10 to 12 minutes, until lightly colored. Transfer to wire racks to cool.

# HAZELNUT FRUIT WREATHS

Formed Cookies

YIELD: *1 to 2 dozen*
TOTAL TIME: *35 minutes*

1 cup vegetable shortening
¾ cup packed light brown sugar
3 large egg yolks
1 teaspoon vanilla extract
2½ cups all-purpose flour
¾ cup hazelnuts, chopped
½ cup candied citron, chopped fine
1 large egg white
1 tablespoon light corn syrup
Glacè cherries, halved, for decoration

**1** Preheat the oven to 325 degrees. Lightly grease 2 baking sheets.

**2** In a large bowl, cream the vegetable shortening and brown sugar. Beat in the egg yolks. Beat in the vanilla extract. Gradually blend in the flour. Fold in the hazelnuts and candied citron.

**3** Pinch off walnut-sized pieces of dough and roll each one into a rope ¾ inch in diameter and 6 inches long. Form each one into a ring, pinching the ends together to seal, and place 1 inch apart on the prepared baking sheets. Combine the egg white and corn syrup and use to brush the cookies. Place a glacé cherry half on each ring where the ends join.

**4** Bake for 18 to 20 minutes, until lightly colored. Transfer to wire racks to cool.

**Baking notes:** To color the wreaths, add a few drops of green food coloring to the dough. You can also frost the cookies with colored icing.

# Hazelnut Fruit Rings

Formed Cookies

YIELD: *1 to 2 dozen*
TOTAL TIME: *35 minutes*

1 cup vegetable shortening
¾ cup packed light brown sugar
3 large egg yolks
1 teaspoon rum
2½ cups all-purpose flour
¾ cup hazelnuts, chopped
½ cup mixed candied fruit, chopped fine
1 large egg white
1 tablespoon light corn syrup
Glacè cherries, halved, for decoration

1  Preheat the oven to 325 degrees. Lightly grease 2 baking sheets.

2  In a large bowl, cream the vegetable shortening and brown sugar. Beat in the egg yolks. Beat in the rum. Gradually blend in the flour. Fold in the hazelnuts and candied fruit.

3  In a small cup, beat the egg white and corn syrup together.

4  Pinch off pieces of dough and roll into pencil-thin ropes about 6 inches long. Form the ropes into circles, pinch the ends together to seal, and place 1 inch apart on the prepared baking sheets. Place a half-cherry on each rope at the point where the ends meet. Brush the cookies with the corn syrup mixture.

5  Bake for 18 to 20 minutes, until lightly colored. Transfer to wire racks to cool.

**Baking notes:**  Sprinkle the cookies with colored sugar crystals before baking if desired.

# Hazelnut Macaroons

Rolled Cookies

YIELD: *2 to 3 dozen*
TOTAL TIME: *40 minutes*

1¼ cups powdered sugar
⅛ teaspoon baking soda
½ cup hazelnuts, chopped
¼ cup almonds, ground fine
2 large egg whites

1  Preheat the oven to 300 degrees. Line 2 baking trays with parchment paper.

2  Combine the powdered sugar, baking soda, hazelnuts, and almonds.

3  In a medium bowl, beat the egg whites until foamy. Gradually beat in the dry ingredients, and beat for 5 minutes longer.

4  Turn the dough out onto a floured surface and dust it with flour. Roll out to a thickness of ½ inch. Using a cookie cutter, cut into shapes and place 1 inch apart on the prepared baking sheets.

5  Bake for 28 to 30 minutes, until firm to the touch. Cool on the baking sheets on wire racks.

**Baking notes:**  This is an adaptation of a very old German recipe; in the original it called for beating the egg white for 15 minutes by hand, of course.

1 cup all-purpose flour
½ teaspoon baking powder
½ teaspoon allspice
¼ teaspoon salt
1 cup vegetable shortening
1 cup packed light brown sugar
1 large egg
1 teaspoon vanilla extract
1 tablespoon grated orange zest
3 cups rolled oats
¾ cup hazelnuts, chopped fine
½ cup currants

**1** Preheat the oven to 350 degrees. Lightly grease 2 baking sheets.

**2** Combine the flour, baking powder, allspice, and salt.

**3** In a large bowl, cream the vegetable shortening and brown sugar. Beat in the egg and vanilla extract. Beat in the orange zest.

Gradually blend in the dry ingredients. Fold in the oats, hazelnuts, and currants.

**4** Pinch off walnut-sized pieces of dough and roll into balls. Place 2 inches apart on the prepared baking sheets.

**5** Bake for 18 to 20 minutes, until lightly colored. Transfer to wire racks to cool.

# HAZELNUT OATMEAL COOKIES

Formed Cookies

YIELD: *3 to 4 dozen*
TOTAL TIME: *35 minutes*

---

4½ cups all-purpose flour
1 cup hazelnuts, ground
2 cups vegetable shortening
2½ cups packed light brown sugar
2 teaspoons sherry

**1** Preheat the oven to 350 degrees.

**2** Combine the flour and hazelnuts.

**3** In a large bowl, cream the vegetable shortening and brown sugar. Beat in the sherry. Gradually blend in the dry ingredients.

**4** Pinch off walnut-sized pieces of dough and roll into small balls. Place 2 inches apart on ungreased bakings sheets. Flatten the balls with the bottom of a glass dipped in flour.

**5** Bake for 12 to 15 minutes, until lightly colored. Transfer to wire racks to cool.

# HAZELNUT SHORTBREAD I

Formed Cookies

YIELD: *4 to 5 dozen*
TOTAL TIME: *30 minutes*

# Hazelnut Shortbread II

Formed Cookies

YIELD: *4 to 5 dozen*
TOTAL TIME: *30 minutes*

4½ cups all-purpose flour
1 cup hazelnuts, ground
2 cups vegetable shortening
2½ cups packed light brown sugar
2 teaspoons vanilla extract

**1** Preheat the oven to 350 degrees.

**2** Combine the flour and hazelnuts.

**3** In a large bowl, cream the vegetable shortening and brown sugar. Beat in the vanilla extract. Gradually blend in the dry ingredients.

**4** Pinch off walnut-size pieces of dough and roll into balls. Place 2 inches apart on the ungreased baking sheets. Flatten the balls with the bottom of a glass dipped in flour.

**5** Bake for 12 to 15 minutes, until lightly colored. Transfer to wire racks to cool.

# Hazelnut Shortbread Cookies

Rolled Cookies

YIELD: *2 to 4 dozen*
TOTAL TIME: *35 minutes*
CHILLING TIME: *8 hours*

2 cups all-purpose flour
1 cup hazelnuts, ground fine
1 cup butter, at room temperature
¾ cup packed light brown sugar

**1** Combine the flour and hazelnuts.

**2** In a large bowl, cream the butter and brown sugar. Gradually blend in the dry ingredients. Cover and chill for 8 hours or overnight.

**3** Preheat the oven to 300 degrees. Lightly grease 2 baking sheets.

**4** On a floured surface, roll out the dough to a thickness of ¼ inch. Using a 1-inch round cookie cutter, cut into rounds and place 1½ inches apart on the prepared baking sheets.

**5** Bake for 20 to 25 minutes, until lightly colored. Transfer to wire racks to cool.

CRUST
1 cup all-purpose flour
¼ teaspoon salt
¼ cup vegetable shortening

TOPPING
2 tablespoons all-purpose flour
¼ teaspoon salt
2 large eggs
¾ cup granulated sugar
1 teaspoon rum
2 cups flaked coconut
1 cup hazelnuts, chopped

**1** Preheat the oven to 350 degrees. Lightly grease a 9-inch square baking pan.

**2** To make the crust, combine the flour and salt in a medium bowl.

Cut in the vegetable shortening until the mixture resembles coarse crumbs. Press evenly into the prepared baking pan.

**3** Bake for 15 minutes.

**4** Meanwhile, make the topping: Combine the flour and salt.

**5** In a medium bowl, beat the eggs and sugar until thick. Beat in the rum. Gradually blend in the dry ingredients. Stir in the coconut and hazelnuts.

**6** Spread the topping over the top of the hot crust. Bake for 15 minutes longer, or until firm to the touch. Cool in the pan on a wire rack before cutting into large or small bars.

# HAZELNUT SQUARES

Bar Cookies

YIELD: *1 to 2 dozen*
TOTAL TIME: *50 minutes*

---

½ cup vegetable shortening
½ cup granulated sugar
1 large egg
2 hard-boiled large egg yolks, chopped
1⅓ cups all-purpose flour
½ cup hazelnuts, toasted and chopped
½ teaspoon ground allspice
1 teaspoon salt

**1** In a large bowl, cream the vegetable shortening and sugar. Beat in the egg and egg yolks. Gradually blend in the flour. Shape the dough into a disk, wrap in waxed paper, and chill for 2 hours.

**2** Combine the hazelnuts, allspice, and salt in a small bowl.

**3** On a floured surface, roll out the dough to a 17 by 6-inch rectangle. Sprinkle the nut mix evenly over the top and press lightly into the dough. Starting at a long end, roll up the dough jelly-roll fashion. Wrap in waxed paper and chill for 1 hour.

**4** Preheat the oven to 350 degrees. Lightly grease 2 baking sheets.

**5** Cut the roll into ¾-inch-thick slices and place 1 inch apart on the prepared baking sheets.

**6** Bake for 12 to 15 minutes, until lightly colored. Transfer to wire racks to cool.

# HAZELNUT STICKS

Rolled Cookies

YIELD: *1½ dozen*
TOTAL TIME: *40 minutes*
CHILLING TIME: *3 hours*

---

½ cup all-purpose flour
¼ cup whole wheat flour
½ cup wheat germ
1 teaspoon baking powder
½ cup vegetable shortening
2 ounces carob squares
1¼ cups honey
2 large eggs
1 teaspoon vanilla extract
½ cup pecans, chopped

**1** Preheat the oven to 350 degrees. Lightly grease a 13 by 9-inch baking pan.

**2** Combine the two flours, the wheat germ, and baking powder.

**3** In a large saucepan, melt the vegetable shortening and carob

with the honey, stirring until smooth. Remove from the heat and beat in the eggs one at a time. Beat in the vanilla extract. Gradually blend in the dry ingredients. Stir in the pecans. Spread the dough evenly in the prepared baking pan.

**4** Bake for 25 to 30 minutes, until lightly colored on top and firm to the touch. Cool in the pan on a wire rack before cutting into large or small bars.

**5** Wrap the bars individually in waxed paper to store.

# HEALTH BARS I

Bar Cookies

YIELD: *2 to 3 dozen*
TOTAL TIME: *35 minutes*

# HEALTH BARS II

Bar Cookies

YIELD: *2 to 3 dozen*
TOTAL TIME: *30 minutes*
SOAKING TIME: *1 hour*
CHILLING TIME: *3 hours*

½ cup dried apple, sliced
½ cup banana chips
4 cups bran flakes
½ cup sesame seeds, toasted
½ cup walnuts, chopped
¼ cup wheat germ
1 teaspoon ground cinnamon
1 cup honey
1½ cups peanut butter
2 tablespoons vegetable shortening

**1** In a medium bowl, combine the apple slices and banana chips. Add boiling water to cover and set aside for 1 hour.

**2** Grease a 13 by 9-inch baking pan.

**3** In a large bowl, combine the bran cereal, sesame seeds, walnuts, wheat germ, and cinnamon.

**4** Drain the apples and bananas. Return to the medium bowl and mash together, then add to the bran mixture.

**5** In a large saucepan, heat the honey until it registers 230 degrees on a candy thermometer. Stir in the peanut butter and vegetable shortening and cook, stir-ring constantly until the temperature returns to 230 degrees.

**6** Add the honey mixture to the dry ingredients and stir to coat. Spread the mixture evenly in the prepared baking pan. Chill for at least 3 hours. Cut into large or small bars. Wrap individually in waxed paper and store in the refrigerator.

**Baking notes:** You can toast the bran cereal in a moderate oven before combining it with the other ingredients. Other dried fruits can be added to the mix, and different nuts can be used.

# HEALTH COOKIES I

Drop Cookies

YIELD: *3 to 4 dozen*
TOTAL TIME: *30 minutes*
STANDING TIME: *4 hours*

2 cups packed light brown sugar
1 cup canola, safflower, or soybean oil
4 cups rolled oats
1 cup shredded coconut
1 cup walnuts, chopped
1½ teaspoons milk
1 teaspoon vanilla extract

**1** In a large bowl, beat the brown sugar and oil together. Stir in the oats, cover, and let stand for 4 hours.

**2** Preheat the oven to 350 degrees. Lightly grease 2 baking sheets.

**3** Stir the coconut and walnuts into the oat mixture. Beat in the milk and vanilla extract.

**4** Drop the dough by spoonfuls 1½ inches apart onto the prepared baking sheets.

**5** Bake for 12 to 15 minutes, until lightly colored. Transfer to wire racks to cool.

1 cup all-purpose flour
1 cup soy flour
¼ teaspoon salt
1 cup canola oil
1 cup packed dark brown sugar
2 large eggs
¼ cup skim milk
3 cups rolled oats
1 cup dried apricots, chopped fine

**1** Preheat the oven to 350 degrees. Lightly grease 2 baking sheets.

**2** Combine the flour, soy flour, and salt.

**3** In a large bowl, beat the oil and brown sugar together. Beat in the eggs. Beat in the skim milk. Gradually blend in the dry ingredients. Stir in the oats and apricots.

**4** Drop the dough by spoonful 1½ inches apart onto the prepared baking sheets. Flatten each cookie with the bottom of a glass dipped in flour.

**5** Bake for 10 to 12 minutes, until lightly colored. Transfer to wire racks to cool.

# HEALTH COOKIES II

Drop Cookies

YIELD: *3 to 4 dozen*
TOTAL TIME: *30 minutes*

---

1 cup all-purpose flour
1 cup whole wheat flour
½ teaspoon salt
¼ cup packed dark brown sugar
½ cup canola oil
⅔ cup skim milk
2 cups rolled oats
2 cups dates, pitted and chopped fine
¾ cup almonds, chopped fine
½ cup sesame seeds, toasted
½ cup flaked coconut

**1** Preheat the oven to 350 degrees. Lightly grease 2 15 by 10-inch baking sheets.

**2** Combine the two flours and the salt.

**3** In a large bowl, beat the brown sugar, oil, and milk. Gradually blend in the dry ingredients. Stir in the oats, dates, almonds, sesame seeds, and coconut.

**4** Divide the dough in half. Place each half on a prepared baking sheet and roll out to a thickness of ⅛ inch, leaving a 1-inch border all around. Prick the dough all over with the tines of a fork. Using a pastry cutter, cut into 3 by 1-inch strips.

**5** Bake for 12 to 15 minutes, until lightly colored. Cool on the sheets on wire racks.

# HEALTH STICKS

Rolled Cookies

YIELD: *4 to 5 dozen*
TOTAL TIME: *35 minutes*

---

¾ cup all-purpose flour
¾ cup whole wheat flour
½ cup wheat germ
1 teaspoon baking soda
¼ teaspoon salt
1 cup vegetable shortening
¾ cup packed light brown sugar
¾ cup granulated sugar
2 large egg whites
2 teaspoons vanilla extract
1 cup (6 ounces) carob chips

**1** Preheat the oven to 350 degrees. Lightly grease 2 baking sheets.

**2** Combine the two flours, wheat germ, baking soda, and salt.

**3** In a large bowl, cream the vegetable shortening and two sugars. Beat in the egg whites. Beat in the vanilla extract. Gradually blend in the dry ingredients. Fold in the carob chips.

**4** Drop the dough by spoonfuls 1½ inches apart onto the prepared baking sheets.

**5** Bake for 10 to 12 minutes, until lightly colored. Transfer to wire racks to cool.

# HEALTHY CAROB CHIP COOKIES

Drop Cookies

YIELD: *3 to 5 dozen*
TOTAL TIME: *30 minutes*

# HEALTHY COOKIES

Drop Cookies

YIELD: *4 to 5 dozen*
TOTAL TIME: *30 minutes*

1 cup all-purpose flour
1 teaspoon baking soda
¼ teaspoon ground nutmeg
¼ teaspoon ground cinnamon
½ teaspoon salt
1 cup vegetable shortening
1 cup packed dark brown sugar
1 cup packed light brown sugar
2 large eggs
½ cup unsweetened applesauce
1 teaspoon vanilla extract
1 cup cornflakes

**1** Preheat the oven to 350 degrees. Lightly grease 2 baking sheets.

**2** Combine the flour, baking soda, spices, and salt.

**3** In a large bowl, cream the vegetable shortening two sugars. Beat in the eggs. Beat in the applesauce and vanilla extract.

Gradually blend in the dry ingredients. Stir in the cornflakes.

**4** Drop the dough by spoonfuls 1½ inches apart onto ungreased baking sheets.

**5** Bake for 12 to 15 minutes, until lightly colored. Transfer to wire racks to cool.

**Baking notes:** Half a cup of wheat germ can be added to the dough, as can nuts and raisins.

# HELEN'S CHEESECAKE BARS

Bar Cookies

YIELD: *1 to 3 dozen*
TOTAL TIME: *45 minutes*

CRUST
2 cups (12 ounces) white chocolate chips
6 tablespoons butter, at room temperature
2 cups graham cracker crumbs
2 cups almonds, chopped

FILLING
1 pound cream cheese, at room temperature
½ cup granulated sugar
4 large eggs
1 tablespoon fresh lemon juice
1 tablespoon Amaretto
¼ cup all-purpose flour

**1** Preheat the oven to 350 degrees. Lightly grease a 15 by 10-inch baking pan.

**2** To make the crust, melt the chocolate chips and butter in a double boiler, stirring until smooth. Remove from the heat and blend in the graham cracker crumbs and almonds. Reserve 1½ cups of the mixture for topping, and press the remaining mixture evenly into the prepared baking pan.

**3** Bake for 12 minutes.

**4** Meanwhile, make the filling: In a medium bowl, beat the cream cheese and sugar. Beat in the eggs, lemon juice, and Amaretto. Beat in the flour.

**5** Pour the filling over the hot crust. Sprinkle the reserved crust mixture over the top.

**6** Bake for 20 to 25 minutes longer, until lightly colored on top and firm to the touch. Cool in the pan on a wire rack before cutting into large or small bars.

**Baking notes:** Slivered or chopped almonds may be added to the topping mixture.

1 cup graham cracker crumbs

1 cup (6 ounces) semisweet chocolate chips

1 cup walnuts, chopped

1 cup shredded coconut

¼ cup butter, melted

One 14-ounce can sweetened condensed milk

**1** Preheat the oven to 350 degrees. Lightly grease a 9-inch square baking pan.

**2** Combine the graham crackers, chocolate chips, walnuts, and coconut in a medium bowl.

**3** Pour the melted butter over the dry ingredients and stir. Press the mixture evenly into the pre-pared baking pan. Drizzle the condensed milk over the top.

**4** Bake for 25 to 30 minutes, until lightly colored on top. Cool in the pan on a wire rack before cutting into large or small bars.

**Baking notes:** Other cookies, such as chocolate or vanilla wafers, can be substituted for graham cracker.

# HELLO DOLLY COOKIES

Bar Cookies

Yield: *1 to 2 dozen*

Total time: *35 minutes*

---

5⅓ cups all-purpose flour

1 tablespoon plus 1 teaspoon baking powder

1 teaspoon baking soda

1 tablespoon ground cinnamon

1 teaspoon ground cloves

1 teaspoon ground nutmeg

1 teaspoon salt

4 cups packed light brown sugar

2 cups vegetable shortening

4 large eggs

⅔ cup milk

1½ cups walnuts, chopped

1⅓ cups raisins

**1** Preheat the oven to 350 degrees. Lightly grease 2 baking sheets.

**2** Combine the flour, baking powder, baking soda, spices, and salt.

**3** In a large bowl, cream the vegetable shortening and brown sugar. Beat in the eggs one at a time. Beat in the milk. Gradually blend in the dry ingredients. Fold in the walnuts and raisins.

**4** Drop the dough by spoonfuls 1½ inches apart onto the prepared baking sheets.

**5** Bake for 12 to 15 minutes, until lightly colored. Transfer to wire racks to cool.

**Baking notes:** For another version of these, add ½ teaspoon almond extract and substitute chopped almonds for the walnuts.

# HERMITS

Drop Cookies

Yield: *5 to 8 dozen*

Total time: *35 minutes*

---

2 cups all-purpose flour

2 teaspoons baking powder

½ teaspoon baking soda

½ cup vegetable shortening

1 cup packed dark brown sugar

2 large eggs

½ cup buttermilk

1 teaspoon vanilla extract

1 cup hickory nuts, chopped (see Baking notes)

**1** Preheat the oven to 375 degrees. Lightly grease 2 baking sheets.

**2** Combine the flour, baking powder, and baking soda.

**3** In a large bowl, cream the vegetable shortening and brown sugar. Beat in the eggs. Beat in the buttermilk and vanilla extract. Gradually blend in the dry ingredients. Fold in the nuts.

**4** Drop the dough by spoonfuls 1½ inches apart onto the prepared baking sheets.

**5** Bake for 12 to 15 minutes, until lightly colored. Transfer to wire racks to cool.

**Baking notes:** Although hickory nuts may be difficult to find, they are delicious in this recipe. If they are unavailable, almost any other nut can be substituted.

# HICKORY DROPS

Drop Cookies

Yield: *3 to 5 dozen*

Total time: *35 minutes*

# HIGH-ENERGY COOKIES

Drop Cookies

YIELD: *3 to 5 dozen*
TOTAL TIME: *30 minutes*
CHILLING TIME: *1 hour*

3 cups rolled oats
½ cup peanut butter
5 tablespoons unsweetened cocoa powder
2 tablespoons vanilla extract

**TOPPING**
2 cups granulated sugar
½ cup vegetable shortening
½ cup milk

**1** Line 2 baking sheets with waxed paper.

**2** In a large bowl, combine the oats, peanut butter, cocoa powder, and vanilla extract and stir until well blended.

**3** Drop the mixture by spoonfuls 1 inch apart onto the prepared baking sheets. Cover with waxed paper and chill for 1 hour.

**4** To make the topping, combine the sugar, vegetable shortening, and milk in a saucepan and bring to a boil, stirring until the short-ening melts. Boil for 1 minute. Remove from the heat and spoon over the chilled cookies. Let cool.

**5** Wrap the cookies individually in waxed paper and store in an airtight container.

# HIKER'S TREATS

Bar Cookies

YIELD: *1 to 2 dozen*
TOTAL TIME: *45 minutes*

¾ cup all-purpose flour
½ cup rolled oats
¼ cup toasted wheat germ
6 tablespoons packed light brown sugar
1 tablespoon grated orange zest
½ cup vegetable shortening

**TOPPING**
2 large eggs
6 tablespoon packed light brown sugar
½ cup shredded coconut
⅔ cup slivered almonds

**1** Preheat the oven to 350 degrees. Lightly grease an 8-inch square baking pan.

**2** Combine the flour, oats, wheat germ, brown sugar, and orange zest in a bowl. Cut in the vegetable shortening until the mixture resembles coarse crumbs. Press the dough, evenly into the prepared baking pan.

**3** To make the topping, in a medium bowl, beat the eggs with the brown sugar until thick. Stir in the coconut. Pour over the dough and sprinkle the almonds over the top.

**4** Bake for 30 to 35 minutes, until lighly colored on top and firm to the touch. Cool in the pan on wire rack before cutting into large or small bars.

**Baking notes:** To enhance the flavor of these bars, add ¼ teaspoon almond extract to the topping. Raisins may be added to the dough.

# HOLIDAY COOKIES

Bar Cookies

YIELD: *1 to 2 dozen*
TOTAL TIME: *50 minutes*

**CRUST**
1 cup all-purpose flour
½ teaspoon ground ginger
¼ teaspoon ground cloves
¼ teaspoon ground nutmeg
½ cup vegetable shortening
½ cup packed light brown sugar

**FILLING**
½ teaspoon baking powder
¼ teaspoon ground mace
¼ teaspoon salt
1 cup packed light brown sugar
2 large eggs
1 teaspoon vanilla extract
1½ cups shredded coconut
1 cup almonds, chopped

**1** Preheat the oven to 375 degrees. Lightly grease a 9-inch square baking pan.

**2** To make the crust, combine the flour and spices.

**3** In a large bowl, cream the vegetable shortening and brown sugar. Gradually blend in the dry ingredients. Spread the mixture evenly in the prepared baking pan.

**4** Bake for 20 minutes.

**5** Meanwhile, make the filling: Combine the baking powder, mace, and salt.

**6** In a medium bowl, beat the brown sugar and eggs until thick. Beat in the vanilla extract. Beat in the dry ingredients. Fold in the coconuts and almonds.

**7** Pour the over the hot crust. Bake for 20 to 25 minutes longer, until lightly colored on top. Cool in the pan on a wire rack before cutting into large or small bars.

**Baking notes:** Nutmeg may be used in place of the mace.

---

# HOLIDAY GEMS

Drop Cookies

YIELD: *2 to 4 dozen*
TOTAL TIME: *30 minutes*

½ cup all-purpose flour
½ teaspoon baking powder
4 large egg whites
2 cups powdered sugar
2 cups almonds, chopped fine
1 cup candied cherries, chopped fine

**1** Preheat the oven to 325 degrees. Lightly grease and flour 2 baking sheets.

**2** Combine the flour and baking powder.

**3** In a large bowl, beat the egg whites until foamy, then beat in the powdered sugar until stiff but not dry. Gradually fold in the dry ingredients. Fold in the almonds and cherries.

**4** Drop the dough by spoonfuls 2 inches apart onto the prepared baking sheets.

**5** Bake for 12 to 15 minutes, until lightly colored and firm to the touch. Cool on the baking sheets, on wire racks.

# HOLIDAY ORNAMENTS

Rolled Cookies

YIELD: *varies with the size of the cookie cutter used*
TOTAL TIME: *30 minutes*
CHILLING TIME: *4 hours*

3½ cups all-purpose flour
1 teaspoon baking powder
½ teaspoon salt
1 cup vegetable shortening
1½ cups granulated sugar
2 large eggs
2 teaspoons vanilla extract
Paper drinking straws, cut into ½-inch lengths

**1** Combine the flour, baking powder, and salt.

**2** In a large bowl, cream the vegetable shortening and sugar. Beat in the eggs one at a time. Beat in the vanilla extract. Gradually blend in the dry ingredients. Cover and chill for 4 hours.

**3** Preheat the oven to 400 degrees. Lightly grease 2 baking sheets.

**4** On a floured surface, roll out the dough to a thickness of ⅛ inch. Using cookie cutters, cut into shapes and place 1 inch apart on the prepared baking sheets. Insert a length of drinking straw through the top of each cookie.

**5** Bake for 8 to 10 minutes, until lightly colored. Transfer to wire racks to cool before removing the straws.

**Baking notes:** Decorate these cookies with icing and/or colored sugar crystals, jimmies, and other candies. The dough can also be colored using food coloring to create a variety of color combinations.

# HOLIDAY WREATHS

Formed Cookies

YIELD: *3 to 4 dozen*
TOTAL TIME: *30 minutes*

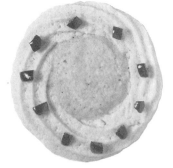

1 cup vegetable shortening
½ cup granulated sugar
1 large egg
1 teaspoon vanilla extract
2½ tablespoons all-purpose flour
¼ cup maple syrup
1⅓ cup walnuts, chopped
Red and green glacé cherries, chopped, for decoration

**1** Preheat the oven to 350 degrees. Lightly grease 2 baking sheets.

**2** In a large bowl, cream the vegetable shortening and sugar. Beat in the egg. Beat in the vanilla extract. Gradually blend in the flour. Transfer one-third of the dough to a medium bowl.

**3** Place the remaining dough in a cookie press or pastry bag fitted with a small plain tip, and press or pipe out rings onto the prepared baking sheets, spacing them 2 inches apart.

**4** Stir the maple syrup into the reserved dough. Stir in the walnuts. Fill the centers of the rings with the maple syrup mix.

**5** Bake for 12 to 15 minutes, until lightly colored. Transfer to wire racks and decorate with the glacé cherries. Let cool.

# HONEY BROWNIES

Bar Cookies

YIELD: *2 dozen*
TOTAL TIME: *35 minutes*

¾ cup all-purpose flour
2 tablespoons unsweetened cocoa powder
¾ teaspoon baking powder
¼ teaspoon salt
⅓ cup plus 2 tablespoons vegetable shortening
¾ cup honey
2 large eggs

**1** Preheat the oven to 325 degrees. Lightly grease an 8-inch square baking pan.

**2** Combine the flour, cocoa powder, baking powder, and salt.

**3** In a saucepan, melt the vegetable shortening with the honey.

Remove from the heat and beat in the eggs one at a time. Gradually blend in the dry ingredients. Spread the batter evenly into the prepared baking pan.

**4** Bake for 25 to 30 minutes, or until a toothpick inserted in the center comes out clean. Cool in the pan on a wire rack before cutting into large or small bars.

2 cups whole wheat flour
1 cup soy flour
1 cup rolled oats
¼ teaspoon salt
1 cup honey
1 cup canola oil
½ cup molasses
1 tablespoon fresh orange juice
½ teaspoon coffee liqueur
1 cup flaked coconut

**1** Preheat the oven to 350 degrees. Lightly grease 2 baking sheets.

**2** Combine the two flours, the oats, and salt.

**3** In a large saucepan, combine the honey, oil, molasses, and

orange juice and heat gently, stirring until well blended. Remove from the heat and stir in the coffee liqueur. Transfer to a large bowl, and gradually blend in the dry ingredients. Stir in the coconut.

**4** Drop the dough by spoonfuls 1½ inches apart onto the prepared baking sheets.

**5** Bake for 10 to 12 minutes, until lightly colored. Transfer to wire racks to cool.

# Honey Chews

Drop Cookies

Yield: *3 to 5 dozen*
Total time: *35 minutes*

---

1¼ cups all-purpose flour
½ teaspoon baking soda
¼ teaspoon salt
⅓ cup butter, at room temperature
½ cup honey
1 large egg
1½ teaspoons apricot flavored brandy
1 cup (6 ounces) semisweet chocolate chips
½ cup almonds, chopped fine

**1** Preheat the oven to 375 degrees. Lightly grease 2 baking sheets.

**2** Combine the flour, baking soda, and salt.

**3** In a large saucepan, melt the butter with the honey, stirring

until smooth. Remove from the heat and beat in the egg. Beat in the brandy. Gradually blend in the dry ingredients. Stir in the chocolate chips and almonds.

**4** Drop the dough by spoonfuls 2 inches apart onto the prepared baking sheets.

**5** Bake for 10 to 12 minutes, until lightly colored. Transfer to wire racks to cool.

# Honey Chippers

Drop Cookies

Yield: *4 to 5 dozen*
Total time: *35 minutes*

---

1 cup all-purpose flour
¼ cup walnuts, ground fine
1 teaspoon baking powder
¼ teaspoon salt
½ cup vegetable shortening
½ cup honey
1 large egg
½ teaspoon crème de cacao
½ cup semisweet chocolate chips

**1** Preheat the oven to 375 degrees.

**2** Combine the flour, walnuts, baking powder, and salt.

**3** In a large saucepan, melt the vegetable shortening with the honey, stirring until smooth. Remove from the heat and beat in the egg. Beat in the crème de

cacao. Gradually blend in the dry ingredients. Stir in the chocolate chips.

**4** Drop the dough by spoonfuls 1½ inches apart onto the prepared baking sheets.

**5** Bake for 10 to 12 minutes, until lightly colored. Transfer to wire racks to cool.

# Honey Chocolate Chips

Drop Cookies

Yield: *4 to 5 dozen*
Total time: *30 minutes*

# HONEY CHOCOLATE-OATMEAL COOKIES

Drop Cookies

YIELD: *4 to 5 dozen*
TOTAL TIME: *30 minutes*

2½ cups all-purpose flour
1 teaspoon baking powder
¼ teaspoon baking soda
1 teaspoon ground cinnamon
¼ teaspoon salt
1 cup vegetable shortening
2 ounces bittersweet chocolate, chopped
1¼ cups honey
2 large eggs
1½ cups rolled oats
1 cup flaked coconut

1  Preheat the oven to 325 degrees. Lightly grease 2 baking sheets.

2  Combine the flour, baking powder, baking soda, cinnamon, and salt.

3  In a large saucepan, melt the vegetable shortening and chocolate with the honey, stirring until smooth. Remove from the heat and beat in the eggs one at a time. Gradually blend in the dry ingredients. Stir in the oats and the coconut.

4  Drop the dough by spoonfuls 1½ inches apart onto the prepared baking sheets.

5  Bake for 18 to 20 minutes, until lightly colored. Transfer to wire racks to cool.

# HONEY COOKIES I

Formed Cookies

YIELD: *2 to 4 dozen*
TOTAL TIME: *30 minutes*

1 cup all-purpose flour
1 teaspoon baking soda
½ cup vegetable shortening
¼ cup honey
¼ cup granulated sugar
1 large egg yolk
Granulated sugar for rolling

1  Preheat the oven to 350 degrees.

2  Combine the flour and baking soda.

3  In a large saucepan, melt the vegetable shortening with the honey, stirring until smooth. Remove from the heat and beat in the sugar. Beat in the egg yolk.

Gradually blend in the dry ingredients.

4  Pinch off walnut-sized pieces of dough and roll into small balls. Roll the balls in granulated sugar and place 1½ inches apart on ungreased baking sheets.

5  Bake for 10 to 12 minutes, until lightly colored. Transfer to wire racks to cool.

# HONEY COOKIES II

Rolled Cookies

YIELD: *3 to 4 dozen*
TOTAL TIME: *30 minutes*

2½ cups all-purpose flour
1 teaspoon baking soda
1 tablespoon ground ginger
½ teaspoon salt
½ cup vegetable shortening
1 cup honey

1  Preheat the oven to 350 degrees. Lightly grease 2 baking sheets.

2  Combine the flour, baking soda, ginger, and salt.

3  In a large saucepan, melt the vegetable shortening with honey stirring until smooth. Remove from the heat and gradually blend in the dry ingredients, stir-ring until the dough is smooth and no longer sticky.

4  On a well-floured surface, roll out the dough to a thickness of ¼ inch. Using a 1½ inch-round cookie cutter, cut into rounds and place the rounds 1 inch apart on the prepared baking sheets.

5  Bake for 12 to 15 minutes, until lightly colored. Transfer to wire racks to cool.

¾ cup all-purpose flour
¾ teaspoon baking powder
¼ teaspoon salt
3 tablespoons vegetable shortening
¾ cup honey
2 large eggs
1 cup dates, pitted and chopped
⅔ cup walnuts, chopped fine
Powdered sugar for coating

**1** Preheat the oven to 350 degrees. Lightly grease a 9-inch square baking pan.

**2** Combine the flour, baking powder, and salt.

**3** In a large saucepan, melt the vegetable shortening with the honey, stirring until smooth. Remove from the heat and beat in the eggs one at a time. Gradually blend in the dry ingredients. Stir in the dates and walnuts.

Spread the mixture evenly in the prepared baking pan.

**4** Bake for 25 to 30 minutes, until lightly colored on top. Cool in the pan on a wire rack.

**5** Cut into large or small bars, and dip half of each bar in powdered sugar.

# HONEY DATE BARS

Bar Cookies

YIELD: *1 to 3 dozen*
TOTAL TIME: *40 minutes*

2¼ cups all-purpose flour
½ teaspoon walnuts, ground fine
1 teaspoon baking soda
½ teaspoon ground allspice
½ teaspoon ground cinnamon
¼ teaspoon salt
½ cup vegetable shortening
1 cup honey
½ cup packed light brown sugar
2 large eggs
3 tablespoons milk
1 cup raisins
1 cup currants
1 cup dates, pitted and chopped fine

**1** Combine the flour, walnuts, baking soda, spices, and salt.

**2** In a small saucepan, melt the vegetable shortening with the honey, stirring until smooth. Transfer to a large bowl and beat in the brown sugar. Beat in the eggs one at a time. Beat in the milk. Gradually blend in the dry ingredients. Stir in the raisins, currants, and dates. Cover and chill for at least 4 hours.

**3** Preheat the oven to 400 degrees. Lightly grease 2 baking sheets.

**4** Drop the dough by spoonfuls 1½ inches apart onto the prepared baking sheets.

**5** Bake for 10 to 12 minutes, until lightly colored. Transfer to wire racks to cool.

# HONEY HERMITS

Drop Cookies

YIELD: *4 to 5 dozen*
TOTAL TIME: *30 minutes*
CHILLING TIME: *4 hours*

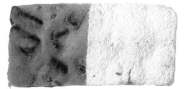

H

# HONEY LACE WAFERS

Drop Cookies

YIELD: *1 to 3 dozen*
TOTAL TIME: *30 minutes*

½ cup all-purpose flour
¼ teaspoon baking powder
⅛ teaspoon baking soda
¼ cup vegetable shortening
2 tablespoons granulated sugar
¼ cup honey
1¾ teaspoons grated orange zest
½ cup flaked coconut

**1** Preheat the oven to 400 degrees.

**2** Combine the flour, baking powder, and baking soda.

**3** In a large bowl, cream the vegetable shortening and sugar. Beat in the honey. Beat in the orange zest. Gradually blend in the dry ingredients. Fold in the coconut.

**4** Drop the dough by spoonfuls at least 3 inches apart onto ungreased baking sheets.

**5** Bake for 10 to 12 minutes, until lightly colored. Roll each warm cookie up around a thin dowel or a pencil to form a cylinder, remove from the round tool, and set on wire racks to cool. (If the cookies become too firm to shape, return them to the oven for a minute or so.)

**Baking notes:** These can be served plain or sprinkled with powdered sugar. For special occasions, fill them with whipped cream, using a pastry bag fitted with a small plain tip.

# HONEY NUTLETS

Drop Cookies

YIELD: *2 to 4 dozen*
TOTAL TIME: *30 minutes*
CHILLING TIME: *2 hours*

4 cups all-purpose flour
2 cups walnuts, ground
½ teaspoon baking soda
1 teaspoon ground cinnamon
1 teaspoon salt
1 cup vegetable shortening
1 cup granulated sugar
1 large egg
1 cup honey

**1** Combine the flour, walnuts, baking soda, cinnamon, and salt.

**2** In a large bowl, cream the vegetable shortening and sugar. Beat in the egg. Beat in the honey. Gradually blend in the dry ingredients. Cover and chill for 2 hours.

**3** Preheat the oven to 350 degrees.

**4** Drop the dough by spoonfuls at least 2½ inches apart onto ungreased baking sheets.

**5** Bake for 12 to 15 minutes, until lightly colored. Let cool slightly, then transfer to wire racks to cool.

3 cups all-purpose flour
1½ teaspoons ground ginger
¾ cup vegetable shortening
½ cup granulated sugar
1 large egg
½ cup honey
2 tablespoons frozen orange juice concentrate, thawed
½ teaspoon orange extract

**1** Combine the flour and ginger.

**2** In a large bowl, cream the vegetable shortening and sugar. Beat in the egg. Beat in the honey. Beat in the orange juice concentrate and orange extract. Gradually blend in the dry ingredients. Cover and chill for 2 hours.

**3** Preheat the oven to 350 degrees.

**4** On a floured surface, roll the dough out to a thickness of ⅛ inch. Using a 1½-inch cookie cutter, cut into rounds and place 1 inch apart on ungreased baking sheets.

**5** Bake for 8 to 10 minutes, until lightly colored. Transfer to wire racks to cool.

**Baking notes:** Flaked or shredded coconut can be sprinkled on these cookies before baking; first brush the cookies with lightly beaten egg whites. Don't underbake these cookies; they should be crisp. For an unusual sweet, spread the cooled cookies with a thin layer of cream cheese and sprinkle with chopped candied citrus peel.

# HONEY ORANGE CRISPS

Rolled Cookies

YIELD: *3 to 4 dozen*
TOTAL TIME: *30 minutes*
CHILLING TIME: *2 hours*

1½ cups all-purpose flour
1½ teaspoons baking powder
¼ teaspoon baking soda
¼ teaspoon salt
½ cup granulated sugar
½ cup honey
¼ cup butter, at room temperature
1 large egg
½ cup milk
1½ cups cornflakes, crushed
1 cup golden raisins

**1** Preheat the oven to 350 degees. Lightly grease a 15 by 10-inch baking pan.

**2** Combine the flour, baking powder, baking soda, and salt.

**3** In a large bowl, beat the sugar, honey, and butter together until smooth. Beat in the egg. Beat in

the milk. Gradually blend in the dry ingredients. Fold in the cornflakes and raisins. Spread the dough evenly in the prepared baking pan.

**4** Bake for 15 to 20 minutes, until lightly colored on top. Cool in the pan on a wire rack before cutting into large or small bars.

# HONEY RAISIN BARS

Bar Cookie

YIELD: *2 to 3 dozen*
TOTAL TIME: *35 minutes*

# Honey Snaps

Formed Cookies

Yield: *4 to 5 dozen*
Total time: *30 minutes*
Chilling time: *4 hours*

**2¼ cups all-purpose flour**
**1 teaspoon baking soda**
**½ teaspoon ground allspice**
**½ teaspoon ground cinnamon**
**¼ teaspoon ground nutmeg**
**½ teaspoon salt**
**1 cup packed light brown sugar**
**¾ cup vegetable shortening**
**¼ cup honey**
**Vanilla Sugar (see Pantry) for rolling**

**1** Combine the flour, baking soda, spices, and salt.

**2** In a large bowl, beat the sugar, vegetable shortening, and honey until smooth. Gradually blend in the dry ingredients. Cover and chill for 4 hours.

**3** Preheat the oven to 350 degrees.

**4** Pinch off walnut-sized pieces of dough and form into balls. Roll balls in vanilla sugar and place 2½ inches apart on ungreased baking sheets. Flatten the balls with the bottom of a glass dipped in flour.

**5** Bake for 10 to 12 minutes, until lightly colored. Transfer to wire racks to cool.

**Baking notes:** This dough can also be rolled out and cut into shapes.

# Honey Spice Cookies

Rolled Cookies

Yield: *3 to 4 dozen*
Total time: *30 minutes*
Chilling time: *2 hours*

**3¼ cups all-purpose flour**
**½ cup hazelnuts, ground**
**½ teaspoon baking soda**
**1 teaspoon ground ginger**
**½ teaspoon ground cinnamon**
**¼ teaspoon ground nutmeg**
**¼ teaspoon salt**
**⅔ cup packed light brown sugar**
**¼ cup vegetable shortening**
**2 large eggs**
**¾ cup honey**
**1 teaspoon grated lemon zest**
**½ cup grated orange zest**

**1** Combine the flour, hazelnuts, baking soda, spices, and salt.

**2** In a large bowl, cream the vegetable shortening and brown sugar. Beat in the eggs. Beat in the honey. Beat in the lemon and orange zest. Gradually blend in the dry ingredients. Cover and chill in the refrigerator for 2 hours.

**3** Preheat the oven to 350 degrees.

**4** On a floured surface, roll out the dough to a thickness of ¼ inch. Using a 1½-inch round cookie cutter, cut into cookies. Place the round on ungreased baking sheets.

**5** Bake for 10 to 12 minutes, until lightly colored. Transfer to wire racks to cool.

1⅓ cups all-purpose flour
1 teaspoon baking powder
¼ teaspoon salt
4 large eggs
1 cup honey
2 teaspoons almond extract
1 cup dates, pitted and chopped
1 cup almonds, chopped
Powdered sugar for sprinkling

**1** Preheat the oven to 350 degrees. Lightly grease a 13 by 9-inch baking pan.

**2** Combine the flour, baking powder, and salt.

**3** In a large bowl, beat the eggs until they are thick and light-colored. Beat in the honey. Beat in the almond extract. Gradually blend in the dry ingredients. Stir in the dates and almonds. Spread the mixture evenly into the prepared baking pan.

**4** Bake for 12 to 15 minutes, until lightly colored on top. Cool 1 to 2 minutes in the pan on a wire rack before cutting into large or small bars.

**5** Sprinkle the bars with powdered sugar when cool.

# HONEY SQUARES

Bar Cookies

YIELD: *2 to 4 dozen*
TOTAL TIME: *30 minutes*

---

2¾ cups all-purpose flour
1 tablespoon baking soda
¼ teaspoon salt
1½ cups butter, at room temperature
¼ cup granulated sugar
4 large egg yolks
1 cup sour cream
1 large egg white, beaten
Granulated sugar for sprinkling

**1** Combine the flour, baking soda, and salt.

**2** In a large bowl, cream the butter and sugar. Beat in the egg yolks. Beat in the sour cream. Gradually blend in the dry ingredients. Cover and chill for 2 hours.

**3** Preheat the oven to 350 degrees. Lightly grease 2 baking sheets.

**4** On a floured surface, roll out the dough to a thickness of ¼ inch. Using a 1½-inch round cookie cutter, cut out cookies and place 1 inch apart on the prepared baking sheets.

**5** Brush with the beaten egg white and sprinkle with granulated sugar.

**6** Bake for 12 to 14 minutes, until lightly colored. Transfer to wire racks to cool.

# HUNGARIAN BUTTER COOKIES

Rolled Cookies

YIELD: *2 to 4 dozen*
TOTAL TIME: *30 minutes*
CHILLING TIME: *2 hours*

# ICEBOX COOKIES

Refrigerator Cookies

YIELD: *4 to 5 dozen*
TOTAL TIME: *30 minutes*
CHILLING TIME: *8 hours*

2½ cups all-purpose flour
1¼ teaspoons baking powder
½ cup vegetable shortening
2 cups packed light brown sugar
2 large eggs
½ cup walnuts, chopped

**1** Combine the flour and baking powder.

**2** In a large bowl, cream the vegetable shortening and brown sugar. Beat in the eggs one at a time. Gradually blend in the dry ingredients. Fold in the walnuts.

**3** Divide the dough in half. Form each half into a log 1½ inches in diameter. Wrap in waxed paper and chill for 8 hours or overnight.

**4** Preheat the oven to 350 degrees.

**5** Cut the logs into ¼-inch-thick slices and place 1 inch apart on ungreased baking sheets.

**6** Bake for 10 to 12 minutes, until lightly colored. Transfer to wire racks to cool.

**Baking notes:** For variety, you can add vanilla extract or another flavoring to this dough. Or roll the logs in crushed or chopped nuts befoore chilling.

# IMPERIALS

Drop Cookies

YIELD: *2 dozen*
TOTAL TIME: *30 mintues*
CHILLING TIME: *2 hours*

¾ cup vegetable shortening
¾ cup granulated sugar
4 large egg yolks
1 cup all-purpose flour
Granulated sugar for flattening
3 ounces semisweet chocolate, chopped

**1** In a large bowl, cream the vegetable shortening and sugar. Beat in the egg yolks. Gradually blend in the flour. Cover and chill for 2 hours.

**2** Preheat the oven to 350 degrees.

**3** Drop the dough by spoonfuls 2½ inches apart onto ungreased baking sheets. Flatten with a glass dipped in water and then in granulated sugar.

**4** Bake for 8 to 10 minutes, until lightly colored. Transfer to wire racks to cool.

**5** Melt the chocolate in a double boiler over low heat, stirring until smooth. Remove from the heat. Spread a thin layer of chocolate over the bottoms of the cooled cookies and let cool until set.

1 cup granulated sugar
1¼ cups water
1 cup nonfat dry milk
1 tablespoon rose water
1 teaspoon ground cardamom
½ cup pistachio nuts

**1** Lightly grease a 9-inch square baking pan.

**2** Boil the sugar and water together until it spins a thread. (230 to 234 degrees). Stir in the rose water and powdered milk. Continue to simmer on low for 3 minutes longer. Stir in the cardamom and pistachio nuts.

**3** Immediately pour into the prepared baking pan and cool in the

pan on a wire rack. When cool cut into small squares or diamonds.

# INDIAN BARFI

Bar Cookies

YIELD: *2 to 3 dozen*
TOTAL TIME: *30 minutes*

2¾ cups all-purpose flour
½ cup almonds, ground
½ teaspoon baking powder
1 cup vegetable shortening
1 cup granulated sugar
1 large egg
3 ounces cream cheese, softened
1 tablespoon grated lemon zest
½ cup raspberry preserves
Powdered sugar for dusting

**1** Combine the flour, almonds, and baking powder.

**2** In a large bowl, cream the vegetable shortening and sugar. Beat in the egg. Beat in the cream cheese and lemon zest. Gradually blend in the dry ingredients. Divide the dough in half, wrap in waxed paper, and chill for 8 hours or overnight.

**3** Preheat the oven to 350 degrees.

**4** On a floured surface, roll out one-half of the dough to a thickness of ⅛ inch. Using a 3-inch round cookie cutter, cut into rounds. With a ½-inch round cutter, cut out the centers of the cookies. Place the rounds 1 inch

apart on the prepared baking sheets. Roll out the remaining dough, cut into 3-inch rounds and place on the baking sheets.

**5** Bake for 8 to 10 minutes, until lightly colored. Transfer to wire racks to cool.

**6** To assemble, spread a thin layer of raspberry preserves over the plain rounds and top with the cut-out rounds. Dust the tops with powdered sugar.

**Baking notes:** For variety, try any one of the many fruit preserves available in grocery stores.

# ISCHL TARTLETS

Rolled Cookies

YIELD: *4 to 5 dozen*
TOTAL TIME: *45 minutes*
CHILLING TIME: *8 hours*

**I**

# ITALIAN ALMOND COOKIES

Bar Cookies

YIELD: *1 to 3 dozen*
TOTAL TIME: *75 minutes*

2⅔ cups all-purpose flour
1 cup almonds, ground
**Pinch of salt**
1 cup vegetable shortening
1 cup granulated sugar
2 tablespoons fresh lemon juice
1 tablespoon brandy
1 teaspoon grated lemon zest

**1** Preheat the oven to 350 degrees. Lightly grease a 9-inch square baking pan.

**2** Combine the flour, almonds, and salt.

**3** In a large bowl, cream the vegetable shortening and sugar. Beat in the lemon juice and brandy. Beat in the lemon zest. Gradually blend in the dry ingredients.

Spread the mixture evenly in the prepared baking pan. (Do not press down on the mixture.)

**4** Bake for 50 to 60 minutes, until lightly colored on top. Cool in the pan on a wire rack before cutting into large or small bars.

# ITALIAN CHRISTMAS COOKIES

Rolled Cookies

YIELD: *2 to 4 dozen*
TOTAL TIME: *30 minutes*
CHILLING TIME: *4 hours*

3 cups all-purpose flour
1 tablespoon baking powder
¼ teaspoon salt
1 cup vegetable shortening
1 cup granulated sugar
2 large eggs
1 teaspoon grated lemon zest
¼ cup pistachios, chopped
**Lemon Glaze (see Pantry)**
**Chipped pistachios for sprinkling**

**1** Combine the flour, baking powder, and salt.

**2** In a large bowl, cream the vegetable shortening and sugar. Beat in the eggs one at a time. Beat in the lemon zest. Gradually blend in the dry ingredients. Fold in the pistachios. Cover and chill for 4 hours.

**3** Preheat the oven to 425 degrees. Lightly grease 2 baking sheets.

**4** On a floured surface, roll out the dough to a thickness of ⅛ inch. Using a 1½-inch round cookie cutter, cut the cookies and place 1 inch apart on the prepared baking sheets.

**5** Bake for 8 to 10 minutes, until lightly colored. Transfer to wire racks to cool.

**6** Frost the cooled cookies with the lemon glaze and sprinkle with chopped pistachios.

**Baking notes:** Traditionally these cookies are made with pistachios, but any type of nut can be used. These cookies are being baked at a high temperature, so watch closely as they bake.

1½ cups all-purpose flour
2 tablespoons granulated sugar
½ teaspoon salt
½ cup butter
1 large egg
1 cup apricot preserves

**1** In a large bowl, combine the flour, sugar, and salt. Cut in the butter. Add the egg and stir to form a soft dough. Divide the dough in half. Wrap in waxed paper and chill for 1 hour.

**2** On a floured surface, roll out one-half of the dough to a 12 by 6-inch rectangle. Trim the edges and place the dough on a microwave-safe baking sheet.

Spread the apricot preserves evenly over the dough. Roll out the remaining dough to a rectangle and place on top of the preserves.

**3** Bake on high for 3 minutes. Cool on the baking sheet on a wire rack before cutting into large or small bars.

# JAM-FILLED STRIPS

Bar Cookies
(Microwave Recipe)

YIELD:: *1 to 2 dozen*
TOTAL TIME: *30 minutes*
CHILLING TIME: *1 hour*

---

CRUST
1½ cups all-purpose flour
¼ teaspoon salt
½ cup butter
2 to 2½ tablespoons ice water

TOPPING
2 each large eggs
½ cup powdered sugar
2½ cups flaked coconut
⅓ cup raspberry preserves

**1** Preheat the oven to 400 degrees.

**2** To make the crust, combine the flour and salt in a medium bowl. Cut in the butter until the mixture resembles coarse crumbs. Add just enough water to make a soft dough. Press the dough

evenly into an ungreased 9-inch square baking pan.

**3** Bake for 20 minutes.

**4** Meanwhile, make the topping: In a medium bowl, beat the eggs until thick and light-colored. Beat in the powdered sugar. Stir in the coconut.

**5** Spread the raspberry preserves over the hot crust. Spread the topping over the preserves.

**6** Bake for 20 to 25 minutes longer, until lightly colored on top and firm to the touch. Cool in the pan on a wire rack before cutting into large or small bars.

# JAM SQUARES

Bar Cookies

YIELD: *1 to 3 dozen*
TOTAL TIME: *50 minutes*

---

CRUST
2 cups all-purpose flour
¼ teaspoon salt
1 cup vegetable shortening
1 cup packed light brown sugar
1 large egg yolk

TOPPING
1 large egg white
1 cup granulated sugar
½ teaspoon ground cinnamon
½ cup walnuts, chopped

**1** Preheat the oven to 375 degrees. Lightly grease a 9-inch square baking pan.

**2** To make the crust, combine the flour and salt.

**3** In a large bowl, cream the vegetable shortening and brown sugar. Beat in the egg yolk. Gradually blend in the dry ingredients. Spread the dough evenly in the prepared baking pan.

**4** To make the topping, in a medium bowl, beat the egg white until stiff but not dry. Gradually fold in the sugar and cinnamon. Fold in the nuts. Spread the topping over the dough.

**5** Bake for 18 to 20 minutes, until lightly colored on top and firm to the touch. Cool in the pan on a wire rack before cutting into large or small bars.

# JAN HAGEL

Bar Cookies

YIELD: *1 to 3 dozen*
TOTAL TIME: *30 minutes*

# JELLY COOKIES

Formed Cookies

YIELD: *3 to 4 dozen*
TOTAL TIME: *45 minutes*

1 cup vegetable shortening
½ cup granulated sugar
1 large egg
1 teaspoon vanilla extract
½ teaspoon fresh lemon juice
2½ cups all-purpose flour
About ¼ to ½ cup grape jelly

**1** Preheat the oven to 350 degrees. Lightly grease 2 baking sheets.

**2** In a large bowl, cream the vegetable shortening and sugar. Beat in the egg. Beat in the vanilla extract and lemon juice. Gradually blend in the flour.

**3** Pinch off walnut-sized pieces of the dough and roll into balls. Place 1 inch apart on the pre- pared baking sheets. Press your finger into the center of each cookie to make an indentation. Fill each cookie with a little jelly.

**4** Bake for 20 to 25 minutes, until lightly colored. Transfer to wire racks to cool.

# JEWEL BARS

Bar Cookies

YIELD: *1 to 2 dozen*
TOTAL TIME: *45 minutes*

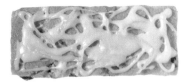

2¼ cups all-purpose flour
1½ teaspoons baking powder
1 teaspoon ground cinnamon
1 teaspoon ground nutmeg
1 teaspoon salt
½ cup vegetable shortening
1½ cups packed light brown sugar
8 ounces cream cheese, at room
    temperature
1 large egg
¼ cup honey
1 cup walnuts, chopped
1 cup mixed candied fruit, chopped
    fine
1 cup raisins
Lemon Icing (see Pantry)

**1** Preheat the oven to 350 degrees. Lightly grease a 9-inch square baking pan.

**2** Combine the flour, baking powder, cinnamon, nutmeg, and salt.

**3** In a large bowl, cream the vegetable shortening and sugar. Beat in the cream cheese. Beat in the egg and honey. Gradually blend in the dry ingredients. Stir in the walnuts, mixed fruit, and raisins. Spread the mixture evenly in the prepared baking pan.

**4** Bake for 30 to 35 minutes, until a toothpick inserted in the center comes out clean. Cool in the pan on a wire rack.

**5** Spread the icing over the cooled cookies and cut into large or small bars.

**Baking notes:** If you prefer, use just one kind of candied fruit, such as cherries.

2 cups all-purpose flour
2 teaspoons bitter almonds, grated
(see Baking notes)
1 teaspoon baking powder
3 teaspoons ground cardamom
½ cup butter, at room temperature
½ cup packed light brown sugar
1 large egg

TOPPING
1 large egg white
2 tablespoons granulated sugar
½ teaspoon ground cinnamon
½ cup butter, melted temperature

**1** Combine the flour, almonds, baking powder, and cardamom.

**2** In a large bowl, cream the butter and sugar. Beat in the egg. Gradually blend in the dry ingredients. Cover and chill in the refrigerator for 6 hours.

**3** Preheat the oven to 375 degrees. Lightly grease 2 baking sheets.

**4** To make the topping, beat the egg white in a small bowl until foamy. Beat in the sugar and cinnamon.

**5** On a floured surface, roll out the dough to a thickness of ⅛ inch. Using a 1½-inch round cookie cutter, cut into rounds and place 1 inch apart on the prepared baking sheets. Brush each cookie with the melted butter and then with the egg white mixture.

**6** Bake for 12 to 15 minutes, until lightly colored. Transfer to wire racks to cool.

# JEWISH COOKIES I

Rolled Cookies

YIELD: *3 to 6 dozen*
TOTAL TIME: *40 minutes*
CHILLING TIME: *6 hours*

---

2½ cups all-purpose flour
½ teaspoon baking soda
¾ cup vegetable shortening
½ cup granulated sugar
1 large egg
1 large egg white, beaten
¼ cup almonds, ground fine

**1** Preheat the oven to 300 degrees. Lightly grease 2 baking sheets.

**2** Combine the flour and baking soda.

**3** In a large bowl, cream the vegetable shortening and sugar. Beat in the egg. Gradually blend in the dry ingredients.

**4** On a floured surface, roll out the dough to a thickness of ¼ inch. Using a 1½-inch round cookie cutter, cut out rounds and

place 1 inch apart on the prepared baking sheets. Brush with the beaten egg white and sprinkle the almonds over the top.

**5** Bake for 10 to 12 minutes, until lightly colored. Transfer to wire racks to cool.

# JEWISH COOKIES II

Rolled Cookies

YIELD: *4 to 6 dozen*
TOTAL TIME: *30 minutes*

# Jewish Cookies III

Rolled Cookies

Yield: *6 to 7 dozen*
Total time: *30 minutes*

4 cups all-purpose flour
2 cups walnuts, ground
1 teaspoon baking soda
1 teaspoon ground cinnamon
1 teaspoon ground cloves
½ teaspoon ground nutmeg
1 cup vegetable shortening
1½ cups granulated sugar
3 large eggs
2 cups candied citrus peel, chopped

**1** Preheat the oven to 325 degrees. Lightly grease 2 baking sheets.

**2** Combine the flour, walnuts, baking soda, and spices.

**3** In a large bowl, cream the vegetable shortening and sugar. Beat in the eggs. Gradually blend in the dry ingredients. Fold in the candied citrus peel.

**4** On a floured surface, roll out the dough to a thickness of ¼ inch. Using a 1½-inch round cookie cutter, cut into rounds and place 1 inch apart on the prepared baking sheets.

**5** Bake for 10 to 12 minutes, until lightly colored. Transfer to wire racks to cool.

# Jodekager

Rolled Cookies

Yield: *3 to 4 dozen*
Total time: *35 minutes*
Chilling time: *8 hours*

2½ cups all-purpose flour
1 teaspoon baking powder
1½ teaspoons ground cardamom
¼ teaspoon salt
1 cup butter, at room temperature
¾ cup granulated sugar
1 large egg

**TOPPING**
½ cup almonds, ground
¼ cup granulated sugar
1 large egg white, beaten

**1** Combine the flour, baking powder, cardamom, and salt.

**2** In a large bowl, cream the butter and sugar. Beat in the egg. Gradually blend in the dry ingredients. Divide the dough into quarters. Wrap in waxed paper and chill for 8 hours.

**3** Preheat the oven to 375 degrees. Lightly grease 2 baking sheets.

**4** To prepare the topping, combine the almonds and sugar in a small bowl.

**5** Work with one piece of dough at a time, keeping the remaining dough in the refrigerator. On a floured surface, roll out the dough to a thickness of ⅛ inch. Using a 2½-inch round cookie cutter, cut out cookies and place 1 inch apart on the prepared baking sheets. Brush with the beaten egg white and sprinkle with the almond-sugar mixture.

**6** Bake for 8 to 10 minutes, until lightly colored. Transfer to wire racks to cool.

4½ cups all-purpose flour
1 teaspoon baking powder
1 teaspoon baking soda
1¼ teaspoons ground ginger
⅛ teaspoon ground cloves
1 teaspoon salt
¾ cup vegetable shortening
1 cup packed light brown sugar
1 cup molasses
½ cup water

**1** Combine the flour, baking powder, baking soda, ginger, cloves, and salt.

**2** In a large bowl, cream the vegetable shortening and brown sugar. Beat in the molasses and water. Gradually blend in the dry ingredients. Cover and chill for 8 hours or overnight.

**3** Preheat the oven to 350 degrees. Lightly grease 2 baking sheets.

**4** On a floured surface, roll the dough out to a thickness of ¼ inch. Using a 3-inch round cookie cutter, cut into rounds and place 1 inch apart on the prepared baking sheets.

**5** Bake for 10 to 12 minutes, until firm to the touch. Transfer to wire racks to cool.

**Baking notes:** This was one of the most popular cookies in my shop in New England.

# JOE FROGGERS

Rolled Cookies

YIELD: *5 to 6 dozen*
TOTAL TIME: *35 minutes*
CHILLING TIME: *8 hours*

---

2½ cups all-purpose flour
1 teaspoon baking powder
½ teaspoon baking soda
1 teaspoon ground cinnamon
½ teaspoon ground cloves
¼ teaspoon ground mace
¼ teaspoon ground cardamom
½ cup vegetable shortening
1 cup granulated sugar
⅔ cup light corn syrup
½ cup brandy
1 cup almonds, chopped fine
½ cup candied citrus peel, chopped
   fine

**1** Combine the flour, baking powder, baking soda, and spices.

**2** In a large bowl, cream the vegetable shortening and sugar. Beat in the corn syrup. Beat in the brandy. Gradually blend in the dry ingredients. Fold in the almonds and candied citrus peel.

**3** Divide the dough in half. Form each half into a log 2 inches in diameter. Wrap in waxed paper and chill in the refrigerator for 24 hours.

**4** Preheat the oven to 350 degrees. Lightly grease 2 baking sheets.

**5** Cut the logs into ¼-inch-thick slices and place 1 inch apart on the prepared baking sheets.

**6** Bake for 12 to 15 minutes, until lightly colored. Transfer to wire racks to cool.

**Baking notes:** You can substitute either honey or molasses for the corn syrup for a slightly different flavor. Nutmeg can be used in place of mace.

# JUBILEE WAFERS

Refrigerator Cookies

YIELD: *5 to 6 dozen*
TOTAL TIME: *35 minutes*
CHILLING TIME: *24 hours*

# JUMBLES I

Drop Cookies

YIELD: *3 to 4 dozen*
TOTAL TIME: *45 minutes*

1 cup all-purpose flour
½ teaspoon baking powder
¼ teaspoon baking soda
¼ teaspoon salt
⅓ cup vegetable shortening
½ cup packed light brown sugar
1 large egg
1½ tablespoons evaporated milk
1 teaspoon vanilla extract
½ cup dates, pitted and chopped
½ cup sliced almonds
½ cup walnuts, chopped
1½ cups cornflakes, crushed

**1** Preheat the oven to 375 degrees. Lightly grease 2 baking sheets.

**2** Combine the flour, baking powder, baking soda, and salt.

**3** In a large bowl, cream the vegetable shortening and brown sugar. Beat in the egg. Beat in the milk and vanilla extract. Gradually blend in the dry ingredients. Fold in the dates, almonds, and walnuts.

**4** Spread the cornflakes in a pie pan. Drop the dough by spoonfuls onto the cornflakes and roll in the cornflakes until well coated. Place them 3 inches apart on the prepared baking sheets.

**5** Bake for 12 to 15 minutes, until lightly colored. Transfer to wire racks to cool.

# JUMBLES II

Formed Cookies

YIELD: *3 to 4 dozen*
TOTAL TIME: *45 minutes*

½ cup vegetable shortening
1 cup granulated sugar
4 large eggs
2 tablespoons heavy cream
3 cups all-purpose flour

**1** Preheat the oven to 350 degrees.

**2** In a large bowl, cream the vegetable shortening and sugar. Beat in the eggs one at a time. Beat in the cream. Gradually blend in the flour.

**3** Pinch off walnut-sized pieces of the dough and roll into pencil-thin ropes about 6 inches long. Form the ropes into horseshoes on ungreased baking sheets, placing them about 1 inch apart.

**4** Bake for 12 to 15 minutes, until lightly colored. Transfer to wire racks to cool.

**Baking notes:** You can also twist 2 ropes together for each cookie and lay them out straight or form them into knots, circles, and other shapes.

# JUMBO OATMEAL CRUNCHES

Drop Cookies

YIELD: *2 to 4 dozen*
TOTAL TIME: *30 minutes*

3 cups all-purpose flour
1 teaspoon baking soda
Pinch of ground mace
1 teaspoon salt
2 cups vegetable shortening
2½ cups packed light brown sugar
2 large eggs
½ cup milk
3½ cups rolled oats
1 cup raisins (optional)

**1** Preheat the oven to 350 degrees.

**2** Combine the flour, baking soda, mace, and salt.

**3** In a large bowl, cream the vegetable shortening and brown sugar. Beat in the eggs. Beat in the milk. Gradually blend in the dry ingredients. Fold in the oats and the optional raisins.

**4** Drop the dough by tablespoonfuls 3 inches apart onto ungreased baking sheets. With the back of a spoon, spread the dough into 2½-inch rounds.

**5** Bake for 10 to 12 minutes, until lightly colored. Transfer to wire racks to cool.

**Baking notes:** Nutmeg can be used in place of the mace.

4 cups all-purpose flour
2 teaspoons baking powder
1 cup vegetable shortening
1 cup granulated sugar
2 large eggs
1 large egg white, beaten
Granulated sugar for sprinkling

**1** Preheat the oven to 350 degrees. Lightly grease 2 baking sheets.

**2** Combine the flour and baking powder.

**3** In a large bowl, cream the vegetable shortening and sugar. Beat in the eggs. Gradually blend in the dry ingredients.

**4** On a floured surface, roll out the dough to a thickness of ¼ inch. Using a cookie cutter, cut into shapes and place 1 inch apart on the prepared baking sheets. Brush the tops with the beaten egg white and sprinkle with granulated sugar.

**5** Bake for 10 to 12 minutes, until lightly colored. Transfer to wire racks to cool.

# KAFFEE ZWIEBACK

Rolled Cookies

YIELD: *5 to 6 dozen*
TOTAL TIME: *35 minutes*

---

3 large egg whites
½ cup powdered sugar
1 cup grated fresh or packaged
    coconut

**1** Preheat the oven to 325 degrees. Line 2 baking sheets with parchment paper.

**2** In a large bowl, beat the egg whites until foamy. Beat in the powdered sugar and continue beating until stiff peaks form. Fold in the coconut.

**3** Drop the mixture by spoonfuls 1 inch apart onto the prepared baking sheets.

**4** Bake for 12 to 15 minutes, or until the edges start to color. Cool on the baking sheets on wire racks.

# KENTUCKY COCONUT DROPS

Drop Cookies

YIELD: *3 to 4 dozen*
TOTAL TIME: *35 minutes*

---

CRUST
1⅓ cups all-purpose flour
1¼ cups packed light brown sugar
½ teaspoon baking soda
½ teaspoon salt
1 cup pecans, toasted and chopped
½ cup vegetable shortening

TOPPING
3 large eggs
⅓ cup granulated sugar
¼ cup butter, at room temperature
3 tablespoons bourbon
1 teaspoon vanilla extract

**1** Preheat the oven to 350 degrees. Lightly grease an 8-inch square baking pan.

**2** To make the crust, combine the flour, brown sugar, baking soda, salt, and pecans. Cut in the vegetable shortening until the mix-

ture resembles coarse crumbs. Press the mixture evenly into the prepared baking pans.

**3** Bake for 15 minutes.

**4** Meanwhile, make the topping: In a medium bowl, beat the eggs until thick and light-colored. Beat in the sugar and butter. Beat in the bourbon and vanilla extract.

**5** Spread the topping over the hot crust. Bake for 20 to 25 minutes longer, until lightly colored and firm to the touch. Cool in the pan on a wire rack before cutting into large or small bars.

**Baking notes:** You can decorate these bars by arranging pecan halves on the topping before baking.

# KENTUCKY PECAN BARS

Bar Cookies

YIELD: *1 to 2 dozen*
TOTAL TIME: *45 minutes*

# KING'S ARMS TAVERN PECAN COOKIES

**K**

Drop Cookies

YIELD: *3 to 5 dozen*
TOTAL TIME: *45 minutes*

1 tablespoon all-purpose flour
Pinch of salt
1 large egg white
1 cup packed light brown sugar
1 cup pecans, chopped fine

**1** Preheat the oven to 325 degrees. Line 2 baking sheets with parchment paper.

**2** Combine the flour and salt.

**3** In a large bowl, beat the egg white until stiff but not dry. Beat in the brown sugar a little at a time. Gradually fold in the dry ingredients. Stir in the pecans.

**4** Drop the mixture by spoonfuls 1½ inches apart onto the prepared baking sheets.

**5** Bake for 12 to 15 minutes, until the edges are lightly colored. Cool on the pans on wire racks.

**Baking notes:** This recipe dates from the early nineteenth century.

# KISSIES

Formed Cookies

YIELD: *3 to 4 dozen*
TOTAL TIME: *30 minutes*

1⅓ cups all-purpose flour
1 teaspoon baking soda
½ teaspoon salt
½ cup vegetable shortening
½ cup granulated sugar
½ cup packed light brown sugar
½ cup peanut butter
1 large egg
1 teaspoon vanilla extract
Granulated sugar for rolling
Chocolate kisses for decoration

**1** Preheat the oven to 350 degrees.

**2** Combine the flour, baking soda, and salt.

**3** In a large bowl, cream the vegetable shortening and the two sugars. Beat in the peanut butter. Beat in the egg and vanilla extract. Gradually blend in the dry ingredients.

**4** Pinch off walnut-sized pieces of the dough and roll into balls. Roll the balls in granulated sugar and place 1 inch apart on ungreased baking sheets.

**5** Bake for 8 to 10 minutes, until just starting to color. Press a chocolate kiss into the center of each ball and return to the oven for 3 minutes. Transfer to wire racks to cool.

3¼ cups all-purpose flour
½ cup hazelnuts, ground
½ teaspoon baking soda
1 teaspoon ground ginger
½ teaspoon ground cinnamon
¼ teaspoon ground nutmeg
¼ teaspoon salt
¼ cup vegetable shortening
⅔ cup packed light brown sugar
¾ cup honey, warmed
2 large eggs
1 teaspoon grated lemon zest
½ cup grated orange zest

**1** Combine the flour, hazelnuts, baking soda, spices, and salt.

**2** In a large bowl, cream the vegetable shortening and brown sugar. Beat in the honey. Beat in the eggs. Beat in the lemon and orange zests. Gradually blend in the dry ingredients. Cover and chill for 4 hours.

**3** Preheat the oven to 350 degrees.

**4** On a floured surface, roll the dough out to a thickness of ¼ inch. Using a 1½-inch round cookie cutter, cut out cookies and place 1 inch apart on ungreased baking sheets.

**5** Bake for 10 to 12 minutes, until lightly colored. Transfer to wire racks to cool.

# KISS-ME-QUICK COOKIES

Rolled Cookies

YIELD: *4 to 5 dozen*
TOTAL TIME: *30 minutes*
CHILLING TIME: *4 hours*

---

2¼ cups all-purpose flour
½ teaspoon salt
1 cup vegetable shortening
8 ounces cream cheese, at room temperature
¼ teaspoon vanilla extract
About ¼ cup jam or preserves

**1** Combine the flour and salt.

**2** In a large bowl, beat the vegetable shortening and cream cheese until smooth. Beat in the vanilla extract. Gradually blend in the dry ingredients. Cover and chill for 2 hours.

**3** Preheat the oven to 350 degrees.

**4** On a floured surface, roll out the dough to a thickness of ¼ inch. Using a 2-inch round cookie cutter, cut out cookies and place 1 inch apart on ungreased baking

sheets. Make a small indentation in the center of each round with your finger and place about ½ teaspoon jam or preserves into the hollow.

**5** Bake for 8 to 10 minutes, until lightly colored. Transfer to wire racks to cool.

**Baking notes:** Lemon extract can be substituted for the vanilla.

# KOLACKY

Rolled Cookies

YIELD: *3 to 4 dozen*
TOTAL TIME: *35 minutes*
CHILLING TIME: *2 hours*

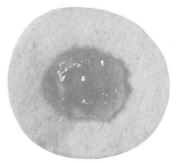

# KRINGLES

Formed Cookies

YIELD: *2 to 3 dozen*
TOTAL TIME: *40 minutes*
CHILLING TIME: *24 hours*

3 cups all-purpose flour
½ teaspoon salt
1 cup vegetable shortening
1 cup granulated sugar
1 large egg
2 hard-boiled large egg yolks, chopped
1 teaspoon vanilla extract
1 large egg white, beaten
Granulated sugar for sprinkling

1  Combine the flour and salt.

2  In a large bowl, cream the vegetable shortening and sugar. Beat in the egg and egg yolks. Beat in the vanilla extract. Gradually blend in the dry ingredients. Cover tightly and chill for 24 hours.

3  Preheat the oven to 350 degrees.

4  Pinch off pieces of dough and roll into pencil-thin ropes about 6 inches long. Form the ropes into pretzels on ungreased baking sheets, placing them 1 inch apart. Brush with the beaten egg white and sprinkle with granulated sugar.

5  Bake for 12 to 14 minutes, until lightly colored. Transfer to wire racks to cool.

**Baking notes:**  Decorate the pretzels with white or Dark chocolate Frosting (see Pantry).

# KRISPIES

Bar Cookies

YIELD: *1 to 2 dozen*
TOTAL TIME: *30 minutes*

1½ ounces milk chocolate
½ cup butter
½ cup corn syrup
1 cup powdered sugar
2 teaspoons vanilla extract
4 cups rice krispies

1  Lightly grease a 13 by 9-inch baking pan. Chill in the freezer.

2  In a large saucepan, melt the chocolate and butter with the corn syrup, stirring until smooth. Remove from the heat and beat in the powdered sugar. Beat in the vanilla extract. Stir in the rice krispies. Press the mixture evenly into the prepared baking pan.

3  Chill in the refrigerator for 20 minutes or until set. Cut into large or small bars.

# KRUMKAKE

Formed Cookies

YIELD: *2 to 4 dozen*
TOTAL TIME: *30 minutes*
CHILLING TIME: *1 hour*

1½ cups all-purpose flour
¼ teaspoon ground cardamom
Pinch of salt
6 tablespoons butter, at room temperature
1 cup granulated sugar
2 large eggs
⅔ cup milk
⅓ cup heavy cream
1 teaspoon vegetable shortening

1  Combine the flour, cardamom, and salt.

2  In a large bowl, cream the butter and sugar. Beat in the eggs. Beat in the milk and cream. Gradually blend in the dry ingredients. Cover and refrigerate for 1 hour.

3  Heat a krumkake iron and brush with the vegetable shortening.

4  Drop a tablespoon of the batter into the center of the iron and cook for 35 to 45 seconds, or until the krumkake is a golden brown. Remove from the iron and immediately roll into a cone or cigar shape. Let cool. Repeat with the remaining batter.

**Baking notes:**  These are delicious filled with whipped cream or a chocolate cream filling, or even a rum–cream cheese filling (see Pantry).

⅓ cup all-purpose flour
½ teaspoon salt
2 large eggs, separated
½ cup powdered sugar
½ teaspoon vanilla extract

**1** Preheat the oven to 350 degrees. Line 2 baking sheets with parchment paper.

**2** Combine the flour and salt.

**3** In a large bowl, beat the egg yolks and powdered sugar until thick and light-colored.

**4** In a small bowl, beat the egg whites until stiff but not dry. Fold in the vanilla extract. Gradually beat the egg white mixture into the egg yolk mixture. Gradually blend in the dry ingredients.

**5** Fill a cookie press or a pastry bag fitted with a large plain tip with the batter and press or pipe out 3-inch-long strips 1 inch apart onto the prepared baking sheets.

**6** Bake for 12 to 15 minutes, until lightly colored. Cool on the baking sheets on wire racks.

# LADY FINGERS I

Formed Cookies

YIELD: *2 to 3 dozen*
TOTAL TIME: *35 minutes*

---

1¾ cups all-purpose flour
½ teaspoon ground cinnamon
¼ teaspoon ground cloves
4 large egg yolks
2 cups powdered sugar

**1** Preheat the oven to 350 degrees. Line 2 baking sheets with parchment paper.

**2** Combine the flour, cinnamon, and cloves.

**3** In a large bowl, beat the egg yolks and powdered sugar until thick and light-colored. Gradually blend in the dry ingredients.

**4** Fill a cookie press or a pastry bag fitted with a large plain tip and press or pipe out 3-inch-long strips 1 inch apart onto the prepared baking sheets.

**5** Bake for 10 to 12 minutes, until lightly colored. Cool on the baking sheets on wire racks.

# LADYFINGERS II

Formed Cookies

YIELD: *3 to 4 dozen*
TOTAL TIME: *35 minutes*

# LEBKUCHEN

Rolled Cookies

YIELD: *3 to 5 dozen*
TOTAL TIME: *45 minutes*
CHILLING TIME: *24 hours*

3½ cups all-purpose flour
½ teaspoon baking soda
1 teaspoon ground cinnamon
1 teaspoon ground nutmeg
½ teaspoon ground allspice
½ teaspoon ground ginger
¼ teaspoon ground cloves
1 teaspoon salt
¾ cup honey
¾ cup packed light brown sugar
1 large egg
3 tablespoons fresh lemon juice
2 teaspoons grated lemon zest
1 cup candied citron, chopped
1 cup almonds, chopped
Glacé cherries, halved

1  Combine the flour, baking soda, spices, and salt.

2  In a large saucepan, bring the honey to a boil. Remove from the heat and beat in the brown sugar. Beat in the egg. Beat in the lemon juice and zest. Gradually blend in the dry ingredients. Fold in the candied citron and almonds.

Transfer the dough to a bowl, cover, and chill for 24 hours.

3  Preheat the oven to 350 degrees.

4  On a floured surface, roll out the dough to a thickness of ¼ inch. Using a 2-inch round cookie cutter, cut out cookies and place 2 inches apart on ungreased baking sheets. Place the cherry halves on top of each cookie.

5  Bake for 10 to 12 minutes, until lightly colored. Transfer to wire racks to cool.

**Baking Notes:** Traditionally these are frosted with white icing and decorated with almonds and cherries.

# LEMON BARS I

Bar Cookies

YIELD: *2 to 3 dozen*
TOTAL TIME: *40 minutes*

2½ cups all-purpose flour
2 teaspoons baking powder
1 teaspoon baking soda
½ teaspoon ground allspice
¼ cup vegetable shortening
2 large eggs
1½ cups frozen lemon juice concentrate, thawed
1 teaspoon lemon extract
1 cup golden raisins
1 cup walnuts, chopped
¾ cup flaked coconut
¾ cup canned crushed pineapple, drained

1  Preheat the oven to 350 degrees. Lightly grease a 13 by 9-inch baking pan.

2  Combine the flour, baking powder, baking soda, and allspice.

3  In a large bowl, cream the vegetable shortening until light and fluffy. Beat in the eggs. Beat in the lemon juice concentrate and lemon extract. Gradually blend in the dry ingredients. Fold in the

raisins and walnuts. Spread the mixture evenly in the prepared baking pan. Sprinkle the coconut and pineapple over the top.

4  Bake for 20 to 25 minutes, until lightly colored on top and firm to the touch. Cool in the pan on a wire rack before cutting into large or small bars.

2 cups all-purpose flour
1 teaspoon baking soda
1 teaspoon ground cinnamon
½ teaspoon ground nutmeg
½ teaspoon salt
¾ cup vegetable shortening
1½ cups packed light brown sugar
2 large eggs
3 tablespoons fresh lemon juice
3 tablespoons grated lemon zest
1 cup raisins

**1** Preheat the oven to 350 degrees. Lightly grease a 9-inch square baking pan.

**2** Combine the flour, baking soda, spices, and salt.

**3** In a large bowl, cream the vegetable shortening and brown sugar. Beat in the eggs one at a time. Beat in the lemon juice and zest. Stir in the raisins. Spread the dough evenly in the prepared baking pan.

**4** Bake for 25 to 30 minutes, until lightly colored on top. Cool in the pan on a wire rack before cutting into large or small bars.

# LEMON BARS II

Bar Cookies

YIELD: *1 to 3 dozen*
TOTAL TIME: *40 minutes*

---

**CRUST**
2 cups all-purpose flour
½ cup powdered sugar
1 cup vegetable shortening

**TOPPING**
4 large eggs
2 cups granulated sugar
⅓ cup fresh lemon juice
¼ cup all-purpose flour
½ teaspoon baking powder

**1** Preheat the oven to 350 degrees. Lightly grease a 13 by 9 inch baking pan.

**2** To make the crust, combine the flour and powdered sugar in a medium bowl. Cut in the vegetable shortening until the mix-

ture resembles coarse crumbs. Press the mixture evenly into the prepared baking pan.

**3** Bake for 20 minutes.

**4** Meanwhile make the topping: In a large bowl, beat the eggs until thick and light-colored. Beat in the sugar. Beat in the lemon juice. Beat in the flour and baking powder.

**5** Pour the topping over the hot crust. Bake for 20 to 25 minutes longer, until lightly colored on top and firm to the touch. Cool in the pan on a wire rack before cutting into large or small bars.

# LEMON BARS III

Bar Cookies

YIELD: *1 to 3 dozen*
TOTAL TIME: *55 minutes*

---

**CRUST**
1 cup all-purpose flour
1 cup soy flour
¼ cup granulated sugar
¼ cup rolled oats
¼ cup walnuts, ground fine
½ cup vegetable shortening

**TOPPING**
4 large eggs
2 cups granulated sugar
¼ cup frozen lemon juice concentrate, thawed
1 tablespoon grated lemon zest
¼ cup all-purpose flour
½ teaspoon baking powder

**1** Preheat the oven to 350 degrees. Lightly grease a 13 by 9-inch baking pan.

**2** To make the crust, combine the two flours, the sugar, oats, and

walnuts in a large bowl. Cut in the vegetable shortening until the mixture resembles coarse crumbs. Press the mixture evenly into the prepared baking pan.

**3** Bake for 30 minutes.

**4** Meanwhile, make the topping: In a large bowl, beat the eggs and sugar until thick and light-colored. Beat in the lemon juice and zest. Beat in the flour and baking powder.

**5** Pour over the hot crust.

**6** Bake for 15 to 18 minutes longer, until lightly colored on top and firm to the touch. Cool in the pan on a wire rack before cutting into large or small bars.

# LEMON BARS IV

Bar Cookies

YIELD: *1 to 3 dozen*
TOTAL TIME: *55 minutes*

L

## LEMON CARAWAY COOKIES

Rolled Cookies

YIELD: *2 to 4 dozen*
TOTAL TIME: *35 minutes*
CHILLING TIME: *4 hours*

3 cups all-purpose flour
½ teaspoon baking soda
½ teaspoon salt
½ cup vegetable shortening
1 cup granulated sugar
1 large egg
2 tablespoons fresh lemon juice
2 tablespoons caraway seeds

1  Combine the flour, baking soda, and salt.

2  In a large bowl, cream the vegetable shortening and sugar. Beat in the egg. Beat in the lemon juice. Gradually blend in the dry ingredients. Stir in the caraway seeds. Cover and chill for 4 hours.

3  Preheat the oven to 400 degrees.

4  On a floured surface, roll out the dough to a thickness of ¼ inch. Using a 1½-inch round cookie cutter, cut out cookies and place 1 inch apart on ungreased baking sheets.

5  Bake for 10 to 12 minutes, until lightly colored. Transfer to wire racks to cool.

## LEMON-COCONUT SOUR BARS

Bar Cookies

YIELD: *1 to 3 dozen*
TOTAL TIME: *45 minutes*

CRUST
¾ cup all-purpose flour
⅛ teaspoon salt
½ cup vegetable shortening

FILLING
2 large eggs
1 cup packed light brown sugar
1 teaspoon grated lemon zest
½ teaspoon vanilla extract
¾ cup flaked coconut
½ cup walnuts, ground fine

GLAZE
¾ cup powdered sugar
2 tablespoons fresh lemon juice

1  Preheat the oven to 350 degrees. Lightly grease a 13 by 9-inch baking pan.

2  To make the crust, combine the flour and salt in a medium bowl. Cut in the vegetable shortening until the mixture resembles coarse crumbs. Press the mixture evenly into the prepared baking pan.

3  Bake for 10 minutes.

4  Meanwhile, make the filling: In a large bowl, beat the eggs until thick and light-colored. Beat in the brown sugar and lemon zest. Beat in the vanilla extract. Stir in the coconut and walnuts.

5  Pour the filling over the hot crust. Bake for 18 to 20 minutes longer, until firm to the touch.

6  Meanwhile, make the glaze: Combine the powdered sugar and lemon juice in a small bowl and stir until smooth.

7  Spread the glaze over the top of the warm cookies. Cool in the pan on a wire rack before cutting into large or small bars.

2¾ cups all-purpose flour
½ cup yellow cornmeal
1 teaspoon baking soda
⅛ teaspoon salt
1 tablespoon grated lemon zest
1 cup packed light brown sugar
2 tablespoons canola oil
¾ cup unsweetened applesauce
1 tablespoon fresh lemon juice
1 large egg white

**GLAZE**
¾ cup powdered sugar
2 tablespoons fresh lemon juice

**1** Combine the flour, cornmeal, baking soda, salt, and lemon zest.

**2** In a large bowl, beat the brown sugar and oil. Beat in the applesauce and lemon juice. Fold the egg white into the applesauce mixture. Gradually blend in the dry ingredients: do not overmix. Cover and chill for at least 2 hours.

**3** In a small bowl, beat the egg white stiff but not dry.

**4** Preheat the oven to 350 degrees. Line 2 baking sheets with parchment paper.

**5** Drop the dough by spoonfuls 1½ inches apart on the prepared baking sheets.

**6** Bake for 8 to 10 minutes, until lightly colored. Transfer to wire racks to cool.

**7** Meanwhile, make the glaze: Combine the powdered sugar and lemon juice in a small bowl and stir until smooth.

**8** Drizzle the white glaze over the top of the cooled cookies.

# LEMON-CORNMEAL COOKIES

Drop Cookies

YIELD: *3 to 4 dozen*
TOTAL TIME: *30 minutes*
CHILLING TIME: *2 hours*

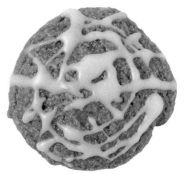

---

**CRUST**
2 cups all-purpose flour
¼ cup granulated sugar
¾ cup vegetable shortening
2 large egg yolks

**FILLING**
1½ cups granola cereal
½ cup almonds, chopped fine
½ cup granulated sugar
1 teaspoon ground cinnamon
3 tablespoons fresh lemon juice
6 medium apples, peeled, cored, and sliced

**GLAZE**
¾ cup powdered sugar
2 tablespoons fresh lemon juice

**1** Preheat the oven to 350 degrees. Lightly grease a 15 by 10-inch baking pan.

**2** To make the crust, combine the flour and sugar in a large bowl. Cut in the vegetable shortening until the mixture resembles coarse crumbs. Work in the egg yolks one at a time until a smooth dough forms. Press the dough evenly into the prepared baking pan.

**3** Combine the granola, almonds, sugar, and cinnamon. Stir in the lemon juice.

**4** Layer the sliced apples on top of the crust. Sprinkle the granola mixture over the apples.

**5** Bake for 55 to 60 minutes, until the top is lightly colored and the apples are soft.

**6** Meanwhile, make the glaze: Combine the powdered sugar and lemon juice in a small bowl and stir until smooth.

**7** Drizzle the glaze over the top of the warm bars. Cool in the pan on a wire rack before cutting into large or small bars.

# LEMON-GLAZED APPLE SQUARES

Bar Cookies

YIELD: *2 to 3 dozen*
TOTAL TIME: *70 minutes*

# LEMON-RAISIN COOKIES

Drop Cookies

YIELD: *4 to 5 dozen*
TOTAL TIME: *30 minutes*

1 cup all-purpose flour
1 teaspoon baking soda
½ teaspoon salt
1 cup vegetable shortening
1½ cups granulated sugar
2 large eggs
¼ cup fresh lemon juice
2 teaspoons lemon extract
1 cup rolled oats
1 cup raisins

**1** Preheat the oven to 350 degrees. Lightly grease 2 baking sheets.

**2** Combine the flour, baking soda, and salt.

**3** In a large bowl, cream the vegetable shortening and sugar. Beat in the eggs. Beat in the lemon juice and lemon extract. Gradually blend in the dry ingredients. Fold in the oats and raisins.

**4** Drop the dough by spoonfuls 1½ inches apart onto the prepared baking sheets.

**5** Bake for 12 to 15 minutes, until lightly colored. Transfer to wire racks to cool.

**Baking notes:** Chopped nuts can be added to this dough. If you substitute undiluted frozen lemon-juice concentrate for the fresh lemon juice, the cookies will have a more tart flavor.

# LEMON ROUNDS

Formed Cookies

YIELD: *4 to 5 dozen*
TOTAL TIME: *40 minutes*

3½ cups all-purpose flour
2¼ teaspoons baking powder
½ teaspoon salt
1 cup vegetable shortening
1⅓ cups granulated sugar
2 large eggs
1 tablespoon fresh lemon juice
2 teaspoons grated lemon zest

**GLAZE**
6 tablespoons powdered sugar
¼ cup water
2 drops yellow food coloring

**1** Preheat the oven to 400 degrees.

**2** Combine the flour, baking powder, and salt.

**3** In a large bowl, cream the vegetable shortening and sugar. Beat in the eggs. Beat in the lemon juice and lemon zest. Gradually blend in the dry ingredients.

**4** Pinch off walnut-sized pieces of dough and roll into balls. Place 2½ inches apart on ungreased baking sheets. Flatten each ball to a thickness of ¼ inch with the bottom of a glass dipped in flour.

**5** To make the glaze, combine the powdered sugar, water, and food coloring in a small bowl, and stir until smooth. Brush over the cookies.

**6** Bake for 6 to 8 minutes, until lightly colored. Transfer to wire racks to cool.

# LEMON SUGAR ROUNDS

Rolled Cookies

YIELD: *1 to 2 dozen*
TOTAL TIME: *30 minutes*
CHILLING TIME: *4 hours*

2¼ cups all-purpose flour
2 teaspoons baking powder
1 teaspoon salt
¾ cup vegetable shortening
1 cup granulated sugar
2 large eggs
1 tablespoon lemon extract
1 tablespoon grated lemon zest
Granulated sugar for sprinkling

**1** Combine the flour, baking powder, and salt.

**2** In a large bowl, cream the vegetable shortening and sugar. Beat in the eggs. Beat in the lemon extract and zest. Gradually blend in the dry ingredients.

**3** Divide the dough in half. Form each half into a log 2 inches in diameter. Wrap in waxed paper and chill for 4 hours.

**4** Preheat the oven to 400 degrees. Lightly grease 2 baking sheets.

**5** On a floured surface, roll out the dough to a thickness of ¼ inch. Using a 3-inch round cookie cutter, cut into rounds and place 1 inch apart on the prepared baking sheets. Sprinkle with granulated sugar.

**6** Bake for 6 to 8 minutes, until lightly colored. Transfer to wire racks to cool.

**Baking notes.** Substitute orange extract and zest for the lemon.

1 cup vegetable shortening
1 cup granulated sugar
4 large egg yolks
2 tablespoons fresh lemon juice
1 tablespoon lemon extract
3 cups all-purpose flour
Orange- or yellow-colored sugar
   crystals for sprinkling

**1** In a large bowl, cream the vegetable shortening and sugar. Beat in the egg yolks. Beat in the lemon juice and lemon extract. Gradually blend in the flour. Cover and chill for 4 hours.

**2** Preheat the oven to 350 degrees. Lightly grease 2 baking sheets.

**3** On a floured surface, roll out the dough to a thickness of ⅛ inch. Using a 1½-inch round cookie cutter, cut into rounds and place 1 inch apart on the prepared baking sheets. Sprinkle with colored sugar crystals.

**4** Bake for 10 to 12 minutes, until lightly colored. Transfer to wire racks to cool.

# LEMON WAFERS

Rolled Cookies

YIELD: *4 to 5 dozen*
TOTAL TIME: *35 minutes*
CHILLING TIME: *4 hours*

---

2 cups all-purpose flour
1 teaspoon salt
1 cup vegetable shortening
1 cup granulated sugar
1 cup packed light brown sugar
2 large eggs
1 teaspoon vanilla extract
1 teaspoon baking soda
1 tablespoon warm water
2 cups rolled oats
1 cup shredded coconut
1 cup gumdrops, chopped
Powdered sugar for rolling

**1** Preheat the oven to 350 degrees. Lightly grease 2 baking sheets.

**2** Combine the flour and salt.

**3** In a large bowl, cream the vegetable shortening and sugars. Beat in the eggs one at a time. Beat in the vanilla extract.

**4** Dissolve the baking soda in the warm water and add the egg mixture, beating until smooth.

Gradually blend in the dry ingredients. Fold in the oats, coconut, and gumdrops.

**5** Pinch off walnut-sized pieces of dough and roll into small balls. Place 1½ inches apart on the prepared baking sheets.

**6** Bake for 10 to 12 minutes, until lightly colored. Transfer to wire racks to cool.

**7** Roll the cooled cookies in powdered sugar.

# LITTLE JEWEL COOKIES

Formed Cookies

YIELD: *2 to 3 dozen*
TOTAL TIME: *30 minutes*

# LITHUANIAN PRESKUCHIAI

Rolled Cookies

YIELD: *4 to 5 dozen*
TOTAL TIME: *30 minutes*

2½ cups whole wheat flour
1½ tablespoons brewer's yeast
1 tablespoon honey
1 teaspoon salt
¼ cup warm water
¾ cup nonfat dry milk

**1** Preheat the oven to 400 degrees. Lightly grease 2 baking sheets.

**2** Combine the flour and yeast.

**3** In a saucepan, stir in the honey, salt, water, and milk. Gradually blend in the dry ingredients.

**4** Form the dough into a rectangle ½ inch thick. Cut lengthwise into ½-inch-wide strips, then cut the strips into ½-inch cubes. Place 1½ inches apart on the prepared baking sheets.

**5** Bake for 8 to 10 minutes, until lightly colored. Transfer to wire racks to cool.

# LIZZIES

Drop Cookies

YIELD: *3 to 4 dozen*
TOTAL TIME: *30 minutes.*

1½ cups all-purpose flour
1½ teaspoons baking soda
1 teaspoon ground cinnamon
¼ teaspoon ground nutmeg
¼ teaspoon ground cloves
¼ cup vegetable shortening
½ cup packed light brown sugar
2 large eggs
⅓ cup bourbon
1½ tablespoons milk
1½ cups raisins
1 cup walnuts, chopped fine
1½ cup glacé cherries, chopped (see Baking notes)
½ cup glacé citron, chopped (see Baking notes)

**1** Preheat the oven to 350 degrees.

**2** Combine the flour, baking soda, and spices.

**3** In a large bowl, cream the vegetable shortening and brown sugar. Beat in the eggs. Beat in the bourbon. Beat in the milk.

Gradually blend in the dry ingredients. Fold in the raisins, walnuts, and glacé fruits.

**4** Drop the dough by spoonfuls 1½ inches apart onto ungreased baking sheets.

**5** Bake for 10 to 12 minutes, until lightly colored. Transfer to wire racks to cool.

**Baking notes:** Candied fruits can be substituted for the glacé citron and cherries.

FILLING
2 large egg whites
¼ cup granulated sugar
½ teaspoon ground cinnamon
1 cup almonds, ground fine
1 teaspoon grated lemon zest
2 cups all-purpose flour
¼ teaspoon salt
¾ cup vegetable shortening
2 tablespoons granulated sugar
4 large egg yolks

**1** Preheat the oven to 350 degrees.

**2** To make the filling, in a medium bowl, beat the egg whites until stiff but not dry. Beat in the sugar and cinnamon. Fold in the almonds and lemon zest. Set aside.

**3** Combine the flour and salt.

**4** In a large bowl, cream the vegetable shortening and sugar. Beat in the egg yolks. Gradually blend in the dry ingredients.

**5** On a floured surface, roll out the dough to a thickness of ¼ inch. Using a sharp knife, cut into 3-inch squares. Place 1 inch apart on ungreased baking sheets. Drop a teaspoonful of the filling into the center of each square and fold the corners into the center like an envelope. Lightly seal the seams.

**6** Bake for 18 to 20 minutes, until lightly colored. Transfer to wire racks to cool.

# LOVE LETTERS
Formed Cookies

YIELD: *4 to 5 dozen*
TOTAL TIME: *40 minutes*

---

1¼ cups all-purpose flour
½ teaspoon baking powder
¼ teaspoon ground nutmeg
2 cups packed light brown sugar
⅓ cup canola oil
2 large egg whites
½ cup skim milk
1 teaspoon almond extract
2 cups rolled oats
1 cup raisins

**1** Preheat the oven to 375 degrees. Lightly grease 2 baking sheets.

**2** Combine the flour, baking powder, and nutmeg.

**3** In a large bowl, beat the brown sugar and oil together. Beat in the egg whites. Beat in the milk and

almond extract. Gradually blend in the dry ingredients. Stir in the oats and raisins.

**4** Drop the dough by spoonfuls 1½ inches apart onto the prepared baking sheets.

**5** Bake for 12 to 15 minutes, until lightly colored. Transfer to wire racks to cool.

# LOW-CALORIE COOKIES
Drop Cookies

YIELD: *2 to 3 dozen*
TOTAL TIME: *25 minutes*

---

2 cups all-purpose flour
½ teaspoon baking soda
1 teaspoon ground cinnamon
1 teaspoon ground ginger
½ teaspoon salt
⅔ cup vegetable shortening
½ cup granulated sugar
1 large egg
½ cup molasses

**1** Combine the flour, baking soda, cinnamon, ginger, and salt.

**2** In a large bowl, cream the vegetable shortening and sugar. Beat in the egg. Beat in the molasses. Gradually blend in the dry ingredients. Cover and chill for 4 hours.

**3** Preheat the oven to 350 degrees.

**4** On a floured surface, roll out the dough to a thickness of ¼ inch. Using a 2½-inch round cookie cutter, cut out rounds and place 1 inch apart on ungreased baking sheets.

**5** Bake for 10 to 12 minutes, until the tops look dry and the edges are lightly colored. Transfer to wire racks to cool.

# LUMBERJACKS
Rolled Cookies

YIELD: *4 to 5 dozen*
TOTAL TIME: *30 minutes*
CHILLING TIME: *4 hours*

# MACADAMIA NUT BARS

Bar Cookies

YIELD: *1 to 3 dozen*
TOTAL TIME: *55 minutes*

**CRUST**
**2 cups all-purpose flour**
**2 cups packed light brown sugar**
**1 cup vegetable shortening**

**FILLING**
**1 large egg**
**1 teaspoon baking soda**
**1 cup sour cream**
**1 cup macadamia nuts, chopped**

**1** Preheat the oven to 350 degrees. Lightly grease a 13 by 9-inch baking pan.

**2** To make the crust, combine the flour and brown sugar in a large bowl. Cut in the vegetable shortening until the mixture resembles coarse crumbs. Press evenly into the prepared baking pan.

**3** To prepare the filling, in a medium bowl, beat the egg until thick and light-colored. Beat in the baking soda. Beat in the sour cream. Pour the filling over the crust. Sprinkle the chopped macadamia nuts over the top.

**4** Bake for 45 to 50 minutes, or until firm to the touch. Cool in the pan on a wire rack before cutting into large or small bars.

# MACADAMIA NUT COOKIES

Drop Cookies

YIELD: *2 to 3 dozen*
TOTAL TIME: *35 minutes*
CHILLING TIME: *4 hours*

**3 cups all-purpose flour**
**2 teaspoons baking soda**
**1 teaspoon salt**
**1½ cups vegetable shortening**
**1½ cups packed light brown sugar**
**⅔ cup granulated sugar**
**4 large eggs**
**1 teaspoon vanilla extract**
**1 teaspoon fresh lemon juice**
**2 cups macadamia nuts, chopped**
**½ cup rolled oats**

**1** Combine the flour, baking soda, and salt.

**2** In a large bowl, cream the vegetable shortening and two sugars. Beat in the eggs one at a time, beating well after each addition. Beat in the vanilla

extract and lemon juice. Gradually blend in the dry ingredients. Fold in the macadamia nuts and oats. Cover and chill for 4 hours.

**3** Preheat the oven to 325 degrees. Lightly grease 2 baking sheets.

**4** Drop the dough by spoonfuls 1½ inches apart onto the prepared baking sheets.

**5** Bake for 15 to 18 minutes, until lightly colored. Transfer to wire racks to cool.

# MACAROON NUT WAFERS

Drop Cookies

YIELD: *1 to 2 dozen*
TOTAL TIME: *35 minutes.*

**2 large egg whites**
**¼ teaspoon salt**
**½ cup powdered sugar**
**1 teaspoon Amaretto**
**1 cup almonds, ground fine**

**1** Preheat the oven to 350 degrees. Line 2 baking sheets with parchment paper.

**2** In a medium bowl, beat the egg whites with the salt until they form stiff peaks. Fold in the powdered sugar. Fold in the Amaretto. Fold in the almonds.

**3** Drop the dough by spoonfuls 1½ inches apart onto the prepared baking sheets.

**4** Bake for 15 to 20 minutes, until lightly colored. Cool slightly on the pans, then transfer to wire racks to cool completely.

2 large egg whites
1 tablespoon cornstarch
½ cup granulated sugar
1 teaspoon vanilla extract
1 cup flaked coconut

**1** Preheat the oven to 300 degrees. Line 2 baking sheets with parchment paper.

**2** In a medium bowl, beat the egg whites until stiff but not dry. Fold in the cornstarch. Transfer to the top of a double boiler and set over low heat. Stir in the sugar and cook for about 3 to 4 minutes, until the edges of the mixture begin to pull away from the pan. Remove from the heat and stir in the vanilla extract. Stir in the coconut.

**3** Drop the dough by spoonfuls 1½ inches apart onto the prepared baking sheets.

**4** Bake for 20 to 25 minutes, until golden brown and firm to the touch. Cool on the pans on wire racks.

**Baking notes:** This dough can be piped out using a cookie press or pastry bag, shaped into mounds or little finger logs.

# MACAROONS I

Drop Cookies

YIELD: *2 to 3 dozen*
TOTAL TIME: *40 minutes*

---

4 large egg whites
¼ teaspoon salt
1½ cups granulated sugar
1 teaspoon almond extract
1 cup shredded coconut
½ cup almonds, ground fine
3 cups cornflakes

**1** Preheat the oven to 350 degrees. Line 2 baking sheets with parchment paper.

**2** In a large bowl, beat the egg whites with the salt until they hold stiff peaks. Fold in the sugar. Fold in the almond extract. Fold in the coconut and almonds. Fold in the cornflakes.

**3** Drop the dough by spoonfuls 1½ inches apart onto the prepared baking sheets.

**4** Bake for 12 to 15 minutes, until lightly colored. Cool slightly on the pans on wire racks before removing from the paper.

# MACAROONS II

Drop Cookies

YIELD: *3 to 4 dozen*
TOTAL TIME: *35 minutes*

---

1½ cups graham cracker crumbs
½ cup butter, melted
1 cup flaked coconut
1 cup (6 ounces) butterscotch chips
1 cup pecans, chopped

**1** Preheat the oven to 350 degrees. Lightly grease a 13 by 9-inch baking pan.

**2** Put the graham cracker crumbs in a large bowl and stir in the butter. Press the mixture into the prepared baking pan.

**3** Combine the coconut, butterscotch chips, and pecans in a medium bowl and toss to mix. Spread this mixture evenly over the graham cracker mixture.

**4** Bake for 25 to 30 minutes, until lightly colored on top. Cool in the pan on a wire rack before cutting into large or small bars.

# MAGIC BARS

Bar Cookies

YIELD: *1 to 3 dozen*
TOTAL TIME: *45 minutes*

**M**

# Magic Moments

Bar Cookies

YIELD: *1 to 3 dozen*
TOTAL TIME: *45 minutes*

½ cup vegetable shortening, melted
1 cup cookie crumbs
1 cup walnuts, chopped
1 cup flaked coconut
6 ounces chocolate chips
One 14-ounce can sweetened condensed milk

**1** Preheat the oven to 350 degrees. Lightly grease a 9-inch square baking pan.

**2** Melt the vegetable shortening in a small saucepan. Remove from the heat.

**3** In a large bowl, combine the cookie crumbs, walnuts, coconut, and chocolate chips. Stir in the melted shortening. Stir in the condensed milk. Spread the mixture evenly in the prepared baking pan.

**4** Bake for 30 to 35 minutes, until lightly colored on top. Cool in the pan on a wire rack before cutting into large or small bars.

**Baking notes:** There are many variations on this recipe; some add raisins, wheat germ, and other ingredients.

# Mandelbrot

Formed Cookies

YIELD: *3 to 4 dozen*
TOTAL TIME: *50 minutes*

3 cups all-purpose flour
1 teaspoon baking powder
¼ teaspoon salt
½ cup honey, warmed
6 tablespoons butter, at room temperature
3 large eggs
½ teaspoon grated lemon zest
½ cup pistachio nuts, chopped
1 teaspoon anise seeds, crushed

**1** Preheat the oven to 350 degrees.

**2** Combine the flour, baking powder, and salt.

**3** In a large bowl, beat the honey and butter together. Beat in the eggs one at a time, beating well after each addition. Beat in the lemon zest. Gradually blend in the dry ingredients. Stir in the pistachio nuts and anise seeds.

**4** Divide the dough in half. Shape each half into a loaf 12 inches long, 3 inches wide, and

1½–2 inches high. Place the logs on an ungreased baking sheet, leaving 1½ inches between them.

**5** Bake for 25 to 30 minutes, until lightly colored and firm to the touch.

**6** Transfer the loaves to a cutting board and cut into ½-inch-thick slices. Place 1 inch apart on the baking sheets and bake for 5 to 7 minutes longer, or until the slices are lightly toasted. Transfer to wire racks to cool.

2 cups all-purpose flour
½ cup almonds, ground fine
⅔ cup vegetable shortening
1 cup granulated sugar
2 large egg yolks, beaten
Vegetable oil for deep-frying

**1** Combine the flour and almonds.

**2** In a large bowl, cream the vegetable shortening and sugar. Beat in the egg yolks. Gradually blend in the dry ingredients. If the dough seems too stiff, add a little water a ½ teaspoon at a time.

**3** In a deep-fryer or deep heavy-pot, heat the oil to 375 degrees.

**4** Pinch off walnut-sized pieces of dough and roll into balls. Fry the balls in the hot oil until golden brown. Drain on paper towels on wire racks.

**Baking notes:** Be sure the oil is hot enough, or the cookies will absorb some oil. After the balls are cool, they can be sprinkled with powdered sugar or be dipped in melted chocolate.

# MANDEL MUTZE

Formed Cookies

YIELD: *5 to 6 dozen*
TOTAL TIME: *35 minutes*

---

2 cups all-purpose flour
⅓ cup unsweetened cocoa powder
1 teaspoon baking powder
½ teaspoon salt
1 cup vegetable shortening
¾ cup packed dark brown sugar
½ cup granulated sugar
1 large egg
⅓ cup water
2 tablespoons butter flavoring
2 tablespoons white crème de menthe
1 tablespoon coffee liqueur
1⅓ cups (8 ounces) white chocolate chips

**1** Preheat the oven to 350 degrees. Lightly grease 2 baking sheets

**2** Combine the flour, cocoa, baking powder, and salt.

**3** In a large bowl, cream the vegetable shortening and two sugars. Beat in the egg. Beat in the water, butter flavoring, crème de menthe, and coffee liqueur. Gradually blend in the dry ingredients. Fold in the chocolate chips.

**4** Drop the dough by spoonfuls 1½ inches apart onto the prepared baking sheets.

**5** Bake for 12 to 15 minutes, until the tops look dry. Transfer to wire racks to cool.

# MANU'S BEST

Drop Cookies

YIELD: *4 to 5 dozen*
TOTAL TIME: *35 minutes*

---

2½ cups all-purpose flour
2½ teaspoons baking powder
1 teaspoon salt
½ cup butter, at room temperature
1 cup maple sugar
2 large eggs
1 tablespoon milk
½ teaspoon lemon extract
Sifted light brown sugar for sprinkling

**1** Combine the flour, baking powder, and salt.

**2** In a large bowl, cream the butter and maple sugar. Beat in the eggs. Beat in the milk and lemon extract. Gradually blend in the dry ingredients. Cover and chill for 1 hour

**3** Preheat the oven to 350 degrees. Lightly grease 2 baking sheets.

**4** On a floured surface, roll out the dough to a thickness of ¼ inch. Using a 2-inch round cookie cutter, cut out the cookies and place on the prepared baking sheets. Dust with sifted light brown sugar.

**5** Bake for 12 to 15 minutes, until lightly colored. Transfer to wire racks to cool.

# MAPLE SUGAR COOKIES

Rolled Cookies

YIELD: *3 to 4 dozen*
TOTAL TIME: *35 minutes*
CHILLING TIME: *1 hour*

# MARBLED CREAM CHEESE BROWNIES

Bar Cookies

YIELD: *1 to 3 dozen*
TOTAL TIME: *45 minutes*

4 ounces cream cheese, at room temperature
5 tablespoons vegetable shortening
1 cup granulated sugar
1 tablespoon cornstarch
3 large eggs
1½ teaspoons vanilla extract
½ teaspoon fresh lemon juice
½ cup all-purpose flour
½ teaspoon baking powder
½ teaspoon salt
⅔ cup semisweet chocolate chips

**1** Preheat the oven to 350 degrees. Lightly grease a 9-inch square baking pan.

**2** In a medium bowl, combine the cream cheese, 2 tablespoons of the vegetable shortening, ¼ cup of the sugar, and the cornstarch and beat until smooth. Beat in 1 of the eggs. Beat in the ½ teaspoon of the vanilla extract and lemon juice. Set aside.

**3** Combine the flour, baking powder, and salt.

**4** In the top of a double boiler, melt the chocolate and the remaining 3 tablespoons vegetable shortening, stirring until smooth. Remove from the heat and stir in the remaining 1 teaspoon vanilla extract.

**5** In a large bowl, beat the remaining 2 eggs and ¾ cup sugar. Beat in the cooled chocolate. Beat in the dry ingredients.

**6** Spread the batter evenly in the prepared baking pan. Pour the cream cheese mixture over the top and swirl a knife back and forth a few times through the mixture to marble it.

**7** Bake for 25 to 30 minutes, until a toothpick inserted in the center comes out clean. Cool in the pan on a wire rack before cutting into large or small bars.

# MASTER COOKIE MIX

Rolled Cookies

YIELD: *23 cups*
TOTAL TIME: *(see below)*

12 cups all-purpose flour
7 cups granulated sugar
2 tablespoons baking powder
1 tablespoon plus 2 teaspoons salt
4 cups vegetable shortening

**1** Combine the flour, sugar, baking powder, and salt in a large bowl. Cut in the vegetable shortening until the mixture resembles a fine cornmeal.

**2** Transfer to an airtight container and store in a cool place or freeze up to 1 year.

**GINGER COOKIES** (sample recipe)

**1** In a large bowl, beat 1 egg and ¼ cup warmed molasses. Beat in 1½ teaspoons ground ginger. Gradually blend in 4 cups Master Cookie Mix. Cover and chill for 2 hours.

**2** Preheat the oven to 350 degrees. Lightly grease 2 baking sheets.

**3** On a floured surface, roll out the dough to a thickness of ¼ inch. Using cookie cutter, cut into shapes and place 1 inch apart on the prepared baking sheets.

**4** Bake for 10 to 15 minutes, until lightly colored. Transfer to wire racks to cool.

**Baking notes:** This dough can be rolled into balls and baked as is or flattened. Or you can roll pieces of the dough into ropes and make rings, twists, or braids. Almost any spice can be used in place of the ginger. Vanilla or almond extract or almost any flavoring can be added. Nuts or raisins can be added to the dough as well.

2 cups all-purpose flour
¼ teaspoon ground cinnamon
¼ cup vegetable shortening
¼ cup butter, at room temperature
¾ cup powdered sugar
1 cup hazelnuts, chopped
Red jimmies for sprinkling

**1** Preheat the oven to 400 degrees.

**2** Combine the flour and cinnamon.

**3** In a large bowl, cream the vegetable shortening, butter, and powdered sugar. Gradually blend in the dry ingredients. Fold in the hazelnuts.

**4** On a floured surface, roll out the dough to a thickness of ¼ inch. Using a 2 inch-round cookie cutter, cut out cookies and place 1 inch apart on ungreased baking sheets. Sprinkle red jimmies over the tops.

**5** Bake for 8 to 10 minutes, until lightly colored. Transfer to wire racks to cool.

# MEASLES COOKIES

Rolled Cookies

YIELD: *2 to 3 dozen*
TOTAL TIME: *30 minutes*

---

1 cup all-purpose flour
1 teaspoon baking soda
½ cup vegetable shortening
¼ cup granulated sugar
1 large egg yolk
¼ cup honey
¼ cup granulated sugar for rolling

**1** Preheat the oven to 350 degrees.

**2** Combine the flour and baking soda.

**3** In a large bowl, cream the vegetable shortening and sugar. Beat in the egg yolk. Beat in the honey. Gradually blend in the dry ingredients.

**4** Pinch off walnut-sized pieces of dough and roll into balls. Roll the balls in granulated sugar and place 1½ inches apart on ungreased baking sheets.

**5** Bake for 10 to 12 minutes, until lightly colored. Transfer to wire racks to cool.

# MEDENI KURABII

Formed Cookies

YIELD: *2 to 4 dozen*
TOTAL TIME: *30 minutes*

---

**CRUST**
1 cup vegetable shortening
⅓ cup granulated sugar
5 large egg yolks
1 teaspoon rum
2½ cups all-purpose flour

**TOPPING**
5 large egg whites
1 cup sugar
3 cups pecans, chopped fine
2 tablespoon Amaretto
About ½ cup black currant jam

**1** Preheat the oven to 350 degrees. Lightly grease a 15 by 10-inch baking pan.

**2** To make the crust, cream the vegetable shortening and sugar. Beat in the egg yolks one at a time, beating thoroughly after

each addition. Beat in the rum. Gradually blend in the flour.

**3** Press the dough evenly into the prepared baking pan. Spread the black currant jam over the crust.

**4** To make the topping, beat the egg whites in a large bowl until they form soft peaks. Beat in the sugar and beat until the whites hold stiff peaks. Fold in the chopped pecans. Fold in the Amaretto. Carefully spread the topping over the jam.

**5** Bake for 35 to 40 minutes, until firm to the touch. Cool in the pan on a wire rack before cutting into large or small bars.

# MERINGUE PECAN BARS

Bar Cookies

YIELD: *4 to 5 dozen*
TOTAL TIME: *50 minutes*

# Meringue-Topped Brownies

Bar Cookies

YIELD: *1 to 3 dozen*
TOTAL TIME: *45 minutes*

2 cups all-purpose flour
1 teaspoon baking powder
¼ teaspoon baking soda
¼ teaspoon salt
¼ cup vegetable shortening
¼ cup butter, at room temperature
½ cup granulated sugar
½ cup packed light brown sugar
2 large egg yolks
1 tablespoon strong brewed coffee
1½ teaspoons crème de cacao
1½ cups (9 ounces) semisweet
   chocolate chips

TOPPING
2 large egg whites
1 cup granulated sugar

1  Preheat the oven to 375 degrees. Lightly grease a 13 by 9-inch baking pan.

2  Combine the flour, baking powder, baking soda, and salt.

3  In a large bowl, cream the vegetable shortening, butter, and two sugars. Beat in the egg yolks. Beat in the coffee and crème de cacao. Gradually blend in the dry ingredients.

4  Spread the batter evenly in the prepared baking pan. Sprinkle the chocolate chips over the top.

5  To make the topping, in a bowl, beat the egg whites until foamy. Gradually beat in the sugar and beat until the whites form stiff peaks. Spread the topping over the chocolate chips.

6  Bake for 20 to 25 minutes, until lightly colored and firm to the touch. Cool in the pan on a wire rack before cutting into large or small bars.

# Mexican Wedding Cakes I

Formed Cookies

YIELD: *3 dozen*
TOTAL TIME: *45 minutes*

¾ cup vegetable shortening
¼ cup granulated sugar
1 teaspoon vanilla extract
2 cups all-purpose flour
½ cup walnuts, chopped
Powdered sugar for rolling

1  Preheat the oven to 200 degrees. Lightly grease 2 baking sheets.

2  In a large bowl, cream the shortening and sugar together. Beat in the vanilla extract. Gradually blend in the flour. Fold in the walnuts.

3  Pinch off walnut-sized pieces of dough and roll into balls. Place 1 inch apart on the prepared baking sheets.

4  Bake for 25 to 35 minutes, or until golden. Roll in powdered sugar and transfer to wire racks to cool.

1 cup vegetable shortening
6 tablespoons powdered sugar
1 teaspoon tequila
2 cups all-purpose flour
1 cup pecans, chopped
Powdered sugar for rolling

**1** Preheat the oven to 350 degrees.

**2** In a large bowl, cream the vegetable shortening and powdered sugar. Beat in the tequila. Gradually blend in the flour. Fold in the pecans.

**3** Pinch off walnut-sized pieces of dough and roll into balls. Place 1 inch apart on ungreased baking sheets.

**4** Bake for 12 to 15 minutes, or until golden brown. Roll in powdered sugar and transfer to wire racks to cool.

# MEXICAN WEDDING CAKES II

Formed Cookies

YIELD: *4 to 5 dozen*
TOTAL TIME: *30 minutes*

---

⅔ cup all-purpose flour
¼ teaspoon baking powder
¼ teaspoon salt
1 cup (6 ounces) semisweet chocolate chips
¼ cup vegetable shortening
¾ cup granulated sugar
2 large eggs
½ teaspoon vanilla extract
½ cup walnuts, chopped

**1** Lightly grease an 8-inch square microwave-proof baking pan.

**2** Combine the flour, baking powder, and salt.

**3** In the top of a double boiler, melt the chocolate chips and vegetable, stirring until smooth. Remove from the heat and beat in the sugar. Beat in the eggs.

Beat in the vanilla extract. Gradually blend in the dry ingredients. Stir in the walnuts. Spread the batter evenly in the prepared baking pan.

**4** Cook on high for 7 minutes, stopping to turn the pan a quarter-turn every 2 minutes until the center is set. Cool in the pan on a wire rack before cutting into large or small bars.

# MICROWAVE FUDGE BROWNIES

Bar Cookies
(Microwave Recipe)

YIELD: *1 to 2 dozen*
TOTAL TIME: *20 minutes*

---

2¾ cups all-purpose flour
⅛ teaspoon salt
¾ cup vegetable shortening
¾ cup granulated sugar
1 large egg
1 large egg yolk
½ teaspoon fresh lemon juice
½ teaspoon grated lemon zest
1 large egg yolk, beaten

**1** Combine the flour and salt.

**2** In a large bowl, cream the vegetable shortening and sugar. Beat in the egg and egg yolk. Beat in the lemon juice and zest. Gradually blend in the dry ingredients. Cover and chill for 1 hour.

**3** Preheat the oven to 375 degrees. Lightly grease 2 baking sheets.

**4** On a floured surface, roll out the dough to a thickness of ¼ inch. Using cookie cutters, cut into shapes and place 1 inch apart on the prepared baking sheets. Brush the beaten egg yolk over the top of the cookies.

**5** Bake for 10 to 12 minutes, until lightly colored. Transfer to wire racks to cool.

**Baking notes:** Traditionally these Christmas cookies are cut into the shapes of reindeer and Christmas trees.

# MILAENDERLI

Rolled Cookies

YIELD: *3 to 4 dozen*
TOTAL TIME: *30 minutes*
CHILLING TIME: *1 hour*

## MINCEMEAT COOKIE BARS

Bar Cookies

YIELD: *2 to 3 dozen*
TOTAL TIME: *35 minutes*

1½ cups all-purpose flour
1¾ cups rolled oats
2 teaspoons baking powder
¼ teaspoon salt
½ cup butter, at room temperature
1 cup packed light brown sugar
1 teaspoon vanilla extract
1 cup prepared mincemeat

**1** Preheat the oven to 325 degrees. Lightly grease a 13 by 9-inch baking pan.

**2** Combine the flour, oats, baking powder, and salt.

**3** In a large bowl, cream the butter and brown sugar. Beat in the vanilla extract. Gradually blend in the dry ingredients.

**4** Spread half of the dough evenly in the bottom of the prepared baking pan. Spread the mincemeat over the top, and spread the remaining dough over the mincemeat. Press down lightly.

**5** Bake for 20 to 25 minutes, until a toothpick inserted in the center comes out clean. Cool slightly, then cut into large or small bars and transfer to wire racks to cool.

## MINCEMEAT COOKIES

Drop Cookies

YIELD: *3 to 4 dozen*
TOTAL TIME: *35 minutes*

4½ cups all-purpose flour
½ teaspoon baking soda
2 cups honey, warmed
1 cup vegetable shortening
3 large eggs
1 cup prepared mincemeat

**1** Preheat the oven to 350 degrees. Lightly grease 2 baking sheets.

**2** Combine the flour and baking soda.

**3** In a large bowl, beat the honey and shortening. Beat in the eggs. Gradually blend in the dry ingredients. Stir in the mincemeat.

**4** Drop the dough by spoonfuls 1½ inches apart onto the prepared baking sheets.

**5** Bake for 12 to 15 minutes, until lightly colored. Transfer to wire racks to cool.

## MINCEMEAT COOKIE SQUARES

Bar Cookies

YIELD: *1 to 2 dozen*
TOTAL TIME: *45 minutes*

3 tablespoons vegetable shortening
1 cup granulated sugar
1 large egg
¼ cup fresh milk
2½ cups packaged biscuit mix
1½ cups prepared mincemeat

**1** Preheat the oven to 350 degrees. Lightly grease a 9-inch square baking pan.

**2** In a large bowl, cream the vegetable shortening and sugar. Beat in the egg. Beat in the milk. Gradually blend in the biscuit mix.

**3** Spread half of the dough in the prepared baking pan. Spread the mincemeat over the dough, leaving a ½-inch border all around. Spread the remaining dough over the mincemeat.

**4** Bake for 25 to 30 minutes, or until a lightly colored. Cool in the pan on a wire rack before cutting into large or small bars.

**Baking notes:** These can be frosted before they are cut into bars.

4 cups all-purpose flour
½ cup walnuts, ground
1 teaspoon baking soda
1 teaspoon ground cloves
1 teaspoon ground nutmeg
¼ teaspoon ground ginger
½ teaspoon salt
1 cup vegetable shortening
2 cups granulated sugar
3 large eggs
1 cup prepared mincemeat

**1** Preheat the oven to 375 degrees.

**2** Combine the flour, walnuts, baking soda, spices, and salt.

**3** In a large bowl, cream the vegetable shortening and sugar. Beat in the eggs. Gradually blend in the dry ingredients. Stir in the mincemeat.

**4** Drop the dough by spoonfuls 1½ inches apart onto an ungreased baking sheets.

**5** Bake for 10 to 12 minutes, until lightly colored. Transfer to wire racks to cool.

# MINCEMEAT GOODIES I

Drop Cookies

YIELD: *5 to 6 dozen*
TOTAL TIME: *30 minutes*

---

3½ cups all-purpose flour
½ cup walnuts, ground fine
1 teaspoon baking soda
1 teaspoon ground cloves
1 teaspoon ground nutmeg
¼ teaspoon salt
1 cup vegetable shortening
1½ cups granulated sugar
3 large eggs
1 cup prepared mincemeat

**1** Preheat the oven to 350 degrees. Lightly grease 2 baking sheets.

**2** Combine the flour, walnuts, baking soda, spices, and salt.

**3** In a large bowl, cream the vegetable shortening and sugar. Beat in the eggs. Gradually blend in the dry ingredients. Stir in the mincemeat.

**4** Drop the dough by spoonfuls 1½ inches apart onto the prepared baking sheets.

**5** Bake for 12 to 15 minutes, until lightly colored. Transfer to wire racks to cool.

# MINCEMEAT GOODIES II

Drop Cookies

YIELD: *4 to 6 dozen*
TOTAL TIME: *30 minutes*

# Mincemeat Squares

Rolled Cookies

YIELD: *4 to 5 dozen*
TOTAL TIME: *35 minutes*

4 cups all-purpose flour
6 tablespoons granulated sugar
Pinch of salt
6 tablespoons vegetable shortening
2 teaspoons active dry yeast
1 cup milk
2 large eggs
6 tablespoons prepared mincemeat
2 large egg yolks, beaten
½ cup almonds, ground fine
Granulated sugar for sprinkling

1  Preheat the oven to 375 degrees. Lightly grease 2 baking sheets.

2  In a large bowl, combine the flour, sugar, and salt. Cut in the vegetable shortening.

3  Put the yeast in a medium bowl. In a small saucepan, heat the milk until tepid. Pour the milk over the yeast and stir to dissolve it. Beat in the eggs.

4  Add the yeast mix to the flour mixture and work to a soft dough. Knead for 3 to 5 minutes.

5  On a floured surface roll out the dough to a thickness of ¼ inch. Using a sharp knife, cut into 2-inch squares. Place a spoonful of mincemeat in the center of half the squares.

6  Cover with the remaining squares, pinch to seal the edges. Place 1½ inches apart on the prepared baking sheets, brush with the beaten egg yolks, and sprinkle with the ground almonds.

7  Bake for 18 to 20 minutes, until golden brown. Sprinkle the tops with granulated sugar. Transfer to wire racks to cool.

# Mint Bars

Bar Cookies

YIELD: *1 to 3 dozen*
TOTAL TIME: *35 minutes*
CHILLING TIME: *2 hours*

1 cup all-purpose flour
½ teaspoon baking powder
½ cup vegetable shortening
1 cup granulated sugar
4 large eggs
2 cups chocolate syrup

TOPPING
½ cup margerine
2 cups powdered sugar
2 tablespoons fresh milk
1 teaspoon crème de menthe
3 drops green food coloring
6 ounces (1 cup) semisweet chocolate chips
½ cup butter

1  Preheat the oven to 350 degrees. Lightly grease a 13 by 9-inch baking pan.

2  Combine the flour and baking powder.

3  In a large bowl, cream the vegetable shortening and sugar. Beat in the eggs. Beat in the chocolate syrup. Gradually blend in the dry ingredients. Spread the dough evenly in the prepared baking pan.

4  Bake for 20 to 25 minutes, until the top is lightly colored. Let cool in the pan on a wire rack, then refrigerate for 1 hour or until chilled.

5  To make the topping, cream the butter and powdered sugar in a large bowl. Beat in the milk and crème de menthe. Beat in the food coloring. Spread evenly over the chilled bars. Chill for 1 hour longer.

6  In the top of a double boiler, melt the chocolate chips and butter, stirring until smooth. Carefully spread this mixture over the chilled cookies and cut into large or small bars.

½ cup vegetable shortening
3 ounces bittersweet chocolate, chopped
2 cups granulated sugar
4 large egg yolks
½ teaspoon vanilla extract
⅛ teaspoon mint extract
1 cup all-purpose flour
1 cup walnuts, chopped

**1** Preheat the oven to 325 degrees. Lightly grease a 9-inch square baking pan.

**2** In the top of a double boiler, melt the vegetable shortening and chocolate, stirring until smooth. Remove from the heat and stir in the sugar. Beat in the egg yolks. Beat in the vanilla and mint extracts. Gradually blend in the flour. Stir in the walnuts. Spread the mixture evenly in the prepared baking pan.

**3** Bake for 25 to 35 minutes, or until a toothpick inserted in the center comes out clean. Cool in the pan on a wire rack before cutting into large or small bars.

# MINT BROWNIES

Bar Cookies

YIELD: *1 to 2 dozen*
TOTAL TIME: *35 minutes*

---

3 cups all-purpose flour
1½ cups walnuts, ground
½ teaspoon baking soda
½ teaspoon salt
1 cup vegetable shortening
1 cup granulated sugar
½ cup packed light brown sugar
2 large eggs
1 teaspoon vanilla extract
14 ounces mint-chocolate wafer candies, such as After Eights or Andies, chopped

**1** Combine the flour, walnuts, baking soda, and salt.

**2** In a large bowl, cream the vegetable shortening and two sugars. Beat in the eggs. Beat in the vanilla extract. Gradually blend in the dry ingredients. Fold in the mint wafers. Cover and chill for 4 hours.

**3** Preheat the oven to 350 degrees.

**4** Drop the dough by spoonfuls 1½ inches apart onto ungreased baking sheets.

**5** Bake for 10 to 12 minutes, until lightly colored. Transfer to wire racks to cool.

**Baking notes:** For a stronger mint flavor, add 2 drops of peppermint oil. Instead of chocolate mint wafers, you can use mint-flavored chocolate chips, or grated chocolate and a teaspoon of mint extract.

# MINT CHOCOLATE COOKIES

Drop Cookies

YIELD: *3 to 4 dozen*
TOTAL TIME: *35 minutes*
CHILLING TIME: *4 hours*

---

3¼ cups all-purpose flour
½ teaspoon baking soda
Pinch of salt
1 cup granulated sugar
½ cup canola oil
1½ teaspoons fresh milk
6 to 8 drops peppermint extract

**1** Preheat the oven to 350 degrees. Lightly grease 2 baking sheets.

**2** Combine the flour, baking soda, and salt.

**3** In a large bowl, beat the sugar and oil together. Beat in the milk and peppermint extract. Gradually blend in the dry ingredients.

**4** On a floured surface, roll the dough out to a thickness of ¼ inch. Using a 1½-inch round cookie cutter, cut out cookies and place 1 inch apart on the prepared baking sheets.

**5** Bake for 10 to 12 minutes, until lightly colored. Transfer to wire racks to cool.

**Baking notes:** Be careful when using peppermint extract: One drop too much can make the cookies inedible.

# MINT COOKIES I

Rolled Cookies

YIELD: *3 to 4 dozen*
TOTAL TIME: *35 minutes*

# MINT COOKIES II

Drop Cookies

YIELD: *4 to 5 dozen*
TOTAL TIME: *30 minutes*
CHILLING TIME: *4 hours*

3 cups all-purpose flour
½ teaspoon salt
1 cup vegetable shortening
1 cup granulated sugar
1 cup packed light brown sugar
2 large eggs
2 tablespoons water
1 teaspoon vanilla extract
1 pound small chocolate mint
  candies

**1**  Combine the flour and salt.

**2**  In a large bowl, cream the vegetable shortening and two sugars. Beat in the eggs. Beat in the water and vanilla extract. Gradually blend in the dry ingredients. Cover and chill for 4 hours.

**3**  Preheat the oven to 350 degrees. Lightly grease 2 baking sheets.

**4**  Drop the dough by spoonfuls 1½ inches apart onto the prepared baking sheets. Press a chocolate mint into the center of each cookie so it is standing on its edge.

**5**  Bake for 10 to 12 minutes, until lightly colored. Transfer to wire racks to cool.

# MIRIORS

Formed Cookies

YIELD: *2 to 3 dozen*
TOTAL TIME: *30 minutes*

**MERINGUE**
4 large egg whites
½ cup granulated sugar

**FILLING**
4 large egg yolks
2 tablespoons vegetable shortening
1 teaspoon rum
½ teaspoon vanilla extract
¼ cup almonds, ground
2 tablespoons all-purpose flour
Granulated sugar for sprinkling

**1**  Preheat the oven to 350 degrees. Line 2 baking sheets with parchment paper.

**2**  To make the meringue, in a large bowl, beat the egg whites to soft peaks. Gradually beat in the sugar and beat until the whites hold stiff peaks.

**3**  Place the meringue in a cookie press or a pastry bag fitted with a medium tip and press or pipe out 1¼-inch mounds onto the prepared baking sheets, spacing them 1 inch apart.

**4**  To make the filling, in a large bowl, beat the egg yolks and vegetable shortening. Beat in the

rum and vanilla extract. Gradually blend in the almonds and flour.

**5**  Place the filling in the (clean) cookie press or pastry bag and press or pipe out small mounds of this mixture into the center of the meringues. Sprinkle with granulated sugar.

**6**  Bake for 12 to 15 minutes, until lightly colored. Cool slightly on the baking sheets, then transfer to wire racks to cool.

2 ounces semisweet chocolate, chopped
⅓ cup vegetable shortening
¾ cup all-purpose flour
½ teaspoon baking powder
¼ teaspoon salt
2 large eggs
1 cup granulated sugar
1 teaspoon vanilla extract
2½ tablespoons instant mocha coffee crystals
½ cup walnuts, chopped

1  Preheat the oven to 375 degrees. Lightly grease an 8-inch square baking pan.

2  In a double boiler, melt the chocolate and vegetable shortening, stirring until smooth. Remove from the heat.

3  Combine the flour, baking powder, and salt.

4  In a large bowl, beat the eggs until thick and light-colored. Beat in the sugar. Beat in the melted chocolate mixture and vanilla extract. Gradually blend in the dry ingredients. Stir in the coffee crystals. Spread the mixture evenly in the prepared baking pan. Sprinkle the walnuts on top.

5  Bake for 20 to 25 minutes, until a toothpick inserted into the center comes out clean. Cool in the pan on a wire rack before cutting into large or small bars.

# MOCHA-COFFEE BROWNIES

Bar Cookies

YIELD: *1 to 2 dozen*
TOTAL TIME: *35 minutes*

---

1 ounce semisweet chocolate, chopped
1 tablespoon instant coffee crystals
1 tablespoon hot water
1½ cups all-purpose flour
2 teaspoons baking powder
½ teaspoon ground cinnamon
2 tablespoons vegetable shortening
½ cup granulated sugar
1 large egg
1 teaspoon hazelnut extract

1  In a double boiler, melt the chocolate over low heat, stirring until smooth. Remove from the heat. Dissolve the coffee in the hot water and stir into the chocolate.

2  Combine the flour, baking powder, and cinnamon.

3  In a large bowl, cream the vegetable shortening and sugar. Beat in the egg. Beat in the hazelnut extract. Beat in the chocolate mixture. Gradually blend in the dry ingredients. Cover and chill in the refrigerator for 8 hours or overnight.

4  Preheat the oven to 350 degrees. Lightly grease 2 baking sheets.

5  On a floured surface roll out the dough to a thickness of ¼ inch. Using a 1½-inch round cookie cutter, cut out cookies and place 1 inch apart on the prepared baking sheets.

6  Bake for 8 to 10 minutes, until the tops look dry. Transfer to wire racks to cool.

# MOCHA TREATS

Rolled Cookies

YIELD: *3 to 4 dozen*
TOTAL TIME: *35 minutes*
CHILLING TIME: *8 hours*

# MOHN COOKIES

Rolled Cookies

YIELD: *8 to 10 dozen*
TOTAL TIME: *40 minutes*
CHILLING TIME: *6 hours*

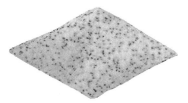

**3¼ cups all-purpose flour**
**2½ teaspoons baking powder**
**½ teaspoon salt**
**1 large egg, separated**
**½ cup butter, at room temperature**
**¾ cup granulated sugar**
**3 tablespoons orange liqueur**
**2 large egg whites**
**¼ cup poppy seeds**

**1** Combine the flour, baking powder, and salt.

**2** In a medium bowl, beat one egg white until foamy.

**3** In a large bowl, cream the butter and sugar. Beat in the egg yolk and liqueur. Beat in the egg whites. Gradually blend in the dry ingredients. Stir in the poppy seeds. Cover and chill for 6 hours.

**4** Preheat the oven to 375 degrees. Lightly grease 2 baking sheets.

**5** On a floured surface, roll out the dough to a thickness of ⅛ inch. Using a cookie cutter, cut into diamond shapes and place the diamonds 1 inch apart on the prepared baking sheets.

**6** Bake for 7 to 9 minutes, until lightly colored. Transfer to wire racks to cool.

**Baking notes:** For variation, leave the poppy seeds out of the dough; then brush the cut-out cookies with milk and sprinkle with the poppy seeds before baking.

# MOLASSES BALLS

Formed Cookies

YIELD: *3 to 4 dozen*
TOTAL TIME: *30 minutes*
CHILLING TIME: *24 hours*

**2¾ cups all-purpose flour**
**1½ teaspoons baking soda**
**1 teaspoon ground cinnamon**
**1 teaspoon ground ginger**
**¼ teaspoon ground cloves**
**¾ cup vegetable oil**
**¼ cup molasses**
**1 cup granulated sugar**
**Granulated sugar for rolling**

**1** Combine the flour, baking soda, and spices.

**2** In a large saucepan, heat the vegetable oil and molasses until warm. Remove from the heat and stir in the sugar. Gradually blend in the dry ingredients. Cover and chill for 24 hours.

**3** Preheat the oven to 350 degrees. Lightly grease 2 baking sheets.

**4** Pinch off walnut-sized pieces of dough and roll into balls. Roll the balls in the granulated sugar and place 1 inch apart on the prepared baking sheets.

**5** Bake for 10 to 14 minutes, until lightly colored. Transfer to wire racks to cool.

**Baking notes:** Any cookies containing ground ginger will be more flavorful if the dough is allowed to chill before forming the cookies. For a tip on measuring molasses, see Hint 16 in pantry.

5 cups all-purpose flour
1½ cups whole wheat flour
1 cup rice flour
2 teaspoons baking powder
2 teaspoons baking soda
2 teaspoons ground cinnamon
2 teaspoons ground ginger
½ teaspoon salt
2 cups vegetable shortening
2 cups granulated sugar
3 large eggs
2 cups molasses
1½ cups hot water

**1** Preheat the oven to 350 degrees. Lightly grease 2 baking sheets.

**2** Combine the three flours, the baking powder, baking soda, spices, and salt.

**3** In a large bowl, cream the vegetable shortening and sugar. Beat in the eggs. Beat in the molasses. Beat in the hot water. Gradually blend in the dry ingredients.

**4** On a floured surface, roll out the dough to a thickness of ¼ inch. Using a 2½-inch round cookie cutter, cut out cookies an place 1 inch apart on the prepared baking sheets.

**5** Bake for 10 to 15 minutes, until lightly colored. Transfer to wire racks to cool.

# MOLASSES COOKIES I

Rolled Cookies

YIELD: *6 to 7 dozen*
TOTAL TIME: *40 minutes*

---

3 cups all-purpose flour
2 teaspoons baking powder
1 teaspoon baking soda
2 teaspoons ground ginger
1 teaspoon ground cinnamon
1 teaspoon ground nutmeg
1 cup molasses
1 cup vegetable shortening
1 large egg
1 cup sour milk
1 teaspoon vanilla extract

**1** Combine the flour, baking powder, baking soda, and spices.

**2** In a large bowl, beat the molasses and vegetable shortening until smooth. Beat in the egg. Beat in the sour milk and vanilla

extract. Gradually blend in the dry ingredients. Cover and chill for 24 hours.

**3** Preheat the oven to 375 degrees. Lightly grease 2 baking sheets.

**4** On a floured surface, roll out the dough to a thickness of ⅛ inch. Using a 2-inch round cookie cutter, cut into cookies and place 1 inch apart on the prepared baking sheets.

**5** Bake for 10 to 12 minutes, until lightly colored. Transfer to wire racks to cool. Store in an airtight container.

# MOLASSES COOKIES II

Rolled Cookies

YIELD: *3 to 4 dozen*
TOTAL TIME: *35 minutes*
CHILLING TIME: *24 hours*

---

2 cups all-purpose flour
2 teaspoons baking soda
1 teaspoon ground cinnamon
½ teaspoon ground cloves
½ teaspoon ground ginger
½ teaspoon salt
¾ cup vegetable shortening
1 cup granulated sugar
1 large egg
⅓ cup molasses
Granulated sugar for rolling

**1** Combine the flour, baking soda, spices, and salt.

**2** In a large bowl, cream the vegetable shortening and sugar. Beat in the egg. Beat in the molasses. Gradually blend in the dry ingredients. Cover and chill for 2 hours.

**3** Preheat the oven to 350 degrees. Lightly grease 2 baking sheets.

**4** Pinch off walnut-sized pieces of dough and roll into balls. Roll the balls in granulated sugar and place 1 inch apart on the prepared baking sheets.

**5** Bake for 10 to 12 minutes, until lightly colored. Transfer to wire racks to cool.

# MOLASSES COOKIES III

Formed Cookies

YIELD: *4 to 5 dozen*
TOTAL TIME: *40 minutes*
CHILLING TIME: *2 hours*

## MOLASSES COOKIES IV

Formed Cookies

YIELD: *2 to 3 dozen*
TOTAL TIME: *35 minutes*
CHILLING TIME: *4 hours*

3½ cups all-purpose flour
1½ teaspoons baking soda
1 teaspoon ground cinnamon
½ teaspoon ground ginger
½ teaspoon salt
1 cup molasses
⅓ cup boiling water
1 tablespoon fresh lemon juice
½ cup vegetable shortening
¾ cup granulated sugar
1 large egg

1 Combine the flour, baking soda, spices, and salt.

2 Combine the molasses, boiling water, and lemon juice in a small bowl.

3 In a large bowl, cream the vegetable shortening and sugar. Beat

in the egg. Beat in the molasses mixture. Gradually blend in the dry ingredients. Cover and chill for 4 hours.

4 Preheat the oven to 350 degrees. Lightly grease 2 baking sheets.

5 Pinch off walnut-sized pieces of the dough and roll into balls. Place 1½ inches apart on the prepared baking sheets. Flatten each ball with the bottom of a glass dipped in flour.

6 Bake for 10 to 12 minutes, until lightly colored. Transfer to wire racks to cool.

## MOLASSES COOKIES V

Rolled Cookies

YIELD: *7 to 8 dozen*
TOTAL TIME: *30 minutes*

5 cups all-purpose flour
½ teaspoon baking soda
1 cup vegetable shortening
1 cup granulated sugar
1 cup molasses
½ teaspoon cider vinegar

1 Preheat the oven to 350 degrees. Lightly grease 2 baking sheets.

2 Combine the flour and baking soda.

3 In a large bowl, cream the shortening and sugar. Beat in the molasses and vinegar. Gradually blend in the dry ingredients.

4 On a floured surface, roll out the dough to a thickness of ¼

inch. Using a 2-inch round cookie cutter, cut out cookies and place 1 inch apart on the prepared baking sheets.

5 Bake for 12 to 15 minutes, until lightly colored. Transfer to wire racks to cool.

## MOLASSES GINGER COOKIES

Formed Cookies

YIELD: *4 to 5 dozen*
TOTAL TIME: *35 minutes*
CHILLING TIME: *4 hours*

2 cups all-purpose flour
2 teaspoons baking soda
2 teaspoons ground ginger
1 teaspoon ground cinnamon
1 teaspoon ground cloves
½ teaspoon ground nutmeg
¼ cup vegetable shortening
¼ cup molasses
⅔ cup granulated sugar
1 large egg
1 large egg white, beaten
Granulated sugar for coating

1 Combine the flour, baking soda, and spices.

2 In a large bowl, cream the vegetable shortening, molasses, and sugar. Beat in the egg. Gradually

blend in the dry ingredients. Cover and chill for 4 hours.

3 Preheat the oven to 350 degrees. Lightly grease 2 baking sheets.

4 Pinch off walnut-sized pieces of dough and roll into balls. Dip half of each ball first in the beaten egg white and then in the granulated sugar and place 2 inches apart, the sugar sides up, on the prepared baking sheets.

5 Bake for 10 to 12 minutes, until lightly colored. Transfer to wire racks to cool.

## MOLASSES JUMBLES

Rolled Cookies

YIELD: *8 to 9 dozen*
TOTAL TIME: *45 minutes*
CHILLING TIME: *24 hours*

3¼ cups all-purpose flour
2 teaspoons baking powder
½ teaspoon baking soda
1 teaspoon ground ginger
½ teaspoon ground cloves
½ teaspoon ground nutmeg
¾ cup vegetable shortening
1 cup packed light brown sugar
1 large egg
¼ cup molasses

TOPPING
Colored sugar crystals, walnuts, chopped, flaked coconut, and/or gumdrops, diced fine

**1** Combine the flour, baking powder, baking soda, and spices.

**2** In a large bowl, cream together the vegetable shortening and brown sugar. Beat in the egg. Beat in the molasses. Gradually blend in the dry ingredients. Cover and chill for 24 hours.

**3** Preheat the oven to 350 degrees. Lightly grease 2 baking sheets.

**4** On a floured surface, roll out the dough to a thickness of ¼ inch. Using cookie cutters, cut into shapes and place 1 inch apart on the prepared baking sheets. Sprinkle with any combination of the toppings.

**5** Bake for 8 to 10 minutes, until lightly colored. Transfer to wire racks to cool.

## MOLASSES SNAPS

Formed Cookies

YIELD: *5 to 6 dozen*
TOTAL TIME: *30 minutes*

2¼ cups all-purpose flour
2 teaspoons baking soda
1 teaspoon ground cinnamon
1 teaspoon ground ginger
½ teaspoon ground cloves
½ teaspoon salt
¾ cup vegetable shortening
1 cup packed dark brown sugar
1 large egg
¼ cup molasses
1 cup golden raisins
Granulated sugar for rolling

**1** Preheat the oven to 350 degrees.

**2** Combine the flour, baking soda, spices, and salt.

**3** In a large bowl, cream the vegetable shortening and brown sugar. Beat in the egg. Beat in the molasses. Gradually blend in the dry ingredients. Fold in the raisins.

**4** Pinch off walnut-sized pieces of dough and roll into balls. Roll in granulated sugar and place 1½ inches apart on ungreased baking sheets. Flatten each ball with the bottom of a glass that has been dipped in water and then in granulated sugar.

**5** Bake for 10 to 12 minutes, until lightly colored. Transfer to wire racks to cool.

## MOLASSES SPICE COOKIES

Drop Cookies

YIELD: *2 to 3 dozen*
TOTAL TIME: *30 minutes*

2¼ cups all-purpose flour
½ cup walnuts, ground fine
1 teaspoon baking soda
½ teaspoon ground ginger
½ teaspoon ground cinnamon
½ teaspoon salt
½ cup vegetable shortening
⅓ cup packed light brown sugar
1 large egg
½ cup molasses
¼ cup fresh orange juice
½ cup currants

**1** Preheat the oven to 350 degrees. Lightly grease 2 baking sheets.

**2** Combine the flour, walnuts, baking soda, spices, and salt.

**3** In a large bowl, cream the vegetable shortening and brown sugar. Beat in the egg. Beat in the molasses and orange juice. Gradually blend in the dry ingredients. Fold in the currants.

**4** Drop the dough by spoonfuls 3 inches apart onto the prepared baking sheets.

**5** Bake for 8 to 10 minutes, until lightly colored. Transfer to wire racks to cool.

# MOLASSES STICKS

Rolled Cookies

YIELD: *2 to 3 dozen*
TOTAL TIME: *35 minutes*

4 cups all-purpose flour
2 teaspoons baking soda
1 teaspoon ground cinnamon
1 teaspoon ground ginger
1½ cups vegetable shortening
1 cup granulated sugar
1 cup packed dark brown sugar
2 large eggs
½ cup molasses
Granulated sugar for rolling

1  Preheat the oven to 350 degrees. Lightly grease 2 baking sheets.

2  Combine the flour, baking soda, and spices.

3  In a large bowl, cream the vegetable shortening and two sugars. Beat in the eggs. Beat in the molasses. Gradually blend in the dry ingredients.

4  On a floured surface, roll the dough out to a thickness of ½ inch. Using a sharp knife, cut into strips ½ inch wide and 3 inches long. Roll the strips into logs, roll in granulated sugar, and place 1 inch apart on the prepared baking sheets.

5  Bake for 12 to 15 minutes, until lightly colored. Transfer to wire racks to cool.

# MOON PIES

Drop Cookies

YIELD: *3 to 4 dozen*
TOTAL TIME: *30 minutes*

2 cups all-purpose flour
6 tablespoons unsweetened cocoa powder
2½ teaspoons baking powder
½ teaspoon salt
⅓ cup vegetable shortening
1 cup granulated sugar
1 large egg
1 cup sour milk
1 teaspoon vanilla extract

FILLING
¾ cup vegetable shortening
1 cup powdered sugar
1 teaspoon vanilla extract
½ cup store-bought marshmallow topping

1  Preheat the oven to 350 degrees. Lightly grease 2 baking sheets.

2  Combine the flour, cocoa powder, baking powder, and salt.

3  In a large bowl, cream the vegetable shortening and sugar. Beat in the egg. Beat in the sour milk and vanilla extract. Gradually blend in the dry ingredients.

4  Drop the dough by heaping tablespoonfuls 3 inches apart onto the prepared baking sheets.

5  Bake for 7 to 10 minutes, or until a toothpick inserted in a cookie comes out clean. Transfer to wire racks to cool.

6  To make the filling, beat the vegetable shortening and powdered sugar in a medium bowl. Beat in the vanilla extract. Beat in the marshmallow topping.

7  To assemble, cut the cookies horizontally in half. Spread a generous layer of the topping over the bottom halves, replace the top halves, and press lightly together.

**Baking notes:**  Metal crumpet or English muffin rings are perfect for making these; it takes 2 heaping full tablespoons of the batter to fill each ring. For Mint Moon Pies, add a few drops of green food coloring to the topping and substitute ½ teaspoon mint extract for the vanilla extract.

# Natural Lemon Drops

Drop Cookies

YIELD: *3 to 5 dozen*
TOTAL TIME: *30 minutes*

2 cups all-purpose flour
½ teaspoon baking powder
2 teaspoons grated lemon zest.
½ cup vegetable shortening
4 large eggs
¾ cup frozen lemon juice concentrate, thawed

**1** Preheat the oven to 375 degrees. Lightly grease 2 baking sheets.

**2** In a large bowl, combine the flour, baking powder, and lemon zest. Cut in the vegetable shortening.

**3** In a large bowl, beat the eggs until thick and light-colored. Beat in the thawed lemon juice concentrate. Gradually blend the eggs into the flour mixture.

**4** Drop the dough by spoonfuls 1½ inches apart onto the prepared baking sheets.

**5** Bake for 6 to 8 minutes, until lightly colored. Transfer to wire racks to cool.

# New England Molasses Cookies

Drop Cookies

YIELD: *4 to 5 dozen*
TOTAL TIME: *35 minutes*

3 cups all-purpose flour
½ teaspoon baking soda
½ cup vegetable shortening
½ cup granulated sugar
2 large eggs
½ cup molasses
¼ cup hot water

**1** Preheat the oven to 350 degrees.

**2** Combine the flour and baking soda.

**3** In a large bowl, cream the vegetable shortening and sugar. Beat in the eggs. Beat in the molasses and hot water. Gradually blend in the dry ingredients.

**4** Drop the dough by spoonfuls 1½ inches apart onto ungreased baking sheets.

**5** Bake for 12 to 15 minutes, until firm to the touch. Transfer to wire racks to cool.

# New Hampshire Fruit Cookies

Drop Cookies

YIELD: *3 to 4 dozen*
TOTAL TIME: *30 minutes*

3¼ cups all-purpose flour
½ teaspoon ground cinnamon
¼ teaspoon salt
1 cup vegetable shortening
1½ cups granulated sugar
3 large eggs
1 teaspoon baking soda
1½ tablespoons warm water
1 cup chestnuts, chopped
½ cup raisins, chopped
½ cup currants, chopped

**1** Preheat the oven to 350 degrees. Lightly grease 2 baking sheets.

**2** Combine the flour, cinnamon, and salt.

**3** In a large bowl, cream the vegetable shortening and sugar. Beat in the eggs one at a time, beating well after each addition.

**4** Dissolve the baking soda in the warm water and add to the egg mixture, beating until smooth. Gradually blend in the dry ingredients. Stir in the chestnuts, raisins, and currants.

**5** Drop the dough by spoonfuls 1½ inches apart onto the prepared baking sheets.

**6** Bake for 12 to 15 minutes, until lightly colored. Transfer to wire racks to cool.

# New Orleans Jumbles

Formed Cookies

YIELD: *4 to 5 dozen*
TOTAL TIME: *35 minutes*

3 cups all-purpose flour
¼ teaspoon salt
1 cup butter, at room temperature
1 cup granulated sugar
1 large egg
1 tablespoon grated orange zest

**1** Preheat the oven to 350 degrees. Lightly grease 2 baking sheets.

**2** Combine the flour and salt.

**3** In a large bowl, cream the butter and sugar. Beat in the egg. Beat in the orange zest. Gradually blend in the dry ingredients.

**4** Pinch off walnut-sized pieces of dough and roll into pencil-thin ropes about 6 inches long. Form the ropes into circles and place 1 inch apart on the prepared baking sheets.

**5** Bake for 12 to 15 minutes, until lightly colored. Transfer to wire racks to cool.

# New Year's Eve Biscuits

Rolled Cookies

YIELD: *3 to 5 dozen*
TOTAL TIME: *35 minutes*

3 cups all-purpose flour
1 teaspoon baking powder
¾ cup butter, at room temperature
1 cup granulated sugar
1 cup warm water

**1** Preheat the oven to 375 degrees. Lightly grease 2 baking sheets.

**2** Combine the flour and baking powder.

**3** In a large bowl, cream the butter and sugar. Gradually blend in the dry ingredients. Add just enough water to form a smooth dough.

**4** On a floured surface, roll the dough out to a thickness of ½ inch. Using cookie cutters, cut into shapes and place the cookies 1 inch apart on the prepared baking sheets.

**5** Bake for 12 to 15 minutes, until lightly colored. Transfer to wire racks to cool.

**Baking notes:** This is a very English recipe. These cookies are like sweet baking powder biscuits and are usually cut into rounds. They can be served for breakfast in place of sweet rolls.

2 cups milk
½ cup granulated sugar
6 cups all-purpose flour
2 tablespoons active dry yeast
½ cup butter, at room temperature
3 large eggs

ICING
1 cup powdered sugar
1 tablespoon water
1 tablespoon vanilla extract
¼ cup chopped nuts

**1** In a large saucepan, heat the milk just until warm (105 degrees); do not overheat. Remove fom the heat and stir in the sugar. Stir in 1 cup of the flour and the yeast. Blend in the butter. Stir in the eggs one at a time, blending well after each addition. Then blend in the remaining flour, ¼ cup at a time until a soft dough forms.

**2** Turn the dough out onto a floured surface and knead for 5 minutes, or until smooth. Place in a large bowl, cover with a clean cloth, and let rise in a warm place for 1 hour, or until doubled in bulk.

**3** Punch down the dough and knead briefly. Let rise for a second time.

**4** Preheat the oven to 375 degrees. Lightly grease 2 baking sheets.

**5** Punch down the dough. Pinch off large pieces and roll into ropes about 30 inches long. Cut smaller ropes, approximately 3 to 4 inches to make the pretzels. Form the ropes into pretzel shapes on the prepared baking sheets, placing them 1½ inches apart. Cover and let rest for 10 to 15 minutes.

**6** Bake for 25 to 30 minutes, until golden brown. Transfer to wire racks to cool.

**7** To make the icing, combine the powdered sugar, water, and vanilla extract in a bowl and stir until smooth. Stir in the nuts.

**8** Spread the icing over the tops of the cooled pretzels.

**Baking notes:** These are the soft-crust pretzels that are so popular. The pretzels can be as big or as small as you want.

# NEW YEAR'S EVE PRETZELS

Formed Cookies

YIELD: *7 to 9 dozen*
TOTAL TIME: *45 minutes*
RISING TIME: *2 hours*
RESTING TIME: *10 minutes*

---

3 cups all-purpose flour
2 teaspoons baking powder
¼ teaspoon salt
1 cup vegetable shortening
1⅓ cups granulated sugar
2 large eggs
1 teaspoon vanilla extract

TOPPING
2 teaspoons ground cinnamon
3 tablespoons granulated sugar

**1** Preheat the oven to 350 degrees. Lightly grease 2 baking sheets.

**2** Combine the flour, baking powder, and salt.

**3** In a large bowl, cream the vegetable shortening and sugar. Beat in the eggs. Beat in the vanilla

extract. Gradually blend in the dry ingredients.

**4** Combine the cinnamon and sugar in a cup for the topping.

**5** Pinch off 1-inch pieces of dough and roll into balls. Roll each ball in the cinnamon sugar and place 1½ inches apart on the prepared baking sheets.

**6** Bake for 10 to 12 minutes, until lightly colored. Transfer to wire racks to cool.

# NIBBLES

Formed Cookies

YIELD: *3 to 4 dozen*
TOTAL TIME: *30 minutes*

# No-Bake Brownies

Bar Cookies

YIELD: *1 to 2 dozen*
TOTAL TIME: *75 minutes*

2 cups (12 ounces) semisweet chocolate chips
1 cup evaporated milk
1 cup granulated sugar
3 cups crushed vanilla wafers
2 cups miniature marshmallows
1 cup walnuts, chopped
½ teaspoon salt

**1** Lightly grease a 9-inch square baking pan.

**2** In a double boiler, melt the chocolate chips with the milk, stirring until smooth. Stir in the sugar to dissolve. Remove from the heat.

**3** In a large bowl, combine the vanilla wafers, marshmallows, walnuts, and salt. Transfer ½ cup of this mixture to a small bowl. Add 2 teaspoons of the warm chocolate mixture and stir to blend.

**4** Add the remaining chocolate mixture to the vanilla wafer mixture and stir to blend. Press the dough evenly into the prepared baking pan, pressing down hard to pack the mixture into the pan. Spread the reserved chocolate mixture on top.

**5** Refrigerate until thoroughly chilled and set. Cut into large or small bars.

**Baking notes:** Graham crackers or chocolate wafers can be used in place of the vanilla wafers.

# No-Bake Chocolate Cookies

Bar Cookies

YIELD: *2 to 3 dozen*
TOTAL TIME: *15 minutes*
CHILLING TIME: *4 hours*

4½ cups puffed wheat cereal
1 cup walnuts, ground
⅔ cup flaked coconut
Pinch of salt
¼ cup vegetable shortening
1 cup powdered sugar
½ cup light corn syrup
⅔ cup unsweetened cocoa powder

**1** Lightly grease a 13 by 9-inch baking pan.

**2** Combine the cereal, walnuts, coconut, and salt.

**3** Melt the shortening in a large saucepan. Remove from the heat and beat in the powdered sugar. Beat in the corn syrup. Blend in the cocoa. Gradually blend in the dry ingredients, coating well. Press the mixture evenly into the prepared baking pan.

**4** Refrigerate for 4 hours, or until thoroughly chilled, then cut into large or small bars.

2 teaspoons instant coffee powder
½ cup hot water
1 cup (6 ounces) semisweet chocolate chips
3 tablespoons light corn syrup
3 cups powdered sugar
1¾ cups graham cracker crumbs
1 cup walnuts, chopped fine
Powdered sugar for rolling

**1** Dissolve the coffee in the hot water.

**2** In the top of a double boiler, melt the chocolate over low heat, stirring until smooth. Stir in the corn syrup. Stir in the coffee. Remove from the heat and beat in the powdered sugar. Gradually blend in the graham crackers and walnuts.

**3** Pinch off 1-inch pieces of dough and roll into balls. Roll each ball in powdered sugar. Store in an airtight container for at least 2 days before serving.

**Baking notes:** For cookies with more of a kick, use ½ cup of coffee liqueur in place of the water and coffee.

# NO-BAKE COOKIE BALLS

Formed Cookies

YIELD: *3 to 5 dozen*
TOTAL TIME: *35 minutes*
STORING TIME: *2 days*

---

3 cups rolled oats
½ cup walnuts, chopped fine
7 tablespoons unsweetened cocoa powder
½ cup flaked coconut
2 cups raw sugar
½ cup vegetable shortening
½ cup evaporated milk

**1** Line 2 baking sheets with waxed paper.

**2** In a large bowl, combine the oats, walnuts, cocoa powder, and coconut.

**3** In a saucepan, combine the sugar, vegetable shortening, and milk and bring to a boil, stirring

until smooth. Pour over the dry mixture and blend thoroughly.

**4** Drop the dough by spoonfuls 1½ inches apart onto the prepared baking sheets. Let cool and set for 1 hour.

**Baking notes:** Raisins or chopped banana chips, or both, can be added to the cookie mixture. Light brown sugar may be substituted for the raw sugar if you prefer.

# NO-BAKE COOKIES

Drop Cookies

YIELD: *3 to 4 dozen*
TOTAL TIME: *30 minutes*
RESTING TIME: *1 hour*

---

3 tablespoons vegetable shortening
3 cups miniature marshmallows
¼ cup honey
½ cup peanut butter
1 cup raisins
¼ cup rolled oats
½ cup peanuts, chopped

**1** Lightly grease a 9-inch square baking pan.

**2** In a large saucepan, combine the vegetable shortening, marshmallows, honey, and peanut butter and heat, stirring, until smooth. Remove from the heat and gradually blend in the raisins, oats, and peanuts.

**3** Spread the mixture evenly in the prepared baking pan. Chill for at least 2 hours.

**4** Cut into large or small bars and wrap individually in waxed paper.

**Baking notes:** You can spread this mixture in a larger pan to make make thinner bars. For a different version, plump the raisins in boiling water while heating the marshmallow mixture. Spread half of the mixture in the prepared pan. Drain the raisins, pat dry, and sprinkle over the marshmallow mixture. Then sprinkle with finely chopped peanuts, and spread the remaining marshmallow mixture on top.

# NO-BAKE OATMEAL BARS

Bar Cookies

YIELD: *2 to 3 dozen*
TOTAL TIME: *20 minutes*
CHILLING TIME: *2 hours*

# No-Bake Peanut Cookies

Drop Cookies

Yield: *2 to 3 dozen*
Total time: *30 minutes*

2 cups granulated sugar
¼ cup vegetable shortening
½ cup milk
3 tablespoons unsweetened cocoa powder
⅓ cup peanut butter
1 teaspoon vanilla extract
3 cups rolled oats
1 cup peanuts, chopped fine

**1** Line 2 baking sheets with waxed paper

**2** In a saucepan, combine the sugar, vegetable shortening, milk, and cocoa powder and bring to a simmer over low heat, stirring until smooth. Simmer for 2 minutes. Remove from the heat and beat in the peanut butter and vanilla extract. Gradually blend in the oats and peanuts.

**3** Drop the dough by spoonfuls 1 inch apart onto the prepared baking sheets. Flatten the cookies with the bottom of a glass dipped in water and then in granulated sugar. Let cool.

# Norske Kröner

Rolled Cookies

Yield: *3 to 4 dozen*
Total time: *35 minutes*
Chilling time: *2 hours*

3 cups all-purpose flour
¼ teaspoon salt
6 hard-boiled large egg yolks
6 large egg yolks
¾ cup granulated sugar
1½ cups vegetable shortening
1 large egg white, beaten
1 cup packed light brown sugar, sifted

**1** Combine the flour and salt.

**2** Force the hard boiled eggs through a sieve into a large bowl. Add the egg yolks and sugar and beat until smooth. Beat in the vegetable shortening. Gradually blend in the dry ingredients. Cover and chill until the dough is very stiff, at least 2 to 4 hours.

**3** Preheat the oven to 400 degrees. Lightly grease 2 baking sheets.

**4** On a floured surface, roll out the dough to a thickness of ¼ inch. Cut the dough into strips ½ inch wide and 5 inches long. Form the strips into rings, over-lapping the ends and pinching them to seal. Dip the cookies in the beaten egg white and then into the brown sugar. Place 1½ inches apart on the prepared baking sheets.

**5** Bake for 8 to 10 minutes, until lightly colored. Transfer to wire racks to cool.

2 large eggs, separated
2 hard-boiled large eggs, chopped fine
1½ cups powdered sugar
¾ cup butter, at room temperature
2 cups all-purpose flour
Powdered sugar for sprinkling

1 In a large bowl, beat the egg yolks and hard-cooked eggs until smooth. Beat in the powdered sugar. Beat in the butter. Gradually blend in the flour. Cover and chill for 8 hours or overnight.

2 Preheat the oven to 350 degrees. Lightly grease 2 baking sheets.

3 In a small bowl, beat the egg whites until stiff but not dry.

4 On a floured surface, roll out the dough to a thickness of ½ inch. Cut the dough into pencil-thin strips about 8 inches long. For each cookie, braid 3 strips together and form into a wreath, placing them 1 inch apart on the prepared baking sheets. Brush the egg whites over the wreaths and sprinkle with powdered sugar.

5 Bake for 12 to 15 minutes, until golden brown. Transfer to wire racks to cool.

**Baking notes:** It is important to let the dough mix sit for 8 hours or overnight. For added taste and texture, combine finely chopped hazelnuts with the powdered sugar for sprinkling.

# NORWEGIAN CHRISTMAS COOKIES

Rolled Cookies

YIELD: *4 to 5 dozen*
TOTAL TIME: *35 minutes*
CHILLING TIME: *8 hours*

---

2 cups all-purpose flour
1 cup almonds, ground
1 cup vegetable shortening
1 cup packed light brown sugar
2 tablespoons Vanilla Sugar (see Pantry)
4 large eggs
½ cup currants

1 Preheat the oven to 350 degrees. Lightly grease a 9-inch square baking pan.

2 Combine the flour and almonds.

3 In a large bowl, cream the vegetable shortening and two sugars. Beat in eggs one at a time. Gradually blend in the dry ingredients. Fold in the currants. Spread the dough evenly in the prepared baking pan.

4 Bake for 18 to 20 minutes, until lightly colored. Cool in the pan on a wire rack before cutting into large or small bars.

**Baking notes:** This dough can be chilled, rolled out ¼ inch thick, and cut into shapes.

# NORWEGIAN COOKIES

Bar Cookies

YIELD: *3 to 4 dozen*
TOTAL TIME: *35 minutes*

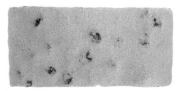

# Norwegian Currant Cookies

Formed Cookies

YIELD: *3 to 4 dozen*
TOTAL TIME: *30 minutes*
RESTING TIME: *1 hour*

1 cup currants
½ cup butter, at room temperature
¼ cup granulated sugar
2 large egg yolks
1 teaspoon vanilla extract
½ teaspoons orange extract
1 cup all-purpose flour
Milk for glazing

**1** Place the currants in a small bowl and add boiling water to cover. Set aside.

**2** Lightly grease 2 baking sheets.

**3** In a large bowl, cream the butter and sugar. Beat in the egg yolks. Beat in the vanilla and orange extracts. Gradually blend in the flour.

**4** Place the dough in a cookie press or a pastry bag fitted with a plain tip and press or pipe out small mounds onto the prepared baking sheets, spacing them 1½ inches apart. Set the baking sheets aside for 1 hour.

**5** Preheat the oven to 375 degrees.

**6** Drain the currants and pat dry between paper towels. Brush the cookies lightly with milk and sprinkle with the currants.

**7** Bake for 8 to 10 minutes, until lightly colored. Transfer to wire racks to cool.

# Norwegian Kringler

Drop Cookies

YIELD: *4 to 5 dozen*
TOTAL TIME: *35 minutes*

3 cups all-purpose flour
¾ teaspoon baking soda
1 teaspoon ground cinnamon
1 teaspoon salt
1 cup granulated sugar
1 cup sour cream

**1** Preheat the oven to 350 degrees. Lightly grease 2 baking sheets.

**2** Combine the flour, baking soda, cinnamon, and salt.

**3** In a large bowl, beat the sugar and sour cream together. Gradually blend in the dry ingredients.

**4** Drop the dough by spoonfuls 1½ inches apart onto the prepared baking sheets.

**5** Bake for 10 to 12 minutes, until lightly colored. Transfer to wire racks to cool.

2 cups all-purpose flour
½ teaspoons baking soda
½ teaspoons salt
⅔ cup vegetable shortening
1 cup granulated sugar
⅔ cup peanut butter
3 large eggs
⅓ cup milk
2 cups rolled oats
1 cup raisins
1 cup walnuts, chopped (optional)
1 cup dates, pitted and chopped
   (optional)

**1** Combine the flour, baking soda, and salt.

**2** In a large bowl, cream the vegetable shortening and sugar. Beat in the peanut butter. Beat in the eggs. Beat in the milk. Gradually blend in the dry ingredients. Fold in the oats, raisins, and the optional walnuts and dates. Cover and chill for 6 hours.

**3** Preheat the oven to 375 degrees.

**4** Drop the dough by spoonfuls 1½ inches apart onto ungreased baking sheets.

**5** Bake for 12 to 15 minutes, or until lightly colored. Transfer to wire racks to cool.

**Baking notes:** Two cups of chopped dried fruit may be used in place of the raisins and dates; instead of adding the chopped nuts to the dough, sprinkle them over the tops of the cookies before baking.

# NUGGETS

Drop Cookies

YIELD: *3 to 4 dozen*
TOTAL TIME: *30 minutes*
CHILLING TIME: *6 hours*

---

5½ cups all-purpose flour
1 teaspoon baking soda
¼ teaspoon baking powder
2 teaspoons ground cinnamon
½ teaspoon ground nutmeg
¼ teaspoon ground cloves
1½ cups packed light brown sugar
4 large eggs
2 cups honey
1 tablespoon plus 1 teaspoon vanilla
   extract
⅔ cup orange peel, zested and
   chopped
1 cup walnuts, chopped fine

**1** Combine the flour, baking soda, baking powder, and spices.

**2** In a large bowl, beat together the brown sugar and eggs until thick. Beat in the honey and vanilla extract. Beat in the orange zest. Gradually blend in the dry ingredients. Stir in the walnuts. Cover and chill for 24 hours.

**3** Preheat the oven to 350 degrees.

**4** Drop the dough by spoonfuls 1½ inches apart onto ungreased baking sheets.

**5** Bake for 8 to 10 minutes, or until lightly colored. Transfer to wire racks to cool.

**Baking notes:** In place of the citrus zest, mixed candied fruit can be used.

# NÜRNBERGERS

Drop Cookies

YIELD: *5 to 6 dozen*
TOTAL TIME: *30 minutes*
CHILLING TIME: *24 hours*

# Nut Bars I

Bar Cookies

Yield: *3 to 4 dozen*
Total time: *25 minutes*

3 large egg whites
1 cup sweetened condensed milk
1 teaspoon vanilla extract
1 teaspoon almond extract
4 cups shredded coconut
1 cup walnuts, ground fine
1 cup dates, pitted and chopped

**1** Preheat the oven to 350 degrees. Lightly grease a 9-inch square baking pan.

**2** In a large bowl, beat the egg whites until foamy. Beat in the milk and vanilla and almond extracts. Gradually blend in the coconut, walnuts, and dates. Spread the mixture evenly in the prepared baking pan.

**3** Bake for 10 to 12 minutes, until lightly colored on top. Cool in the pan on a wire rack before cutting into large or small bars.

**Baking notes:** To make sandwich cookies using this recipe, spread the batter in a 13 by 9-inch baking pan and bake. Cut into bars and fill with a custard or cream filling. This same recipe can be used for drop cookies; drop onto well-greased baking sheets.

# Nut Bars II

Bar Cookies

Yield: *1 to 2 dozen*
Total time: *45 minutes*

½ cup all-purpose flour
1 cup walnuts, ground fine
½ teaspoons baking powder
½ teaspoon salt
½ cup granulated sugar
2 large eggs
½ teaspoon vanilla extract
1 cup prunes, pitted and chopped
Powdered sugar for sprinkling

**1** Preheat the oven to 325 degrees. Lightly grease an 8-inch square baking pan.

**2** Combine the flour, walnuts, baking powder, and salt.

**3** In a large bowl, beat the sugar and eggs until thick and light-colored. Beat in the vanilla extract. Gradually blend in the dry ingredients. Stir in the prunes. Spread the mixture evenly in the prepared baking pan.

**4** Bake for 35 to 40 minutes, until a toothpick inserted into the center comes out clean. Cool slightly in the pan, then cut into large or small bars. Sprinkle the warm bars with powdered sugar before removing from the pan.

# Nut Cookies I

Drop Cookies

Yield: *1 to 2 dozen*
Total time: *35 minutes*

¾ cup all-purpose flour
1 teaspoon baking powder
¼ cup butter, at room temperature
¼ cup vegetable shortening
½ cup granulated sugar
2 large eggs
1 teaspoon vanilla extract
¾ cup walnuts, chopped

**1** Preheat the oven to 350 degrees.

**2** Combine the flour and baking powder.

**3** In a large bowl, cream the butter, vegetable shortening, and sugar. Beat in the eggs. Beat in the vanilla extract. Gradually blend in the dry ingredients.

**4** Drop the dough by spoonfuls 1½ inches apart onto ungreased baking sheets. Sprinkle with chopped nuts.

**5** Bake for 10 to 12 minutes, until lightly colored. Transfer to wire racks to cool.

¾ cup vegetable shortening
¼ cup butter, at room temperature
½ cup powdered sugar
½ teaspoons vanilla extract
2 cups all-purpose flour
1¼ cups pecans, ground

**1** Preheat the oven to 350 degrees. Lightly grease 2 baking sheets.

**2** In a large bowl, cream the vegetable shortening, butter, and sugar. Beat in the vanilla extract. Gradually blend in the flour.

**3** Spread the pecans in a shallow bowl or pie plate.

**4** Pinch off walnut-sized pieces of dough and roll into pencil-thin ropes about 8 inches long. Fold the ropes in half and twist them, roll in the pecans, and place 1 inch apart on the prepared baking sheets.

**5** Bake for 12 to 15 minutes, until lightly colored. Transfer to wire racks to cool.

**Baking notes:** This dough can be formed into crescents, rolled in the pecans, and baked.

# Nut Cookies II

Formed Cookies

YIELD: *3 to 4 dozen*
TOTAL TIME: *30 minutes*

---

3 cups all-purpose flour
¾ teaspoon baking soda
1 cup vegetable shortening
2 cups packed light brown sugar
3 large eggs
1 cup walnuts, chopped

**1** Preheat the oven to 350 degrees.

**2** Combine the flour and baking soda.

**3** In a large bowl, cream the vegetable shortening and brown sugar. Beat in the eggs. Gradually blend in the dry ingredients. Fold in the walnuts.

**4** Drop the dough by spoonfuls 1½ inches apart onto ungreased baking sheets.

**5** Bake for 10 to 12 minutes, until lightly colored. Transfer to wire racks to cool.

# Nut Cookies III

Drop Cookies

YIELD: *4 to 5 dozen*
TOTAL TIME: *30 minutes*

---

2 large egg whites
1 cup powdered sugar
1 cup almonds, ground fine

**1** Preheat the oven to 300 degrees. Line 2 baking sheets with parchment paper.

**2** In a large bowl, beat the egg whites until foamy. Gradually beat in the powdered sugar until the whites form stiff peaks. Fold in the ground almonds.

**3** On a well floured surface, roll out the dough to a thickness of ¼ inch. Using a 2-inch round cookie cutter, cut out cookies and place the cookies 1 inch apart on the prepared baking sheets.

**4** Bake for 20 to 25 minutes, or until light colored. Cool in the baking pans on wire racks.

# Nut Cookies IV

Rolled Cookies

YIELD: *3 to 4 dozen*
TOTAL TIME: *30 minutes*

# NUT COOKIES V

Refrigerator Cookies

YIELD: *5 to 6 dozen*
TOTAL TIME: *35 minutes*
CHILLING TIME: *4 hours*

**2 cups all-purpose flour**
**1½ cups pecans, ground fine**
**½ teaspoon baking soda**
**½ teaspoon salt**
**¾ cup vegetable shortening**
**¼ cup butter, at room temperature**
**1 cup packed light brown sugar**
**1 large egg**
**2 teaspoons vanilla extract**

**1** Combine the flour, pecans, baking soda, and salt.

**2** In a large bowl, cream the vegetable shortening, butter, and brown sugar. Beat in the egg. Beat in the vanilla extract. Gradually blend in the dry ingredients. If dough seems a little dry, add a little water ½ teaspoon at a time.

**3** Divide the dough in half. Form each half into a log 2 inches in diameter. Wrap in waxed paper and chill for 4 hours.

**4** Preheat the oven to 400 degrees.

**5** Cut the logs into ⅛-inch-thick slices and place 1 inch apart on ungreased baking sheets.

**6** Bake for 8 to 10 minutes, until lightly colored. Transfer to wire racks to cool.

**Baking notes:** As an added touch, roll the logs in coarsely ground nuts before chilling. Almost any type of nut can be used for these: peanuts, almonds, hazelnuts, walnuts, brazil nuts, pistachios, etc.

---

# NUTMEG COOKIES

Rolled Cookies

YIELD: *3 to 4 dozen*
TOTAL TIME: *35 minutes*
CHILLING TIME: *4 hours*

**4 cups all-purpose flour**
**2 teaspoons baking powder**
**¼ teaspoon ground nutmeg**
**¾ cup vegetable shortening**
**2 cups granulated sugar**
**2 large eggs**
**¼ cup milk**
**1½ teaspoons vanilla extract**
**1 teaspoon grated lemon zest**

**1** Combine the flour, baking powder, and nutmeg.

**2** In a large bowl, cream the vegetable shortening and sugar. Beat in the eggs. Beat in the milk and vanilla extract. Beat in the lemon zest. Gradually blend in the dry ingredients. Cover and chill for 4 hours.

**3** Preheat the oven to 375 degrees. Lightly grease 2 baking sheets.

**4** On a floured surface, roll out the dough to a thickness of ⅛ inch. Using a 2-inch round cookie cutter, cut into rounds and place 1 inch apart on the prepared baking sheets.

**5** Bake for 10 to 12 minutes, or until lightly colored. Transfer to wire racks to cool.

4½ cups all-purpose flour
1 cup walnuts, ground
1 cup butter, at room temperature
1 cup vegetable shortening
2½ cups packed light brown sugar
2 teaspoons vanilla extract

**1** Preheat the oven to 350 degrees.

**2** Combine the flour and walnuts.

**3** In a large bowl, cream the butter, vegetable shortening, and brown sugar. Beat in the vanilla extract. Gradually blend in the dry ingredients.

**4** Pinch off walnut-sized pieces of dough and roll into small balls. Place 1½ inches apart on ungreased baking sheets and flatten with the bottom of a glass dipped in flour.

**5** Bake for 10 to 12 minutes, until lightly colored. Transfer to wire racks to cool.

**Baking notes:** Almost any type of nut can be used for this recipe; if you use almonds, substitute almond extract for the vanilla extract. Rum or brandy can be very good.

# NUT SHORTBREAD

Formed Cookies

YIELD: *4 to 5 dozen*
TOTAL TIME: *30 minutes*

---

3¾ cups all-purpose flour
1½ teaspoons baking powder
¼ teaspoon salt
1 cup vegetable shortening
1½ cups granulated sugar
2 large eggs
2 teaspoons vanilla extract
1 cup pecans, chopped fine
Colored sugar crystals for sprinkling

**1** Preheat the oven to 375 degrees. Lightly grease 2 baking sheets.

**2** Combine the flour, baking powder, and salt.

**3** In a large bowl, cream the vegetable shortening and sugar. Beat in the eggs one at a time. Beat in the vanilla extract. Gradually blend in the dry ingredients. Fold in the pecans.

**4** On a floured surface, roll out the dough to a thickness of ⅛ inch. Using cookie cutters, cut into shapes and place 1 inch apart on the prepared baking sheets.

**5** Bake for 8 to 10 minutes, until lightly colored. Sprinkle with sugar crystals and transfer to wire racks to cool.

**Baking notes:** For softer cookies, roll the dough out to a thickness of ¼ inch; increase the baking time to 10 to 12 minutes.

# NUTTY SUGAR COOKIES

Rolled Cookies

YIELD: *5 to 6 dozen*
TOTAL TIME: *35 minutes*

# OASIS COOKIES

Rolled Cookies

YIELD: *5 to 6 dozen*
TOTAL TIME: *35 minutes*

4 cups all-purpose flour
1 teaspoon baking powder
1 teaspoon baking soda
1 cup vegetable shortening
½ cup butter, at room temperature
1 cup packed light brown sugar
2 large eggs
1 teaspoon fresh lemon juice
1 cup raisins
1 cup walnuts, chopped
1 cup candied citron, chopped
1 cup prunes, pitted and chopped
½ cup flaked coconut

**1** Preheat the oven to 350 degrees. Lightly grease 2 baking sheets.

**2** Combine the flour, baking powder, and baking soda.

**3** In a large bowl, cream the vegetable shortening, butter, and brown sugar. Beat in the eggs. Beat in the lemon juice. Gradually blend in the dry ingredients. Fold in the raisins, walnuts, candied citron, prunes, and coconut.

**4** On a floured surface, roll out the dough to a thickness of ⅛ inch. Using a 1½-inch round cookie cutter, cut out cookies and place 1½ inches apart on the prepared baking sheets.

**5** Bake for 12 to 15 minutes, until lightly colored. Transfer to wire racks to cool.

**Baking notes:** This is an English recipe; candied citron is particularly popular in England, but mixed candied fruit can be substituted if preferred. Frost the cookies with lemon icing if you like.

# OATMEAL-AND-APPLESAUCE COOKIES

Drop Cookies

YIELD: *3 to 5 dozen*
TOTAL TIME: *40 minutes*

½ cup all-purpose flour
½ teaspoon baking soda
1½ teaspoons ground cinnamon
1 teaspoon ground allspice
¼ teaspoon salt
¼ cup vegetable oil
1 large egg
½ cup unsweetened applesauce
1 teaspoon brandy
½ cup rolled oats
½ cup golden raisins

**1** Preheat the oven to 375 degrees. Lightly grease 2 baking sheets.

**2** Combine the flour, baking soda, spices, and salt.

**3** In a large bowl, beat the oil and egg together. Beat in the applesauce and brandy. Gradually blend in the dry ingredients. Stir in the oats and raisins.

**4** Drop the dough by spoonfuls 1½ inches apart onto the prepared baking sheets.

**5** Bake for 10 to 12 minutes, until lightly colored. Transfer to wire racks to cool.

3 ounces semisweet chocolate, chopped
1 cup all-purpose flour
½ teaspoon salt
⅔ cup vegetable shortening
1 cup packed light brown sugar
½ cup granulated sugar
4 large eggs
2 teaspoons vanilla extract
1 cup rolled oats
1 cup walnuts, chopped

**1** Preheat the oven to 325 degrees. Lightly grease a 13 by 9-inch baking pan.

**2** Melt the chocolate in a double boiler over low heat, stirring until smooth. Remove from the heat.

**3** Combine the flour and salt.

**4** In a large bowl, cream the vegetable shortening and two sugars. Beat in the eggs one at a time, beating well after each addition. Beat in the vanilla extract. Beat in the melted chocolate. Gradually blend in the dry ingredients. Fold in the oats and walnuts. Spread the mixture evenly in the prepared baking pan.

**5** Bake for 25 to 30 minutes, or until a toothpick inserted in the center comes out clean; don't overbake. Cool in the pan on a wire rack before cutting into large or small bars.

**Baking notes:** Raisins can be added to this batter.

# OATMEAL BROWNIES

Bar Cookies

YIELD: *1 to 2 dozen*
TOTAL TIME: *35 minutes*

---

1 cup all-purpose flour
1 teaspoon baking powder
½ teaspoon baking soda
¼ teaspoon salt
¾ cup vegetable shortening
1⅔ cups granulated sugar
2 large eggs
1½ teaspoons vanilla extract
2½ cups rolled oats
1 cup flaked coconut

**1** Preheat the oven to 375 degrees. Lightly grease 2 baking sheets.

**2** Combine the flour, baking powder, baking soda, and salt.

**3** In a large bowl, cream the vegetable shortening and sugar. Beat in the eggs. Beat in the vanilla. Gradually blend in the dry ingredients. Fold in the oats and coconut.

**4** Drop the dough by spoonfuls 3 inches apart onto the prepared baking sheets.

**5** Bake for 12 to 14 minutes, until golden brown. Transfer to wire racks to cool.

# OATMEAL-COCONUT CRISPS

Drop Cookies

YIELD: *4 to 5 dozen*
TOTAL TIME: *30 minutes*

# OATMEAL COOKIES I

Drop Cookies

YIELD: *3 to 4 dozen*
TOTAL TIME: *30 minutes.*

1 cup butter
1 cup packed light brown sugar
2 cups quick-cooking oatmeal
2 large egg whites

**1** Preheat the oven to 375 degrees. Lightly grease 2 baking sheets.

**2** In a large saucepan, melt the butter. Stir in the brown sugar and oatmeal and cook, stirring for 2 minutes. Transfer to a large bowl.

**3** In a small bowl, beat the egg whites until stiff but not dry. Fold the beaten egg whites into the oatmeal mixture.

**4** Drop the mixture by spoonfuls 2 inches apart onto the prepared baking sheets. Flatten the cookies with the back of a spoon dipped in flour.

**5** Bake for 7 to 10 minutes, or until the edges are light brown. Transfer to wire racks to cool.

**Baking notes:** Add chopped dried mango or papaya for a delicious and unusual variation.

# OATMEAL COOKIES II

Drop Cookies

YIELD: *5 to 6 dozen*
TOTAL TIME: *30 minutes*
CHILLING TIME: *5 hours*

**FRUIT-NUT MIX**
1 cup all-purpose flour
1 cup walnuts, chopped
¾ cup raisins, chopped
½ cup candied citrus peel, chopped fine
2 tablespoons brandy
1½ cups all-purpose flour
1¾ cups cooked oatmeal
½ teaspoon baking soda
½ teaspoon ground cinnamon
½ teaspoon ground cloves
½ teaspoon ground mace
½ teaspoon salt
½ cup vegetable shortening
1 cup granulated sugar
1 large egg
¼ cup buttermilk

**1** To make the fruit-nut mix, combine the flour, walnuts, raisins, and candied citrus peel in a medium bowl. Stir in the brandy. Cover and chill for 2 hours.

**2** Combine the flour, oatmeal, baking soda, spices, and salt.

**3** In a large bowl, cream the vegetable shortening and sugar. Beat in the egg and buttermilk. Grad-ually blend in the dry ingredi-ents. Cover and set aside for 2 hours.

**4** Add the fruit-nut mix to the dough and blend thoroughly. Set aside for 1 hour.

**5** Preheat the oven to 350 degrees. Lightly grease 2 baking sheets.

**6** Drop the dough by tablespoon-fuls 2 inches apart onto the pre-pared baking sheets.

**7** Bake for 15 to 18 minutes, until golden brown. Transfer to wire racks to cool.

2 cups all-purpose flour
1 teaspoon baking soda
1 teaspoon ground cinnamon
1 teaspoon salt
¾ cup vegetable shortening
1 cup granulated sugar
2 large eggs
1 cup rolled oats
1 cup raisins

**1** Preheat the oven to 350 degrees.

**2** Combine the flour, baking soda, cinnamon, and salt.

**3** In a large bowl, cream the vegetable shortening and sugar. Beat in the eggs. Gradually blend in the dry ingredients. Fold in the oats and raisins.

**4** Drop the dough by spoonfuls 1½ inches apart onto ungreased baking sheets.

**5** Bake for 10 to 12 minutes, until lightly colored. Transfer to wire racks to cool.

**Baking notes:** You can add vanilla extract or almond extract to the dough to enhance the flavor of these cookies.

# OATMEAL COOKIES III

Drop Cookies

YIELD: *3 to 4 dozen*
TOTAL TIME: *30 minutes*

---

4 cups all-purpose flour
½ teaspoon baking soda
1 teaspoon ground nutmeg
½ cup vegetable shortening
1¾ cups granulated sugar
4 large eggs
½ cup buttermilk
3¼ cups rolled oats
1 cup golden raisins

**1** Preheat the oven to 350 degrees. Lightly grease 2 baking sheets.

**2** Combine the flour, baking soda, and nutmeg.

**3** In a large bowl, cream the vegetable shortening and sugar. Beat in the eggs one at a time, beating vigorously after each addition.

Beat in the buttermilk. Gradually blend in the dry ingredients. Stir in the oats and raisins.

**4** Drop the dough by spoonfuls 1½ inches apart onto the prepared baking sheets.

**5** Bake for 12 to 15 minutes, until lightly colored. Transfer to wire racks to cool.

# OATMEAL COOKIES IV

Drop Cookies

YIELD: *4 to 5 dozen*
TOTAL TIME: *30 minutes*

---

2 cups all-purpose flour
1 cup rolled oats
1 teaspoon baking soda
½ teaspoon ground nutmeg
½ teaspoon salt
1 cup vegetable shortening
1 cup packed light brown sugar
¾ cup milk

**1** Combine the flour, oats, baking soda, nutmeg, and salt.

**2** In a large bowl, cream the vegetable shortening and brown sugar. Beat in the milk. Gradually blend in the dry ingredients. Cover and chill for 2 hours.

**3** Preheat the oven to 350 degrees. Lightly grease 2 baking sheets.

**4** On a floured surface, roll out the dough to a thickness of ¼ inch. Using a 2-inch round cookie cutter, cut out cookies and place 1 inch apart on the prepared baking sheets.

**5** Bake for 10 to 12 minutes, until golden. Transfer to wire racks to cool.

# OATMEAL COOKIES V

Rolled Cookies

YIELD: *4 to 5 dozen*
TOTAL TIME: *30 minutes*
CHILLING TIME: *2 hours*

# OATMEAL COOKIES VI

Formed Cookies

YIELD: *3 to 4 dozen*
TOTAL TIME: *30 minutes*
CHILLING TIME: *6 hours*

1 cup whole wheat flour
½ cup wheat germ
1 teaspoon baking soda
1 teaspoon ground cinnamon
½ teaspoon salt
1 cup vegetable shortening
1 cup packed light brown sugar
½ cup granulated sugar
2 large eggs
1 teaspoon almond extract
1½ cups rolled oats
1 cup almonds, chopped
Granulated sugar

**1** Combine the flour, wheat germ, baking soda, cinnamon, and salt.

**2** In a large bowl, cream the vegetable shortening and two sug-

ars. Beat in the eggs. Beat in the almond extract. Gradually blend in the dry ingredients. Fold in the oats and almonds. Cover and chill for 6 hours.

**3** Preheat the oven to 350 degrees. Lightly grease 2 baking sheets.

**4** Pinch off walnut-sized pieces of dough and roll into balls. Place 1½ inches apart on the prepared baking sheets. Flatten each ball with the bottom of a glass dipped in water and then in granulated sugar.

**5** Bake for 8 to 10 minutes, until golden. Transfer to wire racks to cool.

# OATMEAL COOKIES VII

Drop Cookies

YIELD: *4 to 6 dozen*
TOTAL TIME: *30 minutes*

2 cups all-purpose flour
1 teaspoon baking soda
½ teaspoon salt
1 cup vegetable shortening
1 cup granulated sugar
2 large egg whites
3 tablespoons milk
½ teaspoon vanilla extract
2 cups rolled oats
1 cup golden raisins

**1** Preheat the oven to 350 degrees.

**2** Combine the flour, baking soda, and salt.

**3** In a large bowl, cream the vegetable shortening and sugar. Beat in the milk and vanilla extract.

Gradually blend in the dry ingredients. Stir in the oats and raisins.

**4** In a small bowl, beat the egg whites to soft peaks. Fold the whites into the oat mixture.

**5** Drop by spoonfuls 1½ inches apart on ungreased baking sheets.

**6** Bake for 10 to 12 minutes, until golden. Transfer to wire racks to cool.

# OATMEAL CRISPS

Drop Cookies

YIELD: *2 to 3 dozen*
TOTAL TIME: *30 minutes*

1¼ cups all-purpose flour
½ teaspoon baking powder
½ teaspoon baking soda
½ teaspoon salt
1 cup vegetable shortening
¼ cup granulated sugar
1 cup packed light brown sugar
2 large eggs
¼ teaspoon milk
1 teaspoon vanilla extract
3 cups rolled oats
1 cup (6 ounces) chocolate chips (see Baking notes)

**1** Preheat the oven to 350 degrees.

**2** Combine the flour, baking powder, baking soda, and salt.

**3** In a large bowl, cream the vegetable shortening and two sug-

ars. Beat in the eggs. Beat in the milk and vanilla extract. Gradually blend in the dry ingredients. Fold in the oats and chocolate chips.

**4** Drop the dough by spoonfuls 1½ inches apart onto ungreased baking sheets.

**5** Bake for 10 to 12 minutes, until lightly colored. Transfer to wire racks to cool.

**Baking notes:** You can use semi-sweet chocolate, milk chocolate, or butterscotch chips. If making these for kids, omit the chips and press several M & Ms into the top of each cookie.

# OATMEAL-DATE COOKIES

Drop Cookies

YIELD: *5 to 6 dozen*
TOTAL TIME: *30 minutes*

1 cup all-purpose flour
½ teaspoon baking soda
¼ teaspoon ground nutmeg
1 teaspoon salt
½ cup vegetable shortening
1 cup packed light brown sugar
½ cup granulated sugar
1 large egg
½ cup sour cream
1 teaspoon vanilla extract
3 cups rolled oats
1 cup dates, pitted and chopped

**1** Preheat the oven to 350 degrees. Lightly grease 2 baking sheets.

**2** Combine the flour, baking soda, nutmeg, and salt.

**3** In a large bowl, cream the vegetable shortening and two sug-ars. Beat in the egg. Beat in the sour cream and vanilla extract. Gradually blend in the dry ingredients. Stir in the oats and dates.

**4** Drop the dough by spoonfuls 1½ inches apart onto the prepared baking sheets.

**5** Bake for 10 to 12 minutes, until golden. Transfer to wire racks to cool.

**Baking notes:** Raisins can be used in place of the dates.

# OATMEAL DROPS

Drop Cookies

YIELD: *5 to 6 dozen*
TOTAL TIME: *30 minutes*

¾ cup all-purpose flour
1½ cups rolled oats
½ teaspoon baking soda
½ teaspoon salt
½ cup vegetable shortening
1 cup packed light brown sugar
1 large egg
1 teaspoon rum

**1** Preheat the oven to 350 degrees. Lightly grease 2 baking sheets.

**2** Combine the flour, oats, baking soda, and salt.

**3** In a large bowl, cream the vegetable shortening and brown sugar. Beat in the egg. Beat in the rum. Gradually blend in the dry ingredients.

**4** Drop the dough by spoonfuls 1½ inches apart onto the prepared baking sheets.

**5** Bake for 12 to 15 minutes, or until golden brown. Transfer to wire racks to cool.

# OATMEAL HEALTH COOKIES

Drop Cookies

YIELD: *3 to 5 dozen*
TOTAL TIME: *30 minutes*

1¼ cups all-purpose flour
¼ teaspoon baking soda
¼ cup carob powder
⅓ cup canola oil
2 large eggs
¼ cup skim milk
½ cup mashed bananas
¼ teaspoon fresh lemon juice
1 cup pecans, chopped
⅔ cup rolled oats

**1** Preheat the oven to 350 degrees. Lightly grease 2 baking sheets.

**2** Combine the flour, baking soda, and, carob powder.

**3** In a large bowl, beat the oil and eggs. Beat in the skim milk. Beat in the bananas and lemon juice. Gradually blend in the dry ingredients. Stir in the pecans and oats.

**4** Drop the dough by spoonfuls 1½ inches apart onto the prepared baking sheets.

**5** Bake for 8 to 10 minutes, until golden. Transfer to wire racks to cool.

# OATMEAL LEMONADE BARS

Bar Cookies

YIELD: *1 to 2 dozen*
TOTAL TIME: *50 minutes*

**O**

**FILLING**
12 ounces prunes, pitted
¾ cup water
¾ cup frozen lemon juice concentrate, thawed
⅓ cup granulated sugar
¼ cup all-purpose flour
¼ teaspoon salt

**CRUST**
1 cup all-purpose flour
1 cup rolled oats
¼ teaspoon baking soda
½ cup vegetable shortening
1 cup packed light brown sugar

**1** Preheat the oven to 400 degrees. Lightly grease a 13 by 9-inch baking pan.

**2** To make the filling, combine the prunes, water and lemon juice concentrate in a saucepan and bring to a boil. Cook for 15 minutes, or until the prunes are a puree. Remove from the heat and stir in the sugar, flour, and salt.

**3** To make the crust, combine the flour, oats, and baking soda.

**4** In a large bowl, cream the vegetable shortening and brown sugar. Gradually blend in the dry ingredients.

**5** Spread half of the crust mixture evenly in the bottom of the prepared baking pan. Spread the filling over the crust, leaving a ½-inch border all around. Spread the remaining crust mixture over the filling and press down lightly.

**6** Bake for 18 to 20 minutes, until golden brown on top. Cool in the pan on a wire rack before cutting into large or small bars.

# OATMEAL POWDER PUFFS

Drop Cookies

YIELD: *1 to 1½ dozen*
TOTAL TIME: *35 minutes*

1 cup (6 ounces) semisweet chocolate chips
2 cups all-purpose flour
1 teaspoon baking soda
½ teaspoon baking powder
½ teaspoon salt
1 cup vegetable shortening
1 cup granulated sugar
1 cup packed light brown sugar
2 large eggs
1 teaspoon vanilla extract
2 cups rolled oats
1 cup shredded coconut
16 maraschino cherries, chopped fine

**1** Preheat the oven to 350 degrees. Lightly grease 2 baking sheets.

**2** Melt the chocolate chips in a double boiler over low heat, stirring until smooth. Remove from the heat.

**3** Combine the flour, baking soda, baking powder, and salt.

**4** In a large bowl, cream the vegetable shortening and two sugars. Beat in the eggs. Beat in the vanilla extract. Beat in the melted chocolate. Gradually blend in the dry ingredients. Fold in the oatmeal, coconut, and cherries.

**5** Drop the dough by spoonfuls 1½ inches apart onto the prepared baking sheets.

**6** Bake for 10 to 12 minutes, until lightly colored. Transfer to wire racks to cool.

# OATMEAL THINS

Drop Cookies

YIELD: *2 to 3 dozen*
TOTAL TIME: *30 minutes*

1 cup rolled oats
2 teaspoons baking powder
½ teaspoon salt
1 tablespoon vegetable shortening
1 cup granulated sugar
2 large eggs
1 teaspoon vanilla extract

**1** Preheat the oven to 350 degrees. Lightly grease 2 baking sheets.

**2** Combine the oats, baking powder, and salt.

**3** In a large bowl, cream the shortening and sugar. Beat in the eggs. Beat in the vanilla extract.

Gradually blend in the dry ingredients.

**4** Drop the dough by spoonfuls 2 inches apart onto the prepared baking sheets.

**5** Bake for 12 to 15 minutes, until lightly colored. Transfer to wire racks to cool.

**Baking notes:** Keep a close eye on these cookies; they burn very easily.

# OLD-FASHIONED COOKIES

Rolled Cookies

YIELD: *5 to 6 dozen*
TOTAL TIME: *30 minutes*

3½ cups all-purpose flour
2½ teaspoons baking powder
½ teaspoon salt
1 cup vegetable shortening
1½ cups granulated sugar
2 large eggs
1 tablespoon rum
Vanilla Icing (see Pantry)

**1** Preheat the oven to 350 degrees.

**2** Combine the flour, baking powder, and salt.

**3** In a large bowl, cream the vegetable shortening and sugar. Beat in the eggs. Beat in the rum. Gradually blend in the dry ingredients.

**4** On a floured surface, roll out the dough to a thickness of ¼ inch. Using a 2-inch round cookie cutter, cut out cookies and place 1 inch apart on ungreased baking sheets.

**5** Bake for 10 to 12 minutes, until lightly colored and firm to the touch. Transfer to wire racks to cool.

**6** Drizzle the icing over the cooled cookies.

**Baking notes:** You can decorate these cookies with gum drops or small candies—be creative.

# OLD-FASHIONED SOFT GINGER COOKIES

Rolled Cookies

YIELD: *4 to 5 dozen*
TOTAL TIME: *35 minutes*
CHILLING TIME: *6 hours*

4 cups all-purpose flour
2 teaspoons baking soda
1 tablespoon ground ginger
1 teaspoon salt
¾ cups vegetable shortening
2 cups packed light brown sugar
⅔ cup molasses
⅔ cup boiling water

**1** Combine the flour, baking soda, ginger, and salt.

**2** In a large bowl, cream the vegetable shortening and brown sugar. Add in the molasses and boiling water, beating until smooth. Gradually blend in the dry ingredients. Cover and chill for at least 6 hours.

**3** Preheat the oven to 350 degrees. Lightly grease 2 baking sheets.

**4** On a floured surface, roll out the dough to a thickness of ¼ inch. Using a 2-inch round cookie cutter, cut the cookies and place 1 inch apart on the prepared baking sheets.

**5** Bake for 18 to 20 minutes, until lightly colored. Transfer to wire racks to cool.

**Baking notes:** These cookies may be iced once cool. Store tightly covered to retain their flavor and softness; should the cookies become hard, place half an apple in the cookie container for 8 hours to soften them.

**O**

# ORANGE BARS I

Bar Cookies

YIELD: *2 to 3 dozen*
TOTAL TIME: *35 minutes*

2½ cups all-purpose flour
2 teaspoons baking powder
1 teaspoon baking soda
1 teaspoon ground cardamom
2 large eggs
¼ cup vegetable shortening, melted
1½ cups frozen orange juice concentrate, thawed
1 teaspoon orange liqueur
1 cup cranberries, chopped
1 cup almonds, chopped
¾ cup shredded coconut

**1** Preheat the oven to 350 degrees. Lightly grease a 13 by 9-inch baking pan.

**2** Combine the flour, baking powder, baking soda, and cardamom.

**3** In a large bowl, beat together the eggs, vegetable shortening, orange juice concentrate, and orange liqueur until smooth. Gradually blend in the dry ingredients. Stir in the cranberries and almonds. Spread the mixture

evenly in the prepared baking pan and sprinkle the coconut over the top.

**4** Bake for 20 to 25 minutes, until the top is lightly colored. Cool in the pan on a wire rack before cutting into large or small bars.

# ORANGE BARS II

Bar Cookies

YIELD: *1 to 3 dozen*
TOTAL TIME: *35 minutes*

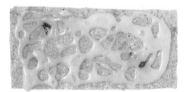

2 cups all-purpose flour
1 teaspoon baking soda
1 teaspoon ground cinnamon
½ teaspoon ground cloves
½ teaspoon salt
¾ cup vegetable shortening
1½ cups packed light brown sugar
2 large eggs
3 tablespoons fresh orange juice
3 tablespoons grated orange zest
1 cup raisins
1 cup walnuts, chopped

**1** Preheat the oven to 350 degrees. Lightly grease a 9-inch square baking pan.

**2** Combine the flour, baking soda, spices, and salt.

**3** In a large bowl, cream the vegetable shortening and brown sugar. Beat in the eggs. Beat in the orange juice and zest. Gradually blend in the dry ingredients. Fold in the raisins and walnuts. Spread the mixture evenly in the prepared baking pan.

**4** Bake for 25 to 30 minutes, until lightly colored on top. Cool in the pan on a wire rack before cutting into large or small bars.

**Baking notes:** Frost if desired when cooled; orange or lemon icing is good with these bars.

**CRUST**
2 cups all-purpose flour
¼ cup walnuts, ground fine
½ cup vegetable shortening
¼ cup granulated sugar

**TOPPING**
¼ cup all-purpose flour
¼ cup rolled oats
½ teaspoon baking powder
2 cups granulated sugar
4 large eggs
¼ cup fresh orange juice

**1** Preheat the oven to 350 degrees. Lightly grease a 13 by 9-inch square baking pan.

**2** To make the crust, combine the flour and walnuts.

**3** In a large bowl, cream together the vegetable shortening and sugar. Gradually blend in the dry ingredients. Spread the mixture evenly in the prepared baking pan.

**4** Bake for 25 minutes.

**5** Meanwhile, make the topping: Combine the flour, oats, and baking powder.

**6** In a medium bowl, beat the sugar and eggs together until thick and light-colored. Beat in the orange juice. Gradually blend in the dry ingredients.

**7** Pour the topping over the hot crust. Bake for 18 to 20 minutes longer, until the topping is lightly colored and firm to the touch. Cool in the pan on a wire rack before cutting into large or small bars.

# ORANGE BARS III

Bar Cookies

YIELD: *1 to 3 dozen*
TOTAL TIME: *60 minutes*

---

2 cups all-purpose flour
1 teaspoon baking powder
½ teaspoon baking soda
1 teaspoon ground cinnamon
¼ cup vegetable shortening
3 large eggs
⅔ cup fresh orange juice
½ teaspoon orange extract
1 cup cranberries, minced

**TOPPING**
⅓ cup almonds, ground fine
¼ teaspoon ground nutmeg

**1** Preheat the oven to 350 degrees. Lightly grease an 8-inch square baking pan.

**2** Combine the flour, baking powder, baking soda, and cinnamon.

**3** In a large bowl, beat the vegetable shortening, eggs, orange juice, and orange extract until smooth. Gradually blend in the dry ingredients. Stir in the cranberries. Spread the mixture evenly in the prepared baking pan.

**4** Combine the almonds and nutmeg and sprinkle over the top.

**5** Bake for 20 to 25 minutes, until golden brown on top. Cool in the pan on a wire rack before cutting into large or small bars.

# ORANGE-CRANBERRY BARS

Bar Cookies

YIELD: *2 to 3 dozen*
TOTAL TIME: *30 minutes*

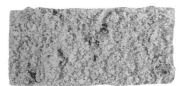

---

3 cups all-purpose flour
1 tablespoon baking powder
¼ teaspoon salt
⅔ cup butter, at room temperature
1½ cups granulated sugar
2 large eggs
¼ cup frozen orange juice concentrate, thawed
1 tablespoon grated orange zest
½ teaspoon almond extract
1 tablespoon water
1 cup raisins, chopped

**1** Preheat the oven to 375 degrees. Lightly grease 2 baking sheets.

**2** Combine the flour, baking powder, and salt.

**3** In a large bowl, cream the butter and sugar. Beat in the eggs. Beat in the orange juice concentrate and zest. Beat in the almond extract and water. Gradually blend in the dry ingredients. Fold in the raisins.

**4** Drop the dough by spoonfuls 1½ inches apart onto the prepared baking sheets.

**5** Bake for 10 to 12 minutes, until lightly colored. Transfer to wire racks to cool.

# ORANGE DROP COOKIES

Drop Cookies

YIELD: *3 to 4 dozen*
TOTAL TIME: *30 minutes*

# ORANGE DROPS

Drop Cookies

YIELD: *3 to 5 dozen*
TOTAL TIME: *30 minutes*

1½ cups all-purpose flour
½ cup whole wheat flour
½ teaspoon baking powder
½ cup canola oil
4 large eggs
½ cup frozen orange juice concentrate, thawed
¼ cup orange-flavored brandy
1 tablespoon grated orange zest

**1** Preheat the oven to 375 degrees. Lightly grease 2 baking sheets.

**2** Combine the two flours and the baking powder.

**3** In a large bowl, beat the oil and eggs until thick and light-colored. Beat in the orange juice concentrate and brandy. Beat in the orange zest. Gradually blend in the dry ingredients.

**4** Drop the dough by spoonfuls 1½ inches apart onto the prepared baking sheets.

**5** Bake for 6 to 8 minutes, until lightly colored. Transfer to wire racks to cool.

# ORANGE-NUT REFRIGERATOR COOKIES

Refrigerator Cookies

YIELD: *5 to 6 dozen*
TOTAL TIME: *40 minutes*
CHILLING TIME: *24 hours*

2¾ cups all-purpose flour
1 teaspoon baking soda
1 cup vegetable shortening
½ cup packed light brown sugar
½ cup granulated sugar
1 large egg
2 tablespoons orange liqueur
2 teaspoons grated orange zest
½ cup walnuts, chopped fine.

**1** Combine the flour and baking soda.

**2** In a large bowl, cream the vegetable shortening and two sugars. Beat in the egg. Beat in the orange liqueur and zest. Gradually blend in the dry ingredients. Fold in the walnuts.

**3** Divide the dough in half. Form each half into a log 2 inches in diameter. Wrap in waxed paper and chill in for 24 hours.

**4** Preheat the oven to 350 degrees. Lightly grease 2 baking sheets.

**5** Cut the logs into ¼-inch-thick slices and place 1 inch apart on the prepared baking sheets.

**6** Bake for 12 to 15 minutes, until lightly colored. Transfer to wire racks to cool.

# ORANGE-PECAN COOKIES

Drop Cookies

YIELD: *3 to 5 dozen*
TOTAL TIME: *35 minutes*

1 cup all-purpose flour
¼ teaspoon baking powder
¼ teaspoon salt
¼ cup vegetable shortening
1 cup granulated sugar
1 large egg
6 tablespoons fresh orange juice
2 tablespoons orange liqueur
¼ cup pecans, chopped fine

**1** Preheat the oven to 375 degrees. Lightly grease 2 baking sheets.

**2** Combine the flour, baking powder, and salt.

**3** In a large bowl, cream the vegetable shortening and sugar. Beat in the egg. Beat in the orange juice and orange liqueur. Gradually blend in the dry ingredients. Stir in the pecans.

**4** Drop the dough by spoonfuls 1½ inches apart onto the prepared baking sheets.

**5** Bake for 12 to 15 minutes, until lightly colored. Transfer to wire racks to cool.

# ORANGE-RAISIN COOKIES

Drop Cookies

YIELD: *4 to 5 dozen*
TOTAL TIME: *30 minutes*

1 cup all-purpose flour
1 teaspoon baking soda
½ teaspoon salt
1 cup vegetable shortening
1 cup granulated sugar
1 cup packed light brown sugar
2 large eggs
¼ cup frozen orange juice concentrate, thawed
2 teaspoons orange liqueur
1 cup rolled oats
¾ cup golden raisins

**1** Preheat the oven to 350 degrees. Lightly grease 2 baking sheets.

**2** Combine the flour, baking soda, and salt.

**3** In a large bowl, cream the vegetable shortening and two sugars. Beat in the eggs. Beat in the orange juice concentrate and liqueur. Gradually blend in the dry ingredients. Fold in the oats and raisins.

**4** Drop the dough by spoonfuls 2 inches apart onto the prepared baking sheets.

**5** Bake for 12 to 14 minutes, until lightly colored. Transfer to wire racks to cool.

**Baking notes:** Half a cup of chopped nuts (any kind) can be added to the dough.

# Orange Sugar Rounds

Rolled Cookies

Yield: *1 to 2 dozen*
Total time: *30 minutes*
Chilling time: *4 hours*

2¼ cups all-purpose flour
2 teaspoons baking powder
1 teaspoon salt
¾ cup vegetable shortening
1 cup granulated sugar
2 large eggs
1 tablespoon orange extract
1 tablespoon grated orange zest
Granulated sugar for sprinkling

**1** Combine the flour, baking powder, and salt.

**2** In a large bowl, cream the vegetable shortening and sugar. Beat in the eggs. Beat in the orange extract and zest. Gradually blend in the dry ingredients. Cover and chill for 4 hours.

**3** Preheat the oven to 400 degrees. Lightly grease 2 baking sheets.

**4** On a floured surface, roll out the dough to a thickness of ¼ inch. Using a 3-inch round cookie cutter, cut out cookies and place 1 inch apart on the prepared baking sheets. Sprinkle with the granulated sugar.

**5** Bake for 6 to 8 minutes, until lightly colored. Transfer to wire racks to cool.

**Baking notes:** Add a few drops of orange coloring to give an orange tint to these cookies if you like.

# Orange Wafers

Rolled Cookies

Yield: *4 to 5 dozen*
Total time: *35 minutes*
Chilling time: *4 hours*

1 cup vegetable shortening
1 cup granulated sugar
4 large egg yolks
2 tablespoons fresh orange juice
1 tablespoon orange extract
3 cups all-purpose flour
Orange colored sugar crystals

**1** In a large bowl, cream the vegetable shortening and sugar. Beat in the egg yolks one at a time, beating vigorously after each addition. Beat in the orange juice and orange extract. Gradually blend in the flour. Cover and chill for 4 hours.

**2** Preheat the oven to 350 degrees. Lightly grease 2 baking sheets.

**3** On a floured surface, roll out the dough to a thickness of ⅛ inch. Using a 1½-inch round cookie cutter, cut into rounds and place 1 inch apart on the prepared baking sheets. Sprinkle with orange sugar crystals.

**4** Bake for 10 to 12 minutes, until lightly colored. Transfer to wire racks to cool.

**Baking notes:** If you do not have orange extract, increase the orange juice to 3 tablespoons. This recipe works equally well with grapefruit juice; use sweetened grapefruit juice.

3¼ cups all-purpose flour
1 teaspoon baking powder
¼ teaspoon salt
1 cup granulated sugar
1 cup vegetable shortening
2 large egg yolks
6 tablespoons milk

**1** Combine the flour, baking powder, and salt.

**2** In a large bowl, cream the vegetable shortening and sugar. Beat in the egg yolks. Beat in the milk. Gradually blend in the dry ingredients. Cover and chill for 2 hours.

**3** Form the cookies using any of the variations below. Bake in a 350-degree oven for 7 to 10 minutes, until lightly colored. Transfer to wire racks to cool.

CHECKERBOARD: Divide the dough in half and work a few drops of food coloring into one half. Divide each half in three pieces and form each piece into a log. Flatten each log into a ½-inch-thick strip. Stack the strips, alternating the colors and brushing each strip lightly with water. Cut the stack lengthwise into ½-inch-wide strips. Lay these strips on their sides and stack them, reversing every other strip to alternate the pattern and lightly moistening each layer as you stack. Slice, place 1 inch apart on ungreased baking sheets, and bake as directed.

PINWHEELS: Divide the dough into 4 pieces and color 2 of them. Form each piece into a log. On a floured surface, roll out each log to a ¼-inch-thick rectangle. Stack the rectangles, alternating the colors and moistening each layer. Starting at a long edge, roll up jelly-roll fashion. Wrap in waxed paper and chill for 2 hours. Cut into ¼-inch-thick slices, place 1 inch apart on ungreased baking sheets, and bake as directed.

RIBBONS: Divide the dough into at least 3 pieces. Color each piece of the dough with a different food coloring. Form each piece into a log. On a floured surface, roll each piece into a 2-inch-wide strip ½-inch-thick. Stack the stips 2 to 3 inches high, alternating the colors and moistening each strip. Trim the edges and chill for 2 hours. Cut into ¼-inch-thick slices, lay 1 inch apart on ungreased baking sheets, and bake as directed.

PUMPKINS: Color about ⅛ of the dough green for the stems and leaves. Color the remaining dough orange. Roll out the orange dough and use a cookie cutter to cut out 3-inch circles. Place 1 inch apart on ungreased baking sheets and cut a small V in the top of each cookie. Roll out the green dough and cut out freehand stems and leaves. Moisten the Vs and attach the stems and leaves. Decorate with chocolate chips and/or raisins for the eyes and mouth—use your imagination. Bake as directed.

# PASTEL COOKIES

Rolled Cookies

YIELD: *3 to 5 dozen*
TOTAL TIME: *30 minutes*
CHILLING TIME: *2 hours*

# Pastiniai Natale

Rolled Cookies

Yield: *2 to 4 dozen*
Total time: *30 minutes*
Chilling time: *4 hours*

3 cups all-purpose flour
1 tablespoon baking powder
¼ teaspoon salt
1 tablespoon lemon zest, grated
1 cup vegetable shortening
1 cup granulated sugar
2 large eggs
¼ cup pistachio nuts, chopped
Lemon Glaze (see Pantry)
Chopped pistachio nuts for
  sprinkling

**1** Combine the flour, baking powder, and salt.

**2** In a large bowl, cream the vegetable shortening and sugar. Beat in the eggs. Gradually blend in the dry ingredients. Fold in the lemon zest. Fold in the pistachio nuts. Cover and chill for 4 hours.

**3** Preheat the oven to 325 degrees. Lightly grease 2 baking sheets.

**4** On a floured surface, roll out the dough to a thickness of ¼ inch. Using a 2-inch round cookie cutter, cut out the cookies and place 1 inch apart on the prepared baking sheets.

**5** Bake for 8 to 10 minutes, until lightly colored. Transfer to wire racks to cool.

**6** Ice the cooled cookies with the lemon glaze and sprinkle chopped pistachio nuts over the tops.

---

# Peanut Blondies

Bar Cookies

Yield: *2 to 3 dozen*
Total time: *40 minutes*

½ cup vegetable shortening
2 cups packed light brown sugar
1 cup peanut butter
4 large eggs
2 teaspoons vanilla extract
1 cup all-purpose flour
2 cups peanuts, chopped

**1** Preheat the oven to 350 degrees. Lightly grease a 9-inch square baking pan.

**2** In a large bowl, cream the vegetable shortening and brown sugar. Beat in the peanut butter. Beat in the eggs. Beat in the vanilla extract. Gradually blend in the flour. Spread the mixture evenly in the prepared baking pan and sprinkle the chopped nuts over the top.

**3** Bake for 30 to 35 minutes, until a knife inserted in the center comes out clean. Cool in the pan on a wire rack before cutting into large or small bars.

**Baking notes:** Chunky peanut butter makes an even nuttier bar.

---

# Peanut Butter-Banana Squares

Bar Cookies

Yield: *2 to 3 dozen*
Total time: *30 minutes*

1 cup all-purpose flour
1 teaspoon baking powder
1 teaspoon baking soda
¼ cup peanut butter
1 cup mashed bananas
¼ cup banana-flavored yogurt
1 large egg
½ cup peanuts, chopped

**1** Preheat the oven to 350 degrees. Lightly grease an 8-inch square baking pan.

**2** Combine the flour, baking powder, and baking soda.

**3** In a large bowl, beat the peanut butter, bananas, and yogurt until smooth. Beat in the egg. Gradually blend in the dry ingredients. Fold in the peanuts. Spread the mixture evenly in the prepared baking pan.

**4** Bake for 18 to 20 minutes, until lightly colored on top and firm to the touch. Cool in the pan on a wire rack before cutting into large or small bars.

1½ cups all-purpose flour
½ teaspoon salt
2 cups packed light brown sugar
1 cup peanut butter
⅔ cup vegetable shortening
3 large eggs
1 teaspoon vanilla extract
Vanilla Icing (see Pantry)

**1** Preheat the oven to 350 degrees. Lightly grease an 8-inch square baking pan.

**2** Combine the flour and salt.

**3** In a large bowl, beat the brown sugar, peanut butter, and vegetable shortening until smooth and creamy. Beat in the eggs. Beat in the vanilla extract. Gradually blend in the dry ingredients. Spread the mixture evenly in the prepared baking pan.

**4** Bake for 30 to 35 minutes, until firm to the touch. Cool in the pan on a wire rack.

**5** Drizzle the icing over the cookies and cut into large or small bars.

# Peanut Butter Bars I

Bar Cookies

YIELD: *2 to 3 dozen*
TOTAL TIME: *40 minutes*

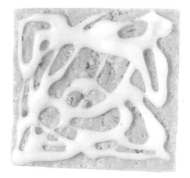

---

1 cup all-purpose flour
½ cup rolled oats
1 teaspoon baking powder
½ teaspoon salt
½ cup vegetable shortening
¾ cup packed light brown sugar
1 cup peanut butter
3 large eggs
½ cup milk
1 teaspoon vanilla extract
1 cup (6 ounces) semisweet chocolate chips

**1** Preheat the oven to 350 degrees.

**2** Combine the flour, oats, baking powder, and salt.

**3** In a large bowl, cream the vegetable shortening and brown sugar. Beat in the peanut butter. Beat in the eggs. Beat in the milk and vanilla extract. Gradually blend in the dry ingredients. Spread the mixture evenly into an ungreased 8-inch square baking pan.

**4** Bake for 25 to 30 minutes, until lightly colored on top. Sprinkle the chocolate chips over the hot crust. Let sit for 1 to 2 minutes to melt the chocolate, then spread it evenly over the top with a spatula. Cool in the pan on a wire rack before cutting into large or small bars.

**Baking notes:** Use peanut butter chips for the topping to add even more peanut butter flavor. Raisins may be added to the dough if desired.

# Peanut Butter Bars II

Bar Cookies

YIELD: *3 to 4 dozen*
TOTAL TIME: *45 minutes*

# PEANUT BUTTER COOKIES I

Formed Cookies

YIELD: *2 to 3 dozen*
TOTAL TIME: *30 minutes*

1½ cups all-purpose flour
1½ teaspoons baking powder
½ teaspoon salt
1 cup packed light brown sugar
½ cup peanut butter
¼ cup vegetable shortening
1 large egg
2 tablespoons fresh orange juice
1½ teaspoons vanilla extract
1½ tablespoons grated orange zest
¾ cup currants

**1** Preheat the oven to 400 degrees. Lightly grease 2 baking sheets.

**2** Combine the flour, baking powder, and salt.

**3** In a large bowl, beat together the sugar, peanut butter, and veg-

etable shortening until smooth and creamy. Beat in the egg. Beat in the orange juice and vanilla extract. Beat in the orange zest. Gradually blend in the dry ingredients. Stir in the currants.

**4** Pinch off walnut-sized pieces of the dough and roll into small balls. Place 2 inches apart on the prepared baking sheets. Flatten each ball with the back of a fork dipped in flour, making a crisscross pattern.

**5** Bake for 12 to 15 minutes, until golden brown. Transfer to wire racks to cool.

**Baking notes:** These taste even better if allowed to age for 1 day.

# PEANUT BUTTER COOKIES II

Drop Cookies

YIELD: *3 to 4 dozen*
TOTAL TIME: *30 minutes*
CHILLING TIME: *4 hours*

2½ cups all-purpose flour
1 teaspoon baking powder
1 teaspoon baking soda
½ teaspoon ground ginger
½ teaspoon ground cinnamon
¼ teaspoon ground cloves
1 cup packed light brown sugar
2 large eggs
½ cup peanut butter
2 tablespoons sour milk

**1** Combine the flour, baking powder, baking soda, and spices.

**2** In a large bowl, beat together the brown sugar and eggs. Beat in the peanut butter. Beat in the sour milk. Gradually blend in the dry ingredients. Cover and chill for at least 4 hours.

**3** Preheat the oven to 350 degrees. Lightly grease 2 baking sheets.

**4** Drop the dough by spoonfuls 1½ inches apart onto the prepared baking sheets. Use a fork dipped in flour to flatten the cookies, making a crisscross pattern.

**5** Bake for 8 to 10 minutes, until golden brown. Transfer to wire racks to cool.

# PEANUT BUTTER COOKIES III

Drop Cookies

YIELD: *4 to 5 dozen*
TOTAL TIME: *30 minutes*
CHILLING TIME: *1 hour*

½ cup corn syrup
1 cup peanut butter
1 cup granulated sugar
6 cups corn flakes

**1** Line 2 baking sheets with waxed paper.

**2** In a medium saucepan, bring the corn syrup to a boil and cook until it registers 234 to 238 degrees on a candy thermometer (soft ball stage). Remove from the heat and stir in the peanut butter and sugar, blending thoroughly.

**3** Place the cereal in a large bowl and pour the warm mixture over the top, stirring until well coated.

**4** Drop the mixture by spoonfuls 1 inch apart onto the prepared baking sheets. Refrigerate until thoroughly chilled.

1 cup all-purpose flour
½ teaspoon baking powder
¼ teaspoon ground cardamom
¼ cup peanut butter
2 tablespoons butter, at room
  temperature
2 large eggs
¼ cup mashed bananas
¾ teaspoon banana-flavored liqueur
1 cup peanuts, chopped

**1** Preheat the oven to 350 degrees. Lightly grease 2 baking sheets.

**2** Combine the flour, baking powder, and cardamom.

**3** In a large bowl, beat the peanut butter, butter, eggs, and bananas. Beat in the liqueur. Gradually blend in the dry ingredients. Stir in the peanuts.

**4** Drop the dough by spoonfuls 1½ inches apart onto the prepared baking sheets. Flatten the cookies with the back of a fork dipped in flour, making a criss-cross pattern.

**5** Bake for 5 to 8 minutes, until lightly colored. Transfer to wire racks to cool.

# Peanut Butter Cookies IV

Drop Cookies

YIELD: *2 to 4 dozen*
TOTAL TIME: *30 minutes*

---

2½ cups all-purpose flour
1 teaspoon baking powder
1½ teaspoons baking soda
2 cups packed light brown sugar
1 cup vegetable shortening
1 cup peanut butter
2 large eggs

**1** Preheat the oven to 350 degrees. Lightly grease 2 baking sheets.

**2** Combine the flour, baking powder, and baking soda.

**3** In a large bowl, beat together the brown sugar, vegetable shortening, peanut butter, and eggs. Gradually blend in the dry ingredients. The dough will be very soft.

**4** Using a serving spoon, drop the dough by spoonfuls 3 inches apart onto the prepared baking sheets. Using the back of a spoon dipped in flour, spread the cookies into large rounds.

**5** Bake for 10 to 12 minutes, until golden brown. Cool on the baking sheets on wire racks.

**Baking notes:** Chunky peanut butter can be used for more crunch.

# Peanut Butter Jumbo Cookies

Drop Cookies

YIELD: *2 to 3 dozen*
TOTAL TIME: *30 minutes*

---

2¼ cups all-purpose flour
¾ teaspoon baking soda
½ teaspoon salt
3½ cups packed light brown sugar
1½ cups granulated sugar
1½ cups peanut butter
1½ cups vegetable shortening
3 large eggs

**1** Combine the flour, baking soda and salt.

**2** In a large bowl, beat together the two sugars, peanut butter, and vegetable shortening until smooth and creamy. Beat in the eggs. Gradually blend in the dry ingredients. Cover and chill for 4 hours.

**3** Preheat the oven to 350 degrees.

**4** Drop the dough by spoonfuls 3 inches apart onto ungreased baking sheets (see Baking notes). Flatten the cookies with the back of a spoon dipped in flour.

**5** Bake for 10 to 12 minutes, until golden brown. Transfer to wire racks to cool.

**Baking notes:** The key word here is "jumbo": For very large cookies, drop the dough from a serving spoon. This cookie spreads, so you may only be able to get 4 or 6 cookies on a baking sheet.

# Peanut Butter Jumbos

Drop Cookies

YIELD: *2 dozen*
TOTAL TIME: *30 minutes*
CHILLING TIME: *4 hours*

**P**

# PEANUT BUTTER REFRIGERATOR COOKIES

Refrigerator Cookies

YIELD: *4 to 5 dozen*
TOTAL TIME: *30 minutes*
CHILLING TIME: *8 hours*

1¾ cups all-purpose flour
2 teaspoons baking soda
¼ teaspoon salt
½ cup vegetable shortening
1 cup granulated sugar
½ cup chunky peanut butter
1 large egg
1 teaspoon vanilla extract
½ teaspoon grated lemon zest

1  Combine the flour, baking soda, and salt.

2  In a large bowl, cream the vegetable shortening and sugar. Beat in the peanut butter. Beat in the egg and vanilla extract. Beat in the lemon zest. Gradually blend in the dry ingredients.

3  Divide the dough in half. Shape each half into a log 2 inches in diameter. Wrap in waxed paper and chill for 8 hours or overnight.

4  Preheat the oven to 350 degrees.

5  Cut the logs into ¼-inch-thick slices and place 1 inch apart on ungreased baking sheets. With a fork dipped in flour, flatten each cookie, pressing a crisscross pattern into the top.

6  Bake for 7 to 10 minutes, until lightly colored. Transfer to wire racks to cool.

**Baking notes:** The logs can be rolled in chopped peanuts before chilling.

# PEANUT BUTTER SHORTBREAD

Bar Cookies

YIELD: *3 to 4 dozen*
TOTAL TIME: *40 minutes*

1⅓ cups all-purpose flour
1 cup rolled oats
1 cup packed light brown sugar
1 cup vegetable shortening
¼ cup peanut butter
1 large egg, separated
1 teaspoon vanilla extract
1 cup peanuts, ground fine

1  Preheat the oven to 300 degrees. Lightly grease a 15 by 10-inch baking pan.

2  Combine the flour and oats.

3  In a large bowl, beat the brown sugar, vegetable shortening, and peanut butter together until smooth and creamy. Beat in the egg yolk and vanilla extract. Gradually blend in the dry ingredients. Spread the mixture evenly in the prepared baking pan.

4  In a small bowl, beat the egg white until frothy. Spread over the dough and sprinkle the ground peanuts over the top.

5  Bake for 25 to 30 minutes, until lightly colored on top and firm to the touch. Cut into large or small bars and cool in the pan on a wire rack.

# PEANUT COOKIES

Drop Cookies

YIELD: *1 to 3 dozen*
TOTAL TIME: *30 minutes*

½ cup all-purpose flour
1 cup peanuts, ground fine (see Baking notes)
¼ cup rolled oats
½ teaspoon salt
1 cup powdered sugar
1 large egg
¼ teaspoon vanilla extract

1  Preheat the oven to 350 degrees.

2  Combine the flour, peanuts, oats, and salt.

3  In a large bowl, beat the powdered sugar and egg until thick and light-colored. Beat in the vanilla extract. Gradually blend in the dry ingredients.

4  Drop the dough by spoonfuls 2 inches apart onto ungreased baking sheets.

5  Bake for 10 to 12 minutes, until golden brown. Cool slightly, then to wire racks to cool.

**Baking notes:** The peanuts should be ground as fine as possible without becoming peanut butter.

---

# PEAR BARS

Bar Cookies

YIELD: *2 to 3 dozen*
TOTAL TIME: *40 minutes*

**FILLING**
½ cup dates, pitted and chopped fine
1½ cups all-purpose flour
2 teaspoons baking powder
¼ teaspoon ground nutmeg
⅓ cup canola oil
2 large eggs
1½ to 2 pears, peeled, chopped and pureed
1 cup rolled oats

1  Preheat the oven to 350 degrees. Lightly grease an 8-inch square baking pan.

2  To make the filling, place the dates in a blender and process to a puree adding just enough water to reach the desired consistency.

3  Combine the flour, baking powder, and nutmeg.

4  In a large bowl, beat the oil and eggs until thick and light-colored. Beat in the pureed pears. Gradually blend in the dry ingredients. Stir in the oats.

5  Spread half of the pear mixture evenly in the bottom of the prepared baking pan. Spread the date filling on top of the batter. Spread the remaining batter over the dates.

6  Bake for 20 to 25 minutes, until lightly browned on the top. Cool in the pan on a wire rack before cutting into large or small bars.

---

# PECAN BARS

Bar Cookies

YIELD: *1 to 2 dozen*
TOTAL TIME: *45 minutes*

**CRUST**
1⅓ cups all-purpose flour
½ cup packed light brown sugar
½ teaspoon baking powder
¼ cup pecans, chopped
⅓ cup vegetable shortening

**FILLING**
3 tablespoons all-purpose flour
½ teaspoon salt
¼ cup packed light brown sugar
2 large eggs
¾ cup light corn syrup
1½ teaspoons vanilla extract
¾ cup pecans, ground fine

1  Preheat the oven to 350 degrees. Lightly grease a 13 by 9-inch baking pan.

2  To make the crust, combine the flour, brown sugar, baking powder, and pecans in a large bowl. Cut in the vegetable shortening until the mixture resembles coarse crumbs. Press the dough evenly into the prepared baking pan.

3  Bake for 10 minutes.

4  To make the filling, combine the flour and salt.

5  In a medium bowl, beat the brown sugar and eggs until thick. Beat in the corn syrup and vanilla extract. Gradually blend in the dry ingredients.

6  Pour the filling over the hot crust and sprinkle the pecans over the top. Bake for 25 to 30 minutes longer, until lightly colored and firm to the touch. Cool in the pan on a wire rack before cutting into large or small bars.

# PECAN COOKIES

Drop Cookies

YIELD: *4 to 5 dozen*
TOTAL TIME: *35 minutes*

1 large egg white
¼ teaspoon salt
1 cup packed light brown sugar
1 cup pecans, ground fine
¼ teaspoon brandy

1  Preheat the oven to 275 degrees. Line 2 baking sheets with parchment paper.

2  In a large bowl, beat the egg white and salt until foamy. Gradually beat in the brown sugar and beat until the whites form stiff peaks. Fold in the pecans. Fold in the brandy.

3  Drop the dough by teaspoonfuls 1 inch apart onto the prepared baking sheets.

4  Bake for 25 to 30 minutes, until lightly colored. Cool on the baking sheets, on wire racks.

# PECAN CRISPIES

Formed Cookies

YIELD: *2 to 3 dozen*
TOTAL TIME: *30 minutes*
CHILLING TIME: *4 hours*

2 cups all-purpose flour
2 teaspoons baking powder
½ teaspoon salt
1½ cups vegetable shortening
1 cup granulated sugar
2 large eggs
1 teaspoon vanilla extract
¾ cup pecans, chopped
Powdered sugar

1  Combine the flour, baking powder, and salt.

2  In a large bowl, cream the vegetable shortening and sugar. Beat in the eggs. Beat in the vanilla extract. Gradually blend in the dry ingredients. If the dough

seems too dry, add a little water ½ teaspoonful at a time. Cover and chill for 4 hours.

3  Preheat the oven to 350 degrees.

4  Pinch off walnut-sized pieces of the dough and roll into balls. Roll in the chopped pecans and place 1½ inches apart on ungreased baking sheets. Flatten each ball with the bottom of a glass dipped in powdered sugar.

5  Bake for 6 to 8 minutes, until lightly colored. Cool slightly on the baking sheets, then transfer to wire racks to cool completely.

# PECAN HEALTH COOKIES

Drop Cookies

YIELD: *3 to 4 dozen*
TOTAL TIME: *30 minutes*

½ cup golden raisins
¼ cup currants
1 cup whole wheat flour
1½ cups rolled oats
¼ cup wheat germ
¼ teaspoon baking powder
½ teaspoon ground nutmeg
½ teaspoon salt
¾ cup vegetable shortening
1¼ cups raw sugar
1 large egg
¼ cup skim milk
¼ cup fresh orange juice
1 cup pecans, chopped

1  Preheat the oven to 350 degrees.

2  Combine the raisins and currants in a small bowl and add just enough water to cover them. Set aside to soak.

3  Combine the flour, oats, wheat germ, baking powder, nutmeg, and salt.

4  In a large bowl, cream the vegetable shortening and sugar. Beat in the egg. Beat in the milk and orange juice. Gradually blend in the dry ingredients. Stir in the pecans. Drain the raisins and currants thoroughly and fold into the dough.

5  Drop the dough by spoonfuls 1½ inches apart onto ungreased baking sheets. Flatten each cookie with the back of a spoon dipped in flour.

6  Bake for 12 to 15 minutes, until golden brown. Transfer to wire racks to cool.

**Baking notes:** For even more texture, sprinkle the cookies with sesame seeds before you flatten them.

# PECAN HEALTH DROPS

Drop Cookies

YIELD: *3 to 4 dozen*
TOTAL TIME: *40 minutes*

½ cup whole wheat flour
½ cup all-purpose flour
¼ cup soy flour
1½ cups rolled oats
¼ cup nonfat dry milk
¼ cup wheat germ
¼ teaspoon baking powder
½ teaspoon ground allspice
½ teaspoon salt
1¼ cups packed dark brown sugar
¾ cup canola oil
1 large egg
¼ cup fresh lemon juice
½ teaspoon vanilla extract
1 cup pecans, chopped

1 Preheat the oven to 350 degrees.

2 Combine the three flours, oats, dry milk, wheat germ, baking powder, allspice, and salt.

3 In a large bowl, beat the brown sugar and oil. Beat in the egg. Beat in the lemon juice and vanilla extract. Gradually blend in the dry ingredients. Stir in the pecans.

4 Drop the dough by spoonfuls 1½ inches onto ungreased baking sheets. Flatten each cookie with the back of a spoon dipped in flour.

5 Bake for 20 to 30 minutes, until lightly colored. Transfer to wire racks to cool.

# PECAN SHORTBREAD

Formed Cookies

YIELD: *4 to 5 dozen*
TOTAL TIME: *30 minutes*

4½ cups all-purpose flour
1 cup pecans, ground
2 cups (1 pound) butter, at room temperature
2½ cups packed light brown sugar
2 teaspoons vanilla extract

1 Preheat the oven to 350 degrees.

2 Combine the flour and pecans.

3 In a large bowl, cream the butter and brown sugar. Beat in the vanilla extract. Gradually stir in the dry ingredients. The dough will be stiff.

4 Pinch off walnut-sized pieces of dough and roll into small balls. Place the balls 1½ inches apart on ungreased baking sheets and flatten the cookies with the back of a spoon dipped in flour.

5 Bake for 10 to 12 minutes, until lightly colored. Transfer to wire racks to cool.

# PECAN SQUARES

Bar Cookies

YIELD: *1 to 2 dozen*
TOTAL TIME: *50 minutes*

CRUST
1 cup all-purpose flour
¼ teaspoon salt
¼ cup vegetable shortening

FILLING
2 tablespoons all-purpose flour
¼ teaspoon salt
¾ cup granulated sugar
2 large eggs
2 teaspoons bourbon
2 cups flaked coconut
1 cup pecans, chopped

1 Preheat the oven to 350 degrees. Lightly grease a 9-inch square baking pan.

2 To make the crust, combine the flour and salt in a medium bowl. Cut in the shortening until the mixture resembles coarse crumbs. Press the dough evenly into the prepared baking pan.

3 Bake for 15 minutes.

4 To make the filling, combine the flour and salt.

5 In a large bowl, beat the sugar and eggs. Beat in the bourbon. Gradually blend in the dry ingredients. Stir in the coconut and pecans.

6 Spread the filling over the hot crust. Bake for 12 to 15 minutes longer, or until lightly colored on top and firm to the touch. Cool in the pan on a wire rack before cutting into large or small bars.

# PENNSYLVANIA DUTCH CHRISTMAS COOKIES

Drop Cookies

YIELD: *7 to 8 dozen*
TOTAL TIME: *30 minutes*
CHILLING TIME: *4 hours*

3½ cups all-purpose flour
¼ teaspoon salt
2 cups vegetable shortening
2¼ cups granulated sugar
6 large eggs
2 tablespoons fresh lemon juice
2 teaspoons grated lemon zest
1½ cups currants
Vanilla Icing (see Pantry)

**1** Combine the flour and salt.

**2** In a large bowl, cream the vegetable shortening and sugar. Beat in the eggs. Beat in the lemon juice and zest. Gradually blend in the dry ingredients. Fold in the currants. Cover and chill for 4 hours.

**3** Preheat the oven to 350 degrees.

**4** Drop the dough by spoonfuls 1½ inches apart onto ungreased baking sheets.

**5** Bake for 8 to 10 minutes, until lightly colored. Transfer to wire racks to cool.

**6** Drizzle the sugar icing over the tops of the cooled cookies.

# PEPPARKAKOR I

Rolled Cookies

YIELD: *6 to 7 dozen*
TOTAL TIME: *30 minutes*
CHILLING TIME: *24 hours*

1⅔ cups all-purpose flour
½ teaspoon baking soda
¾ teaspoon ground ginger
½ teaspoon ground cinnamon
¼ teaspoon ground cloves
¼ teaspoon ground cardamom
½ teaspoon salt
6 tablespoons butter, at room
    temperature
⅓ cup granulated sugar
¼ cup molasses
1 teaspoon grated orange zest
¼ cup almonds, chopped

**1** Combine the flour, baking soda, spices, and salt.

**2** In a large bowl, cream the butter and sugar. Beat in the molasses. Beat in the orange zest. Gradually blend in the dry ingredients. Fold in the almonds. Cover and chill for 24 hours.

**3** Preheat the oven to 350 degrees. Lightly grease 2 baking sheets.

**4** On a floured surface, roll out the dough to a thickness of ⅛ inch. Using cookie cutters, cut into shapes and place the cookies 1 inch apart on the prepared baking sheets.

**5** Bake for 5 to 7 minutes, until lightly colored. Transfer to wire racks to cool.

**Baking notes:** These can be decorated with Vanilla Icing (see Pantry).

3 cups all-purpose flour
2 cups whole wheat flour
1½ teaspoons baking soda
1 teaspoon ground cloves
1 teaspoon ground cinnamon
½ teaspoon salt
1 cup butter, at room temperature
1 cup granulated sugar
1 large egg
1 cup molasses
2 tablespoons cider vinegar

**1** Combine the two flours, the baking soda, spices, and salt.

**2** In a large bowl, cream the butter and sugar. Beat in the egg. Beat in the molasses and vinegar. Gradually blend in the dry ingredients. Cover and chill for 4 hours.

**3** Preheat the oven to 375 degrees. Lightly grease 2 baking sheets.

**4** On a floured surface, roll out the dough to a thickness of ⅛ inch. Using a cookie cutter, cut into shapes and place 1 inch apart on the prepared baking sheets.

**5** Bake for 5 to 8 minutes, or until lightly colored. Transfer to wire racks to cool.

**Baking notes:** These cookies can be decorated with Vanilla Icing (see Pantry) if desired.

# PEPPARKAKOR II

Rolled Cookies

<small>YIELD: *6 to 7 dozen*
TOTAL TIME: *30 minutes*
CHILLING TIME: *4 hours*</small>

---

4 cups all-purpose flour
1 teaspoon baking powder
1 teaspoon ground cinnamon
½ teaspoon ground cloves
1 cup packed light brown sugar
1 cup milk
1 cup molasses
1 cup candied citrus peel, chopped

**1** Preheat the oven to 300 degrees. Lightly grease an 8-inch square baking pan.

**2** Combine the flour, baking powder, and spices.

**3** In a large bowl, beat the brown sugar, milk, and molasses until smooth. Gradually blend in the dry ingredients. Stir in the candied citrus peel. Spread the dough evenly in the prepared baking pan.

**4** Bake for 1½ to 2 hours, or until lightly colored and firm to the touch. Cool in the pan on a wire rack before cutting into large or small bars.

# PEPPARKOEK

Bar Cookies

<small>YIELD: *3 to 4 dozen*
TOTAL TIME: *90 minutes*</small>

---

2½ cups all-purpose flour
¼ cup almonds, ground fine
1 teaspoon baking soda
1 teaspoon ground cinnamon
1 teaspoon ground cardamom
1 teaspoon ground ginger
½ teaspoon ground allspice
½ teaspoon salt
1 cup vegetable shortening
1 cup granulated sugar
1 large egg
½ cup corn syrup
Vanilla Icing (see Pantry)

**1** Combine the flour, almonds, baking soda, spices, and salt.

**2** In a large bowl, cream the vegetable shortening and sugar. Beat in the egg. Beat in the corn syrup. Gradually blend in the dry ingredients. Cover and chill for 8 hours.

**3** Preheat the oven to 350 degrees.

**4** On a floured surface, roll out the dough to a thickness of ¼ inch. Using cookie cutters, cut into shapes and place 1 inch apart on ungreased baking sheets.

**5** Bake for 8 to 10 minutes, until lightly colored. Transfer to wire racks to cool.

**6** Frost with the icing when cool.

# PEPPER COOKIES

Rolled Cookies

<small>YIELD: *3 to 4 dozen*
TOTAL TIME: *30 minutes*
CHILLING TIME: *8 hours*</small>

# Peppermint Delights

Rolled Cookies

YIELD: *4 to 5 dozen*
TOTAL TIME: *30 minutes*

1½ cups all-purpose flour
½ teaspoon salt
1 cup vegetable shortening
1 cup powdered sugar
2 teaspoons vanilla extract
1 cup rolled oats
¼ cup crushed peppermint candies

**1** Preheat the oven to 325 degrees.

**2** Combine the flour and salt.

**3** In a large bowl, cream the vegetable shortening and powdered sugar. Beat in the vanilla extract. Gradually blend in the dry ingredients. Fold in the oats. Fold in the candies.

**4** On a floured surface, roll out the dough to a thickness of ¼ inch. Using a 1½-inch round cookie cutter, cut out the cookies and place 1 inch apart on ungreased baking sheets.

**5** Bake for 10 to 12 minutes, until lightly colored. Transfer to wire racks to cool.

**Baking notes:** Be sure to crush the candy very fine. For a festive look, add a few drops of red food coloring to the dough.

# Peppermint Meringues

Formed Cookies

YIELD: *2 to 3 dozen*
TOTAL TIME: *45 minutes*

3 large egg whites
¾ cup granulated sugar
¾ teaspoon cider vinegar
6 drops peppermint oil
Green food coloring (optional)

**1** Preheat the oven to 200 degrees. Line 2 baking sheets with parchment paper.

**2** In a large bowl, beat the egg whites until foamy. Gradually beat in the sugar and beat until the whites hold stiff peaks. Fold in the vinegar and peppermint oil. Fold in the optional food coloring and beat for 5 minutes longer.

**3** Place the mixture in a cookie press or a pastry bag fitted with a star tip and press or pipe out 1-inch mounds onto the prepared baking sheets, spacing them 1 inch apart.

**4** Bake for 30 to 35 minutes, until firm to the touch. Cool on the baking pans on a wire racks.

# Persimmon Cookies I

Drop Cookies

YIELD: *4 to 5 dozen*
TOTAL TIME: *30 minutes*

2 cups all-purpose flour
1 cup almonds, ground
1 teaspoon baking soda
1 teaspoon ground cinnamon
1 teaspoon ground cloves
1 teaspoon ground nutmeg
⅛ teaspoon salt
½ cup vegetable shortening
1 cup granulated sugar
1 large egg
1 persimmon, peeled and pureed
1 cup raisins (optional)

**1** Preheat the oven to 350 degrees.

**2** Combine the flour, almonds, baking soda, spices, and salt.

**3** In a large bowl, cream the vegetable shortening and sugar. Beat in the egg. Beat in the persimmon puree. Gradually blend in the dry ingredients. Stir in the optional raisins.

**4** Drop the dough by spoonfuls 1½ inches apart onto ungreased baking sheets.

**5** Bake for 10 to 12 minutes, until lightly colored. Transfer to wire racks to cool.

**Baking notes:** Use overripe persimmons for these intensely flavorful cookies. These cookies are delicious but perishable; store in the refrigerator.

2 cups all-purpose flour
1 teaspoon baking powder
½ teaspoon baking soda
½ teaspoon ground cinnamon
½ teaspoon ground cloves
½ teaspoon salt
½ cup vegetable shortening
1½ cups granulated sugar
1 large egg
1 persimmon, peeled and pureed

**1** Preheat the oven to 350 degrees.

**2** Combine the flour, baking powder, baking soda, spices, and salt.

**3** In a large bowl, cream the vegetable shortening and sugar. Beat in the egg. Beat in the persimmon puree. Gradually blend in the dry ingredients.

**4** Drop the dough by spoonfuls 1½ inches apart onto ungreased baking sheets.

**5** Bake for 10 to 12 minutes, until lightly colored. Transfer to wire racks to cool.

# PERSIMMON COOKIES II

Drop Cookies

YIELD: *4 to 5 dozen*
TOTAL TIME: *30 minutes*

---

1¾ cups all-purpose flour
1 teaspoon baking soda
1 teaspoon ground nutmeg
1 teaspoon ground cinnamon
¼ teaspoon ground cloves
1 cup granulated sugar
½ cup canola oil
1 large egg
1 persimmon, peeled and pureed

**1** Preheat the oven to 350 degrees. Lightly grease a 9-inch square baking pan.

**2** Combine the flour, baking soda, and spices.

**3** In a large bowl, beat the sugar and oil. Beat in the egg. Beat in the persimmon puree. Spread the mixture evenly in the prepared baking pan.

**4** Bake for 20 to 25 minutes, until lightly colored on top and firm to the touch. Cool in the pan on a wire rack.

# PERSIMMON BARS

Bar Cookies

YIELD: *4 to 5 dozen*
TOTAL TIME: *35 minutes*

---

3 cups all-purpose flour
½ teaspoon baking powder
1 cup butter, at room temperature
½ cup granulated sugar
1 tablespoon heavy cream
1 teaspoon vanilla extract

**1** Preheat the oven to 350 degrees. Lightly grease 2 baking sheets.

**2** Combine the flour and baking powder.

**3** In a large bowl, cream the butter and sugar. Beat in the heavy cream and vanilla extract. Gradually blend in the dry ingredients.

**4** Turn the dough out onto a floured surface and knead until smooth.

**5** Divide the dough into 6 equal pieces. Roll each piece into ¼-inch-thick round. Using a 1½-inch-round cookie cutter, cut out the centers of the rounds. Cut each round into 6 to 8 wedges. Carefully place the wedges 1 inch apart on the prepared baking sheets. Prick all over with the tines of a fork.

**6** Bake for 12 to 15 minutes, until lightly colored. Cool slightly on the baking sheet, then transfer to wire racks to cool completely.

**Baking notes:** You can frost these with a thin layer of Vanilla Icing (see Pantry). This cookie was created for Queen Victoria.

# PETTICOAT TAILS

Formed Cookies

YIELD: *3 to 4 dozen*
TOTAL TIME: *30 minutes*

# PFEFFERNÜSSE

Rolled Cookies

YIELD: *4 to 5 dozen*
TOTAL TIME: *30 minutes*
CHILLING TIME: *4 hours*
RESTING TIME: *4 hours*

**3 cups all-purpose flour**
**1 teaspoon baking powder**
**½ teaspoon ground cinnamon**
**¼ teaspoon ground nutmeg**
**¼ teaspoon ground cloves**
**¼ teaspoon salt**
**1 cup granulated sugar**
**3 large eggs**
**1½ tablespoons fresh lemon juice**
**1 teaspoon hazelnut syrup (optional)**
**½ teaspoon grated lemon zest**
**¼ cup hazelnuts, chopped**
**About 1 teaspoon brandy**

**1** Combine the flour, baking powder, spices, and salt.

**2** In a large bowl, beat the sugar and eggs until thick and light-colored. Beat in the lemon juice and hazelnut syrup. Beat in the lemon zest. Gradually blend in the dry ingredients. Stir in the hazelnuts. Cover and chill for 4 hours.

**3** Lightly grease 2 baking sheets.

**4** On a floured surface, roll out the dough to a thickness of ½ inch. Using a 1½-inch round cookie cutter, cut out cookies and place 1 inch apart on the prepared baking sheets. Cover the baking sheets with clean towels and leave undisturbed for 4 hours.

**5** Preheat the oven to 350 degrees.

**6** Turn the cookies over and place a drop of brandy in the center of each cookie. Bake for 8 to 10 minutes, until lightly colored. Transfer to wire racks to cool.

# PINEAPPLE-BLUEBERRY BARS

Bar Cookies

YIELD: *2 to 3 dozen*
TOTAL TIME: *35 minutes*

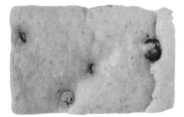

**½ cup canned crushed pineapple, drained**
**½ cup unsweetened pineapple juice**
**1 teaspoon baking powder**
**1 teaspoon baking soda**
**1 teaspoon orange liqueur**
**1 tablespoon vegetable shortening**
**1 large egg**
**1½ cups all-purpose flour**
**½ cup blueberries**

**1** Preheat the oven to 350 degrees. Lightly grease an 8-inch square baking pan.

**2** In a blender, puree the pineapple and pineapple juice.

**3** Transfer pineapple puree to a large bowl and whisk in the baking powder, baking soda, orange liqueur, vegetable shortening, and the egg. Gradually blend in the flour. Fold in the blueberries. Spread the mixture evenly in the prepared baking pan.

**4** Bake for 20 to 25 minutes, until lightly colored on top and firm to the touch. Cool in the pan on a wire rack before cutting into large or small bars.

¾ cup all-purpose flour
¾ teaspoon baking powder
½ teaspoon salt
½ cup vegetable shortening
1 cup packed light brown sugar
2 large eggs
One 8-ounce can crushed pineapple, drained
½ teaspoon rum
¾ cup flaked coconut

**1** Preheat the oven to 350 degrees. Lightly grease a 9-inch square baking pan.

**2** Combine the flour, baking powder, and salt.

**3** In a large bowl, cream the vegetable shortening and brown sugar. Beat in the eggs. Beat in the pineapple and rum. Gradually blend in the dry ingredients. Stir in the coconut. Spread the mixture evenly in the prepared baking pan.

**4** Bake for 25 to 30 minutes, until lightly colored on top. Cool in the pan on a wire rack before cutting into large or small bars.

# PINEAPPLE-COCONUT BARS

Bar Cookies

YIELD: *2 to 3 dozen*
TOTAL TIME: *40 minutes*

---

1 cup all-purpose flour
½ teaspoon baking powder
¼ teaspoon baking soda
½ cup granulated sugar
¼ cup vegetable oil
1 large egg
⅓ cup frozen pineapple juice concentrate, thawed
1 tablespoon orange liqueur
½ cup shredded coconut
½ cup almonds, chopped fine

**1** Preheat the oven to 350 degrees. Lightly grease 2 baking sheets.

**2** Combine the flour, baking powder, and baking soda.

**3** In a large bowl, beat the sugar and oil. Beat in the egg. Beat in the pineapple juice concentrate and liqueur. Gradually blend in the dry ingredients. Fold in the coconut and almonds.

**4** Drop the dough by spoonfuls 1½ inches apart onto the prepared baking sheets.

**5** Bake for 6 to 8 minutes, until lightly colored. Transfer to wire racks to cool.

# PINEAPPLE COOKIES

Drop Cookies

YIELD: *2 to 3 dozen*
TOTAL TIME: *30 minutes*

---

½ cup vegetable shortening
2 tablespoons granulated sugar
2 tablespoons honey
2 tablespoons brandy
1 cup all-purpose flour
¼ cup pine nuts

**1** Preheat the oven to 375 degrees. Lightly grease 2 baking sheets.

**2** In a large bowl, cream the shortening and sugar. Beat in the honey and brandy. Gradually blend in the flour. Stir in the pine nuts.

**3** Pinch off walnut-sized pieces of dough and roll into balls. Place 1 inch apart on the prepared baking sheets.

**4** Bake for 8 to 10 minutes, until lightly colored. Transfer to wire racks to cool.

# PINE NUT COOKIES

Formed Cookies

YIELD: *3 to 4 dozen*
TOTAL TIME: *30 minutes*

# PINE NUT CRESCENTS

Formed Cookies

YIELD: *3 to 4 dozen*
TOTAL TIME: *30 minutes*

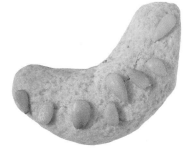

1 cup vegetable shortening
⅔ cup packed light brown sugar
3 large egg yolks
½ teaspoon vanilla extract
1 teaspoon orange flower water
1 teaspoon grated orange zest
2¾ cups all-purpose flour
½ cup pine nuts, chopped
3 tablespoons honey, warmed

**1** Preheat the oven to 325 degrees. Lightly grease 2 baking sheets.

**2** In a large bowl, cream the vegetable shortening and brown sugar. Beat in the egg yolks and vanilla extract. Beat in the orange flower water and orange zest. Gradually blend in the flour.

**3** Pinch off walnut-sized pieces of dough and form into crescents and place the crescents 1 inch apart on the prepared baking sheets. Press a few of pine nuts into each crescent and brush with honey.

**4** Bake for 12 to 15 minutes, until lightly colored. Transfer to wire racks to cool.

# PLÄTTPANNA

Drop Cookies

YIELD: *6 to 10 pancakes*
TOTAL TIME: *40 minutes*

2 large eggs
1 cup all-purpose flour
6 tablespoons butter, melted
½ cup granulated sugar
½ cup almonds, ground fine
2 tablespoons sugar crystals

**1** Preheat the oven to 400 degrees.

**2** Place a plättar pan in the oven to preheat.

**3** In a medium bowl, beat the eggs and sugar. Beat in the melted butter. Gradually blend in the flour.

**4** Combine the ground almonds and sugar crystals.

**5** Spoon ½ tablespoon of the batter into each indentation in the hot pan. Sprinkle the tops with the almonds and sugar crystals and bake for 2 to 3 minutes, until golden brown color. Immediately remove the pancakes from the pan and roll each one up around a broom handle or heavy dowel stick. Repeat with the remaining batter.

**Baking notes:** Plättar pans are available at specialty cookware shops. These are great for desserts, filled with chopped fruit and whipped cream.

# PLAY CLAY

Nonedible Cookies

YIELD: *1½ pounds dough*

2 cups cornstarch
4 cups baking soda
2½ cups water

**1** In a saucepan, combine all of the ingredients and stir until smooth. Turn the mixture out onto a flat surface and cover with a damp cloth until cool.

**2** Knead until the dough is smooth and elastic. Store in a tightly closed container when not in use.

**Baking notes:** Food coloring can be added if desired.

1 cup all-purpose flour
2 cups rice flour
¼ cup unsweetened cocoa powder
1 teaspoon baking powder
¾ cup vegetable shortening
1 cup granulated sugar
1 teaspoon vanilla extract
1 cup raisins, chopped
1 cup peanuts, chopped

**1** Preheat the oven to 350 degrees. Lightly grease 2 baking sheets.

**2** Combine the two flours, cocoa, and baking powder.

**3** In a large bowl, cream the vegetable shortening and sugar. Beat in the vanilla extract. Gradually blend in the dry ingredients. Fold in the raisins. If the dough is not binding, add 1 teaspoon of water at a time to achieve the right consistency.

**4** Pinch off walnut-sized pieces of dough and roll into balls. Roll each ball in the chopped peanuts and place 3 inches apart on the prepared baking sheets. Flatten each ball to a thickness of ¼ inch with the bottom of a glass dipped in flour.

**5** Bake for 10 to 12 minutes, until golden. Transfer to wire racks to cool.

**Baking notes:** Decorate with chocolate icing: Combine 1 cup powdered sugar, 2 teaspoons unsweetened cocoa, and 1 teaspoon of water and stir until smooth. Add a drop or so more water if necessary.

# P-NUTTIES

Formed Cookies

YIELD: *4 to 5 dozen*
TOTAL TIME: *30 minutes*

---

2¼ cups all-purpose flour
½ teaspoon salt
1 cup vegetable shortening
8 ounces cream cheese, at room temperature
¼ teaspoon lemon extract
½ cup fruit preserves

**1** Combine the flour and salt.

**2** In a large bowl, cream the vegetable shortening and cream cheese. Beat in the lemon extract. Gradually blend in the dry ingredients. Cover and chill for 2 hours.

**3** Preheat the oven to 350 degrees.

**4** On a floured surface, roll out the dough to a thickness of ¼ inch. Using a 2-inch round cookie cutter, cut out cookies and place 1 inch apart on ungreased baking sheets. With your thumb, make an indentation in the center of each cookie. Fill the hollow with ½ a teaspoon of fruit preserves.

**5** Bake for 10 to 12 minutes, until lightly colored. Transfer to wire racks to cool.

# POLISH KOLACKY

Rolled Cookies

YIELD: *3 to 4 dozen*
TOTAL TIME: *35 minutes*
CHILLING TIME: *2 hours*

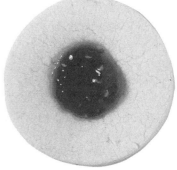

# POOR MAN'S COOKIES

Rolled Cookies

YIELD: *3 to 4 dozen*
TOTAL TIME: *30 minutes*

1 tablespoon powdered sugar
2 large eggs
3 tablespoons evaporated milk
1¾ cups all-purpose flour
Vegetable oil for deep-frying
Powdered sugar for sprinkling

**1** In a large bowl, beat the powdered sugar and eggs. Beat in the milk. Gradually blend in the flour.

**2** On a floured surface, roll the dough out to a thickness of ¼ inch. Using a knife, cut into very large diamonds. Cut a slash across the center of each diamond and pull one tip through the slash.

**3** In a deep-fryer or deep heavy pot, heat the oil to 375 degrees.

**4** Deep-fry the diamonds in batches, turning once or twice, until golden brown on both sides.

**5** Transfer to paper towels to drain and sprinkle with powdered sugar. Let cool, then sprinkle with powdered sugar again.

# POPPY SEED COOKIES

Refrigerator Cookies

YIELD: *3 to 4 dozen*
TOTAL TIME: *25 minutes*
CHILLING TIME: *8 hours*

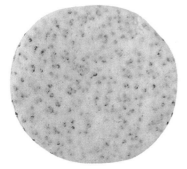

2¼ cups all-purpose flour
½ teaspoon ground nutmeg
¼ teaspoon salt
1 cup vegetable shortening
1 cup granulated sugar
2 large egg yolks
2 tablespoons grated orange zest
2 tablespoons poppy seeds

**1** Combine the flour, nutmeg, and salt.

**2** In a large bowl, cream the vegetable shortening and sugar. Beat in the egg yolks. Beat in the orange zest. Gradually blend in the dry ingredients. Fold in the poppy seeds.

**3** Divide the dough in half. Form each half into a log 2 inches in diameter. Wrap in waxed paper and chill for 8 hours or overnight.

**4** Preheat the oven to 350 degrees.

**5** Cut the logs into ¼-inch-thick slices and place 1 inch apart on ungreased baking sheets.

**6** Bake for 6 to 9 minutes, until lightly colored. Transfer to wire racks to cool.

2½ cups all-purpose flour
1½ teaspoons unsweetened cocoa powder
1 teaspoon baking powder
1 teaspoon ground allspice
Pinch of salt
1 cup vegetable shortening
1 cup granulated sugar
1 cup packed light brown sugar
2 large eggs
1 teaspoon vanilla extract
1½ cups (9 ounces) semisweet chocolate chips

**1** Combine the flour, cocoa powder, baking powder, allspice, and salt.

**2** In a large bowl, cream together the vegetable shortening and two sugars. Beat in the eggs. Beat in the vanilla extract. Gradually blend in the dry ingredients. Fold in the chocolate chips. Cover and chill for 4 hours.

**3** Preheat the oven to 350 degrees. Lightly grease 2 baking sheets.

**4** Drop the dough by spoonfuls 1½ inches apart onto the prepared baking sheets.

**5** Bake for 10 to 12 minutes, until lightly colored. Transfer to wire racks to cool.

**Baking notes:** I created this recipe in 1980 in honor of the city of Portsmouth, New Hampshire. For a different flavor variation, substitute coffee liqueur for the vanilla extract.

# PORTSMOUTH COOKIES

Drop Cookies

YIELD: *4 to 5 dozen*
TOTAL TIME: *30 minutes*
CHILLING TIME: *4 hours*

---

1 cup vegetable shortening
1 cup powdered sugar
1½ cups all-purpose flour
1 teaspoon vanilla extract
1½ cups potato chips, crushed
Powdered sugar for sprinkling

**1** Preheat the oven to 350 degrees.

**2** In a large bowl, cream the vegetable shortening and powdered sugar. Stir in the flour. Beat in the vanilla extract. Fold in the potato chips.

**3** Drop the dough by spoonfuls 1½ inches apart onto ungreased baking sheets.

**4** Bake for 15 to 18 minutes, until lightly colored. Sprinkle with powdered sugar and transfer to wire racks to cool.

**Baking notes:** It is best to use "lite" potato chips because they are less oily. This is a good cookie for children to make. For an after-school snack rather than a sweet treat, substitute water for the vanilla extract and use one of the many flavored potato chips available. Sprinkle with onion powder instead of powdered sugar.

# POTATO CHIP COOKIES

Drop Cookies

YIELD: *3 to 5 dozen*
TOTAL TIME: *30 minutes*

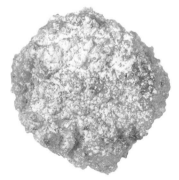

---

2 cups mashed potatoes
3 tablespoon vegetable shortening, melted
½ teaspoon salt
⅔ cup all-purpose flour

**1** Preheat a large nonstick frying pan or griddle.

**2** In a large bowl, add the mashed potatoes. Stir in the melted vegetable shortening and salt. Stir in the flour, a little at a time, so as not to dry out the mixture.

**3** Roll out the dough to a thickness of ¼ to ⅜ inch. Cut out 4-inch rounds, and then cut the rounds into pie-shaped wedges.

**4** Cook the wedges in the pan or on the griddle for 3 to 5 minutes, until the scones are lightly browned on both sides and cooked through. Keep moist by wrapping in a clean towel until ready to serve.

**Baking notes:** If not using a non-stick pan, then grease the pan or griddle to avoid sticking. This is not really a cookie. It is closer to a biscuit. In Britain, scones are often eaten spread with jelly, jam, or cream.

# POTATO SCONES

Rolled Cookies

YIELD: *1 to 2 dozen*
TOTAL TIME: *30 minutes*

# POWER CRUNCH COOKIES

Drop Cookies

YIELD: *2 to 3 dozen*
TOTAL TIME: *30 minutes*

½ cup all-purpose flour
¼ cup whole wheat flour
½ teaspoon baking soda
¼ teaspoon salt
⅓ cup vegetable shortening.
½ cup packed light brown sugar
1 large egg
1 tablespoon warm water
1 teaspoon vanilla extract
1 cup rolled oats
¾ cup bran cereal
½ cup mixed dried fruit, chopped fine

**1** Preheat the oven to 375 degrees.

**2** Combine the two flours, the baking soda, and salt.

**3** In a large bowl, cream the vegetable shortening and brown sugar. Beat in the egg. Beat in the water and vanilla extract. Gradually blend in the dry ingredients. Fold in the oats, cereal, and dried fruit.

**4** Drop the dough by spoonfuls 2 inches apart onto ungreased baking sheets.

**5** Bake for 4 to 6 minutes, until lightly colored. Transfer to wire racks to cool.

# PRIDE COOKIES

Drop Cookies

YIELD: *2 to 3 dozen*
TOTAL TIME: *30 minutes*

2 cups all-purpose flour
1 teaspoon baking powder
1 teaspoon baking soda
¼ teaspoon salt
1 cup butter, at room temperature
1 cup granulated sugar
1 cup packed light brown sugar
2 large eggs
2 teaspoons almond extract
3 cups rolled oats
1 cup flaked coconut
1 cup almonds, chopped fine
½ cup golden raisins

**1** Preheat the oven to 350 degrees. Lightly grease 2 baking sheets.

**2** Combine the flour, baking powder, baking soda, and salt.

**3** In a large bowl, cream the butter and two sugars. Beat in the eggs one at a time, beating vigorously after each addition. Beat in the almond extract. Gradually blend in the dry ingredients. Fold in the oats, coconut, almonds, and raisins.

**4** Drop the dough by spoonfuls 1½ inches apart onto the prepared baking sheets.

**5** Bake for 8 to 10 minutes, until lightly colored. Transfer to wire racks to cool.

# PRUNE COOKIES

Bar Cookies

YIELD: *1 to 2 dozen*
TOTAL TIME: *20 minutes*
CHILLING TIME: *1 hour*

1½ cups vegetable shortening
1½ cups granulated sugar
3 tablespoons corn syrup
½ teaspoon vanilla extract
3 cups prunes, pitted and chopped fine
3½ cup graham cracker crumbs
Powdered sugar for sprinkling

**1** Lightly grease a 13 by 9-inch baking pan.

**2** In a large saucepan, combine the vegetable shortening, sugar, corn syrup, and vanilla extract and cook, stirring until the shortening has melted. Beat vigorously. Remove from the heat and stir in the prunes. Gradually blend in the graham cracker crumbs. Press the mixture evenly in the prepared baking pan.

**3** Cover and refrigerate for 1 hour, or until chilled and set.

**4** Cut the cookies into large or small bars and sprinkle with powdered sugar.

# PUMPKIN BARS

Bar Cookies

YIELD: *1 to 2 dozen*
TOTAL TIME: *45 minutes*

2 cups all-purpose flour
2 teaspoons baking powder
1 teaspoon baking soda
2 teaspoons ground cinnamon
½ teaspoon ground ginger
½ teaspoon ground cloves
½ teaspoon ground nutmeg
¾ teaspoon salt
4 large eggs
2 cups granulated sugar
¾ cup vegetable oil
One 16-ounce can solid-pack
    pumpkin
Vanilla Icing (see Pantry)

**1** Preheat the oven to 350 degrees. Lightly grease a 13 by 9-inch baking pan.

**2** Combine the flour, baking powder, baking soda, spices, and salt.

**3** In a large bowl, beat the eggs and sugar until thick and light-colored. Beat in the oil. Beat in the pumpkin. Gradually blend in the dry ingredients. Scrape the mixture into the prepared baking pan.

**4** Bake for 30 to 35 minutes, until the edges pull away from the sides and the top springs back when lightly touched. Cool in the pan on a wire rack.

**5** Frost the cooled cookies with the icing and cut into large or small bars.

# PUMPKIN COOKIES I

Drop Cookies

YIELD: *3 to 5 dozen*
TOTAL TIME: *30 minutes*

1½ cups all-purpose flour
¾ teaspoon baking powder
¼ teaspoon baking soda
1 teaspoon ground allspice
⅓ cup vegetable shortening
1 cup solid-pack pumpkin
1 large egg
1 cup dates, pitted and chopped
Pecan halves for decorating

**1** Preheat the oven to 350 degrees. Lightly grease 2 baking sheets.

**2** Combine the flour, baking powder, baking soda, allspice.

**3** In a large bowl, beat the vegetable shortening and pumpkin pulp until smooth. Beat in the egg. Gradually blend in the dry ingredients. Stir in the dates.

**4** Drop the dough by spoonfuls 1½ inches apart onto the prepared baking sheets. Push a pecan half into the center of each cookie.

**5** Bake for 8 to 10 minutes, until lightly colored. Transfer to wire racks to cool.

# PUMPKIN COOKIES II

Drop Cookies

YIELD: *3 to 5 dozen*
TOTAL TIME: *30 minutes*

1 cup golden raisins
1½ cups (or enough to cover raisins) brandy
2 cups all-purpose flour
1 teaspoon baking powder
½ teaspoon baking soda
1 teaspoon ground cinnamon
½ teaspoon ground nutmeg
¼ teaspoon ground allspice
1 large egg
1 cup vegetable shortening
1 cup solid-pack pumpkin
1 teaspoon brandy from the raisin bowl
½ cup walnuts, chopped

1 Place the raisins in a small bowl and add enough brandy to just cover. Let soak for 15 minutes. Drain thoroughly, reserving the brandy.

2 Preheat the oven to 350 degrees. Lightly grease 2 baking sheets.

3 Combine the flour, baking powder, baking soda, and spices.

4 In a large bowl, beat the egg until thick and light-colored. Beat in the vegetable shortening and pumpkin. Beat in the 1 teaspoon of the reserved brandy. Gradually blend in the dry ingredients. Fold in the walnuts and raisins.

5 Drop the dough by spoonfuls 1½ inches apart onto the prepared baking sheets. Flatten each cookie with the back of a spoon dipped in flour.

6 Bake for 10 to 12 minutes, until lightly colored. Transfer to wire racks to cool.

# PUMPKIN COOKIES III

Drop Cookies

YIELD: *2 to 3 dozen*
TOTAL TIME: *30 minutes*

2 cups all-purpose flour
½ teaspoon baking powder
½ teaspoon baking soda
½ teaspoon ground cinnamon
½ teaspoon ground ginger
½ teaspoon ground nutmeg
¼ teaspoon ground cloves
½ cup vegetable shortening
1½ cups packed light brown sugar
1 large egg
1 cup solid-pack pumpkin
1 cup almonds, chopped
1 cup raisins, chopped fine

1 Preheat the oven to 400 degrees. Lightly grease 2 baking sheets.

2 Combine the flour, baking powder, baking soda, and spices.

3 In a large bowl, cream the vegetable shortening and brown sugar. Beat in the egg. Beat in the pumpkin. Gradually blend in the dry ingredients. Stir in the almonds and raisins.

4 Drop the dough by spoonfuls 2 inches apart onto the prepared baking sheets.

5 Bake for 12 to 15 minutes, until lightly colored. Transfer to wire racks to cool.

4 cups all-purpose flour
1 cup rolled oats
1½ teaspoons baking soda
2 teaspoons ground cinnamon
1 teaspoon salt
1½ cups vegetable shortening
1 cup granulated sugar
1 cup packed light brown sugar
1 large egg
1 teaspoon vanilla extract
2 cups solid-pack pumpkin

**1** Preheat the oven to 350 degrees.

**2** Combine the flour, oats, baking soda, cinnamon, and salt.

**3** In a large bowl, cream together the vegetable shortening and two sugars. Beat in the egg and vanilla extract. Beat in the pumpkin. Gradually blend in the dry ingredients.

**4** Drop the dough by spoonfuls 2 inches apart onto ungreased baking sheets.

**5** Bake for 18 to 20 minutes, until lightly colored. Transfer to wire racks to cool.

**Baking notes:** These can be drizzled with Vanilla Icing (see Pantry) if desired.

# PUMPKIN COOKIES IV

Drop Cookies

YIELD: *4 to 5 dozen*
TOTAL TIME: *30 minutes*

---

2 cups all-purpose flour
1 tablespoon baking powder
½ teaspoon baking soda
½ teaspoon ground ginger
½ teaspoon ground allspice
½ teaspoon ground nutmeg
¼ teaspoon salt
¼ cup vegetable shortening
3 tablespoons light brown sugar
1 cup solid-pack pumpkin
¼ cup plain yogurt
2 tablespoons sour milk

**1** Preheat the oven to 350 degrees. Lightly grease 2 baking sheets.

**2** Combine the flour, baking powder, baking soda, spices, and salt.

**3** In a large bowl, cream together the vegetable shortening and brown sugar. Beat in the pumpkin, yogurt, and sour milk. Gradually blend in the dry ingredients.

**4** Turn the dough out onto a floured surface, sprinkle with flour, and knead until smooth. Roll out the dough to a thickness of ¾ inch. Using a sharp knife, cut into 2-inch-squares and place 1 inch apart on the prepared baking sheets.

**5** Bake for 12 to 15 minutes, or until lightly colored. Transfer to wire racks, cover with a clean towel, and let cool.

# PUMPKIN SCONES

Rolled Cookies

YIELD: *4 to 5 dozen*
TOTAL TIME: *30 minutes*

---

1½ cups rolled oats
½ cup oat bran cereal
¼ teaspoon salt
⅓ cup canola oil
3 mashed bananas
1 teaspoon vanilla extract
1½ cups dried apricots, chopped
½ cup almonds, chopped fine

**1** Preheat the oven to 350 degrees. Lightly grease 2 baking sheets.

**2** Combine the oats, oat bran cereal, and salt.

**3** In a large bowl, beat the oil, bananas, and vanilla extract until smooth. Gradually blend in the dry ingredients. Stir in the apricots and almonds.

**4** Drop the dough by spoonfuls 1½ inches apart onto the prepared baking sheets.

**5** Bake for 20 to 25 minutes, or until lightly colored. Transfer to wire racks to cool

# PURE FRUIT COOKIES

Drop Cookies

YIELD: *2 to 3 dozen*
TOTAL TIME: *35 minutes*

# Queen Bees

Drop Cookies

YIELD: *3 to 4 dozen*
TOTAL TIME: *30 minutes*

1¾ cups all-purpose flour
1 cup almonds, ground
1 tablespoon baking powder
½ teaspoon ground ginger
½ teaspoon salt
½ cup vegetable shortening
½ cup granulated sugar
1 large egg
½ cup honey, warmed
¼ cup sherry

**1** Preheat the oven to 400 degees.

**2** Combine the flour, almonds, baking powder, ginger and salt.

**3** In a large bowl, cream the vegetable shortening and sugar. Beat in the egg. Beat in the honey and sherry. Gradually blend in the dry ingredients.

**4** Drop the dough by spoonfuls 1½ inches apart onto ungreased baking sheets.

**5** Bake for 10 to 12 minutes, until lightly colored. Transfer to wire racks to cool.

# Queen Elizabeth Cookies

Rolled Cookies

YIELD: *2 to 3 dozen*
TOTAL TIME: *30 minutes*

3 cups all-purpose flour
1 teaspoon baking powder
1 tablespoon vegetable shortening
¾ cup granulated sugar
2 large eggs
½ teaspoon fresh orange juice
Candied citron cut into thin strips

**1** Preheat the oven to 350 degrees. Lightly grease 2 baking sheets.

**2** Combine the flour and baking powder.

**3** In a large bowl, cream the vegetable shortening and sugar. Beat in the eggs one at a time. Beat in the orange juice. Gradually blend in the dry ingredients.

**4** On a floured surface, roll out the dough to a thickness of ¼ inch. Using a 2-inch round cookie cutter, cut out cookies and place 1½ inches apart on the prepared baking sheets. Lay a strip of citron across each cookie.

**5** Bake for 15 to 18 minutes, until lightly colored. Transfer to wire racks to cool.

**Baking notes:** Recipes for this cookie first appeared around the time of the coronation of Queen Elizabeth II.

# Queen Victoria Biscuits

Rolled Cookies

YIELD: *4 to 5 dozen*
TOTAL TIME: *30 minutes*

4 cups rolled oats
1 teaspoon ground cinnamon
¼ teaspoon ground nutmeg
1 cup vegetable shortening
1 cup powdered sugar
1 cup currants

**1** Grind oats finely in a food a food processor.

**2** Preheat the oven to 350 degrees. Lightly grease 2 baking sheets.

**3** Combine the oats, currants, cinnamon, and nutmeg.

**4** In a large bowl, cream the vegetable shortening and powdered sugar. Gradually blend in the dry ingredients. Fold in the currants. If the dough seem very dry, add a little water a teaspoonful at a time.

**5** On a floured surface, roll out the dough to a thickness of ½ inch. Using a 1½-inch round cookie cutter, cut out cookies and place 1 inch apart on the prepared baking sheets.

**6** Bake for 15 to 18 minutes, or until lightly colored. Transfer to wire racks to cool.

3 cups all-purpose flour
½ teaspoon baking soda
½ teaspoon ground cinnamon
¼ teaspoon ground cloves
½ teaspoon salt
1 cup vegetable shortening
¾ cup granulated sugar
¾ cup packed light brown sugar
2 large eggs, lightly beaten
¼ cup fresh orange juice
1 cup raisins
1 cup flaked coconut

GLAZE
¾ cup powdered sugar
1 tablespoon plus 1 teaspoon fresh
    orange juice
1 teaspoon orange zest, chopped

1  Preheat the oven to 350 degrees. Lightly grease a 15 by 10-inch baking pan.

2  Combine the flour, baking soda, spices, and salt.

3  In a large bowl, cream the vegetable shortening and two sugars. Beat in the eggs. Beat in the orange juice. Gradually blend in the dry ingredients. Fold in the raisins and coconut. Spread the mixture evenly in the prepared baking pan.

4  Bake for 20 to 25 minutes, until lightly colored on top and firm to the touch.

5  Meanwhile, make the glaze: Combine the sugar, orange juice, and orange zest in a small bowl and stir until smooth.

6  Drizzle the glaze over the hot crust. Cool in the pan on a wire rack before cutting into large or small bars.

# RAISIN BARS

Bar Cookies

YIELD: *3 to 4 dozen*
TOTAL TIME: *35 minutes*

---

1 cup raisin bran
½ cup granulated sugar
1 apple, peeled, cored, and grated
½ cup milk
1 teaspoon vanilla extract

1  Preheat the oven to 350 degrees. Lightly grease 2 baking sheets.

2  In a large bowl, combine the raisin bran, sugar, and apple. Stir in the milk and vanilla extract and mix well.

3  Drop the dough by spoonfuls 1 inch apart onto the prepared baking sheets.

4  Bake for 12 to 15 minutes, until lightly colored. Transfer to wire racks to cool.

# RAISIN BRAN COOKIES

Drop Cookies

YIELD: *3 to 5 dozen*
TOTAL TIME: *30 minutes*

---

3 cups all-purpose flour
2 teaspoons baking soda
½ teaspoon ground cloves
½ teaspoon ground cinnamon
½ teaspoon salt
1 cup vegetable shortening
2 cups packed light brown sugar
2 large eggs
1 cup sour milk
1 cup walnuts, chopped
½ cup raisins
½ cup golden raisins

1  Preheat the oven to 350 degrees.

2  Combine the flour, baking soda, spices, and salt.

3  In a large bowl, cream the vegetable shortening and brown sugar. Beat in the eggs. Beat in the sour milk. Gradually blend in the dry ingredients. Stir in the walnuts and raisins.

4  Drop the dough by spoonfuls 1½ inches apart onto ungreased baking sheets.

5  Bake for 9 to 12 minutes, until lightly colored. Transfer to wire racks to cool.

# RAISIN COOKIES I

Drop Cookies

YIELD: *4 to 5 dozen*
TOTAL TIME: *30 minutes*

# RAISIN COOKIES II

Drop Cookies

YIELD: *4 to 5 dozen*
TOTAL TIME: *30 minutes*

2 cups all-purpose flour
2 teaspoons baking powder
½ teaspoon ground cinnamon
2 tablespoons vegetable shortening
1 cup granulated sugar
2 large eggs
1 teaspoon vanilla extract
1 cup raisins

**1** Preheat the oven to 350 degrees.

**2** Combine the flour, baking powder, and cinnamon.

**3** In a large bowl, cream together the sugar and vegetable shortening. Beat in the eggs. Beat in the vanilla extract. Gradually blend in the dry ingredients. Fold in the raisins.

**4** Drop the dough by spoonfuls 1½ inches apart onto ungreased baking sheets.

**5** Bake for 10 to 12 minutes, until lightly colored. Transfer to wire racks to cool.

# RAISIN SANDWICH COOKIES

Rolled Cookies

YIELD: *4 to 5 dozen*
TOTAL TIME: *30 minutes*
CHILLING TIME: *4 hours*

3½ cups all-purpose flour
2 teaspoons baking powder
¼ teaspoon salt
½ cup vegetable shortening
1 cup granulated sugar
2 large eggs
½ cup milk

**FILLING**
¼ cup butter
½ cup granulated sugar
½ cup raisins
½ teaspoon grated orange zest
1 tablespoon all-purpose flour

**1** Combine the flour, baking powder, and salt.

**2** In a large bowl, cream the vegetable shortening and sugar. Beat in the eggs. Beat in the milk. Gradually blend in the dry ingredients. Cover and chill for 4 hours.

**3** Meanwhile, make the filling: In a medium saucepan melt the butter with the sugar. Add the raisins and orange zest. Sprinkle in the flour and continue stirring until the mixture thickens.

**4** Preheat the oven to 350 degrees. Lightly grease 2 baking sheets.

**5** On a floured surface, roll out the dough to a thickness of ⅛ inch. Using a 1½-inch round cookie cutter, cut out an even number of rounds. Place half the rounds 1 inch apart on the prepared baking sheets and spread each one with a small spoonful of the filling. Place the remaining rounds on top.

**6** Bake for 10 to 12 minutes, until golden brown. Transfer to wire racks to cool.

**Baking notes:** This recipe is unusual in that the sandwich cookies are assembled before they are baked, so it's essential to roll the dough thin enough to cook through.

CRUST
¾ cup vegetable shortening
¼ cup granulated sugar
2 large eggs, yolks
1½ cups all-purpose flour

TOPPING
2 large egg whites
½ cup granulated sugar
1 cup almonds, chopped fine
1 cup raspberry puree
1 cup flaked coconut

**1** Preheat the oven to 350 degrees. Lightly grease a 13 by 9-inch baking pan.

**2** To make the crust, cream the vegetable shortening and sugar in a large bowl. Beat in the egg yolks. Gradually blend in the flour. Spread the dough evenly in the prepared baking pan.

**3** Bake for 15 minutes.

**4** Meanwhile, make the topping: In a large bowl, beat the egg whites until foamy. Gradually beat in the sugar and beat until the whites hold stiff peaks. Fold in the chopped nuts.

**5** Spread the raspberry puree over the hot crust and sprinkle with the coconut. Spread the topping over the coconut.

**6** Bake for 20 to 25 minutes longer, or until lightly colored on top and firm to the touch. Cool in the pan on a wire rack before cutting into large or small bars.

# RASPBERRY MERINGUE BARS

Bar Cookies
YIELD: *1 to 4 dozen*
TOTAL TIME: *45 minutes*

---

5 large egg whites
2⅔ cups ground almonds
¼ teaspoon almond extract
2⅔ cups granulated sugar

**1** Preheat the oven to 350 degrees. Line 2 baking sheets with parchment paper.

**2** In a large bowl, beat the egg whites until stiff but not dry. Fold in the almonds and almond extract. Fold in the sugar.

**3** Place the mixture in a cookie press or a pastry bag fitted with a medium plain tip and press or pipe out small mounds 1½ inches apart onto the prepared baking sheets.

**4** Bake for 35 to 40 minutes, until lightly colored and firm to the touch. Cool on the pans on wire racks.

# RATAFIAS

Formed Cookies
YIELD: *5 to 6 dozen*
TOTAL TIME: *50 minutes*

---

2 cups all-purpose flour
¼ teaspoon ground cinnamon
½ cup vegetable shortening
¾ cup powdered sugar
1 cup walnuts, chopped
Red jimmies for sprinkling

**1** Preheat the oven to 400 degrees.

**2** Combine the flour and cinnamon.

**3** In a large bowl, cream the vegetable shortening and powdered sugar. Gradually stir in the dry ingredients. Stir in the walnuts.

**4** On a floured surface, roll out the dough to a thickness of ¼ inch. Using a 2-inch round cookie cutter, cut out cookies and place 1½ inches apart on ungreased baking sheets. Sprinkle red jimmies over the top.

**5** Bake for 8 to 10 minutes, until lightly colored. Transfer to wire racks to cool.

# RED RIVER QUEENS

Rolled Cookies
YIELD: *2 to 3 dozen*
TOTAL TIME: *30 minutes*

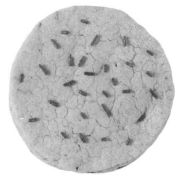

# REFRIGERATOR COOKIES

Refrigerator Cookies

YIELD: *will vary*
TOTAL TIME: *30 minutes*
CHILLING TIME: *2 hours*

3½ cups all-purpose flour
2 teaspoons baking powder
½ teaspoon salt
1 cup vegetable shortening
2 cups granulated sugar
2 large eggs
2 teaspoons lemon extract

**1** Combine the flour, baking powder, and salt.

**2** In a large bowl, cream the vegetable shortening and sugar. Beat in the eggs and lemon extract. Gradually blend in the dry ingredients.

**3** Divide the dough into 4 pieces. Form each piece into a log 2 inches in diameter. Wrap in waxed paper and chill for 2 hours.

**4** Preheat the oven to 350 degrees.

**5** Cut the logs into ¼-inch-thick slices and place 1 inch apart on ungreased baking sheets.

**6** Bake for 10 to 12 minutes, until lightly colored. Transfer to wire racks to cool.

**Baking notes:** These are just some of the possible variations using this basic dough.

BLACK-AND-WHITE COOKIES: Add in 1 tablespoon of unsweetened cocoa powder or melted chocolate to half the dough and ½ teaspoon of mint extract to the other half. Chill, roll out and cut into rounds. Sandwich the cooled cookies with a creamy fudge frosting (see Pantry), using one of each type for each sandwich.

PECAN COOKIES: Add ¼ to ½ cup finely chopped pecans to the dough. Press a pecan half into each cookie before baking.

FILLED COOKIES: Place the cookies on the baking sheets and make a shallow indentation in the centers with your finger. Fill with a filling of your choice.

BANANA COOKIES: Use banana extract in place of the lemon extract.

PEPPERMINT COOKIES: Substitute 3 drops of peppermint oil for the lemon extract.

ALMOND COOKIES: Substitute almond extract for the lemon extract and add ½ cup finely ground almonds to the dough.

# REFRIGERATOR SPICE COOKIES

Formed Cookies

YIELD: *3 to 6 dozen*
TOTAL TIME: *30 minutes*
CHILLING TIME: *8 hours*

2¾ cups all-purpose flour
1 teaspoon baking soda
1 teaspoon ground cinnamon
1 teaspoon ground nutmeg
½ teaspoon ground cloves
1 cup vegetable shortening
½ cup granulated sugar
½ cup packed light brown sugar
1 large egg

**1** Combine the flour, baking soda, and spices.

**2** In a large bowl, cream the vegetable shortening and two sugars. Beat in the egg. Gradually blend in the dry ingredients.

**3** Divide the dough in half. Form each half into a log 1½ inches in diameter. Wrap in waxed paper and chill for 8 hours.

**4** Preheat the oven to 375 degrees. Lightly grease 2 baking sheets.

**5** Cut the logs into ¼-inch-thick slices. Place 1 inch apart on the prepared baking sheets.

**6** Bake for 10 to 15 minutes, until lightly colored. Transfer to wire racks to cool.

3 cups all-purpose flour
½ teaspoon baking soda
½ teaspoon ginger
¼ teaspoon salt
1 cup vegetable shortening
1 cup granulated sugar
1 cup packed light brown sugar
2 large eggs
¾ cup walnuts, chopped

**1** Combine the flour, baking soda, ginger, and salt.

**2** In a large bowl, cream the vegetable shortening and two sugars. Beat in the eggs. Gradually blend in the dry ingredients. Fold in the walnuts.

**3** Divide the dough in half. Form each half into a log 2 inches in diameter. Wrap in waxed paper and chill for 4 hours.

**4** Preheat the oven to 350 degrees.

**5** Cut the logs into ¼-inch-thick slices and place 1 inch apart on ungreased baking sheets.

**6** Bake for 10 to 12 minutes, until lightly colored. Transfer to wire racks to cool.

# REFRIGERATOR WALNUT COOKIES I

Refrigerator Cookies

YIELD: *4 to 5 dozen*
TOTAL TIME: *30 minutes*
CHILLING TIME: *4 hours*

---

2½ cups all-purpose flour
1¼ teaspoons baking powder
½ cup vegetable shortening
2 cups packed light brown sugar
2 large eggs
½ cup walnuts, chopped

**1** Combine the flour and baking powder.

**2** In a large bowl, cream the vegetable shortening and brown sugar. Beat in the eggs. Gradually blend in the dry ingredients. Fold in the walnuts.

**3** Divide the dough in half. Form into a log 2 inches in diameter. Wrap in waxed paper and chill for 4 hours.

**4** Preheat the oven to 350 degrees.

**5** Cut the logs into ¼-inch-thick slices and place 1 inch apart on ungreased baking sheets.

**6** Bake for 10 to 12 minutes, until lightly colored. Transfer to wire racks to cool.

# REFRIGERATOR WALNUT COOKIES II

Formed Cookies

YIELD: *4 to 5 dozen*
TOTAL TIME: *30 minutes*
CHILLING TIME: *4 hours*

# REGAL RICE COOKIES

Drop Cookies

YIELD: *3 to 4 dozen*
TOTAL TIME: *30 minutes*

2¼ cups all-purpose flour
1½ teaspoons baking powder
¼ teaspoon cream of tartar
2 large egg whites
1 cup granulated sugar
1 teaspoon almond extract
1 cup "rice mush" (see Baking notes)

**1** Preheat the oven to 350 degrees. Lightly grease 2 baking sheets.

**2** Combine the flour, baking powder, and cream of tartar.

**3** In a large bowl, beat the egg whites until foamy. Beat in the sugar and almond extract. Beat in the rice mush. Gradually blend in the dry ingredients; the dough will be sticky.

**4** Drop the dough by spoonfuls 1 inch apart onto the prepared baking sheets.

**5** Bake for 12 to 15 minutes, until lightly colored. Transfer to wire racks to cool.

**Baking notes:** To prepare the rice mush, pour 1 quart of low-fat or non-fat milk into a sauce-pan and add ⅓ cup of long-grain rice. Bring to a simmer over low heat and cook until all of the milk evaporates, stirring occasionally. Remove from the heat and let cool. These are pale cookies; press a glacé cherry half into the center of each one before baking to add color; drizzle melted chocolate in various patterns across the tops of the cookies.

# ROCKY ROAD BARS

Bar Cookies

YIELD: *1 to 3 dozen*
TOTAL TIME: *40 minutes*

¼ cup all-purpose flour
½ cup walnuts, ground fine
¼ teaspoon baking powder
⅛ teaspoon salt
1 tablespoon vegetable shortening
⅓ cup packed light brown sugar
½ teaspoon vanilla extract

TOPPING

1 cup miniature marshmallows
1 cup (6 ounces) semisweet chocolate chips
½ cup walnuts, chopped

**1** Preheat the oven to 350 degrees. Lightly grease an 8-inch square baking pan.

**2** Combine the flour, walnuts, baking powder, and salt.

**3** In a large bowl, cream the vegetable shortening and brown sugar. Beat in the vanilla extract. Gradually blend in the dry ingredients. Spread the mixture evenly in the prepared baking pan.

**4** Bake for 15 minutes.

**5** Meanwhile, to make the topping: In a small bowl, combine the marshmallows, chocolate chips, and walnuts and toss to blend.

**6** Spread the topping mixture evenly over the hot crust. Bake for 15 to 18 minutes longer, until the topping is melted and lightly colored. Cool in the pan on a wire rack before cutting into large or small bars.

**CRUST**

½ cup all-purpose flour
½ cup rice flour
1 teaspoon baking powder
1 cup granulated sugar
1 cup almonds, chopped fine
½ cup butter
2 ounces semisweet chocolate, chopped
1 teaspoon almond extract

**FILLING**

6 ounces cream cheese, at room temperature
¼ cup butter, at room temperature
½ cup powdered sugar
1 large egg
2 tablespoons all-purpose flour
¼ cup almonds, chopped
½ teaspoon almond extract
1 cup (6 ounces) semisweet chocolate chips
2 cups miniature marshmallows

**TOPPING**

¼ cup butter
2 ounces cream cheese
1 ounce bittersweet chocolate, chopped fine
3½ cups powdered sugar
¼ cup evaporated milk
2 teaspoons amaretto

**1** Preheat the oven to 350 degrees. Lightly grease a 13 by 9-inch baking pan.

**2** To make the crust, combine the two flours, baking powder, sugar, and almonds in a large bowl.

**3** In a double boiler, melt the butter and chocolate over a low heat, stirring until smooth. Remove from heat and stir in the almond extract. Drizzle over the dry ingredients, stirring to form a crumbly dough. Press this evenly into the prepared baking pan.

**4** To make the filling, in a medium bowl, beat the cream cheese, butter, powdered sugar, and egg. Beat in the flour. Beat in the almonds and almond extract. Spread the filling evenly over the crust. Sprinkle with the chocolate chips.

**5** Bake for 25 to 30 minutes, or until lightly colored. Sprinkle the marshmallows over the top and bake for 2 to 4 minutes longer, until the marshmallows are golden brown.

**6** Meanwhile, make the topping: In a medium saucepan, combine the butter, cream cheese, chocolate, and milk and heat over low heat, stirring until smooth. Remove from the heat and stir in the powdered sugar. Stir in the amaretto.

**7** Pour the topping over the hot bars and swirl the mixture lightly with a knife. Cool in the pan on a wire rack before cutting into large or small bars.

# ROCKY ROAD FUDGE BARS

Bar Cookies

YIELD: *1 to 3 dozen*
TOTAL TIME: *40 minutes*

---

1 cup butter
½ cup powdered sugar
2 cups all-purpose flour
About ⅓ to ½ cup raspberry preserves

**1** Preheat the oven to 375 degrees.

**2** In a medium bowl, cream the butter and powdered sugar. Gradually blend in the flour.

**3** Pinch off large olive-sized pieces of dough and roll into balls. Place 1 inch apart on ungreased baking sheets and make an indent in the center of each cookie with your finger. Fill the hollow with raspberry preserves.

**4** Bake for 15 to 18 minutes, until lightly colored. Transfer to wire racks to cool.

# ROSENMUNNAR

Formed Cookies

YIELD: *4 to 6 dozen*
TOTAL TIME: *30 minutes*

# Rosy Rocks

Formed Cookies

YIELD: *3 to 4 dozen*
TOTAL TIME: *30 minutes*

1¾ cups all-purpose flour
1 teaspoon baking powder
½ teaspoon baking soda
2 teaspoons ground cinnamon
½ teaspoon ground cloves
1 cup vegetable shortening
1⅓ cups granulated sugar
1 large egg
1 cup undiluted canned tomato soup
2½ cups rolled oats
1 cup golden raisins
1 cup pecans, chopped

**1** Preheat the oven to 350 degrees. Lightly grease 2 baking sheets.

**2** Combine the flour, baking powder, baking soda, and spices.

**3** In a large bowl, cream the vegetable shortening and sugar. Beat in the egg and tomato soup. Gradually blend in the dry ingredients. Stir in the oats, raisins, and pecans.

**4** Pinch off walnut-sized pieces of dough and roll into balls. Place 1½ inches apart on the prepared baking sheets. Flatten the balls with the bottom of a glass dipped in flour.

**5** Bake for 10 to 12 minutes, until lightly colored. Transfer to wire racks to cool.

# Rovastinpip-parkakut

Rolled Cookies

YIELD: *3 to 4 dozen*
TOTAL TIME: *30 minutes*
CHILLING TIME: *8 hours*

2½ cups all-purpose flour
¼ cup almonds, ground fine
1 teaspoon baking soda
1 teaspoon ground cinnamon
1 teaspoon ground cardamom
1 teaspoon ground ginger
½ teaspoon ground allspice
½ teaspoon salt
1 cup vegetable shortening
1 cup granulated sugar
1 large egg
½ cup light corn syrup

**1** Combine the flour, almonds, baking soda, spices, and salt.

**2** In a large bowl, cream the vegetable shortening and sugar. Beat in the egg. Beat in the corn syrup. Gradually blend in the dry ingredients. Cover and chill for 8 hours.

**3** Preheat the oven to 350 degrees.

**4** On a floured surface, roll out the dough to a thickness of ¼ inch. Using cookie cutters, cut into 2-inch rounds or shapes and place 1 inch apart on ungreased baking sheets.

**5** Bake for 8 to 10 minutes, until lightly colored. Transfer to wire racks to cool.

**Baking notes:** These cookies are usually decorated with piped Royal Icing (see Pantry).

# Royal Gems

Formed Cookies

YIELD: *3 to 5 dozen*
TOTAL TIME: *30 minutes*

1¼ cups all-purpose flour
1 teaspoon baking soda
¾ cup butter, at room temperature
1 cup granulated sugar
½ cup flaked coconut
Powdered sugar for sprinkling

**1** Preheat the oven to 325 degrees.

**2** Combine the flour and baking soda.

**3** In a large bowl, cream the butter and sugar until fluffy. Gradually add the dry indredients. Blend in the coconut.

**4** Pinch off walnut-sized pieces of dough and roll in to ¾ inch balls. Place 2 inches apart on ungreased baking sheets.

**5** Bake for 10 to 12 minutes, or until lightly colored. Transfer to wire racks to cool. Sprinkle with powdered sugar.

2 large egg whites
2 cups powdered sugar
1 cup pecans, chopped
1 cup almonds, chopped
1 teaspoon distilled white vinegar
1 teaspoon almond extract

**1** Preheat the oven to 300 degrees. Lightly grease baking sheets.

**2** In a medium bowl, with an electric beater beat the egg whites until they hold soft peaks. Gradually beat in the powdered sugar and beat until stiff peaks form. Fold in the two nuts, vinegar, and almond extract.

**3** Drop the dough by spoonfuls 1½ inches apart onto the prepared baking sheets.

**4** Bake for 12 to 15 minutes, or until lightly colored. Transfer the cookies to wire racks to cool.

# RUFFLES

Drop Cookies

YIELD: *2 to 3 dozen*
TOTAL TIME: *30 minutes*

---

1 cup butter, at room temperature
8 ounces cream cheese, at room temperature
6 tablespoons powdered sugar
1 tablespoon raspberry-flavored brandy
2¾ cups all-purpose flour

**FILLING**
¾ cup packed light brown sugar
½ cup almonds, chopped
½ cup raisins, plumped in warm water and drained
1 teaspoon ground cinnamon

**1** Combine the butter, cream cheese, and powdered sugar in a large bowl and beat until smooth and creamy. Beat in the brandy. Gradually blend in the flour. Divide the dough into 4 pieces. Wrap the dough in waxed paper and chill for 4 hours.

**2** Preheat the oven to 350 degrees. Lightly grease 2 baking sheets.

**3** To make the filling, combine all the ingredients in a small bowl and toss to mix.

**4** On a floured surface, roll out each piece of dough into a 9-inch circle. Spread one-quarter of the filling over each round. Cut each round into 8 wedges. Starting at the wide end, roll up each wedge. Place 1 inch apart on the prepared baking sheets, curving the ends to form crescents.

**5** Bake for 20 to 25 minutes, until lightly colored. Transfer to wire racks to cool.

# RUGELACH

Rolled Cookies

YIELD: *2 to 3 dozen*
TOTAL TIME: *40 minutes*
CHILLING TIME: *4 hours*

---

2½ cups crushed gingersnaps
½ cup honey
6 tablespoons rum
1½ cups pecans, ground fine
Powdered sugar for rolling

**1** In a large bowl, combine all of the ingredients and stir to form a sticky dough. Pinch off small pieces of dough and roll into balls. Roll each ball in powdered sugar.

**2** Store in an airtight container for at least 1 week before serving. Before serving, roll the balls a second time in powdered sugar.

**Baking notes:** These cookies are not for children.

# RUM BALLS

Formed Cookies

YIELD: *3 to 5 dozen*
TOTAL TIME: *30 minutes*
AGING TIME: *1 week*

# RUM COOKIES

Drop Cookies

YIELD: *6 to 8 dozen*
TOTAL TIME: *30 minutes*
CHILLING TIME: *4 hours*

2 cups all-purpose flour
2 teaspoons baking powder
½ teaspoon salt
1 cup butter, at room temperature
1 cup packed light brown sugar
3 large eggs
½ cup rum
1 teaspoon almond extract

**1** Combine the flour, baking powder, and salt.

**2** In a large bowl, cream the butter and sugar. Beat in the eggs. Beat in the rum and almond extract. Gradually blend in the dry ingredients. Cover and chill for 4 hours.

**3** Preheat the oven to 400 degrees.

**4** Drop the dough by spoonfuls 1½ inches apart onto the prepared baking sheets.

**5** Bake for 6 to 8 minutes, until lightly colored. Transfer to wire racks to cool.

# RUM-TOPPED GINGER COOKIES

Rolled Cookies

YIELD: *3 to 4 dozen*
TOTAL TIME: *45 minutes*
CHILLING TIME: *30 minutes*

2 cups all-purpose flour
⅔ cup granulated sugar
2 teaspoons ground ginger
Pinch of salt
½ cup butter, chilled and cut into small pieces
½ cup large-curd cottage cheese
1 large egg white, beaten with 2 teaspoons water for egg glaze
Colored sugar crystals

TOPPING
1½ cups butter, at room temperature
3 cups powdered sugar
1 tablespoon minced crystallized ginger
3 tablespoons rum

**1** Preheat oven to 350 degrees. Lightly grease 2 baking sheets.

**2** In a large bowl, combine the flour, sugar, ginger, and salt. Cut in the butter until the mixture resembles coarse crumbs. Blend in the cottage cheese. The dough will be stiff. If the dough is too dry, add a little water 1 teaspoon at a time. Cover and chill for 30 minutes.

**3** On a floured surface, roll out dough to a thickness of ⅛ inch. Using a 2-inch round or 2-inch scalloped cookie cutter, cut out cookies. Place 1 inch apart on the prepared baking sheets and brush with egg glaze. Sprinkle with the sugar crystals.

**4** Bake for 10 to 12 minutes, or until browned around the edges. Transfer to wire racks to cool.

**5** To make the topping, cream the butter and sugar in a small bowl. Beat in the ginger and rum. Spread over the top of the cooled cookies.

**Baking notes:** The ginger flavor will be more intense if the cookies are stored in an airtight container to age.

2¼ cups all-purpose flour
¼ teaspoon salt
1 cup butter, at room temperature
¾ cup powdered sugar
1 teaspoon vodka
¾ cup hazelnuts, chopped fine
Powdered sugar for sprinkling

1  Preheat the oven to 325 degrees.

2  Combine the flour and salt.

3  In a large bowl, cream the butter and powdered sugar. Beat in the vodka. Gradually blend in the dry ingredients. Fold in the hazelnuts.

4  Pinch off walnut-sized pieces of dough and roll into balls.

Place 1½ inches apart on ungreased baking sheets. Flatten each ball with the bottom of a glass dipped in flour.

5  Bake for 12 to 15 minutes, until lightly colored. Sprinkle with powdered sugar and transfer to wire racks to cool

# RUSSIAN TEA BISCUITS I

Formed Cookies

YIELD: *3 to 6 dozen*
TOTAL TIME: *35 minutes*

2¼ cups all-purpose flour
1 cup walnuts, ground fine
¼ cup unsweetened cocoa powder
¼ teaspoon salt
1¼ cups butter, at room temperature
¾ cup powdered sugar
1 teaspoon vodka
Powdered sugar for sprinkling

1  Preheat the oven to 325 degrees.

2  Combine the flour, walnuts, cocoa, and salt.

3  In a large bowl, cream the butter and powdered sugar. Beat in the vodka. Gradually blend in the dry ingredients.

4  Pinch off walnut-sized pieces of dough and roll into balls. Place 1½ inches apart on ungreased baking sheets.

5  Bake for 12 to 15 minutes, until lightly colored. Sprinkle with powdered sugar and transfer to wire racks to cool.

# RUSSIAN TEA BISCUITS II

Formed Cookies

YIELD: *4 to 5 dozen*
TOTAL TIME: *30 minutes*

2 tablespoons vegetable shortening
¼ cup granulated sugar
2 large egg yolks
1 cup sour milk
2½ cups all-purpose flour

1  Preheat the oven to 350 degrees. Lightly grease a 13 by 9-inch baking pan.

2  In a large bowl, cream the vegetable shortening and sugar. Beat in the egg yolks. Beat in the sour milk. Gradually blend in the flour. Spread the mixture evenly into the prepared baking pan.

3  Bake for 10 to 12 minutes, until lightly colored on top and firm to the touch. Cool in the pan on a

wire rack before cutting into large or small bars.

# RUSSIAN TEA COOKIES

Bar Cookies

YIELD: *2 to 3 dozen*
TOTAL TIME: *25 minutes*

# Rye Cookies I

Rolled Cookies

YIELD: *2 to 3 dozen*
TOTAL TIME: *45 minutes*

⅓ cup all-purpose flour
½ cup rye flour
½ cup butter, at room temperature
¼ cup packed light brown sugar
1 teaspoon minced candied orange peel

**1** Preheat the oven to 400 degrees. Lightly grease 2 baking sheets.

**2** Combine the two flours.

**3** Cream the butter and brown sugar. Beat in the orange peel. Gradually blend in the dry ingredients.

**4** Turn the dough out onto a floured surface and knead until it is easy to handle. Roll out to a thickness of ⅛ inch. Using a cookie cutter or knife, cut into diamond shapes and place 1 inch apart on the prepared baking sheets. Prick the cookies all over with the tines of a fork.

**5** Bake for 8 to 10 minutes, until golden. Transfer to wire racks to cool.

**Baking notes:** For a more decorative appearance, cut the diamonds with a pastry wheel or a fluted cookie cutter.

# Rye Cookies II

Rolled Cookies

YIELD: *2 to 3 dozen*
TOTAL TIME: *30 minutes*

2 cups all-purpose flour
1 cup rye flour
½ cup vegetable shortening
6 tablespoons granulated sugar

**1** Preheat the oven to 400 degrees. Lightly grease 2 baking sheets.

**2** Combine the two flours.

**3** In a large bowl, cream the vegetable shortening and sugar. Gradually blend in the dry ingredients. Knead to a soft dough.

**4** On a floured surface, roll the dough out to a thickness of ⅛ inch. Using 3-inch round cookie cutter, cut out cookies. Using a 1 inch round cookie cutter, cut out the center of each cookie and place 1 inch apart on the prepared baking sheets. Prick all over with the tines of a fork.

**5** Bake for 5 to 7 minutes, until lightly colored. Transfer to wire racks to cool.

4 cups all-purpose flour
½ teaspoon baking soda
1 tablespoon plus 1 teaspoon ground cinnamon
½ teaspoon ground nutmeg
½ teaspoon ground cloves
¼ teaspoon salt
2 cups vegetable shortening
2 cups granulated sugar
½ cup sour cream
½ cup walnuts, chopped fine

**1** Combine the flour, baking soda, spices, salt.

**2** In a large bowl, cream the vegetable shortening and sugar. Beat in the sour cream. Gradually blend in the dry ingredients. Stir in the walnuts.

**3** Divide the dough in half. Form each half into a log 2 inches in diameter. Wrap in waxed paper and chill for 8 hours or overnight.

**4** Preheat the oven to 400 degrees. Lightly grease 2 baking sheets.

**5** Cut the logs into ¼-inch-thick slices, and place the slices 1 inch apart on the prepared baking sheets.

**6** Bake for 8 to 10 minutes, or until lightly browned. Transfer to wire racks to cool.

# St. Nikolaas Koekjes

Refrigerator Cookies

YIELD: *4 to 6 dozen*
TOTAL TIME: *30 minutes*
CHILLING TIME: *8 hours*

---

2 cups all-purpose flour
1½ teaspoons baking powder
½ cup butter, at room temperature
1 cup granulated sugar
1 large egg

TOPPING
1 tablespoon granulated sugar
½ teaspoon ground cinnamon
1 large egg white, beaten
About 1 cup whole almonds

**1** Combine the flour and baking powder.

**2** In a large bowl, cream the butter and sugar. Beat in the egg. Gradually blend in the dry ingredients. Cover and chill for 2 hours.

**3** Preheat the oven to 375 degrees. Lightly grease 2 baking sheets.

**4** In a cup, combine the sugar and cinnamon for the topping.

**5** On a floured surface, roll out the dough to a thickness of ⅛ inch. Using a 2-inch round cookie cutter, cut out cookies and place 1 inch apart on the prepared baking sheets. Brush the rounds with the beaten egg white and sprinkle the cinnamon sugar over the top. Press a whole almond into the center of each round.

**6** Bake for 8 to 10 minutes, until lightly colored. Transfer to wire racks to cool.

# Sand Tarts

Rolled Cookies

YIELD: *4 to 5 dozen*
TOTAL TIME: *30 minutes*
CHILLING TIME: *2 hours*

---

3 tablespoons vegetable shortening
1½ cups granulated sugar
3 large eggs
1½ teaspoons almond extract
3 cups rolled oats
1½ teaspoons salt

**1** Preheat the oven to 325 degrees. Lightly grease 2 baking sheets or line with parchment paper.

**2** In a large bowl, cream the shortening and sugar. Beat in the eggs. Beat in the almond extract. Gradually blend in the oats and salt.

**3** Drop the dough by spoonfuls 2 inches apart onto the prepared

baking sheets. Flatten with the back of a spoon dipped in flour.

**4** Bake for 12 to 15 minutes, until golden. Transfer to wire racks to cool.

# Scotch Lace

Drop Cookies

YIELD: *1 to 3 dozen*
TOTAL TIME: *30 minutes*

# SCOTCH QUEEN CAKES

Rolled Cookies

YIELD: *2 to 3 dozen*
TOTAL TIME: *30 minutes*

**4 cups rolled oats**
**1 teaspoon ground cinnamon**
**¼ teaspoon ground nutmeg**
**1 cup butter, at room temperature**
**1 cup powdered sugar**
**1 cup currants**

**1** Preheat the oven to 350 degrees. Lightly grease 2 baking sheets.

**2** Combine the oats and spices.

**3** In a large bowl, cream the butter and powdered sugar. Stir in the dry ingredients. Stir in the currants. If the dough seems a little dry, add a little water ½ teaspoon at a time.

**4** Divide the dough into quarters and work with one piece of dough at a time. On a floured surface, roll out each piece of dough to a 6-inch round. Place the rounds 1 inch apart on ungreased baking sheets and prick all over with a fork. Score each round into wedges.

**5** Bake for 15 to 18 minutes, until lightly colored. Transfer to wire racks to cool, then cut into wedges.

# SCOTCH SHORTBREAD I

Rolled Cookies

YIELD: *2 to 3 dozen*
TOTAL TIME: *30 minutes*
CHILLING TIME: *2 hours*

**2 cups (1 pound) butter, at room temperature**
**1 cup powdered sugar**
**4 cups all-purpose flour**

**1** In a large bowl, cream the butter and powdered sugar. Gradually blend in the flour to make a smooth dough. Divide the dough into quarters. Wrap in waxed paper and chill for 2 hours.

**2** Preheat the oven to 350 degrees.

**3** Work with one piece of dough at a time, keeping the remaining dough in the refrigerator. On a floured surface, roll out each piece of dough to a 6-inch round. Place the rounds 1 inch apart on ungreased baking sheets and prick all over with a fork. Score each round into wedges.

**4** Bake for 12 to 15 minutes, until very dry and lightly colored. Transfer to wire racks to cool, then cut into wedges.

**Baking notes:** Be sure to use unsalted butter. This dough can also be rolled out to a thickness of ½ inch and cut into small rounds. Or it can be pressed into a 13 by-9 inch baking pan, pricked all over with a fork, and scored into bite-sized pieces.

# SCOTCH SHORTBREAD II

Rolled Cookies

YIELD: *2 to 3 dozen*
TOTAL TIME: *75 minutes*
CHILLING TIME: *2 hours*

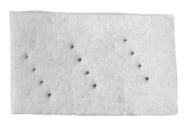

**4½ cups all-purpose flour**
**1½ cups rice flour**
**3 cups (1½ pounds) butter, at room temperature**
**1½ cups powdered sugar**

**1** Combine the two flours.

**2** In a large bowl, cream the butter and powdered sugar. Gradually blend in the flour to make a smooth dough. Cover and chill for 2 hours.

**3** Preheat the oven to 300 degrees.

**4** On a floured surface, roll out the dough to a thickness of ½ inch. Using a small plate as a guide, cut into 6- to 7-inch rounds. Place the rounds 1 inch apart on an ungreased baking sheets and prick all over with a fork. Score each round into wedges.

**5** Bake for 55 to 60 minutes, until very lightly colored. Transfer to wire racks to cool, then cut into wedges.

1¼ cups all-purpose flour
1½ teaspoons baking powder
½ teaspoon salt
½ cup butter, at room temperature
2 cups packed light brown sugar
2 large eggs
1½ cups hazelnuts, chopped

1 Preheat the oven to 350 degrees. Lightly grease 2 baking sheets.
2 Combine the flour, baking powder, and salt.
3 In a large bowl, cream the butter and sugar. Beat in the eggs. Gradually blend in the dry ingredients. Fold in the hazelnuts.

4 Drop the dough by spoonfuls 2½ inches apart onto the prepared baking sheets.
5 Bake for 12 to 15 minutes, until lightly colored. Transfer to wire racks to cool.

**Baking notes:** These cookies have a tendency to stick to the baking sheets; if they do, return to the hot oven for a minute or two.

# SCOTCH WAFERS

Drop Cookies

YIELD: *7 to 9 dozen*
TOTAL TIME: *30 minutes*

---

3 cups cornstarch
1 tablespoon baking powder
2¼ cups vegetable shortening
½ cup granulated sugar
2 large eggs
1 tablespoon grated lemon zest

1 Preheat the oven to 350 degrees. Lightly grease a 12 cup muffin tin.
2 Combine the cornstarch and baking powder.
3 In a large bowl, cream vegetable shortening and sugar. Beat in the eggs. Beat in the lemon zest. Gradually blend in the dry ingredients.

4 Spoon the dough into the prepared muffin tins.
5 Bake for 10 to 12 minutes, until lightly colored. Transfer to wire racks to cool.

# SCOTTISH MORSELS

Drop Cookies

YIELD: *1 to 2 dozen*
TOTAL TIME: *30 minutes*

---

1 tablespoon vegetable oil
1 teaspoon baking soda
½ teaspoon salt
2 cups rolled oats
Boiling water

1 In a large bowl, combine the vegetable oil, baking soda, and salt. Gradually blend in the oats. Add enough boiling water ½ teaspoonful at a time to make a soft dough.
2 Scatter additional oatmeal on a board and knead the dough. Roll out the dough to a thickness of ½ inch. With a sharp knife, cut into 2½- by 3-inch small triangles.
3 Heat a griddle or nonstick frying pan. Cook the triangles turn-

ing only once, until golden brown. Transfer to a plate and cover with a clean towel.

**Baking notes:** The recipe for these oatcakes was created before there were ovens as we know them today. These are Scottish biscuits served warm with preserves or marmalade.

# SCOTTISH OATCAKES

Rolled Cookies

YIELD: *1 to 3 dozen*
TOTAL TIME: *30 minutes*

# SCOTTISH SNAPS

Rolled Cookies

YIELD: *3 to 4 dozen*
TOTAL TIME: *30 minutes*
CHILLING TIME: *4 hours*

6 cups all-purpose flour
1 tablespoon baking soda
1 tablespoon plus 1 teaspoon ground
    ginger
2 cups vegetable shortening
2 cups granulated sugar
2 large eggs
1½ cups molasses
3 tablespoons cider vinegar

**1** Combine the flour, baking soda, and ginger.

**2** In a large bowl, cream the vegetable shortening and sugar. Beat in the eggs. Beat in the molasses and vinegar. Gradually blend in the dry ingredients. Cover and chill for 4 hours.

**3** Preheat the oven to 350 degrees.

**4** On a floured surface roll out the dough to a thickness of ¼ inch. Using a 2-inch round cookie cutter, cut into rounds and place 1 inch apart on ungreased baking sheets.

**5** Bake for 10 to 12 minutes, until lightly colored. Transfer to wire racks to cool.

# SESAME CHEESE WAFERS

Refrigerator Cookies

YIELD: *2 to 3 dozen*
TOTAL TIME: *30 minutes*
CHILLING TIME: *24 hours*

1 cup soft cheese, such as brie
¼ cup vegetable shortening
⅔ cup all-purpose flour
3 tablespoons sesame seeds

**1** In a large bowl, beat the cheese and vegetable shortening until smooth. Gradually blend in the flour. If the dough seems a little dry, add water a teaspoonful at a time. If it seems very soft, add a little all-purpose flour a tablespoonful at a time. Shape the dough into a log and roll the log in the sesame seeds. Wrap in waxed paper and chill for 24 hours.

**2** Preheat the oven to 375 degrees. Lightly grease 2 baking sheets.

**3** Cut the log into ¼-inch-thick slices and place 1 inch apart on the prepared baking sheets.

**4** Bake for 10 to 12 minutes, until lightly colored. Transfer to wire racks to cool.

# SESAME CHIPS

Formed Cookies

YIELD: *2 to 3 dozen*
TOTAL TIME: *30 minutes*

3 cups whole wheat flour
1 cup all-purpose flour
½ teaspoon baking soda
½ teaspoon salt
1 cup vegetable shortening
1 cup granulated sugar
1 large egg
1 teaspoon vanilla extract
2 cups sesame seeds

**1** Preheat the oven to 375 degrees. Lightly grease 2 baking sheets.

**2** Combine the two flours, the baking soda, and salt.

**3** In a large bowl, cream the vegetable shortening and sugar. Beat in the egg. Beat in the vanilla extract. Gradually blend in the dry ingredients.

**4** Pinch off walnut-sized pieces of dough and roll into balls, flouring your hands if the dough is sticky. Roll the balls in the sesame seeds and place 1½ inches apart on the prepared baking sheets. Flatten the balls with the bottom of a glass dipped in flour.

**5** Bake for 8 to 10 minutes, until lightly colored. Transfer to wire racks to cool.

**Baking notes:** Use coarse-ground whole wheat flour for these cookies. If a product called Wheat-a-lax is available in your area, use it.

1 cup all-purpose flour
¼ cup rice flour
¼ teaspoon baking powder
¼ teaspoon salt
¾ cup butter, at room temperature
1½ cups packed light brown sugar
2 large eggs
1 teaspoon vanilla extract
½ cup sesame seeds, toasted

**1** Preheat the oven to 350 degrees. Lightly grease 2 baking sheets.

**2** Combine the two flours, the baking powder, and salt.

**3** In a large bowl, cream the butter and brown sugar. Beat in the eggs and vanilla extract. Gradu-ally blend in the dry ingredients. Stir in the sesame seeds.

**4** Drop the dough by spoonfuls 2 inches apart onto the prepared baking sheets.

**5** Bake for 10 to 12 minutes, until lightly colored. Transfer to wire racks to cool.

## SESAME SEED DROP COOKIES

Drop Cookies

YIELD: *3 to 4 dozen*
TOTAL TIME: *30 minutes*

---

2 cups all-purpose flour
¼ teaspoon baking soda
¼ teaspoon salt
½ cup butter, at room temperature
1 cup granulated sugar
1 large egg
¼ cup sour milk
½ cup sesame seeds, toasted

**1** Combine the flour, baking soda, and salt.

**2** In a large bowl, cream the butter and sugar. Beat in the egg and sour milk. Gradually blend in the dry ingredients. Stir in the sesame seeds.

**3** Divide the dough in half. Form each half into a log 1 inch in diameter. Wrap in waxed paper and chill for 8 hours or overnight.

**4** Preheat the oven the 375 degrees. Lightly grease 2 baking sheets.

**5** Cut the logs into ¼-inch-thick slices and place 1 inch apart on the prepared baking sheets.

**6** Bake for 10 to 12 minutes, until lightly colored. Transfer to wire racks to cool.

## SESAME SEED ICEBOX COOKIES

Refrigerator Cookies

YIELD: *3 to 4 dozen*
TOTAL TIME: *30 minutes*
CHILLING TIME: *8 hours*

---

1 cup vegetable shortening
1 cup cookie crumbs, such as vanilla wafers or Oreos
1 cup (6 ounces) semisweet choco-late chips
1 cup coconut
1 cup almonds, chopped
1 cup (6 ounces) butterscotch chips
One 14-ounce can sweetened con-densed milk

**1** Preheat the oven to 350 degrees.

**2** Melt the vegetable shortening in a small saucepan and pour into a 13 by 9-inch baking pan. Sprinkle the cookie crumbs over the shortening. Sprinkle the chocolate chips over the crumbs, then sprinkle the coconut over the chocolate chips. Sprinkle the almonds over the coconut and the butterscotch chips over the almonds. Drizzle the condensed milk over the top.

**3** Bake for 20 to 30 minutes, until firm to the touch. Cool in the pan on a wire rack before cutting into large or small bars.

## SEVEN-LAYER COOKIES

Bar Cookies

YIELD: *2 to 3 dozen*
TOTAL TIME: *35 minutes*

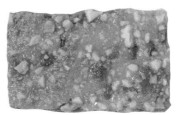

# She-Loves-Me Cookies

Rolled Cookies

YIELD: *3 to 4 dozen*
TOTAL TIME: *30 minutes*

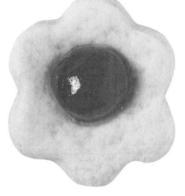

2⅓ cups all-purpose flour
½ teaspoon baking powder
¼ teaspoon salt
1 cup vegetable shortening
⅔ cup granulated sugar
1 large egg
1 teaspoon vanilla extract
1 teaspoon grated lemon zest
Chocolate kisses for decorating

1 Preheat the oven to 350 degrees. Lightly grease 2 baking sheets.

2 Combine the flour, baking powder and salt.

3 In a large bowl, cream the vegetable shortening and sugar. Beat in the egg and vanilla extract. Beat in the lemon zest. Gradually blend in the dry ingredients.

4 On a floured surface, roll out the dough to a thickness of ¼ inch. Using a flower-shaped cookie cutter, cut out the cookies and place 1 inch apart on the prepared baking sheets.

5 Bake for 10 to 12 minutes, until lightly colored. Press a chocolate kiss into the center of each hot cookie and transfer to wire racks to cool.

**Baking notes:** Glacé cherries can also be used for decoration.

# Shrewsbury Biscuits

Rolled Cookies

YIELD: *4 to 5 dozen*
TOTAL TIME: *30 minutes*

3½ cups all-purpose flour
1 teaspoon baking powder
½ teaspoon salt
1½ cups butter, at room temperature
1½ cups granulated sugar
2 large eggs
¼ cup fresh lemon juice
1 tablespoon plus 1 teaspoon grated
  lemon zest
2 cups currants
Milk for glazing
Granulated sugar for sprinkling

1 Preheat the oven to 350 degrees. Lightly grease 2 baking sheets.

2 Combine the flour, baking powder, and salt.

3 In a large bowl, cream the butter and sugar. Beat in the eggs. Beat in the lemon juice and zest. Gradually blend in the dry ingredients. Fold in the currants.

4 On a floured surface, roll out the dough to a thickness of ¼ inch. Using a 2-inch scalloped or fluted round cookie cutter, cut out cookies and place 1 inch apart on the prepared baking sheets. Brush with milk and sprinkle with granulated sugar.

5 Bake for 12 to 15 minutes, until lightly colored. Transfer to wire racks to cool.

8 ounces cream cheese, at room
  temperature
¼ cup butter, at room temperature
3 tablespoons powdered sugar
½ teaspoon vanilla extract
2 cups all-purpose flour
About ¼ cup fruit preserves
  (optional)
Powdered sugar for sprinkling

**1** Preheat the oven to 350
degrees. Lightly grease 2 baking
sheets.

**2** In a large bowl, beat the cream
cheese, butter, and powdered
sugar until smooth and creamy.
Beat in the vanilla extract. Gradually blend in the flour.

**3** On a floured surface roll the
dough out to a thickness of ¼
inch. Using a 2-inch round cookie

cutter, cut into rounds and place
1 inch apart on the prepared baking sheets. If desired, place a dab
of fruit preserves in the center of
each cookie.

**4** Bake for 12 to 15 minutes, until
lightly colored. Sprinkle with
powdered sugar and transfer to
wire racks to cool.

# SIMPLE CREAM CHEESE COOKIES

Rolled Cookies

YIELD: *3 to 4 dozen*
TOTAL TIME: *30 minutes*

---

3 cups all-purpose flour
2 teaspoons baking powder
¼ teaspoon salt
1 cup vegetable shortening
1⅓ cups granulated sugar
2 large eggs
1 teaspoon vanilla extract
3 tablespoons granulated sugar
2 teaspoons ground cinnamon

**1** Preheat the oven to 350
degrees. Lightly grease 2 baking
sheets.

**2** Combine the flour, baking
powder, and salt.

**3** In a large bowl, cream the vegetable shortening and sugar. Beat

in the eggs. Beat in the vanilla
extract. Gradually blend in the
dry ingredients.

**4** In a small bowl, combine the
sugar and cinnamon.

**5** Pinch off 1-inch pieces of
dough and roll into balls. Roll
each ball in the cinnamon sugar
and place 1 inch apart on the prepared baking sheets.

**6** Bake for 10 to 12 minutes, until
lightly colored. Transfer to wire
racks to cool.

# SNICKERDOODLES

Formed Cookies

YIELD: *3 to 4 dozen*
TOTAL TIME: *30 minutes*

---

1 cup all-purpose flour
1 cup walnuts, ground
¼ teaspoon salt
½ cup vegetable shortening
2 tablespoons granulated sugar
1 tablespoon rum
Powdered sugar for sprinkling

**1** Preheat the oven to 325
degrees. Lightly grease 2 baking
sheets.

**2** Combine the flour, walnuts,
and salt.

**3** In a large bowl, cream the vegetable shortening and sugar. Beat
in the rum. Gradually blend in
the dry ingredients.

**4** Pinch off walnut-sized pieces
of dough and roll into balls. Place
1 inch apart on the prepared baking sheets.

**5** Bake for 12 to 15 minutes, until
lightly colored. Roll in powdered
sugar and transfer to wire racks
to cool.

**6** When the cookies are cool, roll
in powdered sugar again. Let sit
for 1 hour and roll in powdered
sugar a third time.

# SNOWBALLS

Formed Cookies

YIELD: *2 to 3 dozen*
TOTAL TIME: *30 minutes*
RESTING TIME: *1 hour*

# SOCKER KAKA

Drop Cookies

YIELD: *2 to 3 dozen*
TOTAL TIME: *30 minutes*

1 cup all-purpose flour
1 teaspoon baking powder
⅛ teaspoon salt
¾ cup granulated sugar
3 large eggs
1 teaspoon vanilla extract
About ¼ pint heavy cream

**1** Preheat the oven to 400 degrees. Lightly grease 2 baking sheets.

**2** Combine the flour, baking powder, and salt.

**3** In a large bowl, beat the sugar and eggs. Beat in the vanilla extract. Gradually blend in the dry ingredients.

**4** Drop by spoonfuls 2½ inches apart onto the prepared baking sheets.

**5** Bake for 8 to 10 minutes, until golden brown. Immediately roll the hot cookies into cone shapes and place seam side down on wire racks to cool.

**6** Whip the heavy cream until it holds soft peaks. Fill the cones with the cream and serve immediately.

**Baking notes:** Watch these cookies carefully; do not overbake. Chopped fruit is a nice addition to the whipped cream.

# SODA CRACKER COOKIES

Bar Cookies

YIELD: *3 to 4 dozen*
TOTAL TIME: *20 minutes*

18 double-packed soda crackers
1 cup butter
1 cup packed light brown sugar
1 cup (6 ounces) semisweet chocolate chips
¾ cup walnuts, chopped fine

**1** Preheat the oven to 375 degrees. Line a 15 by 10-inch baking pan with aluminum foil and grease it well. Line the pan with soda crackers.

**2** In a medium saucepan, melt the butter. Add the brown sugar and cook, stirring until it dissolves. Bring to a boil and cook for about 3 minutes, stirring constantly. Immediately pour the mixture over the soda crackers.

**3** Bake for 3 to 5 minutes, or until the mixture starts to bubble.

**4** Spread the chocolate chips over the hot cookies. Let sit for a minute or so to melt the chocolate, then use a knife or spatula to spread the chocolate evenly over the top. Sprinkle with chopped walnuts. Let cool, then cut into large or small bars.

**Baking notes:** These are an instant favorite of everyone who tries them.

# SOME-MORE BARS

Bar Cookies

YIELD: *1 to 2 dozen*
TOTAL TIME: *30 minutes*

¾ cup vegetable shortening
⅓ cup granulated sugar
3 cups graham cracker crumbs
2 cups miniature marshmallows
1 cup (6 ounces) semisweet chocolate chips

**1** Preheat the oven to 350 degrees. Lightly grease a 13 by 9-inch baking pan.

**2** In a large bowl, cream the vegetable shortening and sugar. Gradually blend in the cookie crumbs. Press half of this mixture firmly into the prepared baking pan. Sprinkle the marshmallows and chocolate chips over the top. Crumble over the remaining crumb mix.

**3** Bake for 8 to 10 minutes, until firm to the touch. Cool in the pan on a wire rack before cutting into large or small bars.

3 cups all-purpose flour
1½ teaspoons baking powder
½ teaspoon baking soda
½ teaspoon ground coriander
½ teaspoon salt
½ cup vegetable shortening
1 cup granulated sugar
1 large egg
½ cup sour cream
½ teaspoon vanilla extract
½ teaspoon almond extract

**1** Combine the flour, baking powder, baking soda, coriander, and salt.

**2** In a large bowl, cream the vegetable shortening and sugar. Beat in the egg. Beat in the sour cream. Beat in the vanilla and almond extracts. Gradually blend in the dry ingredients. Cover and chill for 4 hours.

**3** Preheat the oven to 350 degrees. Lightly grease 2 baking sheets.

**4** On a floured surface, roll out the dough to a thickness of ¼ inch. Using a 2-inch round cookie cutter, cut into rounds and place 1 inch apart on the prepared baking sheets.

**5** Bake for 10 to 12 minutes, until lightly colored. Transfer to wire racks to cool.

# SOUR CREAM AND SPICE COOKIES

Rolled Cookies

YIELD: *4 to 5 dozen*
TOTAL TIME: *30 minutes*
CHILLING TIME: *4 hours*

---

4 cups all-purpose flour
1 teaspoon baking soda
½ teaspoon salt
1 cup vegetable shortening
2 cups granulated sugar
2 large eggs
1 cup sour cream
1 teaspoon lemon extract

**1** Preheat the oven to 350 degrees.

**2** Combine the flour, baking soda, and salt.

**3** In a large bowl, cream the vegetable shortening and sugar. Beat in the eggs. Beat in the sour cream and lemon extract. Gradually blend in the dry ingredients.

**4** On a floured surface, roll out the dough to a thickness of ¼ inch. Using a 2-inch round cookie cutter, cut into rounds and place 1 inch apart on ungreased baking sheets.

**5** Bake for 10 to 12 minutes, until lightly colored. Transfer to wire racks to cool.

**Baking notes:** This is a very old recipe. Some versions brush the cookies with milk and sprinkle them with granulated sugar before baking. Early recipes call for "citrus extract"; lemon is just one of the citrus extracts.

# SOUR CREAM COOKIES

Rolled Cookies

YIELD: *7 to 8 dozen*
TOTAL TIME: *30 minutes*

# SOUTHERN BELLES

Formed Cookies

YIELD: *3 to 4 dozen*
TOTAL TIME: *30 minutes*

1 cup vegetable shortening
½ cup powdered sugar
½ teaspoon vanilla extract
2 cups all-purpose flour
1¼ cups pecans, ground

**1** Preheat the oven to 350 degrees. Lightly grease 2 baking sheets.

**2** In a large bowl, cream the vegetable shortening and powdered sugar. Beat in the vanilla extract. Gradually blend in the flour.

**3** Spread the pecans in a shallow bowl or pie plate.

**4** Pinch off pieces of dough and roll into pencil-thin ropes about 6 inches long. Fold the ropes in half and twist 3 times, then dredge in the ground pecans and place 1 inch apart on the prepared baking sheets.

**5** Bake for 12 to 15 minutes, until lightly colored. Transfer to wire racks to cool.

# SPANISH BUTTER WAFERS

Formed Cookies

YIELD: *4 to 5 dozen*
TOTAL TIME: *30 minutes*
CHILLING TIME: *4 hours*

1¾ cups all-purpose flour
½ teaspoon salt
½ cup vegetable shortening
½ cup butter, at room temperature
1¼ cups granulated sugar
2 large eggs
1 teaspoon vanilla extract
1½ teaspoons anise seeds

**1** Combine the flour and salt.

**2** In a large bowl, cream the vegetable shortening, butter, and sugar. Beat in the eggs one at a time. Beat in the vanilla extract. Gradually blend in the dry ingredients. Stir in the anise seeds. Cover and chill for 4 hours.

**3** Preheat the oven to 350 degrees.

**4** Pinch off walnut-sized pieces of dough and form into balls. Place 1 inch apart on ungreased baking sheets. Flatten the balls with the bottom of a glass dipped in flour.

**5** Bake for 15 to 18 minutes, until lightly colored. Transfer to wire racks to cool.

# SPANISH CHRISTMAS COOKIES

Rolled Cookies

YIELD: *3 to 5 dozen*
TOTAL TIME: *30 minutes*
CHILLING TIME: *2 hours*

1½ cups all-purpose flour
¼ teaspoon ground cinnamon
¼ teaspoon ground allspice
6 tablespoons butter, at room temperature
¼ cup granulated sugar
1 large egg
2 tablespoons canola oil
1½ teaspoons white port
½ teaspoon grated orange zest
¼ teaspoon grated lemon zest

**1** Combine the flour and spices.

**2** In a large bowl, cream the butter and sugar. Beat in the egg and oil. Beat in the port. Beat in the orange and lemon zest. Gradually blend in the dry ingredients. Cover and chill for 2 hours.

**3** Preheat the oven to 350 degrees.

**4** On a floured surface, roll out the dough to a thickness of ¼ inch. Using 2-inch round cookie cutter, cut into rounds and place 1 inch apart on ungreased baking sheets.

**5** Bake for 12 to 15 minutes, until lightly colored. Transfer to wire racks to cool.

**6** Sprinkle the cooled cookies with powdered sugar.

1 cup all-purpose flour
¼ cup unsweetened cocoa powder
1 teaspoon baking powder
1 teaspoon ground cinnamon
½ teaspoon ground cloves
½ teaspoon ground allspice
Pinch of salt
¼ cup vegetable shortening
1 cup granulated sugar
3 large eggs
1 teaspoon vanilla extract
½ cup raisins
½ cup walnuts, chopped

**1** Preheat the oven to 350 degrees. Lightly grease a 13 by 9-inch baking pan.

**2** Combine the flour, cocoa powder, baking powder, spices, and salt.

**3** In a large bowl, cream the vegetable shortening and sugar. Beat in the eggs. Beat in the vanilla extract. Gradually blend in the dry ingredients. Fold in the raisins and walnuts. Spread the dough evenly in the prepared baking pan.

**4** Bake for 20 to 30 minutes, until the tip of a knife inserted in the center comes out clean. Cool in the pan on a wire rack before cutting into large or small bars.

**Baking notes:** If you want to frost these bars, do so while they are still warm.

# SPICE BARS

Bar Cookies

YIELD: *2 to 3 dozen*
TOTAL TIME: *35 minutes*

---

¾ cups all-purpose flour
1½ teaspoons ground ginger
1½ teaspoons ground nutmeg
6 tablespoons vegetable shortening
½ cup packed light brown sugar
¼ cup molasses
1 tablespoon brandy

**1** Preheat the oven to 350 degrees.

**2** Combine the flour and spices.

**3** In a large bowl, cream the vegetable shortening and sugar. Beat in the molasses and brandy. Gradually blend in the dry ingredients.

**4** Drop the dough by spoonfuls 2½ inches apart onto ungreased baking sheets.

**5** Bake for 5 to 6 minutes, until golden brown. As soon as the cookies are cool enough to handle, remove them from the baking sheet and roll up around metal cone shapes. Place seam side down on wire racks to cool.

**Baking notes:** You will need metal cone forms for this recipe; they are available in specialty cookware shops. If the cookies harden before you are able to form them, reheat them for about 30 seconds in the oven. These cones can be filled with many types of dessert topping or ice cream. If you are filling them with ice cream, chill the cones in the freezer for at least 30 minutes before filling them. If you fill the cookies too soon, they will soften before they are served.

# SPICE CONES

Drop Cookies

YIELD: *5 to 6 dozen*
TOTAL TIME: *30 minutes*

# SPICE COOKIES I

Rolled Cookies

YIELD: *4 to 5 dozen*
TOTAL TIME: *30 minutes*
CHILLING TIME: *4 hours*
RESTING TIME: *8 hours*

3 cups all-purpose flour
1 teaspoon baking powder
½ teaspoon ground cinnamon
¼ teaspoon ground nutmeg
¼ teaspoon ground cloves
¼ teaspoon salt
1 cup granulated sugar
3 large eggs
1½ tablespoons frozen orange juice
    concentrate, thawed
½ teaspoon grated orange zest
¼ cup hazelnuts, chopped

**1** Combine the flour, baking powder, spices, and salt.

**2** In a large bowl, beat the sugar and eggs until thick and light-colored. Beat in the orange juice concentrate and orange zest. Gradually blend in the dry ingre-

dients. Stir in the hazelnuts. Cover and chill for 4 hours.

**3** Lightly grease 2 baking sheets.

**4** On a floured surface, roll the dough out to a thickness of ½ inch. Using a 1½-inch round cookie cutter, cut out the cookies and place 1 inch apart on the prepared baking sheets. Cover with clean towels and set aside for 8 hours.

**5** Preheat the oven to 350 degrees.

**6** Turn the cookies over and place a drop of amaretto in the center of each one. Bake for 8 to 10 minutes, until lightly colored. Transfer to wire racks to cool.

# SPICE COOKIES II

Drop Cookies

YIELD: *3 to 4 dozen*
TOTAL TIME: *30 minutes*
CHILLING TIME: *4 hours*

1 cup all-purpose flour
1 teaspoon ground cloves
½ cup vegetable shortening
1 cup granulated sugar
1 large egg
1 teaspoon vanilla extract

**1** Combine the flour and cloves.

**2** In a large bowl, cream the vegetable shortening and sugar. Beat in the egg. Beat in the vanilla extract. Gradually blend in the dry ingredients. Cover and chill for 4 hours.

**3** Preheat the oven to 325 degrees. Lightly grease 2 baking sheets.

**4** Drop the dough by spoonfuls at least 2 inches apart onto the prepared baking sheets.

**5** Bake for 12 to 15 minutes, until lightly colored. Transfer to wire racks to cool.

# SPONGE DROPS

Drop Cookies

YIELD: *3 to 4 dozen*
TOTAL TIME: *30 minutes*

1½ cups all-purpose flour
1½ teaspoons baking powder
½ teaspoon salt
¾ cup granulated sugar
2 large eggs
¼ cup milk
½ teaspoon lemon extract

**1** Preheat the oven to 350 degrees. Lightly grease 2 baking sheets.

**2** Combine the flour, baking powder, and salt.

**3** In a large bowl, beat the sugar and eggs until thick and light-colored. Beat in the milk and lemon extract. Gradually blend in the dry ingredients.

**4** Drop the dough by spoonfuls 1½ inches apart onto the prepared baking sheets.

**5** Bake for 12 to 15 minutes, until lightly colored. Transfer to wire racks to cool.

# SPRITZ COOKIES

Formed Cookies

YIELD: *3 to 4 dozen*
TOTAL TIME: *30 minutes*

2 cups all-purpose flour
⅓ cup almonds, ground fine
1 cup vegetable shortening
½ cup powdered sugar
1 large egg yolk
1 teaspoon almond extract

**1** Preheat the oven to 350 degrees. Lightly grease 2 baking sheets.

**2** Combine the flour and almonds.

**3** In a large bowl, cream the vegetable shortening and powdered sugar. Beat in the egg yolk and almond extract. Gradually blend in the dry ingredients.

**4** Place the dough in a cookie press or a pastry bag fitted with a star tip and press or pipe out into small rings onto the prepared baking sheets, spacing them 1 inch apart.

**5** Bake for 8 to 10 minutes, until lightly colored. Transfer to wire racks to cool.

**Baking notes:** If you do not have a cookie press or pastry bag, roll out the dough on a floured surface. Using a round cutter, cut out cookies, then cut out the centers with a smaller cutter. In Sweden, where the recipe originated, the rings are traditional, but S-shaped cookies are often made from the same basic Spritz Cookie dough.

---

# S-SHAPED COOKIES

Rolled Cookies

YIELD: *3 to 4 hours*
TOTAL TIME: *30 minutes*
CHILLING TIME: *4 hours*

½ cup vegetable shortening
⅔ cup granulated sugar
4 large egg yolks
½ teaspoon grated lemon zest
2 cups all-purpose flour
1 large egg white, beaten

**1** In a large bowl, cream the vegetable shortening and sugar. Beat in the egg yolks. Beat in the lemon zest. Gradually blend in the flour.

**2** Divide the dough into 4 pieces. Wrap in waxed paper and chill for 4 hours.

**3** Preheat the oven to 350 degrees. Lightly grease 2 baking sheets.

**4** Work with one piece of dough at a time, keeping the remaining dough chilled. On a floured surface, roll out the dough to a thickness of ¼ inch. Using a sharp knife, cut into strip ¾ inch wide and 4 inches long. Place the strips on the prepared baking sheets and form into the S-shapes. Brush with the beaten egg white.

**5** Bake for 8 to 10 minutes, until lightly colored. Transfer to wire racks to cool.

**Baking notes:** Sprinkle white or colored sugar crystals over the cookies just before baking.

# STAINED GLASS CUTOUTS

Rolled Cookies

YIELD: *3 to 4 dozen*
TOTAL TIME: *60 minutes*
CHILLING TIME: *24 hours*

3¾ cups all-purpose flour
½ teaspoon baking soda
1 teaspoon ground nutmeg
½ teaspoon salt
½ cup vegetable shortening
1½ cups powdered sugar
1 large egg
½ cup plain yogurt
1 teaspoon almond extract

FILLING
2 cups granulated sugar
1 cup light corn syrup
½ cup water
2 drops flavoring of choice, such as mint or vanilla extract
A few drops of food coloring

1  Combine the flour, baking soda, nutmeg, and salt.

2  In a large bowl, cream the vegetable shortening, powdered sugar, and egg. Beat in the yogurt. Beat in the almond extract. Gradually blend in the dry ingredients. Divide the dough into 4 equal pieces. Wrap in waxed paper and chill for 24 hours.

3  Lightly grease 2 baking sheets.

4  Work with one piece of dough at a time, keeping the remaining dough refrigerated. On a floured surface, roll out the dough to a thickness of ¼ inch. Using cookie cutters, cut into fancy shapes. Using small cookie cutters of different shapes, or a knife, cut out the centers of the cookies. Place 1

inch apart on the prepared baking sheets and chill for 1 hour.

5  Preheat the oven to 350 degrees.

6  Bake the cookies for 10 to 12 minutes, until lightly colored. Transfer to wire racks to cool..

7  To make the filling, combine all of the ingredients in a saucepan and cook over medium heat, stirring, until the sugar dissolves. Bring to a boil and cook until the syrup registers 250 to 265 degrees (hard-ball state) on a candy thermometer. Remove from the heat.

8  Carefully spoon the syrup into the center cut-outs of each cookie. Refrigerate until chilled and set. When cool, carefully twist the cookies to release them and slide them off the baking sheets.

**Baking notes:**  These cookies are designed to be displayed so that "stained glass" can be seen against the light. They can be used as ornaments on a Christmas tree or to decorate presents. In fact, they can be made for almost any holiday of the year. If you wish to make nonedible cookies that will last for several years, use only ½ cup granulated sugar in the dough and add 1 cup of salt. To store, lay them flat in a box so the "stained glass" will not crack.

# STRAWBERRY MERINGUE BARS

Bar Cookies

YIELD: *3 to 4 dozen*
TOTAL TIME: *45 minutes*

CRUST
¾ cup vegetable shortening
¼ cup granulated sugar
2 large egg yolks
1½ cups all-purpose flour

FILLING
2 large egg whites
½ cup granulated sugar
1 cup almond, chopped
1 cup strawberry puree
1 cup flaked coconut

1  Preheat the oven to 350 degrees. Lightly grease a 13 by 9-inch square baking pan.

2  To make the crust, cream the vegetable shortening and sugar in a large bowl. Beat in the egg yolks. Gradually blend in the

flour. Spread the dough evenly in the bottom of the prepared baking pan.

3  Bake for 15 minutes.

4  Meanwhile, make the topping: In a large bowl, beat the egg whites until foamy. Gradually beat in the sugar and beat in until the whites hold stiff peaks. Fold in the chopped nuts.

5  Spread the strawberry puree over the hot crust and sprinkle with the coconut. Spread the topping over the coconut.

6  Bake for 20 to 25 minutes longer, or until the topping is firm to the touch. Cool in the pan on a wire rack before cutting into large or small bars.

5 cups all-purpose flour
1 teaspoon baking soda
1½ teaspoons ground ginger
½ teaspoon salt
1 cup vegetable shortening
1 cup packed light brown sugar
2 cups molasses

**1** Preheat the oven to 375 degrees. Lightly grease 2 baking sheets.

**2** Combine the flour, baking soda, ginger, and salt.

**3** In a large bowl, cream the vegetable shortening and brown sugar. Beat in the molasses. Gradually blend in the dry ingredients. If the dough seems dry,

add a little water ½ teaspoonful at a time.

**4** On a floured surface, roll out the dough to a thickness of ¼ inch. Using a 2-inch round cookie cutter, cut out cookies and place 1 inch apart onto the prepared baking sheets.

**5** Bake for 10 to 12 minutes, until lightly colored. Transfer to wire racks to cool.

# STROOP KOEKJES

Rolled Cookies

YIELD: *8 to 9 dozen*
TOTAL TIME: *30 minutes*

---

3 cups all-purpose flour
2 teaspoons baking powder
½ teaspoon baking soda
½ teaspoon salt
⅔ cup butter, at room temperature
1 cup granulated sugar
2 large eggs
¼ cup buttermilk
½ teaspoon brandy
Milk for glazing
Granulated sugar for sprinkling

**1** Preheat the oven to 375 degrees. Lightly grease 2 baking sheets.

**2** Combine the flour, baking powder, baking soda, and salt.

**3** In a large bowl, cream the butter and sugar. Beat in the eggs.

Beat in the buttermilk and brandy. Gradually blend in the dry ingredients.

**4** On a floured surface, roll out the dough to a thickness of ¼ inch. Using a 2-inch round cookie cutter, cut out cookies and place 1½ inches apart on the prepared baking sheets. Brush with milk and sprinkle liberally with granulated sugar.

**5** Bake for 10 to 12 minutes, until lightly colored. Transfer to wire racks to cool.

# SUGAR COOKIES I

Rolled Cookies

YIELD: *3 to 4 dozen*
TOTAL TIME: *40 minutes*

---

4 cups all-purpose flour
1 teaspoon baking soda
½ teaspoon salt
1 cup vegetable shortening
2¼ cups granulated sugar
2 large eggs
1 cup milk
Milk for glazing
Granulated sugar for sprinkling

**1** Combine the flour, baking soda, and salt.

**2** In a large bowl, cream the vegetable shortening and sugar. Beat in the eggs one at a time. Beat in the milk. Gradually blend in the dry ingredients. Cover and chill for 2 hours.

**3** Preheat the oven to 350 degrees. Lightly grease 2 baking sheets.

**4** On a floured surface, roll out the dough to a thickness of ¼ inch. Using a 1½-inch round cookie cutter, cut into rounds and place 1 inch apart on the prepared baking sheets. Brush with milk and sprinkle with granulated sugar.

**5** Bake for 10 to 12 minutes, until lightly colored. Transfer to wire racks to cool.

# SUGAR COOKIES II

Rolled Cookies

YIELD: *5 to 6 dozen*
TOTAL TIME: *30 minutes*
CHILLING TIME: *2 hours*

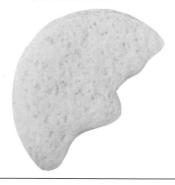

# SUGAR COOKIES III

Rolled Cookies

YIELD: *7 to 8 dozen*
TOTAL TIME: *30 minutes*
CHILLING TIME: *4 hours*

3 cups all-purpose flour
1 teaspoon baking soda
1 cup vegetable shortening
1½ cups granulated sugar
4 large eggs
Milk for glazing
Granulated sugar for sprinkling

**1** Combine the flour and baking soda.

**2** In a large bowl, cream the vegetable shortening and sugar. Beat in the eggs. Gradually blend in the dry ingredients. Cover and chill for 4 hours.

**3** Preheat the oven to 350 degrees. Lightly grease 2 baking sheets.

**4** On a floured surface, roll out the dough to a thickness of ¼ inch. Using a 1½-inch round cookie cutter, cut into rounds and place 1 inch apart on the prepared baking sheets. Brush with milk and sprinkle with granulated sugar.

**5** Bake for 10 to 12 minutes, until golden. Transfer to wire racks to cool.

# SUGAR COOKIES IV

Formed Cookies

YIELD: *3 to 4 dozen*
TOTAL TIME: *30 minutes*

2 cups all-purpose flour
1 teaspoon baking powder
1 teaspoon salt
½ cup vegetable shortening
1 cup granulated sugar
1 teaspoon vanilla extract
Granulated sugar for rolling

**1** Preheat the oven to 350 degrees. Lightly grease 2 baking sheets.

**2** Combine the flour, baking powder, and salt.

**3** In a large bowl, cream the vegetable shortening and sugar. Beat in the vanilla extract. Gradually blend in the dry ingredients.

**4** Pinch off walnut-sized pieces of dough and roll into balls. Roll the balls in granulated sugar and place 1½ inches apart on the prepared baking sheets. Flatten each ball with the bottom of a glass dipped in water and then in granulated sugar.

**5** Bake for 10 to 12 minutes, until lightly colored. Transfer to wire racks to cool.

# SUGAR-FREE COOKIES

Drop Cookies

YIELD: *4 to 6 dozen*
TOTAL TIME: *30 minutes*
CHILLING TIME: *24 hours*

1 cup all-purpose flour
1 cup whole wheat flour
2 teaspoons baking soda
1 teaspoon cream of tartar
1 tablespoon plus 1 teaspoon ground cloves
1 tablespoon plus 1 teaspoon ground nutmeg
½ teaspoon ground cinnamon
1 teaspoon salt
2 cups vegetable shortening
1 cup fructose (see Baking notes)
2 large eggs
1 teaspoon grated lemon zest

**1** Combine the two flours, baking soda, cream of tartar, spices, and salt.

**2** In a large bowl, cream the vegetable shortening and fructose.

Beat in the eggs. Beat in the lemon zest. Gradually blend in the dry ingredients. Cover and chill for 24 hours.

**3** Preheat the oven to 350 degrees. Lightly grease 2 baking sheets.

**4** Drop the dough by spoonfuls 1½ inches apart onto the prepared baking sheets.

**5** Bake for 10 to 12 minutes, until lightly colored. Transfer to wire racks to cool.

**Baking notes:** Fructose is available in health food stores and some grocery stores. It is approximately one and a half times sweeter than granulated sugar.

2 ounces bittersweet chocolate, chopped
¾ cup all-purpose flour
1 teaspoon baking powder
½ cup butter, at room temperature
2 tablespoons plus 2¾ teaspoons nonnutritive sweetener (see Baking notes)
2 large eggs
½ teaspoon vanilla extract
½ cup walnuts, chopped

**1** Preheat the oven to 350 degrees. Lightly grease an 8-inch square baking pan.

**2** Melt the chocolate in a double boiler over low heat, stirring until smooth. Remove from the heat.

**3** Combine the flour and baking powder.

**4** In a large bowl, cream the butter and sweetener. Beat in the eggs and vanilla extract. Beat in the melted chocolate. Gradually blend in the dry ingredients. Stir in the walnuts. Spread the mixture evenly into the prepared baking pan.

**5** Bake for 25 to 30 minutes, until a toothpick inserted in the center comes out clean. Cool in the pan on a wire rack before cutting into large or small bars.

**Baking notes:** Although this recipe was created for diabetics, it should appeal to anyone on a sugar-restricted diet. Several brands of nonnutritive sweetener are available.

# Sugarless Chocolate Bars

Bar Cookies

YIELD: *1 to 2 dozen*
TOTAL TIME: *35 minutes*

---

2 cups all-purpose flour
1 teaspoon baking soda
1 teaspoon salt
1 cup vegetable shortening
1 cup granulated sugar
1 cup packed light brown sugar
2 large eggs
1 teaspoon vanilla extract
2 cups rolled oats
1 cup shredded coconut
1 cup gumdrops, chopped
Granulated sugar for rolling

**1** Preheat the oven to 350 degrees. Lightly grease 2 baking sheets.

**2** Combine the flour, baking soda, and salt.

**3** In a large bowl, cream the vegetable shortening and two sugars. Beat in the eggs. Beat in the vanilla extract. Gradually blend in the dry ingredients. Fold in the oats, coconut, and gum drops.

**4** Pinch off 1-inch pieces of the dough and roll into balls. Place 1 inch apart on the prepared baking sheets.

**5** Bake for 10 to 12 minutes, until lightly colored. Transfer to wire racks to cool.

**6** Roll the cooled cookies in granulated sugar.

**Baking notes:** These can be made as balls or flattened with the bottom of a glass dipped in flour.

# Sugar-Plum Drops

Formed Cookies

YIELD: *2 to 3 dozen*
TOTAL TIME: *30 minutes*

# SWEDISH BUTTER COOKIES

Drop Cookies

YIELD: *3 to 4 dozen*
TOTAL TIME: *30 minutes*

**2 cups all-purpose flour**
**1 teaspoon baking powder**
**½ teaspoon salt**
**¾ cup butter, at room temperature**
**¾ cup granulated sugar**
**¼ cup powdered sugar**
**1 teaspoon vanilla extract**
**1 cup (6 ounces) semisweet choco-**
**late chip**
**½ cup hazelnuts, chopped**

**1** Preheat the oven to 350 degrees. Lightly grease 2 baking sheets.

**2** Combine the flour, baking powder, and salt.

**3** In a large bowl, cream butter and two sugars. Beat in the vanilla extract. Gradually blend in the dry ingredients. Fold in the chocolate chips and hazelnuts.

**4** Drop the dough by spoonfuls 1½ inches apart onto the prepared baking sheets.

**5** Bake for 12 to 14 minutes, until lightly colored. Transfer to wire racks to cool.

# SWEDISH CRISP RYE BISCUITS

Rolled Cookies

YIELD: *4 to 5 dozen*
TOTAL TIME: *45 minutes*

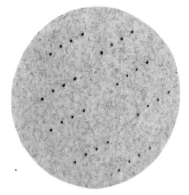

**1¾ cups all-purpose flour**
**2 cups coarse-ground rye flour (see**
**Baking notes)**
**1 teaspoon salt**
**½ cup butter, at room temperature**
**1 tablespoon granulated sugar**
**1 cup cold milk**

**1** Preheat the oven to 375 degrees. Lightly grease 2 baking sheets.

**2** Combine the two flours and salt.

**3** In a large bowl, cream the butter and sugar. Beat in the milk. Gradually blend in the dry ingredients.

**4** On a floured surface, roll out the dough to a thickness of ⅛ inch. Using a 4-inch round cookie cutter or a glass, cut into rounds and place 1 inch apart on the prepared baking sheets. Prick the rounds with the tines of a fork.

**5** Bake for 8 to 10 minutes, or until golden brown. Transfer to wire racks to cool.

2 cups all-purpose flour
1 cup cold butter
¼ cup ice water
About ½ cup fruit preserves
1 large egg, beaten
Sugar crystals for sprinkling

**1** Put the flour in a large bowl and cut in the butter. Add just enough ice water to make a soft dough. Cover and chill for 1 hour.

**2** On a floured surface, roll out the dough to a 14-inch square. Trim the edges. Fold the dough in half and roll to a 21 by 7-inch rectangle. Fold in thirds like a business letter. Roll out to a rectangle and fold up 2 more times. Wrap in waxed paper and chill for 30 minutes.

**3** Preheat the oven to 400 degrees.

**4** On a floured surface, roll out the dough to a 14-inch squares. Trim the edges. Cut into 25 squares. Cut diagonally corner to corner with a pastry wheel. Place 1 inch apart on ungreased baking sheets and put a small spoonful of the preserves in the center of each diagonal. Brush with the beaten egg and sprinkle with crystal sugar.

**5** Bake for 10 to 12 minutes, until lightly colored. Transfer to wire racks to cool.

**Baking notes:** For best results, keep the dough thoroughly chilled at all times.

# SWEDISH PINWHEELS

Rolled Cookies

YIELD: *2 to 3 dozen*
TOTAL TIME: *60 minutes*
CHILLING TIME: *90 minutes*

---

2 cups all-purpose flour
⅓ cup almonds, ground
1 cup vegetable shortening
¾ cup granulated sugar
1 large egg
¼ teaspoon almond extract

**1** Combine the flour and almonds.

**2** In a large bowl, cream vegetable shortening and sugar. Beat in the egg. Beat in the almond extract. Gradually blend in the dry ingredients. Cover and chill for 24 hours.

**3** Preheat the oven to 375 degrees. Lightly grease 2 baking sheets.

**4** On a floured surface, roll out the dough to a thickness of ¼ inch. Using a 2-inch round cookie cutter, cut into rounds and place 1 inch apart on the prepared baking sheets.

**5** Bake for 6 to 8 minutes, until lightly colored. Transfer to wire racks to cool.

**Baking notes:** Traditionally, sand tarts are created by pressing the dough into a sand bakalee mold.

# SWEDISH SAND TARTS

Rolled Cookies

YIELD: *3 to 4 dozen*
TOTAL TIME: *30 minutes*
CHILLING TIME: *24 hours*

---

2½ cups all-purpose flour
¾ teaspoon baking powder
½ teaspoon baking soda
½ cup vegetable shortening
1½ cups packed light brown sugar
2 large eggs
1 cup heavy cream
1 tablespoon cider vinegar
½ cup almonds, chopped

**1** Preheat the oven to 375 degrees. Lightly grease 2 baking sheets.

**2** Combine the flour, baking powder, and baking soda.

**3** In a large bowl, cream the vegetable shortening and brown sugar. Beat in the eggs. Beat in

the heavy cream. Beat in the vinegar. Gradually blend in the dry ingredients. Fold in the almonds.

**4** Drop the dough by spoonfuls 1½ inches apart onto the prepared baking sheets.

**5** Bake for 8 to 10 minutes, until lightly colored. Transfer to wire racks to cool.

# SWEET-AND-SOUR COOKIES

Drop Cookies

YIELD: *3 to 5 dozen*
TOTAL TIME: *30 minutes*

# TASTY HEALTH COOKIES

Drop Cookies

YIELD: *3 to 4 dozen*
TOTAL TIME: *30 minutes*

1 cup all-purpose flour
⅔ cup wheat germ
1 teaspoon baking powder
1 teaspoon baking soda
¼ teaspoon salt
1 cup vegetable shortening
1 cup packed light brown sugar
¾ cup granulated sugar
2 large eggs
2⅓ cups rolled oats
2 cups shredded coconut

1  Preheat the oven to 350 degrees. Lightly grease 2 baking sheets.

2  Combine the flour, wheat germ, baking powder, baking soda, and salt.

3  In a large bowl, cream the vegetable shortening and two sugars. Beat in the eggs. Gradually blend in the dry ingredients. Fold in the oatmeal and coconut. If the dough seems dry, add a little water ½ teaspoonful at a time.

4  Drop the dough by spoonfuls 3 inches apart onto the prepared baking sheets.

5  Bake for 8 to 10 minutes, until lightly colored. Transfer to wire racks to cool.

# TEATIME COOKIES

Formed Cookies

YIELD: *3 to 4 dozen*
TOTAL TIME: *30 minutes*

¾ cup plus 3 tablespoons vegetable shortening
½ cup unsweetened cocoa powder
3 tablespoons powdered sugar
1¾ cups all-purpose flour
1 teaspoon baking powder
½ teaspoon salt
½ cup granulated sugar
1 large egg
1 teaspoon vanilla extract
½ teaspoon almond extract

1  Preheat the oven to 375 degrees. Lightly grease 2 baking sheets.

2  In a small saucepan, melt the 3 tablespoons vegetable shortening. Remove from the heat and blend in the cocoa, and powdered sugar, stirring until smooth. Set aside.

3  Combine the flour, baking powder, and salt.

4  In a large bowl, cream the remaining ¾ cup vegetable shortening and granulated sugar. Beat in the egg. Beat in the vanilla extract and almond extract.

5  Transfer half the dough to another bowl. Add the cocoa mixture and blend well.

6  Drop the dough by spoonfuls 3 inches apart onto the prepared baking sheets. Spread into rounds with the back of a spoon dipped in flour. Drop spoonfuls of the chocolate dough on top of the rounds and use the back of a spoon dipped in flour to spread the chocolate dough to the edges.

7  Bake for 8 to 10 minutes, until firm to touch. Transfer to wire racks to cool.

**Baking notes:**  A whole nut (or half a large nut) can be pushed into the top of each cookie before baking.

½ cup all-purpose flour
1 cup almonds, ground
2 ounces semisweet chocolate, chopped
½ cup vegetable shortening
1 cup granulated sugar
2 large eggs
½ teaspoon almond extract

1 Preheat the oven to 350 degrees. Lightly grease a 9-inch square baking pan.

2 Combine the flour and almonds.

3 In the top of a double boiler, melt the chocolate and vegetable shortening, stirring until smooth. Remove from the heat and beat in the sugar. Beat in the eggs one at a time, beating vigorously after each addition. Beat in the almond extract. Gradually blend in the dry ingredients. Spread the mixture evenly in the prepared baking pan.

4 Bake for 35 to 40 minutes, or until a toothpick inserted in the center comes out clean. Cool in the pan on a wire rack.

5 Frost the cooled cookies with Vanilla Icing (see Pantry) and cut into large or small bars.

**Baking notes:** To make a different version of these cookies, bake in a 13 by 9-inch baking pan for 25 to 30 minutes. Let cool in the pan on a wire rack, then use cookie cutters to cut into fancy shapes and frost.

# TEATIME FAVORITES

Bar Cookies

YIELD: *2 to 3 dozen*
TOTAL TIME: *50 minutes*

---

1 cup vegetable shortening
½ cup packed light brown sugar
2 large eggs, separated
1½ teaspoons vanilla extract
2¼ cups all-purpose flour
1½ cups almonds, ground
About ¼ cup fruit preserves

1 Preheat the oven to 350 degrees. Lightly grease 2 baking sheets.

2 In a large bowl, cream the vegetable shortening and brown sugar. Beat in the egg yolks and vanilla extract. Gradually blend in the flour.

3 In a small bowl, beat the egg whites stiff until stiff but not dry.

4 Pinch off small pieces of dough and roll into balls. Roll the balls in the beaten egg white, then in the ground almonds, and place 1 inch apart on the prepared baking sheets. With your finger,

press an indentation into the center of each ball.

5 Bake for 12 to 15 minutes, until lightly colored. Fill each cookie with a dab of fruit preserves, then transfer to wire racks to cool.

**Baking notes:** These are good filled with preserves; but for a real treat, fill them with a lemon custard or banana custard. Even Jell-O can be used: Chill the cookies, then spoon the Jell-O into the cookies just before it sets.

# THIMBLES

Formed Cookies

YIELD: *3 to 4 dozen*
TOTAL TIME: *30 minutes*

# THIN COOKIES

Drop Cookies

YIELD: *6 to 8 dozen*
TOTAL TIME: *30 minutes*

1 cup vegetable shortening
1 cup granulated sugar
2 large eggs
½ teaspoon vanilla extract
½ teaspoon lemon extract
1 cup plus 2 tablespoons all-purpose
    flour

**1** Preheat the oven to 375 degrees. Lightly grease 2 baking sheets.

**2** In a large bowl, cream the vegetable shortening and sugar. Beat in the eggs one at a time, beating vigorously after each addition. Beat in the vanilla and lemon extracts. Gradually blend in the flour.

**3** Drop the dough by spoonfuls 2 inches apart onto the prepared baking sheets.

**4** Bake for 6 to 8 minutes, until the edges just start to brown. Transfer to wire racks to cool.

---

# THRIFTY COOKIES

Drop Cookies

YIELD: *3 to 4 dozen*
TOTAL TIME: *30 minutes*
CHILLING TIME: *2 hours*

1 cup all-purpose flour
2 cups crushed cookies, such as
    vanilla wafers or Oreos
1 teaspoon baking powder
⅛ teaspoon baking soda
½ teaspoon salt
¼ cup vegetable shortening
½ cup packed light brown sugar
½ cup peanut butter
1 large egg
½ cup sour milk
½ cup raisins

**1** Combine the flour, cookie crumbs, baking powder, baking soda, and salt.

**2** In a large bowl, cream the vegetable shortening and brown sugar. Beat in the peanut butter. Beat in the egg and milk. Gradually blend in the dry ingredients. Fold in the raisins. Cover and chill for 2 hours.

**3** Preheat the oven to 350 degrees. Lightly grease 2 baking sheets.

**4** Drop the dough by spoonfuls 1½ inches apart onto the prepared baking sheets.

**5** Bake for 12 to 15 minutes, until lightly colored. Transfer to wire racks to cool.

---

# THUMBPRINT COOKIES

Rolled Cookies

YIELD:: *5 to 7 dozen*
TOTAL TIME: *40 minutes*

3½ cups all-purpose flour
3 tablespoons baking powder
¼ teaspoon salt
¾ cup vegetable shortening
1 cup granulated sugar
2 large eggs
⅓ cup milk
½ teaspoon vanilla extract
Filling (see Baking notes)

**1** Preheat oven to 400 degrees. Lightly grease 2 baking sheets.

**2** Combine the flour, baking powder, and salt.

**3** In a large bowl, cream the vegetable shortening and sugar. Beat in the eggs. Beat in the milk and vanilla extract. Gradually blend in the dry ingredients.

**4** On a floured surface, roll out the dough to a thickness of about ½ inch. Using a 1½-inch round cookie cutter, cut out the cookies and place 1 inch apart on the prepared baking sheets. Press your fingertip into the center of each cookie to make a shallow depression and fill with the desired filling.

**5** Bake for 12 to 15 minutes, until lightly colored. Transfer to wire racks to cool.

**Baking notes:** The filling for these cookies can range from fruit preserves or jams or jelly to mini-marshmallows or melted chocolate. Be creative.

¾ cup vegetable shortening
1 cup granulated sugar
2 large egg yolks
1 teaspoon grated lemon zest
1½ cups all-purpose flour

GLAZE
½ cup granulated sugar
1 large egg white
1 tablespoon water
⅛ teaspoon salt
1 cup almonds, ground fine
1 tablespoon ground cinnamon
¼ teaspoon ground nutmeg

**1** Preheat the oven to 375 degrees. Lightly grease 2 baking sheets.

**2** In a large bowl, cream the vegetable shortening and sugar. Beat in the egg yolks. Beat in the lemon zest. Gradually blend in the flour.

**3** To make the glaze, beat the sugar, egg white, water, and salt in a medium bowl. Beat in the almonds and spices.

**4** Pinch off walnut-sized pieces of dough and roll into balls. Place 1½ inches apart on the prepared baking sheets. Flatten each ball with the bottom of a glass dipped in flour and brush generously with the glaze.

**5** Bake for 8 to 10 minutes, until lightly colored. Transfer to wire racks to cool.

# TORTELETTES
Formed Cookies

YIELD: *3 to 4 dozen*
TOTAL TIME: *30 minutes*

---

1 cup all-purpose flour
⅓ cup almonds, ground
⅓ cup farina ceral, such as Cream of Wheat
½ teaspoon baking powder
1 cup vegetable shortening
⅔ cup granulated sugar
1 large egg

GLAZE
4 tablespoons butter, melted
6 tablespoons granulated sugar
1 teaspoon corn syrup
⅓ cup slivered almonds

**1** Combine the flour, almonds, farina, and baking powder.

**2** In a large bowl, cream the vegetable shortening and sugar. Beat in the egg. Gradually blend in the dry ingredients. Cover and chill for 2 hours.

**3** Preheat the oven to 350 degrees. Lightly grease 2 baking sheets.

**4** To make the glaze, combine the butter, sugar, and corn syrup in a

small bowl and beat until smooth.

**5** Drop the dough by spoonfuls 1½ inches apart onto the prepared baking sheets.

**6** Bake for 10 to 12 minutes, just until lightly colored. Brush the cookies with the glaze, sprinkle with the slivered almonds, and bake for 5 minutes longer. Transfer to wire racks to cool.

# TOSCA COOKIES
Drop Cookies

YIELD: *3 to 4 dozen*
TOTAL TIME: *30 minutes*
CHILLING TIME: *2 hours*

# TRAIL MIX COOKIES

Drop Cookies

YIELD: *3 to 4 dozen*
TOTAL TIME: *30 minutes*

¾ cup all-purpose flour
½ teaspoon baking soda
½ cup vegetable shortening
1 cup packed light brown sugar
½ cup peanut butter
1 large egg
1 teaspoon vanilla extract
1 cup (6 ounces) semisweet chocolate chips
1 cup raisins
⅔ cup peanuts, chopped

**1** Preheat the oven to 375 degrees. Lightly grease 2 baking sheets.

**2** Combine the flour and baking soda.

**3** In a large bowl, cream the vegetable shortening and brown-sugar. Beat in the peanut butter.

Beat in the egg and vanilla extract. Gradually blend in the dry ingredients. Fold in the chocolate chips, raisins, and peanuts.

**4** Drop the dough by spoonfuls 1½ inches apart onto the prepared baking sheets.

**5** Bake for 10 to 12 minutes, until lightly colored. Transfer to wire racks to cool.

**6** When the cookies are cool, wrap individually and store in an airtight container.

# TROPICAL BARS

Bar Cookies

YIELD: *2 to 3 dozen*
TOTAL TIME: *35 minutes*

¾ cup all-purpose flour
¾ teaspoon baking powder
½ teaspoon salt
½ cup vegetable shortening
1 cup packed light brown sugar
2 large eggs
½ teaspoon rum
8 ounces canned crushed pineapple, drained
¾ cup flaked coconut

**1** Preheat the oven to 350 degrees. Lightly grease a 9-inch square baking pan.

**2** Combine the flour, baking powder, and salt.

**3** In a large bowl, cream the vegetable shortening and brown sugar. Beat in the eggs and rum. Gradually blend in the dry ingredients. Fold in the pineapple and coconut. Spread the batter evenly in the prepared baking pan.

**4** Bake for 25 to 30 minutes, until colored on top. Cool in the pan on a wire rack before cutting into large or small bars.

# TROPICAL FRUIT BARS

Bar Cookies

YIELD: *1 to 3 dozen*
TOTAL TIME: *35 minutes*

1¼ cups all-purpose flour
1 teaspoon baking soda
1 tablespoon canola oil
2 large eggs
1 tablespoon pineapple juice, preferrably fresh
1 teaspoon frozen orange juice concentrate, thawed
1¾ cups crushed fresh (or canned) pineapple, drained
1 cup flaked coconut
¾ cup macadamia nuts, chopped

**1** Preheat the oven to 350 degrees. Lightly grease a 13 by 9-inch baking pan.

**2** Combine the flour and baking soda.

**3** In a large bowl, beat the oil and eggs until thick and light-colored. Beat in the pineapple juice and orange juice concentrate. Gradually blend in the dry ingredients. Fold in the pineapple, coconut, and macadamia nuts. Spread the mixture evenly in the prepared baking pan.

**4** Bake for 15 to 20 minutes, until lightly colored on top. Cool in the pan on a wire rack before cutting into large or small bars.

3½ cups all-purpose flour
2 cups potato flour (see Baking
   notes)
1¾ cups butter, at room temperature
1 cup granulated sugar
2 large eggs, beaten
Powdered sugar for sprinkling
About 1 cup whole almonds

**1** Preheat the oven to 425
degrees. Lightly grease 2 baking
sheets.

**2** Combine the two flours.

**3** In a large bowl, cream the butter and sugar. Gradually blend in
the flour.

**4** On a floured surface, roll out
the dough to a thickness of ⅛
inch. Using a 1½-inch round
cookie cutter, cut out cookies and
place 1 inch apart on the prepared baking sheets. Brush with
the beaten eggs and sprinkle
with powdered sugar. Push a
whole almond into the center of
each cookie.

**5** Bake for 8 to 10 minutes, until
lightly colored. Transfer to wire
racks to cool.

**Baking notes:** Potato flour can
be found at specialty food stores.

You can also use 1 cup of potato
starch in place of the potato flour
and increase the all-purpose flour
to 4½ cups.

# UPPÅKRA COOKIES

Rolled Cookies

YIELD: *4 to 6 dozen*
TOTAL TIME: *35 minutes*

# Vanilla Daisies

Rolled Cookies

YIELD: *3 to 4 dozen*
TOTAL TIME: *30 minutes*

2⅓ cups all-purpose flour
½ teaspoon baking powder
¼ teaspoon salt
1 cup vegetable shortening
⅔ cup granulated sugar
1 large egg
1 teaspoon vanilla extract
1 teaspoon grated lemon zest
About ¼ cup glacé cherries, cut in half

**1** Preheat the oven to 350 degrees.

**2** Combine the flour, baking powder, and salt.

**3** In a large bowl, cream the vegetable shortening and sugar. Beat in the egg and vanilla extract.

Beat in the lemon zest. Gradually blend in the dry ingredients.

**4** On a floured surface, roll the dough out to a thickness of ¼ inch. Using a flower-shaped cookie cutter, cut out cookies and place 1 inch apart on ungreased baking sheets. Press a half-cherry into the center of each cookie.

**5** Bake for 10 to 12 minutes, until lightly colored. Transfer to wire racks to cool.

# Vanilla Hearts

Rolled Cookies

YIELD: *3 to 6 dozen*
TOTAL TIME: *30 minutes*
CHILLING TIME: *2 hours*

4 cups all-purpose flour
½ teaspoon salt
⅔ cup vegetable shortening
1 cup granulated sugar
3 large eggs
1 teaspoon vanilla extract

**1** Combine the flour and salt.

**2** In a large bowl, cream the vegetable shortening and sugar. Beat in the eggs one at a time. Beat in the vanilla extract. Gradually blend in the dry ingredients. Cover and chill for at least 2 hours.

**3** Preheat the oven to 350 degrees. Lightly grease 2 baking sheets.

**4** On a floured surface, roll out the dough to a thickness of ¼ inch. Using a heart-shaped cookie cutter, cut out cookies and place 1 inch apart on the prepared baking sheets.

**5** Bake for 10 to 12 minutes, until lightly colored. Transfer to wire racks to cool.

**Baking notes:** Decorate these cookies with white or pink icing.

# Vanilla Sour Cream Rosettes

Formed Cookies

YIELD: *3 to 4 dozen*
TOTAL TIME: *30 minutes*

1½ cups all-purpose flour
½ teaspoon baking powder
⅛ teaspoon baking soda
¼ teaspoon salt
¼ cup butter, at room temperature
½ cup granulated sugar
1 large egg
¼ cup sour cream
1 teaspoon vanilla extract

**1** Preheat the oven to 350 degrees.

**2** Combine the flour, baking powder, baking soda, and salt.

**3** In a large bowl, cream the butter and sugar. Beat in the egg. Beat in the sour cream. Beat in the vanilla extract. Gradually blend in the dry ingredients.

**4** Place the dough in a cookie press or a pastry bag fitted with a star tip and press or pipe out small rosettes 1 inch apart onto ungreased baking sheets.

**5** Bake for 10 to 12 minutes, until lightly colored. Transfer to wire racks to cool.

2½ cups all-purpose flour
1 teaspoon baking powder
Pinch of salt
1 cup butter, at room temperature
1 cup granulated sugar
2 large egg yolks
1½ teaspoons vanilla extract
Granulated sugar for sprinkling

**1** Combine the flour, baking powder, and salt.

**2** In a large bowl, cream the butter and sugar. Beat in the egg yolks. Beat in the vanilla extract. Gradually blend in the dry ingredients. Cover and chill for 1 hour.

**3** Preheat the oven to 375 degrees. Lightly grease 2 baking sheets.

**4** On a floured surface, roll out the dough to a thickness of ¼ inch. Using a 2-inch round cookie cutter, cut out cookies and place 1 inch apart onto the prepared baking sheets.

**5** Bake for 10 to 12 minutes, until lightly colored. Sprinkle granulated sugar over the hot cookies and transfer to wire racks to cool.

# VANILLA SUGAR COOKIES

Rolled Cookies

YIELD: *3 to 5 dozen*
TOTAL TIME: *30 minutes*
CHILLING TIME: *1 hour*

2 cups all-purpose flour
2 teaspoons baking powder
½ teaspoon salt
⅓ cup vegetable shortening
1 cup granulated sugar
1 large egg
¼ cup milk
1 tablespoon vanilla extract

**1** Combine the flour, baking powder, and salt.

**2** In a large bowl, cream the vegetable shortening and sugar. Beat in the egg. Beat in the milk. Beat in the vanilla extract. Gradually blend in the dry ingredients. Cover and chill for 4 hours.

**3** Preheat the oven to 350 degrees. Lightly grease 2 baking sheets.

**4** On a floured surface, roll out the dough to a thickness of ¼ inch. Using a 1½-inch round cookie cutter, cut out cookies and place 1 inch apart on the prepared baking sheets.

**5** Bake for 18 to 20 minutes, until lightly colored. Transfer to wire racks to cool.

**Baking notes:** To use this dough for drop cookies, add an additional 3 tablespoons milk.

# VANILLA WAFERS

Rolled Cookies

YIELD: *3 to 6 dozen*
TOTAL TIME: *30 minutes*
CHILLING TIME: *4 hours*

3 cups all-purpose flour
1 cup pecans, ground fine
1½ teaspoons baking powder
1½ cups vegetable shortening
1½ cups granulated sugar
2 large eggs
2 teaspoons Tía Maria liqueur
⅓ cup warm water

**1** Preheat the oven to 350 degrees. Lightly grease 2 baking sheets.

**2** Combine the flour, pecans, and baking powder.

**3** In a large bowl, cream the vegetable shortening and sugar. Beat in the eggs one at a time. Beat in the Tía Maria and water. Gradually blend in the dry ingredients.

**4** Drop the dough by spoonfuls 1½ inches apart onto the prepared baking sheets.

**5** Bake for 12 to 15 minutes, until lightly colored. Transfer to wire racks to cool.

# VICEROYS

Drop Cookies

YIELD: *4 to 6 dozen*
TOTAL TIME: *30 minutes*

**V**

# Viennese Crescents

Formed Cookies

YIELD: *4 to 5 dozen*
TOTAL TIME: *45 minutes*

2 cups all-purpose flour
1 cup hazelnuts, ground fine
1 cup vegetable shortening
½ cup granulated sugar
1 teaspoon Gilka liqueur (see Baking notes)
Powdered sugar for rolling

**1** Preheat the oven to 325 degrees.

**2** Combine the flour and hazelnuts.

**3** In a large bowl, cream the vegetable shortening and sugar. Beat in the Gilka. Gradually blend in the dry ingredients.

**4** Pinch off pieces of dough, form into crescents, and place the cres-

cents 1½ inches apart on ungreased baking sheets.

**5** Bake for 25 to 30 minutes, until lightly colored. Roll the crescents in powdered sugar and transfer to wire racks to cool, then roll in powdered sugar a second time.

**Baking notes:** Gilka is a nearly colorless liqueur, highly spiced with caraway seed; Kummel could be substituted.

---

# Viennese Shortcakes

Refrigerator Cookies

YIELD: *3 to 4 dozen*
TOTAL TIME: *30 minutes*
CHILLING TIME: *2 hours*

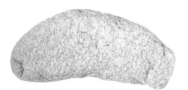

2 cups all-purpose flour
2 tablespoons corn flour
1¾ cups vegetable shortening
1 cup powdered sugar
1 tablespoon plus 1 teaspoon grated orange zest

**FILLING**
2 tablespoons butter, at room temperature
½ cup powdered sugar
1 teaspoon fresh orange juice

**1** Combine the two flours.

**2** In a large bowl, cream the vegetable shortening and powdered sugar. Beat in the orange zest. Gradually blend in the dry ingredients. Form the dough into a log 1½ inches in diameter. Wrap in waxed paper and chill for 2 hours.

**3** Preheat the oven to 350 degrees.

**4** To make the filling, combine the butter, powdered sugar, and orange juice in a small bowl and beat until smooth.

**5** Cut the log into ¼-inch-thick slices and place 1 inch apart on ungreased baking sheets.

**6** Bake for 10 to 12 minutes, until lightly colored. Transfer to wire racks to cool.

**7** To assemble, spread the filling over the bottom half of the cookies and place the remaining cookies on top.

**Baking notes:** For a different filling, beat 2 ounces of softened cream cheese and 1 tablespoon soft butter together.

---

# Virginia Rebels

Drop Cookies

YIELD: *3 to 4 dozen*
TOTAL TIME: *30 minutes*

1 cup all-purpose flour
6 tablespoons unsweetened cocoa powder
½ teaspoon baking soda
½ teaspoon salt
1¼ cups vegetable shortening
1½ cups granulated sugar
1 large egg
¼ cup water
½ teaspoon whiskey
3 cups rolled oats

**1** Preheat the oven to 350 degrees.

**2** Combine the flour, cocoa powder, baking soda, and salt.

**3** In a large bowl, cream the vegetable shortening and sugar. Beat in the egg. Beat in the water and whiskey. Gradually blend in the dry ingredients. Stir in the oats.

**4** Drop the dough by spoonfuls 1½ inches apart onto ungreased baking sheets.

**5** Bake for 10 to 12 minutes, or until lightly colored. Transfer to wire racks to cool.

# WALNUT BARS

Bar Cookies

YIELD: *3 to 4 dozen*
TOTAL TIME: *45 minutes*

### CRUST
1⅓ cups all-purpose flour
½ teaspoon baking powder
½ cup packed light brown sugar
⅓ cup vegetable shortening
¼ cup walnuts, chopped

### FILLING
3 tablespoons all-purpose flour
½ teaspoon salt
¼ cup packed light brown sugar
2 large eggs
¾ cup dark corn syrup
1 teaspoon vanilla extract
¾ cup walnuts, ground fine

**1** Preheat the oven to 350 degrees. Grease a 13 by 9-inch baking pan.

**2** To make the crust, combine the flour, baking powder, and brown sugar in a large bowl. Cut in the vegetable shortening until the mixture resembles coarse crumbs. Stir in the walnuts. Spread the mixture evenly in the prepared baking pan.

**3** Bake for 10 minutes.

**4** Meanwhile, make the filling: Combine the flour and salt.

**5** In a medium bowl, beat the brown sugar and eggs until thick and light-colored. Beat in the corn syrup. Beat in the vanilla extract. Gradually blend in the dry ingredients. Pour the filling over the hot crust. Sprinkle the walnuts over the top. Bake for 25 to 30 minutes longer, until the top is firm to the touch. Cool in the pan on a wire rack before cutting into large or small bars.

# WALNUT BUTTERBALLS

Formed Cookies

YIELD: *2 to 3 dozen*
TOTAL TIME: *30 minutes*

1 cup all-purpose flour
1 cup walnuts, ground fine
¼ teaspoon salt
½ cup vegetable shortening
2 tablespoons honey, warmed
1 teaspoon coffee liqueur
Powdered sugar for rolling

**1** Preheat the oven to 300 degrees. Lightly grease 2 baking sheets.

**2** Combine the flour, walnuts, and salt.

**3** In a large bowl, beat the vegetable shortening, honey, and coffee liqueur until smooth. Gradually blend in the dry ingredients.

**4** Pinch off walnut-sized pieces of dough and roll into balls. Place 1 inch apart on the prepared baking sheets.

**5** Bake for 25 to 30 minutes, until lightly colored. Roll in powdered sugar and transfer to wire racks to cool.

**6** After the cookies have cooled, roll in powdered sugar a second time.

# WALNUT FRUIT RINGS

Formed Cookies

YIELD: *3 to 4 dozen*
TOTAL TIME: *40 minutes*

1 cup vegetable shortening
¾ cup packed light brown sugar
3 large egg yolks
1 teaspoon apricot brandy
2½ cups all-purpose flour
½ cup candied citron, chopped
½ cup walnuts, chopped

**TOPPING**
1 large egg white
1 tablespoon honey
Glacé cherries, halved, for decoration

**1** Preheat the oven to 325 degrees. Lightly grease 2 baking sheets.

**2** In a large bowl, cream the vegetable shortening and brown sugar. Beat in the egg yolks. Beat in the brandy. Gradually blend in the flour. Fold in the candied citron and walnuts.

**3** For the topping, beat the egg white and honey in a small bowl.

**4** Pinch off pieces of the dough and roll into pencil-thin ropes about 6 inches long. Form the ropes into rings, placing them 1 inch apart on the prepared baking sheets, and pinch the ends together. Place a half-cherry on each ring at the point where the two ends join. Brush the egg white mixture over the cookies.

**5** Bake for 18 to 20 minutes, until lightly colored. Transfer to wire racks to cool.

**Baking notes:** Chopped candied red or green cherries can be substituted for the candied citron. The substitution will make the cookie sweeter.

# WALNUT HEALTH COOKIES

Drop Cookies

YIELD: *3 to 4 dozen*
TOTAL TIME: *40 minutes*

1 cup whole wheat flour
¼ cup nonfat dry milk
¼ cup wheat germ
¼ teaspoon baking powder
¼ teaspoon ground cinnamon
1 teaspoon salt
¾ cup vegetable shortening
1¼ cups raw sugar
1 large egg
¼ cup fresh orange juice concentrate, thawed
1½ cups rolled oats
1 cup walnuts, chopped
½ cup raisins

**1** Preheat the oven to 350 degrees.

**2** Combine the flour, dry milk, wheat germ, baking powder, cinnamon, and salt.

**3** In a large bowl, cream the vegetable shortening and sugar. Beat in the egg. Beat in the orange juice concentrate. Gradually blend in the dry ingredients. Fold in the oats, walnuts, and raisins.

**4** Drop the dough by spoonfuls 1½ inches apart onto ungreased baking sheets. Flatten each cookie with the back of a spoon dipped in flour.

**5** Bake for 25 to 30 minutes, until lightly colored. Transfer to wire racks to cool

4½ cups all-purpose flour
1 cup walnuts, ground fine
2 cups vegetable shortening
2½ cups packed light brown sugar
2 teaspoons vanilla extract

**1** Preheat the oven to 350 degrees.

**2** Combine the flour and walnuts.

**3** In a large bowl, cream the vegetable shortening and brown sugar. Beat in the vanilla extract. Gradually blend in the dry ingredients.

**4** Pinch off walnut-sized pieces of dough and roll into balls. Place 1½ inches apart on ungreased baking sheets. Flatten with the back of a spoon dipped in flour.

**5** Bake for 10 to 15 minutes, until lightly colored. Transfer to wire racks to cool.

# WALNUT SHORTBREAD

Formed Cookies

YIELD: *4 to 5 dozen*
TOTAL TIME: *30 minutes*

---

**CRUST**
¾ cup vegetable shortening
⅓ cup granulated sugar
2 large egg yolks
1 teaspoon vanilla extract
1½ cups all-purpose flour

**FILLING**
2 tablespoons all-purpose flour
¼ teaspoon baking powder
¼ teaspoon salt
1½ cups packed light brown sugar
2 large eggs, separated
2 tablespoons evaporated milk
1 teaspoon vanilla extract
1 cup shredded coconut
½ cup walnuts, chopped

**1** Preheat the oven to 350 degrees. Lightly grease a 9-inch square baking pan.

**2** To make the crust, cream the vegetable shortening and sugar in a medium bowl. Beat in the egg yolks and vanilla extract. Gradually blend in the flour. Press the dough evenly into the prepared baking pan.

**3** Bake for 12 minutes.

**4** Meanwhile, make the topping: Combine the flour, baking powder, and salt.

**5** In a large bowl, beat the brown sugar and eggs. Beat in the milk and vanilla extract. Gradually blend in the dry ingredients. Stir in the coconut and walnuts. Pour the topping over the hot crust. Bake for 20 minutes longer, or until the top is firm to the touch. Cool in the pan on a wire rack before cutting into large or small bars.

# WALNUT SQUARES I

Bar Cookies

YIELD: *2 to 3 dozen*
TOTAL TIME: *40 minutes*

# WALNUT SQUARES II

Bar Cookies

YIELD: *2 to 3 dozen*
TOTAL TIME: *40 minutes*

**CRUST**
1 cup all-purpose flour
¼ teaspoon salt
¼ cup vegetable shortening

**FILLING**
2 tablespoons all-purpose flour
¼ teaspoon salt
¾ cup granulated sugar
2 large eggs
1 teaspoon vanilla extract
2 cups flaked coconut
1 cup walnuts, chopped
Granulated sugar for sprinkling

1  Preheat the oven to 350 degrees. Lightly grease a 9-inch square baking pan.

2  To make the crust, combine the flour and salt in a medium bowl. Cut in the vegetable shortening until the mixture resembles coarse crumbs. Press the mixture evenly into the prepared baking pan.

3  Bake for 12 minutes.

4  Meanwhile, make the topping: Combine the flour and salt.

5  In a medium bowl, beat the sugar and eggs together until thick and light-colored. Beat in the vanilla extract. Gradually blend in the dry ingredients. Stir in the coconut and walnuts.

6  Pour the filling over the hot crust. Bake for 15 minutes longer, or until the topping is set. Sprinkle with granulated sugar and cool in the pan on a wire rack before cutting into large or small bars.

# WALNUT STRIPS

Rolled Cookies

YIELD: *3 to 4 dozen*
TOTAL TIME: *30 minutes*
CHILLING TIME: *2 hours*

3 cups all-purpose flour
1 teaspoon ground ginger
¼ teaspoon ground nutmeg
⅛ teaspoon ground cloves
1 teaspoon salt
½ cup vegetable shortening
½ cup packed light brown sugar
1 teaspoon baking soda
¼ cup hot water
½ cup molasses
1½ cups walnuts, chopped

1  Combine the flour, spices, and salt.

2  In a large bowl, cream the vegetable shortening and brown sugar.

3  Dissolve the baking soda in the hot water and add to the brown sugar mixture, beating until smooth. Beat in the molasses. Gradually blend in the dry ingredients. Fold in the walnuts. Cover and chill for 2 hours.

4  Preheat the oven to 350 degrees. Lightly grease 2 baking sheets.

5  On a floured surface, roll out the dough to a thickness of ¼ inch. Using a sharp knife, cut into strips 3 inches long and 1 inch wide. Place 1 inch apart on the prepared baking sheets.

6  Bake for 10 to 12 minutes, until lightly colored. Transfer to wire racks to cool.

1 cup almonds, ground fine
¼ teaspoon ground cinnamon
⅛ teaspoon ground cloves
3 large egg whites
¾ cup granulated sugar
½ teaspoon vanilla extract
½ cup semisweet chocolate chips

**1** Preheat the oven to 350 degrees. Line 2 baking sheets with parchment paper.

**2** Combine the almonds, cinnamon, and cloves.

**3** In a large bowl, beat the egg whites until stiff but not dry. Fold in the sugar. Fold in the vanilla extract. Gradually fold in the dry ingredients. Fold in the chocolate chips.

**4** Drop the dough by spoonfuls 1½ inches apart onto the prepared baking sheets.

**5** Bake for 12 to 15 minutes, until lightly colored. Cool in the pan on wire racks.

**Baking notes:** I created these cookies in the early 1950s; they are named for the way they look when they are baked.

# Wasps' Nests

Drop Cookies

YIELD: *3 to 4 dozen*
TOTAL TIME: *30 minutes*

1½ cups all-purpose flour
1 teaspoon baking soda
1 teaspoon cream of tartar
Pinch of salt
6 tablespoons vegetable shortening
3 tablespoons granulated sugar
⅔ cup milk

**1** Preheat the oven to 375 degrees. Lightly grease 2 baking sheets.

**2** Combine the flour, baking soda, cream of tartar, and salt.

**3** In a large bowl, cream the vegetable shortening and sugar. Beat in the milk. Gradually blend in the dry ingredients.

**4** On a floured surface, roll out the dough to a thickness of ½ inch. Using a cookie cutter or a glass, cut into 3- to 4-inch rounds. Cut the rounds into wedges and place 1 inch apart on the prepared baking sheets.

**5** Bake for 15 to 20 minutes, until lightly colored. Transfer to wire racks to cool.

**Baking notes:** Scones were first cooked on a grill, much like pancakes today. They are traditionally served at teatime, with jams and jellies.

# Welsh Scones

Rolled Cookies

YIELD: *3 to 4 dozen*
TOTAL TIME: *30 minutes*

# WHEAT FLAKE JUMBLES

Drop Cookies

YIELD: *3 to 4 dozen*
TOTAL TIME: *30 minutes*

1 cup all-purpose flour
½ teaspoon baking powder
¼ teaspoon baking soda
¼ teaspoon salt
⅓ cup vegetable shortening
½ cup packed light brown sugar
1 large egg
1½ tablespoons sour milk
1 teaspoon vanilla extract
½ cup dates, pitted and chopped fine
½ cup walnuts, chopped
1½ cups cornflakes

**1** Preheat the oven to 375 degrees. Lightly grease 2 baking sheets.

**2** Combine the flour, baking powder, baking soda, and salt.

**3** In a large bowl, cream the vegetable shortening and brown sugar. Beat in the egg. Beat in the sour milk and vanilla extract. Gradually blend in the dry ingredients. Fold in the dates and walnuts.

**4** Spread the cornflakes in a pie plate.

**5** Drop the dough by spoonfuls onto the cornflakes and roll in the cornflakes until completely coated. Place 3 inches apart on the prepared baking sheets.

**6** Bake for 12 to 15 minutes, until golden brown. Transfer to wire racks to cool.

# WHOLE WHEAT COOKIES

Drop Cookies

YIELD: *4 to 6 dozen*
TOTAL TIME: *30 minutes*
CHILLING TIME: *2 hours*

1 cup all-purpose flour
1 cup whole wheat flour
2 teaspoons baking powder
¼ teaspoon baking soda
¼ teaspoon salt
1 cup vegetable shortening
¾ cup granulated sugar
1 large egg
1 cup mashed, cooked carrots
1 teaspoon lemon extract
½ teaspoon vanilla extract
1 cup walnuts, chopped (optional)
1 cup raisins (optional)

**1** Combine the two flours, the baking powder, baking soda, and salt.

**2** In a large bowl, cream the vegetable shortening and sugar. Beat in the egg. Beat in the carrots. Beat in the lemon extract and vanilla extract. Gradually blend in the dry ingredients. Fold in the optional walnuts and raisins. Cover and chill for 2 hours.

**3** Preheat the oven to 375 degrees. Lightly grease 2 baking sheets.

**4** Drop the dough by spoonfuls 1½ inches apart onto the prepared baking sheets.

**5** Bake for 10 to 12 minutes, until lightly colored. Transfer to wire racks to cool.

3½ cups whole wheat flour
½ cup all-purpose flour
2 teaspoons baking powder
1 teaspoon baking soda
1 teaspoon ground nutmeg
1 teaspoon salt
1 cup vegetable shortening
2 cups granulated sugar
2 large eggs
2 teaspoons sour milk
2 tablespoons granulated sugar
2 teaspoons ground cinnamon

**1** Preheat the oven to 350 degrees.

**2** Combine the two flours, the baking powder, baking soda, nutmeg, and salt.

**3** In a large bowl, cream the vegetable shortening and sugar. Beat in the eggs. Beat in the sour milk. Gradually blend in the dry ingredients.

**4** Combine the sugar and cinnamon in a saucer.

**5** Drop the dough by spoonfuls 1½ inches apart onto ungreased baking sheets. Flatten each cookie with the bottom of a glass dipped in the cinnamon sugar.

**6** Bake for 10 to 12 minutes, until lightly colored. Transfer to wire racks to cool.

# WHOLE WHEAT SUGAR COOKIES

Drop Cookies

YIELD: *3 to 4 dozen*
TOTAL TIME: *30 minutes*

---

2 cups all-purpose flour
6 tablespoons carob powder
2 teaspoons baking powder
½ teaspoon salt
⅓ cup vegetable shortening
1 cup powdered sugar
1 large egg
1 cup skim milk
1 teaspoon crème de cacao
½ cup white chocolate chips

**FILLING**
¾ cup vegetable shortening
1 cup powdered sugar
1 teaspoon coffee liqueur
½ cup store-bought marshmallow
    topping

**1** Preheat the oven to 375 degrees. Lightly grease 2 baking sheets.

**2** Combine the flour, carob powder, baking powder, and salt.

**3** In a large bowl, cream the vegetable shortening and powdered sugar. Beat in the egg. Beat in the milk and crème de cacao. Gradually blend in the dry ingredients. Fold in the chocolate chips.

**4** Drop the dough by heaping tablespoonfuls 3 inches apart onto the prepared baking sheets.

**5** Bake for 7 to 10 minutes, until a toothpick inserted in the center comes out clean. Transfer to wire racks to cool.

**6** To make the filling, beat the vegetable shortening and powdered sugar in a medium bowl. Beat in the coffee liqueur. Beat in the marshmallow topping.

**7** To assemble, cut the cookies horizontally in half. Spread the filling liberally over the bottoms and sandwich with the tops.

**Baking notes:** To make more uniform cookies, you can use crumpet or muffin rings to form the pies.

# WHOOPIE PIES

Drop Cookies

YIELD: *3 to 4 dozen*
TOTAL TIME: *30 minutes*

# ZUCCHINI BARS I

Bar Cookies

YIELD: *2 to 3 dozen*
TOTAL TIME: *45 minutes*

2½ cups all-purpose flour
1 teaspoon ground cinnamon
½ cup granulated sugar
½ cup vegetable oil
2 large eggs
¾ cup finely chopped zucchini
½ cup mashed, cooked carrots
1 cup pecans, chopped
⅓ cup raisins

**1** Preheat the oven to 350 degrees. Lightly grease and flour a 13 by 9-inch baking pan.

**2** Combine the flour and cinnamon.

**3** In a large bowl, beat the sugar and vegetable oil together. Beat in the eggs one at a time. Beat in the zucchini and carrots. Gradually blend in the dry ingredients. Stir in the pecans and raisins. Spread the batter evenly in the prepared baking pan.

**4** Bake for 20 to 25 minutes, until a toothpick inserted in the center comes out clean. Cool in the pan on a wire rack before cutting into large or small bars.

# ZUCCHINI BARS II

Bar Cookies

YIELD: *2 to 3 dozen*
TOTAL TIME: *55 minutes*

1¾ cups all-purpose flour
1½ teaspoons baking powder
½ teaspoon salt
¾ cup vegetable shortening
½ cup granulated sugar
½ cup packed light brown sugar
2 large eggs
2 teaspoons vanilla extract
2 cups shredded zucchini
¾ cup raisins
½ cup dates, pitted and chopped
½ cup flaked coconut

TOPPING
1 tablespoon vegetable shortening
1 cup powdered sugar
1 tablespoon milk
¼ teaspoon ground cinnamon
1 cup walnuts, chopped

**1** Preheat the oven to 350 degrees. Lightly grease a 13 by 9-inch baking pan.

**2** Combine the flour, baking powder, and salt.

**3** In a large bowl, cream the vegetable shortening and two sugars. Beat in the eggs. Beat in the vanilla extract. Beat in the zucchini. Gradually blend in the dry ingredients. Stir in the raisins, dates, and coconut. Spread the batter evenly in the prepared baking pan.

**4** Bake for 30 to 35 minutes, or until a toothpick inserted in the center comes out clean. Cool in the pan on a wire rack.

**5** To make the topping, cream the vegetable shortening and powdered sugar in a small bowl. Beat in the milk. Beat in the cinnamon.

**6** Spread the topping over the cooled bars and and sprinkle with the chopped walnuts. Cut into large or small bars.

1½ cups all-purpose flour
½ cup almonds, ground
1½ teaspoons baking powder
½ cup vegetable shortening
½ cup granulated sugar
2 large eggs
2 teaspoons amaretto

**1** Preheat the oven to 325 degrees.

**2** Combine the flour, almonds, and baking powder.

**3** In a large bowl, cream the vegetable shortening and sugar. Beat in the eggs one at a time. Beat in amaretto. Gradually blend in the dry ingredients.

**4** Shape the dough into a loaf 13 inches long and 2½ inches wide and place on an ungreased baking sheet.

**5** Bake for 18 minutes, or until firm to the touch.

**6** Transfer the loaf to a cutting boards and cut into ½-inch-thick slices. Cut each slice in half diagonally. Place the slices on the baking sheets and bake for 20 minutes. Turn off the oven and leave the cookies in the oven 20 minutes longer; do not open the oven door. Transfer to wire racks to cool.

# ZWIEBACK

Formed Cookies

YIELD: *2 to 3 dozen*
TOTAL TIME: *50 minutes*

# COOKIES BY TYPE

## BAR COOKIES

Almond Awards
Almond Bars I
Almond Bars II
Almond Bars III
Almond Bars IV
Almond Bars V
Almond Bars VI
Almond-Coffee Delights
Almond Cookies V
Almond Crostata
Almond Génoise
Almond Roca Cookies
Almond Shortbread II
Almond Squares I
Almond Squares II
Almond Squares III
Almond Strips I
Ambrosia Bars
Apple Bars I
Apple Bars II
Apple Bars III
Apple Bars IV
Apple Bars V
Apple Butter-Oatmeal Bars
Apple-Oatmeal Cookies I
Apple-Raisin Bars
Apple-Spice Bars
Applesauce Brownies
Applesauce Date Bars
Apple Strips
Apricot Bars I
Apricot Bars II
Apricot Bars III
Apricot Bars IV
Apricot-Cherry Bars
Apricot-Filled Cookies
Apricot-Pecan Gems
Apricot Squares
Apricot Strips
Apricot-Walnut Bars
Arrowroot Cakes
Backpacker's Bars
Baked Cheesecake Bars I
Baked Cheesecake Bars II
Baklava
Banana Bars
Banana-Chip Bars I
Banana-Chip Bars II
Banana-Coconut Bars
Basic Bars
Basic Brownie Mix
Basic Fudge Brownies
Belgian Christmas Cookies
Bienenstich
Big Orange Bars
Bittersweet Brownies
Blackberry Meringue Bars
Blitzküchen

Blond Brownies I
Blond Brownies II
Blueberry Bars I
Blueberry Bars II
Boysenberry Meringue Bars
Brandy Alexander Brownies
Brazil-Nut Bars
Brown-and-White Brownies
Brownies I
Brownies II
Brownies III
Brownies IV
Brownies V
Brownies VI
Brownies VII
Brownies VIII
Brownies (Sugarless)
Brown Sugar Cocoa Brownies
Buttermilk Brownies
Butterscotch Bars I
Butterscotch Bars II
Butterscotch Brownies I
Butterscotch Brownies II
Butterscotch Brownies III
Butterscotch Brownies IV
Butterscotch Cheesecake Bars
Butterscotch Chews
Butterscotch Shortbread
Butterscotch Squares
Caramel Bars
Caramel Sugar Squares
Carrot Coconut Bars
Cashew Bars
Cashew-Caramel Cookies
Cashew Granola Bars
Cheesecake Cookies
Cherry-Almond Squares
Cherry Squares
Cherry Strips
Chewy Pecan Bars
Chocolate Chews
Chocolate Chip Bar Cookies
Chocolate Chip Bars
Chocolate Chip Nut Bars
Chocolate Chip Squares
Chocolate-Coconut Bars
Chocolate-Coconut Tea Strips
Chocolate de la Harina de Avena
    Brownies
Chocolate Delight Bars
Chocolate Oatmeal Bars
Chocolate Pudding Brownies
Chocolate Squares
Chunky Chocolate Brownies
Cinnamon Diamonds
Citrus Bars I
Citrus Bars II
Cocoa Brownies
Cocoa Indians
Cocoa Molasses Bars
Coconut Bars I
Coconut Bars II
Coconut Brownies
Coconut-Caramel Bars

Coconut Chewies
Coconut Chews I
Coconut Chews II
Coconut-Jam Squares
Coconut-Pineapple Squares
Coffee-Flavored Brownies
Coffee Squares
Cookie-Brittle Cookies
Cookie Squares
Cracker Brownies I
Cracker Brownies II
Crackle Brownies
Cranberry Bars
Cranberry Orange Bars
Cream Cheese Brownies
Crème de Menthe Brownies
Crumb Cookies I
Crunchy Chocolate Bars
Currant Bars
Currant-Raisin Bars
Danish Apple Bars
Danish Apricot Bars
Danish Peach Bars
Dark Secrets
Date Bars I
Date Bars II
Date Bars III
Date Brownies I
Date Brownies II
Date-Granola Squares
Date-Honey Fingers
Date Logs
Date-Nut Bars
Date-Oatmeal Bars
Date-Pecan Chews
Date Squares I
Date Squares II
Delicious Fudge Brownies
Dream Bars
Dreamy Squares
Dutch Crunch Applesauce Bars
Dutch Tea Cakes
Edinburgh Squares
English Tea Cakes I
English Toffee Bars
Fresh Plum Bars
Frosted Ginger Creams
Fruit Bars I
Fruit Bars II
Fruitcake Cookies
Fruit Chews
Fruit-Filled Oatcakes
Fruit Meringue Bars
Fruit Squares
Fudge Brownies I
Fudge Brownies II
Fudge Brownies III
Fudgies II
German Brownies
German Honey Cookies
German Molasses Cookies I
Ginger Bars
Ginger Creams
Ginger Shortbread

Graham Cracker Brownies I
Graham Cracker Brownies II
Graham Cracker Prune Bars
Granola Bars I
Granola Bars II
Grape Bars
Grapefruit Bars
Gumdrop Bars
Hazelnut Bars
Hazelnut Bars II
Hazelnut Squares
Health Bars I
Health Bars II
Helen's Cheesecake Bars
Hello Dolly Cookies
Hiker's Treats
Holiday Cookies
Honey Brownies
Honey Date Bars
Honey Raisin Bars
Honey Squares
Indian Barfi
Italian Almond Cookies
Jam-Filled Strips
Jam Squares
Jan Hagel
Jewel Bars
Kentucky Pecan Bars
Krispies
Lemon Bars I
Lemon Bars II
Lemon Bars III
Lemon Bars IV
Lemon-Coconut Sour Bars
Lemon-Glazed Apple Squares
Macadamia Nut Bars
Magic Bars
Magic Moments
Marbled Cream Cheese Brownies
Meringue Pecan Bars
Meringue-Topped Brownies
Microwave Fudge Brownies
Mincemeat Cookie Bars
Mincemeat Cookie Squares
Mint Bars
Mint Brownies
Mocha-Coffee Brownies
No-Bake Brownies
No-Bake Chocolate Cookies
No-Bake Oatmeal Bars
Norwegian Cookies
Nut Bars I
Nut Bars II
Oatmeal Brownies
Oatmeal Lemonade Bars
Orange Bars I
Orange Bars II
Orange Bars III
Orange-Cranberry Bars
Peanut Blondies
Peanut Butter Banana Squares
Peanut Butter Bars I
Peanut Butter Bars II
Peanut Butter Shortbread

Pear Bars
Pecan Bars
Pecan Squares
Pepparkoek
Persimmon Bars
Pineapple-Blueberry Bars
Pineapple-Coconut Bars
Prune Cookies
Pumpkin Bars
Raisin Bars
Raspberry Meringue Bars
Rocky Road Bars
Rocky Road Fudge Bars
Russian Tea Cookies
Seven-Layer Cookies
Soda Cracker Cookies
Some-More Bars
Spice Bars
Strawberry Meringue Bars
Sugarless Chocolate Bars
Teatime Favorites
Torta Fregolotti
Tropical Bars
Tropical Fruit Bars
Walnut Bars
Walnut Squares I
Walnut Squares II
Zucchini Bars I
Zucchini Bars II

**DROP COOKIES**

Almond Cakes I
Almond Cookies I
Almond Dreams
Almond-Flavored Crunchy Cookies
Almond Fruit Cookies
Almond Gems
Almond Health Cookies
Almond Tulip Pastry Cups
Almond Wafer Rolls
American Oatmeal Crisps
Anise Cookies I
Anise Cookies VI
Apple-Bran Cookies
Apple-Coconut Dreams
Apple Cookies
Apple Drops
Apple-Oatmeal Cookies II
Apple-Raisin Drops
Applesauce Cookies I
Applesauce Cookies II
Applesauce Cookies III
Applesauce Cookies IV
Applesauce-Nut-Raisin Cookies
Applesauce-Spice Cookies
Apricot-Bran Cookies
Apricot-Spice Cookies
Arrowroot Biscuits
Aunt Lizzie's Cookies
Back Bay Cookies
Banana-Bran Cookies
Banana Cookies
Banana-Date Cookies
Banana Drops

Banana-Nut Drops
Banana-Oatmeal Cookies I
Banana-Oatmeal Cookies II
Basic Drop Cookies
Bayou Hermits
Beaumont Inn Cookies
Beaumont Inn Drop Cookies
Benne (Sesame Seed) Cookies
Billy Goats
Blackberry Cookies
Black Walnut Cookies II
Blueberry Cookies
Boiled Cookies
Bourbon Chews
Boysenberry Cookies
Brandied Breakfast Cookies
Brandy Cones
Brandy Snaps
Brazil Nut Cookies I
Brazil Nut Cookies II
Brazil Nut Cookies III
Breakfast Cookies
Brown Sugar Cookies II
Brown Sugar Cookies III
Butter Crisps
Butter Pecan Drop Cookies
Butterscotch Cookies I
Butterscotch Drops
Butterscotch-Oatmeal Cookies
Butterscotch–Wheat Germ Cookies
Calla Lilies
Carob Chip Banana Cookies
Carob Chip Oatmeal Cookies
Carob Drop Cookies
Carrot Cookies I
Carrot Cookies II
Carrot Cookies III
Carrot-Molasses Cookies
Cashew Cookies
Cereal Flake Macaroons
Chippers
Chocolate Bonbons
Chocolate Chip Cookies I
Chocolate Chip Cookies III
Chocolate Drop Cookies I
Chocolate Drop Cookies II
Chocolate Drop Cookies III
Chocolate Jumbo Cookies
Chocolate Kisses
Chocolate Hazelnut Cookies
Chocolate Lemon Dessert Cookies
Chocolate Pecan Cookies
Chocolate Raisin Drops
Chocolate Spice Drops
Christmas Cookies I
Cocoa Drop Cookies
Cocoa Pecan Cookies
Coconut Balls I
Coconut Cornflake Cookies
Coconut Discs
Coconut Drop Cookies I
Coconut Drop Cookies II
Coconut Gems
Coconut Homesteads

Anise Drops VII
Aniseed Biscuits
Apricot-Chocolate Spritz Cookies
Austrian Walnut Crescents
Bird's Nest Cookies
Biscotti II
Bohemian Cookies
Bonbons
Bourbon Balls
Brandy Balls
Brandy Cookies I
Brandy Cookies II
Brazil Nut Balls
Brazil Nut Shortbread
Brown-Eyed Susans
Brown Sugar Spritz Cookies
Bulgarian Cookies
Bulgarian Honey Cookies
Butterballs
Butter Cookies IV
Butter Cookies VII
Butternut Drops
Butternuts
Butterscotch Cookies III
Butter Sticks I
Candy Gumdrop Cookies
Cashew Shortbread
Checkerboard Cookies
Cherry-Nut Clovers
Chocolate Chip Cookies II
Chocolate Chip Eggnog Balls
Chocolate Chip Peanut Logs
Chocolate Crinkles
Chocolate Oatmeal Cookies
Chocolate Rum Balls
Chocolate Sparkles
Chocolate Sticks
Christmas Cookies II
Christmas Eve Cookies
Christmas Wreaths I
Christmas Wreaths II
Christmas Wreaths III
Cinnamon Balls
Cinnamon Crisps
Cinnamon-Ginger Wafers
Cinnamon Sticks
Coconut Balls II
Coconut Butterballs
Coconut Classics
Coconut Cookies II
Coconut Dreams
Coconut Macaroons Deluxe
Cookie Pizza
Cookie Twists
Cornflake Cookies I
Cream Cheese Refrigerator Cookies
Cream Cheese Spritz Cookies
Crinkles
Crisp Sugar Cookies
Cuccidatti
Date Balls
Date Newtons
Date-Nut Fingers
Double Peanut-Flavored Cookies

Dreams End
Easy Fudge Cookies
English Tea Cakes II
Fennel Cookies
Finnish Bridal Cookies II
Galaktobouiriko
Galletas de la Harina de Avena
Gazelle Horns
German Almond Wafers
German Bonbons
German Geback Cookies
Ginger Crinkles
Gingersnaps IV
Good-for-You Peanut Butter Cookies
Greek Anisette Cookies
Greek Butterballs
Greek Cloud Cookies
Greek Sesame Cookies
Green Wreaths
Gumdrop Cookies I
Gumdrop Cookies II
Hazelnut Crescents I
Hazelnut Crescents II
Hazelnut Fruit Wreaths
Hazelnut Fruit Rings
Hazelnut Oatmeal Cookies
Hazelnut Shortbread I
Hazelnut Shortbread II
Holiday Wreaths
Honey Cookies I
Honey Snaps
Icebox Cookies
Jelly Cookies
Jumbles II
Kissies
Kringles
Krumkake
Lady Fingers I
Ladyfingers II
Lemon Rounds
Little Jewel Cookies
Love Letters
Mandelbrot
Mandel Mutze
Mendeni Kurabii
Mexican Wedding Cakes I
Mexican Wedding Cakes II
Miriors
Molasses Balls
Molasses Cookies III
Molasses Cookies IV
Molasses Ginger Cookies
Molasses Snaps
New Orleans Jumbles
New Year's Eve Pretzels
Nibbles
No-Bake Cookie Balls
Norwegian Currant Cookies
Nut Cookies II
Nut Cookies V
Nut Shortbread
Oatmeal Cookies VI
Orange-Nut Refrigerator Cookies
Peanut Butter Cookies I

Pecan Crispies
Pecan Shortbread
Peppermint Meringues
Petticoat Tails
Pine Nut Cookies
Pine Nut Crescents
P-Nutties
Ratafias
Refrigerator Spice Cookies
Refrigerator Walnut Cookies II
Rosenmunnar
Rosy Rocks
Royal Gems
Rum Balls
Russian Tea Biscuits I
Russian Tea Biscuits II
Sesame Chips
Snicker-Doodles
Snowballs
Southern Belles
Spanish Butter Wafers
Spritz Cookies
Sugar Cookies IV
Sugar-Plum Drops
Teatime Cookies
Thimbles
Tortas de la Boda del Mexicano I
Tortas de la Boda del Mexicano II
Tortelettes
Vanilla Sour Cream Rosettes
Viennese Crescents
Walnut Butterballs
Walnut Fruit Rings
Walnut Shortbread
Zwieback

## NONEDIBLE COOKIES

Decorator Cookies
Play Clay

## REFRIGERATOR COOKIES

All-Bran Cookies
Almond Cookies II
Almond Cookies III
Almond Cookies VII
Almond Crisps I
Almond Crisps III
Anise Cookies II
Aniseed Refrigerator Cookies
Benne (Sesame Seed) Icebox Cookies
Black Walnut Refrigerator Cookies
Brown Sugar Refrigerator Cookies
Butterscotch Chocolate Pinwheels
Butterscotch Cookies II
Butterscotch Refrigerator Cookies
Butterscotch Slices
Caramel Cookies
Cereal Refrigerator Cookies
Chocolate Refrigerator Cookies I
Chocolate Refrigerator Cookies II
Coconut Cookies I
Cranberry Cookies
Crisp Butter Cookies

Crunchy Cookies
Dutch Sour Cream Cookies
Dutch Wafers
English Tea Cookies
Friggies
Glenda's Favorite Cookies
Grandma's Refrigerator Cookies
Hazelnut Cookies I
Hazelnut Cookies II
Jubilee Wafers
Peanut Butter Refrigerator Cookies
Poppy Seed Cookies
Refrigerator Base for Cookies
Refrigerator Walnut Cookies I
St. Nikolaas Koekjes
Sesame Cheese Wafers
Sesame Seed Icebox Cookies
Viennese Shortcakes

**ROLLED COOKIES**

Abernathy Biscuits
Almond Butter Cookies I
Almond Cakes II
Almond Cakes V
Almond Cakes VI
Almond-Cherry Cookies
Almond Crisps II
Almond Flake Normandy
Almond Strips II
Almond Tea Cookies
American Shortbread
Anise Cookies IV
Anise Cookies V
Apricot Crescents
Arrowroot Wafers
Bannocks
Basic Filled Cookies
Bath Buns
Beaumont Inn Tea Cakes
Berlin Garlands
Biscotti I
Bishop's Pepper Cookies
Black-Eyed Susans
Black Walnut Cookies I
Blushing Cookies
Bohemian Butter Cookies
Border Cookies
Bow Cookies
Brasler Brünsli
Bratislavian Thins
Braune Lebküchen
Brazil Nut Strips
Brown Moravian
Brown Sugar Christmas Cookies
Brown Sugar Cookies I
Brown Sugar Sand Tarts
Brown Sugar Shortbread
Butter-Almond Strips
Butter Cookies I
Butter Cookies II
Butter Cookies III
Butter Cookies V
Butter Cookies VI
Butter Cookies VIII

Buttermilk Cookies
Butter Sticks II
Buttery Caraway Cakes
Cheddar Dreams
Cherry-Almond Kolacky
Cherry Crescents
Chocolate Cookies
Chocolate-Filled Pinwheels
Chocolate Sandwiches
Chocolate Sugar Cookies
Christmas Bells
Christmas Cookies III
Christmas Cookies IV
Christmas Cookies V
Christmas Ornament Cookies
Cinnamon-Cream Molasses Cookies
Coconut Dromedaries
Coconut Sandwiches
Coconut Sugar Cookies
Coffee-Chocolate Kringles
Coffee Cookies
Continental Biscuits
Cookie Faces
Cookie Sandwiches
Cream Cheese Christmas Cookies
Cream Cheese Cushions
Cream Cheese Tasties
Cream Wafers
Crisp Cookies
Crisp Lemon Cookies
Crisp Molasses Cookies
Crumb Cookies II
Cut-Out Hanukkah Cookies
Czechoslovakian Christmas Cookies
Czechoslavakia Cookies
Danish Gypsy Cookies
Danish Oatmeal Biscuits
Date-Filled Cookies
Date Fingers
Date Pinwheels
Date Turnovers
Decorative Cookies
Desert Mysteries
Digestive Biscuits
Dutch Spice Cookies
Eccles Cakes
Edenton Tea Party Biscuits
English Snaps
English Tea Biscuits
Fattigman
Fig-Filled Cookies
Filled Cheese Cookies
Finnish Bridal Cookies I
Finnish Coffee Strips
Finnish Cookies
Finnish Rye Cookies
First Lady Cookies
Foundation Base
Fried Cookies
Fruit Cookies III
Fruit Cookies VI
Fruit Cookies VII
Fruit Dreams
Fruit Fingers

Galette Bretonne
German Christmas Cookies I
German Christmas Cookies II
German Molasses Cookies II
German Puff Pastry Cookies
German Spice Cookies
German-Swiss Holiday Cookies
Gingers
Gingerbread Cookies
Gingerbread Cookies I
Gingerbread Cookies II
Gingerbread Men
Ginger Butter Treats
Ginger Cookies I
Ginger Cookies II
Ginger Cookies III
Ginger Cookies IV
Ginger Cookies V
Gingersnaps I
Gingersnaps II
Gingersnaps III
Graham Crackers
Granny's Cookies
Greek Shortbread
Haman's Pockets (Hamantashen)
Hazelnut Macaroons
Hazelnut Shortbread Cookies
Hazelnut Sticks
Health Sticks
Holiday Ornaments
Honey Cookies II
Honey Orange Crisps
Honey Spice Cookies
Hungarian Butter Cookies
Ischl Tartlets
Italian Christmas Cookies
Jewish Cookies I
Jewish Cookies II
Jewish Cookies III
Jodekager
Joe Froggers
Kaffee Zwieback
Kiss-Me-Quick Cookies
Kolacky
Lebküchen
Lemon Caraway Cookies
Lemon Sugar Rounds
Lemon Wafers
Lithuanian Preskuchiai
Lumberjacks
Maple Sugar Cookies
Master Cookie Mix
Measles Cookies
Milaenderli
Mincemeat Squares
Mint Cookies I
Mocha Treats
Mohn Cookies
Molasses Cookies I
Molasses Cookies II
Molasses Cookies V
Molasses Jumbles
Molasses Sticks
New Year's Eve Biscuits

Norske Kroner
Norwegian Christmas Cookies
Nut Cookies IV
Nutmeg Cookies
Nutty Sugar Cookies
Oasis Cookies
Oatmeal Cookies V
Old-Fashioned Cookies
Old-Fashioned Soft Ginger Cookies
Orange-Sugar Rounds
Orange Wafers
Pastel Cookies
Pastiniai Natale
Pepparkakor I
Pepparkakor II
Pepper Cookies
Peppermint Delights
Pfeffernüsse
Polish Kolacky
Poor Man's Cookies
Potato Scones

Pumpkin Scones
Queen Elizabeth Cookies
Queen Victoria Biscuits
Raisin Sandwich Cookies
Red River Queens
Rovastinpip-Parkakut
Rugelach
Rum-Topped Ginger Cookies
Rye Cookies I
Rye Cookies II
Sand Tarts
Scotch Queen Cakes
Scotch Shortbread I
Scotch Shortbread II
Scottish Oatcakes
Scottish Snaps
She-Loves-Me Cookies
Shrewsbury Biscuits
Simple Cream Cheese Cookies
Sour Cream and Spice Cookies
Sour Cream Cookies

Spanish Christmas Cookies
Spice Cookies I
S-Shaped Cookies
Stained Glass Cutouts
Stroop Koekjes
Sugar Cookies I
Sugar Cookies II
Sugar Cookies III
Swedish Crisp Rye Biscuits
Swedish Pinwheels
Swedish Sand Tarts
Thumbprint Cookies
Uppåkra Cookies
Vanilla Daisies
Vanilla Hearts
Vanilla Sugar Cookies
Vanilla Wafers
Walnut Strips
Welsh Scones